GIVING OURSELVES TO PRAYER

An Acts 6:4 Primer for Ministry

Dan R. Crawford, Compiler

TERRE HAUTE, INDIANA

PrayerShop Publishing is the publishing arm of Harvest Prayer Ministries and the Church Prayer Leaders Network. Harvest Prayer Ministries exists to make every church a house of prayer. Its online prayer store, www.prayershop.org, has more than 600 prayer resources available for purchase.

ISBN: 978-1-935012-12-2

2 3 4 5 6 | 2013 2012 2011 2010 2009

CONTENTS

Section Two: The Personal Passion for Prayer

Section Three: The Corporate Expression of Prayer

Section Four: The Global Impact of Prayer

INTRODUCTION

If I agreed with every paragraph in this book, I could have written it myself. From the birth of its idea, this book was designed to be a collection of short chapters, written by many people, expressing a wide variety of prayer-related subjects. It is a resource book, and as such represents writers from various backgrounds. Some are from the academic community with prayer taught as a part of their academic discipline. Others are from the prayer movement. Still others are persons who have previously written on the subject of prayer. Some of the contributors to this book are from denominations while others are from independent church traditions. There are conservatives and charismatics. Some serve the local church and still others serve through para-church organizations. Thus, the opinions of one contributor do not necessarily reflect the opinions of all the contributors. This much they all have in common—a desire to pray more effectively and lead others to do the same. All have worked without financial remuneration. The royalties from this book will go to the work of America's National Prayer Committee, specifically to its task force for the encouragement of the teaching of prayer in theological education.

Prayer is God's idea. Man's need to communicate with God is a result of God creating that need in man. In the Old Testament, from Adam to Malachi, they experienced that need. The disciples of Jesus learned quickly that they needed to communicate with their Lord. History records that the early Church, having learned from its predecessors in the faith, gave itself "continually to prayer" (Acts 6:4). In an attempt to be biblical, we have drawn the title of this book from the early Church's practice of "giving themselves to prayer." We acknowledge that while this book deals with a human need —communication with God—it is a God-created need. That is why each of the four sections of this book begin with a biblical base chapter.

Each chapter is followed by "Questions for Further Thought or Discussion" which may be used for personal reflection or for group interaction. Should you want to read further on any subject covered in the book, there is a listing of "Suggested Additional Reading" at the conclusion of each chapter.

Further appreciation is expressed to fellow members of the theological education task force from America's National Prayer Committee: Dave Butts, Dennis Fuqua, Daniel Henderson and Phil Miglioratti. Many others, both from within and outside the National Prayer Committee, were instrumental in the birth and implementation of this idea. Genuine appreciation is expressed to all.

I am especially indebted to Phil Miglioratti for assisting with the "Questions for Further Thought or Discussion" and "Suggested Additional Reading" sections as well as helping to compile the Bibliography.

The task of compiling such a book was an awesome one. We knew going into the project that we could not accomplish it except God be with us. Therefore, to God be the ultimate and final glory.

Dan R. Crawford

Head of the Task Force for Encouraging the Teaching of Prayer in Theological Education, America's National Prayer Committee

---

The compiler: Dr. Dan R. Crawford is Senior Professor of Evangelism & Missions and occupant of the Chair of Prayer, Emeritus, Southwestern Baptist Theological Seminary, Fort Worth, Texas. He is the author of fifteen books on prayer, discipleship, evangelism, and the Christian life and also President of Disciple All Nations, Inc. (www.discipleallnations.org) with headquarters in Fort Worth, Texas.

SECTION ONE

THE THEOLOGICAL FOUNDATION OF PRAYER

chapter

1

THE BIBLE AND PRAYER

Gary T. Meadors

Prayer is part of the fabric of the Bible. Genesis 4:26 first mentions that "men began to call on the name of the Lord," and Revelation 22:20 closes the Bible with the prayer, "Come, Lord Jesus" (cf. 1 Cor. 16:22). The entire history of redemption is framed in prayer. In between these terminal references we find a database about prayer that is so large it requires description beyond a simple definition.[1] There are more than 40 extended prayers and hundreds of brief prayer texts in the Bible. Lockyer's classic devotional on prayer treats 355 occurrences.[2] The endeavor to treat "Prayer in the Bible" is like trying to capture the ocean in a bucket. The chapters in this book will merely launch you onto the sea that is prayer.

Why is prayer such a dominant feature in the Bible? Prayer testifies to the basic beliefs of the Jewish and Christian faith. Prayer validates the ultimate belief that the God of the Bible exists. Prayer integrates all the essential elements of faith and life, including our dependence on God, submission to a biblical worldview, our recognition of God's superintendence of all of life, the approachable nature of God as we struggle with life, and all other matters relating to the relationship of humankind to God and His created order.

Prayer reflects God's orchestration of the world. In a conversational manner, the prayers of the key figures of the Old and New Testament illustrate the intimate relationship between God and His people in the flow of redemptive history. We observe Adam and Eve conversing with God in Eden (Gen. 3:9-13). In a similar manner God calls Cain to account for his actions (Chapter 4). The narrative of Noah reflects similar conversation. Abraham continues the conversation but he particularly becomes an intercessor in regard to a number of key events (Chapters 15, 18, 20:17).

Prayer texts cover all aspects of life, but one particular category in the Bible is intercession.[3] A classic text that reflects how the intercession of appointed leaders is crucial in the plan of God is Exodus 32-34. In this text Moses intercedes "face to face" with God (33:11) for wayward Israel in order to reinstate the unique covenant relationship between God and Israel. This event portrays God's chosen, often prophetic, leaders as "the mouth of Yahweh." This unique role of intercessory prayer is imaged in Exodus 4:10-17 although Moses struggled as a spokesman (cf. Num. 12:8; 22:38; 23:5, 12, 16). The role of an Old Testament prophet as intermediary between God and the world is defined in Deuteronomy 18:17-22. In the biblical narrative, the prophet intercedes for the community, receives an answer from God and then becomes God's "mouth"/spokesman to the people concerning the divine will (cf. Gen. 20:7; Num. 11:2; 1 Sam. 7:5; Jer. 7:16, 11:14, 14:11, 42:4; Dan. 9:3).

Jesus continues the tradition of intercession as prophet, priest and king. The plan of God moves forward in consort with Jesus' prayers. The Gospel record contains numerous summary references to Jesus going off alone to pray. John 17 records the classic intercessory prayer of Jesus for the future work of His disciples. Jesus tells Peter that He has prayed for him that his faith would not fail in times of testing (Lk. 22:31-32). Hebrews pictures Jesus as our great high priest who intercedes on our behalf (Heb. 7:23-25). Acts and the epistles continue the tradition of prayer as the intercessory lifeline to God for the community.

Prayer provides a venue for the redeemed community to reflect its view of God and its world. Prayer reflects the creature to creator relationship as conversation with God. Whether we listen in on Adam in the Garden of Eden or the Second Adam (Christ) in Gethsemane, we hear an intimate conversation. The terms that introduce us to prayer texts (e.g. said, spoke, call, cry out, etc.) testify to the personal nature of biblical prayer. This language "largely reflect[s] the emotional state of the one praying rather than a technical vocabulary related to elaborate prayer ceremonies."[4] Consequently, prayer as conversation with God, is the property of all believers regardless of their status or skills.

Prayer reflects the community's struggle with the pain of life. We can listen in on Moses as he struggles with leading a nation to the promise land (Deut. 9:25-29). The various psalmists frame every aspect of human emotion in the struggle of life by their prayers. God is invoked during times of personal distress (Ps. 4:1, 32:6, 102:17), in regard to the stress of feeling abandoned by God in regard to prayer (80:4), as a form of worship (141:2). A significant feature of the psalmists' prayers is how they are framed in regard to God's covenant loyalty toward His people ("steadfast love" 42:8, 66:20, 69:13). The value of the Psalms for the believer today is reflected by how quickly we turn to them in our own times of stress.

The Gospels present Jesus as a model of relating to the Father the issues of life. Jesus praying in the presence of the disciples and His frequent withdrawal to places of prayer dominate the flow of the gospel story. When the disciples requested that Jesus teach them how to pray, the model He gave them turned them first to God and then to their own needs in life (Mt. 6:9-13). The model that prayer connects the believer with God in life's struggle is also captured later by the fact that Jesus was "in all points tempted" like we are as preparation to be our Great High Priest and intercessor (Heb. 2:18, 4:14-16). His model encourages us to approach boldly God's throne in prayer.

Prayer reflects the community's attitude that nothing in life is apart from God. Life is not to be separated into secular and sacred components but is a constant act of dependence on God. The wisdom literature of the Old Testament (certain Psalms, Proverbs, Job, Ecclesiastes) views life without compartmentalizing divine space and human space. All reflection and all life is viewed in terms of God's knowledge and presence.

The New Testament continues this mindset. Prayer images dependence on God and each other in numerous ways. We have a relationship with God because of the work of Christ. Consequently, prayer is now framed "in Jesus name." Prayer is the vehicle of confession to enter the kingdom (Rom. 10:9-15) and a means to maintain a proper relationship to it (1 Jn. 1:9). Our connection to God and dependence upon Him is illustrated in the "Lord's Prayer" (Mt. 6:11) and in the developing life of the early church (Acts 1:24-25, 6:6, 13:2-3; Phil. 4:6). Jesus teaches dependence on God for our internal and external life and the book of Acts portrays how the apostolic community continued Jesus' example. Prayer is our lifeline to heaven.

Prayer is a means to bind the believing community together in its service to God (1 Thess. 5:25). Paul pleads for the Roman church to join in his struggle by praying for his mission (Rom. 15:30-33). This same attitude of community inter-dependence is referenced in Paul's work with the Corinthian church (2 Cor. 1:8-11). Prayer binds the community together in its mutual work for the advancement of God's kingdom on earth.

Community attitudes are fostered in the introduction and closing sections of epistolary literature. These sections are often written in prayer type language. Paul's epistles typically begin with a prayer of thanksgiving and statements of his desires for the church he is addressing (Rom. 1:8-10; 2 Cor. 1:11; Eph. 1:15-16; Phil. 1:3-6, 9-11; Col. 1:9-14; 1 Thess. 1:2-3; 2 Thess. 1:11-12; 2 Tim. 1:3; Phlm. 4; cf. Jas. 1:5-6; 1 Pet. 1:17). Salutations define the church as "those who call on the name of our Lord" (cf. 1 Cor. 1:2). Epistles also usually close with promises and requests in regard to prayer (cf. Eph. 6:18-20; Col. 4:2-6; 1 Thess. 5:17, 25; 2 Thess. 3:1-5; cf. Jas. 5:13ff.). The epistles truly present the early church in terms of prayer. Prayer is not just what they do but who they are. They are a community dependent upon God and each other and prayer seals that bond.

The New Testament language of prayer utilizes a variety of terms to image its multifaceted practice. 1 Timothy 2 lists petitions, prayers, intercession, and thanksgiving. The variety of terms testifies to the fact that prayer is appropriate for every category of life.

Prayer reflects the bewildering fact that God does not always answer our requests. The Apostle Paul presents unanswered prayer as an important experience in his struggle in the Christian life (2 Cor. 12:1-10). All prayer is conditioned by God's sovereign will, a will that is often not immediately known or understood. Prayer is not a means to manipulate God so that our circumstances of life are more acceptable or comfortable. Rather, prayer is our opportunity to struggle with a world that often leaves us bewildered (cf. the Psalms).

Prayer reflects the forwarding of God's agenda and kingdom on earth. Prayer highlights the progress of the history of redemption in the Bible. We observed how God utilized the intercessory prayers of key persons like Moses, Abraham and Jesus in regard to the divine plan. The prayer of Elijah in 1 Kings 18:36 validates the prophet as acting on God's behalf within Israel's history. Likewise, Solomon's prayer of dedication for the temple (2 Chronicles 6). The prophet Daniel repeatedly illustrated the role of prayer in God's program even at the risk of his own life (Daniel 6). Jesus' prayers illustrated how His earthly role was to do the will of the Father in heaven. The major events that unfold the growth of the early church as recorded in Acts are marked by prayer (cf. Acts 1:14; 1:23-26; 6:4, 6; 7:59; 8:15; 9:11; 10:9; 12:5; 13:3; etc.).

God has ordained that prayer be a vital part of how He achieves His purposes in the world. The balance between our pleading that God act in a certain way and our submission to God's will is not easy to define and is even less easy at times to accept. Various religious traditions will address this tension differently in terms of their theological understandings. It is clear, however, that our role is to pray and God's role is to fulfill His plan according to His infinite wisdom. Our prayers are a vital part of the process whether we always understand how it is so or whether we remain puzzled and voice the same sentiments we often hear from the psalmists.

Prayer reflects the believing community's hope. The book of Revelation views earth history from the perspective of prayer and worship. Whether the stress of "How long, O Lord" (Rev. 6:10) or the expectation of "Come, Lord Jesus" (22:20), prayer is the voice of the Church to God to intervene into life's events and culminate earth history.

Prayer in the Bible is truly an ocean of voices captured for the benefit of successive generations of God's people. The current comments can only stand on the shoreline of this testimony and cast an eye to the awesome nature of the ocean before us. The Bible presents prayer as the lifeline between the

Creator and His creation. Prayer captures the relational attitudes internal to the believing community. Prayer in the Bible records every aspect of redemptive history and provides the current believing community with a model for a God-centered life.

Questions for Further Thought or Discussion

1. When a biblical figure intercedes for the community, what are the categories that occur in such prayers? (Read Exodus 32-34 or John 17 as a sample.)
2. How do you or your church model how to pray in reference to Jesus' teaching in "The Lord's Prayer" (Mt. 6:7-15)?
3. Thankfulness is a major theme in biblical prayers. What do you thank God for in prayer?

The author: Dr. Gary T. Meadors is Professor of Greek and New Testament at the Grand Rapids Theological Seminary in Grand Rapids, Michigan. He is the author of *Decision Making God's Way: A New Model for Knowing God's Will* which includes a chapter entitled, "Prayer and God's Will."

SUGGESTED ADDITIONAL READING

Meadors, Gary T. "Prayer and God's Will," in *Decision Making God's Way: A New Model for Knowing God's Will.* Grand Rapids: Baker Books, 2003.

Bloesch, Donald G. *The Struggle of Prayer.* San Francisco: Harper and Row, 1980.

Crump, David. *Knocking on Heaven's Door.* Grand Rapids: Baker Academic, 2006.

"Prayer" in *The HarperCollins Bible Dictionary.* San Francisco: HarperSanFrancisco, 1996.

ENDNOTES

1. Since the reading of a few good dictionary articles on prayer can address the brute facts of prayer in the Bible, the present chapter will only reflect on select aspects of prayer in the Bible.

2. Herbert Lockyer, *All the Prayers of the Bible* (Grand Rapids: Zondervan, 1959).

3. See David Crump, *Jesus the Intercessor.* Grand Rapids: Baker Books, 1992; Gordon P. Wiles, *Paul's Intercessory Prayers.* Cambridge: Cambridge University Press, 1974.

4. "Prayer," in *Dictionary of Biblical Imagery* (Downers Grove: InterVarsity Press, 1998), 659.

chapter

2

JEWISH TRADITIONS OF PRAYER

Jan Verbruggen

The history of Jewish prayer, the practice of Jewish prayers and the various special prayers spoken by the practicing Jew at various occasions, all point to the fact that prayer was and is an important part of being a practicing Jew.

History

Biblical Period: From the earliest records in the Bible, people who believed in God expressed their hopes, joys and sorrows in prayers to God. The scriptures are interspersed with prayer. Some would even say that at least one prayer recorded in the Bible is attributed to every great biblical character from Hannah to Hezekiah. Nevertheless, prayer was, even during the time of the first temple, an entirely voluntary enterprise. The Davidic psalms sung by the Levites and the prayers of repentance which accompanied the sin-offerings were the only obligatory exercises required, although Maimonides argues that at least a prayer a day was offered from the time of Moses on.

The Synagogue: With the destruction of the temple and the exile of the people to Babylon, different modes of worship and places of worship were established. The synagogue came into being as the place to congregate and worship God. After the return of some of the exiles and the restoration of the temple, synagogues became widespread in Israel and the Diaspora as meeting places for those who did not live in the neighborhood of Jerusalem. Especially after the destruction of the second temple and the expulsion of the Jewish people from Jerusalem (70 A.D.) and Judea (135 A.D.), did the prayers come to replace the normal three daily sacrifices of the temple. Possibly, we see the beginning of this in the Bible when Daniel, living in Babylon prayed three times a day on his knees toward Jerusalem (Dan. 6:10) or with David bringing his petitions to God three times a day (Ps. 55:17). Hosea 14:2 is often used as support for this custom: ". . . we will offer the sacrifices of our lips." After the destruction of the temple, the synagogue service was called *avodah*, just as the sacrificial service had been called *avodah*. In the Mishnaic and the Talmudic period, prayer became a commandment and seen as the fulfillment of serving God with the heart. Sections of the Mishna that described the ritual sacrifice were also read during the synagogue service and by reciting them the worshipper participated vicariously in the sacrificial service.

Rabbinical Period (70 CE - 500 CE) and Early Medieval Period (500-1100): Through these years, the study of Torah and Talmud grew in importance somewhat to the detriment of prayer. The study of Torah and Talmud was considered a commandment whose fulfillment was pleasing to God (Psalm 1). Through study of Torah, one could see the world as God sees it. It promised wisdom which would give the student the ability to deal with the problems of this world. It was also a mystical enterprise that allowed men to draw closer to God. Torah study was seen as the key to a long life. The study of Torah became a way of salvation: it was a necessary step in the spiritual growth of a Jewish man, since knowledge of Torah led to right action, and right action showed the people's obedience and reverence for the Lord.

Mysticism: In Jewish mysticism, (Kabala; starting the 2nd century CE, but achieving it biggest following in the $16\text{-}17^{th}$ century) the emphasis was on experiencing an ecstatic religious feeling and the closest possible communion with God. This communion was gained through the understanding of a vast doctrine of theosophical "hidden wisdom" concerning the ultimate mysteries of the word. Prayer was only important in so far as it supported the achievement of the mystical union.

Chasidic Judaism: Only through the rise of Chasidism (beginning of the 18th century) did prayer regain a prominent status.[1] While prayer was valued in traditional Judaism, it was still considered of a lower importance than the study of Torah. Chasidism places prayer back in the center of the Jewish life. Prayer was again the supreme means for communicating with God. Through prayer man can stand before the throne of God without any veil between him and God. Even some kabalistic ideas are intertwined with the Chasidic approach to prayer. In prayer, a man's profane thoughts become sanctified, for in such thoughts, divine sparks were mingled from the time when they were dispersed with the breaking of the vessels.[2]

Prayer was seen as the means of bringing direct practical benefits from God to the individual. Every individual, according to Baal Shem Tov, was able to offer efficacious prayers that could bring about healing, avert misfortune and obtain wealth. The successors of Baal Shem Tov saw only certain individuals capable of offering such efficacious prayers. These men were the Tsaddiks. Still, prayer remains an important element in the Chasidic life of today and in the life of the devout Jew.[3]

Haskalah: In the 19th century under the influence of the Haskalah (a movement under the influence of the Enlightenment that hoped to remove from Judaism those elements that were superstitious or thought to be too offensive to the non-Jews), prayers said in Hebrew and Aramaic were translated in the vernacular language of the land. Prayers for the restoration of the sacrifices, the return to Zion and even the prayers for the coming of Messiah were eliminated in certain congregations, although the more conservative traditions never followed this trend.

The Practice of Prayer

While prayer was and is an important part of the synagogue service, prayer wasn't of course limited to the synagogue. Individuals would offer up prayers voluntarily and spontaneously. We see this already patterned in the Bible.[4] The same freedom is also found in the rabbinical period. Prayer was valued more highly than sacrifices in the Talmud (Ber. 32b). Four types of prayer can be found in Jewish life: (1) Benedictions (2) Private or public petitions related to the dilemma or need that people found themselves in. (3) Prayers of thanksgiving: thanking God for answered prayers or for common grace; (4) Prayers of praise describing God's greatness and goodness, and expressing thankfulness for what God had already done in the life of the petitioner. Prayer was called the service of the heart.

The Morning Prayer was the most important: in this prayer time, the practicing Jew would adorn himself with the prayer shawl, or *Tallit*, and during the week he would strap on the *Tefillin*, boxes containing Bible verses with leather straps attached to them. Rabbi Huna states that the worshipper should have a regular place for his prayers (Ber. 6b). It was customary in prayer to face the east, toward the temple in Jerusalem (this was already anticipated by King Solomon in 1 Kings 8:30, 35, 48).[5] During prayer, the petitioner could stand, sit, bow, prostrate himself, kneel or sway.[6] Fasting, weeping, the wearing of sackcloth and ashes, the rending of the clothes, and the shaving of the head were all possible during prayer depending, on the circumstances or reasons for prayer.

The efficacy of prayer is not questioned either in the biblical period or in rabbinical times although in later periods the spiritual stature of the petitioner was often thought to be of great importance. The social status had no relevance to the worthiness of the prayer, although some thought that the prayers of the poor were more efficacious than others (Ex. 22:27; Ps. 22:24).

A time of prayer was often preceded by a time of preparation, when the faithful would attune their hearts to God (Ber. v. 1) and/or by a time of washing the body before prayer (Y. Ber. iii 4). Posture and dress were also considered important, either by wearing a special mantle, the crossing of the hands (as a servant who awaits the commands of his master), and sometimes by standing (for example, for the special prayer of the *'Amidah*). Prayers were either offered in silence or partly in a plaintive voice (Y. Ber. iv 4), and if one raised his voice to much, he was thought to have too little faith in the efficacy of his prayers. One who prays for others will be answered before the one who only prays for himself. Prayers which are offered as a routine exercise negate the purpose and power of the prayer (Ber. 4:4). Praying with the right state of mind and praying with devotion was important. In Rabbinical Judaism, in times of great trouble, even the dead would be interceded for help by going to the cemetery to pray (Ta'an. 16a). Public prayers were offered when there was a quota of 10 adult men. Women were also expected to pray, although their first responsibility was to their husband and family.

Special Prayers in Present Day Judaism

The *Shema'* (Deut. 6:4): The *Shema'* is the Jewish person's affirmation of faith in one God and is recited every morning. The importance of this prayer is seen in that the Mishna begins with the question: When should or can the *Shema'* be recited? It is also a prayer that is not allowed to be interrupted even if a king would greet you in the meantime. When one recites the *Shema'*, one is to cover his eyes so that one is not distracted by anything. The *Shema'* was also often recited by Jews who were faced with imminent death in the gas chambers of the holocaust.

The *'Amidah*: This prayer is also called *the eighteen*, referring to the number of praises or benedictions that were included in the prayer and is recited three times a day. The Chazzan would read the *'amidah* out loud for those who could not read. It is recited while standing and spoken with a quiet voice. The prayer consists of three parts: the first three benedictions, the last three and the 13 intermediate benedictions that deal with the public and personal welfare. Every *'amidah* contains the first three and concluded by the last three. On the Sabbath and other holy days, the 13 intermediate benedictions are replaced by benedictions that are appropriate for the occasion of the day.

The 18 benedictions were expanded to 19 with the inclusion of the condemnation of those who spoke ill of the congregation, the Jewish faith, so that they could not remain in their midst.

The *Kaddish*: This prayer is a central part of the Jewish prayer service. This is a Talmudic Aramaic prayer, acclaiming the magnification and the sanctification of God's name. It was recited as part of the mourning ritual for a deceased member of the family, to plead for that person's rest in the hereafter. Originally, the prayer was spoken by rabbis when they finished presenting their sermon on the Sabbath, or after finishing the study of a section of midrash or aggadah. There is a slight difference between the version that is spoken by the mourners and the one that is pronounced by the rabbis.

Prayers for Gentiles: On the Sabbath and on holy days, a prayer is said for the ruler of the land the congregation finds itself in. During some holy days, such as Yom Kippur, prayers for the salvation of the Gentiles are being offered as part of the regular liturgy.

Who has not made me: Two controversial daily prayers of thanks made by the Jewish male to God have as their heading, "who has not made me. . . ." The first gives thanksgiving for not being a Gentile and the second one for not being a woman. The Talmud gives as defense for these prayers, that the Jewish male has been awarded great privileges but also great responsibilities. It is both a joy and a burden to keep the commandments of God. Gentiles do not have to keep the commandments because they do not belong to the chosen people, and a woman's duty is to take care of family and home and are thus not obligated to follow the commandments.

The *Siddur*: All the prayers customarily recited in the Jewish services in the Synagogue have been collected in the *Siddur*, the Jewish prayer book. Since not everyone understands the Hebrew and the Aramaic of the prayers, a translation is often included in this book. In various liberal and reformed synagogues, these prayers are only recited in the local vernacular language. Besides the aforementioned prayers, sections from the book of Psalms, and the Torah and the prophets are also included. These *Siddurs* can differ depending on the history of the various congregations (Sephardic vs. Ashkenazi, Reformed, Orthodox, Chasidic, etc.).

Prayer and *Shoa*: In present day Judaism, *Shoa* (the holocaust) is a day (27th of Nissan) that is remembered annually. The holocaust has left a great emotional scar among the survivors and the Jewish people in general. Special meetings are held on this day, and one of the survivors will recite the *Kaddish.*

Conclusion

Practicing Jews pray because it is a commandment but also because they long to have communion with God. Often they pray out of obligation, so that in time of need, despair or distress, there will be a well worn path of going to their Maker to pour out their soul, in order to obtain comfort, guidance and help in need.

Questions for Further Thought or Discussion

1. How have Jewish traditions influenced Christian praying?
2. Select a prayer from the Pentateuch, Psalms, and the Prophets. Compare and contrast their content and style.
3. Describe how each style can be used effectively in discipling believers in the Christian expression of prayer.

The author: Dr. Jan Verbruggen is Professor of Old Testament Language and Literature at Western Seminary in Portland, Oregon. He has recently published a commentary on Deuteronomy in a Dutch commentary series.

SUGGESTED ADDITIONAL READING

Donin, Hayim Halevey. *To Pray as a Jew.* New York: Basic Books, 1980.

Ben-Sasson, H.H. ed. *A History of the Jewish People.* Cambridge, MA: Harvard University Press, 1976.

Millgram, Abraham E. *Jewish Worship.* Jewish Publication Society of America, 1971.

ENDNOTES

1. Israel Baal Shem Tov (the founder of the Chasidic movement) did not esteem the study of Talmud as high as direct communion with God through whatever action a believer would be involved in be it plowing the field, sleeping, eating, etc., as long as all is done with joy, humility and fervor. Murmuring prayer as a routine is meaningless; it has to be done with one's whole being. The lowering of the importance of the study of Talmud was also a reaction against the use of *Pilpul. Pilpul* is a reasoning method where one tries to resolve apparent contradictions by acute logical analysis and reasoning. A century before the rise of Chasidism, this method had gained prominence among Jewish scholars. Men devoted themselves to *Pilpul* not to obtain truth but as a demonstration of mental gymnastics. *Pilpul* became an end in itself.

2. Adam's disobedience caused a disruption in the realm of souls. Good intermingled with evil and as a result, the worst soul is not devoid of good and the best soul is still tainted by evil.

3. See further, J. Verbruggen, *Judaica*, (Heverlee: Evangelische Theolo-

gische Faculteit, 2000), pp. 55-56.

4. Abraham intercedes with God for the salvation of Sodom, he prays for the restoration of Abimelech (Gen. 20:17); Eliezer prays for a successful mission (24:12-14); Isaac prayed on behalf of his wife Rebecca since she was barren (25:21); Jacob prays for deliverance from the hand of his brother Esau (32:11); Moses regularly interceded for the people with God (Ex. 32: 31-32; 33:13; Num. 11:2; Deut. 9:20, 26); Joshua interceded with the Lord after the defeat at Ai (Josh. 7:6-9); Hannah, the mother of Samuel, prayed to God to remove her barrenness (1 Sam. 1:10-12); etc.

5. Even some Christians oriented their churches toward the east, toward Jerusalem.

6. With swaying the whole body was thought to be caught up in prayer.

chapter

3

PRAYER AND THE KINGDOM OF GOD

Ron Walborn

Imagine a football team coming into a locker room at halftime leading 49-0, telling their coach the first half went so well they would not need to play the second half. A good coach would quickly silence the nonsense with the following speech, "The game does not end at halftime. If you stop now, the results will be devastating. We will stop playing when the final gun sounds. Until then, we give it everything we have!"

Two thousand years ago Jesus Christ appeared with an announcement that would change the course of human history. "The kingdom of God is near," He declared, "Repent and believe the good news." He then proceeded to proclaim and demonstrate the present rule and reign of God on an earth that had been held captive by the kingdom of darkness. He healed the sick, bringing the health of God's kingdom, ending the reign of death and disease. He cast out demons, bringing the freedom of God's kingdom, ending the reign of terror over people's lives. He forgave sin, bringing the joy of God's kingdom, ending the trauma of guilt once and for all. He defeated the grave by dying a sinner's death on the cross and then coming out of the tomb on the third day. The glorious truth is this: Jesus Christ struck the decisive blow of history in the first half of this game we call life. The ultimate victor has been decided.

The Now and the Not Yet

At this point some are thinking, *Wait a minute, Jesus may have started that victory, and we certainly believe in the finished work of Christ, but people still get sick, many are still in bondage to the Evil One. Guilt still takes it share of victims. The kingdom of God may be here, but it's certainly not here in all its fullness. We are not in heaven yet.* If those are your thoughts, then you have grasped what many theologians and much of the church has missed. While Jesus brought the rule and reign of God, winning a decisive victory over Satan and his kingdom, the battle is not yet over. In the spirit of our great Coach we hear these words, "The game does not end at halftime. If you stop now, the results will be devastating. We will stop playing when the final gun sounds. Until then, we give it everything we have!"

Christians are called to finish the battle Jesus has started. We are living in a world at war, but our weapons are not of this world. We do not embrace a spirit of violence to accomplish this task. On the contrary, we use spiritual weapons with Divine power to bring down Satan's strongholds (2 Cor.10:3-5). Chief among these weapons is prayer.

Jesus taught His disciples to pray in order to finish the work of extending His kingdom. He taught them to pray with authority: "Your kingdom come, Your will be done, on earth as it is in heaven." Prayer is rooted in the present reality of God's kingdom. Prayer works because God responds to the intercession of His people. We must, however, acknowledge that at present, the kingdom is not yet here in its fullness. Not everything that happens this side of heaven is God's will. Thus, we are called to use prayer as a weapon of warfare to bring His kingdom to the ends of the earth.

Sadly, much of the Church in the West has been lulled to sleep in the midst of the battle. Football is a game played by 22 men on the field, badly in need of rest, being watched by 60,000 people in the stands badly in need of exercise. These extremes illustrate two groups of Christians in the use of prayer in spiritual warfare. Certainly there are a few Christians who need to lighten up from all their frenetic spiritual warfare. Those who find a demon behind every bush need to rest more in the finished work of Christ. The other extreme, however, seems to be the largest group. The vast majority of Christians are not even in the game. They are seated in the stands badly in need of exercising their spiritual authority. Prayer to advance the kingdom of God is a foreign concept to this group.

Some believers have even been taken out of the battle through distorted theologies of impotence. In the past 500 years the church has been infected with a naturalistic rationalism resulting in the lie that the kingdom of God is not really here at all. It is a future realm that will only arrive when Jesus returns. As a result, the tools of the kingdom like the supernatural gifts are spoken against and even "outlawed." Prayer becomes a one-way communication with little expectancy of an interactive God. Interestingly enough, Satan is still using all the weapons in his arsenal, but according to this theology God has decided to handcuff His church until He returns.

There has also been a distortion of the sovereignty of God. In our attempt to cope with powerless prayers we have taken a passive view that if something bad happens, God must have allowed it and therefore it must be His will. This "Christian fatalism" is not the discipleship found in the New Testament. In this distortion, phrases like "God can be trusted," and "God knows best," become pathetic excuses not to pray as Jesus taught us: "Let Your kingdom rule and reign come now, Father. Bring Your will, Your purposes, Your plans on this earth now as in heaven."

So if prayer is to be a primary weapon in this battle to expand the kingdom of God, what are some practical ways we can begin to move in our authority as followers of Christ?

Prayer for Evangelism

In 1 Timothy 2:1-4, Paul urges us to pray for all people with the goal that all might be saved and come to a knowledge of the truth. Every time a person comes to faith in Jesus, the kingdom of darkness loses a subject. All of humanity is being invited to leave the bondage of the enemy and come into the freedom of God's kingdom. Thus, prayer for those who have yet to come to Christ is a priority for disciples.

Several years ago while skiing at a crowded resort I was standing alone in a long lift line. I decided to pray and ask the Father to show me who He had prepared to receive the good news of His kingdom. I noticed a young man in the line ahead who was obviously drunk. He cursed loudly, offending everyone. I sensed God's Spirit say, "Him, Ron. He's the one I have prepared to receive my kingdom." I argued with God pointing out the language the young man was using, but the Holy Spirit was prompting me to speak with him anyway. My final excuse was the inconvenience of a number of people in between us. Instantly, the young man launched a string of vulgarities that so offended the people in between us that they left the line after waiting over 45 minutes. Thirty seconds later I was on a lift with a very drunk, angry young man. Whispering another prayer for protection, I turned and said, "God loves you." I was not expecting much. To my surprise the young man began to weep. "How did you know I was running from God?" Feeling a bit more confident, I explained how in prayer God indicated that he was ready to receive the gospel.

Through his tears he shared how his Christian girlfriend had given him an ultimatum that morning: "Surrender to Christ or we are done." He started drinking in an attempt to run from the conviction of the Holy Spirit. His girlfriend was waiting at the top of the mountain. We knelt in the snow to pray as he entered the kingdom of God. Prayer for salvation is one of the ways God's kingdom comes and God's will is done on this earth.

Prayer for Healing

Adam and Eve never knew the pain of sickness until they ate the forbidden fruit, allowing Satan to usurp control of this fallen world. Sickness is part of the corrupt fruit of the fallen kingdom. Jesus demonstrated the perfect will of God when in response to the Leper asking, "Lord if you are willing, you can make me clean," He declared, "I am willing." With these words, Jesus ended the speculation on whether or not it is God's will to heal the sick (Mt. 8:1-4). Prayer for healing is part of our kingdom mandate as followers of Jesus Christ.

Let me be the first to say that not everyone we pray for in this "now and not yet" season will be healed. One day in the fullness of God's kingdom there will be no more sickness or pain. In the meantime, we war against sickness on a daily basis as the demonstration of the proclamation, "The kingdom of God is near." Not everyone is healed, but God forbid that we should ever stop fighting and praying against sickness as a fruit of evil. Can God use sickness? Certainly, but we must never attribute this manifestation of a fallen world to a good God.

A.B. Simpson addressed those who embraced sickness as the will of God by saying, "If those who urge and claim to practice the suggestion, that it is God's will for them to be sick, would really accept their sickness and lie passively under it, they would at least be consistent. But do they not send for a doctor and do their best to get out from under this 'sweet will of God?'"[1] Prayer for healing is one of the ways God's kingdom comes and God's will is done on this earth.

At the end of a seminary class one day I suggested we have a time of prayer ministry. As we began to pray, a young man named Matt grabbed his crutches and slowly left the classroom. Matt had been raised in a denomination that no longer believed healing was part of God's plan. His wife, on the other hand, was praying for God to heal Matt's torn anterior cruciate ligament.

When Matt reached the parking lot he sensed the Lord saying, "If you will go back, I will heal your knee." To Matt's credit, he hobbled back in and asked for prayer. Laying hands on Matt's knee I prayed, "Father, let Your kingdom come upon Matt's knee. Let Your will be done in Matt's knee now, the way it will ultimately be done in heaven." I began to sense warmth and movement in Matt's knee. I pulled my hand back to observe what was happening. Matt and I watched in awe as things began to move in Matt's knee. I asked, "Matt, are you moving your knee?" He assured me he was not. Jesus was healing him. Matt walked home that day without his knee brace or his crutches. More importantly, Matt went home convinced that healing prayer is one of the ways God's kingdom comes and God's will is done on this earth.

Conclusion

While the winner of this great battle of the ages has been decided, the final score has yet to be determined. There are still many who have never heard the good news of the kingdom of God. In between the Cross and the Second Coming of our Lord, the Church has been commissioned to use the words and the works of Jesus to free the captives and extend the kingdom rule and reign of God. Prayer is a primary weapon in this battle. The Coach is speaking to His team at halftime saying, "We will stop praying when the final gun sounds. Until then, cry out to the Father, 'let Your Kingdom come and let Your will be done, on earth as it is in heaven!'"

Questions for Further Thought or Discussion

1. How will this concept of prayer as a weapon for expanding God's kingdom impact your own spiritual formation process?
2. Where in your life do you need to pray for greater surrender to God's rule and reign? In your church? In your community? In our world? What's holding you back?
3. How does the truth that the kingdom of God is here now but not yet in its fullness comfort you? Frustrate you?

The author: Dr. Ron Walborn is Dean of Bible and Christian Ministry at Nyack College in Nyack, New York. He serves on the Board of Directors for the Christian & Missionary Alliance.

SUGGESTED ADDITIONAL READING

Andrew, Brother. *And God Changed His Mind.* 2nd edition. Grand Rapids: Chosen Books, 1999.

Johnson, Bill. *When Heaven Invades Earth.* Shippensburg, PA: Destiny Image Publishers, 2005.

Ladd, George. *The Gospel of the Kingdom.* Grand Rapids: Eerdmans Publishing, 1959.

Williams, Don. *Signs and Wonders and the Kingdom of God.* Ann Arbor, MI: Servant Publications, 1989.

Wimber, John. *Power Healing.* New York: HarperCollins Publishers, 1991.

ENDNOTES

1. A.B. Simpson, *The Gospel of Healing* (Harrisburg, PA: Christian Publications, 1915 rev.), pp. 57-58.

chapter

4

GOD THE FATHER AND PRAYER

Patricia A. Outlaw

"Father, I stretch my hands to Thee; No other help I know;
If Thou withdraw thyself from me, Ah! Whither shall I go?" [1]

There was a time in my life when I was reluctant to stretch my hands upward to God in humble submission or prayer. I remember attending a Sunday morning worship service with my father at his church in Baltimore City when I was a young adult. Together, we listened to the pastor conclude the service by instructing us to lift our hands up and stretch them heavenward in order to receive the benediction. My father sensed my inner struggle and spiritual conflict as he observed me folding my arms in bold defiance across my chest. He placed his hand on my shoulder and whispered in my ear, "Girl, lift your hands up, so God can bless you."

In response to Daddy's encouragement I stretched my hands to the sky. I believe my close relationship with my biological father has shaped my experience and understanding of "God the Father and Prayer" for a lifetime. My hope is that you will be inspired to reflect theologically and spiritually on the relationships you may have had with your earthly father as a preface to understanding and appreciating the influence the paternal relationship has on your eternal relationship with God the Father.

How one sees, conceptualizes, and/or experiences "father," and the relationship one develops with her father has implications for a lifetime. Not only do the connotations of "father" have implications for a lifetime, they also influence one's perceptions and experiences of God the Father. If "father" is perceived and experienced as a benevolent father, then it is highly likely that God the Father will be viewed as a benevolent Father. Similarly, if one experiences her earthly father as a malevolent father figure, then logic suggests that the individual is likely to transfer those same negative perceptions of father onto God the Father. The individual transfers the positive and/or negative attributes of the significant other, the one she can see in the flesh, onto the Spiritual other, the invisible, immutable God, the one she cannot see or touch.

As I write this chapter, I see an image of my father pop-up in my mind's eye. He is wearing a white shirt with greenish-black, double-knit pants, and he is sitting in a green "easy-chair" listening attentively as I talk to him about all the things that were of concern for me on that day. I remember the chair; because it was the first "big" gift I ever bought my daddy. I paid for that chair in full within the first ninety days so as not to have to pay interest charges. I learned early in life that I could talk to my father about anything and everything. He always made time to listen to me.

Jesus understood the needs of His disciples. He realized that they, too, would need someone to pray to, talk to and address their daily concerns. It should come as no surprise when His disciples asked Him in Luke 11:1-4, "'Lord, teach us to pray, as John also taught his disciples.' So He said to them. 'When you pray, say, Our Father in heaven, hallowed be Your name. Your kingdom come. Your will be done on earth as it is in heaven. Give us day by day our daily bread. And forgive us our sins . . .'"

Jesus directs His followers to pray to, "Our Father." God is our Father, and He is the one who will "supply all your need according to His riches in glory" (Phil. 4:19). God the Father, the creator of heaven and earth is the one who will supply enough bread for today.

Although the disciples asked Jesus to teach them "how to pray," we should not assume that they were unfamiliar with the power of prayer. A closer look at the background of these men will reveal that they already knew how to pray. We only have to look to Jesus and His Jewish cultural context to discover that these men knew how to pray. We know that praying was a daily part of Jewish practice. We know that by New Testament times the custom of praying three times a day was the general rule (Acts 3:1; 10:3, 30). We know that it was the minimum of religious practices to recite the *Shema,* the creed, twice a day, "Hear, O Israel: The Lord our God, the Lord is one" (Deut. 6:4).

Jewish men also prayed the *Tephilla* [a hymn of benediction].[2]

We also know that the custom of praying three times a day was testified to by Daniel in the Old Testament. Daniel had windows in his upper room which opened in the direction of Jerusalem. He knelt three times a day to pray and praise God (Dan. 6:11).

It wasn't that the disciples did not know how to pray. They were devout Jews. Surely they knew how to pray. They had been praying the required prayers since the age of twelve, their Bar Mitzvah or rite of passage. Of course the disciples knew how to pray, but they wanted something more. They wanted their own special prayer, which would distinguish them as followers of a new way. [3]

Jesus tells His disciples in Matthew 6:6, "when you pray, go into your room, and when you have shut your door, pray to your Father who is in the secret place." We pray "Our Father" in heaven, because "Our Father" is the creator of the entire human race and the heavenly realm.

The book of Genesis teaches us that in the beginning God created the heavens and the earth. Thus in my opinion, we should pray to the one who created all things, who knows all things, who sees all things, who can be in Africa and Alabama at the same time. We should pray to God the Father who has the power of life and death in His hands. We should pray to the one who is gracious, kind, beautiful, merciful, and loving. We should pray to the one who knows what we need even before we ask Him.

When we pray to God the Father, we acknowledge that we are dependent on the Lord. We say to God, and to those who may hear our prayer that God is the source of our supply. We humbly submit ourselves to the sovereignty, rule, and reign of the God who created us in His image and likeness. When we pray to God the Father, we say, "Abba" or "Daddy." We prostrate ourselves before the throne of grace as a child does when she sheepishly comes into the presence of her earthy father and sits at the feet of his easy chair making her requests known unto him. When we pray to God the Father, we come into the presence of the one who loves us, knows us, and has our best interests at heart.

We are no stranger to God the Father, and He is no stranger to us. There is a special familiarity that resonates between father and daughter when the relationship has been nurtured and cultivated in love. If the relationship between father and child has been one of love, kindness and trust, the child is likely to reach out for the father with a positive expectation that her requests will be received, heard, and fulfilled. As a result of having a benevolent father-child relationship, there is no fear when we approach God the Father in prayer. However, if the daughter-father relationship has been wrought with negative experiences and unpleasant memories, then it is very likely the adult-child will enter the prayer room of God the Father with trembling and trepidation. In severe cases of paternal trauma or abuse the child/adult may not enter the prayer room to God the Father at all.

As Christian educators, ministers, seminarians, and lay leaders we need to be aware of the fact that not everyone will choose to pray to "God the Father" for the very reasons that I have cited previously. The word "father" has powerful connotations for some people. People who have suffered the effects of traumatic life events involving their biological fathers may need to be encouraged to pray to "the God who heals us" until such time as they are able to enter into a trusting, loving relationship with God the Father.

Those of us who are called out to shepherd the flock, and/or serve as spiritual leaders over others have an added responsibility to make prayer to God the Father a priority in daily life. The apostles determined that it was necessary for them to devote much of their time to prayer. "Therefore, brethren, seek out from among you seven men of good reputation, full of the Holy Spirit and wisdom, whom we may appoint over this business: but we will give ourselves continually to prayer and the ministry of the word"(Acts 6:3-4).

Prayer is essential to the mainstay and growth of the ministry. Prayer keeps us connected to God the Father. Prayer is a two-way conversation. We speak to God and God listens to us. God speaks to us and we listen to

Him, only if we are still long enough to hear what God has to say to us. The apostles recognized that the early church was growing exponentially and that the widows were being neglected in the distribution of food. Government welfare programs were not an option for the first century church; the followers of Jesus took care of their own. Wisdom dictated that a systematic plan be adopted to administer to the needs of women and children who through no fault of their own had lost their means of support. Thus, the ministry of deacons was birthed to assist the apostles in the distribution of food to the needy. This move of the early Church served to release the apostles so they could spend their time in prayer and ministry of the word.

Acts 6:1-4 challenges contemporary pastors to devote much of their time to prayer and ministry of the word. Too often we get caught up in the activity of pastoral ministry to the neglect of our prayer life. Daily we ought to sit at the feet of God the Father and tell Him all about our troubles. Not only should we tell Him about our troubles, but we should spend time thanking Him for what He has already done in our lives. We should carve out time from our technologically, over stimulated schedules to praise God for saving us. I am encouraged by pastors such as Dr. James Massey, Dr. Brad Braxton, and Dr. Eugene Peterson who said they were able to give God the first two or three hours of their work day for prayer and study of the word so that they could be effective preachers of the gospel. Peterson's book, *The Contemplative Pastor* has been a valuable resource for me over the years by helping me to seek balance in the work that God has called me to do.[4] I frequently encourage my seminary students, tomorrow's pastors, who cross the threshold of my pastoral counseling classes to read *The Contemplative Pastor.*

God the Father wants to hear from us in prayer. I believe He wants us to stretch our hands to Him in humble submission to His authority, rule, reign, and loving kindness. He wants to commune with us as a daddy communes with his devoted child. He wants us to surrender ourselves to His godly judgment and will for our lives. God wants to bless us so that we can be a blessing to others. When we pray, let us pray to "our Father who is in heaven; holy is His name, and may His kingdom come." When we pray to God the Father may we be transcended beyond the reality and connotations of our earthly father to an intimate, eternal relationship with the perfect true and benevolent, almighty God.

Questions for Further Thought or Discussion

1. How does Adam's relationship with the Creator introduce us to prayer?
2. Why did Jesus instruct His disciples to begin prayer with "Our Father" and to present our prayers in Jesus' name?
3. How can this understanding of the Father's role in prayer enrich the prayer life of Christ's followers?

The author: Dr. Patricia A. Outlaw is Associate Professor of Divinity at the Beeson Divinity School of Samford University, located in Birmingham, Alabama. She is also an itinerant elder in the African Methodist Episcopal Church.

SUGGESTED ADDITIONAL READING

Peterson, Eugene. *The Contemplative Pastor: Returning to the Art of Spiritual Direction.* Grand Rapids: Wm B Eerdmans Publishing Company, 1993.

Stewart-Sykes, Alister. *Tertullian, Cyprian, and Origen on the Lord's Prayer.* (Popular Patrisitic Series) Crestwood: St. Vladimir's Seminary Press, 2004.

Washington, James Melvin. *Conversations with God: Two Centuries of Prayers by African Americans.* New York: HarperCollins, 1995.

ENDNOTES

1. Charles Wesley, 1707-1788, The Commission on Worship and Liturgy, Bishop Vinton R. Anderson, Chairman, *The A.M.E.C. Bicentennial Hymnal* (Nashville: The African Methodist Episcopal Church, 1984) p. 317.

2. Jeremias Joachim, *The Prayers of Jesus* (Philadelphia: Fortress Press, 1967) p. 73.

3. Patricia A. Outlaw, *Soul Food for Hungry Hearts* (Baltimore: Gateway Press, 2005) p. 30.

4. Eugene Peterson, *The Contemplative Pastor* (Grand Rapids: Wm B Eerdmans Publishing Company, 1993).

chapter

5

GOD THE SON AND PRAYER

James R. Wicker

Jesus' primary mission on earth was His atoning death and resurrection. However, He also served as the perfect example for all Christians to follow. Being the Son of God, He was the model teacher, the consummate leader, the exemplary servant, and the excellent ethicist. His prayer life—as in all other spiritual disciplines—was perfect. So, a Christian desiring to learn about prayer and how to pray should carefully examine and follow the prayer life of Jesus.[1]

What We Learn from Jesus' Motives to Pray

Jesus is divine, and He was filled with the Holy Spirit throughout His earthly ministry. If anyone ever had an excuse for a lax prayer life, it was Jesus! Yet, Jesus prayed frequently (Lk. 5:16),[2] fervently (22:44), and faithfully (John 17)—even rising early to pray after a long day of teaching and healing (Mk.

1:35). It can be tricky to discern His motives for prayer since we are not told; yet, it does seem possible to ascertain some reasons by examining when He prayed.

First, He did so to regularly communicate with the Father via God's appointed method. He prayed for guidance, help, and strength, but He also prayed to thank and praise the Father. Arguably, Jesus did not need to pray because He is God; yet, He incarnated here to live as the perfect man (albeit the God-man). Jesus played by the rules and restrictions of being human while still being divine; He did not cheat. He did no self-serving miracles; He took no spiritual or physical shortcuts.[3]

Second, Jesus prayed as an example for His followers. Even Judas knew Jesus was a man of prayer as he led the mob to arrest Jesus at Gethsemane (Jn. 18:2), a preferred meeting place for Jesus—probably for prayer.

Third, He prayed for needs in times of crisis. On His way to Gethsemane (John 17), three times at Gethsemane (Mt. 26:36-46), and twice at Golgotha (Lk. 23:34, 46)—His most difficult moments on earth—Jesus prayed. Interestingly, most of His crisis prayers were intercessory rather than self-serving petitions.

Fourth, He prayed for guidance prior to major decisions/events, such as at His baptism (3:21) and choosing the Twelve (6:12).

Fifth, the specific needs of others, such as for unity (John 17) and resistance to temptation (Lk. 22:32), motivated His prayers.

A sixth motive is admittedly speculative: Jesus prayed for power prior to or during His miracles. Interestingly, most Gospel records of Jesus' miracles make no mention of Jesus praying! I count fifty-eight different miracles of Jesus, including groups of His predictions. On only six of these occasions do the Gospels specifically mention Jesus prayed: feeding the 5,000, feeding the 4,000, the Transfiguration, healing the convulsive boy (prayer assumed), raising Lazarus from the dead, and at Jesus' atoning sacrifice. However, I believe He prayed at some point during most—if not all—of the miracles He performed. Why? First, He prayed often (5:16). Second, there are many acts Jesus did that the Gospels do not mention (Jn. 21:25). The Evangelists rarely recorded Jesus' daily activities of eating, bathing, sleeping and praying (all of which observant Jews did)—unless something was unusual. Third, Jesus said that He did nothing unless He saw the Father do it (5:19)—which would include doing miracles, and prayer was the most likely way for Jesus to "see." Fourth, He said He could do nothing on His own initiative (5:30, 8:28, 12:49-50), and prayer was the expected way to ask for permission. Fifth, prayer is the likely means by which Jesus asked the Father for the power to do miracles, which manifested His messiahship from God. Therefore, it makes sense that Jesus prayed each time that He performed these mighty works of God.

So, how do we go and do likewise? We should pray because God wants us to do so, and Jesus Himself demonstrated the daily need for prayer. Our motives should emulate our Master's: for routine daily communication, help in crisis situations, and guidance in decisions. Following Jesus' example, we should exercise much intercessory prayer, and we ought to ask for God's power to be demonstrated in our lives for the benefit of others. In addition to prayer motives, what else can we learn from Jesus' example?

What We Learn from Jesus' Example in Prayer

The following examination is illustrative rather than exhaustive. First, Jesus' prayers were passionate and personal. Notice the extensive use of the first person in John 17, the *real* Lord's Prayer. Also, He frequently used "Father" (Greek *pater*, but possibly the Aramaic *abba*)[4] to refer to God both in His teaching about prayer and in His prayers (in thirteen of thirty-five occasions). Second, Jesus had the right attitude in prayer, which included: obedience, persistence, expectancy, respect, honor, love, thankfulness, and praise. Third, many of Jesus' prayers were intercessory, such as when He blessed the children (Mt. 19:13-15[5] [Mk. 10:13-16; Lk. 18:15-17]). Fourth, He prayed extemporaneously rather than using memorized, liturgical prayers, or simply praying for prayer's sake. Even the Model Prayer (Mt. 6:9-13 [Lk. 11:2-4]) appears to be a pattern to be personalized rather than a mantra to be memorized. Fifth, all of His prayers were need driven and purposeful rather than generalized or full of meaningless repetition (which He criticized, Mt. 6:7). Sixth, He prayed honestly and sincerely. He never tried to impress God or anyone else. Seventh, He sometimes used teaching moments in prayer when others were listening (Jn. 11:41-42, 17:2-3).

Some of Jesus' practice in prayer can be assumed. Likely His public prayers were short, as were the ones recorded in the Gospels (Mt. 11:25-26;

Jn. 11:41-42). Since He taught that most prayer should be private and pointed (Mt. 6:5-6), no doubt He demonstrated that. The John 17 prayer was probably semi-public, with eleven disciples within earshot. His private prayers were probably longer (such as in Mk. 1:25; Lk. 5:16; Mt. 14:23; Mk. 6:46; Lk. 9:18; and possibly Lk. 11:1). Luke 6:12 says He prayed all night prior to choosing the Twelve.

The Gospels share little about Jesus' prayer position, and none of His teachings address it. We can assume it was usually standing since that was the common prayer position for Jews at the time. Jesus made passing references to standing in prayer, indicating its commonality among Jews (Mt. 6:5; Mk. 11:25; Lk. 18:11, 13). Jesus likely stood during His prayer in John 11:41-42. Jesus also prayed while reclining at the table (Lk. 24:30)—a regular position for special meals. At Gethsemane, Jesus knelt and even touched His face to the ground—possibly lying prostrate (Mt. 26:39; Mk. 14:35; Lk. 22:41). Interestingly, although the Gospels say little about Jesus' head position in prayer, they mention He lifted His eyes to heaven in prayer on three occasions: feeding the 5,000 (Mt. 14:19; Mk. 6:41; Lk. 9:16; Jn. 6:5), at Lazarus' tomb (Jn. 11:41), and during His longest recorded prayer (17:1). At no time does the New Testament record Jesus bowing His head during prayer except, of course, while prostrate (Mt. 26:39). However, since the Scriptures rarely relate Jesus' bodily position or head position in prayer—and Jesus followed Jewish convention—it seems Jesus' example allows freedom in these areas.

We can also learn from what Jesus did not do in prayer. His prayers were not formulaic (never once saying "in Jesus' name, amen," nor "bless the gift and the giver"!). We have no record of Jesus falling asleep during prayer or ever neglecting to pray when He should have prayed. Jesus did not use prayer to attempt to flatter, bribe, or trick God. As in His motives to pray, Jesus' example gave a perfect pattern for Christians to follow. Yet, in addition to demonstrating this inspiring example, Jesus also took many opportunities to teach about prayer.

What We Learn from Jesus' Teaching about Prayer

Jesus' teachings on prayer included a variety of settings and methods. One way to group them is as follows: (1) sections in the Sermon on the Mount (Mt. 5:44-48, 6:5-8, 7:7-11), (2) Model Prayer in Galilee (Sermon on the Mount,

Mt. 6:9-13, teaching *how* to pray), (3) Model Prayer in Judea (Lk. 11:1-4, teaching the Twelve privately *to pray*), (4) temple cleansing (Mt. 21:12-13; Mk. 11:15-18; Lk. 19:45-48), (5) parables on prayer (Lk. 11:5-13, 18:1-14; Mt. 21:22; Mk. 11:23-25), and (6) various individual teachings (see below).

It is a helpful exercise to summarize Jesus' major prayer teachings. An exegesis of each of these could easily comprise the length of this article. They include: (1) increase in fasting and prayer when the bridegroom (Jesus) departs (Lk. 5:33-39), (2) pray for those who persecute you (Mt. 5:44; Lk. 6:27-28), (3) pray in secret and avoid meaningless repetition (Mt. 6:5-8), (4) pray in the example of the Model Prayer (Mt. 6:9-13; Lk. 11:1-4), (5) use persistent prayer—God loves to answer prayer (Mt. 7:7-11; Lk. 11:9-13, 11:5-8, 18:1-8), (6) prayer is critical in a difficult exorcism (Mk 9:29), (7) agree with others in prayer (Mt. 18:18-20), (8) be poor in spirit, humble, and honest in prayer (Lk. 18:9-14), (9) let everyone have access to God through prayer in His house (Mt. 21:13; Mk. 11:17; Lk. 19:46), (10) ask believing, and you will receive (Mt. 21:22; Mk. 11:24), (11) forgive others before praying (Mk. 11:25), (12) avoid long, showy prayers (Mt. 23:14; Mk. 12:40; Lk. 20:47), and (13) pray in Jesus' will and abide in Him (Jn. 14:13-14; 15:7). Of course, some of the above passages, such as the Model Prayer, contain far more teachings than space permits to share. All of these lessons are still just as essential and applicable today as they were in Jesus' day.

Jesus' Present Ministry of Intercession

Jesus' role in prayer continues into the present! In Romans 8:34 Paul described Jesus' current ministry of interceding on behalf of believers. Hebrews 7:25 echoes this task in Jesus' role as great high priest, and 9:24 says Jesus entered into God's presence in Heaven on our behalf. First John 2:1 mentions Jesus' continuing role of "Advocate with the Father" on behalf of sinful Christians. It's comforting to know our Intercessor/Advocate understands us—He has experienced the same temptations, trials, and difficulties we do. Jesus' same consuming concern for His followers—as displayed in John 17—still continues today!

Should we pray to Jesus? There is occasional precedent mentioned in the New Testament, such as Acts 1:24-25; 7:59-60; 8:14-24; 2 Corinthians 12:8; and in the early Christian prayer *Maranatha*, "O Lord, come!" (1 Cor. 16:22).

So, certainly it is allowed. However, the majority of Scriptures—including Jesus' prayers and teaching on prayer—address praying to the Father. It seems most of our prayers should be to the Father because: (1) Jesus rarely addressed praying to Himself (Mt. 9:38; Jn. 14:13-14), (2) He is already involved in our prayers as Intercessor, and (3) Jesus prayed *only* to the Father—never to the Holy Spirit, another member of the Trinity.

Jesus' teachings on prayer are not comprehensive, but they are crucial for every Christian. Coupling these teachings with His exemplary example, there is much to add to other Scriptures on prayer to teach and inspire Christians of all ages.

Questions for Further Thought or Discussion

1. Jesus told us to be disciplers (Mt. 20:19). How does your prayer life compare with Jesus' as an example for other Christians?
2. How does knowing about Jesus' role as Intercessor affect your attitude and actions in prayer?
3. Explain how Jesus' prayers and teaching on prayer are different than our typical "grocery list" of petitions for our health and comfort?

The author: Dr. James R. Wicker is Associate Professor of New Testament and Director of Web-based Education at Southwestern Baptist Theological Seminary in Fort Worth, Texas.

SUGGESTED ADDITIONAL READING

Crump, David. *Jesus the Intercessor: Prayer and Christology in Luke-Acts.* Tübingen: J.C.B. Mohr, 1992. Reprint, Grand Rapids: Baker, 1999.

Crump, David. *Knocking on Heaven's Door: A New Testament Theology of Petitionary Prayer.* Grand Rapids: Baker Academic, 2006.

Longenecker, Richard N. ed. *Into God's Presence: Prayer in the New Testament.* Grand Rapids: Wm. B. Eerdmans, 2001.

ENDNOTES

1. This study uses verses that contain the Greek words meaning "pray" and

"prayer" as well as verses with "ask," "request," "beseech," "entreat," "praise," "glorify," and "worship" when prayer is clearly or likely involved.

2. "Often" or "frequently" is understood here. Space does not permit an application of textual criticism to the many texts listed here or a careful exegesis of them; however, the reader is encouraged to apply both disciplines in a fruitful examination of the Scripture.

3. He did walk on water (Mt. 14:24-33)—but that was clearly for teaching purposes.

4. Mark 14:36 is the only place in the Gospels to record Jesus saying "Abba" (see Rom. 8:15; Gal. 4:6).

5. Parallel passages that also mention prayer follow the first canonical reference in brackets. Additionally, Scripture listings follow the suggested chronological order of Robert L. Thomas and Stanley N. Gundry, *A Harmony of the Gospels* (San Francisco: HarperSanFrancisco, 1978).

chapter

6

PRAYING IN THE NAME OF JESUS

Randal Roberts

Many Christians appear to believe that the words, "I (or we) ask this in the name of Jesus," merely represent one of the two concluding components required to make a prayer acceptable to God (the other being the "amen" that immediately follows). Biblical precepts and precedents, however, clearly reveal that praying in the name of Jesus has a much richer significance than is commonly recognized. Apart from recognizing this significance, those words can be attached mindlessly to petitions that blatantly contradict the implications of the phrase; conversely, the spirit of the praying in His name can be fully honored even if the words themselves are absent.

Three passages in the Upper Room or Farewell Discourse found in John's gospel provide both the most explicit linkage and the most helpful insight into the relationship between prayer and the name of Jesus. Our goal will be to probe each of these passages for its contribution to a theology and practice of prayer that is distinctively and authentically Christian. This will be followed by a brief survey of how the concept of prayer in Christ's name appears to be understood and applied in the New Testament epistolary literature.

The first key passage is John 14:12-14. Here Jesus links the "greater works" that His disciples will subsequently perform to prayer offered in His name (v. 12; commentators disagree as to how "greater" should be understood, with the primary options being greater in quantity, in geographical impact, or—based on the parallel in Jn. 5:20—in clarity of revelation due to the progressive unfolding of God's redemptive-historical activities). Of interest is that such prayer here is to be offered to Jesus Himself, and He will be the one who responds to it in supporting those who are continuing His work. The intent behind His response is the glorification of the Father in the Son (v. 13), a reaffirmation of His supreme goal in ministry (cf. 7:18, 12:28, et al.). Lest this amazing and encouraging promise of supernatural empowerment be missed, Jesus immediately repeats it (v. 14). The mention of loving Him (confirmed by obedience to His commandments) in v. 15 suggests yet another important linkage in His thoughts The significance of this connection will be developed below.

The second explicit reference to prayer in the name of Christ is found in 15:16. Jesus reminds the disciples that they did not choose Him (it was customary practice in that era for disciples to choose the rabbi whom they would follow), but instead He chose them. The purpose or intention of this choice was that they would bear lasting fruit (viz., additional converts as a result of their missional activity?). The use of "fruit" continues the vine/branch imagery that begins the chapter. This fruit-bearing is then linked to efficacious prayer offered to the Father in the name of the Son. The nature of this linkage depends upon one's understanding of "so that"; does it suggest answered prayer depends upon faithfulness in fruit-bearing, or is the fruit-bearing itself dependent upon answered prayer? The contextual reference to the disciples' helplessness apart from divine enabling in v. 5 suggests the latter is in view, even if the source of empowerment is there identified as Jesus rather than the Father. Nevertheless, the importance of a maintaining a close relationship with Jesus (here described as "abiding in Him") is once again found in the immediate context of efficacious prayer (vv. 4ff).

The third and final important passage is John 16:23-27. As in the preceding passage, confidence in God's positive response to prayer that is offered in the name of Jesus is again engendered (in fact, some suggest that the most natural translation of v. 23 reveals that the Father's answer comes in Jesus' name; in that case the name influences both petition and response). In this instance, the result is fullness of joy for the disciples. This joy replaces the temporary grief and mourning they will experience at His imminent departure from them (the events associated with that departure include His crucifixion, resurrection and ascension). Additional results include a clearer understanding of God's redemptive plan (v. 25 and the use of two different Greek terms for "ask" in v. 23 suggests that this greater understanding will eliminate the need for persistent questions addressed to Jesus Himself. Those decreasing questions will in turn be replaced by increasing petitions to the Father in Christ's name, a name they will now use with greater frequency and understanding), taking advantage of the direct, privileged and intimate access to the loving Father facilitated by Jesus' sacrifice on their behalf (vv. 26-27). This will be actualized by the promised Holy Spirit, whose pivotal role is described elsewhere in the discourse (especially in 16:4ff).

With these references from John in mind, we can now turn our attention to answering the question, what does it mean to pray in the name of Jesus? Answering that question is helped by recognizing that Scripture describes many other activities beyond prayer that can be done in the name of someone or something. For example, Jesus comes in the name of the Father (5:43) and does works in His name (10:25); Jesus' disciples are those who believe in His name (1:12; 1 Jn. 3:23), are justified in His name (1 Cor. 6:11), and perform miracles in His name (Lk. 10:17); the Holy Spirit is sent by the Father in Jesus' name (Jn. 14:26); baptism is administered in the name of the Triune God (Mt. 28:19); etc.

These linkages all make sense when one understands that "name" in Scripture typically represents something significant about the person or thing bearing it. The identity can be so close that to believe in the name of Jesus is essentially synonymous with believing in Jesus Himself (cf. Jn. 1:12 with Jn. 3:36).

To act in the name of someone or something, therefore, means to do it in association or identification with that person or thing. Extra-biblical usage reflects the same dynamic. For example, if I say to you, "Stop in the name of the law," I am appealing to an understanding of what the law represents (i.e., authority to enforce legal standards of behavior) to secure your compliance.

To pray in the name of someone, therefore, is to pray in association or identification with what that person represents. The context typically suggests the intended point of association. Thus, as we have seen above, to pray in the name of Jesus means to pray in a manner consistent with His values and purposes; these values and purposes are revealed in both His practice of prayer (e.g., John 17) and His precepts concerning it (e.g., Mt. 6:9-14). It is to pray with the glorification of God as the supreme motive; it is to pray as Jesus would pray were He in our circumstances; it is to pray as His followers who have been appointed as instruments of fruit-bearing in the outworking of His mission. As such, it is praying with respectful submission to the will of the Father, seeking that His will be done, not ours. It is learning to ask for the good things that He delights to give from the devoted heart that He delights to bless.

W. Bingham Hunter illustrates this latter dimension by seeking elsewhere in Scripture structural parallels with the promises linked to prayer in Jesus' name. By using the structure of "verb for petition" + "statement of scope" + "name phrase" (e.g., "ask" + "anything" + "in My name"), Hunter demonstrates that the concept of abiding in Christ (and having His words abide in us) in Jn. 15:7 is linked to a prayer promise identical to that associated with praying in Jesus' name. Thus abiding in Christ appears to serve as a functional synonym for "asking in My name." When that "abiding" is in turn linked in 1 John 3:24 to obedience to His commandments, the connection between praying in Jesus' name and living in obedience to Him becomes even more clear.[1]

A similar quest for parallel prayer promises leads to 1 John 5:14-15, where "ask anything according to His will" becomes the necessary condition for confidence in God's positive response (cf. as well the related assurances offered in Mk. 11:24 for faith and in Lk. 11:9-10 for continual asking/seeking/knocking). So praying in the name of Jesus, living a life of obedience, and persistently asking in faith according to the will of God are apparently all descriptions of the same essential prerequisite for effective petitions: being "in synch" with God both in how we live and in what we ask Him to do. Those pre-conditions provide important qualifications to the otherwise seemingly open-ended promises attached to prayer. Failure to recognize these conditions will inevitably lead to disappointment and disillusionment.

How do the other authors of the New Testament help us understand further the proper way to apply Jesus' teaching about prayer in His name? Interestingly, the phrase appears in only one epistolary prayer (Eph. 5:20). This suggests that uttering the words is not necessary to honor the spirit behind the words (akin to how the values of the so-called Lord's Prayer permeate the rest of the New Testament without being repeated verbatim). The aforementioned emphasis upon obedience to God's commands and cooperation with His purposes (sustained by faith manifesting itself through importunity in prayer) similarly permeate the New Testament writings.

New Testament data also suggests that the phrase does not represent (at least not primarily) a reference to the unique access to the Father given to believers because of the imputed righteousness of Jesus. While Jesus' role in providing such access is certainly true (and undergirds the popular notion that Christian prayer is typically offered to the Father through the Son in the power of the Spirit), that particular understanding of "in Jesus' name" is difficult to sustain in light of Jn. 14:13 (noting that requests there are made directly to Jesus, not through Him). That concept is instead seemingly emphasized by the construction "through Jesus" rather than "in Jesus' name" (cf. Rom. 1:8, 7:25, 16:27).

Given some contemporary misunderstandings (which themselves reflect more ancient errors), it should also be noted that the mere invocation of Jesus' name in prayer does not compel a response from God. As Hunter notes , any notion that the phrase has some sort of magical power over God is refuted by the botched exorcism in Acts 19:13ff, the lack of any biblical instance where the Father acts in response to the authority of the Son (the opposite is the biblical pattern), and the irrationality of any premise that Jesus is somehow impressed or influenced by the invocation of His own name (remembering again Jn. 14:13-14).[2] As explained above, any influence with God does not come from the words themselves but from the harmony with His sovereign will that they represent.

Questions for Further Thought or Discussion

1. What would be the impact of more frequently reflecting upon the sig-

nificance of praying in Jesus' name before we pray—and allowing that reflection to shape how we pray—rather than merely tacking on the words to the end of our prayers?

2. As you read through the New Testament, what evidence do you see that suggest Jesus' values and purposes indeed influence the content and form of prayer more than an explicit citation of His name?
3. Do you find any patterns in Old Testament prayers that function similarly to prayer in Jesus' name? What are those patterns and how do they relate?

The author: Dr. Randal Roberts is Academic Dean/Provost and Professor of Spiritual Formation at the Western Seminary in Portland, Oregon. He edited *Lessons in Leadership: Fifty Respected Evangelical Leaders Share Their Wisdom on Ministry.*

SUGGESTED ADDITIONAL READING

Carson, D. A. ed. *Teach Us to Pray: Prayer in the Bible and the World.* Grand Rapids: Baker/Paternoster, 1990.

Crump. David. *Knocking on Heaven's Door: A New Testament Theology of Petitionary Prayer.* Grand Rapids: Baker Academic, 2006.

Hunter, W. Bingham. *The God Who Hears.* Downers Grove, IL: InterVarsity Press, 1986.

Longenecker, Richard N. ed. *Into God's Presence.* Grand Rapids: Wm. B. Eerdmans, 2001.

ENDNOTES

1. See also W. Bingham Hunter, *The God Who Hears* (Downers Grove, IL: InterVarsity Press, 1986) pp. 194ff.

2. Hunter pp. 192-93, 219.

chapter

7

THE GOSPEL OF PRAYER

John W. Taylor

Luke's gospel shows the dynamics of the relationship between God and His world. Particularly prominent in this regard is prayer. Luke mentions prayer more than any other New Testament writer. Luke the historian has a profound sense of God working out His purposes in history through prayer. Luke the evangelist, writing to confirm and strengthen Christians, exhorts and encourages them to pray unceasingly. The narrative starts with prayer at the temple (Lk. 1:10), and finishes with the disciples in the temple praising God (24:53).

Jesus at Prayer

The most obvious expression of this emphasis is Luke's depiction of Jesus at prayer at significant times in His ministry. At the baptism (3:21), before theological conflict (5:16), before choosing the disciples (6:12), before the confession of Peter (9:18), at the transfiguration (9:28-29) and in unique prayers on the cross (23:34, 46) Luke records prayer where Mark has none. Add to these the prayer of surrender at the Mount of Olives (22:42), and it is clear that Jesus in Luke is dependent on the Father, and that the revelation and direction He needs come through prayer. Jesus deliberately and habitually takes time away from the crowds to pray.

The words of five prayers of Jesus are given to us. In each case Jesus calls God "Father." Father was an unusual title for God in Jewish prayers. Jesus' frequent use of it shows the intimacy of His relationship with God, and the Lord's Prayer (11:2-4) shows that He intended similar intimacy for His disciples. Jesus is depicted in thanksgiving at the return of the seventy disciples. His prayer focuses on the revelation they have received (10:21-22). Before His trial Jesus agonizes with the Father and accepts His will (22:42). On the cross Jesus prays forgiveness for His own executioners (23:34), and finally commits His spirit to the Father at death (23:46). Through His prayers, Jesus is shown in dependence on the Father, both at moments of joy and at times of the greatest trial.

Prayer as Divine Encounter

To Luke prayer is the place of revelation. When Zechariah goes into the temple to offer incense, and the people are praying outside, he meets the angel who gives him the news of the impending birth of John (1:8-17). Anna is constantly in prayer in the temple before her revelation about redemption coming through Jesus (2:36-39). Likewise at the baptism and transfiguration, Jesus is praying when the visionary experience begins, and the voice of God comes (3:21, 9:28-29). Jesus prays all night before choosing His disciples (6:12), with the implication that He received guidance from the Father in His choice. Jesus is praying when He asks the disciples who they and the crowds said that He was (9:18-20). Peter confesses that Jesus is the Messiah, and this leads to the first revelation to the disciples of the forthcoming suffering of the Son of Man.

In Luke, the Holy Spirit is given in response to prayer. The Spirit comes on Jesus as He is praying after His baptism (3:21). The same idea appears in 11:13: "If you then, being evil, know how to give good gifts to your children, how much more will your heavenly Father give the Holy Spirit to those who ask Him!" Matthew's parallel has "good things" instead of "the Holy Spirit"

(Mt 7:11). But for Luke the Holy Spirit is the good gift, who is received by prayer (See also Acts 1:14, 2:1-4, 4:31, 8:15-17, 19:6).

The praying of Jesus is frequently followed by remarkable miracles. In Luke 5:16-17 Jesus is withdrawing to pray, and then "the power of the Lord was present to heal them." Jesus prays all night (6:12), and subsequently "power went out from Him and healed them all" (6:19). When Jesus came down from praying on the Mount of Transfiguration He was able to deliver a boy whom His disciples could not help (9:42). Jesus is found praying in 11:1, leading to teaching on prayer. His next action is to drive out a dumb spirit with such powerful results that the crowd was amazed (11:14).

Prayer as Relationship

Luke emphasizes prayer as relational, not merely ritualistic. This does not mean that Jesus frowns on traditional forms of prayer. He approvingly describes participation in the temple prayers (1:9-10, 2:27-32, 41-42; Acts 3:1), though more often prayers take place outdoors. What is important is the relational reality of the prayer. It has to be more than one-sided. Prayer in Luke is communion with God and listening to Him. When Jesus is in prayer, we are not often told what He was saying. The emphasis is on His relationship to the Father, on the real presence of God (3:21-22, 6:12, 9:28-36). This is surely part of the reason for Jesus' cleansing of the temple (19:45-46). Ritual worship was taking place, but the temple was nevertheless not the house of prayer God intended. Jesus criticized those who were self-righteous, like the Pharisee of the parable who prayed "with himself" (18:11). Prayer is not meant to be the public show in which the scribes indulged (20:47), though it is often public.

Luke's version of the Lord's Prayer arises when Jesus is praying and one of the disciples asked Jesus to teach them to pray "as John also taught his disciples" (11:1). Jesus' disciples had been attacked for not observing the prescribed fasts and prayers like John's disciples. But Jesus said that they were free (5:33-39). Thus the Lord's Prayer is formulaic but not ritualistic, part of a relationship, and notable for its brevity. It has two sections, the first focusing God and His kingdom and the second on human needs and relationships. The key pronouns in the Lord's Prayer are plural. Prayer in Luke is certainly a communal activity (1:10), and Jesus expected His disciples to pray in community. But it is also very personal. Luke tells of an incident

(9:18) where Jesus was praying *alone* (Greek: *kata monas*)—even while the disciples were with Him!

Much prayer in Luke is spontaneous praise, a joyful response to the work of God. Mary (1:46-55), Zechariah (1:68-79) and Simeon (2:28-32) all praise God after His revelation to them. The angels and shepherds praise God at the birth of Jesus (2:13-14, 20). Jesus' prayer of rejoicing in 10:21 is "in the Holy Spirit." The miracles of Jesus result in outbursts of praise to God (5:26, 7:16, 13:13, 17:15, 18:43). During the triumphal entry the multitudes of disciples praise Jesus (19:37-40). Even—or especially—the centurion at the cross praises God (23:47), and Luke finishes his first volume with the disciples' blessing God (24:53). And since prayer can be spontaneous praise, and divine encounter, it is not mere formalism.

If prayer is relational it cannot leave the participant untouched. For Luke prayer is the relationship where the human heart is changed. The parable of the tax collector's prayer shows that humility is the right way to approach God (18:13). Jesus commands His disciples to pray for those who harass or mistreat them (6:28). To pray this way requires a soft and responsive heart, and much forgiveness, the kind seen in the Lord's Prayer (11:4) and when the dying Messiah prays for forgiveness for His executioners (23:34). The prayer of Jesus on the Mount of Olives (22:41-42) and His final prayer of commitment on the cross (23:46) illustrate the surrender that Luke expects to happen in prayer to the will of God, though not necessarily without struggle.

However, Luke depicts prayer as more than spiritual exercise. In the plan of God there is a genuine divine response to human prayer. The angel assures Zechariah, "Your prayer is heard" (1:13). Jesus teaches His disciples, "Ask, and it will be given to you" (11:9). The parable of the friend at midnight (11:5-8) specifically encourages *anadeia*, or "shamelessness" in prayer. The argument is *a fortiori*. Like that friend God will answer, but how much more. This does not mean that God is the servant of men and women. There is no sense in Luke of prayer as manipulation, persuading God to do something He does not want to do. Rather, as Jesus said, it is the year of the Lord's favor (4.19). Prayer in Luke is not a magic ritual practiced by repetition of the right formula. It is the expression of dependence upon the mercy of God.

But alongside this confidence is a call for persistence in prayer. Anna prays night and day (2:37). The parable of the unjust judge encourages prayer day and night (18:1-8). The tension between the assurance of God's answer and the need for patience reflects the wider tension in the Gospel between the kingdom of God as present reality, and the kingdom of God as future fulfillment.

Prayer and Perseverance

Luke also emphasizes prayer in order to persevere under trial. A key petition of the Lord's Prayer (11:4), "Do not lead us into temptation" (or "into testing"), is echoed twice when Jesus instructs His disciples to pray that they would not enter into temptation (22:40, 46). He prays for Peter's faith not to fail even through Satan's sifting (22:31-32). In 21:36, after the discourse on the destruction of the temple, Jesus exhorts the disciples to watch, praying that they would "have strength to escape the judgments (*Parousia*) coming on the earth and to stand before the Son of Man." Mark has the more basic "pray that your flight may not be in winter" (Mk. 13:18). There is awareness in Luke that they may not be immediate, and that perseverance will be necessary (Lk. 17:22-23, 21:8-9, 19).

Prayer and the Plan of God

When Jesus is shown praying at key moments it suggests that through prayer the purposes of God in the life and mission of Jesus were brought to pass. The repeated teaching on prayer and the prominent use of Jesus as an example suggest that the same also must apply to the disciples. The implication is that God will continue to work out His salvation-historical purposes through the prayers of the disciples of Christ, empowered by the Spirit. And those plans include (1) the perseverance of the church through difficult times to come (18:1, 21:36), and (2) the mission to the world. Jesus tells the disciples about to go out in mission to pray for more workers in the harvest (10:2), and to pray that the kingdom of God will come (11:2).

Prayer and Vindication

One of Luke's main intentions is vindication: to show that the events of the gospel, the "things which have been fulfilled among us" (1:1), were truly from God. Prayer has an integral role in this narrative. It is not directed to any god but the God of Israel, the Savior (1:47, 68) and Father. Prayer to Him is genuine divine encounter, and relationship, not merely ritual. Through the prayers of Jesus and His disciples the redemptive plan is fulfilled, and this glorifies God. But it also says something about Jesus and His disciples. It demonstrates that Jesus was empowered and led by God Himself—and His disciples will be also. It is this Jesus and these disciples whose prayers have been and will be powerfully answered by God, and thus the mission of the church is vindicated, and shown to be divinely ordained (18:7).

Questions for Further Thought or Discussion.

1. What concept of God is communicated through the prayers in Luke 1-2?
2. How can we ensure that our prayer life is relational, not simply ritualistic?
3. If the purposes of God in the mission of God are fulfilled through prayer, what place should prayer have in the ministry of the church?

The author: Dr. John W. Taylor is Assistant Professor of New Testament at Southwestern Baptist Seminary in Fort Worth, Texas.

SUGGESTED ADDITIONAL READING

Crump, David Michael. "Jesus the Intercessor: Prayer and Christology in Luke-Acts." *Wissenschaftliche Untersuchungen zum Neuen Testament*, 2. Rehe 49. Tübingen: J. C. B. Mohr (Paul Siebeck), 1992.

Han, Kyu Sam. "Theology of Prayer in the Gospel of Luke." *Journal of the Evangelical Theological Society* 43 no. 4 (2000): pp. 675-693.

Harris, Lindell O. "Prayer in the Gospel of Luke." *Southwestern Journal of Theology* 10, no.1 (1967): pp. 59-69.

O'Brien, P. T. "Prayer in Luke-Acts." *Tyndale Bulletin* 24 (1973): pp. 110-127.

Plymale, Steven F. "Luke's Theology of Prayer." *Society of Biblical Literature 1990 Seminar Papers*, ed. David J. Lull, pp. 529-551.

Smalley, Stephen S. "Spirit, Kingdom and Prayer in Luke-Acts." *Novum Testamentum* 15, no. 1 (1973): pp. 59-71.

Trites, Allison A. "The Prayer Motif in Luke-Acts." In *Perspectives on Luke-Acts*, Charles H. Talbert, ed. pp. 168-186. *Perspectives in Religious Studies* 5. Edinburgh: T&T Clark, 1978.

chapter

8

GOD THE SPIRIT AND PRAYER

James L. Wakefield

"God is love, and he who abides in love abides in God, and God in him."[1] These few words are the key to understanding "God the Spirit and Prayer." Four simple questions have much to teach us: What is love? How is God love? What does it mean for God to live in us? What does it mean for us to live in God?

What is love?

John's definition of love is grounded in the life and mission of Jesus: "This is how we know what love is: Jesus Christ laid down his life for us. And we ought to lay down our lives for one another" (1 Jn. 3:16, echoing Jn. 15:13). God's kind of love is always self-giving, a going forth or going out of oneself on behalf of another. This understanding of love invites us to consider God as self-giving love.

How is God love?

We pray "Our Father" and we pray to the "Father of our Lord Jesus Christ."[2] One cannot be a father without a child—in this case a Son. Calling God *Father* names God within an enduring relationship of love. We know the Father most directly through the only begotten Son[3] and much of Jesus' life is framed in the language of their relationship.[4] This is no mere academic curiosity for us, because Jesus tells us He has loved us with the Father's love, and the Father loves us as He has loved Jesus (Jn. 14:23, 15:9, 17:23). What then does it mean to say that God as Trinity is self-giving love?

When we read "God is love" as descriptive of Trinitarian relationships, we affirm the following: God as Father gives all He is to the Son. Receiving Himself through the self-donation of the Father, the Son gives all He is in loving response to the Father. The same can be said of Father in regard to the Holy Spirit. The Spirit responds and gives all He is to the Father. In fullness of relationship with the Father, the Spirit and the Son give all they are to one another. God as self-giving love characterizes the oneness of the three persons, who receive themselves as persons-in-relation with each other.[5] The Greek word *perichoresis* has been used since the twelfth century to describe this logic of love—the "round-dance" of self-donation within the Trinity.[6]

The energy of the dance is centrifugal and the world is created, not by necessity, but from the abundance of God's love.[7] God's mission is to create and love the world. Foreseeing humanity's rebellion and sin, God plans for the Son to incarnate the mission and give His life to and for the world (Mk. 10:45; Jn. 10:11-17; Rom. 5:8, 8:32; Gal. 1:4). The Spirit participates in the mission of the Son from the beginning and gives Himself in His own mission as He glorifies the Son (Lk. 1:35; Jn. 16:12-15).

A second movement of energy within the dance is centripetal, for triune persons give themselves in love to be loved. They intend to reconcile all things to themselves (Jn. 12:32; Rom. 8:18-21; 1 Cor. 15:28; 2 Cor. 5:18-21). It is the mission of God the Spirit to begin working this out in this present age (Jn. 16:8-11; Phil. 2:12-13). Much of His work is done in and through us.

What does it mean for God to live in us?

Human beings are created in the image of God as Trinity—God-in-community on a mission.[8] We receive ourselves—we learn our identity—as persons-in-community on a mission.[9] We learn we are loved by God from other believers and from God. We receive the glad command to love God—to respond to God with all we have and all we are—as we grow in community. We image God as Trinity and Jesus as our servant-Lord as we give ourselves to and for others—we love our neighbors as ourselves. Christ is formed in us as the Spirit incarnates the logic and grammar of love within us (Gal. 4:19).

John's Gospel teaches us much about the Spirit and about the logic of love: We must be born of water and the unpredictable Spirit of God (1:33, 3:5-8). God seeks us to worship Him as the Spirit gives us life and teaches us the truth (4:23-24, 6:63, 14:26, 15:26, 16:13-15, 17:3). Like a stream of living water within us (3:34, 4:13-14, 7:37-40, 14:17), the Spirit empowers us to give our lives in worship of God (6:29, 12:25, 13:14-17, 34-35, 14:15, 23-24, 15:9-13, 17, 20:31, 21:15-19). The Spirit convicts the world (and us) of sin, of the need for right relationships, and of judgment (16:8-11). The Spirit models self-giving love as He speaks of Jesus and not of Himself (16:13-15). Our first act after receiving the Spirit is to practice self-giving love by forgiving sin.[10] Our joyful obedience in the midst of tribulation (5:24, 14:21-24, 15:5-14, 17:13, 20-26, 21:15-19) testifies that the present evil age is passing away (1:1-5, 3:16-21, 12:31, 16:11, 16:33, 17:15, 18:36-37). The Spirit incarnates the deep logic and grammar of self-giving love in us, and this prepares us to live in God.

What does it mean for us to live in God?

Prayer is the language of love.[11] The Holy Spirit energizes the logic and grammar of self-giving love within us and brings us profound assurance of new life as we utter our most basic and most intimate prayer, "Abba, Father" (Rom. 8:15; Gal 4:6). Romans 8 has much to teach us about life in Christ and praying in the Spirit.

Applying our Lord's sacrifice to us, the Spirit makes us alive and gives us the ability to live new lives in and with Christ (Rom. 8:1-11). The Spirit leads us to deny the deeds of our sinful nature (vv. 12-13) and testifies to us that we are the children of God (vv. 14-16). As co-heirs with Christ we share His suffering in order that we might share in our Lord's glory (vv. 17-18). All creation—and we are part of creation!—groans and travails together (19). This is according to God's will (v. 20), and will be so until the revelation of the children of God (v. 21). As part of creation, we also groan, awaiting the redemption of our bodies (vv. 22-23). Here we live by faith and not by sight (vv. 24-25). The Spirit groans with us and intercedes for us according to God's will (vv. 26-27). Jesus joins the Spirit in this prayer (v. 34) and this allows us to agree with Paul: "we know that in all things God works for the good of those who love Him, who have been called according to His purpose" (v. 28). As we share Jesus' suffering (v. 17), we are conformed to the likeness (vv. 29-30) of the one who was given for us (v. 32). In all of this, nothing can separate us from the love of God (vv. 37-39).

Having poured the self-giving love of God into our hearts (5:5), and having assured us of our Abba's providential love for us, the Spirit now energizes us to live out this sacrificial love in a needy and broken world. God the Spirit transforms our minds and we learn to seek God's "good, pleasing and perfect will" on behalf of all creation (12:1-2).[12] *Praying in the Spirit is the verbal expression of this life of sacrificial love.* Our first word in prayer—Abba!—grows and reaches to bring all things into an experience of our Father's love. Eugene Peterson puts it crisply: "Prayer, as the Spirit prays within us, recovers our original place in creation, making us capable of ambition-free work in the world (8:19-26). It involves us in the grand reconciliation going on in Christ setting us free for relational intimacies with family and friends (Col. 1:15-23)."[13]

How do we pray in the Spirit? Some Christians believe that "praying in the Spirit" is praying in a private prayer language. How are we to evaluate this claim? In 1 Corinthians 14, Paul is discussing praying and worshipping in the assembly. Paul would like all to speak in tongues (v. 5) and even tells us he prays in tongues more than anyone (v. 18). But in the church, he would rather speak only five words to instruct others than ten thousand words in a tongue (v. 19). The benefits of speaking or praying in a private prayer language mentioned in I Corinthians 14 include speaking to God (v.2), edifying oneself (v. 4), praying with one's spirit (v. 14), singing with one's spirit (v. 15), and praising and thanking God with one's spirit (vv. 16-17). These are substantial benefits for the pray-er. I am glad to testify that when I simply don't know what to pray, praying in prayer language is an act of humility and a great comfort to me. I heartily agree this is one of the ways we pray in the Spirit. But when we follow the Trinitarian logic of self-giving love, we must admit praying in a private prayer language cannot be the whole story.

Ephesians 5:18-20 instructs us to "be continually filled with the Spirit" and then describes some of *how* a Spirit-filled life looks. Paul's brief teaching on spiritual warfare (6:10-18) reaches back to this and concludes with this command in verse 18: "praying always with all prayer and supplication in the Spirit . . . with all perseverance and supplication." Even our warfare prayer is characterized by thanks and praise, because we know Jesus and the Spirit are praying with us, and the mighty power of God will be victorious! When Paul writes "with all prayer and supplication" he shows there is more than just one way to pray in the Spirit. The last part of verse 18 encourages us to expand our vision: "with all perseverance . . . for all the saints."

How do we do this? Paul's earlier prayers model some of how we should be praying "in the Spirit" and "for all the saints." The centerpiece here is once again the profound knowledge and revelation of the self-giving love of Christ (3:14-21). This is the work of the Spirit of wisdom (1:17) that helps us live a life worthy of our calling (4:1-2), and of which the tightest summary is found in Ephesians 5:1-2: "Be imitators of God as dear children, and walk in love, as Christ also has loved us and given Himself for us, an offering and a sacrifice to God for a sweet-smelling aroma." As one of the saints, Paul was not seeking freedom from his chains (6:19-20). He wants to preach the gospel without fear. Like Paul, we pray in the Spirit for what is most important to us. Paul prayed what he lived. And he lived what he prayed.

Paul's many exhortations to prayer and the many prayers in his letters serve as checkpoints for our prayers "in the Spirit." Do our prayers show we too are being transformed by God's self-giving love? Who do our prayers serve? The kingdom of God? Our neighbors and enemies? Or ourselves only? It is certainly not wrong to edify ourselves or to build ourselves up in holy faith (Jude 20). Prayers for our own growth and transformation are part of loving God—Father, Son, and Holy Spirit—with all that we have and all that we are. As we learn to pray with and in the Spirit, we learn to imitate the triune God in self-giving love in our needy and broken world. We pray for God's will—reconciliation—to be accomplished in all creation.[14] Dare we, like Paul and the early church, become what we pray?[15] Revelation 22:17 is one of the last words on prayer in the Bible and it encourages us in our prayers: "The Spirit and the bride say, 'Come!'" We are eager to see Jesus.

We want our thirsty world to flow with real life and join our prayer: "Come, Lord Jesus!

Questions for Further Thought or Discussion

1. Meditate on Galatians 5:25. How do our prayers show we are being transformed by God's self-giving love?
2. If we are obedient to Jesus, and seek the kingdom of God as our first priority (Mt. 6:33), who do our prayers serve?
3. In Revelation 22:17, who are the Spirit and the bride addressing? Why is it important for us to identify this audience?

The author: Dr. James L. Wakefield is Associate Professor of Biblical and Spiritual Theology at Salt Lake Theological Seminary. He is the author of *Jürgen Moltmann: A Research Bibliography*, and *Sacred Listening: Discovering the Spiritual Exercises of Ignatius Loyola*.

SUGGESTED ADDITIONAL READING

Hartley, Fred A. III. *Prayer on Fire: What Happens When the Holy Spirit Ignites Your Prayers.* Colorado Springs, CO: *Pray!* Books, 2006.

Torrey, R.A. *The Presence and Work of the Holy Spirit.* New Kensington, PA: Whitaker House Publishers, 2003.

Goldsworthy, Graeme. *Prayer and the Knowledge of God: What the Whole Bible Teaches.* Downers Grove, IL: InterVarsity Press, 2004.

Peterson, Eugene. *The Jesus Way.* Grand Rapids: Eerdmans, 2007.

ENDNOTES

1. 1 Jn. 4:16 (TNIV). My approach here is grounded in Wolfhart Pannenberg's profound observation: "It is right, then, that the doctrine of God should precede that of prayer and that we should deal with prayer in the context of pneumatology, for the Spirit alone enables us to pray and gives us strength to do so." See his *Systematic Theology*, III (Grand Rapids: Eerdmans, 1998), pp. 202-203.

2. Mt. 6:9; and then Rom. 15:16; 2 Cor. 1:3; Eph. 1:3; Col 1:3; 1 Pet. 1:3.

3. Mt. 11:27; Jn. 1:18, 3:26, 35, 5:19-23, 10:36-38, 12:44-50, 14:6-14, 15:9-17, 16:25-28, 17:1-5.

4. Lk. 2:49; 23:34, 46; Mk. 1:11, 14:36; Jn. 1:32. 20:17; Mt. 16:17, 17:5 and Acts 2:33.

5. Mentors behind this sketch of Trinitarian persons-in-relation, but not behind its faults, include Jürgen Moltmann, Wolfhart Pannenberg, Stanley Grenz, Colin Gunton, Paul Fiddes, Miroslav Volf, John Zizioulas, Eugene Peterson, and many others.

6. See Paul S. Fiddes's fine discussion in *Participating in God* (Louisville: Westminster John Knox, 2000), pp. 71-81.

7. One can begin to understand the *ekstasis* and corresponding *kenosis* of Father, Son, and Spirit within and for creation with Jürgen Moltmann, *God in Creation* (San Francisco: Harper & Row, 1985), pp. 94-103; and Eugene Peterson, *Christ Plays in Ten Thousand Places* (Grand Rapids: Erdmanns, 2005), pp. 21-23, 44-47, 300-309.

8. This dense phrase reminds us good theology is always Trinitarian and always eschatological. The structure of these two sentences recognizes that "Theology and anthropology are involved in a reciprocal relationship." See Jürgen Moltmann, *The Crucified God* (New York: Harper & Row, 1974), p. 267.

9. Jürgen Moltmann, *Theology of Hope* (New York: Harper & Row, 1967), pp. 56, 63, 285-287, 327-329, 338.

10. Jn. 20:22-23. When we pray "forgive us our sins, as we forgive those who sin against us" we dare not bind anyone in their sin.

11. This phrasing owes much to Eugene Peterson's *Christ Plays in Ten Thousand Places*, pp. 272-281.

12. For this reading of verse 2, see Grant R. Osborne, *Romans* (Downers Grove: InterVarsity, 2004), pp. 322-323.

13. Eugene Peterson, *The Jesus Way* (Grand Rapids: Eerdmans, 2007), p. 217.

14. Mt. 6:10; Rom. 1:10, 15:30-32; 2 Cor. 1:10-11, 5:16-21, 13:7-9; Phil. 1:9-10; Col. 1:9, 4:12; 2 Thess. 1:11-12; 1 Tim. 2:1-7.

15. For more on this, see Eugene Peterson's meditation on Acts 4:24-30 in *The Jesus Way*, pp. 264-271.

chapter

9

PRAYER AND THE ACCOMPANIMENT OF ANGELS

David A. Shive

Prayer and angels. Stumbling across the topic of angels in a book devoted to prayer, a reader might have pause for some concern as to where things are headed. Are these two topics actually related? Are angels and prayer significantly related in Scripture to merit a full chapter? What are the implications for both the Church and angels if each is allied with the other by prayer?

Answers to these questions may offer us a clearer understanding of these dual themes. Greater clarity of thinking on the themes of prayer and angels may be what is needed to stoke the flames of the Church's prayer life so that prayer may achieve God's objective.

Let's consider three biblical concepts.

First, the church has an audience of angels and they are active among us.

Paul suggests to Timothy that angelic spectators are somehow watching the church: "I charge you before God and the Lord Jesus Christ and the elect angels" (1 Tim. 5:21). Picture Paul as he writes. He pauses and contemplates angels peering curiously over his shoulder. These creatures are inquisitive about the nature of his musings and are eager to discover the implications of his writings for their own mission.

That angels gain insight from the Church is seen in Eph. 3:10: "the manifold wisdom of God might be made known by the Church to the principalities and powers in the heavenly *places*."[1] This verse makes little sense if angels do not learn by watching the Church. God has chosen the Church as His vehicle to demonstrate the rich complexity of His wisdom to His heavenly host. If believers are to impact angelic understanding of God, the host of heaven must observe the Church. We would do well to envision a mood of expectant excitement among the heavenly host as these creatures have occasion to discover more about God by observing us.

Paul also indicates that angels witnessed his afflictions which he endured for the sake of the gospel: "God has displayed us, the apostles, last, as men condemned to death: for we have been made a spectacle to the world, both to angels and to men" (1 Cor. 4:9). Could the witnessing of suffering for the cause of Christ be a facet of angelic "education"?

Angels do not merely watch believers, however. The Scriptures open a tantalizing window into the attendance of angels by declaring that they are "in our midst" as we go about the business of being Jesus' Church. Hebrews 13:2 warns us: "Do not forget to entertain strangers, for by so doing some have unwittingly entertained angels." This instruction is intended to instill in believers the anticipation that angels might actually show up.

Thus, believers' awareness that God watches His Church should be augmented by the idea that angels also gain admission to the cosmic theater to watch the church "on stage." Since God intends that angels profit from glimpsing the Church's conduct, the congregation should gather with a keen awareness that "we are not alone."

To this is added the testimony of the much-discussed 1 Corinthians 11:1-16, where one conclusion is unambiguous: "the woman ought to have a symbol[2] of authority on her head, because of the angels" (11:10). Regardless of one's view of the veil in this passage, Church practice should be nuanced by alertness to the presence of angels. Invoking the specter of angels hovering over the assembly and watching the women as they pray and prophesy,[3] this verse indicates that these divine messengers are spectators of church life, aware of and affected by the congregation's worship.

This raises a fresh line of inquiry for if, when believers violate God's order in the assembly, angels are present, aware, and potentially influenced by our disobedience, how do angels respond? What consequences might occur? We will return to this question below.

Second, angels deliver answers to prayer though confronted with demonic obstacles. While we have biblical evidence as to God's utilization of angels on our behalf,[4] the narrative of Daniel 10 goes further to divulge that angels are employed by God to deliver answers to prayer (10:10-12). To accomplish their mission, these messengers must overcome hindrances posed by Satan and his minions (i.e., fallen angels; 10:13). This is the essence of spiritual warfare—the advance of the kingdom of God through the prayers of God's people. Satan's intention that *his* kingdom advance requires his aggressive resistance to the prayer-induced progress of God's work. The reports of prayer warriors of increasing life difficulties as they give themselves to serious prayer would suggest that the principal agenda item on Satan's daily planner is his continuous crusade to thwart answers to prayer. After all, if prayer answers are blockaded, God's kingdom does not advance.

The narrative of Daniel 10 need not be viewed as an isolated teaching on the topic of angels and answered prayer. Examples occur often in the Bible:

- As people prayed, an angel came to Zacharias (Lk. 1:11) to inform him that his prayer has been answered.
- Jesus was met by an angel as He agonized in prayer (22:43).
- The angel's appearance in Acts 5:19 to release the apostles from prison to preach the gospel is clearly an answer to the church's prayer of Acts 4:24-30.
- Cornelius was visited by an angel in response to his prayers and alms (Acts 10:4).
- The church's prayers for Peter in Act 12:5 are answered by an angel who sends Peter to the same prayer meeting to report his release.

Might the excitement of bearing answers to human petitions be the most highly coveted of all angelic assignments?

The idea that angels deliver answers to prayer is certainly in keeping with God's preferred method for running His universe. His predilection is to delegate His work to His agents (the church and angels). Prayer is the instrument that God has selected to empower His church to participate in the execution of His mission. As his people approach Him with requests for the needed resources for the campaign, angels are dispatched to deliver His responses (i.e., resources for the battle). Simultaneously, fallen angels stand in God's presence (Job 1:6; 2:1; 1 K. 22:19-22), looking for opportunity to obstruct those responses. Given the importance of prayer throughout Scripture, angelic answering of prayer has phenomenal implications for our ability to be engaged in achieving God's objectives.

Third, wrongdoing among believers may hinder angels in completing their mission of delivering answers to prayer. We return to the question raised above: How might angels be influenced by disobedience in the assembly? One answer to this question is found in an unlikely place, 1 Peter 3:7. Peter's advice to husbands establishes the fact that one's behavior can impact the delivery of answers to prayer. Here Peter indicates that husbands who treat their wives in an honorable way will experience an encouraging result: ". . . your prayers may not be hindered."

The similarity of the contexts of 1 Peter 3:7 and 1 Corinthians 11:10[5] is a salient aspect of this discussion. Both passages are gender-oriented, dealing with the differing roles of men and women in church and family life. In the first (1 Cor. 11:10), the concern is with how <u>women</u> should behave because of "angelic surveillance" of the assembly. In the second (1 Pet. 3:7), the concern is with how <u>men</u> should behave toward their wives. These husbands have the hope extended to them that, should they honor their spouses, answers to their prayers could be speeded on their way in the spirit realm as God's messengers battle to complete their assignment.

Summary observations. Three ideas have been generated: (1) angels are actively present as they observe the church; (2) angelic delivery of answers to prayer happens in the face of Satanic opposition; and (3) angels may be hindered in their mission of answering prayer if they observe disorder among believers.

How might these thoughts shape the thinking of the church in prayer?

First, believers should envision themselves in a reciprocal relationship with angels. God has designed prayer to work in harmony with the ministry of His angels. This is a team effort calculated to facilitate the completion of God's program.

Second, the church should be aware of how our actions might influence the host of heaven. First, there is the positive influence. When godly people live in prayerful obedience, angels are dispatched to convey the answers to our prayers and so advance God's mission. By being conscious of our conduct, we can facilitate the angels in their task.

The negative influence is the reverse of the first. Our bad behavior may erect obstacles to the timely arrival of answers to prayer. In other words, answers to prayer are not assured simply because we pray.

Understanding 1 Corinthians 11:10 and 1 Peter 3:7 can assist believers in grasping how sin impinges on prayer's effectiveness. Since both contexts are dealing with the conduct of men and women, is it possible that the Scriptures are emphasizing gender behavior in home and church so that angels may proceed unfettered in the execution of their duties? Are humans as male and female an enticing spiritual battlefield for the forces of darkness? Could the Church's failure to follow God's simple injunctions about proper gender activities fuel the flames of spiritual warfare, unleashing additional Satanic subordinates to contest the timely delivery of answers to prayer?

Third, the importance of persistence in prayer is highlighted. The message of Daniel 10 seems to be that, when we persist, additional angelic reinforcements are dispatched to ensure the arrival of the answer. Daniel prayed for three weeks, the precise time it took for the angel to deliver the answer. Does Daniel 10 suggest that failure to persevere in prayer may swing the tide of spiritual warfare in favor of the forces of darkness seeking to impede answers to prayer? Perhaps this is the intent behind the frequent admonitions of God's Word to "pray without ceasing."[6]

Fourth, these concepts should compel the church to seriously deal with sin in the congregation. If angels are assisted by our godly behavior and negatively impacted by our disobedience, our passion for God's mission and the need for answered prayer should motivate believers to live obedient lives.

Conclusion. Thus, it appears that the twin topics of prayer and angels are inextricably connected. Prayer is essential to the execution of God's great mission. Angels are required if prayer is to be effective.

The Church relies on the host of heaven to bring God's answers to prayer as angels travel from the throne of God and battle the forces of darkness to fulfill their mission. These messengers (good and evil) serve the Lord by undertaking the assignments given to them. God's angels will intensify their attempts to bring answers to prayer as the Church lives in obedience while Satan's minions ratchet up the force of their resistance when the Church is weakened by disobedience.

As the Church of Jesus Christ, we must consider the implications of our conduct in relation to answered prayer, for the ones who deliver the answers to our prayers are among us, are watching us, and are helped or hindered in their mission by our conduct.

Questions for Further Thought or Discussion

1. Did the linkage between prayer and angels surprise you? If yes, what about it was surprising? Is this possibly a neglected topic in the Church? If yes, why do you think it has been neglected?
2. Can you clearly articulate a biblical connection between the behavior of believers and our expectation that our prayers will be answered?
3. If the assertions in this chapter are true, what implications do you see? How must your personal prayer life be changed? How could this impact church life?

The author: Rev. David A. Shive is Associate Professor of Bible and Theology at the Washington Bible College, located in Lanham, Maryland. He is the author of *Night Shift,* a look at how God uses suffering to make us more useful for the kingdom.

SUGGESTED ADDITIONAL READING

Graham, Billy. *Angels: God's Secret Agents*. Nashville: Thomas Nelson, 2000.

Jeremiah, David. *What the Bible Says About Angels*. Portland: Multnomah, 1998.

Lockyer, Herbert. *All the Angels of the Bible.* Peabody, MA: Hendrickson, 1995.

ENDNOTES

1. In Paul's vocabulary, the terms "rulers and authorities" refer to angelic beings. See also Eph. 1:21.

2. The word "symbol" does not appear in the Greek.

3. Unsaid but safely assumed in 1 Cor. 11:1-16 is the idea that the men are also being observed in worship. The purpose of this passage is not to imply that there are no problems with the men in the assembly, but rather to address a specific problem connected to the women in worship at Corinth.

4. For example, Ps. 91:11, 103:20-21, 104:4; Heb. 1:14.

5. First Corinthians 11:10 was previously introduced to demonstrate that angels are actively present in the assembly.

6. For example, Lk. 18:1ff.; Eph. 6:18; Col. 1:3, 4:2; 1 Thess. 5:17.

chapter

10

THE LORD'S PRAYER

Thomas L. Constable

Jesus taught His disciples the Lord's Prayer—popularly so-called because He gave it to others, not because He prayed it Himself, which He did not—on at least two separate occasions. This seems clear from the contexts in which the teachings appear in the Gospels. The earlier occasion is Jesus' Sermon on the Mount, which He delivered during His major Galilean ministry (Mt. 6:9-15), and the later occasion occurred during His later Judean ministry (Lk. 11:1-4). The repetition of this teaching shows its importance.

While there are many similarities between these two teachings, the differences bear noting. In the Matthew passage, Jesus initiated the instruction in a context of correcting erroneous ideas about praying that were common among His hearers. In the Luke passage, He taught His disciples the prayer in response to their request to teach them to pray. In the Matthew passage, the prayer follows introductory instruction warning against hypocritical praying, with implications concerning the character of God (Mt. 6:5-8). But in the Luke passage, it introduces teaching on prayer that encourages praying, with clarification of the character of God (Lk. 11:5-13). In the Matthew passage, Jesus introduced the prayer as a model prayer, namely, one that reveals subjects about which one should typically pray. He said, "Pray in this way." In the Luke passage, He introduced it as a prayer to be repeated verbatim, a ritual prayer. He said, "When you pray, say."

Since the Matthew passage is the longer of the two, I shall expound it first and then conclude with an additional comment about the Luke passage.

Perhaps the most revolutionary and shocking thing that Jesus taught in the Lord's Prayer is that when His disciples prayed to God they should think of and address Him as their Father. Nowhere in the Old Testament did the prophets instruct the people of God to think of Him in such a familiar way. They did refer to Him as the father of the nation of Israel as a whole, but never as the father of the individual believer. Jesus' statement must have drawn a gasp from His hearers. Was not this sacrilegious? The Jews, after all, did not even *speak* the covenant name of God to avoid becoming overly familiar with the Holy One of Israel. Yet Jesus balanced the familiar concept of God as our Father with the reminder that He is in heaven. He is a heavenly Father, over all, and so deserving of respect more than any earthly father. And in ancient Near Eastern culture, even earthly fathers traditionally received great respect. Qohelet taught his readers to remember that "God is in heaven, and you on earth; therefore let your words be few" (Eccl. 5:2). Because God is the Holy Sovereign, we need to approach Him with due respect, but because He is also the heavenly Father of believers in Jesus we may also pray to Him confident of His loving acceptance and concern.

I have talked to some people who say they don't like to think of God as their Father because they have such horrible memories of their earthly father. Even though one's earthly father may have been abusive or worse, everyone knows how a father should behave. He should provide for, protect, nurture, guide, defend, and encourage his children. And this is how our heavenly Father behaves toward those who are His children by faith in Jesus Christ. So, Jesus taught, as we approach God in prayer, it will be particularly helpful for us to think of God as our heavenly Father, even more than as the Creator, Sustainer, or even Redeemer, though we have examples of people addressing God in all these ways in the Bible as well. Normally we should pray to the Father through the Son with the help of the Spirit (Jn. 14:13-14, 16), though there may be examples of people praying to the Holy Spirit in the New Testament too.

Jesus taught His disciples to pray for seven types of things. The first three, by their priority, all deal with what is most important: our Father's concerns. The last four deal with His children's cares.

"Hallowed be Your name" (Mt. 6:9) expresses a desire that the name (reputation) of our Father be regarded as holy. Holy means different (from us) in the sense of absolutely perfect in every way. As disciples of Christ, our primary concern should be that other people perceive God for who He really is. Much of the error and resultant heartache in the world trace back to a warped concept of God. Praying for the honor of His name will also encourage us to represent Him well in the world.

"Your kingdom come" (6:10) is a petition for the coming rule of God over all of humankind. God is sovereign over all now, but when Jesus Christ returns to the earth to reign, righteousness will prevail from shore to shore, men will study war no more, and the deserts will blossom like roses. We should pray for the coming of that kingdom, even as the Apostle John did at the end of the book of Revelation (Rev. 22:20).

"Your will be done on earth as it is in heaven" (Mt. 6:10) voices our desire for God's will to prevail on earth, even now, as it does in the heavenly realm presently. Really the whole purpose of prayer is not to get our will done but to get God's will done. Too often we pray, in effect, "*My* will be done on earth." Praying as Jesus taught us expresses our submission to the divine will and our desire to see it accomplished worldwide now. Again, praying this way should affect how we live. Jesus' prayer in the garden of Gethsemane is a perfect example of expressing a personal desire but making it secondary to God's will (Lk. 22:42).

So the first three petitions in the Lord's Prayer deal with God's reputation, His rule, and His will. The second set of petitions focuses on our needs.

"Give us this day our daily bread" (Mt. 6:11) is a request for God to provide our needs day by day, one day at a time. "Bread" here represents the basic necessities of life. We still often refer to bread as the staff of life. Jesus promised that if we put God's kingdom and righteousness first He will take care of our needs (6:33). Yet by asking Him regularly for what we need it's easier for us to connect the Provider with the provision and to honor Him when He meets our needs. And James reminds us that we have not because we ask not (Jas. 4:2), though we must watch out for unworthy motives (4:3).

"Forgive us our debts (or trespasses, according to some versions, or sins, in Lk. 11:4)" (Mt. 6:12) acknowledges our need for family forgiveness when we have offended our heavenly Father by failing to give what we owe (a debt) or by overstepping His boundary (a trespass). Both of these errors constitute sin. My friend Ted's mother refuses to pray the Lord's Prayer because she believes she's never sinned. She has redefined sin as gross sin. But does not the Bible teach that God forgives the sins of all who trust in His Son for salvation (Jn. 3:16-18; Rom. 8:1; Col. 2:13-14)? Why then do we need to confess our sins as His children? God does indeed forgive the guilt of our sins when we trust in Christ. He will never condemn us for them because Jesus Christ paid the penalty for them by dying in our place (2 Cor. 5:21; 2 Pet. 2:24). However, as members of His family we still need cleansing from the daily defilement of sin since we commit sins every day (Jn. 13:10; 1 Jn. 1:9). Similarly, when parents adopt a child into their family the child becomes a member of the family forever, but when he disobeys his parents he has to apologize before relationships within the family can be restored. Verses 14 and 15 of our passage, as well as the last part of verse 12, emphasize further that our relationships with one another, horizontally, need to be correct before our relationship with God, vertically, can be.

An acquaintance of mine had a disagreement with his daughter that led him to break off all contact with her. This man's wife reminded him that he couldn't expect God to forgive his sins if wouldn't forgive his daughter. He said he never realized that. So he asked God for the opportunity to make contact with his daughter, who lived on her own, so he could try to straighten things out between them. Shortly thereafter he was driving and saw a young woman whose car had broken down. He stopped to help her only to find out it was his own daughter. This "chance" meeting gave him the opportunity to forgive her and to renew their relationship.

"And do not lead us into temptation" (Mt. 6:13) also raises a question. Does not James say that God tempts no one (Jas. 1:13)? If He tempts no one, why should we ask Him not to lead us into temptation? The expression Jesus used here is a figure of speech called litotes, which expresses a positive idea by stating the negative alternative. For example, sometimes we say, "That's no big deal." What we really mean is that it's a very small matter. When Jesus said, "Do not lead us into temptation," He meant, "Keep us from temptation." God tempts no one in that He never seduces people to sin, but He allows Satan, the world, and the flesh to tempt us (Job 1:12, 2:6; 1 Jn. 2:15-16; Rom. 7:5). By praying this petition we ask God to keep temptation from us and to keep us from falling before it.

The final, seventh, petition, "But deliver us from the evil one" (Mt. 6:13) is the positive statement of the previous request. Since certain forms of temptation will plague us throughout this life, though the forms vary from person to person, we need to pray repeatedly for deliverance. Perhaps that's why Jesus taught us to pray twice for protection from evil.

The ending of the prayer, "For yours is the kingdom and the power and the glory forever. Amen" (6:13), is absent in the earliest manuscript copies of Matthew that we have. It was probably added after Jesus' initial teaching, under divine inspiration, I believe, because it became a customary liturgical ending to the prayer. It certainly is an appropriate way to finish it off.

In summary, Jesus taught His disciples to pray first for the honor of the person and the culmination of the program of God. Next we should petition Him for our provisions, our pardon, and our protection. In Luke's version of the prayer, he omitted the third and seventh petitions, leaving a total of five, which constitute the crucial core of Jesus' teaching on this very important subject.

Questions for Further Thought or Discussion

1. Identify the seven prayer requests in Matthew 6 and the five in Luke 11.
2. Explain the significance of the order in which Jesus arranged the prayer requests.
3. Compare and contrast the Lord's Prayers in Matthew 6 and Luke 11.

The author: Dr. Thomas L. Constable is the Department Chair and Senior Professor of Bible Exposition at Dallas Theological Seminary in Dallas, Texas. He is the author of *Talking to God: What the Bible Teaches about Prayer* as well as numerous articles in *Kindred Spirit* and "What Prayer Will and Will Not Change" in *Essays in Honor of J. Dwight Pentecost*, edited by Stanley D. Toussaint and Charles H. Dyer.

SUGGESTED ADDITIONAL READING

Hughes, R. Kent. *Abba Father: The Lord's Pattern for Prayer.* Wheaton: Crossway, 1986.

Hemphill, Ken. *The Prayer of Jesus.* Nashville: Broadman & Holman Publishers, 2001.

Keller, W. Phillip. *A Layman Looks at the Lord's Praye*r. Chicago: Moody Press, 1976.

Lucado, Max, ed. *A Thirst for God: Studies on the Lord's Prayer.* Nashville: Word Publishing. 1999.

MacArthur, John. Jesus' *Pattern of Prayer.* Chicago: Moody Press, 1981.

Packer, J. I. *Praying the Lord's Prayer.* Wheaton: Crossway, 2007.

Pritchard, Ray. *And When You Pray: The Deeper Meaning of the Lord's Prayer.* Nashville: Broadman & Holman Publishers, 2002.

Towns, Elmer. *Praying the Lord's Prayer for Spiritual Breakthrough.* Ventura, CA: Regal Books, 1997.

chapter

11

PRAYER AND GOD'S RESPONSES

Steve Hawthorne

It may surprise you, but the Bible never says that God answers prayer. In all the books of the Bible, in the original languages anyway, you will never find one time which specifically says that God answers prayer.[1] What you will find are hundreds of times that God responds to people who pray. It may seem like I'm hairsplitting over a trivial bit of semantics. But please take a closer look. I think you'll agree that the distinction between God answering prayers and answering people can be an important one.

God doesn't answer prayer. God answers people.

Here are a few samples of how the Hebrew word, *anah*, usually translated "answer," is used to describe God responding to people who pray.

> "Hear my prayer, O LORD, give ear to my supplications!
> In Your faithfulness answer me, and in Your righteousness." (Ps. 143:1)

Prayers are piled on top of supplications. But the prayers, as such, are not answered. The psalmist himself is the one who is answered. But God's responds personally, not programatically. The response is not yes or no. God moves in the marvel of His faithfulness.

Listen to Elijah's famous prayer that brought down fire from heaven. It may be simpler than you remember: "Hear me, O LORD, hear me, that this people may know that You are the LORD God" (1 K. 18:37).

There are many more times that the Bible says God answers people, having heard them call out to Him. The wonder is not that prayers get answered. What's amazing is that people are heard. Jonah's prayer is typical: "I cried out to the LORD because of my affliction, and He answered me. . . . I cried, and You heard my voice" (Jon. 2:2).

It may seem to be a minor point about words. But I don't think so. Underneath the language of "God answered prayer" could be a mechanical model. For example, in the comedy film *Bruce Almighty*, an everyday guy is given unlimited power from God and temporary responsibility to answer prayers. The scene is significant because it reveals some of our assumptions about how prayer works. The human-playing-God figure sits at a computer, where every prayer appears as a kind of email message. He keys in the answers to the prayers with lightning speed. His fingers fly in a blur. We are made to think that he handles millions of prayers per minute. We are left with the idea that God processes requests like emails or text messages.

What's wrong with this picture? Prayer is reduced to a procedure designed to bring about results. One prominent leader was so extreme in this view that he announced, "We now have the spiritual technology to deal with almost any problem." Wow. If prayer can be considered "spiritual technology," no wonder we are bewildered when our prayer experiments don't seem to work.

You can't blame us for thinking that way. It's how we've been taught. Prayer is usually presented as a procurement process or a problem-solving method that mysteriously "works," but only part of the time. We have somehow thought that we could motivate people to pray by convincing them that prayer works. But by that same logic, if it doesn't work, we should stop praying. And for the most part, we have.

Losing Heart

Jesus knew that we would look for ways to make prayer work. He knew that after long days, weeks or months of praying without seeing the asked-for result, that dismay could easily harden into stone-like disappointment. In short, He knew that we would lose heart. He knew that we would try to master the mechanism of prayer, and it would break us instead. So He told a story that invites us into the reality of how God really does hear our praying. "He spoke a parable to them, that men always ought to pray and not lose heart" (Lk. 18:1).

Luke calls it a parable, but I think it opens up a complete paradigm if you look at it with the rest of the Bible's teaching about God hearing prayer.

You recall the story (found in Lk. 18:1-8). A woman goes to a judge. Day after day, time after time, but nothing happens. It would seem that she's not getting an answer. Or that the answer is no. But she refuses to give up. She keeps coming back and keeps making her case. Finally, the judge gives in.

Notice two things: First, that the woman was heard by the judge. The repeated pleas don't add any new information. She wasn't pleading her case badly. The judge was not deaf. What's wrong was that the judge was not good. He cannot be relied upon to act on what he heard with everyday decency, much less righteousness. Second, there was a delay. Nothing changes day after day after day.

Jesus' point is to compare the reliability of the unrighteous judge with the boundless righteousness of God. All the other variables in the story stay the same. Like the woman who kept requesting, apparently getting no response, God's people, will "cry to Him day and night," often without getting an immediate answer. It may seem like God is not responding. But in fact, we have been heard. And He's not finished.

The parable doesn't explain why God's court doesn't "work" more quickly. Jesus offers no tips, keys or secrets about how to make things happen. The point is that no matter how long it takes to see God complete His work, there is never a moment when we are not being heard by the King and Judge of all the earth who can be utterly trusted to act on everything He hears with magnificent wisdom and inexhaustible love.

Coming to Court: The Greater Paradigm

There are two biblical paradigms of prayer. On one hand, we can find what I call prayer as **enforcement**. In this model, prayer is the direct use of delegated spiritual power to accomplish God's will. In this model, those who pray are portrayed as carrying an intrinsic power to command or to even create by faith, to overwhelm dark evil powers, or to pronounce healing. Those who pray are seen as agents exerting spiritual power on earth as derived from God in heaven. Intercessors are seen as adversaries of evil. The prayers are often confrontational, enemy-oriented declarations or denunciations.

On the other hand we can find prayer as **entreaty** for God to act directly by His power. Those who pray are seen as approaching God's throne in the courtroom of heaven. There is no mysticism needed. Anyone who cries out to God from anywhere on earth is heard by God in heaven. It's not just about petitionary prayer. In this model, every kind of prayer and worship carries weight in the deliberations of the courts of heaven and are described as moving the heart of God in accordance with His purpose. The prayers may seek God's direct action against satanic powers, but the petitions and praises are addressed to God Himself and are more focused on what He desires to accomplish on earth. Intercession is simply serving as an advocate representing other people in heaven's courts.

Both of these models have biblical support. But the vast preponderance of biblical material which describes, teaches, or calls for prayer works within the entreaty paradigm.

I don't think heaven's court and the throne of God are mere imagery. There is too much consistency throughout the Bible to seriously think otherwise. Every time God reveals Himself in full blazing glory in scripture, He reveals Himself seated on a throne, surrounded by angelic majesties, governing all things with astounding righteousness and never-dying love. God's throne is not ancient tribal masculine legend formulated to frighten primitive pre-moderns into submission. Somehow God really does preside over all things, leading and intervening something like a king from his court. We have wrongly regarded heaven as just so much eternal reward, merely some puffy clouds and mansions for our bliss. Heaven in the Hebrew mind is God's throne room. The tabernacle and temple were but training replicas of the throne room that stands eternal in the heavens. We now come to that very throne of grace (Heb. 4:16, 8:1-5, 9:24).

What then is prayer in this paradigm? Prayer is approaching God Almighty as a king who is governing all things in real time. All the cities, peoples, and persons of the earth are open cases before Him. He monitors the story of every breathing person. He doesn't need prayer to accomplish His purposes, but prayer could be His favorite way to glorify Himself and even honor those who pray.

The courtroom model does not promise that any prayer instantly sways the mind of God's counsel. Many appeals are not upheld. Some motions are not sustained. But we can count on God to wisely weigh the lives and words of those who pray in light of His purpose as it unfolds throughout all the earth.

His people are His preferred witnesses, who by their testimony bring shame on evil powers, and move His heart like no angel ever has. We are not heard because of our many words, fervent words, or correct words. Ours prayers might seem silly to onlooking angels. But even the simplest prayer is significant because He helps us. The King we approach is our Father. At our side is heaven's favorite Son and Champion. He sends His Spirit to search out the depths of who we are, aligning our muddled desires with the surpassing majesty of His heart.

Because of His mercy, most of the important cases are taking many generations to unfold. But you can be assured of this: Every single word you have prayed with any kind of sincerity has been heard in heaven. Not a single syllable has been forgotten.

Prayer doesn't work. God works.

I suppose it's okay to say that prayer works. But I think it may be more accurate to say that God is at work. Prayer is His way of getting us to work with Him. He never intended us to think of prayer as a problem-solving, goodie-getting procedure. He has always been summoning people to work as His accomplices in His court. Should you answer His call, He'll probably assign you to serve as a court-appointed attorney for people who can't or won't cry out for themselves.

Keep praying and don't lose heart.

1. God is answering. Are you listening? God is not interested in merely processing your requests or granting your wishes. He knows what you need way before you can think to ask. Instead, God is passionate about answering you. He may have been answering you instead of your prayers for some time. Are you listening?

2. Pray with long-haul hope. Never assume that God has not responded because it seems to be taking a long time. The open cases in God's court are many. Most of the important proceedings are being worked out over many generations. How can we doubt that we are now seeing God's response to prayers offered centuries ago? How dare we cease to pray now for Him to finish all that He's begun? What we pray really matters. Because we are being heard. Never cease to pray.

3. Be assured that you've been heard. Never surmise that because you haven't seen God do exactly what you've asked Him, that He does not care or no longer does miracles. You may daydream how nice it would be to have God do whatever you ask, but think about it: You would not want to pray to a God you would not also want to worship. God's desires and wisdom are far greater than ours. Since He can be trusted, it is enough that we are heard. But since He is for us, let's pray for His purposes in matters great and small.

The oft-quoted verse about God doing exceedingly abundantly beyond all that we can ask or think is really talking about God fulfilling a macro-global, history-encompassing work of glory. It ends with this: "to Him be glory in the church by Christ Jesus to all generations" (Eph. 3:20-21). The last phrase could just as easily be translated "throughout all generations" meaning that the answers to prayer that are beyond our life span have taken the entire expanse of history to come forth. At the last, we will not say, "Look at all the amazing answers to prayer we were able to make happen." We will say, "He has fulfilled everything He has promised."

Questions for Further Thought or Discussion

1. According to the author, "the Bible never says that God answers prayer . . . What you will find are hundreds of times that God responds to people who pray." Explain the difference, then identify and explain three implications to the prevailing approaches or perspectives on praying.

2. Contrast the enforcement and entreaty models of prayer, then explain how they fit into the courtroom paradigm.
3. "Prayer doesn't work." Agree or disagree and explain your reasoning.

The author: Steve Hawthorne is Director of WayMakers, located in Austin, Texas. Along with Graham Kendrick, he is the author of *Prayerwalking: Praying On-Site with Insight*. He is also author of *Seek God for the City*, a forty-day prayer guide published annually by WayMakers, helping people unite and focus their praying for their entire community.

SUGGESTED ADDITIONAL READING

Greig, Pete. *God on Mute: Engaging the Silence of Unanswered Prayer*. Ventura, CA: Regal Books, 2007.

Sittser, Gerald Lawson. *When God Doesn't Answer Your Prayer*. Grand Rapids: Zondervan, 2003.

Smith, Eddie, and Alice Smith. *The Advocates*. Lake Mary, FL: Charisma House, 2001.

Tiessen, Terrance L. *Providence & Prayer: How Does God Work in the World*? Downers Grove, IL: InterVarsity Press, 2000.

Yancey, Philip. *Prayer: Does it Make Any Difference?* Grand Rapids: Zondervan, 2007.

ENDNOTES

1. There are a few times that English translations insert the word "prayer" when the original says that God was entreated. For example, the New American Standard translation for 1 Chronicles 5:20 says that God "answered their prayers because they trusted in Him." In fact, a literal translation of the Hebrew original says that God "was entreated by them" (referring to the people). The word for prayers is nowhere in the verse. Instead, God was moved by the people as they cried out, explicitly because they trusted Him. You'll find the same Hebrew expression in 2 Samuel 21:14, 24:25 and Genesis 25:21.

12

THE ASPECTS, VARIETIES AND KINDS OF PRAYER

Alice Smith

I have always been a warrior at heart. My intercessory prayer friends nicknamed me Bulldog! As a bulldog grabs hold of its victim, and won't let go, I love to take hold of a prayer assignment and hang on to it until I see God move. Thankfully, not all praying people are like me. We have unique personalities, skills, gifts, and callings; and we pray differently.

Concerning the spiritual gifts listed in Romans 12, a person who shows mercy would likely pray more passionately than an administrator, who'd pray in a more structured, organized way. A giver might pray for funds for missions; while a teacher prays the Word. Those mentioned in Ephesians 4 will pray differently as well. A pastor will pray fervently for his people; an evangelist will tend to pray for lost souls. And, as Paul points out in 1 Corinthians 12, the manifestations of the Holy Spirit will vary from one believer to the next.

So some are led to pray for nations; some for leaders. Some prefer to pray prayer lists; others pray as the Spirit leads. There are believers who focus on crisis prayer assignments; and those who focus on spiritual warfare.

For this reason, emulations (trying to be like someone else) is a work of the flesh. (See Galatains 5) Keys to an effective prayer life are to learn who you are (identify your assignment or prayer personality); and to embrace the differences we share. Our strength in prayer is found in diversity; not in uniformity!

Because of our diversity, prayer need never be boring. Though there are many approaches to prayer, there is but one focus: Jesus. Let's take a look at the various aspects of prayer with which each of us, regardless of style, should be familiar.

Confession means to come into agreement with God concerning our sin. When we confess, we acknowledge and admit to our sin, and receive God's forgiveness and cleansing. But confession isn't to be a one-time thing; it's to be a lifestyle of acknowledging and dealing with personal sin. There is one important distinction to make: Confessing a sin *isn't synonymous with* repenting of sin. It's one thing to be awakened at six o'clock in the morning and quite another thing to get up out of the bed. Confession involves a change of heart. Repentance involves a change of behavior. So when conviction comes, whether in prayer or not, confess and repent immediately. Confession brings a sweet release to our humbled soul.

> When Morales, the painter, was invited by Philip the Second to court, he came in such a magnificent costume, that the king, in anger, ordered a sum of money to be paid him, and so dismissed him. The next time they met, Morales appeared in a very different dress, poor, old, and hungry, which so touched the heart of the king, that he immediately provided him with revenue which kept him in a comfort for all the future. So when men come to the throne of grace it is not their magnificence but their very want which touches the heart of God.[1]

I'm not suggesting that we are to live as paupers, but spiritually we are to come before the Lord in humility. Confession of sin is an important part of prayer that many Christians need if they are to move to the next level of spiritual maturity.

Since confession involves agreeing with God concerning sin, we have the joy of agreeing with Him that our sin is eradicated by the blood of Christ. In the Old Testament sin was *covered* (see Ps. 32:1), but in the New Testament sin is *cleansed* (see 1 Jn. 1:9). Rejoice New Testament Christian. Your sin is eradicated! That which is covered can be uncovered. That which is eradicated no longer exists!

Petition means to *earnestly* request something from God without attempting to manipulate Him (see Mt. 7:7-8). Genuine petition comes from a heart of praise and worship. If we lose sight of the Lord's view of what we need and don't need, we will pray sentimentally. In time, our prayers will be reduced to little more than hurling petitions at God's throne telling Him what to do without thought of what He wants. This is an adolescent, selfish and need-driven attitude reminiscent of the once-popular *Burger King* commercial, "we want it our way."

In true petitionary prayer we elevate God's will above our own will. Recognizing our loving heavenly Father desires to give us more than we can ask or think (see Eph. 3:20). The following story illustrated this point.

> During evangelistic services in London the Rev. Douglas Brown saw a boy of fourteen, absorbed in earnest petition, kneeling with clasped hands. Bowing beside the lad, the minister heard him say, "Thank you, Lord Jesus. There's one more now; please save that one." Before the evening closed the lad's parents and his brother and sister were all converted.[2]

The boy prayed for *one* to be saved, but God had greater things in mind. He saved them *all.* Like a good earthly father, our Father longs to bless us with benefits. God honors gratitude. And a grateful heart always receives more than it expects.

Intercession means to mediate or negotiate for something; to intervene in prayer to God on behalf of another person or situation. We can't intercede properly without praying to know the heart of God in a matter. In the old days our grandparents called intercessory prayer, "getting a hold of the altar of God" which implies that you stay in prayer until something happens. Veteran prayer warrior, the late John R. Rice, bluntly expressed the nature of genuine prayer. He said, "Prayer is not a lovely sedan for a sight seeing trip around the city. Prayer is a truck that goes straight to the warehouse, backs up, loads, and comes home with the goods."[3]

Intercessory prayer is standing in the gap between two worlds. What are these worlds? The seen and the unseen worlds. Intercession is standing in prayer between what the Lord wants to do on the earth through our faithfulness to pray for the needs on earth, preventing the devil success. The devil wants to "steal, kill and destroy" (see Jn. 10:10). God's job is to create life. Our ambassadorial assignment is to stand in prayer to represent others and drive away with a truckload of answered prayers.

Jesus said it for us. "Your kingdom come. Your will be done in earth as it is in heaven" (Mt. 6:10). Intercessory prayer is calling for God's kingdom to be done on earth, as it is in heaven.

Spiritual Warfare is the cosmic conflict that rages between the kingdom of God and kingdom of Satan. (Good news! I've read the last pages of the Bible, and we win!)

Prevailing thought is that spiritual warfare consists only of direct frontal assaults against the devil and his demons. This is occasionally necessary, but not always the case. Some of our effective weapons against Satan and his minions are:

- Intercession (Isa. 62:1-2)
- Praise and worship (Ps. 68:1-35)
- Intimacy with God (Ps. 42:1, 7)
- Personal evangelism (Acts. 16:16-40)
- Loving Jesus more than life (Rev. 12:11)
- Giving (Mal. 3:10)

We were born on a spiritual battlefield. Psalms 24:1 declares, "The earth is the LORD's, and all its fullness, the world and those who dwell therein" (this establishes ownership). However, in 2 Cor. 4:4 Satan is described as "the god of this age" (this establishes rulership).

Once born again, we are dressed in the uniform of righteousness and armed for battle by the Lord of Hosts Himself. When engaging in spiritual battles we should exercise caution against becoming enamored with the powers of darkness. This is exactly what they want. Demons want us to misplace our focus on Jesus, and focus on them. The church for too long has erred on both sides. Some have ignored the work of Satan while others have focused on it.

When entering in to direct spiritual warfare, here are some ground rules to consider.

1. If God instructs you to address the demonic world, open your eyes, strengthen your voice, square your shoulders, and announce your command. *This is a declaration to darkness, not a prayer.* Here is an example of what not to do.

> "Father, we come to You in the mighty name of Jesus, thanking You for all You're going to do in the service this morning. We praise You and glorify Your name. *Now Satan, you're a liar and a thief, and we won't have any part of you in this auditorium. Get out.* Thank You Jesus for all your benefits. In Jesus name, Amen."

In this illustration, one is praying to God and to Satan! When you pray—pray. When you proclaim—proclaim. God and Satan are not *equals* battling it out for victory. Absolutely not! Satan is *only* a created being, who has been defeated already at the cross of Christ (see Col. 2:15).

Never forget that Satan and his spirits of darkness, though defeated and disarmed, are still on earth deceiving people, blinding them from seeing the gospel, accusing us to each other, and accusing us before God. For this reason, we are still engaged in combat against the devil as a clean-up operation until the end of the age.

2. Never engage in an assault against darkness without clear instructions from the Lord. How will you know when it's time to move from the prayer closet into the battle zone? Don't fight the devil unless a fire wells up in your belly. You'll know. A righteous indignation will fill you with anger against the devil and what he is doing. If you will wait patiently for the Lord to give you this leading, then He will authorize your authority over the enemy. Authority over darkness is ambassadorial and is meted out one assignment at a time.

Intimacy is a spiritual relationship developed in prayer between you and the Lord. In my book, *Beyond the Veil* I explain, "The Father has no favorites, but He does have intimates. And the Lord wants intimacy (spiritual connectedness) with us more than we want intimacy with Him. However,

He can only share His heart with those who delight to be in His presence in the prayer closet. Many of us want to know the secrets of the Father's heart. We want His anointing upon our lives. Be we are unwilling to make the necessary investment before His throne."[4]

The purpose for experiencing a deeper fellowship with Christ is the mystery Paul spoke of in Ephesians 5:31-32. We are the bride of Christ and as His bride, our desire should be to get to know Him, walk with Him and follow His instructions. Sadly, Jesus Christ is a bridegroom whose bride hardly knows Him and rarely speaks to Him.

After forty-one years of developing this intimate prayer life, there aren't words for me to describe the joy that awaits you in the inner chamber of His presence. Every person who wants more of Jesus will have more of Him. If you long for, linger, and wait patiently without selfish expectation, you will experience intimacy with Christ in prayer.

Our diversity makes our walk with Christ fun. No two Christians will pray the same, nor will they have the same experiences. To limit our prayer life to only one facet, will diminish the fullness of a lifetime of rewarding spiritual tension and glorious breakthroughs. Englishman J. Sidlow Baxter was a pastor, theologian and author of thirty books. He summarized well our need for prayer. "Men may spurn our appeals, reject our message, oppose our arguments, despise our persons—but they are helpless against our prayers."[5]

Questions for Further Thought or Discussion

1. Explain how the inter-play of gifting and passion produces a variety of prayer. List two or three implications for a corporate prayer leader.
2. How would you explain variety in prayer styles and passions to a group of people from a variety of congregations?
3. Write a prayer for each of these topics (healing, salvation, revival of the Church) from four different categories of prayer (for example, praise, confession, petition, spiritual warfare).

The author: Alice Smith is an internationally known conference speaker and author of several books, including *Beyond the Veil: Entering into Intimacy with God through Prayer, Beyond the Lie: Finding Freedom from Your Past, 40 Days Beyond the Veil* and

Delivering the Captives. She is also co-author of five books with her husband, Eddie and Executive Director of Eddie and Alice Ministries in Houston, Texas.

SUGGESTED ADDITIONAL READING

Chester, Timothy. *The Message of Prayer: Approaching the Throne of Grace.* Downers Grove, IL: InterVarsity Press, 2003.

Graf, Jonathan. *The Power of Personal Prayer.* Colorado Springs, CO: NavPress, 2002. (He has a detailed chapter on "Finding Your Prayer Personality" and also chapters on the various types of prayer.)

Packer, J. I. and Nystrom, Carolyn. *Praying: Finding Our Way Through Duty to Delight.* Downers Grove, IL InterVarsity Press, 2006.

Poinsett, Brenda. *Reaching Heaven: Discovering the Cornerstones of Jesus' Prayer Life.* Chicago: Moody Publishing, 2002.

Smith, Alice. *Beyond the Veil.* Ventura, CA: Regal Books, 1997. (Has a more detailed chapter on the relationship between spiritual gifts and prayer styles.)

Smith, Eddie. *How to Be Heard in Heaven: Moving from Need-Driven to God-Centered Prayer.* Minneapolis: Bethany House Publishers, 2007.

_______ Strategic *Prayer: Applying the Power of Targeted Prayer.* Minneapolis: Bethany House Publishers, 2006.

ENDNOTES

1. Aquilla Webb. *One Thousand Evangelistic Illustrations* (New York & London: Harper & Brothers, 1921), p. 60.

2. Bernard Webber. *Choice Illustrations and Quotable Poems* (Grand Rapids: Zondervan Publishing, 1948), p. 95.

3. John R. Rice. *Asking and Receiving* (Wheaton, IL: Sword of the Lord Publishers, 1942), p. 50.

4. Alice Smith, *Beyond the Veil* (Ventura, CA: Regal Books, 1997), pp. 62-63.

5. Helen Hosier. *The Quotable Christian* (Uhrichsville, OH: Barbour Publisher, 1993), p. 181.

13

PRAYER AND THE SOVEREIGNTY OF GOD

Leith Anderson

Millions of wall plaques declare, "Prayer Changes Things!" But is it true? Does prayer really make a difference? Many would be quick to say that "If prayer doesn't change things, then why bother to pray?" Isn't *change* the whole point of prayer?

Numerous scientific research projects are searching for objective proof that prayer can really change anything. Some discount such studies as unscientific, inconclusive or inappropriate. From a Christian point of view attempts at scientific proof of prayer's power introduce an inevitable problem. If they demonstrate that prayer indeed works in a scientific manner, then God has been reduced to a principle of physics. If they fail to show results from prayer, then God's supernatural power is discredited. The truth is that God is far more complex than our scientific methods can understand or explain.

Well, then, does prayer change things—or doesn't it? Before we try to answer this important question, think about what prayer is. Prayer is communion with God. Prayer is communication within relationship. From a biblical standpoint, *change* isn't primarily what prayer is all about. It is more about love and relationship with God.

Prayer is not about making God into a celestial genie in a prayer bottle who will grant our wishes when we ask. It's true that changes do come from a personal relationship with God and that prayer is an important means to change. But that is secondary to what prayer is essentially about. Prayer would be a glorious and wonderful privilege even if nothing changed, just because prayer is our means of connecting with God. Prayer is primarily about *God*, not primarily about *change*. It's against this backdrop of understanding prayer that the main question of whether prayer changes things is broken down into four parts: *Does prayer change God? Does prayer change circumstances? Does prayer change others?* and, *Does prayer change me?*

Does prayer change God?

Recall the story of King Hezekiah, who was diagnosed to die and yet understandably pleaded to God for life. God had said Hezekiah would die. Yet, after he prayed, God said, "I will add to your days fifteen years" (2 K. 20:6). Prayer changed God.

But theologians object to the idea that prayer can redirect God, saying that God cannot change. God is immutable. God is unchanging. God Himself declares, "I am the LORD, I do not change!" (Mal. 3:6). Hebrews 13:8 teaches that "Jesus Christ is the same yesterday, today, and forever." If God can and does change, nothing and no one in the universe is constant. And if there is nothing constant, there are no absolutes. Everything leads to chaos.

The truth is that we don't know exactly *how* this seeming change works. We don't know because God never told us. Either we would not have understood or God didn't want us to know. We do know that it *does* work. People pray and God acts in ways that look to us a lot like change. Hezekiah probably didn't try to trace intricate theological arguments. As far as he was concerned he prayed and God changed the prognosis. That was good enough for him.

Does prayer change circumstances?

The prayer of a righteous man is powerful and effective. "Elijah was a man with a nature like ours, and he prayed earnestly that it would not rain; and it did not rain on the land for three and six months. And he prayed again, and the heavens gave rain, and the earth produced its fruit" (Jas. 5:17-18). The clear teaching of James 5:17-18 is that the prayers of righteous persons are powerful and effective. Elijah prayed and circumstances changed.

"Mere coincidence!" the skeptic insists. Perhaps, although Christians will insist that there are a lot of coincidences when they pray!

Circumstances reflect God's answers to our prayers. They are God's way of speaking His care and closeness to us. I look for God in circumstances. I believe that He is the Lord of everything and that by His power and providence He fulfills His purposes in the billions of circumstances that occur every day. That doesn't mean that every circumstance is God-given or God-pleasing. Certainly evil is fulfilled through circumstances as well.

Yet a world where God never intervenes in response to our requests is hopeless. If God doesn't change circumstances, then prayer becomes absurd. Worse yet, if God doesn't change circumstances, then His very power and presence also become unbelievable and untrustworthy. Believing that God is both powerful and present means that I acknowledge Him to work through circumstances. If not, I am forced to say that God is powerful but too distant to become involved in our world and my life, or that He is involved but too weak to make a difference.

Does prayer change others?

Some of our most impassioned prayers are intercessory prayers—prayers for someone else. Every day there are billions of prayers to change someone else.

The Bible has many examples of prayer for others. It also has many commands to pray for others:

- "Love your enemies . . . and pray for those who . . . persecute you" (Mt. 5:44).
- Pray "that I [Paul] may be delivered from those in Judea who do not

believe, and that my service for Jerusalem may be acceptable to the saints" (Rom. 15:31).
- "Praying always with all prayer and supplication in the Spirit, being watchful to this end with all perseverance and supplication for all the saints" (Eph. 6:18).
- "I [Paul] exhort first of all that supplications, prayers, intercessions, and giving of thanks be made for all men, for kings and all who are in authority, that we may live a quiet and peaceful life in all godliness and reverence" (1 Tim. 2:1-2).

God calls us to prayer for others on the assumption that prayer will make a difference. God will effect change. That is the purpose of intercession.

We must be careful, however, to guard against any notion that our prayers can overrule either the will or sins of another person. God allows people to make bad choices and to sin. If another person chooses to commit murder, to be immoral, to abuse or otherwise to do what is wrong we cannot force them by our prayers to do what is right. They make their own choices. Those choices may be terrible. They may harm others. We can and should pray for God to influence others through circumstances and conscience so that they do what is right. But He leaves each of us to choose for ourselves.

Perhaps the most painful part of praying for others is the lack of guarantees. The responsibility to pray is God-given. God expects us to exercise that privilege. He will answer those prayers by acting with a powerful influence against sin and toward righteousness in the other person's live. Yet God will also allow that person to choose—and to sin.

Does prayer change me?

In practical terms it's the most important question of all. Jesus believed that the answer to this question is an unqualified *yes!* On that night before He was crucified He prayed profusely for Himself. When Jesus took a break from His prayers and talked to His three best friends He told them likewise to pray for themselves—"lest you enter into temptation" (Mt. 26:41). Jesus knew that life is a spiritual battlefield. Praying for ourselves is the best protection. The prayers themselves aren't what protect us. They are the means of deploying the great forces of God in our lives.

Prayer's first goal isn't to change God's mind to do things *my* way. It is to change me to things *God's* way. Every day I need to be realigned with God: my thought with His thoughts; my will with His will; my life with His life. Yes, prayer changes me.

Does prayer make a difference? Absolutely! . . . but, not always as we ask.

(This chapter is adapted from the author's previous work, *When God Says No,* © 1996, and is used by permission of Bethany House, a division of Baker Publishing Group.)

Questions for Further Thought or Discussion

1. How should the truth that "prayer is communion with God" influence our thinking about this chapter's four major questions?
2. Explain within the context of the sovereignty of God, why prayer still matters.
3. Select one of the four questions posed in the chapter and write your response, providing supporting scripture.

The author: Leith Anderson is Senior Pastor of Wooddale Church in Eden Prairie, Minnesota and President of the National Association of Evangelicals headquartered in Washington, DC. He is the author of numerous books including *Dying for Change,* and *Praying to the God You Can Trust, JESUS: An Intimate Portrait.* He can be heard daily on his national radio program "Faith Matters."

SUGGESTED ADDITIONAL READING

Piper, John, "The Sovereignty of God and Prayer." Minneapolis, MN, 1976 (sermon located @ http://www.desiringgod.org/ResourceLibrary/Articles/ByDate/1976/1475_The_Sovereignty_of_God_and_ Prayer/

Yancey, Philip. *Prayer: Does It Make Any Difference?* Grand Rapids: Zondervan, 2006.

Foster, Richard. *Prayer: Finding the Heart's True Home.* San Francisco, CA: HarperCollins, 1992.

chapter

14

CRISIS PRAYING VS. CONSISTENT PRAYING

Bert Downs

My mother became a Christian about the same time I became a teenager. It seemed an unfortunate coincidence. Of our many early clashes over what her Christianity meant for my life, one was the role of *the prayer meeting.* Held weekly in someone's home, the meeting became a point at which her new life regularly collided with my old one. So each week I got instructions: don't fidget, don't be impolite, bow your head, keep your eyes closed, don't look up (I always thought if I did someone would hit me . . . whether I thought it would be God or Mom, I can not remember). So this became our Wednesdays . . . my receiving rules, violating at least a few of them and having to endure an hour or more of people praying about all sorts of things totally foreign to the world of a 13 year old.

The prayer meeting night now in my memory began like all others.

Eventually the group, huddled in Mrs. Robertson's dark and somewhat eerie living room, settled in to their usual prayers . . . for Albert's job, Agnes' illness, Sandy's marriage, Bill's car . . . and on it went. Until it got to a particular guy that to this day I only know as Brother Jackson. When Brother Jackson prayed, he caused me to violate fully half of my mother's rules; I opened my eyes, looked up, and even made an audible sound that initiated a swat to my knee. What had Brother Jackson done that brought that response, even in the face of serious threat? He prayed like he was really talking to someone . . . someone he knew well. The difference made me look, not at him so much as to see the person he was speaking to.

Hundreds of prayer meetings later, I've come to deeply appreciate what happened there. That evening I was in the presence of someone who clearly spent a lot of time with the One to whom he was praying . . . and it made an obvious difference . . . even to a thoroughly pagan teenager. His prayer had a quality of authenticity, transparency, knowledge and comfort that only exists among old friends who have tremendous respect for one another. It made the kid that night think that maybe there is something to this prayer stuff after all. Perhaps prayer is more than simply a recitation of the latest wish list.

So, in the balanced, growing life in Christ, which kind of prayer do we find: crisis or consistent? Well, before we jump to a possible answer, let me insert a disclaimer. As much as we try to define and describe the life of prayer and our engagement with the Lord in that process, we dare not put God's grace in a box. The truth is that we all know of, perhaps have even lived out, situations of God's remarkable responses to what on the surface seem incredibly spontaneous, disconnected and presumptuous requests.

And we've seen those prayers come from highly unlikely people. Call them the "foxhole" variety of prayer from a person whose immediate circumstances have surfaced a long dormant interest in God or at least in what God can do. Surprise of surprises—God answers such prayers. Describe and define as we will, we must nevertheless accept the fact that our feeble attempts will not eliminate those surprises from a God who operates far outside our defining boundaries. However, by contrasting the two extremes—crisis and consistent prayer—we can learn some critical elements about our relationship with the Lord and others, and the role of prayer in those relationships.

Both Kinds of Prayer

What amounts to a brief essay doesn't allow for a detailed examination of how I came to the data which follows. In summary, I looked into the lives of select biblical characters who seemed to use both consistent and crisis prayer. Simplistic perhaps, but I viewed consistent prayer as that kind of prayer that seems relational, more planned than spontaneous, that connects to major themes of life in relationship to God. In contrast, I viewed crisis prayer as those times when the prayer interacts with God on what seems a more immediate circumstance or need. For instance, Nehemiah demonstrates great connection to God and the big themes of God's work as revealed in his longstanding concerns for Jerusalem. He is clearly a consistent prayer. However, when he sees an opportunity that may or may not be from the Lord, he fires up a prayer and then takes action with the king hoping for God's intervention rather than the death that could await him; he practiced crisis prayer as well.

So I looked at the lives of Nehemiah, Esther, Hezekiah, David, Job, Mary (mother of Jesus) and Jesus searching for what might be considered events demonstrating either consistent prayer or crisis prayer. While there is an arbitrary nature to such a search, the differences in those approaches are there to be found. In some cases, they are profound. I believe careful consideration of those differences has the potential to lead to an increasingly powerful, satisfying and effective life of prayer for each of us.

To effectively take advantage of the opportunities this topic affords within the constraints we have, I'll present the contrasts in chart form, providing limited definitions for items in the chart. The focus will center on big picture qualities for each aspect of prayer. Exceptions will exist to my generalizations. If we can allow ourselves to hover over these items so as to see them all from the largest possible view, then the contrasts will lead to connections between the two approaches. Those connections will lead to strategic conclusions about the roles these two approaches to praying fulfill.

Summary Chart: Crisis Prayer vs. Consistent Prayer

Characteristics	**CONSISTENT PRAYER**	**CRISIS PRAYER**
Focus of the prayer	*Relational* – want to know and be known by the One to whom I'm praying	*Task* – want something from the One to whom I'm praying
Connection	*Intimate* – deep connection of heart, mind, theme, journey and destination.	*Less intimate* – a more superficial connection around the result desired
Motivation	*Internal* – as if friends are simply continuing a deep life-long conversation	*External* – a circumstance or need requiring solution has become priority
Driven by	*Calling* – here prayer, like air, is a critical element in the best outworking of life	*Circumstance* – here prayer, like pain, is the response to an external stimulus
Point of view	*Big picture* – built from seeing God and His plan from "10,000 feet"	*Little picture* – built from seeing God and His plan from ground-level need
Preparation for	*Planned and practiced* – as the talk of old friends, has an easy direction and pace	*Spontaneous* – more quick and energetic reflecting the demand of the moment
Dimensions	*Multi-dimensional* – seems to embrace the Lord, His plans, and other people	*One-dimensional* – mostly embraces the required task and desired result
Sense of time	*Long term (eternal)* – a pace and patience clearly connected to eternal themes	*Short term (temporal)* – an urgency clearly connected to immediate need
Pragmatic	*Least pragmatic* – seems pragmatism gives way to long term relationship/goals	*Most pragmatic* – emphasis on the immediately applicable trumps long term
Benefit focus	*Primarily God's* – while having earthly impact, focus is on the heart of God	*Primarily man's* – while engaging God, focus is on the needs of man
Practiced	*Least* – demands discipline and relational commitment rarely pursued or reached	*Most* – natural stimuli easily make this the default position for our prayers

Conclusion

We're back to the earlier question: which is it . . . crisis prayer or consistent prayer? I believe the biblical answer is both. Both practices make up a healthy, developing life in Christ and relationship to the Father. At their functional best, one practice is built on the other; one practice is energized by the other. Consistent prayer builds the knowledge, understanding and confidence in God that makes a foundation for the inevitable crisis. Crisis prayer and God's response energizes our drive to be more consistent, to go deeper in our relationship with the Being who makes communication with Himself possible, invites it and then rewards it.

The relationship of the two practices is seen in the life of Jesus' mother, for instance. In the *Magnificat* Mary reveals herself as a girl with a deep personal knowledge of and relationship with God. Her words point to consistent communication with Him. And it's that relationship that allows her to fend off the initial shock and confusion of the angel's announcement with the simple crisis prayer couched in this statement: "Let it be to me according to your word" (Lk. 1:38).

There you have it. The practice of consistent prayer builds an internal reservoir of faith and understanding of God, His ways and His works within Mary. That reservoir is then drawn upon at her time of crisis to empower what is a powerful, spontaneous request with the full weight of God's will . . . her request that what was said become reality.

Undoubtedly, Brother Jackson would resonate with Mary's approach. Neither she nor he settled for the shallow waters of constant crisis praying as a way of life. Instead, they waded into the deep waters of consistent prayer where the Father of prayer may be found, known and embraced. It's the place where consistent praying and crisis praying come together in an unbeatable team.

Questions for Further Thought or Discussion

1. Using the chart in this chapter, determine which prayer practice dominates your approach and consider ways by which you can gain increased balance and effectiveness.
2. If you agree that crisis praying is the typical default approach, why do you think that's so? What problems do you see arising if that approach dominates?

3. What contribution does an increasingly strong, consistent prayer life make to the effectiveness of crisis praying? What are the characteristics of consistent prayer that cause it to bolster our response to crisis?

The author: Dr. Bert Downs is the President of Western Seminary with campuses in Portland, Oregon and Sacramento and San Jose, California.

SUGGESTED ADDITIONAL READING

Chapel, Bryan. *Praying Backwards: Transform Your Prayer Life by Beginning in Jesus Name.* Grand Rapids: Baker Books, 2005.

Graf, Jonathan. *The Power of Personal Prayer: Learning to Pray with Faith and Purpose.* Colorado Springs, CO: NavPress, 2002.

Smith, Eddie and Hennen, Michael L. *Strategic Prayer: Applying the Power of Targeted Prayer.* Bloomington, MN: Bethany House Publishers, 2007.

chapter 15

PROBLEMS OF SEEMINGLY UNANSWERED PRAYER

Elmer L. Towns

Does God have a problem when Christians pray for the opposite things? Two ball teams pray to win the game, which team does God answer? During the American Civil War, both the North and the South prayed to win the war. Does God have a dilemma because there were praying Christians on both sides? Note some of the following problems and challenges with the nature of God and prayer.

Six Alleged Problems about Prayer

Once Carl Sagan, an agnostic (inability to believe in God) and an atheist (inability to accept the existence of God), was responding to Dr. Joan Brown Campbell, General Secretary to the National Council of Churches, at an environmental exchange. Sagan at one time had believed the existence of an omnipotent and omniscient God. But he came to a place where the evidence in the universe demanded that if such a God existed he should be able to know it. But he did not know if God existed because he couldn't prove it with logic or experimentation. The issue to Sagan was never "to believe," but always "to know."

However Joan Campbell one day asked Sagan a question that he couldn't answer, "Carl, do you believe in love?"

He said, "Of course, I do." He was very much in love with his wife and he knew it. Campbell said, "Can you prove that love exists?"

At first he said, "Well, certainly." But eventually he agreed that love, like faith, was something un-provable at its core, "But that doesn't mean it doesn't exist and you can know when you're in love." Therefore, we don't have to prove God to know that He exists. Also, we don't have to give scientific proof that prayer exists. Yet, the very fact we have answers should be proof enough to the critics.

1. The problem of God's plan and will. How can prayer be allowed to override God's omnipotent and omniscient plan for the world and those He loves?

God is omnipotent (has all power to do all things possible), and God is eternal (has always existed in His present form). So God's power leads to His immutability. But the fact God has all power means He has always existed in an unchangeable existence. The only thing that could change God is God, but He cannot be changed. And since God has no cause, it is concluded that God cannot be changed, therefore He is immutable.

If God cannot be changed, how can our prayers change His mind? How can our prayer cause Him to do something He hasn't already done? Then why pray?

If God has a pre-determined will, it also is immutable. How can you pray for a sick person to be well when God has already determined the end of his life or the day of his death? Does God have to be reminded that someone is sick? Since He is immutable, does it mean He can't do anything about it, even when people ask.

In answer to above, remember that an all-powerful God has created laws that cannot be changed, i.e., the earth's gravity will always draw objects to the core of the earth. However, God who created the law in the first place, can create a higher law to offset the pull of gravity.

When Jesus walked on water, He defied gravity and as C. S. Lewis said, "A miracle is an interference with Nature by a supernatural power."[1]

Also, God has created time and space within His creation where man is allowed to soar above those laws by appealing to a higher law, i.e., God Himself.

When we say that God is omnipotent, eternal and immutable, we must make sure that we are not saying that He is like a machine that cannot change. God is a Person with intellect, emotion and will. He can love individuals, hear and know about their needs; and decide to do something for them.

2. The problem of the impartial nature of God. This argument suggests that when God answers prayer, He is playing favorites with those He likes, but allows others to go through life without His favor or answers to prayer.

God is impartial meaning He must always punish every sin and always reward righteousness. But since man is a sinner in nature and deed, there is nothing in him that God can reward. However, remember we end our prayers, "In Jesus' Name." This means we come to the Father through the forgiveness and Person of Jesus Christ.

A God who has the attributes of love has no choice but to interact with people He has created on the basis of love. Who was it that said, "If God is that involved with me, then I shall be involved with Him"?

Also, a vision of God who perceives and knows the needs of His people, but turns His back on their needs; if anything, an unconcerned God destroys our faith. But God loves the entire world and wants everyone to be His child (2 Pet. 3:4), that's impartiality. Also, God loves His children and looks after their needs; that's an important promise He's made to all of His children. He looks after their needs differently because God loves each and has a wonderful plan for each life.

3. The problem of a sovereign deity who recognizes and caters to the personal and selfish benefits of petitioners. God wants people to worship and obey Him. However, at the very heart of man is "the lust of the flesh, the lust of the eyes, and the pride of life" (1 Jn. 2:16). At the core of all of these is a self-driven individual who thinks first primarily *uno numero* (number one).

God knows individuals put themselves first, but He demands that we love Him with all our hearts (Mt. 22:37) and "You shall love your neighbor as yourself" (Mt. 22:38). When we do this, we get selfish benefits, some directly, and some indirectly. God appeals to our selfish nature so we will enjoy loving God and others.

When we pray for selfish reasons, at times we are trying to manipulate God for personal benefit. At least we think that's what we're doing. But maybe that's why so many of our prayers are not answered. We pray for selfish reasons. James says, "You ask and do not receive, because you ask amiss, that you may spend it on your pleasures" (Jas. 4:3).

However, sometimes our selfish prayers fit into the purpose of God. At other times when God answers our selfish prayers, maybe He does so, so we will trust Him more in the future.

So, when we pray—even for selfish reasons—this can be the beginning of a lifelong prayer-relationship. We go to God with our needs and He answers. Then we know that He loves and cares for us, even in the little things that appear to be selfishly driven.

4. The problem of divine mechanistic power. This raises a question, "Can selfish people manipulate God for their own personal benefit or happiness?" Obviously, not all prayers are for selfish reasons, but many of them are. As a matter of fact, since self is the primary drive for individuals, even when selfish people pray for God to be magnified, they get their selfish ambitions filled by the fact that a sovereign God will listen and give them what they ask.

Nowhere in the Bible is prayer described as a divine vending machine whereby you get what you choose. Only those outside of Christianity look at God as a large warehouse of "goodies" to dispense to the people with the right membership card. In essence, this argument takes away from the personhood of God. When the Christians pray for daily bread, they're not asking God to feed them from His large warehouse, rather they are relating to a personal God who is the Divine Bread Maker.

Remember, prayer is a relationship; the human with the Divine. This is a form of consanguinity that the world has never seen.

In one sense, prayer answers are in the eye of the beholder. And if you had eyes of faith, you can see what God is doing. But if you don't have the spiritual eyes to see God in your heart, you will never understand the answers that He gives to His children.

5. The problem that answers are awarded based on begging and/or constantly annoying God, as when we display the characteristics of importunity. Those who see prayer as begging, also see God as a Divine miser who doesn't want to give anything away without getting something in return. First, they say we must "beg" so that we get God's attention. Second, they say we must "beg" to demonstrate our sincerity, and third, we must "beg" to recognize He is the "gift-giver."

Prayer was not merely a religious soul talking to God in far-away heaven. Jesus said prayer is a child making a request to His father (Mt. 7:11). And Jesus also taught that our prayers always got the loving attention of a kind heavenly Father (Lk. 11:11-13). Jesus taught that the success of prayer was based on the access to the Father that He gave to His children (Jn. 17:19; Heb. 4:14-16, 10:19-22).

6. The problem of a universe governed by scientific laws. This problem says that laws cannot upset or overrule the mechanical ecological system because laws are the controlling power of events. This problem suggests that even the human freedom of praying for divine help could not override or abdicate any law of nature without throwing the entire system into chaos.

The problem with this view is that there is no place for God to intervene in the laws, nor is there any place for humans to make choices about their influence on posterity or history. In essence, there is no place for miracles. Isn't every answer to prayer a miracle?

However when scientists examined the unexplainable phenomena of events in the universal laws, they only explained it as the "misbehavior of nature." The scientists accept their view of the unexplained, but exclude the possibility of Divine intervention. They seek answers only within their limited interpretation.

When doctors see patients get well, even those patients with incurable cancer, they usually explain it as a wrong diagnosis, or a cause that they missed in their original diagnosis. Even if they said their diagnosis was correct, they explain the healing as a result of an *unexplainable cause,* most are never willing to admit that the unexplainable cause might be God.

A few doctors may say that prayers make people feel better. And since hope has therapeutic value for medicinal causes (and psychological causes), then prayer gives people hope and makes them better. When the whole psychological and physical systems of the individual are "up," then the body works better, and heals itself.

However, there are Bible promises that God heals in answer to prayer, i.e., "The prayer of faith shall save the sick" (Jas. 5:15). God will answer prayers for healing when we approach Him properly.

Yes, there are laws that govern the universe, but first let's define law, i.e., law is the extension of God's nature and power that He uses to govern the universe. Since law comes from God, cannot God create a higher power/higher law to override the existing ones? Can't God do anything within His will that He desires to do? And can't God govern His spiritual world by spiritual laws? The answer is YES!

To Take Away

The problem with the *problems* is that most of the times the critics look at the world through their limited eyesight. Those who criticize prayer do not fully understand God, nor do they understand the teachings of the Word of God on prayer. We can all pray more effectively when we pray more intelligently, i.e., according to the Word of God. When we begin with the understanding that prayer is a relationship with God, then we will base our prayers to God on that relationship.

Questions for Further Thought or Discussion

1. Why do most non-Christians have questions or problems with prayer?
2. Why do some Christians have questions about prayer?
3. Since "prayer is a relationship with God," how can a person form a deeper faith-relationship with God?

The author: Dr. Elmer L. Towns is Dean of the School of Religion at Liberty University in Lynchburg, VA. He is the author of numerous books including *Fasting for Spiritual Break Through, How to Pray, Praying the Psalms* and *The Names of the Holy Spirit*, for which he received the Gold Medallion Award from the Evangelical Christian Publishers Association for its book of the year.

SUGGESTED ADDITIONAL READING

Crump, David. *Knocking on Heaven's Door: A New Testament Theology of Petitionary Prayer.* Grand Rapids: Baker Academic, 2006.

Yancey, Phillip. *Praying: Does It Make Any Difference.* Grand Rapids: Zondervan, 2006.

Smith, Michael M. *Nurturing a Passion for Prayer* (Chapter on how to handle the dilemma of unanswered prayer). Colorado Springs, CO: NavPress, 2000.

Towns, Elmer. *Bible Answers for Almost All Your Questions.* Nashville: Thomas Nelson Publishers, 2003. (See section on Prayer, pp. 217-232 for a complete listing of questions/problems and suggested answers.)

ENDNOTES

1. C.S. Lewis, *Scholar and Spiritual Writer* (22 November 1963). Definition of a miracle. http://satucket.com/lectionary/cslewis.htm, (accessed 21 December 2004).

16

CHARACTERISTICS OF GOD-HONORING PRAYER

Arturo G. Azurdia, III

"Prayer is simply talking to God."

Since the earliest days of our Christian discipleship, well-intentioned spiritual mentors have employed this popular cliché in an attempt to simplify the challenge and complexity of prayer. On the one hand, few would argue that it conveys a helpful dimension of truth. On the other hand, does its overuse render it subject to a kind of reductionism; namely, that the attempt to simplify prayer into a single cliché has caused its degeneration into something simplistic? Has its undiscerning use confused our new covenant accessibility to God with the apparent freedom to address Him without intelligent meaning and biblically informed purpose?

The Gospel narratives give us every impression that the men who would eventually become the disciples of Jesus were already faithful Jews prior to meeting Him. As such, prayer was not a foreign spiritual experience, but a familiar expression of their covenant-keeping faith. It is not altogether without surprise, then, when they make the following request of Jesus: "Lord, teach us to pray" (Lk. 11:1). Apparently, by virtue of observing His praying, they deduce that prayer is something more substantive than their prior experiences would demonstrate; something more than "simply talking to God." And Jesus, rather than retreating to a well-worn cliché, exploits this didactic opportunity with a telling response: the provision of six, highly specific imperatives that serve as a definitive pattern for prayer. According to Jesus, therefore, is it accurate to suggest that prayer can be summarized sufficiently as "simply talking to God?"

Prayer is *more* than "simply talking to God." It transcends meaningless chatter, repeated platitudes, and even the artful stringing together of religious sentiments. It is the conversation of adoration, the intimacy of intercession, the dialogue of dependence, and the humility of confession. Simply speaking, *prayer is talk that honors God.* A cursory reading of the Bible's inscripturated prayers steadily reveals this fact. And, among many others,[1] we would do well to give our attention to the opening prayer of Nehemiah the cupbearer, for in it we encounter distinguishing characteristics of God-honoring prayer that can significantly inform the substance of our own praying.

Characteristic #1: *God-honoring prayer is infused with a vision of the character of God.* Nehemiah commences his prayer as follows: "LORD God of heaven" (1:5a). It is a stunning manner of address. To a Jew under the old covenant, the phrase "LORD God of heaven" was a declaration of God's absolute sovereignty; a description that affirmed Yahweh as no mere local deity, confined to the boundaries of Palestine. Rather, it asserts that His authority exercises itself over the entire universe. It is an address designed not primarily to acknowledge God's location, but to affirm God's status; namely, that He is the *universal* Lord. Nehemiah continues by declaring Yahweh to be the "great and awesome God" (1:5b), describing the vast potency and immobilizing dread engendered by Israel's Lord.[2] Finally, Nehemiah recognizes God as one who keeps His "covenant and mercy with those who love" Him and "observe" His "commandments" (1:5c). Yahweh is no fickle or capricious deity. He is a steady and faithful Lord who keeps His promises, always maintaining His loyal love to those who enter into covenantal partnership with Him. Hence, at the outset, Nehemiah's prayer *honors* God with a declaration of His character that will prove essential to the accomplishment of his forthcoming request.

Characteristic #2: *God-honoring prayer is marked by a passion to be right before God.* Subsequent to his declaration of God's character, it is not surprising that Nehemiah turns his attention to confession: "I . . . confess the sins of the children of Israel which we have sinned against You. Both my father's house and I have sinned. We have acted very corruptly against You, and have not kept the commandments, the statutes, nor the ordinances which You commanded Your servant Moses" (1:6-7). Three salient features distinguish this statement: 1) Nehemiah acknowledges his own culpability. Rather than side with Yahweh in self-righteousness, Nehemiah openly affirms his guilt;[3] not only because of his own transgressions, but also by virtue of his solidarity with the disobedient covenant community. 2) Nehemiah acknowledges the comprehensiveness of his sin. His use of the three-fold phrase "commands, statutes, and ordinances" serves as a rhetorical designation for the entire law of God. It asserts that the guilt of the covenant community is thoroughgoing. 3) Nehemiah acknowledges God as the offended party. Similar to David's confession, "Against You, You only, have I sinned, and done this evil in Your sight" (Ps. 51:4), Nehemiah's guilt acknowledgement is radically theocentric in its orientation and, thus, his confession of sin *honors* God.

Characteristic #3: *God-honoring prayer is grounded upon a confidence in the Word of God.* Given the preceding confession, Nehemiah is unable to ground this prayer (and its ultimate request) upon the covenantal faithfulness of his people. His only recourse is an appeal to God's promise, which he summarily recites to Yahweh: "Remember, I pray, the word that You commanded Your servant Moses, saying, 'if you are unfaithful, I will scatter you among the nations; but if you return to Me, and keep My commandments and do them, though some of you were cast out to the farthest part of the heavens, yet I will gather them from there, and bring them to the place which I have chosen as a dwelling for My name'" (1:8-9). To set God's own promise before Him represents no disrespect on the part of Nehemiah, nor does it reflect any attempt to pressure or manipulate God. To the contrary, his appeal to this covenantal promise esteems God by revealing a firm confidence in His faithful allegiance to His word. More personally, it recognizes prayer as a covenantal,[4] filial reciprocity. "Love loves to be told what it knows already . . . It wants to be asked for what it longs to give."[5] Nehemiah's prayer *honors* God by resting its request on the integrity of God and His word.[6]

Characteristic #4: *God-honoring prayer is energized by a heart that finds pleasure in God.* What disposition motivates Nehemiah to pray as he does? "Please let Your ear be attentive to the prayer of Your servant, and to the prayer of Your servants who *desire to fear Your name*" (1:11a). The Hebrew verb, here translated "desire," means "to feel great favor toward something . . . a delight drawn out by the intrinsic qualities of its object."[7] But what is the object of Nehemiah's delight? Is it the anticipated granting of his forthcoming request? For Nehemiah, this is but the penultimate aim. His ultimate pleasure is to revere the name of God. And thus, only secondarily does this prayer honor God by virtue of its ambition. Its primary expression of *honor* is manifested by its doxological motivation.[8]

Characteristic #5: *God-honoring prayer is dependent upon the limitlessness of God.* What is Nehemiah's petition? "Let your servant prosper this day, I pray, and grant him mercy in the sight of this man" (1:11b). To which man, in particular, is he referring? "For I was the *king's* cupbearer" (1:11c, *emphasis added*). Nehemiah seeks compassion from God with reference to the Persian monarch, Artaxerxes. But why, specifically, does he seek compassion? Because of the staggering nature of his request—that Artaxerxes, the unbelieving Persian king, would reverse his previous decree, thereby allowing the returned Jewish exiles to rebuild the walls of Jerusalem. The unstated implication of the text is obvious: to seek favor from God for a matter of such significant proportions exposes a thoroughgoing confidence in His limitless abilities; and thus, God is *honored* by a request for something only He can perform.[9] "The Lord is great and high, and therefore He wants great things to be sought from Him and is willing to bestow them so that His almighty power might be shown forth."[10]

As a father, I derive great pleasure from the various conversations I engage in with my seventeen year-old daughter and fifteen year-old son. It would prove terribly disturbing, however, if their conversation with me had not matured beyond that of a typical toddler, or if their talk did not reflect an increasingly greater understanding of the nature of our relationship. It is within a similar context that we must answer the question: Is prayer "simply talking to God?" *Yes*—if what is implied is a filial freedom to draw near to God in full assurance of faith, owing entirely to the redemptive accomplishments of Jesus Christ. *No*—if the substance of our conversation with God is allowed to remain stunted in self-serving immaturity. Prayer is talk that *honors* God, and a consideration of the prayers in the sacred text consistently demonstrate this, as exemplified by the prayer of Nehemiah the cupbearer.

Questions for Further Thought or Discussion

1. Agree or disagree (and explain why): Not all prayer honors God's ultimate intention of prayer.
2. Explain how the 5 characteristics of God-honoring prayer have potential of shaping the personal prayer lives of Christian believers.
3. Explain how the 5 characteristics of God-honoring prayer have potential of transforming the Church.

The author: Dr. Arturo G. Azurdia, III is Associate Professor of Pastoral Theology/ Director of Pastoral Mentoring at Western Seminary in Portland, Oregon. He is the author of *Spirit Empowered Preaching* and of an article in *Reforming Pastoral Ministry*, entitled, "Reforming the Church through Prayer." He is also the author of an article in *The Compromised Church* entitled, "Preaching: The Decisive Function."

SUGGESTED ADDITIONAL READING

Carson, D.A. *A Call to Spiritual Reformation*. Grand Rapids: Baker Book House, 1992.

Forsyth, P.T. *The Soul of Prayer*. London: Independent Press, 1960.

Bloesch, Donald. *The Struggle of Prayer*. Colorado Springs, CO: Helmers & Howard, 1988.

ENDNOTES

1. Ezra 9; Nehemiah 9; Daniel 9; *et al*

2. One can recall the C. S. Lewis description of the great lion, Aslan: "He is not a tame lion." This description of God/Jesus is noticeably absent in most evangelical circles. One must ponder the extent to which our domesticated views of God have contributed to our correspondingly paltry praying.

3. "The man who really prays never attempts to justify himself. In true prayer, he knows he cannot do so." Karl Barth, *Church Dogmatics*, G.W. Bromiley and T.F. Torrance eds., Vol II, 2 (Edinburgh: T & T Clark, 1957), p. 752.

4. "Because God is the living God, He can hear; because He is a loving God, He will hear; because He is our covenant God, He has bound Himself to hear." C. H. Spurgeon, *The Check Book of the Bank of Faith* (Fort Washington: Christian Literature Crusade, 1960), p. 31.

5. P. T. Forsyth, *The Soul of Prayer* (London: Independent Press, 1960), p. 63.

6. "One way to get comfort is to plead the promise of God in prayer, show Him His handwriting; God is tender of His Word." Thomas Manton in *A Puritan Golden Treasury*, ed. I. D. E. Thomas (Carlisle: The Banner of Truth Trust, 1989), p. 216.

7. R. Laird Harris, Gleason L. Archer, Jr., and Bruce K. Waltke, *Theological Wordbook of the Old Testament,* vol. I (Chicago: Moody Press, 1981), p. 310.

8. "We may have improved a little on the quality of what we ask for, but the deeper question is this: Do we bring these petitions before God both with a proximate goal (that we might receive what we ask for) and with an ultimate goal—that God might be glorified? For that, surely is the deepest test: Has God become so central to all our thoughts and pursuits, and thus to our praying, that we cannot easily imagine asking for anything without consciously longing that the answer bring glory to God?" D. A. Carson, *A Call to Spiritual Reformation* (Grand Rapids: Baker Book House, 1992), p. 203.

9. "It is possible to move men, through God, by prayer alone." J. Hudson Taylor in *Heroes of Faith on Pioneer Trails* (Chicago: Moody Press, 1945), p. 105.

10. *Luther's Works*, Vol. 6, J. Pelikan ed. (St. Louis: Concordia Press, 1970), p. 15.

17

THE ROLE OF FASTING AS AN ACCOMPANIMENT TO PRAYER

Dean C. Trune

Fasting is mentioned throughout the Bible. It appears to have been utilized when people were humbling themselves before God (David in Ps. 35:13 or Ezra in Ezra 8:21) and when people were in an intense time of petitioning God about an important issue in their lives.

Fasting was connected with such activities as:

- solemn assemblies
- weeping
- confessing
- repenting
- appointing leaders

It is possible that the absence of fasting in many churches in the 21st century has also caused the absence of weeping, confessing, and repenting. These activities help redirect our focus and attention back on our heavenly Father and on His purposes.

Jesus' Thoughts on Fasting

Jesus fasted. Jesus answered questions about fasting. Jesus taught about fasting. Here are a couple of Jesus' thoughts about fasting: "When you fast, do not be like the hypocrites, with a sad countenance. For they disfigure their faces that they may appear to men to be fasting. Assuredly, I say to you, they have their reward. But you, when you fast, anoint your head and wash your face, so that you do not appear to men to be fasting, but to your Father who is in the secret place; and your Father who sees in secret will reward you openly" (Mt. 6:16-18).

Here Jesus is not condemning the activity of fasting, He is simply condemning the wrong motives by which proud people fasted. Isaiah did the same in Isaiah 58.

"Then they said to Him, 'Why do the disciples of John fast often and make prayers, and likewise those of the Pharisees, but Yours eat and drink?' And He said to them, 'Can you make the friends of the bridegroom fast while the bridegroom is with them? But the days will come when the bridegroom will be taken away from them; then they will fast in those days'" (Lk. 5:33-35).

The Bridegroom was taken away almost 2,000 years ago. I have to conclude that He expects His present day disciples to fast.

What is a fast and its different types?

Biblically, a fast is abstaining from food, either entirely or partially. Can we benefit from fasting from other things such as television, sports, dating, etc.? Absolutely! In the Bible though, fasting dealt with food.

From my reading about fasting and my personal experience with fasting, I would have to conclude that there are at least five different types of fasts.

1. The Liquid Fast: This type of fast is either water and/or juices only. I have found this fast to be the most beneficial to me. Many people who utilize this type of fast, have fasted for up to 40 days.

2. The Absolute Fast: An individual on an absolute fast will consume no food and no liquids. Our bodies need water and cannot go beyond 72 hours without it.

3. The Partial Fast: Eliminating certain foods or certain meals would be a partial fast. People who are hypoglycemic or who have sugar diabetes can make a partial fast work well. They should consult their physician, however. A couple years ago, God prompted me to fast from desserts for a while because my consumption of them seemed to be out of control. After a few months I concluded this partial fast and the additional self-control (even in other areas) was extremely evident in my life.

4. The Wesley Fast: John Wesley used to fast by consuming whole wheat bread and water only. Apparently this type of fast was a great benefit to him.

5. The Rotational Fast: People utilizing a rotational fast would rotate certain foods and meals in and out of their diets. An example would be to rotate meats, pasta, breads at different times out of my diet or maybe rotate fast a different meal each day out of the diet.

Why do most Christians not fast?

There are three main reasons why most Christians today do not fast.

Most Christians are not taught about fasting. I have attended Sunday morning worship services for more than fifty years and I have never heard a sermon on fasting. My exposure to teachings on fasting has come in the context of seminars or retreats. That is sad. Satan loves to keep us in ignorance about fasting because he knows how fasting can be used to limit his activities and/or defeat him.

Many Christians do not fast because they are addicted to food. This is especially true of Christians in America. We do not do well at handling hunger or other discomforts. If we have a headache, we immediately take something for it. If we experience pain elsewhere, we immediately take something for it. Likewise, we normally follow that pattern when we experience hunger. We "fix" the discomfort right away.

I also believe that many present day Christians do not fast because of spiritual laziness. It is always easier not to go the second mile with God or not to be a passionate pursuer of Him. We allow ourselves to be trapped in our busy lifestyles and, as a result, God receives our "leftovers" instead of our "best."

The Spiritual Benefits of Fasting

There are many spiritual benefits to fasting. Unfortunately we often figure out how to live for God without these benefits. Here are four benefits that I have experienced in my life and in the lives of others who fast:

Humility before God: As mentioned before, David and Ezra stated that they humbled themselves with fasting. Fasting is certainly not the only way to humble ourselves before God, but it is one way. Why should we be interested in humbling ourselves before God? Proverbs 3:34, James 4:6, and 1 Peter 5:5 say the same thing: "God resists the proud, but gives grace to the humble." Fasting done with correct motives will produce humility in our lives. Humility in us gives God the freedom to give us grace. I love God's grace. We all receive it to some extent. I wholeheartedly believe that properly motivated fasting increases His grace.

Joy and Gladness before God: "Thus says the LORD of hosts: 'The fast of the fourth month, the fast of the fifth, the fast of the seventh, and the fast of the tenth, shall be joy and gladness and cheerful feasts for the house of Judah. Therefore love truth and peace'" (Zech. 8:18-19). I have had people approach me during a seminar and confess depression. They typically want to know what they should do. I often recommend fasting. They often get this look on their face that says, "You are an idiot. I am depressed and you want me to go without food?" God has a way of injecting more joy and gladness into our lives through fasting. How God does this is not significant. The fact that He does it is significant.

We will be rewarded by God: Jesus makes this perfectly clear. Matthew 6:18 says, "So that you do not appear to men to be fasting, but to your Father who is in the secret place; and your Father who sees in secret will reward you openly." Our Father desires to reward us through properly motivated fasting. I personally believe that this reward that Jesus speaks of is a spiritual reward. God certainly knows how to draw us into closer intimacy with Him.

We will have a heightened sensitivity to God: This appears to be evident for the leaders at the church in Antioch in Acts 13:2-3. "As they ministered to the Lord and fasted, the Holy Spirit said, 'Now separate to Me Barnabas and Saul for the work to which I have called them.' Then, having fasted and prayed, and laid hands on them, they sent them away." Why is this so significant? Up until this time in Acts, no one had been sent out with the express purpose of taking the gospel somewhere else. Some had been scattered by persecution but no one had been sent on a mission trip. The Holy Spirit directed these church leaders to do something new in order to spread the gospel and He spoke to them during a time of worshipping and fasting.

In 2004, when Impact Ministries (our ministry) sensed God was heading us in a particular direction concerning a retreat center, our staff fasted for direction and God spoke with great clarity. We obeyed and He magnificently blessed us. Sometimes we need a greater sensitivity to the Holy Spirit that God has placed in us. Fasting and worshipping increase that sensitivity.

Can God answer prayer without us fasting? Absolutely! I appreciate my experience with fasting in that it seems to bring my thoughts in line with God's thoughts. For me, prayer alone sometimes attempts to bring God's thoughts in line with my thoughts. I have concluded for my life that I have a greater opportunity to connect with God in prayer and a greater opportunity to pray in a God-centered way when I combine prayer with fasting.

Questions for Further Thought or Discussion

1. What is my biggest hindrance to fasting and why?
2. What lies from Satan have I believed about fasting?
3. What would I expect God to do if I spent more time in prayer and fasting?

The author: Dean Trune is the Executive Director of Impact Ministries International located in Okemos, Michigan.

SUGGESTED ADDITIONAL READING

Wallis. Arthur. *God's Chosen Fast.* Fort Washington, PA: Christian Literature Crusade, 1968.

Fletcher, Kingsley A. *Prayer and Fasting.* New Kinsington, PA: Whitaker House, 1992.

Floyd, Ronnie. *The Power of Prayer and Fasting.* Nashville: Broadman & Holman Publishers, 1997.

chapter

18

PRAYING WITH GOD'S HEART AND MIND

Joel Wilson

Learning to pray with God's heart and mind leads to effectual, answered prayer. Our Lord modeled this prayer foundation in His earthly ministry. Consequently we should grow in this prayer foundation because it is our Lord's will for us to pray and not faint (Lk. 18:1). This involves four interdependent biblical truths associated with abiding in Christ: prayer is a relationship-based practice, is inseparable from the Word of God and worship, is how God gets His work done on earth, and is heavenly energized work. The result will be answered prayer as Jesus promises in John 15:7-8. Learning prayer from our Lord Jesus' words and practice will equip us to pray doxologically from beginning to end.

Prayer is a relationship-based practice.

Jesus denounced the pharisaical practice of prayer in His day because it was activity and performance focused (Mt. 6:5). He redirected His listeners to understand prayer as an intimate, relational interaction between the Father and disciple (Mt. 6:6-7). He next expanded the relational character of prayer by giving His listeners a pattern (not a formula) for relational growth in prayer (6:9-15). His disciple's request to "teach us to pray" should not be an unexpected response (Lk. 11:1) from those who watched their Lord pray while observing the Pharisee's pious display and public performance in the synagogues and at the street corners.

Accordingly, the overarching purpose of prayer demonstrates the non-negotiable dependency of the created on the fully sustaining, sufficiency of the Creator. Prayer reveals the reality of our finiteness in distinction to His infiniteness. Our relationship to our Savior Jesus Christ gives us the opportunity to daily align our lives to be in submission with our heavenly Father's will so that His will is done on earth as it is in heaven. In this understanding, the desires and directions of God our Father become the main focus for why we pray. We learn to pray unceasingly as we work out our salvation with Godly reverence and submission. Praying with God's heart and mind reveals the sovereign kingdom rule of God who works in us to will and do His good pleasure (Mt. 5:10, 16-17, 6:9; 1 Thess. 3:10-11, 5:17; Phil. 2:12-13).

As the fully sustaining, sufficient Creator over His created, God has known and understood all things from eternity to eternity. Nothing surprises Him. He knows what we will say when we shut the door and pray to our Father who is in secret. He knows the answer to our prayers before they are ever voiced as we express our dependence on Him in prayer (Ps. 139:1-6; Mt. 6:8). He delights to give us good things—not a stone but bread, not a serpent but a fish (Mt. 7:9-11).

As our intimate relationship grows with our Heavenly Father, so does our confidence in looking to God for His heart and mind in every situation. Relational confidence in prayer is based on our full acceptance as a new creation in Christ. We were dead in trespasses and sin, but are now alive able to relationally experience and execute our Father's heart and mind (Eph. 2:1, 10). We stand before His throne in His presence (1:6-8, 3:12; Heb. 4:16) through His inseparable, unconditional love (Rom. 8:38-39). God is love! If we apply the type of love God desires among believers expressed in 1 Corinthians 13: 4-8, we learn that our heavenly Father is patient, kind, not boastful and conceited, self-seeking or rude, not easily provoked, does not keep a record of my wrongs, does not rejoice in unrighteousness but in truth, seeks what is best for His own and never gives up. His agape love never fails toward those who have a new covenant relationship with Him in Christ Jesus.

Moreover, this relational confidence aspect of praying with God's heart and mind is likewise expanded by understanding the roles of the other two members of the Trinity, Jesus, our High Priest, and the Holy Spirit, our Comforter. As our High Priest who walked on this earth as we do (1 Jn. 2:16, 4:17), our Lord understands temptation (Mt. 4:1-11; Heb. 2:18), weariness associated with our present fleshly body, the necessity of pressing forward in the kingdom assignments God our Father has led us to complete (Mt. 26:36-46; Heb. 4:15), and looking to God alone for directions about the next step to take (Lk. 6:12-16). Subsequently, the Spirit of God is the one who prompts us to pray even when we cannot adequately articulate a burden (Rom. 8:26-27). He clearly helps believers pray with God's heart and mind by revealing the things that are ours in Christ (Jn. 14:26, 16:12-15) by virtue of our identification in Christ Jesus (Eph. 2:1-10).

In this relationship we do not pray for the purpose of trying to get God to do what we want; that is, get Him to conform Himself to our will. However, He delights in and invites us to pour out our hearts to Him (Ps. 62:8; Jn. 16: 23-24). We can experience His heart and mind (Phil. 2:5-8) in the tribulations we experience in this present world (Jn. 16:33; Gal. 1:4). We are to let the mind of Christ be in us as His servants, who serve as their Lord served (Jn. 4:34). Consequently, most Christians tragically live in prayer that is one-sided—with no enjoyment of relationship in prayer. Many have not learned to listen to God! The center point for listening to God and growing in our prayer relationship and practice is learning how to meditate in His special revelation to us, the Bible. Meditation-based prayer founded in God's inerrant, infallible Word is therefore the central means by which we build our relationship with God and one another. It further affirms our complete dependency on His fully sustaining sufficiency revealed through His heart and mind in prayer (Eph. 6:18; Col. 3:16).

Answered prayer is inseparable from the Word of God and worship.

God communicates as we meditate in His Word and receive the wisdom and spiritual understanding given by the Holy Spirit (Jn. 16:13-15; Col. 1:9-10). We learn His mind and heart and therefore build a genuine relationship with Him. In observing this, we grow more in believing prayer and pray less default prayers tagged with "if it be Your will" as a convenient out. Scripture becomes the framework for expressing the cries of our heart in petitions and supplications to God (Jn. 15:7-8).

As we continue to meditate in Scripture and persevere in prayer three matters transpire in our prayer life. We begin to stand in awe and take pleasure in His presence as we learn God's character and ways (Eph. 3:20-21; Rev. 5:12). Jesus' high priestly ministry and intercession for us becomes a great assurance in our wrestling and burdens (Rom. 8:34; Eph. 6:12-18; Heb. 4:15-16). And the reality of the Spirit's intercession takes place for us when we do not know what or how to pray—for the Spirit knows what is the mind and will of God and He knows how to intercede for us with unspoken groanings that cannot be uttered (Rom. 8:26-27).

Meditating in God's Word transforms our hearts and minds to be in line with our Father's heart and mind (12:1-2). As we reflect on God's will (as expressed in His Word) and compare it to our thoughts and desires (as expressed in our prayers), we often discover that our will does not match God's. He reveals areas in our life needing change and adjustment.

As we obey, these changes and adjustments take place, our desires increasingly line-up with God's will—the way we pray changes. Our prayer focus becomes less self-centered. This in turn affects all of our praying, for we begin to desire what God desires. When we do ask for things, our prayers will cease to be mere "shopping lists" about our own wants and desires. We, instead, become the petitioners and supplicants for others in persevering prayer.

We experience and enjoy intercessory prayer as God moves His will through us to accomplish His work. As a result, we often open and end our intercessory prayer times expressing praise, worship, and thanks to Him because of His greatness. We remain in awe of who He is (Ps. 34:1-8, 37:4; Eph. 1:17-23, 3:20; Col. 1:9-14). Our praying increasingly becomes an expression of God's will—His very mind and heart. We truly advance His kingdom on earth (Mt. 6:9-10). We have what maturing Christians desire and cry out for—answered prayer (Jn. 15:7-8).

Prayer is how God gets His work done on earth.

The Gospel records of Jesus' prayers and the instructions given by Him to us about praying provide a model for the priority of prayer in our personal life, home, and daily walk. Our Lord was focused on one thing—getting God's work done that He was sent to do (Jn. 5:17; 9:4). He actively involved Himself in the Father's kingdom agenda by learning the Father's heart and mind through prayer (3:16; Mk. 8:34-38, 10:45). This often involved misunderstanding and suffering (Jn. 7:1-9). Even in the midst of this, Jesus had joy and desired His disciples have joy in their tribulations in this present evil age (15:11). Jesus learned through His sufferings by offering up prayers and supplications with strong crying and tears to His Father who was able to save Him from death (Heb. 5:7; Lk. 22:39-46). As His servants, we are not greater than our Lord (Jn.15:20). We will experience the same as we obey God's agenda in getting His work done on the earth (Mt. 6:10; Eph. 2:10).

How did Jesus find out what the Father's agenda was? Through prayer! From Luke's gospel, we see this in Jesus' selection of the twelve and in His announcement to them about the Father's agenda concerning His suffering and resurrection the third day. These key events in Jesus' life were preceded by His prayer relationship with the Father (Lk. 6:12, 9:18-22). In fact, in the upper room discourse Jesus makes it very plain about His prayer relationship with the Father. It was the Father initiating and doing the works through the Son. How else could Jesus have known to obey God's agenda except through His vital daily relationship in prayer with His Father? This daily emphasis about Jesus' prayer relationship can be observed in His instructions to His disciples about prayer for their daily bread (Mt. 6:9-15). Jesus desired for His followers to enjoy an abundant prayer life as He did. John records Jesus' upper room discourse invitations for an abundant prayer life in 14:13-14 and 16:23-24.

Answered prayer results from God-energized work.

When we say that prayer is work, this should not be construed as dutiful drudgery. The secret of an abundant prayer life begins with an understanding of what abiding in Christ means to a believer in daily life (John 15). The core of abiding (15:4-8) involves a spiritual understanding of our total inability to do anything of kingdom value apart from Christ abiding in us and we in Him. Abiding leads us to bear fruit, more fruit, and much fruit unto the glory of God. Fruit can be both souls saved and God-honoring responsiveness.

What then does it mean to abide in Christ? Briefly, it signifies learning about and enjoying our "in Christ" relationship as His redeemed (Jn. 14:20; Eph. 2:1-10) and allowing His words to abide in us through meditation (Jn. 15:7-8). The result will be answered prayer mentioned in the beginning of this discussion: "You will ask what you desire, and it shall be done for you" (15:7). We will then be able to enter into the God-energized work of prayer as we watch and persevere with God's mind and heart and bring forth much fruit for the glory of God (Eph. 6:18).

May we be able to say at the end of life on earth as Jesus did: "I have finished the work which You have given me to do" (Jn. 17:4).

Questions for Further Thought or Discussion

1. Use the final scripture (Jn. 17:4) as the beginning of a paragraph explaining the basic premise of this chapter.
2. Why is meditation essential to praying the heart and mind of God?
3. As the leader of a corporate prayer gathering, how would you explain praying from God's perspective?

The author: Dr. Joel Wilson is Assistant Professor of Biblical and Theological Studies at Criswell College in Dallas, Texas.

SUGGESTED FURTHER READING

Bickel, Bruce, and Stan Jantz. *Bruce and Stan's Pocket Guide to Prayer.* Eugene, OR: Harvest House, 2000.

Boa, Ken. *Face to Face: Praying the Scriptures for Intimate Worship.* 2 vols., Grand Rapids: Zondervan, 1997.

Bounds, E. M. *The Compete Words of E.M. Bounds on Prayer.* Grand Rapids: Baker Books: 1990.

Evans, Mike. *The Unanswered Prayers of Jesus.* Minnneapolis: Bethany House Publishers, 2003

Towns, Elmer. *How to Pray When Don't Know What to Say.* Ventura, CA: Regal Books, 2000.

chapter

19

RESPONDING IN PRAYER TO GOD'S CHARACTER

Aida Besancon Spencer

God's character affects one's prayer and one's action and response to one's prayer. Thus, when we pray we should begin with reflecting on God's character because that will help us then pray in accordance with God's character. It should also guide our appropriate action. God's answer to our prayer depends on whether our prayer was consistent with God's character. I would like to illustrate these truths from two prayers: one from the Old Testament and one from the New Testament.

In the tenth century B.C., after King Solomon had the temple built, with the glory of the Lord filling the temple, he prayed before the congregation (1 K. 8:10, 23). Solomon's prayer is unique in that shortly afterwards God appears to him telling Solomon that his prayer had been heard (9:3). It was an effective prayer. Therefore, it can serve as a model prayer for us today. Solomon prayed: "Lord, God of Israel, there is no god like you, in the heavens above and on the earth beneath, observing the covenant and the love to your servants, the ones walking before your face with all their heart" (8:23, my trans.). Every title or characteristic of God mentioned in the opening of this prayer is developed later in the prayer as a basis for a prayer request.

First, Solomon calls God "Lord." The Hebrews would say "Lord," although the Hebrew text itself has the unpronounceable name for God, the consonants YHWH. These consonants are also the consonants in the verb of being: "I will be" (Ex. 3:12-14; 6:2). Thus, this first title tells us that God is mysterious and God "will be" with us. Moreover, the God who "will be" is the God who is always in the process of acting. God is the hope for the future. Consequently, Solomon mentions in his prayer that, although he has built a magnificent house for God to dwell in, in reality "Heaven and the heaven of heavens cannot contain You. How much less this temple which I have built! . . . Your eyes may be open toward this temple night and day" (1 K. 8:27, 29). Solomon acknowledges God's uniqueness and God's omnipresence. Only a God who is always with us can listen to prayers "night and day." We can be assured that God is near to us whenever we call (Deut. 4:7).

Second, Solomon calls God "God of Israel." God had said, "My name shall be there" (1 K. 8:29, 51), calling the Israelites a unique people who God had brought out from slavery in Egypt. In God's reply to Solomon, God confirms that indeed the Israelites are a special people and David and his heirs are unique (9:5, 9). However, God warns Solomon that such special status and favorable response to their prayers is dependent on their obedience to follow God's commands to conform their lives to God's example "if you walk before me" (9:4). "But if you or your sons at all turn from following Me, and do not keep my commandments and My statutes" (9:6). That is why God's character affects people's prayer and action. As we pray based on God's character, God expects us to act in imitation of God's character.

Third, Solomon states, "LORD God of Israel, there is no god in heaven above or on the earth below like You" (8:23). God is unique. As we saw, God can not be contained within a building like gods constructed by humans (8:27). Because God is unique, God expects His followers to embrace and worship only Him and no other god (9:9). Praying to the unique God will be of no effect if we at the same time worship other gods. Because God is unique, God is a jealous God demanding a unique worship.

Fourth, Solomon describes God as observing the covenant. Therefore, Solomon reminds God to keep His promise to His father David by not failing to have a successor to sit on the throne of Israel (8:25). The Lord agrees that He will establish Solomon's throne over Israel, however, He reminds Solomon that this covenant is dependent on Solomon obeying God's commands (9:4-5). God does not answer those who hate good and love evil (Mic. 3:2-4). God's ear is never "too dull to hear," rather human sins block the communication (Isa. 59:1-2).

Fifth, Solomon describes God as "you who keep your covenant of love with your servants who continue wholeheartedly in your way" (1 K. 8:23, NIV). "Love" (*hesed* in Hebrew) can include kindness, goodness, benevolence, mercy, grace, and beauty. The variety of aspects of God's "love" were introduced in Exodus 34:6: "Lord (YHWH) God, compassionate and merciful, slow to be displeased and greatly loving (*hesed*) and faithful" (my trans.). No other deity has God's *hesed* ("steadfast love," 1 K. 8:23; 2 Chron. 6:14). It includes helping someone in difficult circumstances, never giving up on someone recalcitrant, forgiving people's sins, and remaining with someone when times are difficult. Jesus, as God incarnate, was "full of *grace* and truth" (Jn. 1:14, *emphasis added*). Because God is a loving God, Solomon can rely on God to forgive humans who repent of their sins and to respond in compassion to their requests (1 K. 8:30-53).

What can we incorporate from Solomon's prayer into our own prayer lives? We can hope in God when we rely on His character in prayer because God is *Lord*, the mysterious "I will be"; God is the *God of Israel*, but also the God of every individual who acknowledges God as Lord ("walking" before God "with all their heart"); God is *unique*, steadfast in keeping *covenants* and in *loving* us.

In the first century A.D., when Jesus taught His disciples to pray, He taught them to begin prayer by acknowledging who God is and then referencing God's character as evidenced by God's interests. We are to pray to "our Father, the one in the heavens" (Mt. 6:9, my trans.). As with Solomon's prayer, we need to recognize that the one to whom we pray is not a god whom we create nor an earthly father. This is the living, omnipresent God who can hear us wherever we may be and at whatever time, who listens to prayers "night and day" (1 K. 8:29). This is a "Father who is in secret," therefore, we can be "in secret" when we pray (Mt. 6:6). Because our God is also a loving "Father," our model prayer can continue with requests for food and forgiveness and rescuing because a loving God wants us to have food daily and wants us to be forgiven and wants us to be rescued from evil (6:11-13).

Jesus later tells His disciples that if humans "know how to give good gifts to [their] children, how much more will Your heavenly Father" give good gifts, including God's own presence, the Holy Spirit, "to those who ask him!" (Lk. 11:13; Mt. 7:11). Because God is compassionate and omnipresent, we do not need to repeat "vain repetitions as the heathen do." Our Father knows what we need before we even ask (Mt. 6:7-8). God is good. God is loving, as Solomon said, God "observes" love (1 K. 8:23). These qualities are the basis for requests for good and loving things from God.

"Hallowed be (make holy) Your name" next reminds us of God's holy character (Mt. 6:9). As Solomon prayed, God "observes" the covenant (1 K. 8:23). Since God is holy, God does not accept or respond to unforgiven sin (Mt. 6:12). Jesus goes on to teach that, if we forgive others their sins, our heavenly Father will also forgive us (6:14-15). God is just. Therefore, in our prayers we can be assured of God's justice, even if justice may appear to be delayed (Lk. 18:1-7).

"Your kingdom come" (Mt. 6:10) reminds us that our heavenly Father is a ruler (even with an angelic army, e.g. Mt. 26:53; 1 Cor. 15:24-25). This aspect of God certainly affects our actions. A parent is concerned to provide for children. Therefore, we should strive first for God's kingdom and allow God to provide our material needs (Mt. 6:25-33). This also affects the nature of what we pray. We should desire to advance God's reign despite the difficulties involved. For instance, when the religious leaders of their time warned Peter and John not to speak or teach at all in Jesus' name (Acts 4:18, 21), they continued to pray to advance God's reign: "Lord, look on their threats, and grant to Your servants that with all boldness they may speak Your word, by stretching out Your hand to heal, and that signs and wonders may be done through the name of Your holy Servant Jesus" (4:29-30). In response, God shook up the house and filled these disciples with the Holy Spirit and they spoke God's word boldly (4:31)!

Finally, Jesus' prayer begins, "let Your will happen, as in heaven also upon earth" (Mt. 6:10, my trans.). Jesus reminds His listeners that the wise hear His words *and* act on them because then they will be safe from falling (7:24-27). We too are reminded that God wants us to live out on earth lives consistent with God's character "in heaven." God's will will happen, but will we cooperate with it and further it?

Thus, we learn from Jesus' model prayer that we pray to a God who is like a ruling loving Parent and a God who is holy. God's character has not changed from Old to New Testament times.

In the seventeenth century *Interior Castle's* "fourth Mansions" section, the famous Spanish Christian Teresa of Avila gives a beautiful illustration of prayer that flows from Christ's character as a compassionate high priest sympathetic to our human weaknesses.[1] The Book of Hebrews states: "In the days of His flesh, when He had offered up prayers and supplications, with vehement cries and tears to Him who was able to save Him from death, and was heard because of His godly fear, though He was a Son, yet He learned obedience by the things which He suffered. And having been perfected, He became the author of eternal salvation to all who obey Him, called by God as High Priest 'according to the order of Melchizedek'" (Heb. 5:7-10).

Appropriately, St. Teresa of Avila presupposes a God who can empathize when she prays:

> O Lord, do Thou remember how much we have to suffer on this road through lack of knowledge! The worst of it is that, as we do not realize we need to know more when we think about Thee, we cannot ask those who know; indeed we have not even any idea what there is for us to ask them. So we suffer terrible trials because we do not understand ourselves; and we worry over what is not bad at all, but good, and think it very wrong. Hence proceed the afflictions of many people who practice prayer, and their complaints of interior trials—especially if they are unlearned people—so that they become melancholy, and their health declines, and they even abandon prayer altogether, because they fail to realize that there is an interior world close at hand. Just as we cannot stop the movement of the heavens, revolving as they do with such speed, so we cannot restrain our thought. And then we send all

> the faculties of the soul after it, thinking we are lost, and have misused the time that we are spending in the presence of God. [2]

If we concentrate less on ourselves and pray more to the character of our sovereign God who is both completely loving and completely holy, then we will pray with the effectiveness that wise Solomon and God-among-us Jesus did.

Questions for Further Thought or Discussion

1. Pick an attribute or title of God and develop a prayer from that attribute.
2. How does God's title and character affect the nature of the prayer in Luke 10:2 and Matthew 9:37-38?
3. Jesus reminds us that God's will is "as in heaven also upon earth." How does that affect the nature of what you pray for and the manner in which you pray?

The author: Dr. Aida Besancon Spencer is Professor of New Testament at Gordon-Conwell Theological Seminary in South Hamilton, Massachusetts. She is the co-author with her husband, of *The Prayer Life of Jesus: Shout of Agony, Revelation of Love, A Commentary* and co-editor with her husband of and contributor to *The Global God: Multicultural Evangelical Views of God.*

SUGGESTED ADDITIONAL READING

Hunter, W. Bingham. *The God Who Hears.* Downers Grove, IL: InterVarsity Press, 1986.

Littleton, Mark. *Getting Honest with God: Praying as if God Really Listens.* Downers Grove, IL: InterVarsity Press, 2003.

Stone, Nathan. *Names of God.* Chicago, IL: Moody Press, 1944.

Work, Telford. *Ain't Too Proud to Beg: Living through the Lord's Prayer.* Grand Rapids: Eerdmans Publishing, 2007.

ENDNOTES

1. St. Teresa of Avila. *Interior Castle.* Trans., ed. E. Allison Peers. New York: Doubleday, 1989 [originally written 1577].

2. Avila, p. 77.

chapter

20

DOES GOD REALLY NEED OUR PRAYER?

Dutch Sheets

Can our prayers actually change things? Can God's will on earth really be frustrated if we don't pray? Isn't He going to do what He wants to do anyway? Most people, even if only subconsciously, believe just this. And this belief is reflected in their prayer life, or lack thereof.

When God says, "Pray," I want to know that it will matter. If God is going to do something (or not do something) whether I pray or not, then what's the point in praying? If, however, John Wesley was correct when he said, "God does nothing on the earth save in answer to believing prayer," I'll change my lifestyle for that!

The question comes down to this: Why does God want us to pray? Does a sovereign, all-powerful God need our involvement or not? I believe the answer is yes!

God's Plan at Creation

The answer to why prayer is necessary lies in God's original plan at the creation of humankind. The word *adam* means "human being." God made a human and called him "Human." He made an *adam* and named him "Adam." Throughout the Old Testament, the Hebrew word *adam* is often used for "man." Adam represents all of us. What God intended for him, He intended for the entire human race.

Initially, God gave Adam and Eve dominion over the entire earth and all creation: "Then God said, 'Let us make man in Our image, according to Our likeness; let them have dominion . . . over all the earth. . . . So God created man . . . in the image of God He created him; male and female He created them" (Gen. 1:26–27).

"What is man that You . . . crowned him with glory and honor. You have made him to have dominion over the works of Your hands; You have put all things under his feet" (Ps. 8:4–6). A careful look at some of the Hebrew words here and elsewhere will help us see God's plan more clearly. The Hebrew word *mashal*—translated "have dominion" in verse 6 of the Psalms passage—indicates that Adam was God's manager, steward, or governor on earth.

Psalm 115:16 also confirms this: "The heavens . . . the Eternal holds Himself, the earth He has assigned to men" (Moffat Translation). This translation communicates with greater accuracy the meaning of the Hebrew word *nathan*, which is frequently translated "given." God did not give away ownership of the earth, but He did assign responsibility for governing it to humanity.

Humans re-present God on earth.

God's plan was for Adam to be His representative on earth. A representative is one who "re-presents," or presents again, the will of another. Now it's no small task to re-present God. Therefore, God made us so much like Himself that it was like an illusion. The Hebrew word for "image" in Genesis 1:27 is *tselem*, which connotes a shadow or an illusion. The Hebrew word *demuwth*, translated "likeness" in Genesis 1:26, comes from the root word *damah*, which means "to compare." So in a limited sense, Adam was deliberately made similar to or comparable to God. He was not God, but he was made enough like God to be able to represent Him on earth.

The Hebrew word *kabowd* (translated "glory" in Ps. 8:5) literally means "heavy or weighty" and is linked to the concept of authority. We still use this word picture today when we refer to one who "carries a lot of weight." Adam carried the weight on the earth. He represented God with full authority.

To summarize, Adam was comparable to or similar to God—so much like God that it was illusionary. God was recognized in Adam, which meant that Adam "carried the weight" here on earth. Adam represented God, "presenting again" God's will on the earth, as His governor or manager. The earth was Adam's assignment—it was under his charge, or care. How things went on planet Earth, for better or worse, depended on Adam and his offspring.

Think about that. If the earth remained a paradise, it would be because of humankind. If things got messed up, it would be because of humankind. For the serpent to gain control, it had to do it through humankind!

So complete and final was Adam's authority over the earth that he, not just God, had the ability to give it away. And that's what happened in the fall: Adam gave over his authority on earth to Satan. Jesus Himself acknowledged this three times by calling Satan "the prince of this world" (Jn. 12:31, 14:30, 16:11). Satan tried to tempt Jesus with this in Luke 4:6: "All this authority I will give You [the world's kingdoms] and their glory; for this has been delivered to me, and I give it to whomever I wish."

God's decision to do things on earth through human beings cost Him dearly. He had to become human in order to regain what Adam gave away. Nothing is weightier proof of the finality of this "through humans" decision than the incarnation. God clearly intends for humans to be the link to His authority and activity on the earth forever. This is why prayer is necessary. God works through the prayers of His people.

God chose, from the time of the creation, to work on the earth through humans, not independent of them. He always has and always will, even at the cost of becoming human. Though God is sovereign and all-powerful, the Scriptures clearly show He chose to limit Himself (concerning the affairs of earth) to working through human beings.

Is this not the reason the earth is in such a mess? Not because God wills it so, but because He has chosen to work and carry out His will through imperfect people. The story is woven throughout the Scriptures: God and humans, for better or worse, doing it together. God needing faithful men and women, a chosen race, prophets, judges, a human Messiah, human hands to heal, human voices to speak, and human feet to go.

Why else would God tell us to pray for His kingdom to come, His will to be done (Mt. 6:10)? Surely He wouldn't want us to waste our time asking for something that was going to happen anyway! When Paul said, "Pray for us, that the word of the Lord may run swiftly and be glorified" (2 Thess. 3:1), wasn't God already planning to do this?

Are not these things God's will? Why, then, am I supposed to ask Him for something He already wants to do if it's not that my asking somehow releases Him to do it?

Elijah's Fervent Prayers

In 1 Kings 18, we find the account of Elijah's prayers for rain after three years of drought. God told Elijah, "Go, present yourself to Ahab, and I will send rain on the earth" (1 K. 18:1). At the end of chapter 18, Elijah prays seven times, and the rain comes. But according to verse one, whose idea was it to send rain? Whose will? At whose initiation? It was God's, not Elijah's!

Why, then, if it was God's idea and timing, did Elijah's prayers bring the rain? The only logical answer is that God chose to work through a human. Even when the Lord Himself initiates something and earnestly desires to do it, He needs us to ask.

Daniel, a Man of Prayer

Another example of the absolute need for prayer is found in the life of Daniel. While reading Jeremiah's prophecies, Daniel discovered that Israel's captivity was to last 70 years. He realized that it was time for the captivity to end.

At this point, Daniel did something different from what most of us would do. When we receive a promise, we tend to sit and watch for its fulfillment. But Daniel must have known that God needed his involvement, because he turned to the Lord, "to make request by prayer and supplications, with fasting, sackcloth, and ashes" (Dan. 9:3).

No verse in Daniel specifically reports that Israel was restored because of Daniel's prayers, but the insinuation is there. We do know that an angel was dispatched immediately after Daniel started praying, for he tells Daniel, "Your words were heard, and I have come because of your words" (10:12).

God needs our prayers.

God's existence and character are completely independent of any created thing (Acts 17:24–25), and God already has all resources in His hands (Job 41:11; Ps. 50:10–12). But His need of our prayers is shown again in Ezekiel 22:30–31: "So I sought for a man among them who would make a wall, and stand in the gap before Me on behalf of the land, that I should not destroy it; but I found no one. Therefore I have poured out My indignation on them; I have consumed them with the fire of My wrath; and I have recompensed their deeds on their own heads."

The implications are staggering. God's holiness, integrity, and uncompromising truth prevent Him from excusing sin. It must be judged. On the other hand, His love desires always to redeem, restore, and show mercy. The passage clearly says, "While My justice demanded judgment, My love wanted forgiveness. Had I been able to find a human to ask Me to spare this people, I could have done it. It would have allowed Me to show mercy. Because I found no one, however, I had to destroy them."

Our Task

In light of these and other passages, as well as the condition of the world, I can come to no other conclusion: God, in His sovereignty, has chosen to limit Himself on earth to working through humans. Since it's difficult to believe that it's God's will for the earth to be in the condition it's in—or that He's powerless to do anything about it—we can only assume that He is waiting on something from us to bring about the necessary changes.

Let's rise to the occasion and prayerfully ask what that something is. Let's embrace this incredible invitation to be co-laborers with God in prayer. Let's be carriers of His awesome Holy Spirit and ambassadors for His great kingdom as we "re-present" Him on earth!

Awaken us to our destiny, Lord!

(This chapter is adapted from *Intercessory Prayer: How God Can Use Your Prayers to Move Heaven and Earth*, published by Regal Books and was used in *Pray!* magazine, Issue 11, March/April, 1999, entitled, "Does God Really Need Our Prayers." It is used by permission of *Pray!* magazine, the author, and Regal Books.)

Questions for Further Thought or Discussion

1. Why is the question of this chapter ("Does God really need our prayer") important theologically? Practically in church ministry?
2. Clearly state the author's position, then explain why you agree or disagree with his thesis.
3. Based on your position, what are the implications toward developing a church-wide ministry of prayer.

The author: Dr. Dutch Sheets is senior pastor of Freedom Church in Colorado Springs, Colorado and President of Dutch Sheets Ministries. He has traveled extensively, teaching throughout the world and is the author of numerous books including, *Intercessory Prayer; Authority in Prayer; Roll Away Your Stone; Getting in God's Face;* and *Hope Resurrected.*

SUGGESTED ADDITIONAL READING

Tiessen, Terrance. *Providence & Prayer: How Does God Work in the World?* Downers Grove, IL: InterVarsity Press, 2000.

Piper, John. *Desiring God: Mediations of a Christian Hedonist.* Sisters, OR: Multnomah Publishers, 2003.

Hunter, W. Bingham. *The God Who Hears.* Downers Grove, IL: InterVarsity Press, 1986.

SECTION TWO

THE PERSONAL PASSION FOR PRAYER

chapter

21

THE BIBLE AND PERSONAL PASSION IN PRAYER

Earl Pickard

Through my heart's journey of developing a prayer life, pondering and praying the Word, I noticed in the Psalms that David, often, called upon the Lord and cried out to Him. In Psalm 84, I was captivated by David's heart cry for the living God. Through His intimacy with God, yielded and surrendered, he grasped and laid hold of God's strength, turning his inner being into a heart pilgrimage. This burning intensity of zeal, fervor and affection created in David the inner passion for deeper communion with God and a clearer union in Him.

I have not only studied and read the Bible for head-knowing, but I have strived to internalize and live the Word of God for heart-living. It is important, not only to apply the Bible to our lives, but to live the Word of

God in and through our lives. Notice in Ephesians 3:11-21 that Paul, realized that through the Holy Spirit in the inner man, Christ dwelled in the heart, through faith, in order to know the love of Christ which surpasses knowledge, that we may be filled up to all the fullness of God.

Seldom in prayer meetings or gatherings do we participate with others in the burning intensity of heartfelt calling upon and crying out to the Lord. I have wondered, *Why?* Maybe it is because we have not fully comprehended the depth of God's grace and mercy. Or maybe it is because we do not live in personal passion prayer ourselves. Often, David cried out for God's mercy. In Psalm 28, he calls upon the Lord in passion, "O LORD my Rock," and, then, appeals to the Lord, ". . . hear the voice of my supplications when I cry to You, when I lift up my hands toward Your holy sanctuary" (vv.1-2).

I have been at the altar on many occasions alone and with others in deep heart burden, repentance and heart-searching prayer. Sometimes, some people in heartfelt brokenness will cry out to God for His mercy and forgiveness, in conviction from their sinfulness or their deep longings or yearnings. In Romans 9:15-16, "He says to Moses, 'I will have mercy on whomever I will have mercy, and I will have compassion on whomever I will have compassion.' So then it is not of him who wills, nor of him who runs, but of God who shows mercy." No wonder the psalmist or others like Paul cried out to God for mercy (His divine compassion). No wonder I need to cry out to God at the altar for mercy. I do not deserve God's kindness and forgiveness—that is grace. But I need it—that is mercy!

Recently, I was reading Hebrews and allowing it to serve as my outline or framework for intimate prayer, seeking the Lord. I came upon the "draw me" phrase several times. You can look up these three occasions in Hebrews 4:14-16, 7:19-28 and 10:19-26, where we are called to: (1) draw near with confidence to the throne of grace, (2) draw near to God through Christ, and (3) draw near with a sincere heart in full assurance of faith. As I read and pondered these passages and the whole book of Hebrews, I noticed that they are in the context of our Lord Jesus Christ as our High Priest. Hebrews 7:25 indicates the Lord always lives to make intercession for us. His intercession, at the Father's right hand, for me and in me is heard by my heavenly Father.

The closer I draw near to God, the more He is able to reveal and I am able to receive His answers and know His will. The more I meditate upon

God's Word, pondering and praying the Word in passionate prayer, the more God's Word becomes alive in me and takes deep root into my inner being. I begin to internalize and personalize God's ways and His thoughts for my heart pilgrimage and journey. The work of the Holy Spirit in and through me, through God's Word, enables me to know and understand both the ways of God and the will of God.

As I learn to express my heart, in the Word of God and in "heart dump," I increasingly delight and desire to truly be in the presence of God. My heart dump becomes full of passionate and burning zeal to deny myself and be conformed to His image. Paul says it well, "Christ in you, the hope of glory" (Col. 1:27). Not only do I delight and desire to know and understand the Word of God, but I begin to digest and live the Word of God. The inner work, by both the Holy Spirit and God's Word, leads to my deeper communion with the Lord and my clearer union in the Lord.

My perspective about God, the Bible and prayer determines my practice of prayer. The idea that the Creator of the universe desires to communicate with me and have fellowship with Him, gives me more impetus to be in passionate prayer. It is important to know and understand God's attributes of who God is, as it gives me a greater awareness and confidence in the Lord God Almighty. The Bible states that the true and living Lord God Almighty is the God Who was, Who is and Who is to come (Rev. 4:8). He is, then, the Eternal One, the Alpha and Omega, the Beginning and End, the First and Last (22:13).

With this in mind, I have realized how important it is to read, study, ponder and pray the whole Bible. There, I learn much of how God works and sees through eternity, in a moment. In Ecclesiastes 3:11, it states, "He has made everything beautiful in its time. Also He has put eternity in their hearts, except that no one can find out the work that God does from beginning to end." It behooves me to view life, with my passion for God through passionate prayer, having eternity in my heart, by looking in all directions—upward, backward, and forward for the current—the *now* of daily-ness.

This daily-ness of present life, with eternity in my heart, gives me perspective, for a moment by moment relationship with God. Jesus instructed His disciples this way, "If anyone desires to come after Me, let him deny himself, and take up his cross, and follow Me" (Mt. 16:24). This daily denying of self requires my surrender to the Lord, realizing His plans and His will for me are to be mine. This, too, requires me to be consecrated unto the Lord, wholly dedicated and devoted to the Lord, with purity of heart and humility of life.

I must learn to daily abide in Christ, as I follow Him. "If you abide in Me, and My words abide in you, you will ask what you desire, and it shall be done for you. By this My Father is glorified, that you bear much fruit; so you will be My disciples" (Jn. 15:7, 8). As I abide in Christ, soon I desire more and more His will, rather than my own. Through pondering and praying the Word through passionate prayer, increasingly I live and have my being in His presence for His will to be made known and accomplished. I desire, then, to only ask according to His will. "This is the confidence that we have in Him, that if we ask anything according to His will, He hears us. And if we know that He hears us, whatever we ask, we know that we have the petitions that we have asked of Him" (1 Jn. 5:14, 15).

So, as I abide in Christ and ask according to His will, then I believe by faith. "Therefore I say to you, whatever things you ask when you pray, believe that you receive them, and you will have them" (Mk. 11:24). Finally, "Whatever things you ask in prayer, believing, you will receive" (Mt. 21:22). This is simply a flow of God's Word, in my deep, abiding relationship with the Lord, of walking by faith in the power of the Holy Spirit. This power of the Holy Spirit is essentially the work of the Holy Spirit through the Word of God for the will of the Father to be done and for the ways of the Lord to be known, as it is in heaven upon the earth.

Through heart-searching prayer I can live in the presence of God. His presence in my heart manifests His glory in and through me. Heart-searching prayer is another way to explain seeking the Lord wholeheartedly. "You will seek Me and find Me, when you search for Me with all your heart" (Jer. 29:13). The real depth of my spiritual life and walk with the Lord is reflected by my devotion and love for God and my desire and passion to be in His presence through heart-searching prayer, seeking the Lord wholeheartedly. This passion, to be in His presence with personal passion prayer, of heart-searching prayer, is really a passion for our Lord Jesus Christ, above and beyond any desire I may have for a cause, a ministry, a mission or even for others. This passion for the Lord, seeking the Lord wholeheartedly, stimulates and energizes my serving the Lord.

In the midst of this deep abiding in Christ in heart-searching prayer, seeking the Lord wholeheartedly, I must be alert and aware of what is going on and coming forth. I am to be clothed in His righteousness, with putting on the whole armor of God, prepared for spiritual conflict. Moreover, I need to be observant for distractions and deterrents.

I remember the three words that appear to me when I am at a railroad crossing: STOP-LOOK-LISTEN! If I obey this exhortation, it could save my life. Often, though, I can get in too much of a hurry, be impetuous, or I can shortcut the directions or principles, to heed the warnings or to obey the instructions. I should be disciplined enough and instilled deep inside to always STOP-LOOK-LISTEN! That is what is needed when it comes to God's directions and instructions in His Word, to guard our hearts and lives by obeying His Word and Spirit.

- STOP . . . "Be still, and know that I am God" (Ps. 46:10). "I wait for the LORD, my soul waits, and in His Word I do hope" (130:5).
- LOOK . . . "Looking unto Jesus . . . " (Heb. 12:2). "Seek those things which are above, where Christ is . . . " (Col. 3:1-4).
- LISTEN . . . "My sheep hear My voice, and I know them, and they follow Me" (Jn. 10:27). "You shall walk after the LORD your God and fear Him, and keep His commandments, and obey His voice; you shall serve Him and hold fast to Him" (Deut. 13:4).

The book of Proverbs is full of God's wisdom, knowledge and understanding. Proverbs instructs, "Above all else, guard your heart, for it is the wellspring of life" (4:23). The heart is a metaphor for our inner being, the essence of who I really am. It is the dwelling place of my emotions, attitudes and intentions. I am called to be holy, a holy temple in the Lord, according to Ephesians 2:13-22, with Christ Jesus Himself being the cornerstone. This holiness is a result or by-product of my passion for the Lord, in pondering and praying the Word in passionate prayer. My love and passion for God and His Word awakens my heart and increases my awareness of His presence, restoring the fear of the Lord and my hunger and thirst for more of Him.

So, in simplicity and summary, I encourage you to press on in pondering and praying the Word of God in passionate prayer, as you walk in the Spirit by faith, not according to the world, but by the work of the Holy Spirit, in the will of God the Father, in and through the ways of the Lord Jesus Christ, with the Word of God in your heart and mind, as it is in heaven upon the earth.

Questions for Further Thought or Discussion

1. Explain the role of the Bible, the Holy Spirit, and the pray-ers heart in developing a passion for prayer.
2. Word search "cry" in the book of Psalms. Identify 10-12 diverse occurrences; explain the emotional, physical, and spiritual state of the pray-er; and offer a conclusion of the role of passion in personal prayer.
3. Write a prayer, addressing each person of the Holy Trinity, Holy Sovereign God, Holy Savior, and Holy Spirit, asking each for His participation in maturing your personal prayer life.

The author: Rev. Earl Pickard is the National Director of Prayerworks, a ministry of Campus Crusade for Christ housed in Wichita, Kansas. He also serves on America's National Prayer Committee.

SUGGESTED ADDITIONAL READING

Graf, Jonathan. *The Power of Personal Prayer.* Colorado Springs, CO: NavPress, 2002.

"Motivating Your Personal Prayer Life" *Pray!*, Issue 57, November/December 2006.

Chapell, Bryan. *Praying Backwards: Transform Your Prayer Life by Beginning in Jesus' Name.* Grand Rapids: Baker Books, 2005.

chapter

22

A BIBLICAL ROLE MODEL OF PERSONAL PASSION IN PRAYER

Gloria J. Wiese

When I found out that Bethel University had been built on land that was originally a dynamite repository, I began to pray that God would kindle an explosive revival on BU's campus. But could this happen when papers are due and exams must be taken? Would God ever break into our set schedules? Where would He begin? It seemed likely that He would ignite somebody's prayers into an intense impassioned blaze.

The Lord has provided a perfect biblical role model: Daniel. While attending a different BU (Babylon University), Daniel had to get an "A" in REL101: *Interpretation of Dreams* or incur a fate much worse than academic probation. Yet instead of trying to handle the pressure, Daniel became passionate in prayer.

The Daniel model offers four aspects to developing and maintaining passion in prayer. First, passion begins to spark when we nurture a blameless heart before the Lord. Second, passion ignites when we are strategically informed by Him. Third, passion will be sustained when we embrace a continuous attitude of courageous humility. And fourth, passion intensifies as we orient everything in our life toward eternal kingdom realities.

Blamelessness sparks passion in prayer.

After entering BU, Daniel got his student ID card with a Babylonian name on it and began to go to astrology class (Dan. 1:7-16). Apparently, it wasn't these things that troubled him; it was the food! It is true that college cafeterias are notorious for their bland high carb smorgasbord. Was Daniel worried about adding the "freshman 15"? What's wrong with Babylonian cuisine? Ancient tablets indicate that the Mesopotamian elite's discriminating palate reflected their culinary *religious* rituals.[1] To eat of the king's delicacies was to feast with the gods. Daniel "resolved not to defile himself" (1:8; cf. 5:17) and so "no fault" could be found in him (6:4).

What really "defiles" and "corrupts" people? Unfortunately, most societies narrowly define defilement in hygienic terms and corruption in legal terms.[2] But in a biblical sense, if "to be holy" is to be "set apart to God" and enter the sphere of God's being or activity, then (given that holiness emanates from God alone) those who abide in Him will inevitably be transformed by His presence. Contrarily, "to be defiled" is to be "set apart to something that is not God" and thus enter the sphere or activity of a corrupt influence.[3] When Daniel "resolved not to defile himself" he was determined to abide in God's presence while entrenched in a morally bankrupt Babylonian system.

The screws really began to turn when people set Daniel up and railed false accusations against him (6:3-5, 24). Could he stay blameless? Daniel's resolve to abide in God remained steady because "three times a day he got down on his knees and prayed, giving thanks to his God, as was his custom since early days" (6:10-11). If we consistently abide in the Lord's presence in prayer we will bear the fruit of authenticity (Jn. 15:4; 1 Jn. 2:27-28) until the Ancient One pronounces judgment in our favor (Dan. 7:22).

The Daniel model confirms that passion in prayer begins to spark when we nurture a blameless heart. The Hebrew word "blameless" (*tamiym*) means:

"to have integrity; to be completely in accordance with truth" (e.g., Gen. 6:9; 17:1; Deut. 18:13; Job 1:1, 8; Ps. 15; 101). What is truth? Ironically, when Pilate asked Jesus this question he was looking at the face and embodiment of truth (Jn. 18:38; 1:14, 17; 14:6). Naturally, people perceive reality by subjectively interpreting their experiences and making their own conclusions. God, on the other hand, has a different perspective of reality; He calls it The Truth. The Truth (the Word of God) is the "true truth" because it reflects God's will and character. Although people may not understand God's truth (Dan. 9:13) or may even try to "cast truth down to the ground" (8:12), our prayers must be based on the "Book of Truth" (10:21; 9:2). If we do, we will be set free and sanctified by The Truth (Jn. 17:17; 8:32).

God does not reveal great mysteries to the smartest guys in the prayer room (Dan. 2:29-30). He imparts understanding to those who resolve to remain "undefiled" and are entirely aligned with The Truth. Their blameless hearts produce impartial prayer requests that are not only able to *understand* truth, they are willing to *plead* for mercy *and* justice (2:18-23). Can you feel Daniel's passion in the following prayer?

> As it is *written in the Law of Moses*, all this disaster has come upon us; yet we have not made our prayer before the LORD our God, that we might turn from our iniquities and understand your truth. . . . the LORD our *God is righteous in all the works which He does*; though we have not obeyed His voice . . . *we do not present our supplications before You because of our righteous deeds, but because of Your great mercies.* O Lord, hear! O Lord, forgive! O Lord, listen and act! . . . *For Your own sake*, my God." (9:13-14, 18-19, *emphasis added*)

Blamelessness shouts: "Heaven rules" (4:26; cf. 2:18) and appeals to Heaven to expose sin mercifully and appropriately (4:19, 27; 5:23-28).

Strategic information ignites passion in prayer.

For three years professor Ashpenaz taught Daniel all about Babylonian culture: its literature, language, history, and religion (1:4-5). King Nebuchadnezzar wanted to use Daniel's studies to further his own kingdom, but God wanted to utilize it to further His: "*God gave* them knowledge and skill in all literature and wisdom" and in "all matters of wisdom and understanding" (1:17, 20; cf. 5:11-16, *emphasis added*). The study of Babylonian culture was not just an exercise in gathering interesting information, *God wanted to impart His perspective* on what was happening in the land. God wanted more out of Daniel than expertise; He wanted an informed intercessor.[4]

Informed intercession values God's view of history and affirms that history serves God. Each city experiences changes. But the informed intercessor knows that it is the Lord who issues such "times and the seasons"; God desires to give "wisdom to the wise and knowledge to those who have understanding" and to reveal strategic "deep and secret things" for "he knows what is in the darkness, and light dwells with Him" (2:21-22; cf. 5:17-29; 8:15-27). When God sheds His light on our modern day "Babylon" our vision instantly broadens to encompass an eternal perspective (past, present, and future).

Too often, we allow the present circumstances to direct our prayers, ignoring the spiritual history that explains "how-we-got-to-this-point." But diligent, patient, and prayerful research allows us to honor God's sovereignty as it links our present generation with the past and shapes the future. Strategic information requires us to dwell in God's presence long enough to survey the territory, gather the intelligence, and implement the prayer strategy that is necessary to further God's kingdom (e.g., chapters 7-11). Like Daniel we too need to *ask God for His perspective on the history of our land.* Although many run to and fro over the globe as knowledge increases (12:4), only Holy Spirit-led investigations ignite fervency, sharpen discernment, and aid in praying more precisely and more effectively.

Courageous humility sustains passion in prayer.

What will happen when a blameless heart prays with some strategic information? Daniel began to repent (9:3-20)! But notice *how* courageously Daniel repented:

> *We* have sinned and committed iniquity, *we* have done wickedly and rebelled, even by departing from Your precepts Your judgments. Neither have *we* heeded Your servants the prophets . . . O LORD, to *us* belongs shame of face, to our kings, our princes,

> and our fathers because *we* have sinned against You. (9:5-6, 8, *emphasis added*)

Daniel *did not* commit the sins he confessed, but as a representative he humbly identified with and repented of the (generational) corporate sins of others. He is not alone. Moses sought God's forgiveness on a corporate level (Ex. 32:9-14, 34:8-9; Deut. 9:18-29, 10:10-11); Isaiah repented on behalf of Israel (Isa. 6:5); Jeremiah confessed the sins of his generation and his forefathers (Jer. 3:25; 14:7, 20); Ezra's identificational repentance (Ezra 9:6-15) led to corporate repentance (10:1-4); Nehemiah's identificational repentance (Neh. 1:6-9) also preceded corporate repentance (8:9-11, 9:1-2).

To intercede through "identificational" repentance is simply to identify with a particular corporate sin (regional, ethnic, religious, vocational, or family) and represent the perpetrators (or victims) by repenting of (or forgiving) that particular sin. Clearly, identificational repentance is *not* a prayer for the dead (to absolve them of personal accountability before God) nor is it vicarious repentance (to stand as a substitute of others); identificational repentance seeks to release the present generation from the *consequences* of the sins of previous generations (cf. Lev. 26:40; 2 Chron. 7:40).

Passion in prayer is sustained by courageous humility and repentance for it opens the arms of an intensely affectionate God (Ezek. 22:29-30; Isa. 59:15-18). Daniel grasped the need for brokenness among all of God's people when he prophesied:

> When the power of the holy people has been completely shattered, all these things shall be finished. . . . Many shall be purified, made white, and refined, but the wicked shall do wickedly, . . . the wise shall understand. (Dan.12:7-10)

The goal of the Holy Spirit's refining fire is to *set us up* and *complete us.* When our hearts soften about sin in our own lives, we become more sensitive, more aware, and more responsive to bigger issues.

Kingdom-vision intensifies passion in prayer.

Daniel's fervency incited some stunning responses from the Lord. When

Daniel prayed for "X," instead of receiving a simple answer (like "X"), God entrusted to him spectacular truths that went beyond a mere "answer." God's replies were more like "XYZ" overload-type responses! The Daniel model verifies that passion in prayer does not just get results; it totally slants our perspective on life. Such a personal revolution prays from a particular angle: a *kingdom*-angle. Passion in prayer evokes kingdom-based requests.

God's "answers" were always kingdom related; they seem to spotlight His kingdom reign over His people. God's view of us *kingdom people* is not one of millions of personal mandates; according to Daniel's revelations, *kingdom people* must embrace one big prophetic kingdom mandate.[5] Our passion in prayer must fit into the King's prophetic game plan: "Your kingdom come, Your will be done on earth as it is in heaven" (Mt. 6:10). Passion in prayer intensifies because God's kingdom is all about something that actually happens within space and time right here in our neighborhood.

Our passion will be set ablaze when we view life with spiritual binoculars. Although the kingdoms of the world are powerful, they rise and fall according to God's will (2:31-43, 7:2-8, 8:1-26, 10:20-11:45); our passion in prayer will intensify as we focus on God's triumphal kingdom crushing evil as it marches on into eternity (2:44-45, 4:3, 7:9-27, 9:24-27, 12:1-3). In short, personal passion in prayer will inevitably inflame and enlarge our heart to envision the eternal reality of God's manifest kingdom.

Daniel's passion-saturated prayers exposed wicked schemes, confirmed rescue operations, affirmed God's administration of nations, uncovered an invisible war that rages on in the heavenly realm, and clarified God's blessing on the repentant, humble, and broken ones. But the Daniel model does come with one warning: passion in prayer can be very intense; our thoughts may become deeply troubled by some disturbing insights from God (7:15, 28). At times we may feel exhausted or sick (8:27; 10:1-2, 8-10, 15-17). But what did Daniel do? He always asked the Lord to interpret everything (7:16, 19-20; 12:8) and had enough wits about him to keep some matters to himself (7:28).

Daniel is a key model. His blameless, strategically informed humble heart was less interested in interpreting future events than it was in passionately praying in the present reality of God's kingdom reign.

Questions for Further Thought or Discussion

1. Why would blamelessness produce impartial prayer requests?
2. How might God's perspective on your city's history impact your prayers?
3. How would praying from a kingdom-angle ignite passion in your prayers?

The author: Dr. Gloria J. Wiese is Assistant Professor at Bethel University in Saint Paul, Minnesota. She is the author of *Spiritual Reality: Coming to Terms with Our Ancient Spiritual Heritage.*

SUGGESTED ADDITIONAL READING

Elliff, Thomas D. *A Passion for Prayer: Experiencing Deeper Intimacy with God.* Wheaton: Crossway Publishing, 2001.

Thrasher, Bill. *Journey to Victorious Praying, A: Finding Discipline and Delight in Your Prayer Life.* Chicago: Moody Publishers, 2003.

Bickle, Mike. *After God's Own Heart.* Lake Mary, FL: Charisma House, 2004.

ENDNOTES

1. Jean Bottéro, "The Cuisine of Ancient Mesopotamia," *Biblical Archaeology Review* (1985): pp. 36-45.

2. Gordon J. Wenham, *Leviticus*, NICOT (Grand Rapids: Eerdmans, 1985), pp. 171-173.

3. This may explain why Jesus refers to demons as "unclean" spirits.

4. George Otis, Jr., *Informed Intercession* (Ventura: Regal Books, 1999).

5. Sunday Aigbe, "Cultural Mandate, Evangelistic Mandate, Prophetic Mandate: Of These Three the Greatest Is . . . ?" *Missiology* 19 (1991): pp. 31-43.

chapter

23

JESUS AS A ROLE MODEL OF PERSONAL PASSION IN PRAYER

Howard Baker

"What are you seeking?" Those are the first recorded words of Jesus in the Gospel of John (1:38). What we seek reveals our personal passion. Jesus is interested in my passion, what drives me, what motivates me, what fulfills me. Before considering passion in prayer it would be wise to identify what it is I am really seeking through prayer, thus answering Jesus' question.

Jesus' passion was the will of the Father: My food is to do the will of Him who sent me (Jn. 4:34). His prayer flowed from the passion of trust and obedience in that good and loving will. Jesus had no personal agenda for His life or His prayer, did nothing on His own initiative, spoke only what He heard from the Father, and did only what He saw the Father doing (see 5:19, 30; 8:28, 38, 42).

As we observe Jesus at prayer in this chapter, our goal is to catch His passion for intimacy with the Father, which for us becomes personal passion in prayer. But pray-er beware! Jesus' intimacy with the Father incited the religious establishment's desire to kill Him. Intimacy with God is seldom a crowd pleaser. But it ushers us into the great passionate conversation called prayer. Personal passion in prayer is the difference between blowing a kiss and kissing. It is the movement from smelling bread to eating bread, from knowing *about* to true knowing.

We ask, "How?" Jesus says, "Come and see." Come and see where He abides and join Him there. (Compare 1:38-39 with chapter 15.) Jesus, we come. Teach us to pray with passion.

Prayer in the Personal Life of Jesus

The Gospel of Luke presents Jesus as "son of man." It is clear that being fully God does not eliminate for Jesus the fully human need to pray, so twelve of sixteen prayer occasions occur in this third gospel. Let's look first at some of the ways Jesus prayed in private.

Habitual Prayer—"He Himself often withdrew into the wilderness and prayed" (Lk. 5:16). With the small word *often* a gigantic truth is revealed: it was the habit of Jesus to withdraw into solitude and silence in order to pray. The spiritual masters of the past and present speak with one accord when they say that it is virtually impossible to grow spiritually without regular times of quiet solitude with God. Indeed, Jesus' practice harks back to the beginning of time and the principle of Sabbath rest. Following Jesus into His habit of retreat will bring streams of refreshment to dry and thirsty souls.

Listening Prayer—"He continued all night in prayer to God" (6:12). What sort of extended prayer would Jesus have engaged in before choosing the twelve apostles? As one whose passion was to do the Father's will, would He not gladly spend the entire night listening for the Father's voice and direction concerning the decisions He was about to make? Jesus' example shows us that prayer is much more than asking God to bless our plans, rather it is the means of discovering His.

Mystical Prayer—"And while He prayed, the heaven was opened. And the Holy Spirit descended in bodily form like a dove upon Him, and a voice came from heaven which said, 'You are My beloved Son; in You I am well pleased'" (3:21-22). Many are suspect of anything "mystical" associated with prayer. However, "mystical," coming from the same root as "mystery," is simply a descriptor for any sort of direct experience of the mystery that is our God. So, *while* Jesus was praying He experienced direct manifestations of the presence of the Father and the Holy Spirit—mystical prayer. All the while He was seeking God not experiences, but, like our Master, when we seek God passionately, experiences will come. As one of our prayer masters has said, "the end of prayer is to be snatched away to God." Have we allowed our fears, prejudices, and modern rationalism to domesticate the wildness of relationship to the Lion of Judah, to make suburban the frontiers of prayer?

Surrendering Prayer—"Not My will, but Yours, be done" (22:42). "And when Jesus had cried out with a loud voice, He said, 'Father, into Your hands I commit My spirit.' Having said this, He breathed His last" (23:46). Just as the life of Jesus was characterized by surrender, so was His prayer. Passion leads to surrender to the object of one's passion. For Jesus the surrender was to the Father and His will. His earthly life that began with the surrender of divine glory and prerogative ended with the surrender of His spirit into the care of the Father. "Not My will, but Yours be done," is not a caveat that follows a bold prayer request, but an attitude of the heart that is the source of passion in prayer. Without the surrender of our wills to God, prayer becomes a narcissistic tool of self-passion hardly worthy to be called prayer.

Despairing Prayer—"My God, My God, why have You forsaken Me" (Mt. 27:46)? Passionate relationships both ascend to the heights of ecstasy and dive into the depths of agony. Jesus' passion for His Father is revealed in His heart-rending cry of despair from the cross. By praying these words from Psalm 22 Jesus at once shows us His passion and gives us permission to express ours. It is doubtful that passion in prayer can survive without this kind of raw emotional honesty. Throughout the Psalms (which Jesus no doubt prayed often) we find these expressions of despair, pain, lament, confusion, hate, anger, and sorrow brought to God in prayer. To paraphrase C.S. Lewis, by this prayer Jesus has given us the freedom to passionately pray what is in us, not what ought to be in us.[1]

Prayer in the Public Life of Jesus

Prayer is always personal even when offered in public. It is an expression of relationship between persons. Jesus' intimate conversation with the Father often spilled over into His public life and ministry. When our lives are filled with prayer this will happen to us as well.

Praise—"I thank You, Father, Lord of heaven and earth, that You have hidden these things from the wise and prudent and have revealed them to babes" (Mt. 11:25). In the middle of a sermon Jesus' hidden dialogue with the Father is revealed when He can no longer contain the praise that is in His heart over the gracious work of the Father. True praise erupts when we have eyes to see and ears to hear the activity and voice of our Father. The personal forms of prayer lead to this public expression of passion.

Thanksgiving—"Father, I thank You that You have heard Me" (Jn. 11:41). It would be unfathomable to picture Jesus, the only Son of God, as anything but overflowing with gratitude to the Father He is so intimate with. In addition to thankfulness at meals (Jn. 6:11; Mt. 26;26), more significant was Jesus grateful responsiveness to the Father's work and listening ear. The raising of Lazarus was in response to Jesus' petition and even before the request was fulfilled Jesus' gratitude was expressed, knowing that He had been heard. Passion in prayer gives the settled assurance that we have been heard without having to see the answer enacted. It is an example of the mature faith of believing without seeing, of living by faith not by sight.

Intercession—"I have prayed for you, that your faith should not fail" (Lk. 22:32). In some ways this brief expression is a summary of the extended intercession that Jesus makes for His disciples in John 17. Together they represent the blending of His passion in prayer and His passion for the disciples He loves. Jesus' prayer acknowledges the realities of testing, persecution, trouble, and loss, but it also affirms that His peace will overcome all of those if we continue to place our confidence in Him. Slowly and meditatively immerse yourself in Jesus' intercession in John 17 letting His passion for you and for prayer flow into your heart.

Prayer as Union with the Father

Jesus did not simply pray often. He did not only pray regularly. And He did not just pray much. His was a life of constant, continuous, conscious communion with His Father. A life of passion for the Father expressed most clearly in a life of prayer. This is evident not only in the above examples of

His praying, but more so in His own statements regarding this abiding life. He spoke of His

1) Conscious awareness of what the Father is doing—Jn. 5:19-20.
2) Constant hearing of the Father's voice—8:28.
3) Consistent experience of the Father's presence—8:29.

We are invited to follow Him into this life (10:10; 14:6). We can abide in His love, just as He abides in His Father's love (15:10). We are in union with Him just as He is in union with the Father (14:20). We can hear His voice just as He heard His Father's (10:16).

This unceasing passionate prayer, this timeless Trinitarian dance extends into eternity past and eternity future. The writer of Hebrews gives us the pre-incarnation description, "Therefore, when He came into the world, He said, 'Sacrifice and offering You did not desire, But a body You have prepared for Me'" (Heb. 10:5). During His incarnation Jesus "offered up prayers and supplications, with vehement cries and tears to Him who was able to save Him from death, and He was heard because of His godly fear" (5:7-8). Finally, we see that the passionate prayer of Jesus extends for all of eternity as "He always lives to make intercession" (7:25). Herein lies the most important fact of all concerning prayer: Jesus is praying for us. To pray is to join Him in His praying. To pray is to connect with His passion that has and will burn for all eternity.

Questions for Further Thought or Discussion

1. Where does passion in prayer come from?
2. Do you experience more passion in praying alone or praying with others?
3. Do you see constant communion with the Lord as a realistic possibility? What are some initial steps you could take toward unceasing prayer?

The author: Professor Howard Baker is Instructor of Christian Formation and Campus Chaplain at Denver Seminary. He is the author of *Soul Keeping: Ancient Paths of Spiritual Direction* and *The One True Thing* and contributor to *Renovare Spiritual Formation Bible* and to *Transformation of a Man's Heart.*

SUGGESTED ADDITIONAL READING

Bonhoeffer, Dietrich. *Life Together.* San Francisco: HarperCollins, 1954.

Brother Lawrence. *Practicing the Presence of God.* many editions.

Balthasar, Hans Urs von. *Prayer.* London: Geoffrey Chapman, 1963. (Also available in paperback from Ignatius Press.)

Tozer, A.W. *The Pursuit of God.* Camp Hill, PA: Christian Publications, 1948, 1982.

Lewis, C.S. *Letters to Malcolm: Chiefly on Prayer.* New York: Harcourt Brace Jovanovich, 1964.

ENDNOTES

1. C.S. Lewis, *Letters to Malcolm: Chiefly on Prayer* (New York: Harcourt Brace Jovanovich, 1964), 22.

chapter

24

AN HISTORICAL ROLE MODEL OF PERSONAL PASSION IN PRAYER

Karen O'Dell Bullock

In the summer of 2005, I joined a group of friends who traveled to Birmingham, England, for a conference. Along our journey we visited sacred sites associated with our faith heritage and the graves of those heroes whose influence upon us had been most profound. We visited the cobbler shop of William Carey, missionary to India; the parish church of John Newton, converted ex-slaver who wrote "Amazing Grace;" and the ancient grounds of Bunhill Fields, where Isaac Watts, Susannah Wesley, John Bunyan, and thousands more Dissenters were buried.

Perhaps the most amazing discovery of them all was the early morning we climbed through the derelict bars of the old Victorian cemetery in Bristol, wound our way up the overgrown, vine-clad hillside, and found the headstone of George Müller (1805-1898). We encircled that gray chiseled stone and stood in silence and awe. We remembered together Müller's example of passionate prayer. We recalled the orphanages and Christian schools and missionary endeavors he began and how, with great conviction, he declined to solicit funds for any portion of the work. Instead, with childlike faith, he committed daily needs into the providence of the One who keeps His Promises. In that hushed circle we thanked God for George Müller—whose life models for us even today how to live and how to pray: "I live in the spirit of prayer. I pray as I walk, when I lie down, and when I rise. And the Answers are always coming."[1]

What are the spiritual secrets of those Christians of faith across the ages, like Müller, who lived such deeply prayer-infused lives? Is it possible for us to learn and practice these ways of knowing and communing with God today? Can these profound yearnings of our souls be satisfied in the cold and calculating age in which we now live? The fathers and mothers of our faith sing the exultant word, "Yes!" Yet this kind of living with God, Müller said, comes with a price. While it is possible for each child of God to walk the path of passionate prayer, it is not a journey for the fainthearted.

How then, shall we order our lives so that intimacy with the Almighty God is the result? Müller answered this same question in his own day. Toward the end of Müller's life, Albert Sims paid a visit to the vast Ashley Down campus, near Bristol, where more than two thousand children lived in multiple-storied homes. There the elder Müller lived among those he loved best in a house behind a garden gate. The old prayer warrior reflected upon his own experiences as he explained what he had learned in his more than seven decades of walking with God. His words were simple. A life of faith requires that the child of God must be willing to pay a price. What price? Müller identified four costly principles, or secrets, upon which his passionate prayer life depended.

First, Müller's life was grounded in God's Word. He insisted that close communion with the heavenly Father requires the study, meditation, and memorization of the Word of God. He had learned that apart from this essential truth there could be no consistent effectiveness in prayer. His greatest treasure was the revealed Word of God, wherein lay the storehouse of God's riches—His nature and character, His attributes of holiness, justice, grace, mercy, wisdom, faithfulness, and love.[2] His "blessed promises" are also here, whereby the child of God can learn, step by step, how to trust the promises of the Father. For Müller, it was crucial to *know* the promises of God, to *believe* them, and then to *act* upon them.

Müller related that God gave to him a theme verse in December of 1835 for his life's labors—the promise from Psalm 81:10: "Open thy mouth wide, and I will fill it" (KJV). As the orphanage work unfolded and Müller trusted that God would supply even the smallest provision for his children, he was never once, he said, in all of the years that followed, disappointed in God. Müller simply believed the one who had revealed Himself in Scripture and trusted Him to act according to His own nature and character. This unwavering faith in God's *Being* was possible because Müller was thoroughly familiar with God's revealed Word.

The cost of applying this principle lay in Müller's resolution to arise each morning early, to read and meditate upon his daily Bible passage several hours before the rest of the household stirred. His priority of Bible reading and prayer gave him both an orientation toward God's voice throughout the day and the serenity of heart that allowed him to remain attentive in the face of obstacles. This habit of resting upon God's character took the particular form of waiting upon God's answers and timing, both infinitely better than anything he could devise. He said three years before his death,

> I never remember, in all [of] my Christian course . . . that I ever sincerely and patiently sought to know the will of God by the teaching of the Holy Ghost through the instrumentality of the Word of God, but [that] I have always been directed rightly. But if honesty of heart and uprightness before God were lacking or if I did not patiently wait upon God for instruction, or if I preferred the counsel of my fellow men to the declarations of the Word of the living God, I made great mistakes.[3]

Müller had learned to trust that God, through His Word and prayer, would direct his steps.

Müller's second secret to a life of passionate prayer was the determination on one hand to walk uprightly and the equal determination on the other not to indulge knowingly or habitually in anything that may be contrary to the mind of God as revealed in His Word. Müller took seriously the verse in Psalm 66:18: "If I regard iniquity in my heart, the Lord will not hear." Above all else, Müller longed for his relationship with God to be pure. Linking answered prayer with purity of heart in a cause-and-effect equation, George believed that a person's faith was either strengthened or weakened in direct proportion to the measure that the believer was willing to separate himself from known sin. When we consciously ask the Holy Spirit to evaluate our thoughts and intentions, Müller said, the Spirit has the freedom to create within us greater faith and direct us to act in ways that bring honor and glory to Himself. Because Müller was sensitive to God's holy character, and yearned to be made increasingly into the likeness of Jesus Christ, the phrase "Walk uprightly and do not regard iniquity in your heart" became the theme of his meditation, giving rise to his enduring hope that, "My whole life shall be one service for the Living God."[4]

The third of the costly lessons that this passionate prayer warrior acknowledged as essential was that faith must be tried if it is to be strengthened. "Müller's faith was not Jonah's gourd," Sims noted, upon leaving his interview with the aged Müller. Instead, his faith-maturation was sequential. Faith sprouted with his saturation in the Word of God; it flowered in his increasing intimacy with God; and it came to fruition through trials, obstacles, difficulties, and defeats—all of which Müller welcomed as the stepping stones with which his heavenly Father affectionately lined his pathway. He wrote in 1839,

> Should it be supposed . . . by anyone in reading the details of our trials of faith during the year . . . that we have been disappointed in our expectations or discouraged in the work, my answer is . . . such days were expected from the commencement. Our desire is not that we may be without trials of faith, but that our Lord graciously [may] be pleased to support us in the trial.

And again,

> When sometimes all has been dark, exceedingly dark, judging from natural appearances; yea, when I should have been overwhelmed

> indeed in grief and despair had I looked at things after the outward appearances . . . I have sought to encourage myself by laying hold in faith on God's almighty power, His unchangeable love, and His infinite wisdom. [5]

Müller had discovered the costly correlation between mature faith and trials: faith grows incrementally as it engages personal and spiritual opposition.

The last of Müller's four prayer secrets is the simple admonition to confide in God with the trust of a child, and to wait on Him to answer. Miraculous responses to prayer came almost daily as Müller waited for God to answer in His time. Throughout his ninety-three years, eight months, and five days, Müller learned to trust. A favorite text from James 1:4 hung on his memory's walls: "Perseverance must finish its work so that you may be mature and complete, not lacking anything." Müller had asked God to increase his faith and to sustain his patience and God heard and answered. Indeed, he insisted at the very end of his life:

> It is not enough to begin to pray, nor to pray aright; nor is it enough to continue for a time to pray; but we must patiently, believingly continue in prayer, until we obtain an answer; and further, we have not only to continue in prayer unto the end, but we have also to believe that God does hear us and will answer our prayers. *Most frequently, we fail in not continuing in prayer until the blessing is obtained, and in not expecting the blessing.*[6] (*emphasis added*)

Müller found no detail too insignificant to take to the Lord in prayer, believing that Philippians 4:6 is true: "Be anxious for nothing, but in everything by prayer and supplication, with thanksgiving, let your requests be made known to God." Childlike in trust, Müller took to the throne room of God the need for shoes and breakfasts and playgrounds, for teachers and assistants, for jobs for the oldest boys leaving his care, for healing of illnesses, and the provision of financial resources. Prayer became as natural as breathing for Müller who testified that, in more than seven decades of walking hand in hand with God, he had never found the throne vacant nor the supplies exhausted.

The costliness of trusting is multi-faceted. It is found in the discipline required to train the mind and heart to rely solely upon God, instead of devising deliverances or engineering solutions on our own. It is found in being still—even when others misinterpret our waiting on God for a lack of initiative. Müller's model sometimes requires the self-binding of one's own hand or mouth or influence in order to allow God the freedom to work in His way and time. Indeed, in this model the giving away of self is necessary to the process of becoming passionate in prayer. The focus shifts when prayer is not centered as much upon *what we do* but, rather, *who we are.*

Throughout the history of the Christian church, men and women of faith have walked this often-solitary path of deep intimacy with God. It should come as no surprise to us that others have found this possible, for God has promised that "You will seek the LORD your God, and you will find Him if you seek Him with all your heart and with all your soul" (Deut. 4:29). Müller's life teaches us today that if we long to experience a life of passionate prayer, we must take the first costly step . . . and then the next . . . and then another in careful, intentional response to the Holy God's transformation of us. Passionate prayer will become the supernatural characteristic of such a walk with Him.

Questions for Further Thought or Discussion

1. In the life of a believer, what are the connections between a yearning to know the heart of God, a love for the Scriptures, and passionate prayer?
2. How did George Müller's life correspond to the scriptural teaching about effective prayer?
3. What aspect of your life might hinder an effective prayer life according to biblical standards?
4. Who may be other persons from history who lived passionate prayer lives? For further study, explore the passionate prayer lives of other fathers and mothers of the faith, such as Madame Guyon, St. John of the Cross, and Teresa of Avila.

The Author: Dr. Karen O'Dell Bullock is a Fellow and Professor of Christian Heritage at the B. H. Carroll Theological Institute in Arlington, Texas.

SUGGESTED ADDITIONAL READING

Müller, Susannah Grace. *Preaching Tours and Missionary Labours of George Müller of Bristol.* London: J. Nisbet & Co., 1883.

Pierson, Arthur T. *George Müller of Bristol and His Witness to a Prayer-Hearing God.* New York: The Baker and Taylor Company, 1899.

ENDNOTES

1. Albert Sims, ed., *An Hour with George Müller: The Man of Faith to Whom God Gave Millions* (Grand Rapids: Zondervan, 1939), p. 10.

2. Bonnie Harvey, *George Müller: Man of Faith* (Uhrichsville, OH: Barbour Publishing, Inc., 1948), pp. 88-89.

3. George Müller, *The Autobiography of George Müller* (New Kensington, PA: Whitaker House, 1984), p. 183. During the latter years of his life, George read the Bible through four times each year.

4. Sims, p. 4; Harvey, p. 80.

5. Harvey, pp. 147-148.

6. Basil Miller, *George Muller: Man of Faith and Miracles* (Minneapolis: Bethany House, 1972), p. 66.

chapter 25

DISCIPLINES OF PERSONAL PRAYER

Dan R. Crawford

The stress of interpersonal relationships demands that we spend time alone with God. The anxiety of constant exposure to people was evidenced recently by a news story indicating that the Tokyo City Zoo in Japan would be closed for two days each month. The law became necessary because zoo officials discovered the animals were showing signs of extreme emotional distress due to constant exposure to the public. Likewise, there are times in our lives when the "zoo" needs to be closed for a period of time.

Our Lord felt it necessary in His public ministry frequently to withdraw from the crowds for time alone with the Father. In so doing, Jesus may have been communicating to us one of the secrets of interpersonal ministry, namely personal time with the Father. Indeed, the secret to effective praying is effectively praying in secret.

Praying alone, in private is biblical. Isaac went into the fields to pray and meditate. Jacob remained on the eastern bank of the Brook Jabbok. Moses hid in the clefts of the rocks on Mt. Horeb. Elijah withdrew to the lonely crest of Mt. Carmel. Daniel remained on the banks of Hiddekel. On one occasion Paul arranged to go by land while his associates traveled by ship, perhaps to use the time alone for prayer (Acts 20:13). John, though not of his own will, prayed alone on Patmos.

Because it is just you alone, there are disciplines required in personal prayer. You will not have the support of another Christian or a group of Christians to hold you accountable to the task of praying. Therefore, more discipline will be needed.

Among the disciplines needed for personal prayer is *the discipline of time.* In a survey by *Leadership* magazine it was discovered that thirty-four percent felt "time" was the greatest hindrance to personal prayer.[1] A similar survey was conducted by *Evangelical Missions Quarterly,* which reported out of 390 missionaries surveyed, eleven percent spent less than an average of five minutes per day in prayer. Sixty percent spent between eleven and thirty minutes daily in prayer.[2] In contrast consider Andrew Bonar who wrote in his diary, "I work more than I pray. I must at once return, through the Lord's strength, to not less than three hours per day spent in prayer and meditation upon the Word."[3] Or consider Adoniram Judson, who said:

> Arrange thy affairs, if possible, so that thou canst leisurely devote two or three hours every day not merely to devotional exercises but to the very act of secret prayer and communication with God. Endeavor seven times a day to withdraw from business and company and lift thy soul to God in private retirement.[4]

We've seen the time discipline of two of the great prayer warriors in the faith. The difference between their practice and ours is not one of inherent nature. It is simply that they took time to ponder God, to study God in an act of supreme attention. We are too greatly overrun with our own trivial pursuits to find leisure for such time of spiritual pondering.

As to how to spend the disciplined time alone with God, Dick Eastman has helped us by dividing prayer into twelve categories. He suggests that an hour ("keep watch with Me for one hour, Mt. 26:40") be divided into twelve equal parts as follows: (1) Praise (Ps. 63:3); (2) Waiting (Ps. 46:10); (3) Confession (139:23); (4) Scripture praying (Jer. 23:29); (5) Watching (Col. 4:2); (6) Intercession (1 Tim. 2:1-2); (7) Petition (Mt. 7:7); (8) Thanksgiving (1 Thess. 5:18); (9) Singing (Ps. 100:2); (10) Meditation (Jos. 1:8); (11) Listening (Eccl. 5:2); and (12) Praise (Ps. 52:9).[5]

The above reference to "scripture praying" may need a further explanation. In his book, *Touch the World Through Prayer*, Wesley Duewel suggests ten ways to use Scripture in seeking to make your prayer more effective:

(1) Begin your regular prayer times with God's Word.
(2) Apply to your life what you read.
(3) Personalize Scripture passages during your prayer time.
(4) Bathe your soul in Scripture to increase your faith.
(5) Memorize verses of Scripture which will be useful in prayer.
(6) Use Scripture in praising and worshipping the Lord.
(7) Use Scripture to confess your unworthiness.
(8) Use Scripture prayers and prayer expressions.
(9) Claim the Bible promises when you pray.
(10) Use Scripture to rebuke Satan.[6]

Daniel gave us an example of the discipline of time when it was recorded that, "he knelt down on his knees three times that day, and prayed and gave thanks before his God, as was his custom (Dan. 6:10)." Daniel set an appointment with God and kept it faithfully. Whether your appointment with God is early in the morning or late at night, you must set an appointed time and with spiritual discipline remain faithful to that appointed time.

Another discipline needed in personal prayer is *the discipline of place*. The same *Leadership* magazine survey alluded to earlier reported that forty-two percent of those surveyed prayed in their office while twenty percent prayed at home and ten percent prayed at church.[7] Jesus not only had a favorite time for private prayer (early in the morning), but was always able, even in the midst of His travels, to find "a solitary place" (Mk. 1:35) for prayer. Jesus actively sought the solitary place for prayer. In the busiest seasons of His life, Jesus would rob Himself of sleep and needed rest in order that He might have the quiet and unhurried place for prayer.

In His ministry Jesus mentioned the prayer "closet" (KJV) or "a secret place" (Mt. 6:6). The word rendered "closet" signified originally a storeroom and has the same root word as the word "to cut" or "divide." It may have referred to a sectioning-off of a corner of the large room in which the family lived. In that private place supplies were kept for the needs of the family. While this word eventually came to be used for any place of privacy, the "supply room" would also speak to the storehouse of God's resources available to us through personal prayer.

For Jesus the place was not as important as the purpose, namely to get away from the routine and the interruptions and spend time alone with the Father. There are no sacred places, just places that become sacred because of what happens there between a person and God. It will be of great benefit to you if you can designate a location for personal prayer. If you are not able to do this, then, like Jesus, you should seek some temporary, "solitary place."

A third discipline necessary in personal prayer is *the discipline of mind.* You must learn how to relax without your mind shifting into neutral. Perhaps concentrating on a written prayer list will help with this discipline. Personal prayer includes listening as well as speaking to God. Therefore, your must discipline yourself to listen. *The Evangelical Missions Quarterly,* in a survey alluded to earlier, reported that out of 257 missionaries surveyed, sixty-six percent cited "mind wandering" during prayer as a frequent occurrence. Only one said it never happened to him.[8] You and I must discipline our mind to concentrate on prayer in the private place at the private time. W. E. Sangster says:

> Let no beginner in prayer abandon the privilege because of mind wandering. It can be conquered. A brisk, live imagination and a resolute will cannot be denied. Even though, in the early stages, the precious minutes tick away and all the time seems spent in bringing the mind back from its wanderings and fixing it again on prayer, they are not moments lost. Such discipline will exercise the muscles of the will, and the day will dawn when the sweetest meditation and the most earnest prayer will be possible even amid distraction.[9]

The fourth discipline required in personal prayer is *the discipline of continuation.* While in public prayer there needs to be an "amen" to indicate to others that the prayer is finished, in personal prayer you need to learn how to pray without saying "amen." This allows the communication to continue beyond the special time and apart from the special place. Refraining from saying "amen" is a symbolic way of allowing the Lord to continue communication with you throughout the day. It is like parents wanting to stay in touch with their children. How often in your childhood did one of your parents call your name and when you responded they said, "I just wanted to know if you were okay?" The discipline of continuation allows God to continue communication with us.

A final discipline required in personal prayer is *the discipline of organization.* In times of personal prayer you should keep a prayer list, diary, or notebook including a listing of the names for whom and issues for which prayer is being offered. This list might well include government leaders, church leaders, missionaries, friends, and specific needs among associates and colleagues. The list might also record answers to prayers and items of praise. Since no one else is involved with you in personal prayer, you will need to employ your own discipline of organization rather than depending on someone else to be organized on your behalf or hold you accountable.

It has been reported that John Wesley preached 44,000 sermons in his lifetime and travelled on horseback and carriage 290,000 miles. In addition, Wesley wrote an English dictionary, prepared grammars in Hebrew, Latin, Greek, French and English. He wrote several volumes on theology, history, philosophy and medicine. Further, Wesley edited a fifty volume set of books. Yet he had time for personal prayer at 4:00 a.m. each day. How did he accomplish all of this and still have time to pray? Discipline! The exact same prayer disciplines that you and I can employ in our lives.

(The material in this chapter is adapted from the author's previous book, *The Prayer-Shaped Disciple* and is used by permission of Hendrickson Publishers, Peabody, MA.)

Questions for Further Thought or Discussion:

1. Which of the five disciplines in this chapter are the strongest in your present prayer life?

2. Which of the five disciplines in this chapter are the weakest in your present prayer life and thus need the most work?
3. What is one thing you could do this next week to strengthen your personal prayer life?

The author: Dr. Dan R. Crawford is Senior Professor of Evangelism & Missions and Occupant of the Chair of Prayer Emeritus, Southwestern Baptist Theological Seminary, Fort Worth, TX. He is the author of numerous books on prayer, discipleship and evangelism including *The Prayer Shaped Disciple, DiscipleShape, Coping with Conflict: A Measure of Discipleship* and *Night of Tragedy, Dawning of Light.*

SUGGESTED ADDITIONAL READING:

Burr, Richard. *Developing Your Secret Closet of Prayer.* Camp Hill, PA: Christian Publications, 1998.

Cornwell, Judson. *The Secret of Personal Prayer.* Altamonte Springs, FL: Creation House, 1988.

Graf, Jonathan. *The Power of Personal Prayer.* Colorado Springs, CO: NavPress, 2002.

Ogilvie, Lloyd John. *Conversation with God: Experience Intimacy with God through Personal Prayer.* Eugene OR: Harvest House Publications, 1993.

Pilkington, Evan. *Paths to Personal Prayer.* Mystic, CT: Twenty-Third Publications, 1990.

ENDNOTES

1. Terry C. Muck, "Questions about the Devotional Life," *Leadership* 3, no. 1 (Winter 1982), p. 31.

2. Phil Parshall, "How Spiritual Are the Missionaries?" *Evangelical Missions Quarterly* 23, (no. 1 January, 1987): pp. 10-11.

3. James C. K. McClure, *Intercessory Prayer* (Atlanta: reprinted by Home Mission Board, SBC, 1987), p. 17.

4. Reported in *A Treasury of Prayer: The Best of E.M. Bounds on Prayer in a Single Volume,* Compiled by Leonard Ravenhill (Minneapolis: Bethany House Publishers, 1981), p. 103.

5. Dick Eastman, *The Hour That Changes the World* (Grand Rapids: Baker Book House, 1978).

6. Wesley L. Duewel, *Touch the World Through Prayer* (Grand Rapids: Francis Asbury Press, 1986), pp. 147-151.

7. Muck, p. 32.

8. Parshall, pp. 10-11.

9. Warren W. Wiersbe, Compiler, *Classic Sermons on Prayer,* "When I Find It Hard to Pray" by W. E. Sangster (Grand Rapids: Kregal Publications, 1987), pp. 155-156.

chapter

26

HABITS OF EFFECTIVE PRAY-ERS

Dennis Conner

Having spent fifty years within the "world of sports"—either as a competing athlete, college and professional coach, or on staff with a national sports ministry (Fellowship of Christian Athletes) encouraging coaches and athletes in their "spiritual journey with Jesus Christ—I have clearly seen both the benefits of employing good habits and consequences of practicing bad habits. Those practicing good habits always seem to be more effective in their sport than those who do not. Now, in my thirty-eighth year as a praying Christian, I, again, see the effect that good or bad prayer habits can have on my personal prayer life.

Unfortunately, for too long, my own prayer life was much less fulfilling and fruitful than I believe God wanted me to enjoy with Him, simply because I was not practicing good prayer habits. How thankful I am today for God's grace and mercy prevailing, to draw me closer and closer to Him "in prayer," by showing me several good habits to start practicing. These habits made a huge difference. Because "habits" are not user-biased, I share these with you, believing that they will benefit you as they have me, if you choose to use them. Hopefully I can share these with you as if I were your "prayer coach" (encouraging and equipping), but certainly never taking the place of our greatest "prayer coach": Jesus Christ.

First: Be still and hunger for God (Ps. 46:10).

Developing stillness is the most fundamental of all, because without it, there will be no effective prayer. In an American culture that almost worships over-stuffed PDAs and calendars, Satan has many Christians totally distracted—and therefore discouraged—from their personal praying. As I began to study and better understand the prayer life of Jesus, it became obvious that there were some key differences from mine:

JESUS	MINE
1. Done with INTENTION (frequent) and ATTENTION (focus).	1. Done without CONSISTENCY and proper FOCUS.
2. Always MADE time to pray.	2. Always trying to FIND time to pray (unsuccessfully).
3. Sought out prayer time with the Father with DELIGHT.	3. Submitted to prayer time out of a sense of DUTY.
4. Motivated to pray by His PASSION for the Father.	4. Prayed in my PURSUIT of "things" from the Father.

After numerous times of confessing to the Lord my sin of apathy toward praying faithfully, I recognized that the solution was not merely acknowledging my weakness, but my need to ask for His help. Sure enough, He answered my prayer by pointing me to the "cry" of the psalmist in the Bible who prayed with deep sincerity: "As the deer pants for the water brooks, so pants my soul for You, O God. My soul thirsts for God, for the living God. When shall I come and appear before God" (Ps. 42:1-2)? In faith, I began to pray that the Lord would give me that same kind of passion for the

Father; to actually hunger and thirst for time (in prayer) with Him. Slowly but surely I experienced a definite "spiritual transplant" in my heart; so that my prayer time became something I began to eagerly anticipate. With that transformation came a much greater sense of "connecting" with the Lord and fulfillment in seeing many more of my prayers—for myself and others—answered! Once that happened, the habit of being still became a natural part of my daily prayer life; I don't even consider a day to be complete without my prayer time with the Lord. In fact, I literally feel "incomplete" (an uneasy, uncomfortable feeling) if my day has not included a special time "in prayer" with the Lord!

Second: Be kingdom-minded (Col. 3:1-3).

In this post-modern day and "me first" culture, being committed to sincerely praying (i.e. more than just lip-service) in the manner of the "Model Prayer" (Mt. 6:9-13) mode—i.e. for "Your kingdom come, Your will be done, On earth as it is in heaven" (6:10)—is surely not what comes natural to most Christians. Even as a "new creation" (2 Cor. 5:17), my "natural man" spirit (sin nature) fights against any prayer practice—much less allowing a habit to form—that would seek to put my own prayer agenda in a secondary and submissive posture to anyone else's, even God's!

However, as I continued to grow in my Christian walk with the Lord, I began to note the prayer priorities of not only Jesus, but also men like Abraham, Moses, Joshua, David, Elijah, Paul, James, Peter, and John; and women like Hannah, Esther, Ruth and Mary. Time and time again each of these individuals put the agenda and will of God at the top of their prayer list. Unashamedly and unhesitatingly they acknowledged that they preferred God's will for their life more than their own. Additionally I noted—especially obvious in the New Testament—that their prayers for others focused much more often on their spiritual rather than physical needs or desires! The Apostle Paul was totally committed to this "kingdom-minded" prayer habit; opening and closing his nine NT letters to churches in various cities with a "spiritual blessing" prayer. Is there a sweeter or more submissive-to-God's-will prayer than that of the young woman, Mary, who prayed—when she was told of her Holy Spirit conception—"Behold, the maidservant of the Lord! Let it be to me according to your word" (Lk. 1:38). Is that not the same kingdom-minded prayer commitment Jesus expressed in His final Garden of Gethsemane prayer. Knowing the crucifixion was imminent, He prayed: "Father, if it is Your will, take this cup away from Me; nevertheless not My will, but Yours, be done" (Lk. 22:42).

In 1991, through my church's small-group study of *Experiencing God* by Henry Blackaby, I first began to learn what it means to look for God at work more closely in my everyday life, and the real meaning of, "Delight yourself also in the LORD, and He shall give you the desires of your heart" (Ps. 37:4). As I began to live out that admonition, I began to experience an increasing desire to pray more like Jesus—i.e. seeking and submissive of the Father's will in all matters of daily living—and God began to answer my prayers more visibly because He was guiding me in the very things I should be praying!

Over time, my understanding of the *practical* aspect of "kingdom-minded" praying became the commitment to: praying the Word of God—which is the expressed Will of God—that will bring all glory to God and visible growth to His kingdom. Second Corinthians 4:18 is another great biblical reference that exhorts you and me to re-focus our life perspective: from temporal to eternal.

Being fully committed to the habit of kingdom-minded praying (i.e. wanting God's will more than my own) was the key to the career decision I had to make in December 2000. At fifty-eight years old and on the brink of starting my twenty-fifth year on staff with the Fellowship of Christian Athletes—which, for me, was the ultimate assignment from the Lord because it combined the two worlds that were most important in my life (after my family): sports and ministry—I was having to decide whether to stay with the FCA or resign. I sensed the Lord was prompting me to resign and wait ("in the posture of Mary, not Martha" were the exact words He spoke to me) for His new assignment. Since I had not "planned ahead" to resign from the FCA ministry, I had no specific employment awaiting me. To "walk-away" from my existing position—at an age when it is more difficult to find new equal employment—I had to totally desire God's Will (there was no indication or assurance of whatever that would be) more than my own. For the next eighteen months, my primary prayer was: "Show me Your ways, O LORD; teach me Your paths. Lead me in Your truth and teach me, for

You are the God of my salvation; on You I wait all the day" (Ps. 25:4-5). I desperately wanted to be right where He wanted me to be and nowhere else. It was surely a "trial-by-fire," but His faithfulness to lead my wife and me into a new "prayer coaching" ministry (helping pastors and churches grow their "prayer ministry" into a true "house of prayer") has been a blessing far beyond whatever I would have chosen to do! Kingdom-minded praying is a habit well worth your practicing; I promise!

Third: Be praise-focused (Ps. 150:6).

Perhaps our biggest step toward a more effective and fulfilling prayer life comes when we develop the habit of praising (and/or "thanking") God as a natural "first-response" to everything that comes our way in living our daily life! While the psalmist clearly exhorts "whoever has breath" (isn't that every living person) to praise the Lord; and the prophet Isaiah—speaking the word of the Lord—proclaims: "This people I have formed for Myself, they shall declare My praise" (Isa. 43:21). For many years—even as a Christian—my own "natural man" (1 Cor. 2:14) response to many things I encountered was definitely not "praise" to the Father! I was always more into the petitioning—rather than the praising—of God!

The Old Testament account (2 Chron. 19:1-25) of Jehoshaphat's initial response to what looked like sure defeat for the totally out-numbered Israelite army is a tremendous example of what God can and will do when His people choose to praise Him in all circumstances. A classic example in the New Testament is the miraculous testimony of Paul and Silas's release from the jail in Philippi (Acts 16:19-40) after the conversion of the Philippian jailer. It can all be traced back to God's intervention into their unjust incarceration. In response to Paul and Silas's prayer and singing of praise hymns, the jail doors opened and binding chains fell off. Following the conversion and baptism of the jailer's entire household, Paul and Silas walked away free men, at the request of the Philippian magistrates. God not only "saved" an entire family through Paul and Silas's "praising" from their jail cell, but He also changed the hearts of the very authorities who were the ones that ordered them jailed originally.

This prayer habit was never made more real to me than in November, 2005. Having begun our new "prayer coaching" ministry—in obedience to God's clear direction in June, 2002—we were at the very end of our financial resources three and one-half years later. Not trained in the field of accounting, it was still easy for me to see—many months prior to November, 2005—that with our cash outflow being much greater than our income, in a matter of a few months, we would be completely penniless. Firmly believing God had "called" us into this new ministry—and wanting His will and my will to be in complete unity—I had already begun (two years earlier) "praising and thanking God" for His Divine guidance and provision; even though the financial part of that provision was in our "retirement" account that was being slowly and surely exhausted.

With the same perfect timing as He did with the opening of the Red Sea for the safe passage of the Israelite nation, in November, 2005—when our financial resources were within thirty days of depletion—Jehovah Jireh (God the Provider) sent us a major gift from a unexpected donor (who had never given to our ministry in twenty-seven years) The gift came without any solicitation and it carried us for several months.

Now, even when I do not understand "what or why" I am experiencing certain difficult circumstances, my "praise-focused" prayer habit comes forth much more naturally, because I have experienced the faithfulness of God: "For the word of the LORD is right, and all His work is done in truth" (Ps. 33:4).

All three of these habits have impacted my personal and corporate prayer life. They have become a natural part of my journey with Jesus. I am no longer plagued with feelings of doubt and frustration as I pray, but rather I am filled with confidence and peace. I heartily encourage you to practice these until they become life-changing prayer habits for you!

Questions for Further Thought or Discussion

1. Are you still trying to find time to pray regularly, or have you begun making regular times to pray? What steps can you take to make this a habit?
2. Have you reached a point of praying from an eternal perspective rather than temporal (i.e. desiring God's will to prevail more than your own agenda)?
3. Is there anything hindering you from praising God more than you petition Him?

The author: Dennis Conner is Co-Founder and President of the Called to Serve Prayer Ministry of Richardson, Texas. He is a member of America's National Prayer Committee and a former executive with the Fellowship of Christian Athletes.

SUGGESTED ADDITIONAL READING

Pritchard, Ray. *Beyond All You Could Think or Ask: How to Pray Like the Apostle Paul.* Chicago: Moody Publishing, 2004.

Reapsome, James. *Effective Prayer: Studies on Prayer Skills.* Grand Rapids: Zondervan Publishing, 1992.

White, John. *Daring to Draw Near: People in Prayer.* Downers Grove, IL: InterVarstiy Press, 1977.

chapter

27

THE USE OF SCRIPTURE IN PERSONAL PRAYER

Larry Ashlock

Prayer concerns a relationship with God and reflects His active choice to communicate with us. Communicating with God involves our thoughts, words, and gestures as we reach beyond our earthly limitations toward His transcendence. In short, prayer helps us to experience God in all of His fullness. Furthermore, practicing daily prayer *and* Bible reading is like having two arms that reach longingly toward the heavenly Father. Such a "praying person" receives God's loving embrace as He answers through prayer and the Scripture.

Unfortunately, the daily practice of *intentionally blending* prayer and the reading of the Scriptures into one voice as one listens actively and communicates scripturally with God remains unknown to many believers. There are indeed many types of prayer and methods for praying but the use of scripture in prayer or, *praying the scripture*, has provided me with the deeply satisfying benefit of knowing God's powerful transforming inner presence and recognizing His voice as He directs my daily Christian walk. Many believers, however, are unacquainted with the meaning of this approach to prayer.

What is "praying the scripture"?

Richard Foster states, "to pray is to change."[1] Indeed, God uses prayer to change us, and, even though we might not comprehend fully the scope of such a claim, the results of prayer are life-changing. It also is widely recognized that Bible reading and study enhances our prayer lives. As important as Bible reading and prayer are, the use of scripture in prayer—*praying the scripture*—will, at times, involve more than a simple combination of the two. Praying the scripture involves a different focus that permits a person to enter deeply into a specific biblical text with a wholehearted desire to receive a personal word from God.[2]

One of my heroes of the Christian faith, George Müller (1805-1898), modeled this sort of prayer. He learned that "the safe guide in every crisis is believing prayer in connection with the Word of God."[3] Müller discovered that the power for spiritual empowerment lay in Bible reading and that once his soul was filled with God's Word, he was able to test his daily walk with the principles from God's Word.[4] What was true of a crisis in his life, was true in every detail of his life. He literally walked throughout his day with scripture and prayer on his lips. His example of scriptural praying gives critical insight into this approach to prayer.

Like Müller, we also recognize the value of prayer and study of the scripture as two core inward spiritual disciplines that we practice in order to comprehend and to apply the will of God. Yet, his attitude in such prayer informs me. He seemed to pray always with his entire soul opened before God. I believe "praying the scripture" includes a vital attitudinal difference; namely, that something more is longed for in my inner person. *Praying the scripture* refers more to *being* than to *doing* and the application of the scripture's "two-edged sword" (Heb. 4:12) with prayer to my life implies that I long for the Spirit's moral activity to be operative within my heart in dramatic ways. The result of this attitude of prayer provides me with a *holistic* approach where my entire being is linked to God in Christian communication.[5]

Where is this evident?

Some believers hold a mistaken idea that a holistic encounter with God falls upon them without "intention" or "consideration" and is somewhat akin to a magical experience.[6] They believe that the Christian devotional life requires little planning and lacks the use of formative disciplines such as prayer, scripture study, and self-denial.[7] I dispute this view of Christian spiritual formation and I have discovered that I require discipline in order to grow into the image of Christ. I do not want to miss anything that God may offer to me in my daily walk with Him, so I eagerly seek to learn methods for successful spiritual formation. Generally, a discipline is a particular rule or method or set pattern of behavior with an intended purpose to shape one's moral character.[8] Therefore, encountering God requires me to pursue well-established, *precise* paths. Praying the scripture has become for me one of those paths to hearing God's voice in my life.

Thankfully, praying the scripture is not a new phenomenon or fad. This approach to prayer has been a part of the successful devotional life of great souls throughout Christian history.[9] One particular woman, however, provided renewed instruction in the method of such prayer and her approach has influenced the lives of generations to follow. Her name was Madame Jeanne Guyon (1648-1717) and a rich history of Christian men and women have been influenced by her approach to praying the scripture.[10] Her method of praying the scripture is based upon the desire of a believer to move into a "living experience of Jesus Christ."

"Moving" into such a spiritual union with Christ might seem to mean that one possesses a mind and a heart to *actively pursue* spiritual things. But this form of prayer requires a *willingness to wait* patiently for God to speak and to move in the heart. The nature of this prayer approach also requires an individual *to discipline oneself* to wait upon God. While learning to wait has been a growth process for me, I have discovered that it yields wonderful results.

How is praying the scriptures practiced?

Guyon teaches us that praying the Scripture is a process that begins with reading God's Word and praying. She states that a believer should turn to a simple and practical passage and enter before the Lord "quietly and humbly." As a person reads the passage he or she should take care to read it slowly while seeking to take its meaning into one's being as though he or she were "tasting" and "digesting" the Word of God. The key is not to rush this process. I have made it a practice throughout my Christian life to read large portions of scripture at a time, but in this instance she teaches me to *sense* the innermost meaning of a shorter passage that I am reading.

At this point I take the passage and turn it into prayer. A single verse or a phrase often becomes the particular focus throughout my day. Over and over again God speaks to my innermost being through His Word in the circumstances of my day. As a person senses he has extracted the deeper sense of a passage he may move on to the next passage where he slowly encounters the text in the same way as before.[11] I make sure that I read daily prescribed passages throughout the entire scriptures and while I make certain to read extensively and broadly, I do not fail to pray the scriptures in order to experience the deep inner presence of God in my life.

Praying the scripture is gauged not by *how much* I read but the *way* I read. Guyon likens such things to a bee that either skips from flower to flower barely experiencing it or to one that penetrates deeply into the depths of the flower. Praying the scriptures enables one to taste its deepest "nectar." She is quick to point out that there is a way to read the scripture for scholarship and study but this sort of reading will not help a person when it comes to "divine" matters. Her desire was for the sweet aroma of God's word to break out upon the life of a believer who prays the scripture.[12] Additionally, I have discovered though that scriptural scholarship has greatly enhanced my encounter with God when I pray the scripture.

Guyon is not the lone example of this type of deep approach to spiritual formation. Charles Haddon Spurgeon once remarked: "I would rather lay my soul asoak in half a dozen verses [of the Bible] all day than rinse my hand in several chapters."[13] The German Pietist, Jacob Philip Spener (1635-1705) also believed that it was not enough to pray outwardly with one's mouth but that true prayer, and the "best prayer" occurred in *the inner man*. It was his aim for the word of God and prayer to penetrate to this level of a believer's life. He likewise advocated a holistic spiritual and devotional life where both the Word of God and prayer commingled in the inner person and was reflected in spiritual fruit in daily living.[14] Spener's example reminds me to take care to seek an *accurate* understanding of God's Word in order to know *clearly* His voice in my life.

Praying the scripture applied as a spiritual discipline offers God the daily opportunity to bring us into a "more effective cooperation with Christ and His kingdom."[15] As a result, "scripture praying" bears lasting implications for the lives of believers.

What are the implications of praying the scripture?

There are *individual* implications for praying the Scripture. This is not solely a prayer approach for the mature believer but for any and every child of God. *Every believer*, no matter the age or level of spiritual knowledge may engage in such prayer. I like the universal appeal and benefit of such an approach to spiritual formation. The Scriptures are the guide and support for every believer as he or she seeks God's counsel in prayer (Ps. 119:105).

There are *moral* implications as well. The moral transformation that will occur in a believer's life is readily discernible when the word of God and prayer are conjoined within the life of a believer. Such prayer yields an ever-deepening spiritual maturity and an ever-growing Christian usefulness in God's kingdom.

The *corporate* implications for churches also are significant. Individual scriptural praying followed by open reflection upon and discussion of the scripture and its application will surely benefit the people of God.[16] I believe sincerely that praying the scripture will strengthen significantly the typical church "prayer meeting" and will provide the Holy Spirit with an important medium to plant the Word of God in the hearts of His people.

Why is scriptural praying important?

Scriptural praying is important because it *opens widely all of my life to recognize and respond to God's will.* Much Bible reading and prayer is rooted in the mind alone, and does not permeate the whole life of a believer. Sadly, I have often approached spiritual formation more with my head than I have with my whole being—heart and hands (24:3-4). The union of the penetrating Word of God and prayer at the level of my entire being can only bring assist the Spirit's work to change me into the likeness of Christ. It is from this wellspring that the activity of God flows throughout my whole life.[17]

Scriptural praying *directs my thoughts and actions* upward toward God and ultimately outward toward the purposes God has for me in His world. Praying the scripture enables me to *experience* the activity of God in "real time" and enables me to become involved effectively[18] in His work without groping about searching for His divine presence and activity. Scriptural praying *centers my life directly into the movement of God* like a computer guidance system enables a space craft to dock with an orbiting space station. Such prayer is precise and accurate and effective not only in my devotional life but also in the whole of life.

Conclusion

The goal of the Christian disciple is to be completely transformed into the image and likeness of Christ. Praying the scriptures produces mature disciples of Jesus Christ and enables His Spirit to speak clearly into the daily context of individual life. Continual, consistent growth into the likeness of Christ results from such spiritual discipline. This approach to prayer has been modeled throughout my life by Christian saints who have gone before me and by mature Christian mentors. I have discovered that a secret to successful Christian living and ministry resides in such an approach to prayer.

Questions for Further Thought or Discussion

1. What ways do you believe you have set the agenda for God in prayer? Explain.
2. Discuss ways that *holistic* praying of the scripture can lead you to a more fulfilling Christian life. Dallas Willard's *Renovation of the Heart* will be especially helpful in this discussion. Compare pp. 27-44.
3. In what fresh ways has this approach to prayer enabled you to "behold the Lord?"

The author: Dr. Larry Ashlock is Director of Baptist Center for Global Concerns located in Arlington, Texas. He is also a Resident Fellow and Professor of Pastoral Leadership and Ethics at B.H. Carroll Theological Institute in Arlington. He taught Spiritual Formation as a former Professor, Director and Dean at both Dallas Baptist University and Southwestern Baptist Theological Seminary.

SUGGESTED ADDITIONAL READING

Howard, Evan B. *Praying the Scriptures: A Field Guide for Your Spiritual Journey.* Downers Grove, IL: InterVarsity Press, 1999.

Campbell, Wesley and Stacey. *Praying the Bible: The Pathway to Spirituality.* Ventura, CA: Regal Books, 2003.

Butts, David and Kim. *Pray Like the King: Lessons from the Prayers of Israel's Kings.* Terre Haute, IN: PrayerShop Publishing, 2007.

ENDNOTES

1. Richard Foster, *Celebration of Discipline: The Path to Spiritual Growth* (San Francisco: Harper & Row, Publishers, 1978), p. 30.

2. Adele Ahlberg Calhoun, *Spiritual Disciplines Handbook: Practices That Transform Us* (Downers Grove, IL: InterVarsity Press, 2005), p. 246. "Words and verses that catch our attention become invitations to be with God in prayer." The Word of God provides a vital foundation for such praying because the scriptures remind us that we are prone to "maintain control" and seek to get God to endorse our personal agendas. Praying the scriptures can return us to a "simpler state of openness and attentiveness to God."

3. Bonnie Harvey, *George Müller: Man of Faith* (Uhrichville, Ohio: Barbour Publishing, Inc., 1998), p. 27.

4. Harvey, pp. 53-54. Müller did more than simply "read" the Bible daily. He " . . . learned to look to God's Word and His promises to supply his daily needs . . ." This dependence upon prayer and God's Word and His promises indicates that he had acquired a clear understanding of the meaning and application of God's Word applied *directly* to his own life through prayer.

5. Much prayer and Bible reading is cognitive alone.

6. See John R. Tyson, ed., *Invitation to Christian Spirituality: An Ecumenical Anthology* (New York: Oxford University Press, 1999), p. 46. A hindrance to a commitment to praying the scriptures holistically is the false belief that knowing God is much like "falling in love."

7. Tyson, p. 46.

8. Keith Beasley-Topliffe, ed. "Discipline," in *The Upper Room Dictionary of Christian Spiritual Formation* (Nashville: Upper Room Books, 2003), p. 84. One also might adopt a discipline in order to ". . . train, to correct or to perfect one's mental facilities . . ."

9. Richard J. Foster and James Bryan Smith, eds., *Devotional Classics: Selected readings for Individuals and Groups* (San Francisco: HarperSanFrancisco, 1993), p. 320.

10. Foster, p. 320. Madame Guyon spent nearly 25 years imprisoned in Vincennes and the Bastille where she wrote some of the world's most profound devotional works on the experience of living in Jesus Christ. Watchman Nee saw that her work, *A Short and Very Easy Method of Prayer* was translated into Chinese and made available to new believers in the "Little Flock." Francoise Fenelon, John Wesley, and Hudson Taylor all recommended her method to the believers of their day.

11. Foster, pp. 320-321.

12. Foster, pp. 320-321.

13. Charles Haddon Spurgeon, *The New Park Street Pulpit and Metropolitan Tabernacle Pulpit* (London: Passmore and Alabaster, 63 vols., 1855-1917), 1578: p. 42. See also Mary Ann Jeffreys, "Sayings of Spurgeon," in *Christian History* (Issue 29, 1991): p. 12.

14. Philip Jacob Spener, *Pia Desideria,* Translated, edited, and with an Introduction by Theodore G. Tappert (Eugene, OR: Wipf and Stock Publishers, reprint ed., 2002), p. 117.

15. Dallas Willard, *The Spirit of the Disciplines: Understanding How God Changes Lives* (San Francisco: HarperSanFrancisco, 1st paperback ed., 1991), p. 156.

16. Spener, *Pia Desideria*, pp. 89-90.

17. See Dallas Willard, *Renovation of the Heart*: *Putting on the Character of Christ* (Colorado Springs, CO: NavPress, 2002). Willard believes that believers must experience a "pervasive inner transformation" in order to experience the divine life that God desires each believer to know.

18. See Christ's call for His disciples to be "salt" and "light" in Matthew 5.

chapter

28

PERSONAL PRAYER RETREATS

Cynthia Bezek

Most of us start out in ministry full of vision, passion, and energy. Sure we've heard stories of burnt out pastors, missionaries, and other Christian ministry leaders, but that won't happen to us . . . will it? Can we protect ourselves from becoming the next casualties? With God's help, we can. Even more importantly, we can minister to others from hearts overflowing with God's wisdom, love, and power. How? By developing a habit of regular extended times with the Lord.

When I assumed the leadership of *Pray!* magazine, I had already enjoyed occasional personal prayer retreats. But I knew that the requirements of this demanding position combined with my responsibilities to care for a critically ill husband and a home-schooled teenage son, would stretch me beyond anything I'd ever experienced before. So I asked our publisher if I might have one day each month off for prayer as part of my job description. He graciously agreed.

Those days set apart for God alone have been my lifeline. During these times God has shown up and kept me sane (well, *mostly* sane!). He's kept me creative and productive in leadership. He's refreshed me physically, spiritually, mentally, and emotionally. He's helped me to keep my vows of "for better or worse, in sickness or in health." He's helped me heal and forgive from the bumps and bruises of life and ministry. He's directed me, corrected me, and given me His perspective on things.

Pastor Jack Hayford says that times of solitude and waiting on the Lord are the "hallmark of people who walk steadfastly with the Lord—people who experience trials and come through with faithfulness, stability, and strength of character."[1] But how can something so simple be so powerful?

Ministering from the Overflow

Have you ever tried to deliver a life-changing talk, pray a heart-healing prayer, or speak words of compassionate comfort when you're depleted yourself? We all have. But that's not what God intends for us. He intends to be our Source, refreshing us so we in turn can refresh others.

Jesus said that we speak out of the overflow of our hearts (Lk. 6:45). He promised us living water that would flow out of us and into other people (Jn. 7:37). Through His Spirit, He wants to enable us to be streams of water in the desert for those around us who are parched (Isa. 32:2).

The problem is, we view refreshment as a luxury rather than a necessity. We say, "A day alone with God sounds *wonderful* but I can't do it because I've got meetings and appointments and projects and commitments and responsibilities." So we minister on empty.

Jesus looks at things differently. No one can argue about having more demands on His time than Jesus. Yet to Him, it was impossible *not* to spend extended time with the Father. Luke tell us that Jesus frequently took extended time alone with His Father (see 5:16, 6:12, 21:37, 22:39-40).

Jesus had to protect that time and make it a priority, just as we do. Mark gives us just a glimpse of how hard it was sometimes: "Very early in the morning, while it was still dark, Jesus got up, left the house and went off to a solitary place, where he prayed. Simon and his companions went to look for him, and when they found him, they exclaimed: 'Everyone is looking for You!'" (Mk. 1:35-37).

Nevertheless, Jesus *did* make time alone with God a priority, and taught His disciples to do the same. Later in Mark, we see Him addressing His ministry-weary friends. "The apostles gathered to Jesus and told Him all things, both what they had done and what they had taught. And He said to them, 'Come aside by yourselves to a deserted place and rest awhile' For there were many coming and going, and they did not even have time to eat. So they departed to a deserted place in the boat by themselves" (Mk. 6:30-32).

So, if prayer retreats are to be part of our lives, like Jesus, we'll need to be intentional about it. It might mean taking a day off work or out of our weekend. It may mean hiring a baby sitter. Some churches and ministries give or even require their staff to take a day off with God. Husbands can watch the kids so their wives can get away. Friends can help each other by offering their home, cabin, or condo for a retreat location. But whatever it takes, it will be worth it in terms of your own spiritual health and that of the people to whom you minister.

You know it's time for a prayer retreat when . . .

Some people make prayer retreats a regular part of their schedules. Others take them "as needed." Here are signs that it's time for a prayer retreat:

- You're dry and out of touch with the Lord.
- You feel overwhelmed, overworked, stressed, or scattered.
- You feel mechanical in your devotion and service.
- You have an important decision to make.
- You have a sinful habit to overcome.
- You have a person or people you need to forgive.
- You need God's perspective on a situation.
- You have a strategic ministry event or season ahead.
- You need insight about an unanswered prayer.
- You're behind in intercession and others are depending on you.
- Your spouse, teenager, roommate, colleague or dog tells you that you need one.

How will I spend the time?

Some people wonder how they could possibly spend *an entire day* in prayer.

This difficulty is easily addressed, however, when we consider that our relating to God takes many forms. During a full day of prayer—overnight, if possible—we have the luxury to linger with God and to try new forms of expression. Here are some ideas that many people enjoy trying on prayer retreats. There are far more here than you could possibly do during one day or even two. So ask the Holy Spirit to help you pick from this list and give you other ideas of how to spend your time together.

- Prayerfully and meditatively read a short book from the Bible such as Ephesians, Philippians, James, or 1 John.
- Play a worship CD and sing to God.
- Take a walk with God and talk to Him about what you see.
- Pray some of the great prayers of all time—start with Psalms or some of the prayers of the Apostle Paul.
- Ask the Lord to refresh you spiritually and physically. Meditate on these Scriptures: Ps. 23:2-3, 62:1-5, 91:1; Prov. 11:25; Isa. 30:15 Mt. 11:28-29; Acts. 3:19; Heb. 4:1-11.
- Dialogue with the Lord about a specific burden. Ask Him for comfort, perspective, direction, correction or help with it. Listen to His responses.
- Read a *short* portion of a devotional classic on prayer and talk to the Lord about it.
- With the Holy Spirit's help, spend time in extended intercession for those for whom you have committed to pray.
- Ask God what *He* would like to say regarding your life, ministry, relationships, and so on. Then listen carefully.
- Read about and try a new-to-you type of praying. For example, you might experiment with prayerwalking, lectio divina,[2] listening prayer, or different forms of worship.

Where will I go?

There are many options for a retreat spot. Look for a place that's quiet, comfortable, and free from distractions. The fewer amenities (phone, television, Internet) the better. Following are some possibilities. Some will work better for a nine to five kind of retreat. Ideally, plan to stay overnight.

Free

- A friend's cabin, condo, or cottage, or their residence
- A chapel or church during the week

Inexpensive

- Catholic retreat centers. These are usually available to anyone, Catholic or not. Call a local Catholic church to ask, or try this website: www.catholiclinks.org/retirosunitedstates.htm.
- Christian camp/retreat center. Many Christian camps are happy to accommodate a personal prayer retreat. Try www.cciusa.org or www.retreatsonline.com/guide/christian for leads. Or check with your own denomination.

Pastors Only

Several ministries offer retreats for pastors, their spouses, and sometimes for other full-time Christian workers very inexpensively or free. Try www.pastorsretreatnetwork.org. Or do a "Google" search for "pastors retreats" for options in various locales and within various denominations.

Other Ideas

- Spend the day at a nearby park
- Go camping
- Find a quiet corner of a library
- Rent a cabin or cottage
- Splurge and go to a resort or spa

Should I fast?

Sometimes the Lord may direct you to fast during your retreat. Other times He may invite you to fellowship with Him over food. Don't feel guilty if for health or other personal reasons you cannot abstain from food during your prayer retreat. Ask Him for guidance, and consider the following guidelines.

Reasons to Fast

Hunger for God. Fasting has a way of helping us really to understand what it means for our souls and flesh to yearn for God (Ps. 63:1). Every time we feel a pang of hunger, we can direct it into a craving for deeper intimacy with the Lord.

Repentance and humility. The only regular fast God required of His people under the Old Covenant was on the Day of Atonement. That day—essentially a prayer retreat on a grand corporate scale—was a day of fasting, repentance, and deep humility. We, too, can benefit when we humble [our souls] with fasting (Ps. 35:13).

Power over temptation. Jesus fortified Himself against temptation with a 40-day fast in the wilderness. Most of us won't be called to fast for that long (and if we are, we should consult a doctor first); however, fasting is a great way to subject our bodies to our spirits. People who struggle with sins of the flesh may especially benefit from a time of extended prayer combined with fasting.

In Crisis. There are many occasions of crisis in Scripture when people were called to extended prayer combined with fasting (see 2 Chron. 20:1-4; Neh. 1:4; Est. 4:15-16; Dan. 9:3; Jon. 3:6-9).

For wisdom. When Daniel sought to understand a perplexing vision he fasted (Daniel 10). Similarly, when the church in Antioch needed to know who to send out as missionaries, and later who to appoint as elders in the missionary churches, they met together for prayer, worshipping, and fasting (Acts. 13:1-2, 14:23).

Reasons Not to Fast

In times of exhaustion. When Elijah burned out from ministry he retreated to the desert to be alone with God. There, God miraculously provided him with warm bread and fresh water (1 K. 19:4-9). The Lord delights in restoring us. He does this spiritually, but also physically.

When Jesus invites you to deeper intimacy. Revelation 3:20 paints a poignant picture of a Friend knocking on the door of His loved one's heart. Jesus longs for us invite Him into our deepest confidence to eat with us and have us eat with Him. Consider taking bread and grape juice or wine along on your prayer retreat to make the experience of this fellowship more meaningful.

In times of thanksgiving and celebration. The Hebrew feast days were times set apart for corporate prayer, worship, thanksgiving, and celebration of God's faithfulness (e.g. The Feast of Tabernacles, Pentecost, Passover and Purim).

Similarly, there are times when we will want to retreat with the Lord to reflect on and celebrate His goodness. These are not times for deprivation.

Passing It On

After I'd experienced prayer retreats for myself, I found myself wanting to share this blessing with those I lead and serve. Exposing people to this soul-restoring gift makes our ministry easier. As they make prayer retreats part of their lives, the people we minister to will be increasingly in touch with the Lord for themselves, experiencing the joy of His love, guidance, comfort, encouragement, and help. And that's another way to protect ourselves from burnout. So how can we lose?

Questions for Further Thought or Discussion

1. What should characterize the ministry we are called to provide to others? How does the Lord equip and supply us for such ministry? Read Isa. 32:1-3, 55:1-2; Jn. 7:37; and Lk. 6:45 as you consider your answer. How might a discipline of regular prayer retreats help us with this calling?
2. What objections or concerns come to mind when you think about making prayer retreats a regular part of your life? Ask the Lord how you might overcome these. How would you answer others who have similar objections?
3. Prayerfully put together a tentative outline for how you might spend a day alone with God. What scriptures might you meditate upon? How could you include worship, thanksgiving and celebration in your day? Would you try a new style of prayer? Which one? How might you develop your skills of listening to and hearing from God? Don't forget to include time for rest, walks alone with the Lord, and other refreshment in His presence. Now, with this plan available to help you structure your day, set a date for a personal prayer retreat.

The author: Cynthia Bezek is the Editor for *Pray!* magazine in Colorado Springs, Colorado. She is author/compiler of *Come Away with Me: Pray! Magazine's Guide to Prayer Retreats.*

SUGGESTED ADDITIONAL READING

Arensen, Shel. *Come Away: How to Have a Personal Prayer Retreat.* Grand Rapids: Kregel Publishers, 2003.

Bezek, Cynthia. *Come Away with Me: Pray! Magazine's Guide to Prayer Retreats.* Colorado Springs, CO: *Pray!* Books, 2008.

Rubietta, Jane. *Resting Place: A Personal Guide to Spiritual Retreats.* Downers Grove, IL: InterVarsity Press, 2005.

Griffin, Emilie. *Wilderness Time: A Guide for Spiritual Retreat.* New York: HarperCollins, 1997.

ENDNOTES

1. Jack Hayford, *Living the Spirit-Formed Life* (Ventura, CA: Regal Books, 2001), p. 151.

2. *Lectio divina* is a centuries-old Christian practice of meditating on Scripture with the help of the Holy Spirit. We do this by reading a text slowly, sitting for a few moments in silence and then reading again. The following books offer helpful discussions about this prayer discipline: *Sacred Rhythms: Arranging Our Lives for Spiritual Transformation* by Ruth Haley Barton, pp. 45-61 (InterVarsity Press 2006), *Sacred Listening: Discovering the Spiritual Exercises of Ignatius Loyola* by James L. Wakefield, pp. 22-23, 34-43 (Baker Books, 2006), and *Eat This Book: A Conversation in the Art of Spiritual Reading* by Eugene H. Peterson, pp. 81-117 (Wm. B. Eerdmans Publishing Co 2006).

chapter

29

PRAYER JOURNALS/ DIARIES

Gary Waller

One of the most important influences to seeing people pray more is the encouragement that comes from answered prayer. All too often, as individuals and churches we pray for things, but never hear what happened. We never get a chance to praise God for answered prayer, and see our faith built through remembering God's grace and mercy. That is why as a pastor, it is important to look for ways to record what is being prayed for and the answers that come.

One only needs to do a "Google search," to find that there are a number of journals that are published in which you can record petitions and note when they are answered for individuals or circumstances being faced. When we pray in general for everyone or all the missionaries it is difficult to know if our prayer has been answered or if our prayer had any part in the answer. If we believe God hears and answers our prayers then it is important to give proof to such. The way we can give proof is by writing down our specific requests and the dates they were answered. Keeping a journal of our prayer interaction with God can have a profound affect on us and our congregations.

Keeping a Prayer Journal

A quick visit to a dictionary would tell you that a journal is an account of daily transactions and events. A diary is a record of personal experiences or observations. Many people today that are recording experiences or observations would say "they are journaling." We will use journal and diary as synonymous.

What is a prayer journal? "Prayer" means one is going to focus on a regular time of prayer where we go before Christ and offer our petitions. This time of prayer is more than a habit; it is going before the living Lord. "Journal" would mean it is a guide and a record of our time with Him in prayer.

A prayer journal is a document that allows one to keep track of one's journey with God. Most journals include blank sections to write down what you are praying and what you sense God saying to you. But another focal point of many journals will be a section that helps organize your prayer life and that allows you to record the names of individuals, ministries, and events for which you are praying.

Creating a Prayer Journal

Data collection or record keeping is an important part of assessing our progress and makes us accountable. Before creating, or buying a journal, you need to decide what kind of daily records you wish to keep. Do you want a lot of space to write about what you are sensing from the Lord as you pray? Do you plan to have different categories of requests that you pray for each day? Your journal should help you stay focused in your prayer time. Without guidance it is easy for our minds to wander and we end up repeating the same prayer we did yesterday. You will want it organized in a way that you can go back months or years later and see how God faithfully answered your requests.

How often will you pray for your prayer list? You may have individuals or needs you pray for each day, some weekly, and others monthly. If you choose this approach then your journal should have sections for daily prayer, weekly, and monthly.

What method will you use for your journal? Do you prefer a notebook that allows you to use a pen? Would you prefer your journal online? Several advantages of keeping your journal online would be: it is easier to search and you can copy and move things around. Regardless of the method consider adding pictures to your prayer requests.

Personal Use

Keeping a personal journal will help you to stay focused. You will be blessed as you record your interaction with the Lord and as you see answers to prayer. You can use a blank notebook and organize it yourself, or purchase any of a myriad of journals that are currently available.

The important things to record are prayer sections for family and friends, the lost, missionaries, church needs, etc. Make sure you date when you first pray for something. Then any time you see signs of God's moving in that situation, record that.

Here are two journals that are currently available.

The 2959 Plan—Newly revised, this journal is designed to be used in an individual's quiet time. It pushes the individual to spend twenty-nine minutes and fifty-nine seconds in prayer. It was originally developed by Dr. Peter Lord, but was revised recently with Dr. Daniel Henderson. There are seven sections, one for each day of the week. Each day the individual is encouraged to write down on the special form personal prayer requests and the date of the first time they began lifting this petition to the Lord. There is space allotted for the individual to enter the date the prayer was answered. Specific days are designated to pray for the following: Sunday—church leaders, Monday—fellow believers, Tuesday—the lost and those out of fellowship with the Lord, Wednesday—those in authority, Thursday—fellow believers, Friday—missionaries, and Saturday—God's blessings.

The Pray! Prayer Journal. Developed by *Pray!* magazine, besides the usual characteristics of a journal—places to record requests, answers, and what you are hearing from the Lord—this includes much more. Every two-page spread includes a helpful idea from *Pray!* magazine to enhance your prayer life. There are also 12-scripture based prayer guides, one per month, and a daily Bible reading plan that will take you through the Bible in a year.

Community Use

Small groups and churches find that utilizing a prayer journal can be an enriching experience for the spiritual development of their members. Here are several ways that I have observed journals being effectively used by groups.

Church Journal. Many churches have a weekly prayer service that involves a time of intercessory prayer. Usually a prayer list (a form of a journal) is published containing names from the week before and a few new ones that were added to the list during the previous prayer service. Weekly, individuals are asked to update the congregation on the condition of the prayer requests. Usually the church list will contain a section for the sick that are in the hospital, sick at home, shut-ins, those looking for work, and missionaries.

Unfortunately, in some of the churches more time is spent updating than praying for the individuals on the prayer list. Two observations about the church prayer journal are (1) usually there is no date of when the church began praying for the specific need and, (2) when the prayer is answered, instead of letting anyone know of God's blessing so praise and thanksgiving can result, the request is simply dropped off the list.

Some progressive and astute churches actually record the flow of prayer in the weekly prayer meeting within the pages of its journal. In other words a scribe listens to what is being prayed for by each person and jots notes down about the prayers. This can be helpful to show a pattern or a Holy Spirit guided direction within a given prayer meeting.

Deacon/Elder Meetings. The monthly deacon's meeting, at one of the churches I served, had a special time of prayer, usually at the conclusion. For this group the prayer journal was a blackboard. They would ask for prayer concerns and three names always appeared on the list. These three men had families active in our church but they never attended. For over twenty months these men were prayed for by the deacons that they might come to know Christ as their personal Savior. One by one all three received Christ into their lives and became active followers of Him. Again, though, if written on an erasable board, someone should record them in a book so you have a record of what was prayed for.

Small Groups. Small groups that meet on regular bases should consider having their own prayer journal. Meeting weekly or bi-weekly these groups usually set aside a special time of prayer. It would enhance the group experience if they documented the special requests they lifted to the Lord and recorded the answer to their petitions.

Prayer Room. Some churches make use of a 24/7 prayer room. They seek to enlist people that will serve in the prayer room for one hour a week. In the prayer room they provide a prayer list for the 168 prayer warriors. Some use a metal file, others a notebook, and some just lined paper to list prayer requests.

During your assigned hour for the week you are to lift up the names in the file. You write down anything you might sense God saying to you about the request. When you finish your hour you indicate the last request for which you prayed. The next person then would begin at the next request on the list. There usually is a form for the prayer team members to update information on a prayer request or to add someone to the prayer list. Once a day someone will collect the completed forms and update the list in the prayer room. When the prayer request is answered the date and the answer is placed on the prayer list so the prayer team can rejoice.

Online. One of the most effective ways I have found to use the prayer journal concept is with the online classes I teach. At the start of a term I will set up a "Prayer Room" for students to enter prayer requests. Other students will post their prayers, online, that they offer up to the Lord on behalf of the request. The student's request which is being prayed for is easily updated to share the answer to the prayers. I have noticed there is a relationship between the number of times the request is prayed for and the number of answers that are reported.

Concerning online prayer one can find prayer rooms that have been established on the web. Some will be prayer sites for specific requests. Other sites will allow for anyone to post a request.

Keep a list and be blessed.

While keeping lists of our prayer concerns is important for organization sake, by far the biggest blessing is having a history of the working of God in your life and in your church. While it might seem tedious or boring to take the time to record everything, you will be amazed at what it can do when you clearly know God's activity in your midst and share that with your congregation.

Questions for Further Thought or Discussion

1. What should be included in a prayer journal?
2. What is the best way to organize your prayer journal?
3. What method will work best for you?

The author: Dr. Gary Waller is Co-founder and Vice President of Learning Management at Rockbridge Seminary in Springfield, Missouri.

SUGGESTED ADDITIONAL READING

Briggs, Edward. *A Pilgrim's Guide to Prayer.* Nashville: Broadman Press, 1987.

Hanks, Billie. *If You Love Me.* Waco: Word, 1985.

Parkhurst, Louis. *The Believer's Secret of Intercession.* Minneapolis: Bethany House, 1988.

Water, Mark. *Prayer Made Easy.* Peabody, MA: Hendrickson Publishers, 1999.

The Online Prayer Journal: A Christian internet journaling resource http://prayer-journal.com.

chapter

30

HOW TO ADDRESS GOD IN PRAYER

William David Spencer

"When you pray, do not use vain repetitions as the heathen do" warned Jesus in Matthew 6:7-8. What did He mean? What was so wrong about the way His contemporaries were praying that God-Among-Us commanded His hearers not to follow their example? What exactly were these many words they were babbling?

Gentiles in Jesus' day were often engaged in a form of power religion, using prayer to attempt to enlist a god to fulfill their requests. Many would write their prayers on a piece of papyri, roll it up, and insert it into the mouth of an idol of the god they were beseeching. One might say they were literally stuffing their prayers down their gods' throats!

Hans Dieter Betz has compiled a collection of these prayers, *The Greek Magical Papyri in Translation, including the Demotic Spells*. Some appear composed in complex patterns as talismans or charms. Prayers would often include a string of vowels as an ululation, followed by a reference to the god's sacred story, and the particular petition the supplicant wanted, couched in terms of that god's story, followed by the plea "immediately, immediately, quickly, quickly." Strong-arming their god was apparently not a breach of divine protocol. But, what is so striking about many of these prayers is the abnormally long section devoted to naming the god. One example, PGM xi xa 1-54, is basically devoted to flattery and summoning up the god's various names and titles, such that the request, when it finally comes, appears like a tag on to the end.[1] One thinks of a child wheedling a reluctant parent, cajoling and heaping on the purr words.

While the true and only God does honor genuine praise and particularly appreciates expressions of gratitude (e.g., see Ps. 100:4), such flattery is what Jesus condemns as "babbling." God does not relish being preened and coaxed with flattery.

In contrast, the model prayers Jesus provides seem stark. He merely tells us to address God as "our Father." He Himself refers to God as "My Father," since God was His Father on earth. He extends that familial privilege to believers collectively, since, among other redemptive tasks, He came to earth to do what Adam and Eve failed to do: set the example of what a perfect child of God looks like. Jesus buys us back from our sin, while exhibiting perfect filial obedience to us, so that in His earthly incarnation He is our elder brother, the heir of God. And He includes us in His inheritance of God's grace as ourselves children and heirs of God. So, although "Father" is rarely used as a prayer address in the Old Testament,[2] it becomes the recommended form of address in Jesus' teaching. Paul indicates both he and the Romans follow Jesus' example, when he comments on their crying the Aramaic word Abba and the Greek words *ho Pater*, both of which mean "Father," in their prayers (Rom. 8:15).

But, what is similar in the Old Testament is the non-flattering manner and the sheer simplicity with which God is addressed. The early chapters of Genesis basically record conversations where an address for God is not recorded, until Abraham calls on the name of "the LORD" in Genesis 12:8. "The Lord" is the English translation of the four consonants from the Hebrew verb *yhwh* ("to be"), often called "the Tetragrammaton" (or four letters), that God gave to Moses to tell to Pharaoh in Exodus 3:14. When the vowel points for the Hebrew word for ruler and master, *adonai*, were substituted by pious scribes for the actual vowels of the name, the result became unpronounceable (sometimes called in literature the unpronounceable name of God). The combination of consonants and vowels literally transliterates into English as *Jehovah*, but ancient believers never used that construction as a name. They simply saw the vowel points for *adonai* adorning the four consonants for the verb "to be" and called God "*Adonai*" or "Lord." Abraham even uses the word *Adonai* along with the Tetragrammaton in Genesis 15:2 to emphasize the rulership of God. We translate this name "Lord God."

Throughout the Hebrew Bible, this is the preferred form of address: to call God ruler or master = the Lord. But, built, as it is, from the verb "to be," it signifies the one who lives, or who has been, is, and will be (as God told Moses (literally), "I am existing that I am existing" [Ex. 3:14]). When we employ it to address God in prayer, we acknowledge God's eternity, omnipotence, and gift to us of the breath of life.

Melchizedek praises God as "God Most High," "God Supreme," or "God Exalted" (*'el 'el'yon*) in his blessing of Abraham, underscoring God's supremacy, and Abraham adopts that designation (see Gen. 14:18-22).

Sometimes *'elohim*, the great plural word for God, is added, as Abraham's servant does in Genesis 24:12, "O LORD (singular) God (plural) of my master Abraham," echoing, I believe, the triune nature of our Deity—one God with three distinct faces (*prosopon*) or in three distinct coeternal and coequal personalties or persons. That is why *Adonai*, which equals the Greek word *kurios*, the title given for God throughout the Bible, is applied to Jesus in prayer, as the dying Stephen did, when he cried out in a loud voice, "Lord Jesus, receive my spirit" (Acts 7:59). Peter also appears to apply the title to the Holy Spirit, when he is given the vision of unclean animals and ordered to "stand up, Peter, kill and eat!" and he replies, "Not so, Lord!" (Acts 10:13-14). Acts 10:19 reveals he is in conversation with the Holy Spirit (cf. Acts 13:2, where the believers are fasting and ministering [or worshipping, *leitourgeo*] "to the Lord," and the Holy Spirit replies).

Sometimes, God is identified in prayer by an action God does, as when Hagar, having fled into the wilderness to escape Sarai, is shown water by God's messenger and cries to God, "You-Are-the-God-Who-Sees!" (Gen. 16:13).

God is also addressed with images, as Asaph does in Psalm 80:1, "Give ear, O Shepherd of Israel, You who lead Joseph like a flock; You who dwell between the cherubim."

Often God uses a relationship to a predecessor to self-identify to an individual, as "I am the God of Abraham your Father" to Isaac (Gen. 26:24), or "I am God, the God of your father [Isaac]" to Jacob (46:3), and of all three to Moses (Ex. 3:6). So, to identify God accordingly honors God's covenantal nature. We even see Abraham's servant praying to the "LORD God of my master Abraham," for success in his quest for a wife for Isaac (Gen. 24:12). God honors and answers that prayer with success. God is even identified as the "LORD God of the Hebrews" (Ex. 3:18), "the God of Israel" (Josh. 24:2), and even the God of all people, Jews and Gentiles alike (Rom. 3:29). God can identify with a place (see "God of Bethel" in Gen. 31:13) or with all places as the "LORD God of heaven, who made the sea and dry land" (Jon. 1:9).

Of course, Jesus teaches us to pray to the "Father in Heaven" in His model prayer (Mt. 6:9). Therefore, when persecuted, the disciples in the book of Acts roll all these prayers and prayer designations into one great covenantal prayer in Acts 4:24-30. They begin by addressing God as LORD (*Despotes*), You are God, who made heaven and earth and the sea, and all that is in them." Then they quote God's words through King David, point out their opposition, ask God to give themselves boldness to preach the gospel, and request God to perform once again in their time the signs and wonders God did in the days of the Old Covenant. God says yes: the house they are in is shaken; they are filled with the Holy Spirit; and they begin preaching forth God's word boldly. Covenantal prayers are powerful prayers!

What, then, can we learn about the proper way to address God in prayer, so God will be pleased?

- Be simple. Flattery is not effective with God. Our God is the one being who knows us inside and out and insincerity will not work. If you are overwhelmed with love of God or gratitude or a response of praise, by all means extol God. God loves the praises of God's people (see, for example, 1 Tim. 1:17). But, faith is not magic, so simplicity is always a good rule.
- Be familial. God is our creator, the great Parent who loves us perfectly and has bought us back at a great price. We are precious to God who is our heavenly Father. We are adopted as heirs, so, if you are a believer in Jesus, you can call God your Father, too.
- Be respectful. "Lord," "Sovereign God," "Almighty One," terms as these

are all appropriate, and addressing God as completer of an action, or the giver of a gift, as Hagar did, has a biblical precedent. So, we can call God our Healer, our Divine Physician, the One who loves us, the One who caretakes us—the list seems endless.

- Be biblical. Generational blessing of God as the One who succors the faithful, or even the One who sustains our individual family—especially when we do it by reviewing God's great actions in Scripture—is a powerful way to honor and invoke God. If you remember the specific place where God called you to salvation, you can even identify God as the God who visited you in that place and speaks to you in all places, while ruling us all from heaven.

In all things, being simple, but sincere, familial but respectful, biblical and personal, loving and grateful are keys when addressing God.

Questions for Further Thought and Discussion

1. Do you ever babble superfluous words to God, seeking to cajole God into giving you what you want (especially when you sense it may not be God's will for you)? How can you use Jesus' model to pray more in the way God would want you to pray?
2. Try to list five new titles you can use for God in prayer you may not have used before. See if addressing God with them will enrich the quality of your prayers.
3. Do you have a family member who is a devout Christian and perhaps led you to the Lord? Try a familial prayer mentioning God as the God of that person. If you have no one like that in your history, try a covenantal prayer identifying God as the God of some faithful believer in the Bible and see if doing so connects you more deeply to the family of God, the body of Christ on earth, even as you connect with God.

The author: Rev. Dr. William David Spencer is a Ranked Adjunct Associate Professor of Theology and the Arts at Gordon Conwell Theological Seminary, Boston Campus Center for Urban Ministerial Education. He has authored or edited ten books, including the two he co-authored with his wife, on prayer: *The Prayer Life of Jesus* and *Joy Through the Night: Biblical Resources on Suffering.*

SUGGESTED ADDITIONAL READING

Towns, Elmer, *My Father's Names: The Old Testament Names of God.* Ventura CA: Gospel Light, 1991.

Torrey, R.A. *How to Pray*. Chicago: Moody Publishing, 2007.

White, John. *Daring to Draw Near.* Downers Grove, IL: InterVarsity Press, 1977.

ENDNOTES

1. Hans Dieter Betz, ed., *The Greek Magical Papyri in Translation, including the Demotic Spells* (Chicago: University of Chicago, 1986), see particularly pp. 323, 256-57, 314.

2. Joachim Jeremias, *The Prayers of Jesus* (Philadelphia: Fortress, 1978), pp. 11-15.

chapter

31

TO WHOM DOES GOD LISTEN?

W. Bingham Hunter

Psalm 65:2 describes God as, "You who hear prayer" and Psalm 77:1 confesses: "I cried out to God with my voice . . . and He gave ear to me." That "God hears prayer," is foundational to biblical faith (Deut. 4:7; Ps. 4:3, 34:17, 55:17; Mt. 7:7-8; 1 Pet. 3:12). Christians know this, but many secretly wonder, *Is God really listening to me?*

Why are we unsure whether God hears us? The issues include:

- I don't get what I ask and wonder, "Did my request get through?"
- If God hears prayer, then, "Just whose prayer is getting heard? He sure isn't listening to me."

Not receiving what I seek produces doubt God really cares for me, and anxiety something's wrong with me or how I'm praying. This chapter provides biblical perspectives on such questions.

What does "*listen*" mean?

Psalm 139 says God knows everything about us: all our thoughts and activities. Before a word is on our tongue God knows it completely. God, by definition, is omniscient. So, it's correct to say God hears any prayer offered by anyone—godly believer, hardened skeptic or plaintive pagan. But He makes no promises to non-believers, and hence is under no obligation to respond to their prayers. Some say in a life-threatening crisis (such as a battlefield, or in a raging storm), their desperate, "God save me!" was heard. Such deliverances reflect God's common grace and can result in increased reflection ("I must still be alive for a reason"), which God may use to draw people to Christ. But even if it's theologically correct to say, "God listens to everybody," most of us aren't thinking about God's omniscience. What we mean is, "If God *is* listening, He should give me what I ask." At just this point, confusion about many aspects of prayer often reigns.

What exactly *is* prayer?

People often talk as if prayer is the way we get God to give us what we want. Those who think this way seek prayer promises, techniques, locations, mediators and other methods they believe will influence God or place Him under obligation. But Scripture points in virtually the opposite direction, indicating prayer, *communication with the living God, is a means He uses to give us what He knows we need.*

On what *basis* can we approach God in prayer?

Many assume we exchange personal accomplishments for the prayer-answers we seek. People argue their piety, morality, discipline, passion, sacrifice, service, offerings and faith provide the basis by which God will listen to their prayers. Yet Scripture teaches us access to God in prayer *cannot* be earned (Lk. 18:9-14). Every human effort falls short: "All our righteousnesses are like filthy rags" (Isa. 64:6). Access to God comes only through faith in Jesus Christ: "I am the way, the truth and the life. No one comes to the Father, except through Me" (Jn. 14:6). Only Jesus' blood can secure confident access to a Holy God (1Tim. 2:5; Heb. 10:19). By God's grace alone, received through faith alone, can we become His spiritual children (Jn. 1:12) and receive the right to pray to Him as *Abba*, "Dear Father" (Rom. 8:15-16; Eph. 2:14-19). *Abba* defines the context of Christian prayer.

What is the *context* of prayer?

Christians often embrace pragmatism (pursuing "what works"). This mindset may be coupled with the widespread assumption prayer (like math or physics) is a *system*: Discover the spiritual formula governing how prayer functions, and you can make the system work and get the desired answers.

Those with this perspective think of prayer in a mechanical context. Sin, for example, is said to "interfere" or "block" prayer. Therefore, if you repent of sin and confess it (removing the obstruction), answers to prayer should be forthcoming. This understanding is common, but profoundly unbiblical: Our Heavenly Father is not a vending machine.

Scripture says the context of prayer is living interpersonal relationship with God (Jn. 14:23; 15:4-11). Prayer is one aspect of our relationship with another personal being. It takes place in a setting where on-going communication deepens and enriches understanding and develops intimacy, disclosure, trust and commitment. There is far more than conversation and petition going on in such a relationship. As does any truly loving father, God "listens" to the entire life of His child. (And none of us is an only child. God cares about how we treat our spiritual brothers and sisters: Mt. 18:21-35; 1 Pet. 3:7; 1 Jn. 3:16-23.)

In this relationship, sin grieves the Holy Spirit living in every believer. And it alters the priorities of the Spirit, who motivates and guides us in praying according to the Father's will. Living in willful disobedience, we pray selfishly, seeking our will, not God's (Jas. 4:3). Our Lord, who loves us too much to reward our rebellious independent spirit (Num. 11:4-33 and Ps. 106:14-15 are instructional), uses the discipline of unanswered prayer to stimulate reflection, conviction and repentance, as well as longing for fellowship and desire for intimacy. When His promptings are ignored, the Spirit is "quenched" and genuine estrangement results. Although the Father-child relationship is legal, eternal and unbreakable (Jn. 10:28-29; Rom. 8:35-39), the warmth of fellowship cools, and communication becomes strained and uncomfortable. Eventually we may avoid prayer altogether. Repentance, confession, forgiveness and restitution don't instantly "fix" the relationship and immediately "switch answers to prayer back on." It takes time to restore fellowship and intimacy, and to rebuild trust (reflect on Num. 12:13-14). Answers to prayer will follow, in proportion to the Father's discernment of our commitment to the relationship and the priority of His will.

What is the *goal* of prayer?

The goal of prayer is to get what we pray for, right? Wrong. The goal of Christian prayer is to *glorify the Father* through His Son, the Lord Jesus Christ (Jn. 14:13). God is glorified through accomplishment of His will and advancement of His kingdom on earth (Mt. 5:16, 6:9-10; 1 Cor. 10:31), as well as by our obedience, spiritual growth and deepening relationship with Him (Jn. 15:8). Since we often ask for things outside of His will—because they will not advance His kingdom, develop our spiritual maturity or enrich our relationship with Him—*unanswered prayer is a part of the normal Christian life* (2 Cor. 12:7-10). It's not an indication that God isn't listening to us. Nevertheless, most of us persist in thinking, *There must be some way to get Him to give me what I ask.*

Popular *Misconceptions* about Prayer

More than a few are convinced that good works, offerings, vows, extreme discipline, praying at "holy" places, using blessing cloths, oil, icons, candles, petitioning saints, persistence (repetition), and getting large numbers to intercede will incline God to listen to their prayers. Such ideas assume there are ways to get "spiritual leverage" and apply "power" or "authority" to facilitate receiving positive answers. There is no evidence in Scripture this is the case. (Mt. 18:19 relates especially to pray for wisdom in dealing with matters of discipline.[1])

Think about it: Does God lack, or is He dependent on, anything we might give, devote, vow or sacrifice to/for Him? The Bible says God doesn't need anything we promise or give to Him (Job 35:7; Acts 17:25). Is there any way we can obligate Him? Scripture clearly says, "No." His creatures can never obligate, manipulate or control their Creator. "'Who has been his counselor? Or who has given a gift to him that he might be repaid?' For from him and through him and to him are all things" (Rom. 11:34-36, ESV).

Jesus said pagans—not the people of God—"think that they will be heard for their many words" (Mt. 6:7). His command is: "Do not be like them." We persist in urgent prayer not to impress or wear God down, but because Jesus said don't lose heart (Lk. 18:1); and to express *complete dependence* on God: "Whom have I in heaven but You?" (Ps. 73:25). We fast, not to gain a hearing in prayer, but to express humility (Ezra 8:21), to discipline ourselves to focus on, and devote ourselves to the One who gives all good gifts. Reliance on mediators (praying to a "saint," for example) is not rational. Scripture repeatedly says the dead cannot pray (Ps. 30:9, 115:17). And let's be absolutely clear: No saint (dead or alive) offers more effective intercession than Christ and the Holy Spirit (Rom. 8:26-27, 34). The Bible never says the prayers of many are more effective than prayer offered by a single child of God. Prayer does not take place on a teeter-totter with God on one end and me and my intercessors on the other.

So . . . just what does it take for God to listen to a Christian's prayers?

The Apostle John approaches this question from two directions. First, he connects God's listening to prayer with obedience: God hears those who hear Him. "We know that God does not hear sinners; but if anyone is a worshipper of God and does His will, He hears him" (Jn. 9:31). "Beloved, if our heart does not condemn us, we have confidence before God; and whatever we ask we receive from him, *because we keep his commandments and do what pleases him*" (1 Jn. 3:21-22, ESV, *emphasis added*).

If we claim the privilege of access to God on the basis of our relationship with Him by grace through faith in Christ, we must live like His spiritual children—act like Jesus' true disciples. Obedience does not earn a hearing with God, even less, enable us to "trade" obedience for answers to prayer. Rather, obedient Christian behavior identifies those who love Christ and have access to their Heavenly Abba through faith in Christ. As Jesus said, "Why do you call me 'Lord, Lord,' and do not the things which I say?" (Lk. 6:46). "If you love Me, keep my commandments" (Jn. 14:15).

Second, John links being heard with asking according to God's will: "this is the confidence that we have toward him, that *if we ask anything according to his will he hears us*" (1 Jn. 5:14, ESV, *emphasis added*). In short: God hears those who pray according to His will. This is *the* bottom line. No matter how much passion we put into prayer, we cannot wrestle God into granting petitions contrary to His will. But be encouraged: We *can* learn to pray according to God's will.

The Prayer-Obedience Relationship

It begins when we receive Christ as Savior. In thankful response for His gift of salvation, our love for God grows and we long to know Him better. His Word becomes precious because it reveals His heart, character and will. We read, study and memorize it; and express love to Christ by obeying His commandments. As we obey God's will, the Spirit trains us to think in terms of God's will; and He reveals Jesus and the Father to us (Jn. 14:21). We increasingly see life God's way, and learn to think His thoughts after Him: We come to understand what the will of God is (Rom. 12:2). The outcome? We more frequently pray according to God's will.

The experience of God's love in salvation

↓

God's child desires to respond in love and thankfulness to the Father

↘

The child desires to read God's Word and know Him more fully

↘

The child is helped by the Holy Spirit to understand God's Word

↓

The child's desire to live in a way that pleases God increases

↓

The Spirit helps the child to live according to the Father's will

↙

In the obedient child's life, an atmosphere develops which encourages fellowship with the Father and the Lord Jesus Christ

↙

The Holy Spirit lives comfortably in the child; and through the Spirit, the child grows in understanding the mind and will of God

↖

The child begins to think about life as God thinks about life. Events and decisions are evaluated from God's point of view: According to His will

↖

The child begins to think like the Father, thinking His thoughts after Him

↑

The child begins to understand what the Father might want in a particular situation

↑

The Spirit enables the child to pray in terms of God's thoughts: According to His will

↗

The Father answers prayer that is in accord with His will

↗ (back to: God's child desires to respond in love and thankfulness to the Father)

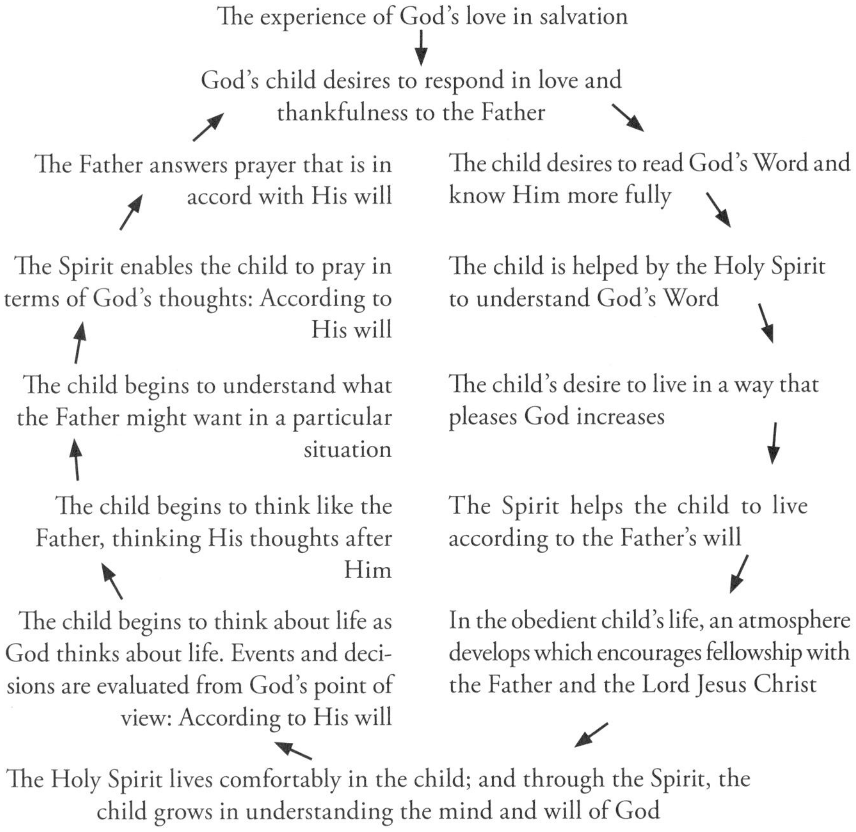

The prayer-obedience relationship is not a system." It describes how the Holy Spirit develops the "mind of Christ" in us. Nor can it support claims obedient believers always receive what they ask. Rather, it explains why "righteous" people often pray effectively (Jas. 5:16) and reveals what's behind the promise, "Delight yourself also in the LORD, and He shall give you the desires of your heart" (Ps. 37:4). Righteous people delight in God and His will. Their lives are committed to doing God's will. It comes as no surprise they frequently pray according to God's will.

So . . . to whom does God listen? He "listens" to the entire life of His obedient child. Do you long to be heard? Become passionate about discipleship: Run in the path of His commandments . . . and He *will* give you the desires of your heart.

Questions for Further Thought and Discussion

1. If "access to God in prayer cannot be earned," as the author claims, then how can we know that God hears our prayers?
2. The writer claims that there is *nothing* that makes our prayers "work better." He mentions oil, candles, icons, etc. In 2 Kings 5:17, Naaman, who had been cleansed of leprosy, wanted to take some of the earth of Israel back to Aram (Syria)—apparently so he could "make burnt offerings and sacrifices" to the true God on it. Does this show the writer is right or wrong? What does it indicate about Naaman? Do people have similar attitudes today? Describe some of them.
3. Have you ever "made a deal" with God: "Lord, just give me _______, and I will _______?" What happened? Do you think the author is right when he says, "God doesn't need anything we can promise Him"? Why or why not?

The author: Dr. W. Bingham Hunter is a former Professor and Academic Dean at Talbot School of Theology and Trinity Evangelical Divinity School. He is the author of *The God Who Hears, Praying When Life Hurts*, and "Prayer," an article in: Gerald F. Hawthorne, Ralph P. Martin & Daniel G. Reid (eds.) *Dictionary of Paul and His Letters*. He lives in Deerfield, Illinois.

SUGGESTED ADDITIONAL READING

Cowart, John W. *Why Don't I Get What I Pray For?* Downers Grove, IL: InterVarsity Press, 1993.

Piper, John. *A Hunger for God: Desiring God through Prayer & Fasting.* Wheaton, IL: Good News Publishers/Crossway, 1997.

Spear, Wayne R. *Talking to God: The Theology of Prayer.* Pittsburg, PA: Crown & Covenant Publishers, 2002.

Whittaker, Colin. *Seven Guides to Effective Prayer—Secrets of Intercession and Spiritual Warfare from Seven Great Prayer Warriors: George Müller, Hudson Taylor, Praying Hyde, Charles Finney, David Brainerd, Reese Howells, Madame Guyon.* Minneapolis: Bethany House, 1987.

ENDNOTES

1. William Hendriksen, *The Gospel of Matthew,* (Edinburgh: Banner of Truth Trust, 1973), p. 702. Hendriksen rightly says, "The assurance is given that even though at a certain place the fellowship of believers consists of only two persons, even these two, when in agreement with each other, can definitely figure on the guidance for which they have made request. It should hardly be necessary to add that such a prayer must be in keeping with the characteristics of which Jesus revels elsewhere."

chapter

32

HOW TO HEAR FROM GOD IN PRAYER

Calvin A. Blom

"Playing the piano helped me pray!" The surprised student pondered, "How does playing the piano relate to prayer?" Why, or how, could the playing of music enhance hearing from God? Enhanced hearing from God while playing the piano does not readily or logically integrate into one's thinking about prayer, and particularly about "hearing" from God in the process. Herein lays mystery, a wonderful mystery that defies and goes beyond what the gray matter between the ears can explain or understand; mystery that is foreign to the head but at home with the heart. At the deepest and most intimate level, God is heard with the heart, the inner essence of a person's reality. Hearing God with the heart is not a revolutionary concept for much has been written down through the centuries espousing this reality. But in these latter days there seems to be a dearth of thought about "how" the heart hears. Practical processes for helping the heart to hear from God are the core thrust of this reflection.

"Hearing" from God is a real possibility because God is inherently revelatory! Creation was designed to declare God's glory. The inspired Word of God is God's revelatory gift to humanity, and finally there comes the Incarnation, God's ultimate revelation underscoring God's revelatory nature. The Apostle John writes that the Word became flesh to "explain" God (Jn. 1:18).

Within orthodox Christendom hearing God through Scripture and creation is commonly accepted, and considerable credence is also given to believing that God can and does speak in mystical ways through visions, dreams, intuitions and induced thoughts. That God speaks and reveals is inextricable intertwined with the nature and essence of God. "How" God speaks is His sovereign choice. God can communicate in any fashion at anytime, and it is neither the prerogative nor the obligation of mere mortals to define how God should make Himself known. Furthermore, there is nothing done on the human side to "make" God talk to us. God initiates all God/human communication. God is neither a reluctant revealer, nor an unclear communicator. But, as with all communication where humans are involved, perfect clarity by the one speaking does not mean that the hearers always hear and understand clearly. God undoubtedly speaks absolutely clearly, but we do not always hear clearly. Because of human limitations we must always be humble in attitude when declaring how we have "heard" God. This reality ought not frighten us away from seeking to hear the Lord, but we must consciously live in the reality of our limitations.

Why do we not hear God clearly? Why do we sometimes seem not to hear God in any manner? A few weeks ago my mother-in-law awoke essentially deaf in one ear. Her hearing, which was relatively good on one day, was gone the next day. In reality her hearing loss did not happen overnight, but there was a climatic point in time when the wax that was slowly building up totally shut down her ability to hear. When the wax was removed, her hearing returned, it was like a miracle! What "wax" in our spiritual ears needs to be removed? How do we remove that wax so we might hear?

Unconfessed Sin

The most common spiritual wax is the wax of un-confessed sin. Habitual sin renders the ears of the heart deaf to God. In any age where there is a lack of corporate encouragement to seriously deal with sin and where personal piety is discounted, hearing from God will be difficult at best. Specific verbal confession cleanses the wax of sin and opens the ears to hear the Lord.

Reluctance

Then there is the strange and subtle "wax of reluctance" present in the people of faith. This reluctance to bend the ear to God seems rooted in a basic fear and distrust of God. I have had seminary students openly admit being afraid of solitude time there they would be one-on-one with God. What disturbing, distressing, or disheartening thing might God say if we really listened for a word from Him? Fear and distrust of God can cause people to pull back, to stay distant, and hence to miss hearing God's still small voice. For such people learning to hear from God will have to be preceded by simply learning to know God better. Behind and beyond the sin of distrust there is simply a void of real knowledge about the love and grace of God. We learn to hear God better by learning to know Him better.

But beyond those spiritually deaf because of sin, or reluctant because of fear, there are those who really want to hear the Lord, but they are simply unaware that their hearing is hindered. Their hearts are open to hear, but at the same time their hearts are too full and too cluttered with other stuff to receive a message from God. What opens such a heart to hear more clearly what God the revealer is declaring? Is playing the piano the key? No, playing the piano is not "the" key to hearing God with the heart, but quite plausibly there is a crucial connection between playing the piano and hearing from God. Consider some of the key dynamics involved in hearing from God.

First, as already noted, God is a revealer who wants to communicate. Second, the human heart has been created with a capacity to hear God's voice. The human heart also has the capacity to consciously or unconsciously screen out God's voice. Unconsciously the presence of many "voices" coming from the cultural, or one's own inner thoughts, makes hearing God quite difficult. God, of course, can speak with a voice "as the sound of many waters" (Rev. 1:15), and if God so deems people simply must listen. But while God has the power to break into and override other voices that are screaming messages to the heart, God seems to be a respecter of the heart's privacy. Thus Jesus stands at the door of the heart and knocks seeking a welcome that would allow Him entrance (Rev. 3:20). Such a sad passage, Jesus the Son of God knocking at a door of a house He already owns. Jesus is kept out not because He cannot break down the door or shout through it, but Jesus is kept out because of internal resistance. Jesus could knock down the door and legitimately demand admittance, but consistent with the nature of God, there is the waiting to be invited into what is His. God initiates communication with a tender knock on the door. Then God waits for His people to open the door rather than forcefully invading the heart's privacy with an irresistible shout. If we are to open the door and hear God, then we must make room for His voice to be heard. The din and clamor of our environment must be toned down so that God's still small voice can be heard. Here is where the disciplines of silence and solitude serve us well. Being alone and still, quiet and silent before God are volitional actions the believer can take to open the doors to God's voice.

Openness before God

But beyond silence and solitude, there is the necessity of mind-clearing openness before God. The heart is opened to hear from God when the heart is opened to God. At first glance that statement may seem like an oxymoron, but there is actually a necessary order of action. First, the heart must be opened to God. There must be a response to His knocking. But the opening of the door is not as simple as just saying "come on in" because in a sense when the door is initially opened, the heart is often too full of other voices to receive anything new from God. The heart makes room for God when ideas, thoughts, emotions, sins, dreams and desires of the heart are poured out to God. The heart is opened to hear from God when there is a pouring out to God what is in the heart. When the one praying exposes his or her heart to God, then his or her heart becomes open to receive what God wants to communicate.

But there is often fear about such utter openness to God, particularly if there are unseemly and embarrassing heart-issues that seem contrary to the spirit of godliness. Strange though it may seem, even people who believe in an all-knowing God somehow feel that there are secrets of the heart that God does not know. Hence there is the "wax of concealment," an attempt to hide from God what God already knows. We must realize that as the heart is totally open and transparent before God, nothing that comes out of the heart shocks or surprises God. There are no real inner-heart secrets hidden from God's all-knowing nature, and these supposed barriers to hearing God are only barriers because we keep them in place. If we want to hear God with our heart, then our heart must be consciously and openly exposed to Him.

Perhaps a case study would best illumine the point. Michael, a true believer in Christ, has received a series of hard knocks. Financially his ship is fragile; anger and confusion plague his relationship with his wife, and he really dislikes his job. Deep inside Michael's heart are two basic thoughts about God. For Michael there is much doubt about God's love for him, and right now Michael often feels like he literally hates God. Nonetheless, Michael is praying, crying out to God for help. He wants to hear from God and hopes to get some relief from all the pressures of life. But as he prays and expresses the "right" words of faith and trust and even love for God, he hears nothing, which further frustrates and aggravates.

In sane moments Michael actually thinks right thoughts about God and "knows" God loves him, but deep within there is a hollow echo that questions God's reality. One day, in a very unguarded moment, Michael explodes to God. "God I hate you, you are cruel, unfair and you don't care for me at all!" Remarkably, as he opens his heart and pours out his heart to God, he begins to hear God's voice speaking words of love and comfort. Nothing Michael has said surprises or shocks God, though Michael is a bit shocked. Without any real cognizance of the reality, those doubts, fears and self-recriminations in his heart have diminished Michael's ability to hear God's voice. The issue was not, and is not, God's reluctance to speak. The issue is that the ears of his heart were closed because his heart was so full of noises and voices from the world and self that misconstrued God and left him deaf to God's voice. When the heart is opened to God by emptying the heart to God, then the voices of the world are diminished and God's steady, small quiet voice can be heard.

But how does playing the piano help one hear God? For the musician, music is an open channel of the heart. Via music the emotions and deep feelings of the heart can be poured out even without words. Through the keys on the piano sorrow, sadness, anger or joy and happiness freely flow forth. But music is just one medium for an emptying of the heart to God. Different personalities with different gifts and abilities must discover the medium that allows them to hear the sweet voice of God speaking to the soul. We must become consciously aware of utilizing whatever medium is good for us to open our heart to God. Openness may come through painting, journaling, writing, hiking, meditating, whatever else allows the heart to express itself in an unedited fashion. When we consciously and volitionally enter into activities that open our hearts to God we can become receptive to hearing the voice of God. The simple principle is that the heart poured out to the ears of God becomes a heart prepared to hear from God.

Questions for Further Thought or Discussion

1. Can you explain in your own words how bending God's ear with the realities of your heart enables you to hear God's heart with your spiritual ears?
2. What practices or spiritual disciplines open you up and allow you to express your whole heart to God and why do you see these processes as being helpful for you?
3. What are some ideas about God in your mind that may be making you reluctant to really want to hear His voice?

The author: Dr. Calvin A. Blom is Associate Professor of Spiritual Formation at Multnomah Biblical Seminary and co-host with his wife Evelyn of the Shepherd's Rest, Pastor's Retreat Center (www.shepherdsrest.org). He lives in Battle Ground, Washington.

SUGGESTED ADDITIONAL READING

Blackaby, Henry and Richard Blackaby. *When God Speaks: How to Recognize God's Voice and Respond.* Nashville: LifeWay Publishers, 1995.

Deere, Jack S. *Surprised by the Power of the Spirit: Discovering How God Speaks and Heals Today.* Grand Rapids: Zondervan, 1996.

Shirer, Priscilla Evans. *Discerning the Voice of God: Recognizing When God Speaks.* Chicago: Moody Publishing, 2007.

chapter

33

CONTEMPLATIVE PRAYER

Reg Johnson

"Prayer should be an enjoyable and fulfilling experience." I remember the day that sentence popped suddenly into my mind. It jolted me and started me thinking. Of the many adjectives I would have used to describe prayer, "enjoyable" and "fulfilling" were not at the top of my list. In fact, prayer was more closely connected to guilt than to bliss because of my frustrations with it. By "frustrations" I mean that I knew prayer should have greater priority in my life, but it wasn't; and I knew that I ought to be spending a lot more time praying, but I didn't. Fresh resolutions, new systems for organizing my prayer time, or the latest inspirational resources, might help temporarily, but before long I would be right back where I had started. Was my problem one of motivation? Discipline?

One day I came across Henri Nouwen's, *The Way of the Heart.* In a couple of pages near the end of the book I discovered a freeing insight.

Nouwen's diagnosis: sometimes we neglect prayer because we are disappointed with it.[1]

Frustrations with Prayer

Nouwen observed how we often approach prayer as a purely mental exercise, formulating thoughts and emotions into words that we speak, aloud or silently, to God. The very process has all of the look and feel of a monologue and, if we succumb to that notion, we end up with a sense that we are "talking into the dark," explained Nouwen, wasting time talking to ourselves when we could spend our time much more productively, doing the practical things that demand our attention.

Nouwen continued with a second observation: sometimes we are disheartened with prayer because we have mainly viewed it as a mental activity of "thinking about God." Labeling this activity "meditation," it doesn't make it any easier. It still looks like work to people who are not reflective by nature, or those who are mentally fatigued, driven to distraction by the constant bombardment of life. When prayer starts feeling like a heavy homework assignment, we tend to avoid it.

This is not to say that our intellect is to be parked outside the prayer room. God has given us the gift of our rational faculties and they are very important in our Christian lives. But we are missing the healthy balance taught by our ancient mothers and fathers in faith. They knew that "active prayer," with its emphasis on the use of our cognitive capacity to express our deepest thoughts into well-chosen words, needs the balance of more "receptive" ways of deepening our faith that God is near.

In receptive prayer the agenda is God's and we are ready to receive whatever He offers. We "delight" in Him (Ps. 37:4, NIV), enjoying everything that expresses Him. We may immerse ourselves in a gospel story, captivated by Jesus' love; stand in rapt silence by the crib of a newborn, amazed at the miracle of this precious life; listen to the thunder of a cascading waterfall, enthralled by the magnificence of God's creation; or simply look back over an ordinary day, remembering so many occasions of unexpected grace. Moments like these are crucial for replenishing our faith. They furnish fresh reasons for casting ourselves unreservedly on God's mercy, living by His promises, and depending on Him for our daily strength.

Prayer as Receiving

Jesus was familiar with this more receptive approach to prayer. He spoke Aramaic and the word for prayer in that language is *shela* (pronounced sha-lu) and meaning "to open oneself" or "to listen to." Seen in this way, prayer was the very breath of His life. Turn the pages of the Gospels and notice His appreciation for God's goodness all around: a gentle breeze, soaring birds, fragrant flowers, freshly ploughed fields, vines laden with grapes, nothing escapes His notice. When a child brought Him a gift of loaves and fish, His immediate response was to lift the little lunch toward heaven and bless it, because He knew that everything good comes from God. We can be sure that in the long nights He spent praying, He not only talked conversationally with His Father, He also listened. Being lovingly attentive to God was just as much "prayer" as pouring out His heart through the words of a psalm.

The Catholic monk and spiritual writer, Thomas Merton, described contemplation as "spiritual wonder," "spontaneous awe at the sacredness of life," and "gratitude for life." He refers to it as "a gift of awareness," "awakening to what is real," and being "touched by God."[2] Contemplation is not something we can produce on our own; it is always God's gift. He is communicating every moment and in each event, the only question is whether we are prepared to notice and respond.[3]

Opening to Love

Picture the story of Christ's encounter with the two disciples on the road to Emmaus, found in Luke 24. The lives of these two friends of Jesus had been in a tailspin ever since receiving the devastating news of Jesus' crucifixion three days earlier. Now they were heading away from Jerusalem, back to their home a few miles away, rehearsing yet again the heartbreaking chain of events, and trying to make some sense out of it all. A stranger came alongside and joined in their conversation, asking them questions, and reminding them of scriptures promising that these days would come, and explaining the meaning of these events for the salvation of the race. Their hearts were touched by what he said and when they reached home, they pleaded with him to come in and stay the night, because darkness was already falling, besides, they didn't want this evening with him to end. He accepted their invitation. Later, when dinner was served, he took his place at the head of the table, blessed the bread, broke it, and gave it to them. He, their *guest,* became the *host.* They were in the presence of Divine Love. He offered them hospitality, cared for their needs, showed them His lavish kindness. By His simple actions, faith was awakened and they realized the real identity of this mysterious Person.

This historical event is, at the same time, a helpful metaphor of what happens in contemplative prayer. The Risen Christ comes to us continually, in the experiences of our lives, in scripture, in relationships with others, and so forth. We may have an inkling of His presence in any given moment, but we must choose to respond. Like the disciples Jesus met on the road, we also long for His companionship, but Jesus awaits our invitation. He treasures unrushed moments with us. They are important, not just because of the love He receives from us, but because of the love He longs to give.

When we awaken to God's presence in some passing moment, or step aside from our endless activities to carve out some space for Him, we are actually opening the door of our heart to our deepest Friend. We may have thought of Him as our guest, and we His host, orchestrating these moments. But soon we experience the great reversal. It is not so much that *we* welcomed *Him*; *He* invited *us*. Our conscious turn in His direction, our prayer, was actually our response to His Spirit's nudge. When invited, Christ assumes His place as host, because our heart is actually *His* home and we, *His* invited guests. He invites us because He wants to meet our needs, show us His love, nourish our fainting hearts, and share His unfathomable peace.

Writing about contemplative praying, Teresa of Avila put it simply: "In my view it is nothing but a friendly intercourse, frequent solitary converse with Him Who we know loves us."[4]

Renewing our Relationship

It is so easy to slip into the pattern of treating a loved one very functionally in terms of a role he fulfills, or the chores for which she is responsible. When living in that mode our conversations with the other person tend to be more logistical than personal, and more focused on getting things done than with enjoying one another's company. But we also know how suddenly our perspective can shift.

A man took his wife of many years on a "date" to a quiet restaurant. It was a special occasion, so they chose a relaxing setting. Their window table overlooked a beautiful garden. Romantic music played in the background. The meal was delicious and they took their time. As they relaxed and talked he gradually became aware that he was no longer looking *at* his wife, but was actually *seeing* her. He noticed how her mouth always looked on the verge of a smile, her soft eyes sparkled with life and intelligence, and her personality was etched into those fine, almost invisible, wrinkles at the corners of her eyes. He was taking the time to notice, appreciate, and treasure her presence. He remembered how much they'd been through, the challenges they'd faced as well as all the joys they shared. He realized afresh how much he loved her. And when they rose to leave the restaurant they were both surprised to discover that they had been sitting there for over two hours! Sometime during the course of the evening, supper had turned into an experience of communion. Immersing themselves in the experience of being together that evening had renewed them both.

Cultivate Contemplative Praying

Someone once defined contemplation as a "long and loving look at another." It is a good definition and keeps us from thinking of it as only a tool to use or technique to master, otherwise we would be preoccupied with the methods, rather than focused on this Person, and on upon our relationship of love. Having said this, there are some practical ways we can practice this way of opening to God's love.

- Try deep breathing. Exhale, saying: "I breathe out my tensions;" inhaling say: "I breathe in Your peace."
- Go out on your porch or deck on a summer's night, and there, away from the demands of the day, let the canopy of a starry night remind you of God's immensity and the immediacy of His surrounding presence.
- Look at Jesus as He appears in a gospel story, become absorbed with what He is like, the feelings He shows, and what He does.
- Take a few moments for quiet before starting your day. Place a symbol before you such as a lighted candle, a cross, or a Bible. Treat it as a reminder that you are no longer your own, but His beloved child, and be silent before Him.
- Take time to enjoy the beauty of a flower, allowing God to reveal Himself as

its creator, and knowing He is pleased as you enjoy what He has made.

- Gaze at the reproduction of some great piece of art, or at an icon. Let it become like a window into the unseen realm. Become aware that this "window" works both ways. Not only are you "seeing into" the unseen by becoming aware of God's presence, God also looks lovingly upon you.
- Focus on Him by lifting His name: "Jesus;" praying a short prayer, "Holy Spirit, fill me;" or a scripture phrase, "Lord, You are my Shepherd," as a way of carrying a consciousness of His presence with you all through the day.

Enjoying the Pleasure of His Company

Contemplative praying is God's gift for deepening intimacy and exchanging love. Sometimes we may feel that we are not so much "spending time" in God's presence, so much as we are "squandering time" doing absolutely nothing. When this happens we recall that Jesus waits to be invited and relishes unhurried moments with us, and we remember that God wants us to learn to "wait," "listen," and "be still." We offer God the gift of our attentive presence, not demanding that He do something for us in return, but simply for the pleasure of His company. What on earth could be more enjoyable and fulfilling than that?

Questions for Further Thought or Discussion

1. Talk about the notion that we neglect prayer because we are disappointed or frustrated with it.
2. Discuss reasons we may need a balance of both active, as well as receptive prayer.
3. Share an experience from your week when you became conscious of God's goodness or nearness.

The author: Dr. Reg Johnson is the Dean of the School of Theology and Formation and occupies the Chair of Prayer & Spiritual Formation at Asbury Theological Seminary in Wilmore, Kentucky.

SUGGESTED ADDITIONAL READING

Nouwen, Henri. *The Way of the Heart.* San Francisco: Harper, 1981.

Keating, Thomas. *Open Mind, Open Heart: The Contemplative Dimension of the Gospel.* Rockport, MA: Element, 1986.

Muto, Susan and Adrian van Kaam. *Practicing the Prayer of Presence.* Mineola, NY: Resurrection Press, 1980.

Johnson, Jan. *When the Soul Listens.* Colorado Springs, CO: NavPress, 1999.

ENDNOTES

1. Henri Nouwen, *The Way of the Heart* (San Francisco: Harper 1981), pp. 72-73.

2. Thomas Merton, *New Seeds of Contemplation* (New York: The Abbey of Gethsemani, Inc.: New Directions Books, 1961), pp. 1-2.

3. Merton, p. 12.

4. Teresa of Avila, *The Life of Teresa of Jesus*, E. Allison Peers, translator (New York: Image Books, 1960), p. 110.

chapter

34

DEVELOPING A LIFESTYLE OF PRAYER

Gerald Schmidt

All of us pray, either consciously or unconsciously. If this is plausible then developing a lifestyle of prayer involves inviting this spiritual and psychological reality into increasing consciousness supported by *apophatic* and *kataphatic*[1] practice and awarenessa praying without ceasing (1 Thess. 5:17).

I wish to define prayer as the conscious and unconscious connection between our self and God. As such, prayer is part of our soul's DNA. It is the honest speech of the soul, that part of us created in the Divine image. It is our most basic form of discourse. Prayer is "primary speech."

> It is that primordial discourse in which we assert, however clumsily or eloquently, our own being. . . . Sometimes the honesty comes because we are confident that nobody can overhear us, not the God in whom we have such shaky faith or no faith at all, not anybody we

> know, perhaps not even ourselves as we grunt or moan or shout or sob our prayers. Sometimes the honesty comes because we do know who it is that is listening, because we feel sure that there is a listener somewhere in us or outside us, because we know from experience that what we have said in prayer or not quite said but somehow expressed, has been heard. . . . For if prayer is primary speech then it is everybody's speech and even those who do not know they speak that language and want nothing to do with anything that can be called prayer have something to say to us about this subject.[2]

God's desire for connection pervades the scriptures beginning with the creation saga. Yet, this desire for connection lovingly honors free choice. This freedom of choice is reflected in Eden's invitation, "Of every tree of the garden you may freely eat" (Gen. 2:16-17). Freedom is also reflected when animals and birds are created with God lovingly bringing them to the human seeking to connect as the human names each one. Throughout the creation God is the playful initiator who invites connection, never the controlling manipulator demanding it. A delighted God, daily reflecting on that creation, calls all that is created "good, very good."

Much of my current play with my four young granddaughters involves showing them an object and asking, "What's this?" I am delighted when they can name the object or picture. Even before they were able to name things I brought objects to them, often with cooing sighs of delight. I experience pleasure as their eyes follow the object and then return my gaze. Those first smiles of recognition and connection are forever etched in my soul. This repetitive interaction is a form of basic speech and connection. It is both kataphatic and apophatic (spoken and unspoken adoration). It is "primary speech."

God creates us in His image, then invites us to notice, name, and respond to that Divine image as God's desire for connection. As we increase this awareness, we also increasingly connect with that part of us that is God breathed, our spiritual DNA. Developing a lifestyle of prayer is increasingly attending to this inner image of the Divine, as well as to the reflection of God in the whole creation.

However, free choice also necessitates an alternative to God's desire and intent for connection. One restriction! "Of every tree of the garden you may freely eat; but of the tree of the knowledge of good and evil you shall not eat, for in the day that you eat of it you shall surely die (2:16-17). All the trees, including the tree of life were given to invite connection. I often wonder what would be different had we chosen the tree of life?

This is another aspect in developing a lifestyle of prayer—daily eat of the fruit of the tree of life, rather than the fruit of the tree of the knowledge of good and evil! The tree of life especially reflects the divine image in the natural creation. From this perspective we see Eden as the central locale of God's creation, the tree of life as a unique symbol of the divine image in the natural order, and primary speech as an expression of the divine image placed in each of us—placed there to invite connection.

Too good to be true? Too simple? Adam and Eve thought so.*There must be more required for connection with this Being that we occasionally notice in the garden!* So they fell to the tempter's deception of increased understanding and clarity, "You will not surely die. For God knows that in the day you eat of it your eyes will be opened, and you will be like God, knowing good and evil" (3:4-5). And see more clearly they did. They saw themselves and didn't like what they saw—nakedness, vulnerability, inadequacy, self-doubt, and fear. They experienced their fear of God as coming from God's self, this overwhelming Mystery. The contrast between their experience of self and their experience of the Holy was overwhelming. So they covered it up and went into hiding—hiding from the very God whose image they carried. Longingly, accompanied by an evening breeze, God walks into the garden, seemingly wishing connection, and finds them hiding and clothed. "Where are you?'[7] God asks. This new knowledge of good and evil—what they hoped would open their eyes—filled them with fear.

Developing a lifestyle of prayer is developing a life that seeks to come out of hiding. Every moment God is nearby asking, "Where are you?" When we hide, cover up, deny, justify, and blame others, our primary speech is overshadowed and interrupted by shame and guilt. Sometimes we go back to the tree of the knowledge of good and evil, thinking if we eat a little more our vision might clear. It never works! Guilt-ridden, we again hear God's question, "Where are you?" as a judgment rather than an invitation from a God who is closer to us than we are to ourselves—a God whose kingdom is within us!

There are so many ways in which we are tempted to return to the tree of the knowledge of good and evil, hoping to make ourselves more presentable. We hone our "glittering image," we get yet another degree, we read another book, we seek to be identified with important people, we acquire wealth, power, and good public relations. We do the due diligence required of our roles. We become adept at putting a "spin" on our image. We stand on the corners of life grateful that we are not like others. None of this is negative in and of itself; however, these identity attachments so easily become a false identity and the only identity we will allow. Any new fruit from the tree of the knowledge of good and evil separates us from our actual selves and the reality of God in us.

In my counseling and spiritual direction practice I have never met a minister/seminarian/priest/religious worker who does not have an intention to be close to God. However, my notes are full of individual stories where the gap between this intention and the person's actuality (experience) is wide and widening. The sheer weight of ministry/study/busyness seems to increase this gap. Ironically success in these endeavors only increases the feedback from others to encourage this busyness. Inevitably a soul-role split occurs as the individual says, "I can't honor my intention to be close to God, so I will at least look like I can."

Karen Horney has demonstrated that this can lead to a neurosis which occurs to the extent that the ideal self—the glittering image—overtakes or obliterates the *real self.* When this occurs the "glittering image" is the only reality the priest or clergy-person/self will allow. The ideal image has become god. Listen to Karen Horney's words from her book *Our Inner Conflicts.*

> He holds before his soul his image of perfection and unconsciously tells himself: "Forget about the disgraceful creature you *actually are;* this is how you *should be;* and to be this idealized self is *all that matters.* You should be able to endure everything, to understand everything, to like everybody, to be productive" . . . *the tyranny of the should.*
>
> But regardless of how much fantasy is woven into the idealized image, for the neurotic himself it has the value of reality. The more firmly it is established the more he *is* his idealized image, while his real self is proportionately dimmed out . . . As long as his image

> remains real to him and is intact, he can feel significant, superior, and harmonious, in spite of the illusory nature of those feelings. He can consider himself entitled to raise all kinds of demands and claims on the basis of his assumed superiority. *But if he allows it to be undermined he is immediately threatened with the prospect of facing all his weaknesses, with no title to special claims, a comparatively insignificant figure or even—in his own eyes—a contemptible one.* (*emphasis added*)[3]

Developing a lifestyle of prayer acknowledges these identity attachments and humbly accepts that we are loved in our actuality, our nakedness, our vulnerability! This is life lived with an attitude of repentance and confession. Our self-aggrandizement (*our origin in sin*) tempts us to take our identity from what we do, what others say about us, or from what we control—our glittering image. These identity attachments might be the necessary clerical or sacred clothing we wear, however they are not who we are—we are the beloved of God. When we become the image, we begin to require all those around us to help us maintain that image. The consequence is a narcissism that no longer sees its actuality, and loses its sense of naked belovedness. "I am what I do, I am what others say about me, I am what I control," becomes secondary speech, a speech cut off from the primacy of the divine image within.

In fact, many clergy I talk to have lost any ability to honor their intention to be close to God. As the gap between intention to be close to God and their actual experience of God widens, this gap creates shame and guilt. As one pastor shamefully said to me, "I no longer feel like I can be close to God, and so I settle for looking like I am! As Thomas Merton suggests honoring our intention is the recognition that even our desire and intention to be close to God, *is God.*[4] How tragic that guilt and shame often make us avoidant of that which we intend! Developing a lifestyle of prayer includes noticing the gap between our intention and experience, then realizing that even our intention to be close to God is God, and then seeking ways to honor that intention. Again confession and repentance bring us to reconciliation with self and God.

Kierkegaard's writings paradoxically suggest that *it is a consoling idea that before God we are always in the wrong.*[5] "Wrongness" is consoling only when repentance and confession bring us back to our actuality and belovedness, back from the inner and cultural temptations to maintain our glittering image. This is a daily "paschal mystery." Daily, perhaps moment by moment, our temptation toward falsity must die, so that God-in-us can again live in our experience. This is why developing a lifestyle of prayer is often so difficult. Jesus said it well when He said, "He must increase, but I must decrease." This is not "worm such as I" theology. Rather it is an acknowledgment, a confession that I most experience the reality of God when I acknowledge my actuality. In psychological terms this is what it means to live a self-actualized life. In theological terms this is a constant attitude of attentiveness (*knowing where you are)* repentance *(agreeing with God about your identity attachments)* and reconciliation (*renewing awareness of your belovedness*).

Developing a lifestyle of prayer invites divinely given courage. Knowing I am absolutely loved makes it easier to acknowledge my temptation toward falsity—the temptation toward maintaining my glittering image at all cost. My spiritual director once told me that "courage is fear that has said its prayers." This kind of courage isn't overcome by the fear of not measuring up.

I have suggested that developing a lifestyle of prayer is part of our souls DNA. Consequently a lifestyle of prayer is about attentiveness to self in God and God in self. However our false self and our culture often tempt us to hide or cover up to maintain the semblance of adequacy. This is the human condition Christ's atonement rectifies. We are loved!

All *kataphatic* and *apophatic* forms and practices of prayer serve to support a lifestyle of prayer. They invite the courage to confess and repent of falsity and move us to our actuality where the reality of God in us becomes the hope of our salvation. Developing a lifestyle of prayer makes us willing to ask, "Teach us to pray."

Questions for Further Thought or Discussion

1. Mother Teresa suggests that "we are not called to be successful; we are called to be faithful." What does a faithful life look like? How might developing a lifestyle of prayer support and encourage that faithfulness?
2. As you imagine developing a lifestyle of prayer, are there *kataphatic* and *apophatic* prayer practices that you would like to practice more consistently? What blocks, resistances, fears, interruption interrupt that consistency?
3. Alan Jones says that in life and ministry we "either manipulate or we con-

template." Discuss the implication of this statement for your life, ministry, and prayer.

The author: Rev. Gerald (Garry) Schmidt is Director of Admissions and Adjunct Faculty in Spiritual Formation and Pastoral Care at Salt Lake Theological Seminary. He also serves as Certified Spiritual Director/Pastoral Counselor and Retreat Leader. His research interest is clergy self-care.

SUGGESTED ADDITIONAL READING

Hands, Donald R and Wayne Fehr. *Spiritual Wholeness for Clergy: A New Psychology of Intimacy with God, Self, and Others.* New York: Alban Institute, 1993.

Linn, Dennis, Sheila F. Linn and Matthew Linn. *Sleeping with Bread: Holding What Gives You Life.* New York: Paulist Press, 1995.

Palmer, Parker. *Let Your Life Teach: Listening for the Voice of Vacation.* San Francisco: Jossey-Bass, 2000.

Palmer. Parker. *A Hidden Wholeness: The Journey Toward an Undivided Life.* San Francisco: Jossey-Bass, 2004.

Paulsell, William O. *Rules for Prayer.* New York: Paulist, 1993.

ENDNOTES

1. *Kataphatic* prayer employs thoughts and images, often with a verbal expression in private or in community, e.g. The Lord's Prayer. *Apophatic* prayer is silent contemplative prayer, reflected in the phrase, "Be still and know that I am God." For a brief discussion of *kataphatic* and *apophatic* prayer and the relationship between them see Frederick G. McLeod: "Apophatic or Kataphatic Prayer?" in *Spirituality Today,* Spring 1986, Vol. 38, pp. 41-52.

2. Ulanov, Ann and Barry, *Primary Speech* (Atlanta: John Knox, 1982), pp. vii-viii.

3. Horney, Karen, "Our Inner Conflicts," from *The Collected Works of Karen Horney*, Vol. 1. (New York: Norton & Co., 1945). p. 109.

4. Merton, Thomas, *Thoughts in Solitude*, (New York: Farrar, Straus & Giroux), p. 20, p. 79, p. 102.

5. Kierkegaard, Soren. *Either/Or,* Vol. II, p. 287.

chapter

35

THE PROBLEM OF PRAYERLESSNESS

MaryKate Morse

Prayer is probably the core spiritual practice of the Christian faith. Yet, despite the example of Jesus and the early church it is often an anemic part of our lives. A common response to this reality is to label prayerlessness—not taking time to pray—a sin problem. Jesus told us to pray, so we should pray. If we are not praying, the solution is to confess and repent, and then start praying. "Start praying" usually means attending prayer groups, keeping prayer notebooks, and interceding on behalf of others during one's daily quiet time. However, in all my years of teaching prayer in seminary and in churches, I have found that prayerlessness truly grieves people. It is not easily resolved with a sin label. People usually feel shame that they are not as devoted to prayer as they believe they should be. So, if it is not sin, what might it be, and can anything be done about it?

The spiritual life is both a hardy and a fragile thing. It is hardy because the God of the universe put in us a God-shaped hole that yearns for fellowship with our Maker. It is fragile because the God-shaped hole is in a dust-to-dust body. For that reason, prayerlessness is more often than not the result of a perception that one's spiritual life isn't going anywhere, that it is stagnant or meaningless. When people say they are too busy to pray, distractions are often a cover-up for this hidden fact: When they do pray, there is no sense of God's presence or of any response to their prayer. When that happens, people often get anxious and stop praying. Emotionally, prayerlessness comes out of fear and not out of hope. It happens when we are thinking: *What if God isn't really there? What if God isn't really there for me? What if instead of living water I only find a dry well? What then?*

Prayerlessness and the Dry Well

Most believers try to have a meaningful connection with God through prayer. But something happens along the way, and the life of prayer often drifts into a dead zone of prayerlessness. I want to suggest that prayerlessness doesn't need to mean that we are stuck or that our spiritual lives are empty. Instead, prayerlessness can be a signal that it is time to begin an authentic adventure. And the journey begins with first naming one's reality: Prayer is dry and empty for me. Metaphorically, this is called the dry well experience. The well is there. The bucket. But when you come thirsty, the bucket comes up empty.

Naming the reality can be difficult because people believe they will be judged or lose status in their faith community, or look stupid. Prayerlessness is often perpetuated in churches because we create a culture of shame rather than spiritual adventure. Instead of seeing it as an opportunity for growth and being open about it, we treat it like a disease. As long as the problem is hidden, it cannot be resolved. The only way to move from prayerlessness to prayerfulness is to start where we know we are. Once we have been honest with ourselves, the next step is to understand why one might be in a prayerless state. The following are some possible reasons.

Exhaustion

Exhaustion can be physical, mental, or emotional. Exhaustion brought on by stress caused by unending deadlines and life upheavals is a common Western problem. After finishing a marathon, many runners cross the finish line and collapse to the ground heaving for air. They stretch out their arms and revel in non-movement. When the body has given its full capacity to some event, it is difficult to be in a prayerful frame. When my stepmother died, who had been the first real mother I ever knew, I was exhausted. The months of care because of her debilitating cancer, the emotional drain of serving her complex needs, standing by her death bed for hours, put me in an empty space for months. I was emotionally and physically exhausted. Elijah in 1 Kings 18 is an example of how even after spiritual and physical success one can feel depressed and empty. Exhaustion is the most common reason why people feel dry in their prayer life. They are dry in their life.

Narrow View of Prayer

Prayer practices and types are as varied as an artist's color palette, but most people are only exposed to one or two ways. In 1 Samuel 3, young Samuel did not recognize the voice of God and three times he ran to Eli thinking Eli had called him. Whenever I teach prayer, I find that someone is profoundly impacted by a type of prayer they hadn't experienced before. This is why teaching prayer in churches is so important. Not just one type of prayer, but all types. Temperaments and personalities lead us toward certain forms of prayer that are more meaningful than others. Liturgical prayers are living water to some and muddy waters to others. Silence is profound for some and music feeds the souls of others. In all of Scripture and the history of the church there is not one "sacred" way to pray. The church carries the honor of teaching people how to pray.

Desert Experience/Dark Night

In Luke 4 Jesus was led by the Holy Spirit into the desert for forty days of prayer and fasting. In the desert Satan sifted the underlying motivations for His sacrificial life. Desert experiences are traditionally those periods of time when God feels absent from our lives. Among the saints, the experience of God's absence is referred to as the dark night. If you experienced God for years in ecstatic worship, for instance, and then for week after week you feel nothing, experience nothing, it might be the dark night. The dark night comes when God is giving us an opportunity to stand in faith no matter what life brings.

The whole of creation tells the story of birth, growth, decline, and death. Our seasons, our need for sleep, the way all of nature has an "on" time and a "down" time is God's design. The music of life has pauses in it. These are the negative spaces where we are still and nothing is gained, known, or felt. God commanded a period of rest in Genesis 2:2. That life of rest is both physical and spiritual. This is different from the dark night which is often a unique experience of deep shaping. The natural rhythm of rest is simply downtime. Sometimes a dry well is our fallow time.

Sin or Disorder in Your Life

In a few instances the dry well is the result of sin in your life. John wrote in 1 John 1: 6 "If we say that we have fellowship with Him, and walk in darkness, we lie and do not practice the truth." It is not possible to relate to a God of love, if in the heart there is gossip, bitterness, or self-indulgence. Despising others in our heart is walking in darkness. Believing that the self-indulgence of pornography, over-eating or excessive shopping is due us because of how hard we work for God is the ultimate of deceptions. If these behaviors, thoughts, and feelings are not kept in the light of Christ for His healing will on them, a dry well is the first outcome. Sincerity before God is the beginning of relationship with God.

Lack of Attention/Distractions

In Jesus' last conversation with His disciples He said in John 15:5, "I am the vine, you are the branches. He who abides in Me, and I in him, bears much fruit; for without Me you can do nothing." Abiding in Christ carries the core notion of connection and non-activity. A branch does no work except to receive from the vine the nutrients and pass them along. For Westerners one of our greatest failures as Christ followers is a lack of attentiveness to the vine. Our busy lives consume our energies, creativity, and time so there is little space to be with God. We make the mistake of equating God's will with kingdom accomplishments rather than quiet attentiveness. Finding ways to be still allows for the Spirit to work naturally in our souls without expectation of gain. Sometimes a dry well is an invitation to simply sit quietly with God.

From Dryness to Living Water

Prayerlessness is a normal experience. We are used to being entertained, getting instant feedback, and having our needs immediately met, so we forget how ordinary a dry well is in our faith journey. If we believe it is not ordinary, the dry well can be a confusing time. If we are not feeling something or doing something or accomplishing something, we can begin to fear that God is absent from us. And when we begin to fear God's absence, we become ashamed of the dry place. We think it is caused by our failure or spiritual weakness, rather than an ordinary part of the journey. The temptation is to drop one's practice of prayer when the experience becomes dry.

A way to avoid this temptation is to mentor and disciple followers so that when we find ourselves in a dry place we recognize it, consider the causes for it, and then take steps to stay connected to the vine rather than drift into continual prayerlessness. Following are some suggestions for moving through the dryness:

1. Healthy Lifestyle—Examine your lifestyle and reorder it so that you can experience rest again. Restore a Sabbath experience. Let the natural nourishments our bodies need be the beginning platform for new waters.
2. Ritual of Space for God—Find a time and place that allows you simply to be present with God. This might mean observing the offices (traditional times of prayer), painting or sculpting, walking in the woods or down a busy street. The goal is to be with God with no expectation of gain or the accomplishment of spiritual work.
3. Breath Prayer—Create a short prayer or use a Scripture verse as a companion during the dry well. A breath prayer is a prayer of 6-8 syllables usually consisting of a name for God and a request. The Jesus Prayer, "Lord Jesus Christ, have mercy on me, a sinner," is used world-wide as a solace during hard times.
4. God in the Everyday—Accept the presence of God in the everyday, especially in nature, music, or art. Sitting in a park or at the beach, listening to a great piece of music, all can speak of God's grace. God in the everyday is a descent into the ordinary wonder of creation that can keep you during dryness.

5. God in Others—Allow God to come to you through others. I have spiritually directed people who have said, "God has never shown up in my life." And then they would tell an extraordinary story of someone who sacrificially served them in a dark time. Spiritual friends or a spiritual director are often the face of God during dry times.

A dry well is a place where water was once drawn regularly. Prayerlessness, drifting away from attachment to God, does not need to be the final response. Instead, the dry well can be the desert before the Promised Land, the cross before the open cave, the crossroads to a new well.

Questions for Further Thought or Discussion

1. Have you ever been in a state of prayerlessness? Tell the story of that time. How did it impact your thinking about God? What did you feel?
2. Which of the listed reasons for the dry well have you experienced? Tell the story of it. Would you add any others?
3. If you are at the dry well in your prayer life right now, which of the suggested ways through might help you?
4. If you have been in a dry well but then moved out, what other suggestions do you have for helping persons stuck at a dry well?

The author: Dr. MaryKate Morse is the Director of Masters Programs and Professor of Pastoral Studies and Spiritual Formation at the George Fox Evangelical Seminary in Portland, Oregon.

SUGGESTED ADDITIONAL READING

Cronk, Sandra. *Dark Night Journey: Inward Re-patterning Toward a Life Centered in God.* Wallingford, PA: Pendle Hill Publications, 1991.

Griffin, Emilie. *Clinging: The Experience of Prayer.* New York, NY: McCracken Press, 1994.

Green, Thomas H. *When the Well Runs Dry: Prayer Beyond Beginnings.* South Bend, IN: Ave Maria Press, 1979.

chapter

36

INTIMACY WITH GOD THROUGH PRAYER

John Franklin

Intimacy with God could take a whole book—and I only have a few pages; therefore I will focus on a less discussed, but monstrously important requirement for intimacy. This understanding will radically revolutionize the prayer lives of those who practice it: God designed intimacy to be founded upon fulfilling the work He has assigned us.

This discovery started with a rather innocuous Sunday school class one morning—nothing about that day seemed unusual. I had just concluded five busy weeks of travel and my focus that morning was more toward a relaxing Sunday afternoon than revolutionary truth. Somewhere about thirty minute mark the question was raised, "What was the first thing God did with Adam the moment He breathed breath into his nostrils?" Immediately I thought, *now that's an important question* because I knew two truths about the garden. 1. God planned the relationship between Him and Adam to be one of intimacy. 2. Since a perfect God can only do things in a perfect order, what He did first would reveal the foundations for how He designed intimacy with Himself to occur.

In my mind I answered *He had Adam name the animals* (Gen. 1:20). Fortunately I kept my mouth shut because that answer turned out to be wrong! Genesis 2:15 states, "Then the LORD God took the man and put him in the garden of Eden to tend and keep it." Much to my surprise the first thing God did the moment He created Adam was to put Him to work! That morning I sat in my chair stunned. Do you see the implications?! Would it really be true that the warp and woof of intimacy with God is bound up in the work God assigns us? Is first base in intimacy sharing our hearts with God in open communication or working with God? What would this do to my prayer life? How would that change how I spent time in prayer? How would it alter my focus?

I began searching the Scriptures to identify God's pattern and quickly saw two truths:

1. The moment God entered into relationship with someone He did indeed assign them work just like with Adam. For example, at the seashore of Galilee, Jesus invitation was, "Follow me, and I will make you become fishers of men." In other words, "Sign up, and I'll put you to work. First Peter 4:10a reads, "As each one has received a gift, minister it to one another." It does not say, "*If* each one of you has received a gift," but "*as* each one of you." Many Protestants can quote Ephesians 2:8-9 that we are saved "by grace . . . not of works," but very few can quote verse 10, "For we are His workmanship, created in Christ Jesus for good works, which God prepared beforehand that we should walk in them." So, we are not saved by works, but the moment God saves us He immediately assigns us work—work which He has prepared for us before our conversion.

2. Jesus specifically linked the intimacy He shared with His Father to their working together. "But Jesus answered them, 'My Father has been working until now, and I have been working . . . For the Father loves the Son, and shows Him all things that He Himself does; and He will show Him greater works than these, that you may marvel'" (Jn. 5:17, 20).

In verse 17 Jesus commented that He and His Father were both working. He then interpreted what that meant—the Father was expressing His love to Him by showing Jesus His work. This greatly challenged my belief system because most of what I had read on intimacy related to quiet time alone with God, honest communication, or sensing His still, small voice. In this passage Jesus squarely founded His intimacy on the fellowship of participating with His Father in His work. He did not speak of His Father's love in the form of His provision, deliverance, or meeting needs, but rather the privilege of working with His Father. The others are indeed an expression of God's love, but they were not what Jesus chose to highlight. The fuel of His relationship lay in serving the Father by fulfilling His work (Jn. 4:34, 5:36, 9:4, 17:4, 19:30), not in what the Father did for Him.

I'm not trying to deny that other avenues enhance intimacy, but I am asserting that you cannot put the cart before the horse. If you don't build on a foundation of participating in His work, the other means prove wanting. Perhaps this explains why in the Gospels Jesus' favorite paradigm of the nature of our relationship with Him was that of Master/King/Lord to servants. Unfortunately, some Protestants have emphasized salvation by grace not works in such a way that many Christians do not have an orientation toward working with God. The result is that millions are sitting in pews deprived of a dynamic, book of Acts relationship with God.

How This Impacts Your Prayer Life

The evidence above set the stage for an important discovery about prayer—your prayer life will be intimate to the degree that your prayers lead you to fulfill the work God has assigned you. Before you can have consistent intimacy with God through any other arena, your prayer life must lead you to do the work He has delegated you. This is true for very logical reasons. The work generates the experiences with God that lead to the understanding about and participation with God that creates intimacy.

I noticed some time ago that all great prayer warriors in the Bible had similarities, yet uniquenesses in their prayer life. Moses did not pray exactly like David, nor David like Moses. Moses seemed to have deeper understanding of God in some areas than David did, David in ways that excelled Moses. Moses' prayers of intercession stand apart, whereas David's prayers of dependence on God are in a league of their own. Wouldn't you think that if they were encountering the same God, that they should turn out alike?

Shouldn't they all progress through the same stages with the same result? It took me some time to figure out the reason why they did not turn out cookie-cutter alike. The differences in their intimacy levels were determined by their assignment. Because Moses' assignment demanded he intercede repeatedly for such a wicked generation, He came to know God's holiness and mercy to an unprecedented degree. Because David's assignment to be king led to constant danger he came to understand God's deliverance and love in amazing ways. Moses' intimacy with God excelled David in some arenas, whereas David excelled Moses in others. The determining factor was decided by the experiences they had with God through fulfilling their assignments.

How You Ought to Organize Your Prayer Life

Therefore, the focus of your petition and intercession ought to relate first to your assignment. For too long in my own prayer life, I allowed the needs of others to dictate my prayer agenda. If I heard of someone sick or in crisis, they were who I typically interceded for. This did not follow the pattern of Scripture. Jesus taught us in the Lord's Prayer to petition first "Your kingdom come, Your will be done." The needle of His compass pointed toward what God wanted to advance His kingdom. Not surprisingly the majority of Jesus' recorded prayer times relate to His next step in ministry (Lk. 3:21, 6:12-13, 9:28-31, 10:2, 22:41-43). He particularly prayed about His assignment.

The importance of praying for our assignment hit home when I discovered that fulfilling our assignment will be the basis of rewards in eternity (1 Cor. 3:13-15). On the Day of Judgment God will not ask whether I was a good Christian or not, i.e. read my Bible, prayed, witnessed, tithed, etc; rather He will hold me accountable for the work He assigned me. Whatever superfluous activities I pursued will be considered wood, hay, and straw. Fire will consume them. I myself will escape, but I will have nothing to show from this life for all eternity. This means I must clearly know and do my assignment. This truth carried tremendous implications for organizing my prayer life. I had to make my assignment the first thing for which I interceded.

You can identify your assignment in two ways. First, if God has given you a position of authority, everyone under you is your assignment. You are to be their servant in presenting them perfect in Christ (Col. 1:28). Second, you should identify what you do that blesses everyone around you. If you are a blessing, then it is actually God who is working through you to impact others. Once you identify your assignment you know the direction in which to focus your prayers.

Often our prayer times experience interruption. We must pray about our assignment so that we complete first things first. This does not mean we should ignore praying for people and things not in our assignment. I'm merely saying that if push comes to shove, we need to have prayed for those in our assignment first.

Conclusion

In my early 20s I was in a state of spiritual crisis. I had doubted for six years whether or not I was saved. In December of my 25th year God pulled back the curtains and revealed to me that I was indeed saved, but I didn't know Him. In a defining season of my life God taught me how to hear Him and He immediately put me to work organizing prayer on my seminary campus. Before twelve months were finished I had come to know God as my provider, my deliverer, my healer, my Father, and He assigned me to be a pastor. For the first time I experienced the joy and intimacy with God that I had longed for as I began to do the will of God. In subsequent years I would discover the waning or deepening of intimacy with God was connected to the rising and falling of my passion and obedience to "do His will . . . and finish His work." (Jn. 4:34).

I discovered two great threats to intimacy exist.

1. A heart that cools in its passion to serve God and see His kingdom come. Too often our heart turns the leaves of its affections toward the sunshine of lesser things. Comfort and ease may beckon us; perhaps the siren call of financial security entices us, or status and prestige set up stumbling blocks in our paths. When this happens, we increasingly begin making decisions in our own favor instead of His. We reduce the amount of time and energy in seeking His kingdom. This begins to create a wall of separation. His voice will become faint, His presence elusive, His guidance muddy.

2. Busyness in doing many good things, but not the non-negotiable things required to fulfill our work. Our heart may not cool, in fact, it may be precisely because we are so desirous to serve that we add on one responsibility after another. We may see good causes and try to respond; however,

God did not call us to do everything, only what He assigned us. Jesus never let the needs of the people dictate His direction. He was not called to meet needs, but to do the will of His Father. We can lose a close connection with God when we become so busy doing good things that fulfilling our assignment suffers.

My concluding advice is to beware of a prayer life that does not seek first the kingdom but merely asks good things for others. Seek instead a heart whose entire existence burns with passion to do His will. Then roll up your sleeves, get to work, and enjoy an intimate relationship with God!

Questions for Further Thought or Discussion

1. Can you explain why praying for God's work leads to greater intimacy with God?
2. Does the majority of your intercession and petition revolve around asking for God's kingdom to come, particularly as it relates to the responsibility you have for your part in it, or do you mostly pray for others' needs?
3. Is either one of the two great threats to intimacy a challenge to your life right now? What can you do to overcome it?

The author: John Franklin is President of John Franklin Ministries in Nashville, Tennessee and former National Prayer Consultant, with Lifeway Christian Resources. He is the author of *And the Place Was Shaken: How to Lead a Powerful Prayer Meeting, A House of Prayer: Prayer Ministries in Your Church, By Faith: Living in the Certainty of God's Reality*, and *Spiritual Warfare: Biblical Truth For Victory.*

SUGGESTED ADDITIONAL READING

Hunter, W. Bingham. *The God Who Hears.* Downers Grove, IL: InterVarsity Press, 1986.

DeMoss, Nancy Leigh. *A Place of Quiet Rest: Finding Intimacy with God through a Daily Devotional Life.* Chicago: Moody Publishers, 2002.

Hunt, T.W. and King, Claude. *In God's Presence: Your Daily Guide to a Meaningful Prayer Life.* Nashville: Lifeway 1994.

chapter

37

HINDRANCES TO EFFECTIVE PRAYER

Sammy Tippit

"Husbands, likewise, dwell with them with understanding, giving honor to the wife, as to the weaker vessel, and as being heirs together of the grace of life, that your prayers may not be hindered" (1 Pet. 3:7).

The Apostle Peter clearly taught that there are certain attitudes and behavioral patterns that act as hindrances to effective praying. As I have traveled around the world, I've met scores of Christians who testify to the truth of Peter's statement. Many have asked, "Why do my prayers seem to hit the ceiling and bounce back?"

Before that question can be answered, we need a clear understanding of the nature of prayer. Only then can we comprehend what constitutes effective praying. We can then identify hindrances to effective praying.

Prayer in its most basic form is intimacy with God. It's the communion of two hearts—the heart of God and the heart of man. Prayer takes place when man shares the deep inner thoughts and feelings of his mind, soul and spirit with his Creator, his Redeemer and his Friend. However, it is much more than a follower of Jesus pouring his heart out to God. That's only half the equation. The other half is the Father pouring out His heart to His child.

Effective praying presumes that a deep and meaningful relationship exists between the two parties. Anything that hinders the intimacy of that relationship becomes a hindrance to the effectiveness of prayer. The Bible clearly identifies hindrances to intimacy with God.

Religion without a Relationship with God

Much religious praying stands on display around the world today. Muslims pray religiously. Hindus take pilgrimages to find peace with their gods. Christians repeat well worn phrases over and over. However, Jesus taught His disciples that religious praying is not effective praying. He told His disciples not to be like the religious leaders of His day who prayed to be seen of men. To the contrary, His disciples were to go into their closets where the heavenly Father would meet with them in privacy.

Jesus knew the folly of religious praying. He asserted that religion could never give access into the presence of an almighty, eternal, holy God. That could only take place through a personal relationship with Him. That's why Jesus told His disciples, "I am the way, the truth, and the life. No one comes to the Father, except through Me" (Jn. 14:6). Such a relationship with God would only be made possible by the death, burial and resurrection of Jesus.

If you would have asked me as a high school student if I prayed, I would have given you a positive response. However, I had no personal relationship with God. My concept of prayer was attempting to get out of the "Man Upstairs" what ever He would give me. Prayer was centered in my wishes, my thoughts, and my needs. I understood religious praying, but had no comprehension of prayer being the expression of a deep and intimate relationship with God.

It was only when I came to know Jesus as my personal Lord, Savior, and Friend that I grasped the true meaning of prayer. When I placed my faith in Jesus, He forgave my sins and placed me in a right relationship with the

Father. Immediately the nature of prayer changed from ritual to adventure; from duty to love; and from self centeredness to God centeredness.

Sin

The second hindrance to effective praying is sin. Isaiah 59:2 says, "But your iniquities have separated you from your God; and your sins have hidden His face from you so that He will not hear."

When we come into the presence of God, we will always behold one outstanding characteristic of His nature: His holiness. There is not a blemish in God; purity and impurity do not mix. If we are to have intimate fellowship with a holy God, then we must be clean before Him. David asked a question in Psalms 24, "Who may ascend into the hill of the LORD? Or who may stand in His holy place?" He then answered his own question saying, "He who has clean hands and a pure heart, who has not lifted up his soul to an idol, nor sworn deceitfully" (24:3-4). Only the pure in heart will be able to enter into the presence of God and discover intimacy with Him.

Sin in the life of the believer hinders intimate fellowship with God. God is holy. When sin resides within the heart of a disciple of Jesus, it's impossible for that disciple to walk in deep intimate fellowship with one who is absolute purity. We must confess our sins, and "He [will be] faithful and just to forgive us our sins and to cleanse us from all unrighteousness" (1 Jn. 1:9).

Pride

The third obstacle to effective praying is pride. James 4:6 says, "God resists the proud, but gives grace to the humble." The word "resists" used in some translations means "opposes." It is an old military term. It denotes that God has set Himself in military opposition to those who are proud in heart. Thus, there is no room for pride in the heart of the one who seeks to be intimate with God.

Pride compares us to others. Humility compares our lives to Jesus. When we look at others, we can always find a reason to boast. We may not be what we ought to be. However, we think that we're better than the other brother or sister in Christ. But when we see Jesus, we can only fall on our face and cry out, "Oh, God, have mercy on me. I have failed so miserably. I am so unlike the Savior."

Pride compares us to others to find someone that has not lived up to our standards. But humility does not look upon men. It only looks on God. Therefore, a praying heart will always be a humble heart. There is no room in the inner chamber of prayer for pride.

On the other hand, God's grace is extended to the humble of heart. There's only one way that any of God's creation can experience intimacy with Him—by God's grace. Amazing grace. Marvelous grace. Because God is absolute purity, none of us can stand in His presence outside of grace being applied to our hearts. We have the ability to draw near to a holy God because of His grace. That grace is applied to the heart that is rooted and founded upon humility.

Broken Relationships

Another reason for the lack of effectiveness in our prayer lives might be a broken relationship. Many view prayer as an escape from everyday life. They view prayer as mystical and of no practical value. They see no correlation between prayer and interpersonal relationships. However, Peter told husbands to live with their wives "with understanding, giving honor to the wife . . . and as being heirs together of the grace of life, that your prayers may not be hindered" (1 Pet. 3:7).

True prayer draws our attention to the nature and character of God. We become like Him as we recognize His attributes. When we emerge from the inner chamber of prayer we will love with a revolutionary love—the love of the Father. Our capacity to love will be broadened and deepened. Consequently, prayer and interpersonal relationships are interwoven. Prayer affects our relationships, and our relationships affect our ability to pray. Many times I have needed to ask my wife and my children to forgive me. I could not be in harmony with God when I was out of tune with my family.

A heart that is finely tuned to the heart strings of God will produce a symphony of music that builds loving relationships. When those relationships are broken, the music may still be able to play, but not with the same kind of beauty. Broken relationships hinder our intimacy with God.

Self Centeredness

The fifth impediment to prayer is selfishness. James 4:3 says, "You ask and do not receive, because you ask amiss, that you may spend it on your pleasures." Prayer should submit our lives to the lordship of Christ. How then can we bring our own selfish desires and activities to God's throne and expect His blessing?

One of our greatest problems is that we have a generation of self-seeking, manipulative Christians. We have learned the methods of the world and tried to mingle them with the method of God. Many well-meaning believers initiate an idea or ministry without consulting the Father. Mass marketing techniques and appeals for funds are used to launch ministries. Things often go well until we reach the limits of human ability. Then we begin to pray fervently for God's assistance.

But God refuses to answer. He had nothing to do with our self-motivated and self-initiated prayer in the beginning and He has nothing to do with it now. The windows of heaven are only open to prayer that is centered in the will of God rather than the will of man.

In his book, *The Root of the Righteous,* A. W. Tozer says, "If I mingle some pet religious enterprise of mine with the will of God and come to think of them as one, I can be hindered in my religious life."[1]

Effective prayer discovers the will of God and passionately pursues it. Anything that would direct us away from His plans and maneuver us in the direction of our own ways will hinder our intimacy with God.

Busyness

The final hindrance that I would mention is that of "busyness." Paul writes in Ephesians 5:16, "[Redeem] the time for the days are evil."

We live in exciting times. More people are alive today than any previous generation. The opportunity to impact our world for Christ has never been greater. We have all the resources we need. But there's one disturbing question, "Where are the workers?"

Jesus said that the solution to enough workers for the harvest is found in prayer (Mt. 9:37-38). But that presents another problem. Where are the men and women of prayer?

Too many of us have become so busy that we have no time for God. It's impossible to have an intimate relationship with anyone without sufficient time with that person. How much more true is that with God? We long to spend time with those we love. Therefore, if you truly love God, you will desire to spend time alone with Him sharing your heart and allowing Him to share His heart with you.

This may be the greatest hindrance of this generation. We have become "professional" ministers and learned well how to produce "quality" programs. But we've forgotten the secret chamber of prayer. We often entertain but seldom convict. We draw crowds to our buildings but few to our Savior. We've learned the art of developing partnerships, but lost the passion to know the one Partner that really matters. The Father longs to spend time with His children. He calls to us. Steal away and make time to meet with Him. If there is any hindrance to your intimacy with God, identify it, confess it, and repent of it.

Determine in your heart that you long to know Him, really know Him, more than anything in life. He will come to you. He will meet with you. Don't allow any obstacle to keep you from such intimacy with God.

Questions for Further Thought or Discussion

1. What are the implications to how we teach and model prayer of the author's perspective that prayer is hindered because it is a relationship?
2. Choose three of the hindrances identified by the author, discuss why they are harmful to both individuals and congregations, then offer biblical solutions to removing the hindrances.
3. Design a prayer format (an outline of the sequence of topics focused on during a prayer meeting) for a group that has gathered to seek God but must first deal with various hindrances. Include scripture and a song (lyrics directed to God as a prayer) for each segment.

The author: Sammy Tippit is President of Sammy Tippit Ministries, located in San Antonio, Texas. As an international evangelist, he has preached all over the world. He is the author of several books including *Praying for Your Family, God's Secret Agent, Victorious Living, Fit for Battle* and *The Prayer Factor.*

SUGGESTED ADDITIONAL READING

Hybels, Bill. *Too Busy Not to Pray.* Downers Grove, IL: InterVarsity Press, 1988.

Moore, Beth. *Living Free: Learning to Pray God's Word.* Nashville: LifeWay Church Resources, 2001.

van Deusen Hunsinger, Deborah. *Pray without Ceasing: Revitalizing Pastoral Care.* Grand Rapids, Eerdmans Publishing, 2006.

ENDNOTES

1. A. W. Tozer. *The Root of the Righteous.* (Harrisburg, PA: Christian Publications. 1955), p.130.

chapter

38

HOW TO PRAY WITHOUT CEASING

Cornell (Corkie) Haan

The biblical admonition to "Pray without ceasing" demands that listening be a major part of prayer. Children learn how to pray by adults telling them to "Bow your head, close your eyes, and fold your hands." Then, all prayers started with "Dear" and ended with "Amen." To this day the majority of Christians bow their head, close their eyes, fold their hands and pray prayers starting with "Dear" and ending shortly thereafter with "Amen." While that is a good model, it makes prayer or talking to God a soliloquy. Communication 101 taught that good communication is two-way. Imagine walking into the very throne room of God in Heaven and talking non-stop, not letting Him get a word in edgewise. When I'm in His presence all I want to do is listen—listen to what the King of Kings and Lord of Lords has to say to me.

The only way to pray without ceasing is to understand prayer as an on-going two-way conversation that doesn't start with "Dear" and end with "Amen." Prayer listening is often defined as some unusual and special technique or event. Praying without ceasing makes prayer normal when it includes a two-way conversation with the Lord. We have made normal prayer a one-way communication.

God speaks when we need to hear from Him.

Listening became part of my "pray without ceasing" experience the night after two surgeons sat on either side of me and told me that my wife of thirty-four years was completely impacted with Ovarian Cancer and would not live another three weeks. After both of us talked about her death, I went home late that evening. I should not have been driving. Through my tears I did two theologically foolish things. First, I told God that I was ticked. He was getting an angel and I was losing one. Second, I told God that if He wanted her He could have her—like she was mine! As a pastor I knew better, but I needed to say those things to the Lord.

That night I tried to pray a "Dear" and "Amen" prayer. I couldn't. I'd get two sentences out, and all I heard was "your wife is dying . . . your wife is dying!" Since I couldn't pray a "Dear" and "Amen" prayer, I learned that if I listened, God would talk to me. This went on for months. Now I still talk to Him, but I have learned to make listening part of my personal prayer life, thus praying without ceasing.

Questions

What does God say? Only on rare occasions does He speak audible English words. Most often God speaks in thoughts that I can only understand in my mind as English words because I speak English and think in English. Generally He talks to me about His kingdom's business. He shares with me His heart and desires. Most often I don't tell anyone else. I'd be somewhat embarrassed to share with anyone what God and I talk about. It's personal. Again and again I asked Him about my wife. Would she live and how long? He never answered me. He did say that it would not be good for me to know.

How do you listen to the King of Kings and the Lord of Lords? The Bible gives much illustration of God's people interacting with God. He spoke to Daniel through visions, Balaam through a donkey, Peter through a rooster, and Moses out of a shrub. There are thousands of people, like Augustine,

Mother Teresa, Joan of Arc, and Brother Lawrence, to whom God spoke.

Praying without ceasing is not . . .

Listening to God is not meditation or practicing the lifestyle of a monk or mulling things over in your mind. Jesus said, "Therefore take heed how you hear" (Lk. 8:18). Prayer listening is not special revelation. Prayer listening should be as common as other parts of praying, as it is part of your communication with the Lord. I find that God talks to me at the most unusual times and places. He does not talk to me only in the closet, or while I'm on my knees or in any typical "Dear" and "Amen" prayer mode.

Some suggest keeping a journal of the things that the Lord says. That would be good, but He doesn't conveniently talk to me when the journal is handy. My DNA will not let me pray a "Dear" and "Amen" prayer for hours on end. I have longed for that ability to be in a closet for hours. For the longest time I was ashamed that I could not do that.

All my life I have been disappointed that I didn't have a very personal relationship with God. While I had my devotions and read my Bible and prayed my "Dear" and "Amen" prayers, I found them to be very routine for my DNA. I found I could talk to my friends by the hour, but I had a hard time praying "Dear" and "Amen" prayers for ten minutes. Then I learned that prayer listening is as common as prayer itself. It is not some special gift, it is your everyday communication with the King of Kings. It is, in fact, a way to pray without ceasing.

Learning to Listen

So how do you learn to listen? For me it started with a need to hear from God. Good listening starts with the desire to learn. If you can handle life without Him, you will not hear from Him. It is not a matter of setting aside more time, albeit, that would be good. "Be silent . . . before the Lord" (Zech. 2:13) does not mean actual decibel silence, but silence in your mind. The world can be very loud around me, but I can still quiet my heart and mind whether in an airport or in the woods.

Remaining silent before God does not mean that you will have no thoughts or reflections. It does mean you will stop telling God your needs, and say with Samuel, "Speak. Lord, for Your servant hears" (1 Sam. 3:9). To pray without ceasing, it will be necessary to stop one-sided chatter.

The Bible Speaks about Listening

The verb "to listen" appears more than a thousand times in the Old Testament and 425 times in the New Testament. "Hear, O Israel" (Deut 5:1 and many other places) is the repeated preamble to the divine call in the Old Testament. "He who has ears to hear, let him hear" (Mt.11:15) is Christ's constant message. In this context "to hear" means "to listen with attention," not distractedly.

- God speaks through the Bible (2 Tim. 3:15-16).
- God speaks through the Son, Jesus Christ (Mt. 17:5; Jn. 1:14; Heb. 4:12).
- God speaks through the Holy Spirit (Acts 9:11-15; 1 Cor. 14:26; Rev. 2:7, 11, 17, 29; 3:6, 13, 22).
- God desires us to listen (Gen. 28:16; Isa. 55:3; Jer. 33:3; Mt. 11:15; Jas. 1:5; Rev 3:20).
- God is displeased when we don't listen (Zech. 7:11-13; Acts 28:26-27).
- God makes the *logos* word a *rhema* word: the written word becomes a specific word for that situation (Hab. 2:1; Mt. 4:4; Rom. 10:8, 17).
- God's speaking is to lead to obedient action (Jn. 2:5; Heb. 3:7-8; Jas. 1:22-25).
- God communicates what to do and say when people listen (Isa. 50:4-5; Jn. 5:19; 8:28; 12:49-50).

Both the Old and New Testaments provide illustrations of prayer listening, including . . .

- Samuel "Speak, for Your servant hears" (1 Sam. 3:10).
- Mary "Mary . . . sat at Jesus' feet and heard His word" (Lk. 10:39).
- Paul "What shall I do, Lord?" (Acts 22:10).

A Theology of Listening

C. S. Lewis warns against egoistic subjectivism or when self talks to the self:

"The prayer preceding all prayers is: May it be the real I who speaks. May it be the real Thou that I speak to."[1]

The more we understand the Scriptures the more likely it is that God will speak to us. The Bible is the message of God to mankind. Why should its author speak to you if you have not read His main message?

God speaks to those whose life is a clear channel ready for reception. The message would be poorly received and garbled if the receptacle were un-prepared. God speaks when we are ready to listen.

Prayer without ceasing is not meditation, special revelation, or receiving a prophetic word of knowledge. It is one's normal communication with the Father.

Conclusion

If you are hungry to pray without ceasing, God will speak to you. If you desire a personal relationship with the Father, then communication is foundational to that relationship and all relationships. Each of us need to see for ourselves that God, our heavenly Father, wants to talk with us. So LISTEN! Spend as much or more time listening than speaking.

Imagine sitting at a table with a group of friends, but God himself is sitting at the head of the table. How much talking would you do? It would be extremely rude for you to talk non-stop and never let God speak. Or imagine that you have just come into the very presence of God to speak to your heavenly Father. Since you are a child—a very little child—He picks you up onto His lap and you talk together. As a Grandfather, my granddaughter comes to sit in my lap. Typically she plays with my face or hands and jabbers on in sweet words. I love to hear her talk to me. She is full of questions some of which I can answer. Our communication is two-way. We enjoy speaking and listening to each other. So it is with God and His children.

So talk together with your heavenly Father and listen to Him talk to you. We have become experts at talking types of praying, but talking is only a part of prayer. Let's try listening more. Then, perhaps we will be able to pray without ceasing.

Questions for Further Thought or Discussion

1. Agree or disagree (and explain why): Prayer that does not include genuine

listening is not truly prayer without ceasing.

2. List and explain four or five biblical benefits of the listening dimension of praying.
3. How would you disciple someone in the listening dimension of praying? How would you help a group develop the ability to listen corporately?

The author: Dr. Cornell (Corkie) Haan serves as a National Facilitator for the Mission America Coalition, president of Kingdom Connections, and founder/co-founder of several ministries, including the Presidential Prayer Team. He is the author of *The Lighthouse Movement,* and *The Lighthouse Prayer Journals* as well as Editor of *The Lighthouse Devotional Guide.* He lives in Cave Creek, Arizona.

SUGGESTED ADDITIONAL READING

Huggett, Joyce. *Listening to God.* London: Hodder and Stoughton, 1986.

Payne, Leanne. *Listening Prayer: Learning to Hear God's Voice and Keep a Prayer Journal.* Grand Rapids: Baker Books, 1994.

Stanley, Charles. *How to Listen to God.* Nashville: Thomas Nelson Publishers, 1985.

ENDNOTES

1. C.S. Lewis, *Letters to Malcolm: Chiefly on Prayer* (New York: Harcourt, Brace & World, Inc., 1964), p. 82.

chapter

39

THE SECRET OF SINGLE-MINDED PRAYER

Eddie Smith

Would you pray if you thought God wouldn't answer you? Hardly. You'd consider it a waste of time. James 1:5-8 promises that unless we pray single-mindedly, we *should not expect answers* to our prayers. Do you pray single-mindedly? Don't answer too quickly. Let's take a closer look.

Prayer Should Be Congruent

The power of single-minded prayer is about congruency. Because doubt is "double-mindedness," which is contrary to God's nature—it's incongruent!

I recently wrote a check incorrectly. Immediately I wrote "VOID" across the face of the check. Prayer is like writing a check on your heavenly account. Assuming certain criterion are met, that check is then due and payable in heaven.

However, it's possible to inadvertently write "VOID" on that check when you leave the prayer room. Let's look at some of the ways this happens.

Many Christians *believe* they are praying in faith, but when you put them under God's CAT scan, it reveals they are not single-minded at all. Let's examine four aspects of prayer that must be in alignment (congruent) if we are to be heard. They are our request, our meditation, our conversation, and our behavior.

Our Request

Pray without anxiety. In Philippians 4:6, Paul warns us not to pray anxiety-ridden, worry-filled prayers because worry is calling into question God's integrity. It's questioning whether or not God means what He's promised; or whether or not He can do what He says. Instead, we are to pray faith-filled prayers, and make our petitions (requests of God), with thanksgiving. Gratitude and anxiety cannot coexist. One will always displace the other.

An anxious person is double-minded. He believes in prayer, and believes that God answers prayer, but he's just not certain he can trust God to answer his prayer. Prayer with thanksgiving is an expression of our faith. Praise in prayer is the door that allows thanksgiving and faith to meet.

Pray according to God's will—His purposes. Shape your prayers according to God's will, His purposes, and His ways. He will answer according to His will. He will never lay aside His purpose to answer your prayer.

For example, a wife's problem-centered prayer for her lost husband might sound like this: "Oh Lord, I'm begging you to save my husband. He's such a good man . . . " Whoa, hold on! Jesus didn't die for "good men." He came to seek and to save lost sinners. In this prayer, the wife is suggesting to God that, because her husband is so decent (good in a natural sense), that *he deserves* to be saved. *God saves people for His own glory.* It's about filling the Father's house with children. While it's true that God loves us, His plan, purpose, and glory are what move Him to answer our prayer and solve our problems (see 1 Jn. 5:14).

To pray for her lost husband, she might pray: "Lord, I thank You that Jesus has died for every sin that my husband has ever committed. Like me, Lord, he deserves nothing from You. Thank You for extending Your grace to him. Establish Your kingdom in his heart and glorify Your name in his life. Fill him with all that You are, so he can accomplish the purpose for which

You created him. Thank You for saving him for Your own glory."

Too often we focus our prayers on either our problem or our perceived solution. God wants us to focus on Him! When we focus on Him, our hearts are kept in perfect peace, as promised in Philippians 4:7. Our focus on God is evidence that we are walking by faith; leaving both the problem and the solution to Him.

What problem are you facing today? Rather than pray frantically, pray for a solution; why not submit your problem to God's purposes in prayer? God wants to do more than simply solve your problem. He wants to demonstrate His miraculous, creative power *for His own glory*—thank Him in advance for doing so!

Pray with thanksgiving. It's hard for us to thank God while making our requests, for two reasons. First, because we are so focused on the need, we often wrestle with anxiety. Secondly, we typically thank someone after they've done something, not before. When it comes to effective prayer, thanksgiving is to both precede and follow God's response.

Thanking God in advance for doing what you're asking Him to do is an expression of your expectancy. It's evidence that you're anticipating measurable results from your prayer. When my wife Alice was pregnant with our children, we said, "She is expecting." When you are praying in faith with pre-thanksgiving, you are praying expectantly. You expect to see God answer your prayer in an observable, verifiable way.

Our faith and thanksgiving are not based on what we see. They are based upon God's character (who He is, what He's done in the past, and what He's promised to do in the future). We're to walk by faith, not by sight. (See 2 Cor. 4:18).

King David often began his prayers with tears, but finished them with celebration. He believed God was a faithful, promise-keeping God. He often thanked God *in advance* for what He was about to do! Celebration is sometimes a shout of victory; and sometimes a declaration of war. As long as we whine to God about our problems, we'll see nothing. We *celebrate* the answer; then *we see* the answer!

- Praise preceded the fall of Jericho's walls. (The shout preceded the falling of the walls.)

- Praise preceded Jehoshaphat's victory. (The praise team preceded the army.)
- Praise preceded the feeding of the five thousand. (Jesus thanked the Father for feeding the people with a lad's lunch.)
- Praise preceded the resurrection of Lazarus. (Jesus thanked the Father for hearing Him.)
- Praise preceded the earthquake and jailbreak in Philippi. (Paul and Silas celebrated.)

Build the track, the train will follow.

There is a world-famous scenic railway over the beautiful snowcapped Alps. It stretches from Venice to Vienna; and it has an amazing history. For several years crews laid the track through the icy mountain passes, across the Alpine Mountains, which in itself was thought to be impossible. But stranger still, the track was laid before a train was built that could actually make the trip! When we pray with praise and thanksgiving, as Paul instructs us to do in Philippians 4:6, we are "building a track." At that point, it's God's job to "build the train!"

We are to be ever mindful of His benefits, not only for the things we want but also for the things we have. "Bless the LORD, O my soul, and forget not all His benefits" says Psalm 103:2. *God never responds to ingratitude.*

Our Meditation

Our *request* is how we present our prayer to God. What about our *meditation*? It's not just crazy people who talk to themselves. We all do. The question is, "What are we telling ourselves?"

You can "void" a perfectly made prayer request by allowing your thoughts to run *contrary* to it. The psalmist prayed that both the words of his mouth *and* the meditations of his heart would be acceptable to God (see Ps. 19:14). If we are saying one thing and thinking another, we are double-minded—unstable—as James 1:8 says.

We speak out of the abundance of our hearts (see Mt. 12:34), and we are as we think (see Prov. 23:7, KJV). The words of our heart can *undo* the words of our prayer.

Our Conversation

James points out that fresh and salty water cannot come from the same fountain (see Jas. 3:11). Our tongues are powerful. It's important that *what we say* lines up with *what we pray*.

Try this. Listen to the things you say throughout the course of an average day. You may discover that although the prayers you are praying sound "faith-filled," in agreement with God's will, and you are expressing gratitude to God in advance, your conversation belies your praying.

Here's an example. Janice needs rent money. She prays fervently, believing, thanking God in advance for His provision. So far, so good. Thirty minutes later someone asks about her situation. She replies, "I don't know. Things look pretty bleak. I don't know what I am going to do. I'm out of options." In one unguarded conversation, Janice writes "VOID" across the prayer she just prayed. Why did she do that?

She exposed an underlying issue of unbelief. Although she prayed the right words, she wasn't actually praying them in faith. She didn't truly believe them in her heart.

If we could search her heart, as God does, we might discover that Janice is still looking for a "backup source" (other than God). By telling another person her need, and showing a bit of desperation, she unconsciously hopes that he or she will assist . . . in case God doesn't come through. It's like having a "Plan B." She's likely not even aware that she does this, but it's a classic case of double-mindedness.

Or perhaps there is an underlying problem with something else she has not yet dealt with—her spending habits. If she's not tithing, or has wasted what God has given her, she subconsciously knows that God can't bless her. It would be hard for her to really believe, and pray in faith, that God would provide for her, knowing in her heart that she has "robbed" Him according to Malachi 3:9-10.

Rather than confess her sin, make restitution, and be restored, she sweeps that under the carpet and expects God to bless her regardless of her past behavior. And it ain't gonna happen! (Pardon the slang.) She needs her financial house in order if she expects God to hear and answer her.

The words we say should match the words we pray. Our conversations with others should reflect the faith with which we've prayed. To pray one thing about a person, place, or circumstance, and confess the opposite is classic double-mindedness and produces nothing. When someone asks Janice about her rent situation, she should respond, "I still don't know how God will do it, but I'm convinced that He is my source and that He's working now to supply all my needs according to His riches in glory, by Christ Jesus (Philippians 4:19). And for that, I give Him praise."

Our Behavior

There's one more way we can "void" our prayer. It's with our behavior. If we behave in a manner inconsistent with our request, our meditation, and our conversation, we are double-minded. The following example should be helpful in illustrating this principle.

Mary prayed for her husband, Ben, for twenty-four years. Ben has no time for God and shows no interest in coming to Him. The problem is, although Mary prays faithfully for Ben's salvation, she treats him like her "spiritual junior." She must begin to treat Ben like the man she *wants him to be*, instead of the man *he currently is*, if she's going to convince Ben, God, and others that she already sees him (with the eyes of faith) saved! When she begins to show Ben the respect due a spiritual man, God will move according to her expectation.

James Stewart (not the American actor) was a Welshman God greatly used in the famed Welsh revival of the nineteenth century. His mother was a praying woman. James, a teenager, hadn't trusted Christ as his Savior. As you can imagine, this greatly concerned his mother.

One day she said to James, "Son, I've asked our youth pastor at the church to make room in the next youth service for you to share your testimony for Christ."

"Testimony for Christ?" he gulped. "What are you talking about? I have no testimony for Christ, Momma. I tell you, I'm going to hell and play football" (his word for soccer).

Undaunted by his insolence, she continued praying and believing God. Every other day or so she would lovingly remind him, "Son, don't forget the youth service. We're counting on you to give your salvation testimony."

He would blurt back his now typical response, "Momma, I've told you, I'm going to go to hell and play football."

One day at soccer practice James was running across the field when he tripped, slipped, or perhaps was pushed to the ground by the Holy Spirit. All he remembered was that, with his face in the sod, he met God. In a mere moment, his life was instantly and eternally changed!

James jumped up. Without explanation to anyone, he ran off the field and down the street to his home. Up the sidewalk he darted, across the porch, and through the house toward the kitchen, all the while screaming, "Momma, Momma, I got saved, I got saved!"

With hardly any expression of surprise, she looked up from her dishes and said with a smile, "Why son, I've been trying to tell you that for the past month."

James' mother was no worrier, she was a warrior. She believed God's promises and His intention and power to keep them. She prayed congruently!

Questions for Further Thought or Discussion

1. Write a definition of single-minded prayer then explain why this type of praying is vital for individual believers. For congregations.
2. Agree or disagree (and explain your reasoning): Our prayers should begin with praise.
3. How does our conversation and behavior affect our prayers?

The author: Eddie Smith is Co-Founder and President of Eddie and Alice Smith Ministries in Houston, Texas. An internationally known conference speaker and author of *How to Be Heard in Heaven: Moving from Need-Driven to God-Centered Prayer* and other books, he has more than 7400 students from more than 100 nations in his online school of prayer at www.teachustopray.com.

SUGGESTED ADDITIONAL READING

Crump, David. *Knocking on Heaven's Door: A New Testament Theology of Petitionary Prayer.* Grand Rapids: Baker Academic, 2006.

Hallesby, O. *Prayer.* Minneapolis: Augsburg/Fortress, 1994.

Smith, Eddie and Michael Hennen. *Strategic Prayer: Applying the Power of Targeted Prayer.* Bloomington, MN: Bethany House, 2007.

chapter

40

ABIDING PRAYER

Tony Twist

I was dying. Call it what you want. Burnout. Fatigue. Stress. Whatever. I was not yet forty with a growing international ministry and dreaming about shuffleboard and bingo. And, I don't even like shuffleboard and bingo!

I knew something had to change.

So, I began looking for a mentor. Perhaps someone to provide spiritual direction. I did not really need answers. Just someone older and wiser who had "been there" and would just be "with me" and "for me." A welcoming listener who would provide hospitable space for me. But, with travel schedule, responsibilities, demands, etc., it just did not happen.

It was about that time that the TCM International Institute needed someone to teach a course on prayer. And, I drew the short straw. "Okay," I reasoned, "nobody is really qualified to teach this, but I'll give it my best shot." That began a three-year time of preparation. Not wanting to be a hypocrite, I determined to follow the disciplines before teaching them to my students. It took three years of growth to (somewhat) consistently practice what I wanted to preach. There was also much to learn about and from believers throughout Central and Eastern Europe. How was I to teach people who had been in prison for their faith? Especially how was I to teach them how to better abide in His presence? A daunting and humbling task!

I took inspiration from Psalm 131 which encourages us to rid ourselves of pride and haughty eyes and not concern ourselves with great matters. Then, as verse 2 urges, "I have calmed and quieted my soul, like a weaned child with his mother; like a weaned child is my soul within me." A beautiful, safe place to begin.

And from the exhortation of Jesus in John 15:4, "Abide in Me, and I in you. As the branch can not bear fruit of itself, unless it abides in the vine, neither can you, unless you abide in Me."

I soon discovered that abiding prayer is a journey together. Like the two who trudged the weary path toward a place they called home. Downcast, they told their tale to a traveler who fell in step. A friend had been murdered. A good man, stricken down in his prime. His destroyed potential, a tragic loss to many, left behind a crushing grief. They, like many of us, trudged onward toward the night.

Their heavy hearts wept for hope aborted. Their burdened spirits found no relief. Their sagging faith explored the bottom. The traveler spoke, but preoccupations kept him distant. He was present but they were not.

They wanted to hear His words of consolation. The best they could do was invite Him into the place they called home. And to their humble table. Then, He blessed their bread. His grace, fitting and good, touched their hearts. Their downcast hearts finally looked upward. And, they beheld Him for the first time.

In His grace, the dikes protecting their fragile spirits crumbled. In flooded a healing torrent. And they rushed back to the path.

This time, however, the journey was brighter. They saw better. Even the darkness could not dim their spirits. Their soaring spirits hastened them forward. Faith lifted them to live in scorn of consequences. They sought community. They needed a place with others to joyfully confess the good news: "The Lord is risen indeed, and has appeared to Simon" (Lk. 24:34).

Even with dust from the Emmaus path on our exhausted feet, we can welcome His good blessing. In His grace, He will resurrect our lives. The weary trudge then becames a majestic march toward community. This is Abiding Prayer. Passive? At times. Active? At times. Relational? Always!

As I learned to abide in His presence with brothers and sisters from Eastern Europe, radical changes occured in me. Things difficult to put into words. And, both in scripture and the history of Christian spirituality, we find that many others throughout the ages have blazed trails for us to follow. And their experiences give us helpful perspective.[1] Not formulas. But, perspective.

One amazing fact we learn from the spiritual lives of men and women through the ages is that none experience our Father in exactly the same way.[2] Same Mentor, but different experiences of Him. Like the blind men discovering the elephant, our limited experiences are not the whole story.

So, there can be no "one size fits all" formula for spiritual fitness. No straitjacket spirituality. Just a simple commitment to a relationship with Him. A relationship that is not only different with each of His children, but one that must also shift as we journey through the stages of life.

The devotional life of a child will not sustain a teenager. Nor that of a teenager, a young adult. Nor that of a young adult, a mature adult. We are committed to a relationship that must grow as we mature. Like children learning to walk. As soon as we take our first small steps, our parent moves away from us. Instead of hugs, we experience distance. This is our reward for learning? A bigger challenge? We then learn several new steps. And the parent moves again. And again. Throughout the dance we call life.

The Christian believers who self-destruct along the way are often not committed to such a growing, dynamic relationship with Him. They either want to cling to past experiences, imitate the relationship of others, or slide down the undemanding path of non-growth. But, authentic relationship moves us. Even when just "muddling through" the dark nights, depressed days, changing times and unexplainable events. Remaining in Him, whether tempted by success or tested by adversity. He tabernacles among us. And, when He is ready, the cloud rises above the camp. We must move to remain with Him.

I have learned that abiding in relationship is all about relationship. Because, He is One. We're learning that everything that is really good began between Them, where love has always lived. The Father, like the sun, radiating beams of love. The Son, glorious reflection, mirroring the Father. The Begetter and the Begotten. Eternally. In the strong bond of the Spirit.[3] All three forever in true love.

It is this loving relationship which birthed you and me (along with all else). I love my parents and will be eternally grateful for family, teachers, friends and adversaries who helped form me along the way. They were mentors for a season. They all participated (and still participate at times) in His conception of me. But, *He* is our rightful Father (Mt. 23:9).

We're chosen, adopted into His eternal family (Eph. 1:5). This family of those who do His will (Mt. 12:46-50). God's strong right-hand Word formed us from frail dust, while His powerful left-hand Spirit energized us into being.[7] We are now sons and daughters of Abraham, called out of Egypt, given the Law and Prophets, the Incarnate Word, the Written Word, martyrs, trailblazers, guides, friends and witnesses all though the ages.

And that's not all. Formed by His many beams of love,[5] we are now being transformed into Him (2 Cor. 3:18). We're being re-created to live in our heart's true home: This eternal relationship of love that painted the first supernova, smiled at the first sunrise and welcomes children home. This relationship we call the Trinity is our eternal destiny.

Knowing where we came from and where we're headed makes all the difference when we are in life's wilderness. The desert becomes a place of instruction rather than destruction. A place where, as we draw life from Him, we grow up. Listening deeper. Feeling healthier. Thinking clearer. Doing better. Loving more.

Through abiding we are being re-created. When quiet before Him, His Word reaches transforming fingers into our hearts, this inner chamber from which we live.[6] From which thoughts and feelings emerge. He brings order into this vast restless heartland which no psychologist can reach. We find soul food by abiding in the true Vine (Jn. 15:1-17). Willing to follow in spite of distracting thoughts and feelings.

It is a journey with no perfect roadmap. Simply a commitment to becoming more cultured by our Father on the way home.

When we first fall in love with Him, we journey with Him to a lakeside bench anticipating the sunrise. Abiding begins. We speak tenderly to each other. Listening attentively. Reading carefully all verbal and non-verbal cues. Even enjoying the silence. Our communication extends to all levels and involves our entire being. We read each other, not for information alone. But, attentively for relationship. Heart waiting, like a moist field receiving life-giving seed. In love, we receive and then slowly meditate upon the Word He gives.

Then we respond to Him whole heartedly, right mindedly, entire soul and strength. Awaiting insight, love, formation and direction.[7] Letting the relationship unfold through times of adoration, confession, thanksgiving and intercession. Before long, as we all know, the journey gets complicated because life intrudes.

Thanks be that the Ancient of Days wants to share all of our journey (Mt. 28:20). However, He will not come uninvited. So, we just say "yes." Inviting Him to form the relationships that form us and those we love. Turning to Him when sleep eludes us in the night. Driving to work with Him instead of some deeply diverted disc jockey. Observing His reaction as He watches television with us and goes along to the movies we consume. Fasting, for His sake, from ball games, shopping, food, friends, vacations, or anything else that intrudes between us. Faithfully keeping the morning, afternoon, evening and/or late night appointments with Him. Having and helping His children. Taking care of His little ones.[8] The more we obediently share life with Him, the better we become. The better we become, the more we want to share with Him.

As our relationship with Him develops, its health is seen in our deepening love for Him and others (Mt. 22:34-40). Going through life's tasks in His powerful and sustaining Presence, mindful of our heritage and destiny, life becomes a "process of being conformed to the image of Christ for the sake of others."[9]

We do this by journeying alongside and toward the Ancient of Days. The One who brought Adam into existence. Who led Abraham out of Ur in search of a place to really live. Who spoke to Moses face to face.[10] Who sent His Son to reveal Himself (Jn. 14:8,9). Who gives His Spirit to make us whole. Who alone is our eternal abiding place (14:1-4).

And, in the autumn of life, we are committed to the same lakeside bench. Still journeying with Him and enjoying the sunset. Still speaking tenderly to one another after all the years. Hearing deeply beneath the few words being spoken. Knowing verbals and non-verbals without even looking at each other.

Libraries of love back and forth, especially in the silence. Looking back on the fruit of a life of love together. While looking forward to the time when we stand before His throne with family from every nation, tribe, people and language (Rev. 7:9-12).

Questions for Further Thought or Discussion

1. How is John 15:4 an invitation and exhortation to prayer?
2. What is the role of prayer in abiding in Christ?
3. What are the implications of this approach to prayer to your personal prayer life? Your corporate prayer experience?

The author: Dr. Tony Twist is President and Professor of Leadership and Spiritual Formation at the TCM International Institute, headquartered in Indianapolis, Indiana with a European campus near Vienna, Austria. TCMII provides graduate theological education for Christian leaders throughout Europe, Russia and Central Asia.

SUGGESTED ADDITIONAL READING

Mulholland Jr., M. Robert. *Invitation to a Journey.* Downers Grove, IL: InterVarsity Press, 1993.

Packer, J. I., and Carolyn Nystrom. *Praying (Finding Our Way through Duty to Delight).* Downers Grove, IL: InterVarsity Press, 2006.

Willard, Dallas. *Renovation of the Heart.* Colorado Springs, CO: NavPress, 2002.

ENDNOTES

1. If you would like a list of books and resources I have found helpful, please send an e-mail requesting the list to Tony@tcmi.org.

2. I would recommend *The Study of Spirituality* edited by Cheslyn Jones, Geoffrey Wainwright and Edward Yarnold (Oxford University Press, 1986) for a good survey of the history of spirituality. Also, Louis Bouyer, *A History of Christian Spirituality*, 3 Volumes (New York: Seabury Press 1963-1968).

3. These ideas of light, reflection and begetting are used frequently in the works of the early church fathers.

4. The early church father, Irenaeus, used this wonderful illustration in

his catechetical summary of Christian belief entitled *Proof of the Apostolic Preaching.* See *The Study of Spirituality*, pp. 107-109 for reference.

5. This lovely image from William Blake is adapted for use by Thomas Merton in several of his works.

6. Dallas Willard, in *Renovation of the Heart: Putting on the Character of Christ*, (Colorado Springs, CO: Navpress, 2002), provides a good introduction to the process of inner transformation accessible to all Christians.

7. See M. Robert Mulholland, Jr., *Shaped by the Word: The Power of Scripture in Spiritual Formation* (Nashville: Upper Room, 1985) for a fuller treatment of spiritual reading. The classical progression of lectio divina is silencio, lectio, meditatio, oratio, comtemplatio and incarnatio.

8. John 21 gives us this abiding lesson. The last breakfast was more than a wonderful spiritual experience. Direction was given regarding what connecting (or re-connecting) with Jesus really means.

9. I like very much this definition of spiritual formation given by Mulholland in his book *Invitation to a Journey*,

10. Kenneth Leech makes the point that the God of the Old Testament is the God of the wilderness and it was in the process of wandering that Abraham and his children encountered the living God. See *Experiencing God, Theology as Spirituality*, (Eugene, OR: Wipf and Stock Publishers).

SECTION THREE

THE CORPORATE EXPRESSION OF PRAYER

chapter

41

THE BIBLE AND CHURCH PRAYER

J. Chris Schofield

Throughout history, prayer or in many cases, the lack thereof, has been a central concern for the Church. Most ecclesial traditions have at some juncture in their existence placed a priority on the practice and need of prayer. Many denominations and church traditions have responded to this need by producing books of common prayer, training courses on prayer, resources on prayer, seminars on prayer and even organizing conferences on prayer. Yet, from a North American perspective, local church prayer beliefs, priorities and practices are stale and in many instances declining in their fervency and effect. Why is that the case?

Bible-based prayer is needed.

In his work, *A Cry for the Kingdom*, Stanley Grenz makes the following statement relating to prayer and the Church. He says,

> The church of Jesus Christ faces many challenges today. Yet the greatest challenge is not what might initially come to mind. The greatest challenge is not that of urging Christians to speak out on the great social issues of the day . . . Nor is our greatest challenge that of encouraging each other to be more fervent in evangelizing the world, . . . Rather, the greatest challenge facing the church of Jesus Christ today, and therefore every local congregation, is motivating the people of God to engage in sincere, honest, fervent prayer.[1]

Grenz is on target with this statement, but only partially. He is correct in that he believes churches need to be about the task of prayer. I have never heard a church say that it spent too much time in prayer—but many have said the opposite. Grenz is also correct in that honest, fervent prayers are needed. Yet, I would add to his assessment that the greatest need is for churches today to return to the Christ of the Bible through heartfelt *Bible-based* prayer. Biblical prayer that focuses on relationship with Christ and His kingdom/mission-centered desires is the greatest need facing the Church today!

Church Prayer—and the God of the Bible

In Genesis 1:1 the Bible begins "In the beginning God . . . ." The Bible is a book about God. In Genesis 3:9 the Lord called to man and said to him, "Where are you?" God's interest in man is relationship and the Bible records God's redemptive work to provide relationship with sinful man through Jesus the Christ (see Jn. 3:16).

When churches allow the Bible to shape their prayer beliefs and practices in relationship and intimacy with Christ, they allow God's agenda and presence to permeate their life of prayer. Why is that? Edmund P. Clowney explains,

> The Bible is God's Word; it is His story of His work in bringing rebellious men and women back to Himself. It tells, not of man seeking a lost God, but of God seeking lost men. The Bible does not present an art of prayer; it presents the God of prayer, the God who calls before we answer and answers before we call (Isa. 65: 24). . . . prayer is personal address to a personal God.[2]

Thus, church prayer begins in faith-based intimacy and relationship with the revealed God of the Bible.

The Bible's Role in Church Prayer

The church that does not keep its prayer beliefs and practices moored to Holy Scripture will soon find itself astray in a myriad of popular, counterfeit prayer beliefs and experiences. This will choke the praying life out of the church. It will poison the free flowing work of the Spirit's life through and in the church. The Bible's role in church prayer is multifaceted to say the least, but in the remaining pages I will attempt to discuss that role as it relates to church prayer beliefs and practices.

The Bible and Church Prayer Beliefs

The Bible ensures a proper theological foundation for church prayer. It provides the appropriate standard or paradigm for beliefs, instructions and models relating to local church prayer (see 2 Tim. 3:16-17). Biblical prayer beliefs help churches understand to whom they are praying and why they need to be holy people of prayer with biblical prayer priorities, focus, motives and expectations.

The Bible reveals a proper prayer relationship with the triune God. Biblical prayer beliefs anchor a church to the triune God in relationship and intimacy. Thus, a church prays to the holy-other, omniscient, omnipresent, and omnipotent God of the Bible who is Father and the great initiator of prayer (see Mt. 6:9; Isa. 45:5; Ps. 27:8; Jn. 15:16).

The Bible also reveals the need to pray through Jesus and in His name (see Jn. 16:23-24). Praying in Jesus' name keeps a church praying in God's character, will, intimacy and desires. This allows for the experience and promotion of the glory of God's name as churches pray.[3] Through Jesus, believers and churches experience communion and fellowship with the God of the universe and they fulfill their role as priests in His kingdom (see 1 Pet. 2:1-9; Rev. 1:6). This means they have confident access into His presence and eternal advocacy through Jesus' blood to ask with boldness and confidence (Heb. 7:25; 10:19-24).

Bible-based church prayer also involves Spirit-controlled and Spirit-aided prayer (see Eph. 6:18; Jude 20; Eph. 5:18). Prayer in God the Spirit allows for a life of prayer that is focused, filtered and fashioned by the Holy Spirit (see Rom. 8:26-27). This ensures Spirit-led and empowered church prayer that is God-centered and accomplishes God's agenda.

Biblical church prayer is characterized by lifestyles of holiness and godliness. James 5:16 says, "The effective, fervent prayer of a righteous man avails much" (also see Ps. 66:18 and 1 Pet. 1:15-16). David's prayer in Psalm 51:10-13 also shows a proper understanding of a holy life of prayer as it relates to relationship and service. The people of Israel were defeated in battle until the sin of Achan was confessed and dealt with (see Joshua 7). Corporate prayer power and effectiveness in mission are greatly affected by personal and corporate holiness.[4]

The Bible provides instruction on prayer's priority and foundational role in the body of Christ. Moses, Nehemiah, David, Isaiah, Ezekiel, Daniel and many of the Minor Prophets all demonstrate their belief in prayer's priority in personal and corporate life (see Ex. 33:1ff; Neh. 1:1-11; 2 Sam. 24:25; Isaiah 1, 6:1-9; Ezk. 37:1-11; Daniel 9). Paul urged Timothy to make Great Commission-centered prayer for all men first place in His ministry and in the church (see 1 Tim. 2:1-8). Jesus expects prayer to be foundational and teaches/models prayer's priority to His followers (see Mt. 6:5-13, Jn. 17:1-24 and Lk. 11:1-6).

Luke's summary statement in Acts 2:42 shows the early church modeled and maintained the priority of prayer. Theirs was a lifestyle of prayer that seemed to permeate everything they did (e.g., 1:14, 6:1-6). This created a ripe environment, a "tropical climate" or "atmosphere" for fruitful, God-centered prayer.[5]

The Bible ensures a proper missional and kingdom focus in prayer. In Acts, the early Church demonstrates a life of prayer-permeated witness where prayer was not only a core belief, but was also vital component or "prime-necessity" for the evangelistic mission (see Acts 1:14, 2:42, 4:23-33, 13:1-3).[6] The temptation in church prayer is to turn inward and focus on selfish temporal desires and agendas. The Bible constantly points churches toward a prayer life that is kingdom-focused and missional at its core (see Mt. 6:9-10; John 17).

The Bible challenges the church to examine its motives in prayer. James 4:3 says, "You ask and do not receive, because you ask amiss, that you may spend it on your pleasures." Proper motives allow the community of faith to grow in "boundary dissolution" rather that in "boundary maintenance."[7]

Bible-centered prayer beliefs allow for proper prayer expectations. This is seen in Acts 4:23-33 as early believers exercised a vibrant faith and trusted their Creator God to grant them boldness to preach while facing great opposition. Their expectations were based upon their faith and trust in the sovereign, providential work of Christ in their midst and not upon any preconceived assumptions related to their present situation.[8]

The Bible and Church Prayer Practices

As with prayer beliefs, the Bible sets appropriate standards, paradigms or examples relating to local church prayer practices. Below, I will examine four primary areas where the Bible provides helpful guidance and instruction relating to church prayer practices.

The Bible presents the need for both personal and corporate prayer practices within the local church. People of prayer will produce congregations that pray. Praying people who practice a lifestyle of prayer will lead the church toward unceasing "one-accord" prayer (see Acts 4:23).[9] Personal and corporate prayer practices permeate the Old Testament. Jesus prayed alone, with and for His followers. The early Church, as seen in Acts and in the epistles, practiced individual and corporate prayer (see Acts 1:14; 2:42). Prayer community and culture should always be the goal (i.e., house of prayer motif, Mk. 11:17). Grenz correctly comments, "Prayer that occurs in solitude reaches outward to the communal prayer that we share together. At the same time, our participation together in communal prayer lays the foundation for the praying that we do alone. . . . even in the solitude of our private 'prayer chamber' we continue to say 'Our Father.'"[10]

The Bible teaches churches correct prayer forms, methods and expressions. Biblical prayer involves both monologue and dialogue prayer. Biblical characters and communities practiced unceasing prayer through intimacy, fellowship and relationship. Biblical prayer expressions for personal, community, and congregational prayer should therefore include talking prayers of adoration (Mt. 6:9), confession (1 Jn. 1:9), petition (Rom.10:1-2; Neh. 4:9), intercession (1 Tim. 2:1-4), consecration (Jon. 2:1-10), lamentation (Lam. 3: 41-55) and thanksgiving (Ps. 100:4-5). Listening prayer forms such as contemplative, abiding and "being still" prayer patterns should also be practiced (Ps. 46:10). Biblical prayer patterns show that different prayer postures including sitting, standing, walking, lying and kneeling to pray are appropriate. The Bible also demonstrates that there are no location or place requirements or limitations placed on the practice of prayer. Praying is done in gardens, boats, in synagogues, on the cross, on the roadways and in small group and corporate worship settings.[11]

The Bible teaches and models strategic prayer practices. Old Testament characters prayed strategic prayers. Moses prayed (with Aaron and Hur's assistance) strategically for Joshua's defeat of Amelek in Rephidim (Ex. 17:8-13). Ezra (Ezra 9), David (Psalms 40, 51) and Isaiah (Isa. 6:1-11) also prayed strategic prayers at pivotal moments when God's mission through their lives was being hindered, halted or slowed. These prayers were therefore very specific and focused on current situations or scenarios and were need-based toward the fulfillment of Divine purposes and plans.

The New Testament is also replete with examples of strategic prayer patterns. Jesus prayed strategically outside the tomb of Lazarus and while on the cross (see Jn. 11:41-42; Lk. 23:34).[12] Jesus also prayed for the completion of His mission in John 17. This prayer serves as a model for strategic prayer toward the mission of the Church as He prayed for His followers to be kept in His name, from the evil one, sanctified in the truth, unified in mission and present with Him in His mission and future glory (see Jn. 17:11-24).

Paul prays strategic prayers for the rapid advance of the gospel and for open doors and protection to share effectively with the lost (see Col. 4:2-6; 2 Thess. 3:2). The early church models strategic prayer for the advancement of the mission through persecution and in missionary endeavors (Acts 4:23-33). These examples demonstrate the need for churches to practice strategic prayer patterns where specific need-based prayers are prayed as they relate to the fulfillment of God's purposes in and through the church.[13]

The Bible provides content and guidance for the practice of church prayer. Praying the promises of God's Word keeps churches grounded in prayer toward God's will. This produces powerful, effective prayers because they are based on God's promises, purposes and desires. Ezra prayed the Word of God after arriving in Israel (see Ezra 9:5-15). Nehemiah's prayer in Nehemiah 1:1-11 was shaped and guided or by several Old Testament texts (see Lev. 26:33; Deut. 12:5-7 and 30:1-5). The same is true of many of David's prayers in Psalms.[14] In the New Testament Simeon prayed toward the arrival of the Messiah in Luke 2:32 (compare Isa. 9:2, 42:1-6, 49:5-6). Jesus used Old Testament scriptures in His prayers (see Mt. 27:46; Heb. 10:1-10) as did the early Church (Acts 4:23-31).

Conclusion

In this brief treatment we have examined the Bible as it relates to church prayer beliefs and practices. We have shown that church prayer beliefs and practices need to be shaped or molded by biblical prayer beliefs and practices. This ensures a proper grounding, so that the winds and waves of theological heresy and experiential aberrations will not consume a church's life of prayer thus producing counterfeit prayer beliefs and practices which are ineffective, self-centered or misguided.

Questions for Further Thought or Discussion

1. Why is it important for leaders to grow and develop biblical prayer beliefs and practices within the life of the church? Share personal examples and /or experiences where prayer practices have been or need to be shaped by biblical teachings?
2. Give one example of a strategic Bible-based prayer? How might a congregation incorporate strategic biblical prayer practices into its praying life?
3. How are you or your congregation doing regarding missional/Great Commission prayer patterns? Are your personal/corporate prayer efforts focused on temporal, felt needs or on kingdom, eternal needs? Are you praying God's prayer list for your world?

The author: Dr. J. Chris Schofield is Director of the Office of Prayer for Evangelization and Spiritual Awakening, Baptist State Convention of North Carolina. He is the author of numerous works including *The Gospel for the New Millennium; Prayerwalking Made Simple;* and *Prayer Prompts for Prayer Groups* as well as articles in *Journal of the American Society of Church Growth and Church Administration.*

SUGGESTED ADDITIONAL READING

Carson, D. A., ed. *Teach Us To Pray: Prayer in the Bible and the World*. Eugene, OR: Wipf and Stock Publishers, 1990, 2002.

Crump, David. *Knocking on Heaven's Door.* Grand Rapids: Baker Academic, 2006.

Franklin, John. *And the Place Was Shaken.* Nashville: Broadman & Holman Publishers, 2005.

Grenz, Stanley J. *Prayer: The Cry for the Kingdom*, rev. ed. Grand Rapids: William B. Eerdmans Publishing Company, 2005.

Martin, Glen and Ginter, Dian. *Power House: A Step-By-Step Guide to Building a Church That Prays.* Nashville: Broadman & Holman Publishers, 1994.

ENDNOTES

1. Stanley J. Grenz, *A Cry for the Kingdom*, rev. ed. (Grand Rapids: Wm. B. Eerdmans, 1988, 2005), p. 1.

2. Edmund P. Clowney, "A Biblical Theology of Prayer," in *Teach Us to Pray*, ed. D. A. Carson (Grand Rapids: Baker Book House, 1990), p. 136.

3. See Andrew T. Lincoln, "God's Name, Jesus' Name, and Prayer in the Fourth Gospel," in *Into God's Presence*, ed. Richard N. Longenecker, (Grand Rapids: Wm. B. Eerdmans, 2002), pp. 177-179.

4. Selwyn Hughes comments, "God does not just answer prayer, He answers you!" See Selwyn Hughes, *Everyday With Jesus* (Nashville: Broadman & Holman, 2004), p. 15.

5. G. F. Oliver says that "Prayer is the tropical climate of the soul." P. T Forsyth says that prayer is the "atmosphere of revelation" for the believer and thus for the church. The praying church is a place where "God Encounters" through His Word are common occurrences. See G. F. Oliver, *Soul-Winner's Secrets* (Cincinnati: Jennings and Pye, 1902), p. 38; and P. T. Forsyth, *The Soul of Prayer* (3d. ed. Vancouver: Regent College Publishing, 1916), p. 31.

6. See Michael Green, *Evangelism in the Early Church* (Grand Rapids: Wm. B. Eerdmans, 1970, 1991), p. 235.

7. This refers to the stretching of the churches vision. Motive in prayer will greatly influence a church's willingness to reach its community and the world with the good news. Motive flows out of proper relationship and understanding of purpose and function. For more see Timothy Chester, "The Message of Prayer," Derek Tidball, ed. in *The Bible Speaks Today* (Downers Grove, IL: InterVarsity Press, 2003).

8. The followers of Christ understood the risks and demonstrate here a

healthy perspective toward prayer. They knew that all things were possible with God—but in the same way they understood that all things may not be permissible or within the realm of God's purposes. For more on this see David Crump, *Knocking on Heaven's Door* (Grand Rapids: Baker Books, 2006), pp. 56-58.

9. Young Christians will learn a great deal about prayer as they pray with more mature believers in corporate prayer experiences. For more on this see Daniel Henderson, *Fresh Encounters* (Colorado Springs: NavPress, 2004), pp. 108-111.

10. Grenz, *A Cry for the Kingdom,* p. 106.

11. For more on biblical prayer forms, expression and methods see, Howard Peskett, "Prayer in the Old Testament Outside the Psalms," in *Teach Us to Pray*, pp. 19-34; D. A. Carson, *A Call to Spiritual Reformation* (Grand Rapids: Baker, 1992).

12. Many of these prayers are intercessory wish petitions. For more on Paul's intercessory wish prayers see Crump, *Knocking on Heaven's Door*, pp. 231-235 or see Gordon P. Wiles, *Paul's Intercessory Prayers* (New York: Cambridge University Press, 1974).

13. Strategic prayers should include both immediate and long-term prayer needs. Also, in the New Testament strategic prayers are often, but not always, associated with the use of *deomai*. See Matthew 9:35-38; Romans 10:1-2; Acts 4:23-31 and compare Matthew 6:9-13 and 2 Thessalonians 3:1-2.

14. For more see Rick Shepherd, *Praying God's* Way (Chattanooga: AMG Publishers, 2003), pp. 79-82. For a brief but excellent look at prayer in Psalms see Howard Peskett, "Prayer in the Psalms," in *Teach Us to Pray*, pp. 35-57.

chapter

42

THE PLACE OF PRAYER IN THE EARLY CHURCH

Steve Booth

In trying to understand the place of prayer in the early Christian Church, we would do well to remember that the Church was born in the cradle of Judaism. Over the centuries the Church has developed its own forms and practices, but it did not have to invent new ones *ex nihilo*. The apostles, like their Master, were all steeped in the Jewish faith and shaped somewhat by the religious life of the temple and the synagogue. The first converts were drawn in large from this milieu, whether in Palestine or throughout the Diaspora. So it would be safe to surmise that the earliest Christians understood and practiced prayer from a context of Jewish traditions.

Of course, Christianity and Judaism had distinct differences from the start, the most significant perhaps being the centrality of Jesus and

His reinterpretation of the Jewish religion. Jesus participated in temple worship, but in some sense He also replaced the temple and the sacrificial system. Jesus attended and preached in synagogues throughout His Galilean ministry, but He called out a new people, which would soon include both Gentiles and Jews, to be the people of God.

In addition to Jesus' teaching on prayer His own personal example set the tone and pattern for prayer in the early Church. As the believers devoted themselves to the apostles' teaching, we can assume that this included Jesus' instructions on how we should pray (Mt. 28:20; Acts 2:42). We note also that the role of the Holy Spirit in every aspect of the life of the Church, including and especially its prayer life, marks a new age that has dawned with the birth of the Church (Acts 2:1ff; 13:2).

The place to begin our survey of prayer in the early Church is the book of Acts. If we can say that the Church was born in the cradle of Judaism, it is equally true that the first breath drawn by the Church—and every breath since—is the breath of prayer. Immediately after Christ's ascension the eleven apostles returned from the Mount of Olives to the upper room where they were staying in Jerusalem. Luke records that these men, along with Jesus' mother and brothers and some other women, were continually united in prayer (Acts 1:14). This was surely the setting of the meeting shortly thereafter when Peter led the group to fill the vacancy left by Judas. After two candidates were put forward, those gathered prayed and then cast lots. (In 1:24-25 the prayer itself is recorded.)

Peter exhorted the crowd on the day of Pentecost to call on the name of the Lord to be saved. A prayer of repentance would lead to the forgiveness of sin (2:21, 38). A hallmark of these new kingdom citizens was their commitment to prayer (2:42). At this time there was still some measure of participation in the scheduled prayer times at the temple (3:1) but also more spontaneously in each other's homes (2:46-47, 5:42) where fellowship and teaching were also enjoyed. At meal times we can be sure that prayers of thanksgiving to God were offered, even if it occurred on a ship in the midst of a storm (27:35)!

It was natural for the early Christians to respond in prayer whenever their hearts were full of thanksgiving or praise to God. The lame man who was healed praised God (3:8) as did all those who witnessed the miracle (4:21; cf.11:18, 21:20—where people glorified God because people were being saved).

The swell of support after this very public miracle led to Peter and John's arrest and interrogation by the Sanhedrin. Subsequently they were released because there were no grounds for punishment. Luke records the response of the believers to their testimony, which includes the longest recorded prayer in Acts (4:24-30). Having seen the boldness of Peter and John, they prayed for more boldness to proclaim the gospel. God heard and answered their prayer, for the place where they had gathered was shaken (v. 31)!

Prayer continued to play an important role in the early Church especially when leaders were being appointed or singled out for special service. The apostles in Jerusalem realized the necessity of narrowing their duties to prayer and the ministry of the word (6:4), while others were appointed to the ministry of meeting the physical needs of the widows (6:3). When the seven were chosen, the apostles prayed for and laid hands on these co-laborers (6:6).

In Antioch Paul and Barnabas were sent off on their first missionary journey after the church fasted, prayed, and laid hands on them (13:3). As a strategy Paul and Barnabas initially engaged the synagogues in order to proclaim the gospel. We can assume that they participated in prayers that were held there, as well as in designated places of prayers in cities that did not have synagogues (13:5; 16:13, 16). As churches were established, they appointed elders and committed them to the Lord by prayer and fasting (14:23).

Another occasion when prayer is found in conjunction with the laying on of hands is in Acts 8. When the apostles in Jerusalem heard that the Samaritans had received the gospel, they sent Peter and John to verify the news. These new believers had been baptized but had not yet received the Holy Spirit. Peter and John prayed for them and laid hands on them and they received the Spirit (vv. 15, 17). Paul also laid hands on and prayed for the healing of Publius' father on the island of Malta (28:8).

On a number of occasions in Acts we find visions in connection with prayer. Saul of Tarsus had a vision on the road to Damascus and conversed with the risen Lord. Afterwards, in his state of blindness, Paul prayed while waiting to learn what to do next. The Lord then appeared to Ananias in a vision and informed him that Saul too had had a vision of a man named Ananias coming in and placing hands on him to regain his sight (9:11-12). Paul later testified that after his conversion he returned to Jerusalem and was at the temple praying when he had another vision of the risen Lord. In this encounter Paul received his commission to be the Lord's messenger to the Gentiles (22:17-21).

This is not unlike the account of both Cornelius in Caesarea and Peter in Joppa. Cornelius is described as a devout God-fearer who did many charitable deeds and always prayed to God. It was during a time of prayer in his home when an angel of God appeared to him and informed him that God had heard his prayers (10:1-4; 30). The very next day Peter also was praying on the roof of the house where he was staying, when he too had a vision from the Lord (vv. 9-10, 11:4). One common element in these visions is that the person both speaks to and receives instructions from a heavenly messenger.

As we might expect, times of crisis for the church or for individuals were times of prayer. A key prayer passage in Acts is found in chapter 12. After Herod Agrippa I executed the Apostle James, Peter too was arrested and placed on death row. Luke records that "constant prayer was offered to God for him by the church" (v. 5). An all-night prayer vigil was held at the home of Mary, the mother of John Mark. In this instance God's will lined up with the prayers of God's people, and Peter was miraculously sprung from the prison (vv. 6-10). Of course the irony and humor in the story is that initially the Church was too busy praying to realize that God had already answered their prayers (vv. 11-17)!

In contrast when Paul and Silas were imprisoned for disturbing the peace in Philippi, the prayer meeting was conducted within the jail cell. What a concert their fellow inmates must have witnessed as the two missionaries prayed and sang hymns to God until midnight (16:25). While an earthquake gave them opportunity to escape as Peter had, they remained where they were, which led to the conversion of the jailor and his entire household. Obviously there were prayers of repentance and rejoicing offered that night in Philippi.

When Stephen faced his personal crisis, he also responded by praying. Just as Jesus had prayed at His approaching death, Stephen prayed, "Lord Jesus, receive my spirit!" He also followed his Lord's example by asking that the Lord not charge his executioners with this sin (7:59-60). What is significant in this instance is that Stephen prayed directly to Jesus rather than to God the Father. In a similar way, Peter instructed Simon the sorcerer to pray to the Lord for forgiveness when he tried to purchase the power of dispensing the Holy Spirit (8:22, 24).

A final observation made about prayer in the early church is that on a number of occasions kneeling is mentioned as the posture taken. Stephen knelt to pray as he was being stoned (7:60). When Peter was informed of the death of Dorcas in Joppa, he knelt to pray alone in the upper room where her body had been placed (9:40). After Paul gave his farewell address to the Ephesian elders at Miletus, he knelt down and prayed with them before boarding his ship (20:36). Later on that same journey, after staying with the disciples in Tyre for a week, men, women and children from the church escorted Paul to the beach, where they all knelt to pray before he departed (21:5). Early Christians didn't always fall to their knees in prayer, but on certain occasions it seems that it was most fitting.

In summary, we can say that prayer has been the life-breath of the Church from its inception. From the earliest days believers have devoted themselves to prayer, individually and corporately, just as Jesus intended. In Luke's history of the expansion of the church as in his gospel, prayer plays a key role. In the pages of Acts we discover all types of prayers—prayers of repentance, thanksgiving, rejoicing, praise and more. We see the Church praying in times of decision making and in times of crisis. We see them fasting, laying on hands, and kneeling. On occasion God spoke to his people through visions as they prayed. Both leaders and members in the early Church were committed to prayer as an indispensable part of the Christian life. Their example has challenged believers of every generation to be a people devoted to prayer.

Questions for Further Thought or Discussion:

1. What can be learned about prayer in the early Church from Paul's Epistles?
2. What can be learned about prayer in the early Church from Acts?
3. What is the significance of the three Aramaic words that are closely tied to the prayer life of the early Church—abba, amen, and maranatha?

The author: Dr. Steve Booth is Academic Dean and Professor of New Testament and Greek at the Canadian Southern Baptist Seminary in Cochran, Alberta, Canada. He is the author of *Selected Peak Marking Features in the Gospel of John* and is a regular contributor to *Biblical Illustrator* (LifeWay)

SUGGESTED ADDITIONAL READING

Martin, R.P, *Worship in the Early Church.* Grand Rapids: Eerdmans, 1974.

Fisher, Fred L. *Prayer in the New Testament.* Philadelphia: Westminster Press, 1964.

Bradshaw, Paul F. *Daily Prayer in the Early Church: A Study of the Origin and Early Development of the Divine Office.* New York: Oxford University Press, 1982.

Carson, D. A, ed. *Teach Us To Pray: Prayer in the Bible and the World.* Grand Rapids: Baker, 1990.

chapter

43

THE MEANING OF "A HOUSE OF PRAYER"

Dennis Fuqua

One of the wonderful movements throughout the church today is an increase in the conviction on the part of pastors and others that God wants His church to be a "house of prayer." This is a desire that crosses theological and denominational lines, racial lines, generational lines, and stylistic lines. It is demonstrated by new prayer campaigns, fresh approaches to prayer, the growth of conferences, books, and programs dealing with prayer, and the number of congregations hiring full-time prayer pastors. It is a grass-roots movement that cannot be traced or stopped. As this movement increases it becomes more important to have a clear understanding of the desired outcome.

What is a "house of prayer?" What did Jesus and Isaiah mean when they referred to it? "He taught, saying to them, 'Is it not written, "My house shall be called a house of prayer for all nations"? But you have made it a den of thieves'" (Mk. 11:17).

Jesus cared deeply about His Father's house. When He was as young as twelve years old, it was already a topic He had evidently spoken of with His parents (see Lk. 2:49). Early in His earthly ministry a zeal for it caused Him to make a whip of chords and drive out people who were misusing it (see Jn. 2:14-17). Then toward the end of His earthly ministry He cleansed it a second time, overturning tables and benches, causing major upheaval. His explanation for His actions was that what God had intended as a house of prayer had become a den of robbers (see Mk. 11:15-17). Jesus cared about what happened in God's house and He cared about how people viewed it.

In the Mark 11 passage above, please notice the five words immediately following Jesus' quote from Isaiah 56. They are very telling. Read them slowly. "But you have made it . . . " "But" draws a contrast between what God intended and what had occurred. "You" refers to the people who were supposed to make God's house a house of prayer. "Have made it" speaks of the ability people have to shape God's work into something other than what He had in mind. In that context God's house had become a "den of thieves." Whenever we alter God's plan with our plans both God and people are robbed. We have made His house a house of teaching, a house of activities, a house of fellowship, a house of music, etc. These are good things, but God still desires His house to be a house of prayer. To make this point, Jesus quotes the last line of Isaiah 56:7: "Also the sons of the foreigner who join themselves to the LORD, to serve him, and to love the name of the LORD, to be His servants—everyone who keeps from defiling the Sabbath, and holds fast My covenant—even them I will bring to My holy mountain, and make them joyful in My house of prayer. Their burnt offerings and their sacrifices will be accepted on My altar; for My house shall be called a house of prayer for all nations."

A key to understanding how Jesus thought about God's house in Mark 11 is to understand the context of Isaiah 56. The context of these two verses begins in verse 3 where God addresses two groups of people: foreigners and eunuchs. God says the foreigners should not say, "The Lord has utterly separated me." And the eunuchs should not say, "Here I am, a dry tree." He goes on in verses 4 and 5 to explain that the eunuchs who follow God will have a memorial and a name better than physical children. Then, in verses 6 and 7, God addresses the foreigners.

When this text was written a foreigner was someone who was not part of the Hebrew culture. Foreigners today would be those who are not part of our Christian culture; those who are unfamiliar with how to develop a meaningful relationship with Jesus. The essence of God's message to these *foreigners* who seek to follow Him is that they will not be excluded! The way God communicates this wonderful (and radical) message is by inviting them into His house.

The invitation to come to God's house is open to all foreigners who meet certain conditions. It is an open invitation in that it is not limited to any one group of people. But it is a conditional invitation in that those who respond must respond in ways prescribed by God. These are people who *join themselves* (commit themselves) to the Lord. This commitment is expressed in three specific ways. They commit to *serve Him*, to *love His name*, and to *worship Him*. As we respond to this invitation, each of them become blessings not burdens.

They are also people who *keep His Sabbath*. From Hebrews 3 and 4, I believe this means they continuously live in a state of remembering what God has done, they rest in His finished work, and they live a reverent life-style that is different from others who are not following the Lord.

Finally, they are people who *keep His covenant*. The New Testament application of this would be for us to live in the wonder of the new covenant where we embrace what God has done us rather than seek to fulfill any code of external standards. It is the difference between God saying to us, "You shall not (or shall)" which is the essence of the first covenant (see Ex. 20:1-17) and Him saying to us, "I have" and "I will" which is the essence of the new covenant (see Jer. 31:31-34).

Those who meet these three conditions can claim three divine promises. They can anticipate God bringing them to *His holy mountain*. God's holy mountain is a reference to the place where God met Moses just after the Exodus (see Exodus 19). In a sense this was the first "house of prayer." He is the one who will bring them to a place where they can meet with Him in a powerful way. It is not dependant upon them and their ability, it is dependant upon God and His ability to get them from where they are to God's holy mountain.

These people can also anticipate great *joy* in the process. According to

Psalm 16 there is great and lasting joy at God's right hand. The process of developing a closer relationship with Jesus through prayer is one that yields great joy because it is a place where we see the growth of the fruit of the Spirit (Gal. 5:22-23) and the kingdom of God (Rom. 14:17). Those who seek Him regularly and gaze upon His beauty are radiant and always have their deepest requests met (Ps. 27:4 and 34:5). This joy is something that God gives to those who respond to His invitation to come to His house.

And these foreigners who seek Him will also have the assurance that their *offerings and sacrifices* will be accepted by the Lord. Offerings and sacrifices were not about ritual, they were about relationship. They were and are about presenting ourselves and those things we value to Him. The promise that God would accept their offerings and sacrifices is the promise that they would have a deeper relationship with Him. If they draw near to Him, He will draw near to them (see Jas. 4:8).

Buildings and People

God's house is referred to three times in Isaiah 56:7 ("my house of prayer," "my house," and "a house of prayer"). The most obvious meaning of this phrase is the place where God lives, or dwells. I live in my house, you live in your house, God lives in His house. Throughout Scripture there are two kinds of places where God has lived and does live; in His buildings and in His people.

The reason God instructed Moses to build the tabernacle was so He would have a dwelling place, that is, a place to live, among His people. Exodus 25:8 says, "Let them make Me a sanctuary, that I may dwell among them." What an amazing thought that Moses and the people built a place where God's omnipresence became His manifest presence. Everything about this structure pointed toward communication with God. Primarily referred to as the Tent of Meeting, it was also known as the house of the Lord from the time of Moses to the time when Solomon built the temple (see 1 Chron. 9:23). This was the place of God's dwelling on earth. It was to be treated differently than all other places.

After several centuries, David still understood the special significance of the house of the Lord. He rejoiced to go there (Ps. 122:1), he longed to spend his days there (27:4) and he looked forward to spending eternity there (23:6).

It would have been his greatest delight to build the Lord a permanent house but that assignment belonged to Solomon, his son. David received detailed plans from the Lord and he passed them on to Solomon (see 1 Chron. 28). He also gave a huge amount of his personal fortune (including 110 tons of gold and 260 tons of silver) for its construction (see 1 Chron. 29) and considered it a great privilege (v. 14).

Solomon also understood this special assignment and gave himself diligently to fulfill it. He employed over 153,000 men for seven years to construct the temple (see 1 K. 6:38 and 1 Chron. 2:2). When it was dedicated, fire from heaven, representing the glory of the Lord, came into that place (see 1 Chron. 7:1-3).

This temple was the physical place Isaiah referred to when he said that God's house would be called a house of prayer for all nations. And, though it had been destroyed and rebuilt, this was the place Jesus referred to as well.

The house Isaiah and Jesus referred to was this special, physical place where God's manifest presence was very evident. This was the place where people from all nations who had a heart to be with this living and loving God would be able to come and enjoy deeper relationship with Him through prayer.

But God not only dwelt in the tabernacle and the temple, He also dwelt in people. Even in the Old Testament, God said, "I dwell in the high and holy place, with him who has a contrite and humble spirit, to revive the spirit of the humble and to revive the heart of the contrite ones" (Isa. 57:15). People have always been God's most desired dwelling place.

In fact, in the New Testament believers are referred to as being the temple of God, the place where His Spirit lives today. Paul, understanding the significant role of the tabernacle and the temple, said that we, individually (1 Cor. 6:19-20) and collectively (3:16-17), are the dwelling place of God today. A shift has taken place. God's primary dwelling place (His primary house) was once a building, now it is people.

So now, when we think of the comments of both Isaiah and Jesus about God's house being a house of prayer for all nations, we no longer need to look for a special place, nor are we to point people to a special place. As His people, whether we are gathered or scattered, we are to *be* that place. We are to be His house. We are to be a place where relationship with God flows very naturally through prayer. And we are to be a place where others ("foreigners") are invited and assisted to a relationship with God through prayer. Our individual lives and our congregational activities are to be an invitation to the joy, the assurance, and the acceptance that God offers those who want to commit themselves to Him, to serve Him, to love His name, and to worship Him. We are to make it easy for "foreigners" to find their way into greater relationship with God.

Questions for Further Thought and Discussion

1. Prior to reading this chapter, how would you describe your understanding of the phrase "A house of prayer for all nations?"
2. What are some differences between God dwelling in a building and God dwelling in people?
3. How can an individual and a congregation demonstrate that they are a house of prayer?

The author: Dennis Fuqua is President of International Renewal Ministries (Prayer Summits Network) of Portland, Oregon.

SUGGESTED ADDITIONAL READING

Glasser, Arthur. *Announcing the Kingdom: The Story of God's Mission in the Bible.* Grand Rapids: Baker Academics, 2006.

Peters, George. *A Biblical Theology of Missions.* Chicago: Moody Press, 1972.

Franklin, John. *A House of Prayer.* Nashville: LifeWay Press, 1999.

Tekyl, Terry. *Encounter: A Blueprint for the House of Prayer.* Muncie, IN: Prayer Point Press, 1997.

chapter

44

HOW TO BUILD A HOUSE OF PRAYER

Dave Butts

Knowing that God's house is to be a house of prayer is one thing. Knowing how to build that house is another. The Bible tells us that unless the Lord builds the house, those who labor, labor in vain. That is especially so when we are speaking of a local congregation that becomes so impacted and driven by prayer that it truly could be called a house of prayer.

God's Word contains no blueprints for building a house of prayer. Looking about at various congregations that are known for their strong focus on prayer also leaves us without a clear pattern. Each of these churches seem to have grown and developed in prayer according to its own corporate personality and distinctiveness. Most of us who work in helping churches grow in prayer have studiously avoided any cookie-cutter methodology. The Divine Builder seems to be custom-building His houses of prayer.

Still, there are principles that are true in all prayer-driven churches. Discovering and implementing those principles should help any congregation move toward the goal of seeing prayer become pervasive throughout the Body.

Pray about prayer.

The simplest and most basic of those principles is that we should pray about prayer. Several years ago I was with a group of prayer leaders who met with the staff of the Brooklyn Tabernacle, certainly a fine example of a house of prayer. In the midst of the conversation, the question arose of how the congregation had begun and continued this journey of prayer. The answer was swift: "We asked God to pour out a spirit of prayer." Though we tried to talk about methodologies, the staff of Brooklyn Tabernacle were adamant in their answer: "We must pray about prayer." If we truly believe that the Lord is the Builder of His house of prayer, then it makes sense that we come to Him first.

The formation of a prayer team to simply pray about the church becoming a house of prayer may well be the most important step to transform a local Body. In Zechariah 12:10 we read of a spirit of prayer being poured out upon a whole city: "And I will pour on the house of David and on the inhabitants of Jerusalem the spirit of grace and supplication." Use that passage to begin to pray for that spirit of prayer to fall upon your congregation.

Pastors must lead the way.

It is difficult, if not impossible to find a passionate, praying church without also finding a congregation that has come to understand the role of the pastor as the key person in becoming a house of prayer. Pastors cannot lead people where they themselves have not gone or are at least in the process of moving to. This is especially so in prayer. The praying pastor is a prerequisite for a church becoming a house of prayer.

In a very real sense, God will not allow it any other way. If a pastor is not a person of prayer, and is not desirous of the congregation growing in prayer, then a movement of prayer within the church actually begins to look and feel like rebellion. God isn't in the business of blessing rebellion against legitimate leaders, even if they are leaders who don't understand the importance and centrality of prayer for a healthy church. This is why it is so important for prayer leaders to consistently pray for their pastors.

It also speaks to the role of the seminary and Bible college in training church leaders regarding the importance of leading the church in prayer. Those of us who attended Bible college or seminary are grateful for the tools we received for ministry. But one tool that was consistently neglected by the vast part of our educational institutions was that of prayer ministry. It was assumed that pastors would pray, and most of us do. But the role of prayer in church growth, shepherding, and spiritual transformation was absent from our instruction. The Church today is paying a price for that neglect as we focus more on human methodologies and less on the power of God released through prayer.

Leaders must be engaged.

It is not only pastors who must lead out in prayer. There must be an ownership of the concept of becoming a house of prayer by the total leadership of the church. To become a praying church will require structural changes that can only be achieved as a local leadership moves together under the leadership of the Holy Spirit.

A very practical way to build this concept into leaders is to slowly but clearly bring more and more prayer into the leadership and business meetings of the church. This will take patience as well as creativity as prayer is made an integral part of how business is done in the Lord's church.

One of the most important steps for leadership is to develop the biblical foundation upon which a house of prayer must be built. Rather than viewing this as the latest "church fad," it is vital that leaders understand the biblical imperatives of a praying church. Perhaps the best study would be to examine the book of Acts and see how pervasive prayer was in the life of the early Church. A desire to move in apostolic direction should lead us to the apostolic secret of much prayer.

A Functioning Prayer Ministry Team

Most praying churches have developed a team of people whose responsibility is to call the church to prayer and keep prayer in the forefront of the church's activities and consciousness. The particular job description of a prayer ministry team will vary from church to church, but will often include:

- planning prayer meetings.
- overseeing prayer education and training events.

- developing intercessory prayer teams for church leaders.
- assisting other church ministries with their prayer focus.
- connecting the church to larger prayer events outside the scope of the local church.
- organizing Sunday morning prayer teams to cover worship services in prayer.

One of the most critical decisions for a church is the formation of a prayer ministry team. A common mistake is to fill that team with those whose major passion and ministry is that of intercession. These dear people are basically being asked to operate outside of their gifting and calling. The prayer ministry team is essentially an organizing, serving and administrative group. Look for those who believe in the power of prayer and have gifts of organization and serving.

This team needs to work closely with the administrative leadership of the church. Its members should see themselves as the team that carries out the desires of church leadership to make the church a house of prayer. Rather than an "outsiders" group that is trying to infiltrate the congregation with prayer, it needs to be seen as the ultimate "insiders" group that has received its commission from the church's leadership to bring prayer into every aspect of church life.

Prayer Meetings that "Pop"

One of the reasons that people don't go to prayer meetings is that they've already gone to one . . . and don't want to go back. Most prayer meetings are poorly attended, poorly planned, and lacking in enthusiasm and effectiveness. This should never be the case. Prayer meetings ought to be the highpoint in the life of believers . . . a time to be ushered into the throne room of God to worship Him and present our requests before Him.

There are several keys to a good prayer meeting that "pops" with excitement. One very basic shift is to move from a need-based prayer meeting to a worship-based meeting. A traditional need-based meeting begins with someone asking the dreaded question, "Does anyone have any prayer needs?" That typically leads to a long period of discussing needs of people rather than praying.

Daniel Henderson, in his excellent book, *Fresh Encounters*, teaches about moving prayer meetings from need-based to worship-based. Prayers that emerge out of times of worship are typically much more God-centered than man-centered. These times of prayer stay fresh and dynamic because of their focus on God.

Another powerful prayer meeting style can be developed around themes. For instance, a church could announce that on a certain night, they would meet to pray about the missions program of the church. The prayer ministry team meets in advance with the missions team and they plan an evening that engages the senses and pulls people into times of serious prayer for missionaries. Maps on the wall, pictures of missionaries, scriptures that focus on the Great Commission, appropriate lighting, music, and décor can give attendees a powerful prayer experience.

Both the worship-based prayer meeting and thematic prayer meeting are based on one assumption . . . someone is planning the prayer meeting. Somehow we have allowed prayer meetings to degenerate into an unplanned, disorganized event in which not a lot gets accomplished for the kingdom. When I am asked to lead a prayer meeting, I feel a solemn responsibility to prepare myself spiritually and to plan carefully. Why? Because I am leading people into the presence of God! What an awesome responsibility. Good planning may be the most spiritual thing you can do as you lead a prayer meeting.

A Pervasive Prayer Strategy

Becoming a house of prayer is far more than adding a prayer meeting to an already hectic church calendar. It is a church in which prayer has become pervasive in all aspects of church life. Leaders and members of the congregation cannot imagine prayer not being a part of everything they do.

This will not happen automatically. It must be an intentional decision made first by leaders and then carried out systematically in the life of the church. There can be a basic church-wide accountability system in which, for every proposal made or program initiated, the question is asked, "Where is prayer in this?"

One way to organize this is to make sure that there is a prayer leader on every ministry team in the church. This is the person who, in a sense, advocates for prayer within that area of the congregation. For example, if a church has a worship team that oversees what takes place in worship services, there would be a prayer leader in that team who is monitoring the quality and quantity of prayer during the worship services. That person would have the freedom to work with the rest of the worship team to build prayer into the services.

This same system of organization could be used for the Christian education, youth, evangelism, and other ministry teams within a local congregation. In this way, prayer is not dependent upon one group of people, but permeates the church. The prayer ministry team in such a church will become the resource group for other teams as they build prayer into their respective areas.

Summary

The local congregation that begins to move toward becoming a house of prayer is changing more than methods and techniques. It is honoring the Lord by turning to Him first and by depending upon His power and might released through prayer. There is a spiritual dynamic that is unleashed within the body that cannot happen in any other way than through God's people bringing everything to the Lord in prayer.

Questions for Further Thought or Discussion

1. Have you ever attended or visited a church that you would consider a house of prayer? What was it about the church that caught your attention?
2. What was the most exciting prayer meeting you've participated in? What made it exciting?
3. How would you define a house of prayer? Write out a succinct definition that could give guidance to a church seeking to move in this direction.

The author: David Butts is the Chairman of America's National Prayer Committee and also President of Harvest Prayer Ministries of Terre Haute, Indiana. He is the author of *The Devil Goes to Church* and co-author with his wife, Kim of *Pray Like the King: Lessons from the Prayers of Israel's Kings.*

SUGGESTED ADDITIONAL READING

Sacks, Cheryl. *The Prayer Saturated Church.* Colorado Springs, CO: NavPress, 2004.

Graf, Jonathan, and Lani Hinkle, eds. *My House Shall Be a House of Prayer.* Colorado Springs, CO: *Pray!* Books 2001.

VanderGriend, Alvin. *The Praying Church Sourcebook.* Grand Rapids: CRC Publications 1997.

chapter

45

PRAYER MEETINGS AND REVIVAL IN THE CHURCH

Joel R. Beeke

"We shall never see much change for the better in our churches in general till the prayer meeting occupies a higher place in the esteem of Christians," wrote Charles Haddon Spurgeon in his famous address, "Only a Prayer Meeting."[1]

By "the prayer meeting" Spurgeon meant a formal meeting of members of a Christian congregation at stated times for the purpose of engaging in united prayer. Such meetings are the focus of this chapter. I choose to use "corporate prayer" below to refer to these meetings in distinction from formal worship services.

Prayer meetings in America have fallen on hard times. Less than ten percent of members now meet for prayer in churches that once had vibrant, Spirit-led meetings. In many churches, prayer meetings have become cold and boring. Other churches have never developed the tradition of meeting regularly for corporate prayer.

Lewis Thompson rightly wrote, "If it is true that the active piety of a church rises no higher than it manifests itself in the prayer-meeting, so that here, as on a barometer, all changes in spiritual life are faithfully recorded, then certainly too much attention cannot be given by both pastor and people to the conducting of the prayer-meeting."[2]

It is time to reassess the importance of prayer meetings, for the church that does not earnestly pray together cannot hope to experience revival and renewal. Have we forgotten that the Reformation era churches often held daily morning and evening services for preaching and prayer? Is it surprising that the Reformed faith has experienced more revival in Korea than anywhere else in the world in the last half-century when Christians there gather 365 mornings a year for prayer (at 5 a.m. in the summer and 6 a.m. in the winter)? Let us take a closer look at the history of prayer meetings in conjunction with revival.

Prayer meetings were influential in times of revival. The 1620s revival in Ireland was spurred on by prayer meetings.[3] So were awakenings in the 1740s. Two generations prior, Josiah Woodward had published *An Account of the Rise and Progress of the Religious Societies in the City of London,* which described forty distinct prayer groups in London.[4] As the awakenings spread, prayer meetings multiplied. Thomas Houston writes in his *The Fellowship Prayer Meeting,* "The awakenings which took place in various parts of England, under the ministry of Wesley and Whitefield, led to the establishment of social prayer-meetings; and, at this period, when *within* the pale of the National Establishment, and *without* it, all was under the torpor of spiritual death, this organization was a powerful means of exciting earnest minds to pursue after eternal concerns."[5]

Prayer meetings were also influential in eighteenth-century revivals in Scotland. Prior to the awakening in 1742, numerous prayer societies had sprung up. One society was established in Kilsyth in 1721; it flourished for some years, then died out in the 1730s, but was resurrected in 1742 just before revival broke out. During the meetings, there were public prayers, psalm-singing, Scripture reading, and discussion based on questions from Thomas Vincent's study of the Shorter Catechism.[6]

During the Great Awakening in Scotland, prayer meetings often began with children, then spread to adults. For example, a schoolteacher in the parish of Baldernock allowed four students to meet on their own for prayer and psalm singing. According to *The Parish of Baldernock*, "In the course of two weeks, ten or twelve more [children] were awakened and under deep convictions. Some of these were not more than eight or nine years of age, and others twelve or thirteen. And so much were they engrossed with the one thing needful as to meet thrice a day-in the morning, at mid-day, and at night." Adults then began holding prayer meetings two or more times a week. There were many conversions at both the adult and the children's meetings.

The fervor soon spread to other parishes. *The Parish of Kirkintillock* reports: "In the month of April, 1742, about sixteen children in the town were observed to meet together in a barn for prayer. Mr. Burnside [their pastor] heard of it, had frequent meetings with them, and they continued to improve. And this being reported, many more were impressed. Soon after, about a hundred and twenty [children] were under a more than ordinary concern, and praying societies, as usual, were formed."

Johnston's reaction to that awakening was to affirm and support the prayers of children. "Why not encourage children's prayer-meetings? Why may not God still perfect praises to the glory of his grace, out of the mouth of babes?" he asked.[7]

Jonathan Edwards also encouraged children's prayer. In answering objections some critics had raised to children's prayer meetings, he wrote, "God, in this work, has shown a remarkable regard to little children; never was there such a glorious work amongst persons in their childhood, as has been of late in New England. He has been pleased, in a wonderful manner, to perfect praise out of the mouths of babes and sucklings; and many of them have more of that knowledge and wisdom that please him, and render their religious worship acceptable, than many of the great and learned men of the world. I have seen many happy effects of children's religious meetings; and God has seemed often remarkably to own them in their meetings, and really descended from heaven to be amongst them. I have known several probable instances of children being converted at such meetings."[8]

In 1747, Edwards published *An Humble Attempt to Promote an Explicit Agreement and Visible Union of God's People through the World, in Extraordinary*

Prayer, for the Revival of Religion and the Advancement of Christ's Kingdom on Earth. Usually referred to thereafter as *An Humble Attempt,* this book was reprinted by Christian Focus in 2003 as *A Call to United, Extraordinary Prayer.* Edwards said he was motivated to write on "a concert of prayer" for two reasons: first, he realized that the revivals of the mid-1730s and the early 1740s would not recur until God's people engaged in earnest prayer for revival. Second, he wanted to provide additional theological support for a document written by some Scottish pastors simply entitled *Memorial.*

David Bryant tells us the story of *Memorial:* "Rising out of scores of prayer societies already functioning in Scotland around 1740, especially among young people, by 1744 a committee of ministers determined it was time to do more. They decided to try a two-year 'experiment,' uniting all prayer groups and praying Christians in their nation into a common prayer strategy. They called for focused revival prayer on every Saturday evening and Sunday morning, as well as on the first Tuesday of each quarter. By 1746 they were so gratified by the impact of their experiment that they composed a call to prayer to the church worldwide, especially in the colonies *(Memorial).* However, this time the 'concert of prayer' was to be for *seven* years."[9]

Citing Zechariah 8:20-22, Edwards said that God's rich promises encourage us to expect great success from corporate prayer. He said: "That which God abundantly makes the subject of His *promises,* God's people should abundantly make the subject of their *prayers."* He concluded that when believers persevere in united, concerted prayer, God will grant a fresh revival, which "shall be propagated, till the awakening reaches those that are in the highest stations, and till whole nations be awakened."[10]

Edwards's book had a limited influence during his lifetime. Republished late in the eighteenth century in England, it influenced William Carey (1761-1834) and his prayer group. It also affected John Sutclif (1752-1814), a well-known Baptist pastor in Olney, who led weekly prayer meetings for revival in the Baptist churches of the Northamptonshire Association, to which his church belonged. Those prayer meetings spread throughout the British Isles, particularly impacting eighteenth century revivals in Wales. Heman Humphrey writes in his *Revival Sketches,* "One of the most important revivals of religion, when the effects are considered, is that which occurred in the 'Principality of Wales' under Howell Harris and Daniel Rowlands; and this was carried forward and fostered by means of private societies for prayer and religious conference."[11] In the end, tens of thousands were converted throughout Britain from the 1790s to the 1840s.[12]

Edwards's treatise became a major manifesto for the Second Great Awakening around the beginning of the nineteenth century. It also fueled other awakenings in the late 1850s. Samuel Prime's *The Power of Prayer,* published by Banner of Truth Trust, explains how corporate prayer ushered in the famous 1857-1859 revival (sometimes called the Third Great Awakening) along the eastern coast of the United States, then spread west, resulting in the conversion of hundreds of thousands of people.

Beginning in the fall of 1857, six men gathered at noon every day for corporate prayer in the consistory room of a Reformed church in New York City. Prayer was the Spirit's means to germinate the seeds of revival. By early 1858 more than twenty prayer groups were meeting at noon in New York City. In Chicago, more than 2,000 people gathered daily for prayer at the Metropolitan Theatre. The movement spread to nearly all the major cities of America, then made its way to the British Isles and around the world. Prayer meetings sprang up everywhere: in churches, on college campuses, in hospitals, among sailors, on mission fields, and at orphanages and colleges. To mention only one example, at Hampden-Sydney College, one student found another student reading Joseph Alleine's *Alarm to the Unconverted,* and told him that there were two other students who were also in favor of such literature. The four students held a prayer meeting, while fellow students harassed them. When the president heard that the four young men were accused of holding a prayer meeting, he said with tears, "God has come near to us," and joined them himself at their next meeting. A remarkable revival swept through the college and into the surrounding area. Soon, more than half the college was attending prayer meetings.[13] Scholars estimate that two million or more were converted in the revivals of the late 1850s, while hundreds of thousands of professed Christians were deeply affected.

In the 1860s, Charles Spurgeon organized prayer meetings at the Metropolitan Tabernacle. People met at 7 a.m. and 7:30 p.m. every day. More than 3,000 came to the meeting on Monday evenings. One evening a visitor asked Spurgeon what accounted for the success of these meetings. Spurgeon walked his visitor to the sanctuary, opened the door, and let him watch the participants. Nothing more needed to be said.

The great revivals of the twentieth century were likewise inspired by prayer. The Welsh revival of 1904-05, the revival in Riga, Latvia, in 1934, and more recent revivals in Romania and Korea were all born and nurtured in prayer.[14] Today, most evangelical churches hold weekly prayer meetings, but there seems to be so much lukewarmness in prayer. We desperately need churches to unite in the kind of prayer that the Spirit may use to produce world-wide revival.

Praying together is often the means God uses to initiate or increase revival and renewal in the church. Let us treasure prayer meetings. Let us engage in them with all our heart, remembering that revivals usually begin with prayer meetings. As one divine put it, "The Holy Spirit loves to answer petitions that are appended with many signatures."

Let us keep praying. Let us pray without ceasing. God is able to do "exceedingly abundantly above all that we ask or think" (Eph. 3:20). Who can tell what He will do?

Questions for Thought or Discussion

1. Do the Scriptures provide us with divine warrant for prayer meetings? If so, where and why?
2. In addition to promoting revival, what other purposes do prayer meetings serve?
3. What could you do to enhance the level of participation at your church prayer meetings?

The author: Dr. Joel R. Beeke is President and Professor of Systematic Theology at Puritan Reformed Theological Seminary and Pastor of Heritage Netherlands Reformed Congregation in Grand Rapids, Michigan. He is the editor of *Banner of Sovereign Grace Truth* and author of many books including, *Meet the Puritans* and *Striving Against Satan*.

SUGGESTED ADDITIONAL READING

Chambers, Talbot W. *The New York City Noon Prayer Meeting: A Simple Prayer Gathering That Changed the World*. Wagner Publications, 2002.

Edwards, Jonathan. *A Call to United, Extraordinary Prayer*. Scotland: Christian

Focus, 2003.

Spurgeon, C. H. *Prayer-Meetings: A Sermon.* August 30, 1868. http://www.biblebb.com.

ENDNOTES

1. Charles Spurgeon, *Only a Prayer Meeting* (Ross-shire: Christian Focus, 2000), p. 9.

2. Lewis O. Thompson, *The Prayer-Meeting and Its Improvement* (Chicago: W. G. Holmes, 1878), p. 16.

3. J. B. Johnston, *The Prayer-Meeting, and Its History, as Identified with the Life and Power of Godliness, and the Revival of Religion* (Pittsburgh: United Presbyterian Board, 1870), pp. 110, 145; cf. Thomas Houston, *The Fellowship Prayer-Meeting,* pp. 80-84.

4. Cf. F. W. B. Bullock, *Voluntary Religious Societies, 1520-1799* (London, 1963).

5. Johnston, p. 154.

6. Arthur Fawcett, *The Cambuslang Revival* (London: Banner of Truth Trust, 1971), pp. 71-72.

7. Johnston, pp. 165-66.

8. Johnston, p. 173.

9. Jonathan Edwards, *A Call to United, Extraordinary Prayer* (Ross-shire: Christian Focus, 2003), pp. 16-17.

10. Edwards, p. 18.

11. Heman Humphrey, *Revival Sketches and Manual* (New York: American Tract Society, 1859), p. 55ff.

12. Erroll Hulse, *Give Him No Rest: A Call to Prayer for Revival* (Durham: Evangelical Press, 1991), pp. 78-79.

13. Johnston, pp. 185-87.

14. Hulse, pp. 103-107.

chapter

46

PRAYING TOGETHER VS. PRIVATE PRAYER

Bruce M. Hartung

Shingles is an odd disease. The symptoms are an outbreak of rash over one half of the head and/or torso following the lines of the nerves which are virally infected. The potential for shingles remains in the body during one's lifetime following the illness of chickenpox. People over sixty are especially vulnerable because of the gradual weakening of the immune system. Generally speaking, symptoms last for two to four weeks.

I was teaching an intensive two-week course, "Faith, Health, and Pastoral Care," when shingles struck. While I had mild symptoms that were diagnosed as an ear and eye infection earlier in the week, a more full-blown range of symptoms emerged toward the end of the week. Classes that I teach begin with a meditation and prayer. The seminarian opening one of the classes began reading from James 4.

> Is anyone among you suffering? He should pray. Is anyone in good spirits? He should sing praise. Is anyone among you sick? He should summon the presbyters of the church, and they should pray over him and anoint with oil in the name of the Lord, and the prayer of faith will save the sick person, and the Lord will raise him up. If he has committed any sins, he will be forgiven. Therefore, confess your sins to one another and pray for one another that you may be healed. (5:13-16, NAB)

The seminarian then challenged the class to, essentially, put our action where our study was, and asked members of the class to share prayer requests. I was one of those who shared, in this case, my shingles diagnosis. Members of the class came as a group, put their hands on me, and prayed for my healing. As I write this essay I am still quite symptomatic, but intend, conserving my strength otherwise, to facilitate the second week of the course. Thus, I am not writing on the other side of the illness, but rather in its midst.

Growing up in a Germanic household in the 40s and 50s, and in perhaps prototypical American fashion, I learned how to tough it out. The idea was to keep things personal to oneself. To bring people into my struggles by talking about them, or into the struggles of my family, was considered not only out-of-bounds but, in the case of family issues, disloyal. The norm was really an individual norm. While extended family members were there to provide times of social connection and helpfulness when asked, the dominant culture was to take care of things oneself.

Sharing of one's concerns could be seen as complaining, attention-getting, or pleas for sympathy. To come to church was a time to show oneself off at one's best. In public worship some of the expectation was to look good, as if everything was all right even when it was not.

In this context, the notion of the church as a community was not fostered in my own spiritual life. "We share our mutual woes, our mutual burdens bear, and often for each other flows the sympathizing tear"[1] was not as normative as "Before our Father's throne, we pour our ardent prayer; our fears, our hopes, our aims are one, our comforts and our cares."[2] Dominant was the sharing of personal concerns with God possible through the work of Christ, private prayer; much less fostered was the notion of sharing concerns with the community and having the community also pray on behalf of the person (praying together). Of course, when someone was in the hospital, the prayer of the community was formally offered. But in my day-to-day life, most everything of a deep personal nature was between me and God.

Essentially, two things happen when we become followers of Christ, as, in the Lutheran tradition, we are baptized. We are placed, through the life, death, and resurrection of Jesus, into a new relationship with God, and truly become His redeemed daughters and sons. What happens, though, is not just vertical, the healing of one individual relationship. We are also placed, through the life, death, and resurrection of Jesus, into a community of people that Saint Paul calls the "Body of Christ." "I believe that I cannot be my own reason or strength believe in Jesus Christ, my Lord, or come to Him; but the Holy Ghost has called me by the gospel, enlightened me with His gifts, sanctified and kept me in the true faith; even as He calls, gathers, enlightens, and sanctifies the whole Christian Church on earth, and keeps it with Jesus Christ in the one true faith, in which Christian Church He daily and richly forgives all sins to me and all believers, and will at the Last Day raise up me and all the dead, and give unto me and all believers in Christ eternal life."[3] This reality brought about by the redemptive work of Jesus Christ, makes prayer together and prayer privately never oppositional. It is expected that private intercessions move into the public arena and that public prayer move into the private arena. Both/and become the theme within the Body of Christ.

At times, prayer and praise is an individual response. At other times, it is a response within the community. Mutual confession of sins and prayer for one another is considered to be a vehicle God in Christ uses for healing.

God's Word, the voice of the Church, and our prayers belong together. So we must now speak of common prayer. "If two of you agree on earth concerning anything that they may ask, it will be done for them of Me in heaven" (Mt. 18:19). There is no part of common devotions that raises such serious difficulties and trouble as does common prayer, for here we must ourselves begin to speak. We have heard God's Word, and we have been permitted to join in the hymn of the Church; but now we are to pray to God as a fellowship, and this prayer must really be *our* word, *our* prayer for this day, for our work, for our fellowship, for the particular needs and sins that oppress us in common, and for the persons who are committed to our care."[4]

The martyred Dietrich Bonhoeffer helps us understand the place and function of the fellowship, of the community. "The fact simply remains that where Christians want to live together under the Word of God they may and they should pray together to God in their own words. . . . Here all fear of one another, all timidity about praying freely in one's own words in the presence of others may be put aside where in all simplicity and soberness the common, brotherly prayer is lifted to God. . . . It is in fact the most normal thing in the common Christian life to pray together."[5]

Is there reluctance of Christians to pray together (except when led by a worship leader in a formal worship service)? Perhaps in the traditions and experience of some of the readers, the answer is "No." Yet I see considerable reluctance, even in some group prayer, to move very deeply into significant prayer issues. If my perception is correct (as well as my own reluctance), why? There are likely as many responses as there are people, each with particular concerns and discomforts.

But one set of possible reluctances based on my own life and ministry experience, seems relatively clear to me. If we stay in our individual prayer modes, we, while we share with God, have little or no personal vulnerability to others in the community of Christ. Thus, our classically American individuality is preserved, as are both our exaggerated view of privacy and a sense of the preservation of our personal space.

The core issue is personal vulnerability to each other. While I know that I am vulnerable to God, who knows my most inward being, I, frankly, am less likely to share that vulnerability with someone else, even if that someone is a member of Christ's Body. Praying together—or at least prayer together in some depth—requires the presentation of myself as less than ideal, less than piously all together, less than whole. It requires the presentation of myself as who I really am rather than who I would like others to believe that I am. It requires as much honesty before others as it requires before my God.

This is a difficult task, possible, I believe, only by the work of the Holy Spirit in our hearts. David Hilton, a psychiatrist, pastor, and former missionary, says somewhere that the task of the contemporary church is to change from being communities of pretense to communities of authentic encounter. I believe that he is correct. What place does authentic encounter, person-to-person, occur more clearly than when two or three are gathered together in the name of Christ with Christ present as promised, where they share their struggles realistically and personally together and where they pray together in the name of Christ, at the foot of His cross and with the power of His empty tomb?

Thus, the question is more than praying together vs. private prayer. I have tried to demonstrate that it is both/and. Additionally it is the personal vulnerability and depth of individual sharing that takes praying together from pious soliloquies, surface chatter, and religiously correct formal language to the deeper areas of personal risk (and therefore deeper personal healing) made possible by personal vulnerability, openness, and authenticity.

Jeffrey Levin, in *God, Faith, and Health: Exploring the Spirituality-Healing Connection*, suggests that "regular religious fellowship benefits health by offering support that buffers the effects of stress and isolation."[6] While not speaking from even a Christian perspective, Levin, as a researcher, begins to understand the emerging research evidence that social support is a significant contributor to health, and that a lack of social support is disease-producing or, at least, disease enhancing. The involvement of people in religious activities is a form of social support that "provides both tangible and emotional resources that buffer or reduce our experience of stress,"[7] that "increases the likelihood that when stressful situations arise, they are put in a larger context that offers greater meaning,"[8] and that "increases our access to people who can offer us assistance when we are in need."[9]

If this is true for all secular social supports, how much more so it is, in this age and the next, for those who are followers of the Truth, Jesus Christ, and are gathered in His name. Medical researchers are just beginning to understand what the early Christian community understood: "Is anyone among you sick? Let him call for the elders of the church, and let them pray over him, anointing him with oil in the name of the Lord, and the prayer of faith will save the sick, and the Lord will raise him up. And if he has committed sins, he will be forgiven" (Jas. 5:14-15).

Questions for Further Thought or Discussion

1. What do you consider to be your personal reluctancies to engage in deep and personal prayer with others in the Body of Christ?
2. If you do not currently engage in personal prayer with others, what strate-

gies might you develop to identify those who might join you in this and to implement such a prayer group?

3. What ways do you believe fellow Christians can engage in prayerful as well as behavioral support of their brothers and sisters?

The author: Rev. Dr. Bruce M. Hartung is Dean of Ministerial Formation at Concordia Seminary, St. Louis, Missouri. He is a past President of the American Association of Pastoral Counselors, and writes a monthly column, "Pressure Points" for the *Lutheran Witness Reporter.*

SUGGESTED ADDITIONAL READING

Crabb, Larry. *The Papa Prayer: The Prayer You've Never Prayed.* Nashville: Thomas Nelson, 2006.

Rick Richardson. *Experiencing Healing Prayer: How God Turns Our Hurts into Wholeness.* Downers Grove, IL: InterVarsity Press, 2005.

Suggs, Rob. *Christian Community: LifeGuide Bible Studies.* Downers Grove, IL: InterVarsity Press, 2003.

ENDNOTES

1. "Abide with Me," *Lutheran Worship* (Saint Louis: Concordia Publishing House, 1982) #295, v. 3.

2. "Abide with Me," v. 2.

3. Martin Luther, "Small Catechism," *Lutheran Book of Worship* (Saint Louis: Concordia Publishing House, 1982), p. 302.

4. Dietrich Bonheoffer, *Life Together,* John Doberstein, translator (New York: Harper and Brothers, 1954), p. 62.

5. Bonheoffer, p. 62.

6. Jeffrey Levin, *God, Faith, and Health: Exploring the Spirituality-Healing Connection* (New York: John Wiley and Sons, 2002), p. 13.

7. Levin, p. 60.

8. Levin, p. 60.

9. Levin, p. 61.

chapter

47

LEADING/FACILITATING CORPORATE PRAYER

Phil Miglioratti

"Let's pray. Everyone bow your head, close your eyes . . ." And so begins a standard, down-the-list, around-the-circle prayer meeting. Unfocused prayers. Unenthused pray-ers.

The day when good intentions or strong emotions were enough to set the table for a strong and successful prayer gathering are long gone. Today's prayer group, whether a class or committee, a study or fellowship group, or a congregation of many or few, desperately needs a leader with the ability to facilitate an "experiential"—an activity during which every person has an authentic, meaningful encounter, both with the ones they pray with and the one they pray to.

The solution is not to make the prayer experience more entertaining, educational, or expressive. Each of these elements is vital to a comprehensive prayer experience but without the engagement of those gathered with one another and the Holy Spirit, the time spent is more a human than a spiritual activity. Those who have the privilege of leading Christ followers in praying need first a new way of thinking about the process rather than a new program or set of methods and ideas.

A New Way of Thinking

Who are You? Yes, prayer starts with God and praying is ultimately about the glory of God ("Your kingdom come on earth . . .") but the role of the person He has selected to lead is vital to the process. Pastors and prayer leaders must realize the difference between their role in leading and how to operate when facilitating. Leadership relates to casting vision, setting clear direction, providing compelling action steps. Leaders direct the process step-by-step, declare solutions to problems or hindrances, exert influence over a group or team to achieve a specific agenda or to take a particular action. Leaders are like symphony conductors; they select the music, determine the tempo, and stand front and center for all to see and follow.

Facilitators perceive their function differently. Facilitators have a clear focus and have prepared an anticipated format but are constantly submissive to the leading of the Holy Spirit as the corporate praying unfolds. They perceive themselves as an assistant to the Holy Facilitator, seeking the mind of Christ then guiding, even redirecting, the praying in that direction.

Facilitators think about the type of authority the group recognizes them to have, as it will make a difference in their readiness to follow, especially if new methods are being employed. Is the person facilitating a self-imposed leader (never a good idea), is he or she operating with delegated authority (for example, the pastor has selected him or her to lead the gathering) or has he or she been officially appointed to an ongoing role (the congregation's prayer coordinator, for example)? The best scenario is to be recognized by those gathered as the one with the heart and skills necessary to facilitate rather than dominate the praying experience. Permission to experiment is related to the extent of trust the facilitator has built with the people gathered to pray.

What is the purpose? The purpose of every prayer meeting is, well, to pray, of course. But, since prayer is never an end in itself, the prayer facilitator must always discern the here-and-now reason for the group to dedicate its time, whether a few minutes or a few hours, to listening and talking with the Lord.

Facilitators ask a series of questions as they prepare and pray toward the meeting in order to recognize the unique-to-this-gathering focus or spiritual assignment. A group which meets weekly and follows a similar format each week should still have a sense that the prayers of this meeting are not merely the prayers of the past 51 weeks. God's Spirit has placed into our hearts and minds the praises and promises, the problems and petitions that are fresh for this particular time and place of praying.

Where are you meeting? Even though we can pray anytime and anywhere, the effect of the environment is often overlooked. In an emergency, a group of people can pray effectively at the scene of an accident on a busy highway in the pouring rain but in normal circumstances, a facilitator will consider the room setting and do what is necessary to maximize its potential.

A small group, whether in a home, a classroom, or a large auditorium can easily and quickly form a circle and create a sanctuary feel that crowds out other noise or activity. Groups of several dozen or more, depending on the purpose of that day, may pray best in circles of six to eight chairs. If the only setting available is pew or fixed seating, the facilitator will need to instruct participants to move into pairs or stand in triplets or kneel at their seat in order to engage all who have come.

If the gathering is multi-church, the facilitator needs to do pre-meeting homework. Does the hosting congregation have local protocol? What is the dress code, at least for the facilitator? As a guest facilitator, should you recognize the host pastor or guest leaders from other congregations? Think carefully through how you will explain the guidelines for praising ("It is fine to raise your hands while we sing or as you pray.") and offering prayers ("Please wait to introduce a new subject or focus until several have prayed over a topic."). Offer guidelines that give both freedom ("You may kneel at any time or come to the altar area . . .") and boundaries ("If you have a message you believe God wants you to speak to the entire group, please bring that to me before you speak it aloud").

Practical matters, such as lighting, sound amplification, competing noise, access, seating arrangement, and room temperature, all impact the praying experience. The extra effort to provide the best possible setting is always well worth the time and energy invested.

When are you meeting? Unless the meeting time is fixed, the facilitator needs to consider how the choice of the day and the time impact participation. Every choice makes it feasible for some and difficult for others. Consider posting both start and stop times as this may benefit parents with young children who have early bed times (Are children welcome, as a way to disciple them in praying?). Time of day may also determine the style of songs selected; does it feel like time for rejoicing or quiet meditation?

Why is this person praying? In order to guide and guard the entire group (whether six or six hundred), the facilitator must be both a praying participant and a prayer observer. Total participation on the part of the facilitator makes it difficult to steer or stop the process. Observation without participation turns the facilitator into a director and methods become manufactured or mechanical. In a small group, the facilitator sits with the group but in a larger gathering, the facilitator needs to be visible to all (and accessible, if many small groups are scattered across the room.)

This active participation is important to the task of reading the prayer dynamic. The facilitator must be able to discern if silence is a sign of listening and contemplation or an indication the topic of prayer has been completed. When unsure, the facilitator should simply ask the group for feedback, such as "Does anyone else have a prayer for this need before we move to our next focus?" Then he or she should wait until someone prays or the silence continues (indicating it is time to introduce a new topic).

Listening to the prayers of the people is a vital task for the facilitator. It enables you to gauge how well participants understand your instructions. Is someone beginning with a petition when you have asked for a time of praise (extolling God for who He is) or thanksgiving (expressing gratitude for what He has done)? If you direct the group to pray from a specific passage of scripture, are the prayers offered based on the text? Is some instruction needed?

The goal in asking oneself "Why is this person praying?" is not to control nor is it to squelch anyone but rather to guide the praying back to the previous instruction or to discern a new leading of the Holy Spirit. Facilitators should neither quench the Spirit (saying no to a new leading because they are not sensitive) nor grieve the Spirit (moving in a direction not intended by the Spirit or moving prematurely).

Discerning the leading of the Spirit is a combination of spirit and skill. The spiritual component requires ongoing dialogue between the Holy Spirit and the facilitator. (Are we ready to move into a new topic? How do I encourage others to participate? The person praying is sad, even tearful. Is that a sign of God's heart for those we are praying for?). The skill component requires the facilitator to listen carefully, communicate clearly, and confidently guide the process.

- Listen to the prayers from a continuity perspective. Are we at the beginning, middle or conclusion of a prayer focus or topic?
- Communicate by giving the group clear instructions. Is it obvious what you are asking them to do and have you repeated the instruction using synonyms for the key words?
- Guide with brief comments ("We've moved too quickly from simple praise . . ." "When your group is done, please wait in silence for the others . . ." "Remember to begin your prayer with a word or phrase from the scripture passage.")

This type of leadership in a prayer context is a paradigm shift for those accustomed to a start-and-stop style. Start-and-stop leaders are only responsible to tell the group when to begin praying and when or how to stop ("I'll say the first prayer, others pray, then Deacon Hernandez will conclude our time."). Facilitators not only give clear instruction at the beginning but as needed, throughout the experience. These interruptions, rather than distracting, are welcomed by those who want a corporate conversation instead of a down-the-list, around-the-circle routine.

How can the focus be formatted for full engagement? Even if the purpose of the gathering is to pray over a list of congregational requests, a format should be utilized. Nothing is more boring (possibly to God as well as those praying) than simply rehearsing a list of names or needs without the discipline of seeking to pray out God's heart for the situation.

A format helps focus the prayers of the saints and allows the prayer leader to disciple the group into biblical praying. Biblical praying utilizes scripture to provide the text (such as using John 3:16 as the basis for evangelism praying), the topic (like Nehemiah pleading for his city), or the themes. Acts 1:8 offers an outward format: Jerusalem (our community), Judea (our state and nation), Samaria (our enemies far and near), the earth (other nations across the globe).

Formats may also be designed from acrostics, such as:

- P—Praise
- R—Repent
- A—Ask
- Y—Yield

Or:

- Upward—Praise
- Downward—Confession
- Inward—God's will for my life
- Outward—God's will for others (healing, evangelism)
- Backward—Remembering God's faithful actions in scripture and the past
- Forward—Declaring our hope in God's faithful action in and through our obedience

Facilitating a small or large group though such a format may be enhanced through power point slides that indicate the primary focus and/or present the scripture that serves as the basis of prayer. Intersperse the format slides with the lyrics of a song that will be sung as a transition. These lyric slides help move the focus of prayer from, say a section of adoration praying into a focus on confession. Simply begin to sing (a capella or with instrument or even CD background), for example, "Change My Heart O God" reminding the group the song is a prayer of petition set to music.

A New Way of Leading

Leading prayer as a facilitator requires:

- A new role: You are a facilitator rather than a director
- A new routine: Unscripted, dynamic, corporate conversation with the Holy Spirit
- A new result: An uncommon prayer experience

"The Helper, the Holy Spirit, whom the Father will send in My name, He will teach you all things, and bring to your remembrance all things that I said to you" (Jn. 14: 26).

Questions for Further Thought or Discussion

1. Explain how this corporate description of facilitation applies to the function of a prayer facilitator:

   "Smoothing the way. That's what facilitate means: to make things easier, to smooth the progress of and to assist in making things happen. Like so much of our work, we think that facilitation is about moving things forward. It's about allowing and creating an environment where things can move forward. It isn't about pushing or forcing things." Impact Factory

2. Explain how each of these components can be used in a prayer gathering:
   - Song—Singing to God, not merely about God
   - Scripture—Praying God's Words back to Him
   - Story—Sharing success and struggles
   - Silence—Seeking, meditating, listening
   - Spoken—"All types of prayers"

3. Design a prayer format that includes:

   - Foundation—A biblical passage or theme
   - Focus—A specific application or topic
   - Format—A road map for praying

The author: Phil Miglioratti is Director of the National Pastors Prayer Network and Facilitator for the Church Prayer Leaders Network. He is the author of several chapters in compiled books including "Creative Ideas for Prayer Ministry" in *A House of Prayer* and "Pastor's Strategies for Mobilizing Men to Pray" in *Fight on Your Knees.* Phil also has six blogs for Christian leaders (www.nppn.org).

SUGGESTED ADDITIONAL READING

Franklin, John. *And the Place Was Shaken: How to Lead a Powerful Prayer Meeting.* Nashville: Broadman & Holman Publishers, 2005.

Henderson, Daniel with Margaret Saylar. *Fresh Encounters: Experiencing Transformation through United Worship-based Prayer.* Colorado Springs, CO: NavPress, 2004.

Henderson, Daniel. *PRAYzing! Creative Prayer Experiences from A to Z.* Colorado Springs, CO: NavPress, 2007.

Small, P. Douglas. *Transforming Your Church into a House of Prayer.* Cleveland, TN: Pathway Press, 2006.

Sacks, Cheryl. *The Prayer Saturated Church.* Colorado Springs, CO: NavPress, 2004.

chapter

48

PRAYER IN THE CORPORATE WORSHIP SERVICE

Jonathan Graf

The early Church in Acts did four things when it gathered together. "They continued steadfastly in the apostles' doctrine and fellowship, in the breaking of bread and in prayers" (Acts 2:42). I don't think that means 25 percent of the time was given to each, but it clearly shows a significant importance was put on each element. If our church gatherings were measured against those four things, where would we stand?

Clearly corporate prayer was given a significant place in early Church meetings. In our day, most churches relegate prayer to a pastor or leader praying once or twice in a service, maybe a worship leader offering a simple prayer amid a song set, perhaps there is a time for people to come forward and be prayed for. While these are important expressions of prayer, they do not usually constitute powerful, corporate prayer.

Instead, corporate prayer has been relegated to the weekly prayer meeting, certainly an important service and event for a church. Unfortunately many churches have disbanded these due to lack of interest or sheer boredom. Most prayer meetings have become a few sitting around in a circle, taking requests about all the physical and personal needs of the church's members, then praying until each one has been mentioned. It is hardly a dynamic time of powerful corporate prayer.

Congregations need to experience powerful, dynamic, earth-changing corporate prayer. And the best place to experience it is in the Sunday morning worship service. Why? Three reasons:

1. Because prayer is not truly corporate unless it is done with all your people. The morning worship is the only place where you have most of your people each week. Acts 12:5 tells us that "Peter was therefore kept in prison, but constant prayer was offered to God for him by *the church*." We can have good times of people praying together at other moments, but the value of an entire congregation calling out to God in agreement is extremely powerful. When a congregation agrees on something and prays, it is effective!
2. It teaches your people how to pray. These days, most believers never participate in times of praying with others. They may observe prayer a few times in a worship service, but they are never required to try it. As a result, most believers do not have any confidence to pray. When they can see and hear others pray, that can grow their own prayer lives as well.
3. It is easier to have a leader-led prayer time in the morning worship service than at a less formal weeknight meeting. This is important for prayer to be truly effective. In the midweek service, often times well-meaning pray-ers will take the prayer meeting away from a leader to pray about their own agendas. This will not happen in a worship service. As a result you can better "manipulate" prayer to operate with the biblical principles of corporate prayer.

Biblical Principles of Corporate Prayer

There are five biblical principles of powerful corporate prayer. The more of these elements are present in our prayer times (during worship or other times), the more powerful the prayer.

Desperation. Ezra 8:22-23 records a time of corporate prayer surrounding a three-day fast. The priest Ezra was taking a group of Jews back to repopulate Israel. They were going to cross dangerous terrain and needed protection. The interesting thing here, however, is that Ezra had a solution—the king would have likely given them soldiers to go along—but he refused to take it. He refused to do the obvious thing in favor of relying on God.

We need to learn from that. The more desperate we are about something, the more vibrant our prayers. When going to prayer corporately, look for ways to impress a sense of desperation in your people. Remember what happened in churches following 9/11? Prayer meetings were full for several weeks. Why? Desperation. As you pick the focus about which to pray, figure out a way to build in desperation. We can't solve this, God. We need You.

One Focus. Powerful prayer is focused prayer. It is not a shotgun approach—giving prayer requests and praying for ten different things. Effective corporate prayer is topical. The leader explains, "now we are going to pray for . . ." We see this played out in the story of Peter's imprisonment (Acts 12). Verse 5 tells us of a prayer meeting for Peter. Not everything under the sun, and "oh yeah, don't forget Peter." In the morning worship service, picking one subject for which to pray is all you need to do—and it is powerful.

One Voice. One voice is a numerical principle. As was mentioned above, the same chapter in Acts tells us that *the church* was earnestly and constantly praying to God. *Everyone.* Not five people in a little room on Wednesday night. A powerful dynamic occurs when an entire congregation prays on the same theme. Again, the only place you will have the entire congregation together is Sunday morning worship.

Invoking the Presence. In 2 Chronicles 6-7 at the dedication of Solomon's Temple, we see God's glory indwelling His temple so much that everyone fell with their faces to the ground. No one went inside. In Solomon's dedication prayer, he invited God to come and dwell. "Now therefore, arise, O LORD God, to your resting place . . ." (2 Chron. 6:41).

We often just take comfort in the presence spoken of in Matthew 18:20: "Where two or three are gathered together in My name, I am there in the midst of them." But there is another presence of God—His manifest presence. It is a presence you can literally sense. It is a transforming presence. We need to look for ways to encourage that presence of God into our midst. He comes by invitation and He comes through praise. Psalm 22:3 tells us that God inhabits the praises of His people. There is no better place to regularly experience the manifest presence of God than the worship service. When we pray in the middle of, or following a time of intense worship—worship that is entirely focused upward, on Jesus Christ rather than on us—we more readily sense His presence and our prayers become more kingdom focused.

Agreement. The last element of powerful corporate prayer is praying in agreement. This is different than focus. It is where everyone knows and agrees with what they are asking God. Often when a congregation prays about an issue in a church there is not agreement. We all have a different idea of what should be done. So when we pray, we often just pray our own agendas. (Just as an aside—agreement will come in any issue if people pray together. As we pray with others, we become more open to God's agenda and we let go of our own.)

In a leader-directed prayer time during a morning worship service it is easier to be in agreement. The leader simply gives direction as to what they will ask God to do. He might say something like this, "After seeking God, the leaders of our church feel that God is moving us to look for a piece of property on which to build. Let's ask God to reveal that piece of land to us."

Ways to Incorporate Prayer in the Service

When incorporating group prayer into the morning worship service several principles are important. First until your people are used to it, keep it fairly short. Never let them go more than five minutes in a prayer group on one topic. Two to three minutes is plenty. Second, put prayer points and even a simple prayer on power point or in the bulletin. Instruct those who are nervous about joining in that they are not being forced to pray, but if they would like to, here is a prayer or some thoughts to use when they pray. Third, when you start doing this, and perhaps a few times afterward, give them some prayer protocol instructions. Remind them that they should not pray like they do when they are by themselves. All prayers should be short, 30-45 second maximum, to give everyone a chance to participate and so no one is intimidated. People can pray multiple times in a group.

Pray the thoughts of a song. Many songs—especially contemporary ones—are prayers themselves, focused on Christ. If we mean what we are singing, then we are praying when we sing. But, another benefit is that songs can be catalysts to dynamic prayer.

For example, a song like "Touching Heaven, Changing Earth" can foster in a time of prayer for revival. A song like "Breathe" can generate prayer for spiritual hunger in each other. A song like "Crown Him with Many Crowns" or "O for a Thousand Tongues to Sing" can move into times of corporate praise where we spontaneously shout out praises to God.

To do it, a worship leader simply guides the people into groups of three to six and instructs them on what to pray. The musicians keep playing to provide some background music. After two to three minutes end the time by moving into the next song.

Set aside a 7 to 10 minute prayer time. Pick a topic of importance to your church or leaders. An upcoming outreach event, a special program, a deep need in the church, the nation, etc. The more the topic relates to the people, the more dynamic the time will be. Have people pray in groups over this topic. But again, offer clear direction and ideas of things to pray.

Pray the Sermon Application. A pastor often has something in the sermon that needs to get across to the people. Why not have a time (two to three minutes) where people get into groups of three or four and pray that application into each other. The pastor needs to give specific instructions so they understand what they are to pray. A bulletin insert or power point slide with the important points are all that is needed.

Pastor Guided Prayer. Another excellent way to incorporate prayer is to have the people pray a prayer in unison at the end of the message. The pastor can put a prayer together that reflects exactly the truths and applications with which the people are to walk away. Instruct them to pray out loud after you. You say a phrase and give them time to repeat it. Not only will this do something powerful by praying the application into them, but people learn to pray. They hear their pastor pray and they begin to understand the kinds of spiritual things they can ask God for in prayer.

A Time to Pray for Needs. While this is not corporate prayer in the truest sense, it can be a wonderful time of blessing for your people. Simply put, you set aside time in the service where people can pray for others. It can be done a number of ways.

During worship or at the end of a service have prayer teams (teams of two people—a husband/wife team or two males, two females) come forward or line up around the church. As you sing, people can come forward, walk up to a team and be prayed for. The book *Praying Grace* (PrayerPoint Press) by Terry Teykl and the DVD set *Upfront* (PrayerShop Publishing) are excellent training resources on this subject.

In a smaller congregation it can be meaningful to have people with a need stand where they are. Then have groups gather around them to pray for their need. The congregation keeps worshipping while this is going on.

Conclusion

If your people won't come to prayer meeting, take prayer meeting to the people. Having times of corporate prayer in the morning worship service can have a profound affect on your people and church. People learn to pray and develop a heart to pray what is on God's heart.

Questions for Further Thought or Discussion

1. What are three or four hindrances that keep prayer minimized in corporate worship? Provide a biblical example or teaching that confronts each barrier.
2. Identify and explain five or six different methods of turning an audience into participants.
3. Design a corporate worship experience that incorporates several diverse prayer opportunities

---

The author: Jonathan Graf is President of the Church Prayer Leaders Network located in Terre Haute, Indiana. He is also founding editor of *Pray!* magazine, author of *The Power of Personal Prayer* and editor of *My House Shall Be a House of Prayer.*

SUGGESTED ADDITIONAL READING

Franklin, John. *And the Place Was Shaken.* Nashville: Broadman & Holman, 2005.

Henderson, Daniel. *Fresh Encounters: Experiencing Transformation Through*

Untied Worship-based Prayer. Colorado Springs, CO: NavPress, 2004.

Teykl, Terry. *Praying Grace: Training for Personal Ministry.* Muncie, IN: PrayerPoint Press, 2002.

Butts, David. *Upfront: Training Prayer Teams for Ministry* (DVD). Terre Haute, IN: PrayerShop Publishing, 2007.

chapter

49

PRAYER PARTNERS, PRAYER TRIPLETS, SMALL PRAYER GROUPS

Daryl Eldridge

Ginger held back her tears as long as she could. She and her husband Tom had been coming to the small group for about three months. They were quiet, reserved, and had not requested personal prayer. One evening, the dam of emotions broke and she told the group how the couple wanted children, but medical problems caused by a car accident had so far prevented her from conceiving. The couple had consulted doctors and undergone several medical procedures, all to no avail. She felt like a failure and was angry with God. Ginger exposed her pain and vulnerability before the group. How the group dealt with the pain would be critical to her spiritual journey and continued involvement in the group. How should the group respond? What would be an inappropriate response to this cry for help?

One of the most powerful aspects of small groups is the opportunity to receive prayer requests, pray for one another, and see how God responds to the prayers. It is amazing to watch God answer prayers and change the hearts and lives of those in a small group. Prayer with another person or a small group may be the most intimate connection we can experience with someone other than a spouse. Sacred information handled poorly can break fragile souls. This young couple was not looking for quick remedies, platitudes, or trite answers. They needed the comfort and spiritual support of others through prayer.

Small prayer groups, prayer triplets, and prayer partners are excellent opportunities to teach believers how to pray. Many people are hesitant to pray in public, but with prayer partners or small groups of 6-10, they can learn to participate in prayer. Praying in smaller groups draws people together and meets personal and spiritual needs. Leaders can have a powerful impact on the groups they lead by showing how much they care about the personal concerns of others and modeling a life of communication with the Almighty.

Small Groups

Unfortunately, many ministers are more comfortable speaking before thousands of people than praying with a small group. Spiritual formation in small groups, accountability partners, and the counsel of spiritual directors should be spiritual practices of all ministers. Henri Nouwen identifies this gap in ministry preparation:

> It is a painful fact indeed to realize how poorly prepared most Christian leaders prove to be when they are invited to be spiritual leaders in the true sense. Most of them are used to thinking in terms of large-scale organization, getting people together in churches, schools, hospitals, and running the show as a circus director. They have become unfamiliar with, and even somewhat afraid of, the deep and significant movements of the Spirit. I am afraid that in a few decades the Church will be accused of having failed in its most basic task: to offer men creative ways to communicate with the source of human life.[1]

As with most things, developing a vibrant prayer life in small groups doesn't just happen. Here are some tips on developing prayer in small groups:

1. Center the prayers on God. Teach your small group how to begin prayer by adoring the creator of the universe. Enjoy the experience of crawling up into the lap of our heavenly Father and expressing as a small group our love for Him. Ask your small group to read Paul's prayer in Ephesians 1:15-23 and discuss what God would like to see from your small group prayer time.

2. Focus on praise. Unfortunately, most prayer groups center on what I call the "liver lists," which are prayers for Harry's ingrown toe nail, a friend of Aunt Martha who has cancer, or Tom's unreasonable boss. Our prayers should be more than a Christmas list of things we want corrected. God is more concerned about changing us into His likeness than changing our circumstances. Read James 1:2-4 from *The Living Bible* as a prayer, "Dear brothers, is your life full of difficulties and temptations? Then be happy, for when the way is rough, your patience has a chance to grow. So let it grow, and don't try to squirm out of your problems. For when your patience is finally in full bloom, then you will be ready for anything, strong in character, full and complete." Turn difficult circumstances into opportunities for praise.

3. Provide opportunities for confessional prayer. Spiritual transformation does not occur without confession. James 5:16 is explicit: "Confess your trespasses to one another, and pray for one another, that you may be healed." We have all seen confession done poorly, but that doesn't mean it should be avoided all together. The leader of a small group can teach and model how to appropriately confess sins. Confession requires trust and it will not happen quickly in a group, but once it begins lives will be changed. In a small group it is not necessary that confessors elaborate on the specific details, but they can share the issue for which they need forgiveness and help.

4. Handle each prayer request as a sacred trust. Much gossip occurs in the church under the guise of prayer concerns. Unless permission has been granted, personal prayer concerns voiced in the group must remain in the group.

5. Don't use prayer requests as opportunities to give advice or solve the person's problems. Small prayer groups are not therapy groups. Small prayer groups can be destroyed when one or more persons seek to fix the problem. Most problems brought before the group are spiritual in nature and can only be solved by a higher power. In the case of Ginger in the opening paragraph, the group could have destroyed her trust if someone had told her she hadn't conceived because she didn't have enough faith, or that she should learn to deal with the inability to have children because this was God's will for her life. She doesn't need to be told about options to adopt or what doctors she should try. The appropriate response is to join her in communicating her pain and faith to the Father.

6. Use variety. Don't allow your small group to get in a rut with its methods of praying. Use different positions for prayer. Pray on your knees, stand, sit in circles, hold hands, raise hands, or walk while you pray. Change the form of prayer. Quote or read Scripture as a prayer. Use fill-in-the-blank prayers, such as "Father, thank You for ___________" (this is particularly good with new believers in teaching them how to pray, because they only need to voice a few words).

Refrain from going around the circle and praying; rather, allow the Holy Spirit to guide the order and person praying. This may seem awkward at first, but it prevents someone from feeling pressure to pray aloud that may not want to, and it also allows God to guide the conversation. Allow time for silence and reflection. Use a theme to guide the session's prayers.

In small groups, often the sharing of the prayer requests is longer than the time actually spent praying for those requests. For a change of pace, ask members to share their requests as a prayer to God. Others may join in praying for that person aloud, or the leader can simply say, "Thank You, God, for hearing this prayer." Be sure to have someone recording the prayer requests as they are prayed.

Use Scripture in your prayer time. Read selected passages from the Bible. Ask each person to think about one thing they sensed God speaking to them through His Word. Allow a moment of silence. Then have them share what they were hearing from God. The variety of form and expression will promote spiritual renewal and guard against staleness.

7. Assign someone to keep a group prayer diary. The diary may contain the following information: the date of the prayer, the person making the request, the nature of the request, and the date and the way it was answered.

Some small groups find it helpful to establish a covenant or agreement on behaviors that are acceptable and not acceptable. The covenant doesn't have to be elaborate, but by establishing ground rules and expectations you can help your small group experience intimacy with one another and prevent misunderstanding in the group. Occasionally, you will need to remind the group of the expectations, since new members may join your small group.

Prayer Triplets

There are many adaptations of prayer triplets, but the most common use is three believers linking together to pray for unbelievers. Each person identifies three unbelievers for prayer, making a total of nine lost persons who are targeted for prayer on a regular basis. Unbelievers may include friends, neighbors, co-workers, employers, or relatives. The triplet prays daily for the nine unbelievers and then meets weekly to pray for the list and give a progress report. Prayer triplets can be used in conjunction with cell groups or small group Bible studies. They provide an excellent opportunity to focus on the lost and provide accountability and motivation for sharing our faith. It is remarkable to see what transpires in your own life when you pray for the salvation of others.

Prayer Partners

Another important weapon in the spiritual arsenal is prayer partners. In larger congregations, the church will want a coordinated plan to link and train members in this valuable ministry. Prayer partners can exchange prayer requests by email or phone, or choose to meet regularly for accountability and prayer.

Bible study groups may ask for members to write a prayer request on a card with the date of the request and submit it to the group. When members leave, each person is encouraged to pick up one of the prayer request cards and pray for that concern during the week. When members arrive the following week, they return the prayer request card. The process is repeated for a month, when it is determined if the request should remain in circulation. This method is a great way to introduce the concept of prayer partners.

Because of the intimacy factor, I have found it best when partners are physically praying together that women pray with women and men pray with men.

One day in my personal prayer time, I was prompted to start a small group at the school in which I was a faculty member. Later that morning a student asked if I led a prayer group with students. I replied I didn't, but related what I had sensed earlier in my prayer time and I said, "Let's start one." At chapel the two of us were making plans when another student overheard the conversation and asked if he could join the group. By the end of the day, God had assembled our first group. We met weekly to pray for one another, our churches, and our witness to the lost. We held each other accountable for moral purity. We typically closed the prayer time with these words, "Lord, keep us close and clean."

Each year students graduated from the school and went to various fields of ministry, but God always brought us new prayer partners. Some remained in church positions in the area and continued to attend the prayer group. We have all moved off to other ministries now, but we still meet occasionally for a prayer retreat. Members of that original group continue to lead small prayer groups in their own ministry context. The most important thing I may have done in my teaching ministry was starting a small prayer group with students. I attribute the vitality of my spiritual life to the small groups of men and women that I pray with each week. Invest in small prayer groups, use prayer triplets to pray for the lost, enlist prayer partners, and experience the spiritual vitality that will come to your life and ministry.

Questions for Further Thought or Discussion

1. Do you agree or disagree with Nouwen's statement that Christian leaders are poorly prepared for the basic task of offering people creative ways to communicate with the source of human life?
2. What guidelines for confession would you incorporate in a small prayer group ministry?
3. After reading this chapter, what do you feel God would have you do in regards to small group prayer, prayer partners, or prayer triplets?

The author: Dr. Daryl Eldridge is President of Rockbridge Seminary, located in Springfield, Missouri. He is the Editor of *The Teaching Ministry of the Church.*

SUGGESTED ADDITIONAL READING

Bonhoeffer, Dietrich. *Life Together.* New York: Harper & Row Publishers, 1954.

Maxwell, John. *Partners in Prayer.* Nashville: Thomas Nelson, 1996.

Bunch, Cindy, ed. *Small Group Idea Book.* Downers Grove, IL: InterVarsity Press, 2003.

ENDNOTES

1. Henri Nouwen, *The Wounded Healer* (New York: Doubleday, 1972), pp. 37-38.

chapter

50

ACCOUNTABILITY IN PRAYER

John D. Floyd

Accountability and responsibility are synonymous. Accountability or responsibility in prayer can cover a wide range of topics. Since the basis of God's operation in churches and individuals is prayer, the responsibility stemming from prayer interfaces with every area of our lives. E. M. Bounds, the great Methodist apostle of prayer, asserted that this world is shaped by our praying. Wesley Duewel acknowledged the unusual power in united prayer. The principle of Ecclesiastes 4:12 applies in spiritual life and prayer warfare: "Though one may be overpowered by another, two can withstand him, and a threefold cord is not quickly broken." God's children can unite in prayer even though they may not be meeting together. The work of national and local government and church leaders, fellow Christians, holiness in corporate and personal lives, revival, and the spread of the gospel around the world are only a few of the areas impacted by our responsibilities in prayer. The first strategy for world evangelization is prayer. I sincerely believe things happen all over the world every day purely as an answer to my prayers. If I did not believe this, I would not pray. This makes the accountability in prayer huge. I will elaborate on a few of these responsibilities for the body of Christ.

Accountability to God. The ultimate prayer accountability is to God because He has determined that so many things depend on prayer. His covenants and promises put this responsibility on His people. Jesus said, "Men always ought to pray, and not lose heart" (Lk. 18:1). F. J. Hugel reminded us:

> What seems an absurd admonition becomes an easy and unspeakably delightful experience when we take into account the glory of the Christian's position before God. Here, praying without ceasing becomes a thing as natural as breathing, something which springs from the very nature of things.[1]

At the coronation of Saul as king over Israel, Samuel reminded the people how they had rebelled against the Lord. He rehearsed their history of rebellion, then told them they had added to that the desire for a king. They then cried out to the Lord, confessing their rebellion and the sin of requesting a king. They asked Samuel to pray for them that God would be merciful. Samuel responded, "Far be it from me that I should sin against the Lord in ceasing to pray for you" (1 Sam. 12:23). James reminded the Jewish believers, "You do not have because you do not ask" (Jas. 4:2). What a disappointment it will be to learn of things that would have been, but were not—because we did not pray.

Jesus did not do many mighty works in Nazareth because of their unbelief (Mt.13:58). When churches do not believe, do not ask, God does not work. We are accountable to God for the demonstration of His person and His power through our praying. J. Oswald Sanders said it well: "True prayer is not asking God for what we want, but for what He wants." [2] We limit what God will do by our failure to ask. God certainly has the power to do whatever He wills, but He has decided to do some things only as an answer to prayer. We are accountable to pray.

Accountability to the Nation and the World. Paul said, "I exhort first of all that supplications, prayers, intercessions, and giving of thanks, be made for all men; for kings and all who are in authority, that we may lead a quiet and peaceable life in all godliness and reverence" (1 Tim. 2:1-2). Good government and civil peace and order are the result of praying. Abraham's prayer power had a dynamic impact on the destinies of those with whom he came into contact. Prayer in his life demonstrates the royal prerogative to influence the destinies of kings, cities, and individuals and the will of God which rules them. The prayers of the church in Jerusalem released Peter from the prison as did Paul's and Silas's prayers in the jail in Philippi. It is easy enough to criticize political leaders for poor decisions, but how much better to help them make good decisions by interceding for them. God can enable leaders to make good and right decisions—even if they are unaware of why—but you will know.

Anne Graham Lotz told of the evenings in the Graham home as she grew up. It was a regular practice for all to sit and listen to the evening news. Her dad, Billy Graham, would make a list of things going on around the world for which they would later pray as a family. God said to Solomon: "If My people who are called by My name will humble themselves, and pray and seek my face, and turn from their wicked ways, then I will hear from heaven, and will forgive their sin and heal their land" (2 Chron.7:14). Ezekiel had the challenging duty of telling Israel that her prophets had spoken when the Lord had not spoken; her princes were destroying the people like wolves; and the people had oppressed and robbed one another. God's message to them was, "So I sought for a man among them who would make a wall, and stand in the gap before Me on behalf of the land, that I should not destroy it; but I found no one" (Ezk. 22:30). When there is no one to intercede for the land, God will pour out His indignation on it. My, what a responsibility, what accountability, to pray for the nation and the world.

Accountability to Church Leaders. Prayer can build a hedge of protection around church leaders. Their lives can be protected from "unreasonable men" who by a careless remark can destroy a ministry, or make them the object of a joke, or a vicious rumor on a blog site. Paul asked for prayers that opportunities for witness would be available as well as boldness in preaching. God's people are responsible for interceding for spiritual leaders. We should pray for their walk and their work, and that they will be filled with the knowledge of God's will as they lead His people (Col.1:9-10). It is always heartbreak when a spiritual leader falls to a moral failure. We are responsible for helping to prevent such by intercession for them. That is part of the church at work.

Accountability to Churches. This is a corporate responsibility as well as an individual responsibility. Fellow Christians depend on intercession for a personal understanding of God's will, a holy walk, and an understanding of sound doctrine. Inner strength, endurance, and joy are all fruits of intercession. Churches have the prayer-power resource for overcoming spiritual darkness and demonic resistance for the purpose of spreading the gospel around the world and for total obedience to the Great Commission. J. Oswald Sanders remarked:

> Is there any wonder that the voice of the Church is so muted and her influence is nominal in the councils of the world when she neglects the primacy and divinely ordained method of influencing national and world affairs. If prayer could not so influence the course of the world events, Paul's exhortation would be without point.[3]

Since prayer so obviously undergirds the work of the churches, we have accountability in prayer to the churches. The Bible is replete with examples of the power of prayer in the body of believers. Paul's admonition to pray for all men (1 Tim. 2:4) and his example for praying for entire churches in Rome, Colosse, Ephesus, Galatia, and Philippi certainly indicate this responsibility. Peter said the apostles would give themselves continually to prayer and the ministry of the word (Acts 6:2). Their prayers doubtless included the body of believers. Through prayer God gave Peter directions to go to Cornelius and to Paul to go to Macedonia. The work of churches is governed through prayer.

Accountability for Holiness and Revival in Churches. Both personal and corporate holiness result from the praying of God's people. Andrew Murray put it forcefully: "And let our hearts be ashamed of our prayerlessness, through which we make it possible for God to impart His holiness to us. . . . No one can expect to understand and receive the holiness of God who is not often and long alone with God"[4]

God commanded, "Be holy, for I am Holy" (1 Pet. 1:16). Merely thinking, reading, and hearing about holiness may be refreshing, but do we dare to think that alone will produce holiness either corporately or individually? What folly! No amount of learning can make up for a failure to pray. Andrew Murray was correct when he urged, "May we begin to thank God that we have a private prayer room, a place where we can be alone with Him. There may we pray, 'Let your holiness, O Lord, shine more and more into our hearts that we may become holy.'"[5]

Personal and corporate holiness are the seedbed of revival. Historically the beginnings of revival have not been songs of joy, but prayers of repentance. Purity and power are not identical. We need both. God's desire is that His people have a heart cry for revival, an intimacy with Him that that is so real they are walking and working in the power of His Spirit. A pure life with sins confessed can appeal for God's blessing of revival to His people. His call remains, "If my people . . ." (2 Chron. 7:14). We live without revival because we are satisfied to live without revival.

Accountability to Be Thankful. God expects us to voice our thanksgiving to Him in prayer, both corporately and individually. We must ask our Lord for our needs, but in all our asking, let us remember to be thankful. It is not wrong to ask God for our needs as a body of believers or as individuals. Some say we should move beyond asking to praising. Both are expected. The Psalms are filled with admonitions, even commands, to offer praise to the Lord. I have made it a practice to record what I ask in a prayer journal. Then I indicate when the request is answered. That helps me to thank God for His answers when I receive them, as well as praising Him as I review them from time to time.

Accountability to Raise up an Army of Intercessors. One of the greatest responsibilities of a church today is to exercise the God-given privilege of praying. People need to be taught to pray, and how to pray. Prayer ministries in local churches are essential to the impact a church makes on its community, the nation, and the world.

Questions for Further Thought or Discussion

1. Do you agree or disagree (and why) with the author's primary motivation to be accountable in prayer?
2. Identify the factor that is your strongest motivation and explain why.

3. Describe how you would seek to develop accountability in prayer for a men's or women's group, a Bible study class, a weekly prayer gathering, a congregation.

The author: Dr. John D. Floyd is Professor of Missions at Mid-America Baptist Theological Seminary in Cordova, Tennessee.

SUGGESTED ADDITIONAL READING

Chapell, Bryan. *Praying Backwards: Transform Your Prayer Life by Beginning in Jesus' Name.* Grand Rapids: Baker Books, 2005.

Thrasher, BIll. *Journey to Victorious Praying: Finding Discipline and Delight in Your Prayer Life.* Chicago: Moody Publishing, 2003.

Towns, Elmer. *How to Pray When You Don't Know What to Say.* Ventura, CA: Regal Books, 2006.

ENDNOTES

1. F. J. Hugel, *The Ministry of Intercession* (Minneapolis: Bethany House Publishers, 1941), p. 22.

2. J. Oswald Sanders, *Prayer Power Unlimited* (Chicago: Moody Press, 1977), p. 132.

3. Sanders, p. 139.

4. Andrew Murray, *The Believer's Prayer Life* (Minneapolis: Bethany House Publishers, 1983), p. 63.

5. Murray, p. 63.

chapter

51

CHURCH PRAYER MINISTRIES AND PRAYER ROOMS

Elaine Helms

Jesus said in Luke 19:46, ". . . My house is a house of prayer . . ." A prayer ministry reinforces the vision and goal of the whole church being a praying church. It undergirds the work of the church with prayer, so that the church can fulfill its part in the Great Commission. God loves to help a church that recognizes its dependence on Him (see 2 Chron. 16:9).

Having a prayer ministry allows a church to experience total prayer saturation. It can cover the personal, corporate and kingdom elements of prayer. Prayer requests for specific ministry can be organized in a systematic way so that the most effective prayer support is given, to seek God's provision to accomplish what He has called the church to do. God answers specific prayer with specific answers and the church begins to see that it is God and God alone who is leading and providing for ministry that is happening.

When we see that our prayers make a difference, that draws us to pray more and God gets the glory in the church.

A prayer ministry can also play a major role in teaching people to be "houses of prayer." "Do you not know that you are the temple of God and that the Spirit of God dwells in you?" (1 Cor. 3:16). Teaching on prayer assists church members to focus their efforts on praying for kingdom issues and seeking what is on the heart of God. Knowing God's Word and keeping the Bible central to prayer is important. In addition, exposing church members to Spirit-filled and Spirit-led corporate prayer gives them a balance while enlarging and enhancing their relationship with the God of prayer.

It is easy for churches to do the work of church with a degree of success and begin to feel self-sufficient. Without meaning to, we can leave God out and begin to trust in our own understanding. However, there is no lasting fruit for the kingdom when we work in the flesh. Having a ministry that helps to keep the church focused on God through believing prayer can prevent that slippery slide into working in our own strength.

We learn to pray by praying, so in addition to teaching, to supplying resources on prayer and to giving help to begin quiet times with the Lord, the prayer ministry can offer opportunities to put prayer into practice. By offering avenues for people in the church to get involved in praying for something that is an interest or sometimes a passion, the prayer ministry can help transition Christians from a dry or non-existent prayer life to a healthy, active and growing prayer life.

A church is not limited to one kind of praying. God will lead you to fashion your prayer ministry according to His design and the interests of your people. The best place to start is on your knees seeking God's plan for your particular church, then obey Him. Form a task force or prayer committee of interested people to meet together weekly to study prayer from a biblical perspective and to pray together for God's direction. Ask God for His vision for prayer in the congregation. God's timing is vital to the establishment of any prayer ministry, so seek His guidance first.

Include in this group, representation from all program ministries of your church such as: Sunday Bible studies, discipleship studies, deacons, elders or board members, music and finance. Include men, women, old, young, singles, married, senior adults and especially those led to pray. The main thing is to keep a balanced group that represents the church at large.

Some examples of the types of prayer opportunities to consider include, prayer groups focused on praying for: church staff especially the pastor; missionaries; salvation; elected officials and civic affairs; schools—teachers and students; military; revival and spiritual awakening; or city, state and nation; prayer during worship—both as part of worship and in a separate place on behalf of the pastor; prayer chains—telephone and/or e-mail; prayer retreats, prayerwalks, prayer conferences/training, prayer vigils, corporate prayer meetings; or a prayer room.

Prayer Rooms

A dedicated room for prayer can be used effectively to minister to members and the community at large, while offering opportunities for Christians to grow spiritually. There are two types of prayer rooms that you can set up for ministry. One is a public prayer room, where anyone in the church may go to spend time with the Father. The other is a private prayer room, manned only by trained intercessors in the church. You will need to determine which kind your church prayer ministry should have (perhaps you will eventually have both).

A public prayer room should be filled with prayer guides and helps that stimulate both personal prayer and prayer for the church, community, nation, etc. Perhaps you will put prayer stations around the room for this purpose. It should be a quiet place where a person can meet God in solitude.

For this chapter, I will spend the most time explaining a private prayer room. A private prayer room is a working room where information is filed in a way that can be easily accessible for use in intercession. The room is locked to keep prayer requests confidential, available only to trained, scheduled intercessors. The purpose of the prayer room is to pray comprehensively for God's concerns as well as for the concerns of church members and others.

There will be people in a church whose spiritual gifts are strong in or include intercession. The prayer room offers a way for their gifts to be used. Those people who are called by God to spend longer times in prayer can also be a valuable asset to the church that desires to be in the center of God's will. However, every member can be invited to participate. As prayer becomes foundational in a congregation, their awareness of a lost world is heightened.

The prayer room with a phone line can offer hope to those who are hurting and need prayer for illness, bereavement, job loss and other serious situations. (If available, ask for your local prefix with PRAY (7729).) An answering service can be available for those times when no intercessor is present. People will call for their felt needs, but they often encounter their real need for a Savior in Jesus Christ. As members experience the power of God in their situation and the caring compassion of the intercessors, many will be led to pray for others also. When they experience prayer on their behalf, many just want to give back to help others. Prayer increases and the ministry grows.

You may need to allow between nine to sixteen weeks to lay the foundation, set policies, promote, offer training, and be ready to begin use of the room. If you do not have an existing room that can be used as it is, you may be able to adapt an existing room. Since an outside entrance is convenient and provides security for the rest of the church building, you might consider converting a window into a door. A keyless combination lock makes it easy for many different people to gain access.

Before opening, it is important to establish a record keeping system and forms to use for the variety of requests that will be attracted. Plan ahead for how prayer requests will be updated as this is a big area of encouragement when done well. A plan for the use of the time in the prayer room is the foundation for training the ones who will serve in the room.

Paper work is a necessary part of any prayer ministry. Recording prayer requests so that intercessors know how to pray is one key need. Keeping records will also help you see where you have been, and where you are going. God's wonderful miracles in answer to prayer can be shared for the encouragement and motivation of intercessors. The follow-up contacts, to update prayer requests, help the people who had asked for prayer feel that you do care about them, and that you are concerned. Without documentation much praise to our Lord would be lost.[1]

Prayer rooms—either kind—can be have a powerful impact in a church. They provide places for people to be stimulated into deeper levels of intercession and connection with God. Plus they can be an excellent outlet for covering the needs of the people in a church, so prayer meetings do not need to get bogged down with those kinds of requests. Finally a prayer room, if operated effectively, can provide your congregation with a visible statement of prayer's importance to your church.

Questions for Further Thought or Discussion

1. Prepare an outline for teaching a group how to pray kingdom focused prayers. What Scriptures will you use?
2. Prepare a plan and timeline for setting up and implementing a prayer room. You may want to read *If My People . . . Pray, Steps to an Effective Church Prayer Ministry.*
3. Make a list of Scriptures that you would include in a prayer service to begin worship of God for who He is. Make a list of Scriptures for praying for salvation.

The author: Elaine Helms is the Manager of Prayer and Spiritual Awakening at the North American Mission Board of the Southern Baptist Convention in Alpharetta, Georgia. She is the author of several books including *Prayer 101, What Every Intercessor Needs to Know* and *"If My People . . .Pray."*

SUGGESTED ADDITIONAL READING

Small, P. Douglas. *Transforming Your Church into a House of Prayer.* Cleveland, TN: Pathway Press, 2006.

Teykl, Terry. *Making Room to Pray: How to Start and Maintain a Prayer Room.* Muncie, IN, 1993.

Franklin, John. *And the Place Was Shaken: How to Lead a Powerful Prayer Meeting.* Nashville: Broadman & Holman, 2005.

Franklin, John, *A House of Prayer,* Nashville: LifeWay Christian Resources, 1999.

Trine, Steven. *Creative Prayer Stations.* Self-published 2007. (Available from www.prayershop.org).

ENDNOTES

1. For more in-depth coverage of setting up, developing and maintaining a prayer room, see *If My People . . . Pray: Steps to Effective Church Prayer Ministry* by Elaine Helms, or Chapter Three, "Intercessory Prayer Room" by Elaine Helms in *A House of Prayer* published by LifeWay Christian Resources.

chapter 52

PRAYER AS CREATIVE EXPRESSION

Gary W. McCoy

What is creative expression? "In the beginning, God created . . ." and humankind, being created in God's own image, has been involved in creative discovery ever since. God is Creator, and the human consequent, *imago Dei*, is an important principle in understanding creativity and creative expression. Humankind, being created in the image of a creator God, is made to create.

Creative expression means to communicate, or in some way, to express meaning via a method that utilizes some kind of creative endeavor. Thus, *prayer as creative expression* means to communicate (pray) to God through some aspect of a creative process. In its most basic understanding, it means using artistic activity to communicate with God. The term "art" or "the arts" is used to refer to art in the broadest sense of the word. While all art can be seen as creative expression, it would hold true that all creative expression may not result in art. Prayer as creative expression emphasizes *process over product.* While the emphasis is on the process of creative endeavor, it cannot be denied that creative activity does usually result in some kind of viewable artifact, that is something that can be seen, heard and experienced by others.

The Narrative Arts

Works of art that tell a story are called "narratives." The subject matter may incorporate scripture, history, current happenings or personal stories. In praying, these narratives may be designed to teach, enlighten, or inspire. The biblical books of history, prophecy, Psalms, and the Gospels are rich in language that gives credence to the use of narrative art within prayer. All art forms embody the possibility of functioning as narrative. Some may include auditory experience, or they may be purely visual. Though the following list is not complete, picture how each of these art *genres* can be used to tell a story:

- Literary Arts—poetry, prose writing, drama
- Musical Arts—vocal and/or instrumental music
- Performance Arts—dance, mime, acting, drama, tableau
- Visual Arts—painting, sculpture, stained glass, architecture, fashion, photography, mosaic, pottery.
- Home crafts—sewing, quilting, needlepoint, scrapbook, carpentry, culinary art, etc.

Creative Expression and Imagination

In prayer, there is one thing that each believer must supply for himself—his or her *imagination.* Creative expression requires imaginative engagement. In fact, it is at the intersection of imagination and faith that we gain a fuller understanding of the Christ Event—the incarnation, life, death and resurrection of God's beloved Son. In prayer we can determine any connections between His work in the world and the spiritual happenings in our own lives. Understanding those connections is a key to building our faith. And faith, while it happens in the mind, always imagines and envisions future outcomes.

Pretending is a part of any child's life. As a small boy I loved playing with blocks and miniature cars creating houses, roads, towns and whole communities. With my brothers and sisters we became imaginative characters acting out made up scenarios that were a part of a fantasy life. I became a hero to my sisters, saving them from horrible consequences, while pantomiming atrocious, life threatening hand-to-hand combat with invading space aliens (who were usually played by my brothers). For children, imagination is a way of life.

Prayer is an exercise of the Christian's reborn imagination. While we work within the cognitive understandings of faith-based theology, when we pray, we are communicating thoughts and desires to God that have come from the part of ourselves that is imagining God's actions—past, present or future. We are not pretending or play-acting, but we are using the God given ability to visualize past happenings or future possibilities. Within our creative capacity humankind is capable of thinking in numerous time-related dimensions all at the same time. We speak to God, remembering past happenings, we recall sights, words, sounds, and even tastes and smells. We also have the gift of anticipation—of looking forward to the future. God has given humankind not only the five sense-gates that open the world of sensory experience, but via imagination, He has given us the ability to recall and to re-experience life's wonderful or traumatic happenings. Likewise, this also allows us a foretaste of things that are beyond the now.

Prayer and Creative Expression as Spiritual Formation

The primary purpose of prayer is not to change God's mind, but to change us so that we are more aligned with the mind of God. Spiritual formation is the term that is used to describe the continuing work of the Holy Spirit in our lives as we who are believers seek to conform more and more to the image of Christ. Second Corinthians 3:18 says, "We all, with unveiled face, beholding as in a mirror the glory of the Lord, are being transformed into the same image from glory to glory, just as by the Spirit of the Lord." This work of God's Spirit is possible because we have been divinely reborn through Christ, and thereby set apart for God. We are drawn by the Holy Spirit to walk in Christ, setting our hearts on "things which are above" (Col. 3:1). We seek to follow scripture, being like Christ, even while we are still human. Within our fallen human condition we are prone to sin, but we do have choices. God has provided salvation through Christ, and therefore also provides, through the Holy Spirit, empowerment to fulfill His command: "be holy, for I am holy" (1 Pet. 1:16).

Creative Expression as Prayer

We are what we experience. Whether we are aware of it or not our identity is formed from our daily lives—by what we see, hear, say, think, and do. One basic premise of prayer and creative expression is that what we experience through our sense-gates shapes us. Prayer that utilizes various artistic or creative expressions can guide you into another type of experience in your Christian life—hopefully, one that will contribute further toward discovery that leads to forming your identity in Christ.

More than reading about it, embarking on an actual experience in prayer as creative expression will guide you into discovery about its meaning. In using your imagination and your five senses, what creative exercise appeals to you? Is it painting, writing poetry, learning a new song that you can use as a prayer, creating a teaching plan for a Bible study, writing a sermon, or taking a walk? As you can tell by this list, your imagination, your senses, and your engagement can guide you into many kinds of creative prayer outlets.

Thoughts about Art as Creative Expression in Prayer

Look first for the obvious. Ask yourself what about the work engages you? What is skillfully involved in the work? C. S. Lewis commented that we should not loose the ability "to respond to the central, obvious appeal of an artistic expression."

Ask, "Why was this work created?" What is the creator trying to express through this artistic work? What about life does the work clarify for you.

What about the work stimulates your imagination? T.S. Eliot said, "It is a function of all art to give us some perception of an order in life, by imposing an order upon it."[2] Usually a work of art is a *distillation* of life or of a life event. In being so it helps us to discern something about life with heightened clarity. Art can divert us from life and transport us to the world of imagination.

An artistic expression should not be viewed as a static event, but as a happening. The narrative art illustrates a story. Look for movement in the art. Movement is shown by how the artist chooses to reflect light, postures of individuals, movement through natural sources such as wind, or moving water, the look in the eye of a person, and how the artistic expression moves your focus from one thing to another.

Identify yourself with the creative process in two ways. First, try to relive the experience and then try to identify with the one who created the artistic expression. You may not be able to do this in all circumstances, but perhaps you will connect and be stimulated to the extent that you experience growth and change occur in your spiritual understandings.

There are a few warnings that I would give on prayer as creative expression:

1. If you view creative expression in prayer only for the purpose of re-affirming what you already know, you will miss the main point. Do not assume that you know the final destination of your praying. Be open to God's voice and to the movement of His Spirit.
2. Prayer is not performance. Prayer as creative expression, while it planned, scripted, or spontaneous is for God alone.
3. Do not view creative expression as overly serious or stuffy. Sometime a particular incident or expression could be humorous.
4. Do not "over-interpret" creative expression. While we should use our imaginations to speculate and to infer meaning in the artistic expression, we need to be aware that it is, in fact, only speculation or inference. Try to understanding of what is current what the present contexts could imply.

In Closing

Let me close by saying that participation in prayer as creative expression is not an easy experience. It requires balance as various ingredients of one's Christian experience—theology, scriptural understanding, background experiences, religious culture, education, values and many other competing forces—each seek their own place of primary focus as we seek to give creativity to our praying. The fullest opportunity for growing faith through the creative experience will come as the Holy Spirit brings these areas into balance within our lives.

The Christian writer C.S. Lewis said, "The first demand any work of art makes upon us is surrender. Look. Listen. Receive. Get yourself out of the way."

"Then when this is done," Lewis says, "art will admit us to experiences other than just our own."[3] This does not mean that you will not bring forth Christian discernment, theological understanding and the right to assess truth and morality within the work that you are doing. In fact, as you do so, this journey of artistic [creative] discovery will help you to know Christ even better.

Questions for Further Thought or Discussion

1. What are some of the most effective uses of prayer as creative expression that you have experienced?
2. What artistic expressions are already being actively included as prayerful expressions, and what areas would you like to develop?
3. What might the differences be between prayer as creative expression for private use or if it were meant for a gathering of believers?

The author: Dr. Gary W. McCoy is Professor of Worship and Music and Chair of the Deptartment of Leadership Skills Formation at Golden Gate Baptist Seminary in Mill Valley, California. He served in Korea as a music missionary and has authored a number of published works, including *Look to the Manger; Easter Praises; Jesus, the Very Thought of Thee;* and *His Only Son: God's Gift at Christmas.*

SUGGESTED ADDITIONAL READING

Best, Harold. *Unceasing Worship: Biblical Perspectives on Worship and the Arts,* Downers Grove, IL: InterVarsity Press, 2000.

Dillenberger, John. *A Theology of Artistic Sensibilities.* New York: The Crossroad Publishing Company, 1986.

Dyrness, William A. *Visual Faith: Art, Theology, and Worship in Dialogue.* Grand Rapids: Baker Academic, 2001.

Ryken, Leland. *Culture in Christian Perspective: A Door to Understanding and Enjoying the Arts.* Portland: Multonomah Press, 1986.

__________. *The Liberated Imagination: Thinking Christianly about the Arts.* Grand Rapids: Baker Book House, 1992.

Webber, Robert E. *The Younger Evangelicals: Facing the Challenges of the New World.* Grand Rapids: Baker Books , 2002.

ENDNOTES

1. As quoted in *Realms of Gold: The Classics in Christian Perspective.* (Wheaton, IL: Harold Shaw Publishers, 1991), p. 3.

2. T.S. Eliot, *On Poetry and Poets* (London: Faber, 1957), p. 87.

3. C.S. Lewis, *An Experiment in Criticism* (Cambridge University Press, 1961), pp. 18-19.

chapter

53

FAMILY PRAYER

Kim Butts

"'A family without prayer is like a house without a roof, open and exposed to all the storms of heaven.' . . . Excuses against the discharge of this sacred duty are idle and worthless. Of what avail will it be when we render an account to God for the stewardship of our families to say that we had not time available."[1]

Finding families who pray together regularly other than at meals or bedtime in our culture is rare! A troubling trend shows that most parents have abdicated the responsibility for the spiritual nurturing of their children to the church. "We're too busy" is the prevalent justification for not discharging the biblical mandates of Scripture in the home.

After teaching on this topic for many years, I have found that busyness is actually a defensive smokescreen for an underlying problem. Parents have often told me that they don't pray together as a family because they don't feel competent in their own prayer lives. They don't want to appear foolish or inept to their children, nor do they wish to seem hypocritical since their prayer lives are weak at best. Recent generations have not been trained in prayer at home or in the church; therefore, they lack important spiritual depth and skills with which to teach their own children. From personal experience of teaching families how to pray together, it appears that there is a huge difference in the spiritual climate of homes where seeking the face of the Father is built into the structure of the family.

The reality of the power of prayer, and the faith in God's ability to hear and answer has been lost in most homes. Most parents think of prayer as a devotional act that Christians are supposed to engage in, or that is usually used as a last resort in times of crisis. Most of them had parents who either kept their prayer lives to themselves, or who did not model and encourage prayer in the home. Therefore, another generation is currently struggling with family prayer. The families of pastors, Sunday School teachers, youth workers, etc. are not immune in this area, which is why families who expect and assume that their children will learn everything they need to know about prayer in church are often mistaken.

What Children Need

Children need two important things in order to develop and grow in prayer: example and opportunity. It is vital that parents demonstrate lives of right relationship with Jesus and that they not only model prayer for their children, but teach and train them, stretching their experiences beyond simple memorized mealtime or bedtime prayers. Parents need to develop a mindset that they don't have to be prayer experts in order to teach their children. It is true of prayer that more is caught than taught; however, learning together is a powerful experience. If we model prayer in the home, it will become a natural part of the DNA of our families. As parents, our prayer lives must be part of our lifestyle, lived out before our children. A woman once told me that her earliest memory of prayer was when she listened through a crack in her mother's bedroom door to hear her name being lifted before the Lord. Another friend's early memories were of crawling over maps of the world, laying hands upon nations whose names she couldn't yet pronounce. Yet, she developed a passion for interceding for the lost.

Another vital component for strong family prayer is spouses who pray together. This practice may truly be the most divorce-proofing activity in an age when Christian marriages are failing at astonishing rates. If you aren't praying together, consider beginning, even if it is only five minutes daily. If you are uncomfortable praying out loud together, then begin by praying silently, pray short sentence prayers. Try praying Scripture out loud to the Lord together—the Psalms is a wonderful place to begin. There are also many wonderful devotionals available. Pray together for your children. If you aren't praying for them, who is? Get comfortable praying together as husband and wife, and it will be an easy transition to family prayer. If you are a single parent, find at least one other prayer partner of the same sex who with whom you can pray for your children. What a blessing for children to know that their parents pray for them and that they are receiving the heritage of a praying family.

It is important to develop a time for family prayer that is as consistent as a busy household can make it. Although it's a great place to begin, don't confine the prayer experience for your family into one 10 to 15 minute segment per day. If prayer is to become a natural outflow of our relationship with God, it must be a continual conversation. Of course, we should take time to thank Him for our meals, but that should not be the only contact with the Lord that we teach our children to engage in.

Opportunities to teach prayer to children are constant. Family prayer should be a natural part of everyday family life! Deuteronomy 6:4-9 states that the Lord's commands are to be impressed upon our children. We are to talk about them when we sit at home and when we walk along the road, when we lie down and when we get up. This is a perfect picture of how natural prayer should be in our homes. Every opportunity to draw attention to the fact that the Lord is in control of every aspect of our lives is important. Teachable moments in prayer are at hand continually. Look for every possible chance to draw your children into conversation with Jesus! Perhaps someone in your family is sick or needing to find work. Pray! When you are grateful for something that has happened in your lives, He is the one to whom we direct our thanks! If you see a beautiful sunset, praise the Creator for it! When we worship, we are communicating with God. In fact, the Father has ordained praise from the lips of children and infants to silence the foe and the avenger (see Ps. 8:2). When children praise, the enemy is silenced! That is a powerful assignment!

When you are driving and come upon the scene of an accident . . . pray!

If you notice a homeless person . . . pray! Talk about things happening in the news and pray! Perhaps you have neighbors on your street who are unbelievers . . . pray that they will have the eyes of their hearts open to receive Christ. One important thing to remember as you pray: teach your children to always be ready to be the answer to the prayers they pray. For example, the Lord may stir one of your children to take a blanket or a meal to the homeless person . . . or to develop a relationship with a neighborhood family that does not attend a church, etc. Prayer is a divine *activity*! We pray and He acts . . . and sometimes He acts through us! Teach children to always be listening to the voice of the Holy Spirit who may be urging them to respond.

The prayers of children are often perceived by most adults as "cute" instead of the way God hears them—as powerful! Children are not practicing when they pray—their prayers are active communication with the Father. They are capable of praying with great faith and boldness . . . sometimes better than many adults. Children do not have a junior Holy Spirit! They are fully enabled to communicate with the Father. Children are never too young to pray! I have witnessed children as young as 18 months of age actively engaged in prayer.

Parents are only going to pass on the heritage that was given to them. If prayer was not a part of the culture in which they grew up, they will not naturally pray as a family. It is critical that those who have grown up in praying homes model this spiritual discipline for others. We need to recruit and train family prayer coaches in the church, and it is especially important that pastors, church leaders and their families are modeling prayer! Train family members together so that prayer becomes part of what a Christian family is! Parents need to be taught what Scripture teaches about prayer, and its significance in the personal devotional life, as couples, and in the family. Family prayer is only limited by a lack of creativity: praying Scripture, family prayer parties, prayerwalking, creative prayer stations, involvement in local, national and global prayer events as well as training in fasting, journaling, intercession for the world, governments, children, state and local officials, schools, etc.

I have great hope that the Church will begin to see the return of the daily practice of family prayer that used to be more commonplace than it is today. One key act would be corporate and personal repentance by parents and churches for largely ignoring this spiritual discipline. Parents, especially fathers, must accept the mantle of responsibility placed upon them by the Lord to train up their children. Pastors and church leaders must take the lead to see that prayer is front and center in their own homes. If it isn't happening at the level of leadership, prayerless families will continue to perpetuate and reproduce themselves. Those who have a successful track record of family devotion and prayer need to be encouraged to come alongside those who are struggling. Families need to have access to resources that can help them to develop a lifestyle of prayer in their homes.

If you are reading this chapter, you may be preparing for ministry, or at least interested in the topic for the benefit of your family or church. Be aware that most bodies of believers are untrained and uncommitted to the practice of prayer—as individuals and as families. It is important for parents and church leadership to realize that children are the Church of Now—not tomorrow. Their hearts are already uniquely prepared to seek the heart of God and to intercede for the things that are on the heart of their heavenly Father. The only way children will learn to grow in prayer is if their experience is stretched through learning to pray in their homes and in their extended church family. May you be a man or woman of prayer who recognizes the urgency of the hour, and the importance of training families in powerful, world-changing prayer! Praying families will lead to praying churches filled with the power of the Spirit!

It is quite clear from the Bible, that the real engine room of a united worshipping church is the united worshipping family. The whole stress on God's covenant promises and man's covenant responsibility is evidence of that. It is equally clear, that this is something which must continually be pressed on each successive generation by patient and loving example and instruction.[2]

Questions for Further Thought or Discussion

1. For the sake of evaluation, what is the current state of: Your personal prayer life? Your prayer life with your spouse? Your family prayer life?
2. Can you attribute your answers above to the state of prayer in your family as you were growing up, and is there a correlation?
3. Consider the current state of prayer in the church you attend. Do you agree with the premise that strong praying families translates into a strong

praying church based upon this evaluation? Why or why not?

The author: Kim Butts is Co-founder of Harvest Prayer Ministries of Terre Haute, Indiana. She is the author of *The Praying Family: Creative Ways to Pray Together,* and along with her husband, Dave, is the co-author of *Pray Like the King: Lessons from the Prayers of Israel's Kings.*

SUGGESTED ADDITIONAL READING

Fuller, Cheri. *Loving Your Spouse through Prayer: How to Pray God's Word into Your Marriage.* Nashville: Thomas Nelson, 2007.

Almquist, Jenny. *KidsGap: Training Children to be Kingdom Intercessors.* Terre Haute, IN: PrayerShop Publishing, 2007.

Sacks, Cheryl and Arlyn Lawrence. *Prayer-Saturated Kids: Equipping and Empowering Children in Prayer.* Colorado Springs, CO: NavPress, 2007.

ENDNOTES

1. From "Family Worship" by A.W. Pink. (www.apuritansmind.com.)
2. Graham Nicholson's introduction to *The Directory for Family Worship,* 1647 (Modernised).

chapter

54

MOBILIZING YOUTH TO PRAY

Mike Higgs

There was a holy hush! The sun dropped behind the towering buildings of the cityscape as the young people assembled in Pioneer Courthouse Square on a warm September evening. We had booked the venue, described as "Portland's living room," for a citywide gathering called "One Night: Prayer in the Square" and didn't really know what to expect in terms of turnout. Perhaps the thousands who had shown up that morning as part of See You At The Pole[1] to pray for their schools felt like their mission for the day had been accomplished. Maybe the commute was too long for a 1-1/2 hour gathering on a school night that was completely devoted to worship and prayer, with no "hot" bands or big-name speakers. But as light-rail transit cars and church buses continued to pull up to the Square and spill out excited students, we sensed that something was up.

By Portland's standards, the 2,500 that showed up comprised a pretty sizable prayer meeting. And since the venue is open to the public, we were not the only ones there; street kids, the homeless, and quite a cast of other characters who use the venue as a gathering place mingled around the edges. Some were not all that excited about us praying in their "living room" and were not hesitant about expressing their displeasure. We had anticipated them, though; they were treated with kindness and respect by the kids, our worship pretty much drowned out their more vocal comments, and policemen stood nearby in case things got out of control.

Who was, indeed, in control became evident through the course of the evening. We moved into a season of repentance, asking the students to kneel as a sign of humility and to confess, on behalf of both themselves and the Church in general, our failure to consistently live in a way that incarnated the love of Christ to a lost world. As we knelt before our God in the midst of our city, the Square suddenly became absolutely quiet. It was as if a holy hush descended on the place. For a few minutes, there was zero heckling, zero shouting, zero commotion around the edges; just several thousand kids on their knees in complete silence before their God.

Stories like this, involving praying youth, are not at all uncommon. See You At The Pole started in 1990 with a handful of teenagers in Texas and grew to what prayer leader Steve Hawthorne called "the largest united prayer gathering in history,"[2] with literally millions involved worldwide on a designated Wednesday morning each September. Hundreds of thousands of young people assembled in Washington, DC for The Call in 2000, over 70,000 came to The Call Nashville in July of 2007, and tens of thousands showed up at one of the many other related gatherings across the country for "massive prayer and fasting." You may have your own local stories involving smaller numbers of youth but a similar passionate expression of prayer. There is something about praying youth that strikes a resonant cord.

It is instructive to note that this is one of the few age-specific chapters you will find in this book. There is no chapter entitled, "Mobilizing Senior Citizens to Pray," (although it would make a great chapter!) or one targeting any other age group. Why is that so? I think I have an answer: because youth are cool! OK, there are other, more rational reasons to make youth a chapter focus. Most of us realize the tremendous prayer potential that exists among youth. I would like to discuss some ways to mobilize that potential, but before we go there, we need to define our target audience.

Who are "youth"?

While "youth ministry" in the American church usually targets those of middle school, junior high, or high school age, in many non-western cultures the scope of "youth ministry" may also include children, college students, and/or young adults up to their late twenties. I would like to suggest that for the purposes of this chapter, we embrace this more global definition, for two important reasons. First, the broader definition is important if we are to be accurate in our portrayal of the past. While it is true that the many well-known revivals and spiritual awakenings of the past began among young people (someone aptly observed, "the youth are the kindling that set fire to the old logs") in many cases the ages of those "young people" ranged from late teens to late twenties or beyond, which is a little older that what we today tend to label as "youth." Second, experience tells me that while all young people are strategic in terms of prayer mobilization, it is the collegians and young adults in their early twenties who are most easily mobilized to pray. Two of the larger globally visioned, locally expressed prayer movements of our day, the International House of Prayer[3] and 24/7[4], have the most spiritual traction among this age group. Additionally, it is probably safe to assume that the majority of those who have attended the various gatherings associated with The Call[5] over the past decade are of a similar age. It's just a whole lot easier for collegians or young adults, unencumbered by the need for parental/adult supervision, to grab a flight or hop in the car on short notice for a cross-country "road trip" to a one-day event. So, from here on, when you read "youth," think teenagers *and* collegians *and* young adults in their early twenties.

Harnessing the Passion

Louis Giglio and his friends have appropriated what I believe is an incredibly descriptive ministry name for a movement involving young people: Passion.[6] Youth is a season of life characterized by passion. When that passion is misused or misdirected, the results are disastrous; when it is harnessed and directed by the Holy Spirit, the results are explosive, life-changing, and world-impacting. A passionate, fired-up youth group can transform a local church; a cadre of passionate praying kids can transform a public high school; an auditorium or stadium full of passionately worshipping and praying young people can help transform a city, a region, or even a nation.

So how do we harness that prayer potential? How do we direct the passion of youth so that passionate praying *and* passionate pray-ers are the result? How do we mobilize this emerging "nameless, faceless generation"[7] to storm heaven for sake of their own intimacy with Christ as well as for the sake of the coming of the kingdom of God and the fulfillment of the Great Commission? I believe the two most important ways we can do so are by *modeling* a lifestyle of prayer, and intentionally *mentoring* in prayer. When youth are recipients of both modeling and mentoring, I believe the mobilizing is an almost inevitable by-product!

Modeling a Lifestyle of Prayer

When I was a "youth" (teens and early twenties) I had a very short run as a competitive amateur golfer. In retrospect, what was likely obvious to others became so to me: my golfing style—swing, mannerisms, on-course disposition, putting style—was very much like that of my father. Since he was the one who put a sawed-off golf club in my hand at age 18 months, and since I caddied for or played with him literally thousands of times over the years, his influence was obviously profound. As he liked to say, "the apple doesn't fall far from the tree."

Prayer, along with a number of other spiritual disciplines, is also like that—it is better caught than taught. Certainly, Jesus taught His followers about prayer (i.e., Mt. 6:3-15; Lk. 18:1-8), but even more so, He modeled prayer for them (i.e., Lk. 5:16; 6:12; 9:28ff; 11:1ff; 22:31-32, 39-46). I have *many* books on prayer in my library, but exposure over the years to the prayer habits of a relatively small number of prayer warriors (a few you would recognize, most you would not) has shaped my own praying more than any library of books or seminary course could. As a brand new Christian, I learned to pray through the modeling of a small group of guys in my college fraternity. As a youth pastor in training, I learned to pray by intentionally hanging around a few pastors and youth pastors who I know "had the goods" when it came to prayer. As a budding prayer ministry leader, I sought veteran prayer leaders, watched them in action, and then bought them meals and peppered them with questions. Their answers were invaluable.

For the vast majority of folks reading this chapter—youth pastors (remember my broad definition of "youth"), volunteer youth workers, senior pastors, seminary students, parents—the most significant influence you can have on the emerging generations when it comes to prayer is to model a lifestyle of prayer.

Mentoring

Modeling with intentionality becomes mentoring. Mentoring is modeling on steroids; you can also think of it as discipleship, which is the biblical word for a decision to invest in and impart to others. Jesus modeled a lifestyle of prayer for all to see, but He was much more intentional with His disciples, mixing teaching and training with His modeling. Today, while the numbers of young people turning out for the prayer big events is impressive, I think we older folks still need to be more intentional about mentoring young people in prayer; in many cases, we *do* have something of value to impart to the next generation!

Here are some brief mentoring suggestions that I have gleaned from prayer leaders Lee Brase and Candy Abbott, among others, as well as from my own experiences:[8]

1. Pray often with and for the person you are mentoring.
2. Use the prayers found in the Bible—there are many!
3. Help others "unlearn" bad prayer habits, such as lengthy, wordy praying; praying about surface issues rather than the underlying ones; prayers directed to the people in the room rather than to God; prayers that focus primarily on asking rather than devotion and praise.
4. Young people often have a fear of praying out loud. (Many adults share this fear as well!) The reasons are varied, the most prominent being a lack of confidence. Encourage this kind of praying, but be patient and gentle. Don't place young people in a situation where they have to pray out loud in a group setting unless you know they have some measure of comfort in doing so. The resulting embarrassment can be counterproductive to prayer mentoring.

5. Prayer works because of the volume of faith, not the volume of prayer. The Lord's Prayer, which Jesus gave to us as a model, is remarkably short and succinct. And while there is nothing wrong with shouting in prayer, a loud voice does not do a better job of getting God's attention.
6. Asking is the easy part of prayer; knowing what to ask is the difficult part. (This is a *profound* prayer principle that will likely be covered in other chapters!)

Mobilizing a Passionate Generation

Why did 2,500 young people show up at Pioneer Courthouse Square? Why do millions gather around school flagpoles on a Wednesday morning each September? Why have hundreds of thousands responded to The Call and convened around the country for massive prayer and fasting? Because they know their God (see Daniel 11:32); because they have a childlike faith that God will keep His promises and do what He says in His Word (see 2 Chron. 7:14); because they believe that God answers prayer (see Mt. 21:21-22).

If we build upon that childlike faith by *modeling* a lifestyle of prayer and intentionally *mentoring* in prayer, young people *will* respond to calls for mobilization! They *will* pray for their churches (if the church prayer meetings don't put them to sleep); they *will* pray for their schools; they *will* pray for their cities; they *will* pray for the nations! They are doing so already; with our help and encouragement, they will follow us, they will pass us, and eventually, they will lead us.

And if we are wise, we will let them infect us with their passion.

Questions for Further Thought or Discussion

1. Who are the people who have been your models and mentors in prayer? (You might prayerfully consider thanking them for their investment in your life!)
2. If you were asked to make a list of three "prayer pointers" that you would consider important to share with others, what would be on your list?
3. Ask God to show you some young people (perhaps just one to start with) within your sphere of influence (church, school, ministry, marketplace) who you could mentor in prayer. Then prayerfully consider making that investment in the emerging generations!

The author: Mike Higgs is President of LINC Ministries and Executive Director of the Portland Youth Foundation. He is the author of *Youth Ministry On Your Knees* and *Youth Ministry from the Inside Out.*

SUGGESTED ADDITIONAL READING

Sacks, Cheryl. *The Prayer Saturated Church.* Colorado Springs, CO: *Pray!* Books, 2004.

Foster, Richard. *Prayer: Finding The Heart's True Home.* San Francisco: HarperSanFrancisco, 1992.

Sheets, Dutch. *Intercessory Prayer.* Ventura, CA: Regal Books, 1996.

Duewel, Wesley. *Mighty Prevailing Prayer.* Grand Rapids: Francis Asbury Press, 1986.

ENDNOTES

1. See www.syatp.com.

2. While worldwide attendance at See You At The Pole has been estimated at between three and four million, that figure has of late been far eclipsed by involvement in Global Day of Prayer, (www.globaldayofprayer.com), which takes place annually on Pentecost Sunday and in 2007 involved more than 200 nations!

3. www.ihop.org.

4. www.24-7prayer.com.

5. www.thecall.com.

6. www.268generation.com.

7. Lillian Poon used this prophetic phrase during her 2001 Commencement address at Simpson College.

8. Adapted from my book *Youth Ministry on Your Knees*, pp. 99-100.

chapter

55

PRAYER COMPONENTS FOR CITY-WIDE MOVEMENTS

Tom White

"Prayer is the slender nerve that moves the muscle of omnipotence."[1] Ministering to the worldwide Body of Christ, particularly in emerging movements of unity and collaboration, I have often wondered, do we really believe a statement like this? Prayer privileges us to partner with God in fulfilling His highest purposes. Discerning and agreeing with God's will in prayer releases power to change people and places. Jesus' model prayer, "Your kingdom come, Your will be done, on earth as it is in heaven" (Mt. 6:10), best captures this axiom.

In September, 2006, I facilitated a Leaders Prayer Summit at Lanka Bible College in Kandy, Sri Lanka. Prompted by the Holy Spirit, I brought instruction on prayerwalking, spiritual warfare and intercession. Many local pastors were in the mix. At 6 PM, around twenty-five packed into vans and cars for a "prayer-drive" around the massive Buddhist temples at city center. I was clear that we would neither rebuke men or rail against demons. Through praise and prayer, we would proclaim the favor of Yahweh over Kandy, pronouncing words of redemption and announcing the victory of Jesus Christ over counterfeit deities. Our prayer appeal: "Lord, increase the influence of Your name, Your word and Your people in this dark place. Manifest Your mercy in greater measure." Around 7 PM, we ended up at a high point overlooking Kandy, continuing our proclamations.

I was stunned when we returned around 9:00 PM. Two groups had stayed behind, one to intercede for the "prayer-vanners," another to sustain worship. Arriving back, we were met by sounds of singing and shouting pouring out of the prayer tower. Pastors, pray-ers and worshippers had labored together for three hours storming heaven on behalf of a city known as a stronghold of Buddhist religion. A *"slender nerve"* moving *"the arm of omnipotence."*

I believe prayer is the "irrigation system" that floods a city or region with the favor and presence of the Lord. I want to identify and illustrate some core components of prayer that advance the kingdom of God in the city context. I like how Mission Ottawa (Canada) defines what it is about: "Authentic Relationships engaged in Transformational Prayer resulting in Intentional Mission."[2] Let me caution against three common pitfalls. First, prayer among Christian leaders can focus exclusively on building relationships and praying for personal needs. Pastors prayer groups can become "cul-de-sacs." Second, cities can fall into an obsessive mode of prayer fixated on revival, to the exclusion of ever doing anything concrete to impact the city. Third, well-meaning people are prone to plunge into outreach events, service projects and activities that may bring some results, but often end up exhausting energy, time and resources. As city movements emerge and grow, I believe we are to engage in what I call "anointed activism," serving people's tangible needs, i.e., good deeds soaked in the incense of prayer. Nehemiah embodies this balance. He carefully sought the will of God at every turn. He prayed before every move. He prayed in response to opposition. But he acted decisively, implementing a God-initiated project.

The Jeremiah 29 Challenge

Let's first glean a principle from the Lord's word to the exiles in Babylon. Clearly, this was not their "home town." God exhorts them to "settle down, build houses, plant gardens, have kids, etc." But here's the challenge: "seek the peace of the city where I have caused you to be carried away captive. and pray to the LORD for it; for in its peace you will have peace" (Jer. 29:7). In short, "Ask me to manifest my *shalom* (well being, blessing, prosperity) in this place," which has mutual benefit for both unredeemed and redeemed alike. This, I believe, is the overarching, broader role of intercession in cities where kingdom leaders call God's people to united worship and witness.

Leadership Prayer Groups ("LPGs")

One of the most vital components is leaders committed to pray together. Prayer foci may be multi-faceted, e.g., sharing personal needs, praying blessing on one another's ministries, interceding for the city, etc. Sustainable over time, such groups spread the incense of prayer throughout a city. Personally, I believe an annual prayer summit[3] or extended retreat serves as the "*agape* cement" to break theological and personal barriers between leaders, build trust and hold "living stones" together. There is no substitute for spending extended, unhurried time in God's presence with colleagues. LPGs typically spring up among youth pastors, worship leaders, marketplace leaders, campus ministry leaders, compassion ministry leaders, etc.

Houses of Prayer

When Jesus cleared the temple of moneychangers, he declared, "My Father's house shall be called a house of prayer" (Mt. 21:13). A pastor or prayer champion may catch a vision for their particular fellowship. Similarly, mission organizations often set aside a prayer room or ministry, calling it a "house of prayer." The International House of Prayer in Kansas City has forged a model of "24/7" prayer balanced by a mix of "harp" (worship) and "bowl" (intercession) ministry. The book *Red Moon Rising* documents the emergence of "24/7" prayer among youth in the U.K. Other expressions of this among youth include "the Furnace," and "Boiler Room." While many city movements are initially inspired by these models, I have found few with the leadership and resources to both initiate and sustain such "24/7" intensity.

But many movements *are* setting aside a home or office space dedicated to serve as a house of prayer. Twelve hour, all-night gatherings for worship and prayer are now quite common. In 2003, leaders in Santa Rosa, CA called the Body to participate in "Vertical Call," ten days of sustained worship, praise and intercession. I encourage city leadership teams to seek the Lord on what this looks like locally, assess personnel assets, start slowly, build momentum, and watch for the Lord's favor.

Intercession

Distinct from LPGs, I believe leaders must engage the spiritual labor of offering intercessory prayers for their city or region. Paul is clear in 1 Timothy 2:1. He urges prayer for people of influence, releasing God's favor to make that place conducive for gospel witness and work. In my home city of Corvallis, OR, we call this "CitiPrayer," one hour of intercession every Thursday at 11 AM, with a mix of pastors, women in ministry, youth pastors and marketplace leaders. This is united, fervent, faith-filled prayer that is externally focused on the needs of our city. We have a simple format that has been sustained for five years. The point leader takes ten to fifteen minutes to explain the prayer target, then facilitates a minimum of forty-five minutes of intercession. We aim at staying flexible and Spirit-led. Sometimes we begin in worship. We may invite in a school principal, the mayor or the chief of police. While we strive to keep the "10/50" maxim, we welcome creativity, keeping a door open for other leaders to bring their facilitation ideas and skills to the mix.

Watchmen on the Walls

Another component that undergirds various activities of the movement: the "watchmen" (men and women) intercessors called by the Lord to stand in the gap on behalf of the city. The word of the Lord through Isaiah: "I have set watchmen of your walls, O Jerusalem; they shall never hold their peace day or night" (62:6). God Himself raises these "watchmen." And He gives them permission to pester Him around the clock with the needs of the city, "till He establishes and till He makes Jerusalem a praise in the earth" (Isa. 62:7). This seems to me a divine pattern. Could it be that our Father selects and empowers prayer warriors to release the blessings of heaven in particular spots on earth? I believe so. I do not believe there is any special gift of intercession. All mature kingdom leaders should engage in a deeper life of sacrificial prayer. But clearly there are men and women appointed and anointed to pray perseveringly for God's highest purposes to be released into a city, region or nation.

There are significant differences in the calling and spiritual "DNA" of pastors and intercessors. Thus, there is typically misunderstanding, often conflict between the two. Watchmen are prophetic, pastors practical. Pastors spend most of their time leading, feeding and leading, watchmen most of their time on their knees. Bringing these two callings together in a city is plain hard work, but worth it.

Intercessory leadership that is mature and seasoned is vital, but in many cases not available. Any man, woman or couple equipped to lead intercessors scattered throughout congregations and organizations, is a huge gift. Meeting regularly to pour incense into the bowl (Rev. 5:8) on behalf of their city, these men and women pray:

- for God's blessing on His servants and their ministries.
- for protection and empowerment of pastors and leaders and their families.
- prophetically, discerning and agreeing with God's sovereign purposes and destiny for both the Christians and non-Christians in that city.

Though this ministry is for the most part literally hidden in a "closet," and though intercessors often endure misunderstanding and opposition from both men and devils, their role undergirding and covering the city movement is vital.

Harvest Prayer

Building a healthy movement of unity and prayer in a city can create its own energy, and, frankly, enjoyment. It can be so fulfilling breaking out of old paradigms of isolation and theological separatism that prayer stays centered around our own needs and ministries. *It is imperative that prayer evangelism become the on-going value and lifestyle of a majority of leaders.* For example, I serve the Mission America Coalition as a coach for three of nine pilot cities seeking to implement a Prayer, Care, Share strategy, "Loving our Community to Christ." Of course a city is free to collaborate on an evangelistic outreach, festival or target specific affinity groups with the gospel. Many cities also mobilize their congregations for serving the city's practical needs (Little Rock's "Sharefest," Santa Rosa's "Spring Clean," and "Reach Out Tuscaloosa"). But in the midst of all of our activities, we must cultivate a life of prayer that keeps us attuned to Spirit-led appointments and opens doors for personally sharing Jesus with others. The clear, biblical bottom line of any city movement must be names written in the book of life, and increased numbers of men, women and young people following Christ as disciples.

Spiritual Warfare Prayer

A final, unavoidable component: discerning and dealing with enemy resistance to building unity and battling for souls. Here's an essential truth: you cannot get darkness out of a room, but you can turn on a light. We must not get fixated on driving the devil out of "Dodge City." But we *can and must* obey Jesus'command to love one another, give witness to His saving mercy, and practically touch the felt needs of hurting people. Here's the strategy: "to the intent that now the manifold wisdom of God (unity in Christ!) might be made known by the church to the principalities and powers in the heavenly places" (Eph. 3:10). When we truly worship, walk and witness together, the powers of darkness are ultimately defeated.[4]

Paul wraps up his warfare theme with this admonition: "Praying always with all prayer and supplication in the Spirit" (Eph. 6:18). Prayer is a potent weapon of warfare. But let's give this admonition its context. Stepping back and looking at Ephesians as a whole, I see a progression: ***humility*** (4:2) enables us to walk with one another in ***unity*** (4:3-6). Our unity must also be evidenced by ethical ***purity***, walking in righteousness (4:14-5:21). When we do our best to obey the word of God by walking together in humility, unity and purity, we are then able "to be strong in the Lord" (6:10) and "stand against the wiles of the devil" not as lone rangers, but by standing in corporate ***authority.***

"Just do it!"

In the early 1980s, Corvallis hosted Armin Gesswein, noted prayer statesman. During a teaching seminar, Armin paused frequently, stared at his audience, and said, "If you're smart, you'll do it" (i.e., "pray!"). He shared this in the context of Philippians 4:9: "The things which you learned and received and heard and saw in me, these do, and the God of peace will be with you." If leaders of emerging and developing city movements take this admonition to heart, and put these components in place, God will gladly answer their prayers, pour out favor and advance His kingdom with power. Prayer *is* the slender nerve that moves the arm of divine omnipotence.

Questions for further Thought or Discussion

1. Agree of disagree (and explain why): The quality of life in the community is in direct proportion to the extent to which the Church is praying for the community.
2. Describe three biblical examples of prayer that extend beyond personal need and explain how this perspective can impact the prayer lfie of a congregation.
3. Identify three or four barriers that keep Christians from various congregations from praying together, then describe how those barriers can be overcome.

The author: Tom White is Founder and President of Frontline Ministries, Corvallis, Oregon. He conducts an international ministry facilitating prayer summits and developing citywide prayer movements and is author of *The Believer's Guide to Spiritual Warfare, Breaking Strongholds: How Spiritual Warfare Sets Captives Free* , and *City-Wide Prayer Movements: One Church, Many Congregations.*

ADDITIONAL SUGGESTED READING

Delph, Ed. *Church @ Community.* Orlando, FL: Creation House Publishers, 2005.

Pier, Mac and Sweeting, Katie. *The Power of a City at Prayer.* Downers Grove, IL: InterVarsity Press, 2002.

Hawthorne, Steve and Kendrick, Graham. *Prayerwalking: Praying On Site with Insight.* Lark Mary, FL: Creation House, 1993.

ENDNOTES

1. This often used quote has been attributed to various people. In *The Tremendous Power of Prayer* by Charlie Jones and Bob Kelly (Howard Books, 2000) this quote is attributed to Edwin Hartsill (http://www.simonsays.com/content/book.cfm?tab=1&pid=521734&agid=2). *The Brainy Quotes* website (and many other websites) attributes the quote to Martin Farquhar Tupper, an English writer, and poet, and the author of *Proverbial Philosophy*. (http://www.brainyquote.com/quotes/quotes/m/martinfarq158341.html). The United Methodist Church website attributes the quote to Charles H. Spurgeon (http://www.umc.org/site/c.gjJTJbMUIuE/b.1518745/k.F11F/Commentary_Prayer_event_brings_unity_to_community.htm). A Greek Orthodox website attributes the quote to Archbishop Seraphim of Johannesburg and Pretoria, Greek Orthodox Patriarchate of Alexandria and All Africa. (http://www.greece.org:8080/opencms/opencms/HEC_Organizations/gopatalex/sa/Prayers/Some_thoughts_about_Prayer_xHis_Eminence_Archbishop_Seraphimx.html). Tradition attributes the quote to Jonathan Edwards. Variations of the quote are to be found in many books such as *31 Days of Prayer* (Multnomah, 2005) by Ruth and Warren Myers, changing "the muscle of omnipotence" to "the mighty hand of God."

2. See also my book, *City-Wide Prayer Movements*, (Servant Publications 2001, for additional practical helps.

3. For more information on prayer summits, go to www.prayersummits.net.

4. See my two books on spiritual warfare for further teaching, *The Believer's Guide to Spiritual Warfare,* (Ventura, CA: Regal Books 1990) and *Breaking Strongholds*.

chapter

56

PASTORAL PRAYERS OF INTERCESSION

Stan May

Pastors are busy people. No honest, full-time pastor works less than forty hours a week in the ministry, and numerous pastors log many more hours regularly. The demands on the pastor are numerous as well: pastoral visitation, hospital ministry, sermon preparation, time with family, rest for the body, and the pastor's own spiritual life and enrichment. Since pastors are inundated continually by these genuine pressures, they may be tempted to neglect crucial spiritual responsibilities.

Prayer, and especially intercession for the flock, falls into this category of omission. One survey of North American pastors recorded that "eighty percent of pastors surveyed spend less than fifteen minutes a day in prayer."[1] This lamentable statistic highlights a major failing in pastoral ministry. While contemporary pastors generally see prayer as a non-essential, the apostles thought otherwise. They devoted themselves to "prayer and the ministry of the word" (Acts 6:4). Prayer is so vital that one can safely posit this statement: *The key to the rest of our life and ministry will be the investment of prayer we make in the lives of others.* This chapter examines biblical intercessors, considers the exhortations of notable pastors, and then offers some concrete suggestions from a fellow pastor who prays for his people regularly.

Biblical Examples

The Bible is replete with examples of intercessors. One of the earliest books in the Bible introduces Job as a righteous man who feared God, hated evil, and prayed for his family. He rose early in the morning to offer burnt offerings for each of them regularly (Job 1:5). Abraham interceded for Sodom, not because he loved the Sodomites (Genesis 14 shows that), but on behalf of his nephew Lot. The psalmist tells us that Moses the intercessor "stood . . . in the breach" (Ps. 106:23) when the people of God sinned, and his intercession averted their destruction. Hezekiah prayed for the Jews who had not purified themselves so that they could eat the Passover (2 Chron. 30:19). Perhaps Samuel most compellingly demonstrated what it means to be a praying man. When he concluded his public service to the nation, he assured them of his continued care, "As for me, I vow that I will not sin against the Lord by ceasing to pray for you. I will teach you the good and right way" (1 Sam 12:23, HCSB).

Two other Old Testament passages provide insights to intercessory prayer by leaders. The garments Exodus 28 describes portray the high priest's principle role as intercessor for the children of Israel. On the ephod that covers his shoulders he wears two onyx stones engraved with the names of the twelve sons of Israel. On his heart, he wears a breastplate with twelve stones, each individually engraved with a name of one of the sons of Israel. The high priest ministers by bearing the names of the children of Israel on his heart out of love, and on his shoulders out of responsibility and burden (for regular intercessory prayer *is* a burden). Intercession, moreover, is the duty of prophets as well as priests. Jeremiah rebukes the false prophets and calls them to cease lying and start praying, "If they are indeed prophets and if the word of the Lord is with them, let them intercede with the LORD of Hosts . . ." (Jer. 27:18, HCSB).

The New Testament differs not at all from the Old in exemplifying intercessory prayer. Epaphras, the church planter at Colossae, labors fervently for those Colossian Christians "in prayers, that [they] may stand perfect and complete in all the will of God" (Col 4:12). Paul prays regularly for the congregations under his care and tells them he does so (Rom. 1:9; Phil. 1:4; Col. 1:3; 1 Thess. 1:2; 2 Thess. 1:11). The fear of the Lord motivates Paul (2 Cor. 5:11). In fact, Kenneth Boa observed, "The apostle Paul had only two days on his calendar: today and that day (the day he would stand before Christ), and he lived every today in light of that day."[2] John the Elder prays for Gaius (3 Jn. 2). The Holy Spirit also intercedes for the saints according to the will of God (Rom. 8:26-7). Preeminent among prayers (as He is in all things) is Jesus. He prays for His disciples all night before He chooses the twelve (Lk. 6:12-13). He prays for Peter before Satan sifts him (22:31-32). He prays for the apostles and all who would believe on Him through their Word that they would be one (Jn. 17:9, 20-21). Even in heaven, the Lord Jesus presently intercedes for His own (Heb. 7:25); thus pastors who intercede for their people show great likeness to Christ.

Pastoral Examples

Perhaps pastors find it difficult to pray because they lead such busy lives. Records abound, however, of the prayer lives and habits of those whose ministries marked this world. Men who touched the world for God learned first to touch the throne of God for the world. They were preeminently men of prayer.

John Wesley stated, "I have so much to do that I spend several hours in prayer before I am able to do it."[3] Charles Haddon Spurgeon lectured his students eloquently about the need for prayer, "The fact is, the secret of all ministerial success lies in prevalence at the mercy-seat."[4] He also wrote, "If you are a genuine minister of God you will stand as a priest before the Lord, spiritually wearing the ephod and the breast-plate whereon you bear the names of the children of Israel, pleading for them within the veil."[5] W. A. Criswell, speaking of the pastor's duty of ministering to people, noted as first priority, "Pray for and be concerned for the welfare of your flock."[6] Ron Dunn wrote of the time when he served as pastor:

> When I was a pastor I carried in my pocket a little black book listing the names of church members I was praying for especially—

> individual needs, special requests, things like that. Inadvertently, I mentioned my little black book in a sermon one Sunday morning. Afterward I was deluged with people asking two questions: Were their names in my book? And, Would I add the name of a person they were concerned about?[7]

These men, and countless others, testify to the fact that the effective pastor must be an effectual intercessor.

Personal Example

I served as a missionary in the country of Zimbabwe from 1989-95. While there, Tom Elliff vicariously influenced me to pray for God's people. He had written a brief book on prayer[8] that chronicled his own journey to becoming an intercessory pastor. This book challenged me to pray regularly for others. As my wife and I began to intercede together for our work, we saw barriers to the gospel begin to fall, and we also saw a renewed work among the churches of the city of Bulawayo. God began to work in momentous ways; we saw churches planted, pastors renewed, and specific prayers answered.

When we returned to the United States (after the Zimbabwean government refused to renew our work permits), I began work on my Ph.D. At the same time, I had the honor of serving as interim pastor of several churches. I started praying for the members weekly. I used the pictorial directory that some of the churches had published and prayed through them. This practice allowed me to pray for the individuals in the family by name and call them by name when I saw them. Once when I spoke to a woman as I moved down the aisle, she asked how I knew her name. I responded, "I pray for you every week." She began to weep, and she then told me, "No one's ever done that for me before."

I currently serve as a part-time pastor (if there is such a thing), and have developed the habit of praying through the entire church roll weekly. I also attempt to pray for most of our faithful members by name daily. The benefits of this habit have been incalculable: I know and love my people; God has knitted hearts in the flock; people are encouraged and blessed to know that their pastor prays for them; and, God allows us to see fruit of all kinds in the body.

Developing an Intercessory Lifestyle

How does a pastor develop a lifestyle of intercession for his people? First, he must understand the purpose of intercession. The intercessors of Scripture and church history stood between God and men to seek God's work in human lives for His glory. Elliff discussed the purpose of intercession, "The proper purpose of intercession is seeking to secure the grace of God for an individual, or individuals, so that fellowship with God or usefulness for God will be established and maintained."[9] Since prayer is primarily cooperating with God to see His purposes come to pass on earth, intercessors must learn to pray for people biblically. I have learned to pray Scripture back to God as I intercede for others, asking for their growth in grace (2 Pet. 3:18), their walk with God (Col. 1:9-14), their surrender to Him (Rom. 12:1-2), and their love for Him (Mk. 12:30). Scripture expresses God's will, and as Elliff noted, "The major issue of intercession is God's will."[10]

Second, the pastor must set aside the time necessary for intercession. An intriguing verse describing the life of the Lord Jesus states, "Yet He often withdrew to deserted places and prayed" (Lk. 5:16, HCSB). Luke uses the imperfect verb tense, so the text clearly teaches that Jesus "was withdrawing" habitually. Time for intercession is not as lengthy as one might suppose; when the pastor develops the practice of intercession, he can pray effectively for hundreds of people in one hour.

After the pastor sets a time, he should develop a list of his members, perhaps even breaking up the list by the days of the week. He may use the church directory, a copy of the church roll, or some other method (such as a PDA). He should revise the list regularly as new members join and others drop from the roll and pray over it faithfully. He can keep it in his vehicle and pray for his members while driving.

As he prays for his people, he may use Scripture to pray generally for the church, requesting Christ's preeminence in the body (Col. 1:18), unity in the church so that the world will believe in Jesus (Jn. 17:21), finances for the church, and laborers for the harvest (Mt. 9:38). When he prays for each member, the pastor can ask God to bless that person as he calls out the member's name before God.

I once asked Dr. B. Gray Allison, the founding president of Mid-America Baptist Seminary, how he was able to pray for so many people daily. "First," he said, "I don't pray for myself. I thank God for saving me, calling me into the ministry, and putting me at Mid-America. Then I pray for people by name, asking God for any specifics I know about them, such as salvation, healing, or finances; if I don't know anything special, I ask God to bless them, because the blessing of God is everything that they need."

Last of all, the pastor should tell his people regularly that he prays for them. Paul did so, Jesus told people that he had already prayed for him, and Samuel told the Israelites that he was praying for them. Telling the congregation endears the pastor to the people. My members tell me that they genuinely feel loved and cared for, even though I do not have the time to visit, because they know that I pray for them. Telling them also holds them accountable to continue in prayer. If the pastor tells his flock that he is praying, he had better do it. He will sense the burden both from the hearts of the people and from the Lord.

Intercession focuses the pastor on the essentials. Jesus was preeminently a man of prayer. For the apostles, prayer was priority one. Paul breathed heaven's air because he breathed heaven's prayers. Faithful pastors must intercede for their people if they desire to impact the kingdom of God and invest significantly in their members' lives. If the key to the rest of our life and ministry is the investment of prayer we make in the lives of others, then pastoral prayers of intercession are both necessary and ultimately rewarding.

Questions for Further Thought or Discussion

1. In what sense is intercessory prayer an "investment in the lives of others"?
2. If intercessory prayer is so significant, why is it so neglected?
3. What positive and immediate steps will you make now to begin to integrate the practice of intercessory prayer into your ministry?

The author: Dr. Stan May is Professor and Chairman of the Missions Department as well as Director of Church Relations and Practical Ministries at Mid-America Baptist Theological Seminary, located in Cordova, Tennessee.

SUGGESTED ADDITIONAL READING

Boa, Kenneth. *Conformed to His Image: Biblical and Practical Approaches to*

Spiritual Formation. Grand Rapids: Zondervan, 2001.
Dunn, Ron. *Don't Just Stand There, Pray Something.* Nashville: Thomas Nelson, 1992.
Elliff, Thomas D. *A Passion for Prayer: Discovering Deeper Intimacy with God.* Wheaton, IL: Crossway, 2001.

ENDNOTES

1. http://www.bethesdarenewalcentre.org/PastorStatistics.html (accessed 2 July 2007).

2. Kenneth Boa, *Conformed to His Image: Biblical and Practical Approaches to Spiritual Formation* (Grand Rapids: Zondervan, 2001), p. 141.

3. http://www.tentmaker.org/Quotes/prayerquotes.htm (accessed 9 July 2007).

4. Charles Haddon Spurgeon, *Lectures to My Students* (Lynchburg, VA: The Old-Time Gospel Hour, 1894 rep.), p. 49.

5. Spurgeon, p. 46.

6. Wally Amos Criswell, *Criswell's Guidebook for Pastors* (Nashville: Broadman, 1980), p. 363.

7. Ron Dunn, *Don't Just Stand There, Pray Something* (Nashville: Thomas Nelson, 1992), p. 101.

8. Thomas D. Elliff, *Praying for Others* (Nashville: Broadman, 1979).

9. Elliff, p. 51.

10. Elliff.

chapter

57

WORSHIP BASED PRAYER VS. LIST BASED PRAYER

Dick Eastman

Prayer has many facets, functions and focuses. Sometimes we wonder if we're getting it just right when we pray and fear our petitions may be negated because we're not sure we're praying properly. But I recall hearing a lady-preacher from Harlem in New York City once say, "God can take what we say backwards and hear it forwards."

I thought of that statement when preparing this chapter. The very title "Worship Based Prayer vs. List Based Prayer" seems to suggest some type of contradiction or conflict. The preposition versus means "against; in contrast to; as an alternative." Yet, I see both types of prayer as potentially combining to become some of the most powerful praying available to believers today. But first let me define the differences.

Worship Based Prayer: Intercessory Worshippers

Worship based prayer might be defined as prayer that is saturated in worship or offered in an atmosphere of worship. In recent years a new term has surfaced in Christ's body to define this: intercessory worship. It's a term I first heard from worship strategist Mike Bickle who founded International House of Prayer in Kansas City, Missouri.

Here it may be helpful to provide a personal definition of worship. To me, in a sentence, worship is: Any act, thought or expression of willful adoration that exalts and enthrones God, thereby defeating and dethroning Satan. Think of this in terms of its impact on corporate prayer as our intercession is bathed in an atmosphere of pure worship.

When intercession (i.e., prayerful intervention in the needs of others) is saturated with fervent worship, we have "worship based prayer," or intercessory worship.

More specifically, intercessory worship pictures concentrated worship that becomes intercessory in nature because it carries the prayers of God's people, like the fragrance of incense, before God's throne, and in so doing releases His power and purposes upon earth, particularly regarding the end-time harvest. (See Rev. 5:8-10 and 8:1-6.) I see this kind of praying as "worship based prayer."

A unique picture of worship based prayer can be seen in the harp and bowl symbols described in Revelation 5:8-10. Here we read: "And when he [the Lamb] had taken it [the scroll], the four living creatures and the twenty-four elders fell down before the Lamb. Each one had a harp and they were holding golden bowls full of incense, which are the prayers of the saints" (Rev. 5:8, NIV, brackets added).

Interestingly, the worshippers coming before the Lamb with harps in one hand (symbols of worship) and bowls in the other (symbols of prayer and intercession) seem to combine these two symbols in the release of a song never sung before. It is a song of global harvest. The text continues: "And they sang a new song: 'You are worthy to take the scroll and to open its seals, because you were slain, and with your blood you purchased men for God from every tribe and language and people and nation' " (5:9, NIV).

It is not without significance that the harp and bowl symbolism here, including the singing of a "new song," is linked to the redeemed coming from every tribe, language, people and nation. This clearly is a harvest song.

Later, in Revelation 8:1-6, we see "the prayers of all the saints" (a picture of intercession) being released with "much incense" (a picture of worship) at the throne. This release results in the final unfolding of God's plan through the sounding of seven trumpets. It is the last of these trumpet blasts (11:15) that releases a shout in heaven, declaring: "The kingdoms of this world have become the kingdoms of our Lord and of His Christ, and He shall reign forever and ever" (11:15).

But all of this follows the release of what might be described as "worship based prayer." Worship, thus, becomes a vital key. Especially helping me understand the role of worship in gathering in the last days harvest (I had already seen the significance of intercession) was John Piper's timely book *Let the Nations Be Glad*. In it Piper wrote:

> Missions is not the ultimate goal of the church. Worship is. Missions exists because worship doesn't. Worship is ultimate, not missions, because God is ultimate, not man. When this age is over, and the countless millions of redeemed fall on their faces before the throne of God, missions will be no more. It is a temporary necessity. But worship abides forever.[1]

But what might we say of the importance of "list based prayer" and how might it be strengthened by combining it with that aspect called intercessory worship?

List Based Prayer: Intercessory Aarons

Regarding the issue of "list based prayer" there is a unique, symbolic picture for today's intercessors in studying God's dress code for Aaron, ancient Israel's high priest, when he entered God's presence (Ex. 28:2-20.) Aaron's vestments were to include twelve precious stones upon which were engraved the names of Israel's twelve tribes.

Of Aaron's ministry before the Lord on behalf of Israel (a clear picture of intercession) Scripture says, "Aaron will regularly carry the names of the sons of Israel on the Breastpiece of Judgment over his heart as he enters the

Sanctuary into the presence of God for remembrance" (Ex. 28:30, MSG). The paraphrase adds, "They [the names of the tribes] will be over Aaron's heart when he enters the presence of God. In this way Aaron will regularly carry the Breastpiece of Judgment into the presence of God" (28:30).

I had read this passage recently during a time of prayer just as I was about to hold before the Lord pictures of several families I pray for daily, including our immediate family, as well as praying over my usual prayer list with numerous names on it.

As I held these pictures in prayer, specifically mentioning each person pictured by name, I realized afresh the significance of such symbolism, including the value of keeping an up-to-date prayer list for practical intercession. The same might apply for those who meet regularly in corporate settings. They become, in a sense, intercessory Aarons.

I do believe there is both a biblical basis and a practical significance for "list based prayer" when it comes to meaningful intercession, even including the praying over objects like pictures of family or friends (or weekly church bulletins or missionary newsletters). We recall how King Hezekiah took a threatening letter from his enemy Sennacherib, carrying it into God's presence and spreading it before Him in prayer, seeking God's intervention (2 K. 19:14). God did intervene, and soon a single angel destroyed 185,000 enemy troops of this evil king (19:35). (I've often jokingly told attendees at my prayer seminars that if they get in really big trouble, ask God to send this specific angel!)

Note also the biblical symbolism of praying specifically over a map as we see in an experience of the prophet Ezekiel. God tells him, "Son of man, take a clay tablet and lay it before you, and portray on it a city, Jerusalem. Lay siege against it" (Ezk. 4:1-2). God's siege directive to Ezekiel follows, including a list of specific prophetic assignments the prophet is to engage in "over" the map of Jerusalem.

Of course, in ancient Bible days a clay tablet was the equivalent today of our drawing a rough sketch of one's city on paper. To me, God was saying, "I have a specific plan for Jerusalem, but before I carry it out, I want you to declare it over your map." Often in my travels to distant nations where I've conducted prayer conferences, I've had participants draw a map of their country on blank paper and then pray in groups over their maps. I would put this in the category of list praying in a corporate setting.

Some may question if simply "praying" a list (or "making mention" of names of others before the Lord in prayer), really counts as meaningful prayer, whether in a personal or corporate prayer setting. Early on in my prayer life I was significantly impacted by the Apostle Paul's various references to "making mention" of his converts and colleagues in regular prayer.

Note several examples:

- "For God is my witness, whom I serve with my spirit in the gospel of his Son, that without ceasing I make mention of you always in my prayers" (Rom. 1:9).
- "Therefore I also, after I heard of your faith in the Lord Jesus and your love for all the saints, do not cease to give thanks for you, making mention of you in my prayers" (Eph. 1:15-16).
- "We give thanks to God always for you all, making mention of you in our prayers" (1 Thess. 1:2).
- "I thank my God upon every remembrance of you, always in every prayer of mine making request for you all with joy" (Phil. 1:3-4).
- "I thank my God, making mention of you always in my prayers" (Phlm. 1:4).

True, one might interpret Paul as saying he prayed generically for all these groups (a kind of "Bless 'em all, oh God" prayer). But we particularly note that Paul told Philemon (who had to have been but one of numerous close friends and contacts) that he specifically made mention of him, by name, in prayer. Surely Philemon was not the only one!

I personally believe "making mention" of friends, loved ones, pastors, missionaries, and government leaders, etc., whether in personal or corporate prayer, is honored by God.

To me, there is something akin to one bringing a prayer list before God (i.e., making mention of each person on one's list) to that of Aaron wearing his jeweled vestments containing Israel's tribes as he entered God's presence. Aaron was, after all, going into God's presence on behalf of these tribes which was a clear act of intercession.

Certain prayer strategists of our day, in seeking to categorize different gifts in prayer, have inadvertently suggested "list intercessors" as those who have some sort of gift to do this. To me, it's not a gift but a discipline. Anyone who wants to remember specific people in prayer on a regular basis would find it helpful to keep a list. It's just good common sense. The more one has to purchase at the grocery store the larger is his or her list. Further, the longer the list, the more time spent at the store. Some intercessory Aarons spend whole days shopping!

A More Excellent Way

In sharing these thoughts I feel there is a "more excellent way" in our corporate praying than trying to decide whether worship based prayer is better than list based prayer. It is obviously to combine the two. It's as simple as saturating our lists with much worship, enthroning God, through worship, in our lists.

What does it mean to enthrone God in our prayer lists? King David sang to the Lord, "you are enthroned as the Holy One; you are the praise of Israel" (Psalm 22:3, NIV). The literal Hebrew translation of this passage reads, "You are enthroned, O God, upon the praises of Israel" (NIV margin note). The King James Version translates it, "thou art holy, O thou that inhabitest the praises of Israel." The Hebrew word translated "inhabitest" here, *yawshab*, comes from a root word meaning "to sit." Of course, the place God sits is His throne, thus leading to the use of the expression "enthroned."

The thought here is that God literally dwells (manifests Himself) where His people praise Him. He inhabits that very place. I am told the literal Japanese translation of this verse reads, "When God's people praise Him, He brings a big chair and sits there."[2]

Imagine, then, God bringing a big chair and sitting in our midst, responding to our very lists as we worship Him! This is the power of "worship based prayer" combined with "list based prayer."

Questions for Further Thought or Discussion

1. How would you define the difference between "worship based prayer" and "list based prayer?"
2. What do you believe it means to enthrone God in our praying over a list of requests?
3. How might our corporate (or personal) times of prayer incorporate more intentional worship?

The author: Dick Eastman is President of Every Home for Christ in Colorado Springs, Colorado. He is the author of many books including *The Hour That Changes the World, No Easy Road: Discover the Extraordinary Power of Personal Prayer, A Celebration of Praise, Beyond Imagination, Heights of Delight, Pathways of Delight, Rivers of Delight,* and *The Change the World School of Prayer.*

SUGGESTED ADDITIONAL READING

Teykl, Terry. *The Presence Based Church.* Muncie IN: Prayer Point Press, 2003.

Bickle, Mike. *Passion for Jesus: Growing in Extravagant Love for God.* Lake Mary, FL: Creation House, 1993.

Henderson, Daniel. *Fresh Encounters: Experiencing Transformation through United Worship-Based Prayer.* Colorado Springs, CO: *Pray!* Books, 2004.

ENDNOTES

1. John Piper, *Let Nations Be Glad: The Supremacy of God in Missions* (Grand Rapids: Baker Book House, 1993), p. 11.

2. Joseph Garlington, *Worship: The Pattern of Things in Heaven* (Shippensburg, VA: Destiny Image Publishing Inc., 1997), p. Introduction.

chapter

58

PRAYING VS. BEING "DEVOTED TO PRAYER"

Steve Loopstra

Is there really a difference between praying and being devoted to prayer? Ask most people what comes to their minds when you say "prayer," they would usually respond with words indicating that praying is something that we do. It might be seen as an activity at a particular time in the church calendar. It might be the idea of turning to God for help in times of trouble, or for direction in life. In order to help us to understand the distinctiveness of being devoted to prayer it is helpful to study the word used in the New Testament for "devoted"

Being Devoted to Prayer

The word that is used for "devoted" in the New Testament is the word, *proskar-*

tereoo. Before looking at the definition of this word, it would be helpful to look at some of the ways that it is used. The first instance of this word is found in Mark 3:9, where Jesus is preaching to the crowds and He told His disciples to have a small boat **ready** for Him. That word "ready" is what we are focusing on. A second instance of this word is found in Acts 1:14 where we find the disciples in the upper room. It states that they all joined together **constantly** in prayer. This was the attitude of the disciples as they waited on the promised gift of the Holy Spirit. Then in Acts 2: 42-46, this word is found twice. Once in verse 42 where it says, they **devoted** themselves to the apostles' teaching, and to the fellowship, to the breaking of bread, and to prayer. And in verse 46 where it states every day they **continued** to meet together.

In Acts 6:4 there is a revealing use of this word when the apostles, confronted with a ministry issue, deferred the leadership of that issue to other qualified leaders so that they will give our **attention** to prayer and the ministry of the word. Notice that for them as leadership in the church, it was not only the ministry of the word, but they were to be "devoted," *proskartereoo* to prayer first in order of importance. Two other references in the book of Acts give further light into the use of this word. In Acts 8:13 it talks about Simon who was following Phillip everywhere, and in Acts 10:7, this word is used of one of Cornelius' solders who waited on him continually. The next instance of this word, *proskartereoo* is found in Romans 12:12, in Paul's instructions to the church that they were to be "faithful" in prayer. Romans 13:6, mentions public officials who give their "full time" to public service. Finally, in Colossians 4:2, Paul instructs the Colossian church with the short verse telling them to **devote** themselves to prayer, being watchful and thankful.

The definition of *proskartereoo* is very instructive now that we have seen some of its uses. Strong's defines the word in this way: "to be earnest towards, that is, to persevere, be constantly diligent, or to attend assiduously all the exercises, or to adhere closely."[1] In case you missed the definition of "assiduously," it means: "marked by careful unrelenting attention, persistent application."[2]

Praying vs. Devoted

So from the use and the definitions of just this one word that is translated "devoted," we see that there is a much higher standard in being "devoted" to prayer than simply "doing" or "saying" our prayers. Being devoted means that it takes us to a whole new level of commitment, and persistence. Being devoted to prayer carries with it these ideas of persistence, purposefulness, constancy, and unrelenting attention. Those are not the characteristics of simply saying prayers or having a once a week prayer meeting. There is built into the very essence of being devoted a lifestyle component. One could say that the main difference between praying and being devoted to prayer is that being devoted to prayer is the manifestation of a lifestyle lived in a constant state of prayerful connection with God.

Consider these contrasting thoughts on praying and being devoted to prayer:

- **Praying**—fits into my schedule, at my convenience. **Devoted to prayer**—is a vital part of everything I do and am.
- **Praying**—is something I do. **Devoted to prayer**—it something I am.
- **Praying**—is an obligation to fulfill. **Devoted to prayer—**is a delightful outflow of my life with God.

What makes the difference?

The cultural influences that weigh upon us, even in the areas of ministry remind us that we are used to "doing" things ourselves, and really do not need God most of the time. Those influences push us toward thinking of prayer as just another one of the "things we need to do" in our Christian life, or one of the many programs that we need to run to keep the church healthy. That mentality leads us to see prayer as another one of the programs that we run in the church, or one of the many "plates" that we must keep spinning in order to be a successful Christian.

In addition, our difficulty in understanding the ways of God adds to our confusion of what prayer is really all about.

Dr. Ronald Goetz says it well, when he writes in *The Christian Century*:

> It is difficult for modern Christians to pray precisely because we carry within ourselves the very questions about how God works in the world—or makes any difference in the world—that cause the so-called atheists among us to turn their backs on God in melancholy outrage. Further, we wonder, are we constantly to go through

> the motions of asking—when we know we can do for ourselves? Weren't we created to be creative, hardworking beings? Aren't our talents given to us precisely so that we can produce? And is it not an embarrassing fact that because we generally don't need God to bail us out, when we do become desperate and could indeed use help we are almost ashamed to ask? We don't want to be like the shameless son who never visits his parents except to hit them for a loan.[3]

How to be Devoted to Prayer

If we see God as a theological abstract or our Christian faith as a duty to be fulfilled and prayer as one of the many duties to fulfill, we will miss entirely the secret to being devoted to prayer. How is it that the early church could gather together "attending assiduously" to prayer in constant dedication? How could the early apostles commit themselves to being devoted to prayer over the duties of ministry? How could Paul charge the Church to live a life of giving constant, unrelenting attention to the matter of prayer? One reason, I believe, is that fact that they understood that prayer, rather being a duty to be fulfilled was a relationship to be lived. It was a living vital relationship with a living, passionate, loving Redeemer God. In any human relationship, where there is true mutual love and a deepening, growing affection, that relationship is not seen as a "duty" but a delight. Being with that other person, spending time, hearing their voice, all are a natural outgrowth of a genuine relationship.

Why should we not think of prayer in the same manner? If we have a vital, intimate, mutually loving relationship with the Holy, Eternal God of the universe, prayer would be a natural response of the heart to that relationship. We would delight in times of prayer, not seeing them as a duty or an obligation. We would seek times of prayer, not be forced into them through duty of necessity. From our "normal" Western church mindset, those terms of unrelenting, continuous, and attending assiduously all seem a little "extreme." However, from an understanding of relationship, being devoted to prayer in those ways begins to seem quite normal.

How does that look?

If we were to accept the premise that we need to learn to be devoted to prayer and not just "do" our praying, what would that look like? How would that be seen in the individual life, and in the corporate life of the local congregation?

This is now where we begin to talk about "culture" and "lifestyle." Individually, if we are devoted to prayer, it will be a part of every area of our lives. Instead of being an occasional duty, prayer would permeate every area of our lives, because we would exercise it as our vital relational link with our heavenly Father. Decisions would be made only after seeking the Lord in prayer. Prayer would become a natural response to the challenges and the frustrations of life. In this regard, think of prayer as like "Gator-Aid." The commercials for this sports drink show a group of guys playing basketball or football. A close up reveals one person sweating, only the drops of sweat are green or orange, the colors of Gator-Aid. The tag line at the end of the commercial asks, "Is it in you?" That is the question we must ask ourselves as we look at what being devoted to prayer would look like. Is it in you? It is not something that you put on for special occasions, like a suit jacket, it is a part of the very essence of who we are.

The same analogies can be used of being devoted to prayer in the local church. Each of the passages cited above in relation to the church are corporate in their expression. Being devoted to prayer is a corporate identity for us a people of God. Is prayer a living vital, growing passion in the lives of the senior pastors and leadership of the church? Prayer will never become a culture in the church without the express, determined, persistent leadership of the senior pastor and staff. Is every program and move in the church birthed in prayer, covered in prayer, and empowered through prayer? Is consulting the Lord in prayer "in" the leadership and staff at every level, so that all activities of the church come, not from the latest how to manual, but from hearing the heart of the Father?

In conclusion, it is evident that being "devoted to prayer" is vastly different in its depth and scope than just "saying prayers." Being "devoted to prayer" means that we, *to be earnest toward, that is, to persevere, be constantly diligent, or to attend assiduously all the exercises, or to adhere closely.* The challenge then is to not hedge around what this word clearly means, to honestly examine our own lives to see whether we are living a life, devoted to prayer, and then to seek the Lord about what that means in building a *culture of prayer* in our local congregations. Dealing with being devoted to prayer means that we will need to be "counter-cultural" in much of our current thinking about how we view prayer, and be willing to move into new areas, and learn new ways of living and thinking. The standard is set by God. The response is up to us.

Questions for Further Thought or Discussion

1. List the three most compelling differences between praying and devotion to prayer and explain the implication of each toward personal prayer and corporate prayer.
2. Discuss the impact of American cultural influences on prayer, giving several examples.
3. How would you disciple an individual toward becoming devoted in prayer? A congregation?

The author: Steve Loopstra is Executive Director of Prayer Transformation Ministries in Minneapolis, Minnesota.

SUGGESTED ADDITIONAL READING

Duewel, Wesley L. *Mighty Prevailing Prayer.* Grand Rapids: Zondervan Publishing House, 1990.

Bounds, E.M., *The Complete Works of E.M. Bounds on Prayer: Experience the Wonders of God Through Prayer.* Grand Rapids: Baker Books, 2006.

Hughey, Rhonda, *Desperate for His Presence: God's Design to Transform Your Life and Your City.* Minneapolis: Bethany House, 2004.

ENDNOTES

1. James Strong. *The New Strong's Expanded Exhaustive Concordance of the Bible* (Nashville: Thomas Nelson Publishers, 2001). *Greek Dictionary of the New Testament,* p. 214.

2. *Webster's Random House College Dictionary.* (New York: Random House, 1991), p. 83.

3. Ronald Goetz, "Lord, Teach Us to Pray (Luke 11:1-4)" *Christian Century,* November 5, 1986, p. 974.

chapter

59

THE RELATIONAL AFFECTS OF CORPORATE PRAYER

David Livingstone Rowe

We had come to know the charm of our Sunday evening moments on the mountain, we few friends in faith who headed up once again to love on Jesus. Not quite a dozen strong this particular evening, we piled in the car and ascended from our house to where pavement ends and the quarter-mile hike begins. Having settled into our usual hillside sanctuary, blankets and water bottles in place, guitar uncased, we took deep breaths and contemplatively gazed around the northern Salt Lake City valley with the closer participants like hummingbird moths who had come to attend our leisurely prayer time. Chatter waned, songs began, stars emerged, a sweet wind caressed our cheeks. Pleasant it was and heartful, but tonight something enormous would transpire to astound us, something to make angels weep for joy.

It's a lovely, meditative place, and I'll start here in my reflections on the relational affects of our practice of corporate prayer. Something in the very environment communicates to us and evokes a response. Imagings and palpable messagings come to strike the heart in their wordless ways of divine love and we of the "little flock" lift up our responses in prayer, returning our love. For the ritual of our corporate prayer attaches itself to a sense of place and that sense of place so profoundly affects us, we come to realize it is of a piece with the ritual itself—good ritual, not dead ritual, for it breathes and exudes life. In these places God whispers lovingkindness and provident care to us, and we know what it means to sing "This is my Father's world and to my list'ning ears, all nature sings and round me rings the music of the spheres."

Places of prayer are many, mind you, and each has its own imagings and messagings in the grand semiotic bearing God's love to His creatures and in particular to His redeemed people. Augustine, that granddaddy of Christian rhetoricians, contended this: a thing in nature is never just a thing, for it also functions as a sign which carries a message from the Creator. "The heavens declare the glory of God," says the psalmist (19:1-2), "the heavens declare the glory of God; and the firmament shows His handiwork. Day unto day utters speech; night unto night reveals knowledge." But while Black slaves met in forests and Celtic Christians also met under trees (hearing, perhaps, as "the trees of the field will clap their hands") or at the coast to hear the words of the waves, others met in richly symbolic cathedrals and sparsely symbolic meeting houses or even in homes, each place bearing its environmental word to the praying people.

The First Level

I want to argue this elemental factor of corporate prayer, this *human-to-world* relationship, becomes a *first level* of relational affect we may experience. Whether it's a natural environment or a built environment and whether it happens subconsciously or consciously, the place has a communication of its own which evokes affective responses of God's people at prayer. Light comes beaming in the window or through the dappling leaves of a tree saying "God is light" and "He makes His sun rise on the evil and on the good" (Mt. 5:45) and our hearts warm to the Creator's purity and grace: the Holy One in whom is "no darkness" yet smiles on us and even cleanses our sin so we can "walk in the light as He is in the light" (1 Jn. 1:7). Or consider this: is it any accident that both Eden and Gethsemane are garden places in which we see profoundly intimate and impassioned prayer evoked? In one the first Adam walks and talks with his beloved Father in the cool of the evening with undarkened bliss. In the other, the second Adam kneels and sweats as if it were blood in the dark night as He cries out agonistically to the same Father. A draped cross, a tree, a stained glass nativity, a howling coyote, a raised pulpit, an ebb tide, an advent wreath and myriad other signs will charm and call to us in the person-to-world relationship that stirs wonder, awe and love. This way we learn to love God through His world.

We had sung—praying, as I like to put it, with notes attached—for an undefined while that evening as again we witnessed the passing of twilight and brightening of the stars and moon. The "we" was a ragtag bunch of mostly university students, members of a handful of different churches. Some who met in our kitchen those times before and after we would "ascend the hill of the Lord" ended up married; some bonded in ways that have lasted over the years; some have become involved in missions to the far corners of the earth like Ethiopia, China and Nepal.

The songs continued, then a time of spontaneous spoken prayer happened and we bore our hearts before the throne on behalf of one another. Then another song or two broke out before it happened. In the gap between songs a one-anothering occurred over a familiar favorite: "I think we should hear Hazel do 'Wayfaring Stranger,'" said our friend Chris, and a clamor of affirmative voices ensued. Now Hazel, my dear wife whose voice is simply seraphic, usually tries to get out of this assignment because it's a very demanding piece for a serious vocalist like herself. So she counteroffered: "I'll sing it if Charity will sing with me." Concord having been reached, I started the familiar picking pattern on the guitar and the two women began to sing. None of us wayfarers that night even dreamed how it would end.

One-anothering like this characterizes good corporate prayer wherever it breaks out. Friends in Christ begin to own the concerns and the gladnesses of others. Vulnerability sets in, and mutual enjoyment—even laughter in prayer! We become one in heart as Ephesians 5:18-20 pictures: notice the filling of the Spirit leads us to "speaking to one another in psalms and hymns and spiritual songs" and yet we make music in our "heart" (singular) to the

Lord. Sometimes Hazel and I, praying in song like Paul talks about, simply reach a blend of voices that transports us to the court of heaven—and not us alone. Others have been transported also: one friend said "When you and Hazel sing, I live through you." This oneness of God's people takes hold during jubilant worship processions (Psalm 42) and also in times of lamenting as during the Babylonian captivity (Psalm 137). And Jesus says anything we disciples ask for in His name we will receive and our joy "will be complete" (Jn. 16:19-24). Corporate prayers of petition are directly connected to corporate affects of joy, our Lord teaches.

My friend Mac does not know Hazel and I are present in his congregation one particular Sunday morning. The people of his church, Keystone Baptist in Chicago, begin a time of corporate prayer before the Lord's Supper gets served, one African American voice and then another speaking out their praises and supplications that rise as incense before the throne. Sometimes the incense is more shouted than spoken so perhaps it rises a little faster. Then Mac, "a White guy with a Black heart" as some of the folks would say, begins his prayer and about two sentences in, his voice starts to tremble. A prayer of corporate lament and confession he offers, his heavy-burdened heart choking its way out through his throat as he adds to the incense phrases like "we love You so much, Lord, but we're just poor children who fall so short of Your righteous will. . . . We've sinned against You and we need Your mercy! . . ." We, the rest of the flock that morning, I'm sure, lived through Mac by feeling and thus owning the weight of our acknowledged sin—and certainly no less, the lightness of our absolution in Christ! What a healing "magic" settled on our souls, let me tell you! One heart with him, we confessed and we were freed.

The Second Level

This way we learn, loving God, to love each other—and through each other, to love God. We become friends around such rituals—friends in Christ. This second level of corporate prayer affect, then, we'll call human-to-human relationship. It's about loving God's people, about one-anothering in joy and sorrow.

So my wife, Hazel, and our daughter, Charity, began to sing the soulful Black spiritual with one another—"I am a poor, wayfaring stranger, a-traveling through this world of woe. . . ." A rather odd turn this seemed, with mother leaning on daughter after all these years; soon we'd realize both in actuality were leaning on Another beyond us all and yet in the midst. Charity did not join us every week, often opting for time with her boyfriend. We her parents had come to know the familiar distance well, though something was afoot lately to give us a modicum of hope. She'd received Jesus by faith as a child, but now had been running from Him for nine years. She'd hung out with druggies, been through rehab, given birth to a son out of wedlock, broken our hearts again, again, again. ". . . but there's no sickness, toil nor danger in that bright land to which I go. I'm going there to see my Father . . ."

Hazel and I had become acquainted with grief and quite familiar with "groanings which cannot be uttered" (Rom. 8:26-27). Strangely, we had known the holy collusion of this level of prayer—the experience of crying out of the depths to God for our precious daughter, now worded, now wordlessly, now only choking out "Jesus, oh Jesus!" and somehow finding Another, indeed the Comforter Jesus sent, joining us in our groanings born of helplessness. Just so, Paul's text says "the Spirit *helps* us in our weakness" even when we haven't a clue what we ought to pray: the verb "helps," a word picture in the Greek tongue, literally means "takes hold on the other side" as a strong man picking up the other end of a log far too heavy for just one to carry. Have you not known the intimate power of this ministry of divine partnering before our Abba, Father, when a river flows through you, a solace takes hold of your heart, a saintly friend who "dreams dreams and sees visions" gives you a personal word they got from the Lord?

The Third Level

This *third level* of affect in prayer, then, we'll call the *human-to-God* relationship. It draws us into Trinitarian movements of relating: "in Christ" (to use that richest of Paul's phrases) we pray as Son-to-Abba, having by grace entered the Triune "family circle." This deepest level is about loving God, our All-in-all, above all. When in prayerful affection we learn to love God's world and also to love God's people we always end up here, learning to love God's very Being.

"I'm going there to see my Savior! I'm going there, no more to roam . . ." When the two women finished the song, a holy silence took hold of us all until

I said "We must pray." Then another silence, very long, was at last interrupted by Charity's voice. For nine interminable years we had not heard our daughter pray out loud. "Lord, I can't pray beautiful prayers like all those preachers," she started. "Thank You for giving me all the gifts you put inside me. I can't keep running from You because I just can't deny anymore that You really rose from the dead. I'm giving my life back to You right now, and . . . well, amen for me." When she began I was on my feet; when she ended I was kneeling, bent to the ground, a quivering mass of sobbing jelly. And in the holy brightness of that moment our joy filled the night sky and all the stars grew dim as angels began their dancing. Never, never had I heard a prayer so beautiful.

Questions for Further Thought and Discussion

1. Name a favorite place of corporate prayer, whether built or natural, in your own experience, and tell what imagings and messagings in that place evoke an affective response from you. How do these work to help shape your prayer experience?
2. On the human-to-human level, explore what affective elements get added to your prayer experience when you pray with others rather than praying alone. Incidentally, don't rule out the concept of praying "with notes attached."
3. Can you tease out even further than the commentary above how corporate prayer at the third level actually takes us into the affective life of the Triune God? What does this mean theologically as well as experientially?

The author: Dr. David Livingstone Rowe is Dean of Spiritual Life at Salt Lake Theological Seminary, serving there in partnership with Missions Door. He is the author of *I Love Mormons: A New Way to Share Christ with Latter-day Saints.*

SUGGESTED ADDITIONAL READING

Merton, Thomas. *Contemplative Prayer.* New York, NY: Doubleday, 1996.

Mottola, Anthony, Transl. *The Spiritual Exercises of St. Ignatius.* New York, NY: Doubleday, 1989.

Tozer, A. W. *The Pursuit of God.* Camp Hill, PA: Christian Publications, Inc., 1993.

Wakefield, James. *Sacred Listening.* Grand Rapids: Baker Books, 2006.

chapter

60

HOW TO EVALUATE THE PRAYER LIFE OF A CONGREGATION

Daniel Henderson

Some years ago I attended a conference at a very large church in a western state. The subject was "church transitions." One staff pastor caught my attention when he told of the dynamic prayer ministry of the congregation. I was intrigued by his glowing commentary on their highly mobilized laity that engaged in powerful 24/7 prayer, 365 days a year.

Providentially, I sat next to a couple at the evening meal that identified themselves as the prayer coordinators of the church. As I reflected on the wonderful account of the prayer ministry described earlier in the day, their faces filled with dismay. They began to speak of their deep discouragement. Thy commented about the "disconnect" between their efforts and the awareness and participation of the pastoral staff. They described a completely different prayer ministry, full of gaping holes and plagued by significant apathy.

The Need for Accurate Diagnosis

This experience illustrates the sad but common problem in many churches. Pastors can easily embrace an exaggerated sense of the prayer participation in their church. Sometimes we elaborate because of our desire to see more than really exists. Other times, we are just unaware of the true condition of the prayer ministry because we are far removed from actual involvement in the heart and soul of the praying.

On one hand, this misdiagnosis can lead to a false notion of the congregation's spiritual health and vitality. Much like a doctor who misreads and X-ray or blood test, we can miss some key indicators that would normally alert us to some significant needs. On the other hand, underestimating the prayer life of our church can lead to discouragement. Feeling pressure to do more, we can tend to "drive" our people to prayer, rather than graciously lead them to rich experiences of the presence of Christ.

A Four Dimensional Evaluation Process

Ultimately, only the Lord knows the truth about the sincerity and substance of our prayers. Still, any appraisal on our part needs to be multi-dimensional. I am learning that it is important to evaluate the height, width, breadth and depth of the prayer culture of a congregation. Here's how it might work.

1. Evaluating the Height—The Example of the Praying Leadership

The best place to begin an authentic assessment of the prayer life of the church is with the church leadership. You will find that the prayer life of a church seldom rises any higher than the personal commitment and example of the senior pastor. Here are some key evaluation questions for pastoral leadership.

Am I leading by example? If we want a praying church, we cannot point the way; we must lead the way. We cannot just preach sermons but must lead God's people in balanced, biblical and transformational prayer experiences. This does not mean that pastors have to manage and organize the prayer ministry. There are others with administrative gifts to do this. It does mean that the pastors must lead by example. It is not necessary that they attend every prayer time each week, but they must be visible, passionate and consistent in their participation.

Am I cultivating a consistent private prayer life? At the core of every praying pastor is a hunger for God and a delight in His presence. This will be evidenced, not just in public venues, but in the place of private communion on a consistent basis.

Am I incorporating prayer into the leadership culture? A praying pastor must also lead and nurture a praying leadership team. This is best accomplished as the leadership team collectively studies the priority and possibilities of prayer. This must lead to engaging times of prayer together as a major component of leadership gatherings. Special evenings of prayer, prayer retreats and prayer summits can ignite a fresh love for prayer as part of the leadership culture.

Over my years of pastoral leadership, I have embraced Acts 6:4 as a primary definition of biblical leadership as we give our primary attention to "prayer and the ministry of the word." This allows us to focus our efforts and delegate trustee and administrative duties to other people. As part of our growth in the priority of prayer our leaders have enjoyed multiple three-day prayer summits and embraced prayer and the word as the best use of our collective leadership time.

Are we teaching on prayer in various venues? A church leadership team should evaluate their proactive commitment to instruct in prayer. They should consider a regular plan to provide comprehensive, practical and motivational instruction on prayer—starting with the pulpit and implemented in classes, small groups and discipleship relationships.

Do we share personal stories about the power of prayer? The congregational prayer life is encouraged by personal stories about prayer. The pastoral team should be looking for these "satisfied customers" who can become missionaries of prayer as they share their motivational stories of God's work in their lives.

Am I training other prayer leaders to help mobilize prayer? I learned many years ago that if I did not train other motivated church members to lead in balanced biblical prayer, the prayer level might not grow beyond my ability to show up at all the prayer gatherings. I also realized that the quality of the prayer times would suffer.

So I took time to clarify everything I had learned (and was still learning) about leading effective prayer times and keeping prayer meetings out of the ditch. I thought about the personal characteristics of an effective and enduring prayer leader. Then I began to gather current and potential prayer leaders for 6-8 weeks of training, coupled with opportunities to practice the principles we were learning.

I've taught these principles to hundreds of local church leaders over the years. Eventually it became a book, *Fresh Encounters,* which is designed to help church leaders understand how prayer should function in a church setting.

2. Evaluating the Width—The Variety of Prayer Activities

When pastors lead by example and train others to facilitate biblical, balanced prayer times the prayer activities of the church can grow. This provides a variety of options from which participants can choose.

Width of Quantity. People connect with one another and the Lord in different ways and times. It is important that a church offer options for prayer-motivated members. Some are "roosters" and enjoy early morning opportunities while others are "owls" and like evening gatherings. Some need to connect around areas of common interests like parenting, youth ministry, men's interests or women's concerns. Some prefer prayer partners, others like small groups and many enjoy a large gathering for prayer. A highly directed prayer format will work for some while a more spontaneous and participatory mode suits others.

In evaluating the prayer life of a church it is important to consider the variety of practical options offered to allow people from a variety of backgrounds, interests and schedules to participate.

Width of Quality. Of course, the quality of the prayer activities must remain solid if the quantity is going to be effective. This requires trained leaders who provide capable, committed coordination for each prayer gathering. A church should have an ongoing training strategy to raise up competent and committed prayer leaders.

These leaders should meet, at least periodically, to share information about the effectiveness of the prayer times offered. Some will need to be discontinued, some should be strengthened.

3. Evaluating the Breadth—The Substance of a Prayer Culture

Often in a church, prayer is relegated to a faithful few, or a few activities. These churches often are not largely affected by the prayer efforts. The goal is not to develop a prayer program that functions like a silo and is isolated from the rest of the church. The goal is a praying church where prayer permeates all the activities and gatherings in every department.

When I first came to Grace Church in Eden Prairie, the congregation seemed eager for me to start a weekly church-wide prayer time. We called it *Fresh Encounter*. However, after a number of months it became apparent that we had the program of prayer ahead of the leadership in prayer. Most of the elders and staff were not attending regularly and I realized we needed to slow the program until the leadership culture had developed more fully around the priority of prayer.

So, we augmented the prayer programming but still worked to grow the prayer culture. We cut the Fresh Encounter service to a once-a-month event. At the same time, we recruited more people to become active in the prayer room during the morning worship services. In this way we were able to adjust the prayer program but still grow a prayer culture with different and more helpful entry points.

A church is growing in a prayer culture when prayer is the default response of the leaders and people throughout the church. As I often say, "prayer is not the only thing we do, it is just the first thing we do." This is the mark of a breadth in prayer. The commitment to prayer far exceeds the organized activities in prayer.

Genuine worship-based prayer is incorporated into every department of the church and most gatherings of the people. You see people engaging in spontaneous prayer in the midst of conversations, while talking on the phone or during fellowship times in the lobby on Sunday.

4. Evaluating the Depth—The Habits of Praying People

Ultimately the prayer life of a church is evidenced in the lifestyles of the people attending the church. Of course, this dimension is hard to quantify but the goal is that prayer becomes as comfortable as breathing and eating in the daily activities of congregational participants. Prayer is integrated into marriage, home, work and virtually every activity. It has broken beyond the walls of the church building and become fully integrated into the life patterns of the saints.

Again, a great way to fuel this commitment to depth in prayer is to teach about it, feature testimonies of those who are enjoying it and emphasizing it as the exciting "norm" for all Christians.

Key Questions and the Vital Outcome

If we could boil all of this down to some basic, penetrating evaluation questions, it might look like this:

- **HEIGHT:** To what degree is the senior pastor and leadership team modeling prayer, cultivating prayer among their ranks, teaching on prayer, highlighting stories about prayer and training others to lead in prayer?
- **WIDTH:** How are we raising up other leaders to provide a broad variety of prayer opportunities that appeal to various interests and that are sustained by consistent and competent leadership?
- **BREADTH:** Are we helping our people understand the need for a prayer culture beyond prayer "activities" as we encourage and highlight prayer as a pervasive reality in all we do as a church?
- **DEPTH:** Are we encouraging and equipping our people to develop a depth in private prayer that will also be evidenced in marriage, family, work and community relationships?

Ultimately, this kind of evaluation should lead us back to the Throne of Grace where we appeal to the Savior again, "Teach us to pray." The evaluation should not cause guilt or pride, depending on the outcome. The goal is a resolve to grow higher, wider, broader and deeper in our dependence on Christ and our supernatural impact on the culture around us through the power of His life within us.

Questions for Further Thought or Discussion

1. Explain why an accurate diagnosis of the congregation's prayer life is so vital and how you would communicate your diagnosis to the congregation you are leading.

2. Summarize each of the four dimensions of the evaluation process and give an example of a step you would take to bring improvement.
3. Create a sermon/teaching outline: The Vital Outcome. Identify each point, provide a scriptural reference, and an action point for the church.

The author: Dr. Daniel Henderson is President/Founder of Strategic Renewal International. He is also Assistant Professor of Leadership and Church Renewal at Liberty University and Seminary and Pastor of Renewal at Thomas Road Baptist Church, both in Lynchburg, VA. He has authored numerous books including *Fresh Encounters* and *PRAYzing!* and speaks regularly at pastor's conferences and renewal events.

SUGGESTED ADDITIONAL READING

Lawless, Chuck. *Serving in Your Church Prayer Ministry.* Grand Rapids: Zondervan Publishing, 2003.

Franklin, John. *House of Prayer: Prayer Ministries in Your Church.* Nashville: Lifeway Publishing, 1999.

Higley, Sandra. *A Year of Prayer Events for Your Church.* Terre Haute, IN: PrayerShop Publishing, 2007.

Miglioratti, Phil. *A Diagnostic Tool to Assess the Prayer Life of Your Congregation.* http://nppn.org/articles/article062.htm.

SECTION FOUR

THE GLOBAL IMPACT OF PRAYER

chapter

61

THE BIBLE AND GLOBAL PRAYER

Henry Blackaby

Where God's heart is, there our heart must also be. We must be especially careful to consider what He commanded us concerning His heart for the world and our responsibility regarding this. But we must also give careful attention to God's eternal plan to redeem the world. When we read how Jesus prayed to the Father in John 17:9, "I do not pray for the world . . .", we are immediately stopped in our tracks. Then we ask, "If this is so, then Father, how did Jesus pray and affect the world?" The answer to this question will be our focus as we explore "The Bible and Global Prayer." God has a clear plan that is revealed all through the Scripture. He knows exactly how He wants to reach the nations of the world. As God's children, when we pray for the world we must do so according to God's plan.

To many people, the heart of the Bible is John 3:16: "God so loved *the world (my emphasis)* that He gave His only begotten Son, that whoever believes in Him should not perish but have everlasting life." God does love the world! The cost to God to love the world was immeasurable—the life, death, resurrection and reigning of His Son. God planned that we, His children, are to *reign with Him* as He redeems our world (Gal 2:4-6). So, as we will see, God's focus is on His people, in redeeming a lost world.

Peter wrote: "The Lord is . . . not willing that any should perish but that all should come to repentance" (2 Pet. 3:9). God does not want one person to *perish.* He desires for all *to have eternal life*! This truth must be firmly fixed in our hearts, as we think through our role, in God's plan for the world.

In addition, Jesus commanded His disciples: "Go into all the world and preach the gospel to every creature" (Mk. 16:15). (See also Mt. 28:18-20; Lk. 24:47-49.) Notice, God does not tell us *to pray* for the world. His instructions are very clear: 1. go into all the world; 2. preach the gospel; 3. to every person. On this command rests the prayer life of Jesus for the world! There is no question that God's heart is for the world. However, we must note carefully how He purposes to provide salvation for every person, and therefore how we should pray accordingly.

John 17 is the significant prayer of Jesus to the Father, at the close of His three-and-a-half-year ministry doing the Father's will for the world. The focus of Jesus' obedience to the Father's plan was to pray "for these" disciples the Father had given Him (Jn. 17:9). Jesus also prayed: "Father . . . I have finished the work You have given Me to do" (17:11). What had God asked Jesus to do? The Father gave Jesus twelve men (all businessmen). He was to teach them that the Father had sent Him into the world and to help them understand why His Father had sent Him. Jesus faithfully told them all the Father told Him to tell them, and they believed. They understood that the Father sent Him because the Father loved the world (17:6-8). The rest of Jesus' prayer focuses on what He had done with the twelve men God had given to Him, and what He asks the Father to do for them. *Herein lies the key to our praying for the world.*

It appears that the Father's heart to redeem the world would rest on these twelve men and all those who would believe through their preaching. They were to be sanctified, set apart for God, and remain absolutely faithful to their assignment. Therefore, the heart of Jesus' prayer was not for the world, but for His disciples. This prayer of Jesus clearly helps us know how we are to pray—not for the world—but for God's people.

Jesus said He would no longer be in the world, but these disciples for whom He was praying would remain behind to fulfill the assignment. Jesus concluded His prayer with these significant words: "O Righteous Father! The world has not known You, but I have known You; and these have known that You sent Me. And I have declared to them Your name" (17:25, 26). By the Father's command Jesus prayed for these disciples and did not pray for the world. The focus of His prayer is vital, for it shows us how we are to pray, so that like Jesus our praying will affect the world.

Jesus prayed to the Father for His disciples as follows:

1. "Sanctify them by Your truth. Your word is truth" (17:17).
2. "As You sent Me into the world, I also have sent them into the world" (17:18).
3. "I do not pray that You should take them out of the world, but that You should keep them from the evil one" (17:15).

Then came the key to the plan by which God purposed to save the world: "[I pray] that they may be one, as You, Father are in Me, and I in You, that they also may be one *in Us, that the world may believe that You sent Me* " (17:21, *emphasis added*). The world would believe the truth of John 3:16—as the disciples remained in a love relationship with Jesus and the Father, the Father's heart for redeeming a lost world would become the life work and passion of the disciples. As we read Scripture we see that the disciples did remain in the Father's will, just as Jesus prayed for them, and the entire Roman empire was radically changed as a result (Acts 17:6).

Then, in an amazing statement, Jesus said to His Father: "And the glory which You gave Me, I have given them, that they may be one just as We are one: I in them, and You in Me; that they may be made perfect in one, and that the world may know that You have sent Me, and have loved them as you have loved Me" (Jn. 17:22, 23).

God's pattern for saving the world *is His own*! In the Old Testament, when God purposed in His heart to save Nineveh, He called Jonah to go and preach to them. When Jonah finally obeyed, after God severely disciplined him, all Nineveh repented (Jon. 3:5-10). Down through history when God wanted nations to hear of His love, He chose, called, and sent prophets.

It is no different in our day. God's people still hold the key to reaching a lost world. So, the biblical pattern in praying for a lost world is to pray for God's people, as Jesus did. How do we practically implement this? When God places a burden on our heart for a nation, we need to pray for:

- The missionaries in that nation, using Jesus' prayer for His disciples in John 17 as our guide
- The national believers and the churches in that nation
- Mission ministry groups
- Denominations
- For God's people

The salvation of the nations rests with God's people. Missionaries have shared the testimony that when they preached the gospel in some villages who had never heard before, these same villagers upon believing asked the missionaries: "How long have you known this good news? Why have you taken so long to come to us? Why did you not come before now? Our parents and others are in an eternity without God and without hope! If only you had come earlier!"

It has been mathematically calculated that if one person discipled another, and they in turn witnessed and discipled one each, and if this continued to multiply and each one hearing remained faithful to sharing with one other each week, it would take a short number of years for all 6.25 billion people in the world to be hear the gospel and to be saved. We must pray for the world, by praying as Jesus did, for God's own people.

God entrusts His children with His plan to reach the nations of the world. In Psalm 2:7, 8 God gives us a powerful invitation and promise. Speaking to His Son, God invites Him: "Ask of Me, and I will give You the nations for Your inheritance, and the ends of the earth for Your possession." He precedes this invitation by declaring, "You are My Son; today I have begotten You." My heart then goes to Romans 8:16, 17. Paul asserts: "The Spirit Himself bears witness with our spirit that *we* are children of God, and if children, then heirs—heirs of God and joint heirs with Christ, if indeed we suffer with Him, that we may also be glorified together" (*emphasis added*).

On the strength of these verses I have the freedom to search the Scriptures to notice what God has granted to His Son. This includes Psalm 2:7, 8. The Spirit then *bears witness with my spirit*, that as a child of God, I too, am invited to "ask of God" concerning the nations of the world that He places on my heart, in order to accomplish His purposes for them. I need to be aware that asking this of God may be costly for me, just as it was for Jesus. It may well require my suffering with Him in the process of seeing a nation turn to God.

Over the years God has laid nations on my heart, both personally and in the heart of churches I have pastored. There has always been a cost involved in asking God for these nations. When He has granted them to us, we have had to be willing to become involved with them and obediently follow through with God regarding His plans for them. Asking God for the nations has also had an effect upon our children as they too have acquired a heart for the nations: one serving in Norway, one in Germany and two others making their way into the nations of Africa. Although this has been "costly," it has brought much joy with Jesus (Jn. 15:9-16). Jesus said the reason He told them all this was so His joy would be in His disciples and their joy would be full. This has been preeminently true in our family; even as I write, two of my sons and my wife and I are ministering in Africa.

Our involvement with God in the redemption of the world is vital. Again, it must be as God has eternally purposed it. God loved the world and sent His Son into the world. But we are reminded that "God was in Christ reconciling the world to Himself" (2 Cor. 5:19). God was working in and through His Son to redeem the world. Gethsemane's, "not My will, but Yours be done" (Lk. 22:42) was preeminently the Father's moment of victory. All the Father had purposed and accomplished over the centuries now rested in His Son's total obedience. The Father, in Christ, now completed His work to redeem the world.

This is still true today. The salvation of the world now rests on us, His children. It rests on our total denial of self, then picking up of our cross, and our obedience in following our Lord.

This is why Jesus prayed for His disciples, and not the world. As goes His disciples, so goes the redemption of the world. We pray more effectively for the world by praying not for the world, but *for God's people.*

Questions for Further Thought or Discussion

1. Using this statement: "Passionate, prayer for the lost, whether across the street or around the world, is not an option for the church it is God's revealed will," construct a simple teaching/preaching outline you could use to cast vision for global praying.
2. Identify and explain three or four components of a congregational or prayer group strategy that casts vision and increases focus on global praying.
3. Agree/disagree and explain your reasoning: "We pray more effectively for the world by praying not for the world, but *for God's people.*

The author: Henry Blackaby is Founder and President Emeritus of Blackaby Ministries International located in Atlanta, Georgia (www.blackaby.org). He is also author and co-author of many books including, *Experiencing God, Fresh Encounter: Experiencing God Through Prayer, Humility and a Heartfelt Desire to Know Him, The Power of the Call,* and *Experiencing God Day-by-Day.*

SUGGESTED ADDITIONAL READING

Johnstone, Patrick, and Jason Mandryk. *Operation World: When We Pray God Works.* Carislile, UK: Paternoster, 2005.

Winter, Ralph, and Steve Hawthorne. *Perspectives on the World Christian Movement, A Reader.* Pasadena, CA: William Carey Library, 1991.

Moore, Beth. *Voices of the Faithful.* Nashville: Integrity Publishers, 2005.

chapter

62

PRAYER AND SPIRITUAL AWAKENINGS

Glenn Sheppard

"When God intends great mercy for His people, the first thing He does is to set them a' praying.[1]

I stumbled in the "backdoor" of revival as a seminary student in 1970. Nearby Asbury College[2] experienced revival, and God sent a few "mercy drops" to Southern Seminary in Louisville, KY. Everything changed for me.

It was several years later that I learned that revival comes to the saved. One must have been *alive,* then died to be *revived.* Spiritual awakening, however, occurs among the lost as their hearts and minds are suddenly drawn to spiritual matters.

In 1972, while pastoring First Baptist Church in Blakely, GA, God visited us with revival. When the Lord began to move, I was as surprised as everyone else. Soon the church was packed and services sometimes lasted past midnight. When Baptists are at church at one a.m., the community notices.

Someone had prayed the revival in—and it wasn't me. We believe that it was an elderly woman in the church who had experienced revival earlier in her life. Before long, the entire region experienced spiritual awakening and people came from across the nation to witness it. Jack Taylor, Bertha Smith and others helped us understand the revival and the spiritual awakening that was happening in our midst.

Later, the Lord called me to Lawrenceville, an Atlanta suburb, to pastor. The Lord met us again, one Sunday, as members were asking forgiveness of one other. The revival lasted for several years and the church overflowed. Newspapers carried stories of the revival as it spread throughout the area. The local public high school would call for the church calendar before making theirs because the students would skip school functions to come to church. Hundreds of youth gathered hour after hour, caught in His presence.

Again, I couldn't take credit for the revival. We believe it was prayed in by Mrs. Jeannette Harris, a member, who knew the difference between being a church member and having an intimate relationship with Jesus.

In 1978, I was invited to the Home Mission Board, SBC, to pioneer the Office of Prayer and Spiritual Awakening. During those years I met J. Edwin Orr and the saints of the Shantung Revival who were in their eighties and nineties—Charles Culpepper, Martha Franks, Katie Murray and Olive Lawton. They became our closest and dearest intercessors until the Lord called them home.

I traveled and preached with Dr. Orr many times over the next decade as he mentored me and I was with him when he died. The greatest researcher and writer of our time on revival and awakening, he said historical research proves that prayer precedes revival and awakening. Evangelism and social justice follow close behind.

Biblical Awakenings

The Old Testament includes ten or more awakenings occurring in answer to prayer. From Jacob to Asa, Johoash, Hezekiah, Josiah to Zerubbabel, Haggai, Zechariah, Nehemiah, Ezra, Jonah and Jehoshaphat as well as Moses,

Samuel and Elijah, we read of awakenings as prophets, priests and people prayed, meeting the pre-requisites of 2 Chronicles 7:14.

The New Testament continues with awakenings accompanying Jesus. Then, in Acts, thousands were added in a day. The fledgling Church continually met for prayer. They prayed in agreement ("in one accord" the old King James described it) and the Holy Spirit empowered the Church to reach the world.

Post Biblical

Throughout Christian history, fires of awakening have burned, lighted by praying people. The Waldensians, 300 years before the Reformation (an awakening in itself), spread the gospel and preserved the Holy Scriptures. By the early 1700s, the line of prayer could be traced.

The First Great Awakening 1726-1756

Crime and immorality increased as Deism grew in England, Europe and the New World. Protestant refugees fled to America or hid in Europe. Count Nicholaus Zinzendorf had given refuge to Moravian Protestants, but much of his time was being spent in settling conflicts among them. On May 12, 1727 the refugees determined to bury differences and pray, a last resort. The Spirit met them. By July, the Moravian Revival and the Herrnhut prayer watch that lasted 100 years had begun.[3] In this day, both the 24/7 prayer movement that began in England and the International House of Prayer in Kansas City, MO were inspired by Herrnhut. Beginning independently in September 1999, they have prayed without ceasing since then.

The 18th Century Revival in Britain—The Evangelical Awakening

Awakenings followed the Moravians as prayer brought heaven close. John Wesley came under their influence while sailing to Georgia as a missionary. Aboard ship he found a personal faith in Christ. John, his brother Charles, and George Whitefield became the voices of the awakening that reached masses from all classes of society. The Methodist Church was born along with thousands of prayer groups and schools that helped bring a spiritual consciousness to the governing authorities. Many believe a bloody uprising, like the French

Revolution, was prevented by a spiritual awakening in Britain.

In America, fervent prayer by Dutch Reformed Pietists, David Brainerd, and others spread. By the time Jonathan Edwards preached his famous sermon "Sinners in the Hands of an Angry God" in Northampton, Massachusetts in 1734, the awakening had begun. Whitefield's second visit brought additional waves of awakening. Thousands were saved. The quickening to train Christian workers for the harvest birthed Princeton, Brown, Columbia, Dartmouth, University of Pennsylvania and Rutgers, all born from awakening as had been Harvard and Yale in the previous century.[4]

The Second Great Awakening (1776-1810)

Following in the wake of the Awakening, concern for Native Americans and slaves birthed strong evangelistic efforts initiating convictions against slavery in England and America. Many, however, in Britain and Europe turned to rationalism and apostasy. With awakening blazing in America, Britain in 1776, was described by Trevelyan in contrast as "marked by infidelity and laxity of doctrine."[5]

Following the War of Independence, immorality, infidelity and debauchery brought by French Revolutionists, threatened the New Republic. Drunkenness and lawlessness were common. Colleges were cesspools of atheism and rationalism. Churches were empty. Latourette says "it looked as though Christianity . . . were about to be ushered out of the affairs of men."[6] At Williams College, five students met secretly to pray. Overtaken by rain, they continued under a haystack. God met them. The impetus for the missionary efforts of Adoniram Judson, Samuel Mott, Luther Rice, Gordon Hall and Samuel Newell and perhaps the beginning of the Great Awakening can be traced back to the Haystack Prayer Meeting.[7]

Pastors Andrew Fuller and John Sutcliffe and layman William Carey called Christians to extraordinary prayer in response to the re-publishing of Jonathan Edward's treatise on prayer. Before long, denominations set aside the first Monday evening of each month for prayer. This concert of prayer movement spread across the world bringing to the front Charles Finney, Devereux Jarrett, Peter Cartwright, Isaac Backus and Timothy Dwight, President of Yale. The awakening turned the tide at many colleges and many students prepared for Christian service.

Thousands of lawless frontiersmen and society's elite found common ground at the foot of the cross, black and white alike. Camp meetings convened to handle the numbers. Waves of awakenings flowed across Europe, Britain, South Africa, the South Sea Islands and South India. When de Tocqueville visited America in 1831, he said, "America is a nation with the soul of a church."[8]

However, by the 1840s, denominations were splitting and an emphasis on the Second Coming left many disillusioned.[9] Apathy and complacency began taking a toll.

The Prayer Meeting Revival of 1858-1859

Once again, God's people were reduced to prayer. Jeremiah Lanphier and five others called for noonday prayer in New York City. Crowds grew from six to six thousand. By 1858, the newspapers were reporting "an extraordinary movement of prayer."[10]

In Britain, the awakening brought a sixty percent increase in believers.[11] It spread to Australia, New Zealand and South Africa where Andrew Murray came under its power. In India, multitudes were won. Charles Spurgeon and William Booth in Britain, Dwight Moody in America, Hudson Taylor of the China Inland Mission, David Livingston in Africa and hundreds of prayer, mission and social justice organizations such as the Y.M.C.A. emerged in the fire and afterglow of the Prayer Meeting Revival.

Spiritual Awakenings following 1860

The Civil War in America, famine in Ireland, wars in Europe, Africa, China and massive immigration slowed down awakening, but millions still came to Christ, especially through student and mission efforts. Around the world, revival and awakening fires followed concerted prayer, but by the end of the century, formalized Christianity had become entrenched.

The Welsh Revival of 1904

By 1900, phenomenal revival was reported by Boer prisoners of war. Japan experienced awakening just prior to the Japanese-Russian war. In Wales, a group of coal miners prayed for 14 months, often through the night. One evening, Seth Joshua prayed, "Bend us." Evan Roberts was there and prayed, "Bend me!"

Within a few weeks, Roberts' Sunday School class burst into revival, crowding churches for more than two years. A hundred thousand were converted cutting drunkenness in half and causing taverns to go bankrupt. Crimes were so few that judges had no cases to try. The mules in the mines had to be re-taught because the miners quit using profanity. It was genuine spiritual awakening. The Welsh Revival touched America, Britain, Europe, Africa, Latin America, the South Seas and the Far East. Church membership in America increased by two million in five years. It was common for stores to close for hours for prayer. In Los Angeles, the Grand Opera House was filled at midnight with drunks and prostitutes seeking salvation.[12]

Azusa Street Revival and Awakenings of the 20th Century

On Azusa Street in Los Angles, during 1906, an African American preacher, William Seymour and a small group sought a deeper infilling of the Holy Spirit. Joined later by Charles Parham, great crowds came. For three years, the movement gained momentum birthing the modern Pentecostal movement that now crosses all denominational lines.

By 1912, World War I began, taking millions to their deaths, crashing homes and churches. Liberalism and emphasis on education accompanied a growing apostasy. In Ireland, Catholics and Protestants killed each other in the Name of the Lord. But God extended mercy by bringing forth men like J. Sidlow Baxter, Roy Hession, J. Edwin Orr, Alan Redpath, James Stewart and Ian Thomas who marked their generation for God. In America, Billy Sunday preached to millions. By 1934, young Billy Graham heard the message of Christ from Mordecai Ham.

In Russia, singing and preaching could be heard in the parks and streets before the Bolshevik seized power. The Communists, alarmed over the influence of the Church, began crushing it in 1929.

In China, during the Boxer Rebellion of 1900, persecuted Christians prayed for babies in the womb of Chinese mothers to become evangelists. Jonathan Goforth and others were deeply influenced by the Welsh and Korean Revivals and missionaries begged to receive a "coal from the altar." In 1927, a group of missionaries in Shantung awaiting evacuation decided to spend their time praying. Urgent prayer took over as repentance and confession of sin spilled out. The Spirit fell. The missionaries were so changed that when they returned to their villages, the Chinese thought they had been saved.[13]

By 1930, young men like Andrew Gih, John Sung, Watchman Nee and Wang Ming Dao were leading the awakening. Begun in prayer, the Chinese awakening was sustained by prayer through the Communist take-over, persecution and martyrdom. When news finally came out of China in 1978, the Church had grown by multi-millions.

World War II doused the flames of awakening, leaving embers. When it was over, Europe and Japan needed to be rebuilt. In America, awakenings were breaking out in colleges and in Hollywood among the stars. Young Bill and Vonnette Bright and others there were being discipled by Henrietta Mears.[14]

In 1949, in the Hebrides, islands off the coast of Scotland, a remarkable awakening was being prayed in by two unlikely women. Peggy Smith, 84 and blind, and her sister, Christine, 82, crippled by arthritis,[15] prayed until they received a vision of evangelist Duncan Campbell coming to their island. Campbell refused the invitation as he was due to speak at Keswick. Just before speaking, the Lord told him to go to Lewis. He obeyed. Arriving by ferry, he was told the people had already gathered to hear him. Following the service, as the people left, they were struck down in the heather by the power of the Lord.[16] Loren Cunningham, Founder of Youth With A Mission, was greatly influenced by Duncan Campbell in the early days of the mission.

The fifties saw amazing growth; the sixties, amazing spiritual decline. Once again, it seemed Christianity was losing ground. For some, a deep hunger for something more that just Sunday church gnawed at the soul. Near the end of the sixties, Winds of the Spirit blew strong enough that many prayed, as never before, Holy Spirit, Breathe on Me.[17]

The powerful awakening of the seventies came touching hippies in California birthing The Jesus Movement. The Asbury Revival and other revivals and sparking awakenings across America and the world. By 1984, the first International Prayer Assembly was held in South Korea with 74 nations present. Since then, thousands of prayer groups and organizations have been formed to promote prayer. Revivals and awakenings have continued, including Brownsville and Toronto and many others, but the greatest awakening of all time still awaits the Wind of the Spirit.

As the 21st century unfolds, we face a broken world with war, terrorism and rampant iniquity. Yet, we don't have to convince an unwilling God to come and refresh us with His presence. He's for it. But, He cannot be manipulated. But when sincere hearts who know they cannot do His work nor His will without Him, humbly pray, He will answer. Times of refreshing will flow from the hand of God (Acts 3:19). We've learned enough to know He will come, but have we learned enough to pray until He does?

"From the day of Pentecost, there has not been one great spiritual awakening in any land which has not begun in union of prayer."[18]

Questions for Further Thought or Discussion

1. Reflect on the statement: "When God desires to do a work in His people, He sets them a' praying." What are the implications of this insight to the prevailing culture of Christian congregations and ministries?
2. Identify three to four principles from this chapter's survey of biblical and historical awakenings.
3. Design a plan for raising awareness and interest in spiritual awakening in a local congregation.

The author: Glenn Sheppard is Co-founder and President of International Prayer Ministries in Greenwood, Missouri. He served as Senior Associate for Prayer for the Lausanne Committee for World Evangelization for eight years and is a founding member of America's National Prayer Committee. He wrote *My African Diary* and with his wife, Jacquelyn, co-authored *The Global Prayer Strategy Manual.*

SUGGESTED ADDITIONAL READING

Coleman, Robert. *One Divine Moment.* Old Tappan, NJ: Fleming Revell, 1970.

Edwards, Brian H. *Revival! A People Saturated with God.* Durham, England, 1990.

Prime, Samuel. *The Power of Prayer: The New York Revival of 1858.* Edinburgh, Scotland: Banner of Truth Trust, 1991.

ENDNOTES

1. J. Edwin Orr, *Conditions for Revival.* Online sermon. www.1248revival.org.

2. The story of the Asbury Revival is told in *One Divine Moment* by Robert Coleman (Old Tappan, NJ: Fleming Revell, 1970).

3. J. Edwin Orr, *The Re-study of Revival and Revivalism* (Los Angeles: The Oxford Association for Research in Revival or Evangelical Awakening, 1981), p. 1.

4. Orr, *Re-study,* p. 7.

5. Orr, *Re-study,* p. 8

6. Orr, *Re-study,* p. 9

7. Malcolm McDow and Alvin L. Reid, *The Role of Prayer in American Revival Movements, 1740 to 1860* (Nashville: Broadman & Holman Publishers, 1997), p. 231.

8. *The Hay Stack Revival,* www.windandfire.org.

9. William Miller and others thought the Second Coming would occur during 1843. When it did not, many became disillusioned with religion altogether.

10. Orr, *Re-study,* p. 4.

11. Orr, *Re-study,* p. 30.

12. Orr, *Re-study,* p. 45.

13. Olive Lawton, interview, 1980.

14. Orr, *Re-study,* p. 58.

15. Brian H. Edwards, *Revival! A People Saturated with God* (Durham, England 1990), p. 82.

16. Personal interviews in the Hebrides, 1993.

17. Edwin Hatch, *Breathe on Me,* 1878.

18. Edwards, p. 84.

chapter

63

PRAYER AND EVANGELISM

Alvin L. Reid

As I write this I sit in the hill country of Texas where I am speaking at a youth camp. Two days ago I awoke about 4:30 AM greatly burdened for the students. We had more than a few radically unchurched students come, and by Day 2 some were scratching their heads, sitting as they were in the middle of a church youth camp like refugees in a foreign land. I awoke, not because I awake that early to spend time with Jesus. I probably should, but regardless I found myself overwhelmed with a burden for the students. Much of the day was spent in prayer, in particular for the most resistant. My prayer: that God would move in such a way that day, that no one could say it was anyone but God!

That night the service was amazing. And, as our great God faithfully does, He moved in power. One young lady, the most resistant perhaps, met Jesus gloriously. Many met Christ. The next night another unchurched high schooler sought me out. With a serious look on his face, he said, "I want to become a Christian."

I know how to communicate to teenagers. I know how to share the gospel. But there is something about the chemistry of prayer when mixed with evangelism that forms a solution for the problems of lost people that our gifts and ingenuity alone can never provide. When prayer and evangelism come together, the power of God is manifested. It brings conviction to the empty and passion to the unconcerned.

The great man of prayer, E. M. Bounds, said, "Prayer does not stand alone. . . . It lives in fellowship with other Christian duties."[1] This is particularly true about evangelism. You cannot evangelize effectively on a consistent basis without prayer. In his research of growing churches, Thom Rainer discovered prayer ranked with biblical preaching and teaching as one of the major reasons churches in the survey reached lost people.[2]

Too often believers compartmentalize their faith, separating prayer from evangelism in an unhealthy manner. I have met people passionate for prayer who seem to have little if any concern for those without Christ. I have also known believers who burn for the salvation of the lost, but whose focus rarely notes the place of prayer. While prayer and evangelism are separate disciplines at one level, they both gain vitality when linked together.

Prayer and Evangelism in Scripture

Notice this prayer of the early Church that links prayer and evangelism: "Now, Lord, look on their threats, and grant to Your servants that with all boldness they may speak Your word, . . . And when they had prayed, the place where they were assembled together was shaken; and they were all filled with the Holy Spirit, and they spoke the word of God with boldness" (Acts 4:29, 31).

Chris Schofield made a vital point about this passage. "The prayer for 'boldness' (from *parrhesia),* which has already been associated with the apostolic witness in 4:13, is significant in at least two ways. First, notice that the apostles are not seeking revenge or the end of the opposition but rather courage and freedom of speech. Second, they were seeking this boldness that they might proclaim the gospel. . . . Their motive was centered on God's redemptive work."[3]

Another key passage is Ephesians 6:18-20. Paul followed his discussion of the armor of God with a request for believers to pray for bold proclamation of the gospel. Prayer is seen as an indispensable part of the armor of God. Praying "in the Spirit" refers to prayer "in the presence, control, help, influence, and power of God's Spirit."[4] Paul exhorted the Ephesians to pray for "utterance," or *parrhesia,* an openness to preach the gospel, the same expression translated "boldness" in Acts 4:29, 31. Paul was in prison as he wrote these words, asking for courage to share Christ.

Certain truths emerge from these two chapters, Acts 4 and Ephesians 6:

- Boldness to proclaim the gospel is a legitimate request to bring before God.
- Such boldness comes only from God. It cannot be "worked up."
- Such boldness comes through the prayers of God's people.

Prayer and Evangelism in History

The history of evangelism cannot be separated from the history of prayer. This is particularly obvious when one studies historical spiritual awakenings. The Evangelical Awakening in England, where John and Charles Wesley, George Whitefield, and others ministered in a sea of conversions and a rebirth of spiritual life, saw its birth in prayer. What some term the "Methodist Pentecost" came in the early hours of January 1, 1739, when about 60 believers prayed through the night and saw the power of God come. On several occasions following that event these young men and others prayed through the night. Soon their reluctant venture into preaching in the fields led to a movement of God that changed the spiritual landscape of England. This movement of evangelism saw its birth in prayer. A few years earlier on the European continent the Moravian Prayer Revival came through the human instrumentality of Count Zinzendorf, initiating an amazing movement of missions. Over and over when one reads the history of awakenings, one sees the chemistry of prayer and evangelism working together.

A bedridden woman in London, England, had been able to cultivate the life of prayer. She had read in the papers about evangelist D. L. Moody's work in Chicago. She didn't know Moody or anyone associated with him. Placing that paper under her pillow, she began to pray, "Lord, send this man to our church." Moody did go to London in 1872 when his church building was in ashes back in Chicago.

While Moody was speaking to the YMCA, a pastor invited him to preach to his congregation. Nothing happened the Sunday morning Moody preached. After the service, the sister of that invalid woman had informed her that a Mr. Moody of Chicago had preached and that he was to speak again that evening. The invalid woman declared, "Oh, if I had known, I would have eaten no breakfast, I would have spent all the time in prayer. Send me no dinner, leave me alone, lock the door. I'm going to spend the whole afternoon and evening in prayer."[5]

That evening the building was packed to hear Moody. The atmosphere was different, and the power of God fell on that place. Five hundred people gave their lives to Christ. Great revival began, and Moody's career as an evangelist multiplied because of that sick woman's prayer.

Robert Speer, a Presbyterian missionary leader, said, "The evangelization of the world . . . depends first of all upon a revival of prayer. Deeper than the need for men; deeper, far, than the need for money; deep down at the bottom of our spiritless lives, is the need for the forgotten secret of prevailing, worldwide prayer."[6]

Prayer and Evangelism in Practice

Pray diligently. Older writers use the term "importunity" to refer to the importance of persisting in prayer. Praying for the lost involves serious spiritual warfare and must include patience. Sometimes it may take years to see the fruit of one's labor in prayer for lost friends and family.

Pastor Charles Sullivan tells of a time when he gave the invitation and a man in his seventies came forward to give his life to Christ. His wife came down the aisle behind him with the glow of God on her face. After Sullivan counseled the man and prayed with him, he reached for a membership card to fill out, as we Baptists do, but the wife stopped him. She told Sullivan that he wouldn't need a card. She reached in her Bible and pulled out an old, yellow, tattered card.

"Forty years ago, I made a commitment to pray for my husband's salvation daily," she explained. "As a sign of my commitment, I filled out a membership card with my husband's name, and checked 'profession of faith' and 'baptism.' The only thing we need to complete is the date." God had answered her prayer.

Pray passionately. I served a small church in Texas as pastor during my seminary days. I was basically ignorance on fire, I had so much to learn. But I had just taken a course on prayer. Our church had baptized about eight new believers in the previous eight years, and none for several years. I knew God had to intervene. I scheduled an evangelistic meeting and secured a faithful evangelist. Then I led our church to pray. I became convicted that although Jesus spent all night in prayer before calling His disciples, I had never followed His example. So we callled an all night prayer meeting, knowing it would take God to awaken our church and reach those around us. That week we saw ten people come to Christ including some amazing accounts of unchurched people meeting Jesus. Ten may not sound like many, but in that little church it was a movement of God! I witnessed early in ministry the importance of passionate, broken prayer. I often tell my students that no matter how long you serve God, no matter the wisdom you gain and the theological insights you master, you will always have to pray passionately and with a broken heart to see God move in the lives of the lost.

Pray specifically. The following suggestions on praying for the lost come from a resource called *Praying Your Friends to Christ* and can help give focus to praying for the lost we know:

- Ask God to open their spiritual eyes (2 Cor. 4:4).
- Ask God to set them free from spiritual captivity (2 Tim. 2:25–26).
- Ask God to give them ears to hear (Mt. 13:15), faith to believe (Acts 20:21), and will to respond (Rom. 10:9).
- Ask God to send people into their lives to witness to them (Mt. 9:38).
- Ask God for ways to build caring relationships (1 Cor. 9:22).
- Ask God for opportunities to witness (Col. 4:3).
- Ask God for boldness to witness (Acts 4:29).
- Ask God for an opportunity to invite them to a harvest event (Lk. 14:23).[7]

Prayer can give us a yearning to share the gospel with others. A student of mine was taking his son to preschool one morning when he noticed a man walking along the side of the road. The student, named Joel, was prompted to pray for that man. He promised that he would share Jesus with this man if he were still on this road on his return. However, after leaving the preschool complex, he thought nothing of the man.

After a stop at the grocery store, Joel headed home. As he neared home, he saw the young man again. As he pulled into his driveway, Joel realized all the seminary training in the world didn't matter if his faith was silent. "I returned to the young man," Joel recalled, "and gave him a ride."

As Joel drove the stranger home, he remarked that "the man upstairs" had looked out for him. Joel began to share with him the good news of Jesus. The conversation flowed freely as God opened the man's heart to the gospel truth. They stopped along the road, and he repented of his sin and asked Jesus to save him. God will use us in witnessing for him *if* we walk with him in communion through prayer.

Do you spend time both in prayer and in personally sharing your faith? Do you discipline yourself in one to the neglect of another? Do you see both as part of a greater whole in your own spiritual disciplines and in the lives of those you lead?

Questions for Further Thought or Discussion

1. Agree or disagree (and support your conclusion): Prayer is more than evangelistic praying and evangelism is more than praying for lost persons, but prayer evangelism combines the two spiritual disciplines in a biblical and practical way that empowers both the Christian's and the congregation's witness.
2. Design your own outline for a workshop on prayer evangelism (include: thesis statement, several main teaching points, scriptural basis for each, and a learning [experiential] activity).
3. Devote thirty minutes to evangelistic praying: five to ten minutes to listening prayer, asking the Lord for the names of persons He wants you to petition for salvation; five to ten minutes writing down each name and indicating the specific request the Spirit directs you to pray about (possible bridges into a spiritual discussion); ten to twenty minutes petitioning God on behalf of each person and the issue or circumstance

you identified. Return to this prayer list several times in the next week, adding further direction you receive as you pray.

The author: Dr. Alvin L. Reid is the Associate Dean of Proclamation Studies and Professor of Evangelism and occupies the Bailey Smith Chair of Evangelism at Southeastern Baptist Theological Seminary Wake Forest, North Carolina. He is the author of many books including *Join the Movement: God Is Calling You to Change the World* and *Radically Unchurched.*

SUGGESTED ADDITIONAL READING

McDow, Malcolm and Alvin L. Reid. *Firefall.* Emunclaw, WA: Pleasant Word, 1997.

Reid, Alvin L. *Join the Movement: God Is Calling You to Change the World.* Grand Rapids: Kregel, 2007.

________. *Radically Unchurched: Who They Are and How to Reach Them.* Grand Rapids: Kregel, 2002.

ENDNOTES

1. E. M. Bounds, *The Necessity of Prayer* (Springdale, PA: Whitaker House, 1984), p. 31.

2. Thom S. Rainer, *Effective Evangelistic Churches* (Nashville: Broadman & Holman, 1997), pp. 11–17.

3. Chris Schofield, "Linking Prayer and Bold Proclamation: An Exegetical Study of Acts 4:23–31 and Ephesians 6:18–20 with Implications for Contemporary Church Growth," *Journal of the American Society of Church Growth,* 8 (Winter 1997): p. 67.

4. Schofield, 71. Other passages include Mt. 9:35-38 (praying for laborers), Mt. 6:9-10 (praying for the reign of Christ in people), and 1 Tim. 2:1-5.

5. W. Stanley Monneyham, "Getting More Hooks in the Water Is Not Enough," *Christianity Today,* XXV, No. 16 (18 Sept. 1981): p. 20.

6. J. G. Hallimond, *The Miracle of Answered Prayer* (New York: The Christian Herald, 1916), pp. 69–71.

7. *Praying Your Friends to Christ* (Alpharetta, GA: North American Mission Board, 1998).

chapter

64

LIGHTHOUSES OF PRAYER

Alvin J. VanderGriend

A Lighthouse of Prayer is any person, family or group of people who commit to pray for, care for and share Jesus Christ with their family members, friends, schoolmates, neighbors or co-workers as God directs. Praying, caring and sharing are the core realities in Lighthouse praying. By means of prayer God's power and grace are released into peoples' lives. Through acts of caring and kindness they are loved and lifted. Through sharing the gospel, their lives can be transformed. This three way Lighthouse approach, it turns out, is a very effective form of outreach.

Why Praying, Caring and Sharing?

First, each of the three core Lighthouse activities—praying, caring and sharing—is scripturally mandated. Every Christian is commanded to pray for others. The Apostle Paul urges Timothy and his congregation to "make requests, prayers, intercession and thanksgiving . . . for everyone." "Everyone" includes our neighbors, coworkers and classmates as well as family and friends. Paul ends his injunction by saying, "This is good, and pleases God our Savior, who wants all people to be saved" (1 Tim. 2:1, 3-4, TNIV). Paul clearly links salvation to prayer. Believers are also obligated to lovingly care for those around them. Jesus instructed us to "love your neighbor as yourself" (Mt. 22:39). And, believers have a responsibility to share the good news as witnesses for Christ (Acts 1:8) and to "make disciples of all the nations" (Mt. 28:19).

Second, bringing praying, caring and sharing together provides a holistic approach to evangelism. Praying leads to caring. Prayerful caring leads to faith sharing. The recipient of prayer, on the other hand, touched by the Spirit of God and moved by the caring concern of a Christ-follower, becomes more and more open to the gospel. Leave out any one of these three and what remains is a truncated approach to outreach.

Third, praying, caring and sharing provide three different ways in which God's power touches human lives—the power of prayer, the power of love and the power of the gospel. James alludes to the power of prayer when he says, "The effective, fervent prayer of a righteous man avails much" (Jas. 5:16). Paul stresses the power of caring love by noting that love "bears all things, believes all things, hopes all things endures all things, [and] never fails" (1 Cor. 13:7-8). Paul also underscores the fact that the gospel "is the power of God to salvation for everyone who believes" (Rom. 1:16). It's no wonder that lives are changed when Lighthouse Christians pray, care and share.

The Merits of Lighthouses of Prayer

Lighthouse evangelism is all about God working. In fact it is more about God working than us. It's His power that is released from heaven through our prayers. It's His love that is conveyed to people through our caring. It's His gospel that is "the power of God to salvation" (Rom. 1:16). In prayer-care-share evangelism we co-labor with God. I like to think of prayer evangelism as evangelism in which God does what only He can do, when we do what He has called us to do. Only God can prepare the soil of human hearts. Only God can break through barriers of resistance. Only God can cleanse hearts and give new life. But He chooses to do His work in cooperation with us as we do our part—praying, caring and sharing.

Lighthouse evangelism is relationally based. Most people are drawn to Christ through a relationship with a person who already knows Jesus and is well-connected to a church. As many as 80-90 percent of new church members report that they came to Christ and came to church because of the influence of another person. Prayer is a relational gift, a gift of love. The minute a believer seriously begins to pray for the well-being of another person, relationship begins. Relationship turns to friendship as Lighthouse Christians invest time and effort in the relationship. And friendship leads to faith-sharing opportunities. It all happens along relational lines.

Lighthouses harness the lay-power of the church. The church's task of bringing the gospel to the ends of the earth will never be accomplished if the work is left to evangelists, pastors and the minority of people with the gift of evangelism. Every believer is meant to witness, to be a light in the world (Mt. 5:14). Lighthouses give ministry back to ordinary Christians. Through Lighthouse ministries the whole church gets involved in reaching out. Everybody does their part and the job gets done. The church becomes effective and fruitful. That's the way it is meant to be.

Lighthouses are culturally correct. People today are open to prayer. It's rare for a person in our country to turn down the offer to be prayed for. This cultural phenomenon has opened a door of opportunity for God to reach into their lives. When people open themselves up for prayer, they are opening themselves up to God. And God, moved through the prayers of faithful intercessors, goes to work in their hearts and lives. Prayed for people, seeing God move in their lives in unexpected ways, are open to the gospel.

Lighthouses are simple. Complex approaches to ministry are often a put-off for the average Christian. But Lighthouses of Prayer are simple enough for any Christian to do. Every Christian can pray. Every believer, having experienced God's love, can love others. Every child of God, who knows the power of the gospel, can share that good news with others. It's not all that complicated. Lighthouse pray-ers don't need weeks of training, manuals full of instructions, huge amounts of time, or special spiritual gifts. They simply need to talk to God about their neighbors and be available to Him as instruments of His love and witnesses of His grace. Ed Silvoso describes

Lighthouse ministries simply as "talking to God about my neighbor, before talking to my neighbor about God."[1]

Some Basic Requirements for Lighthouse Ministry

Lighthouse ministries are effective, not primarily because of a method, but because of people who understand prayer, and love, and the gospel and who share God's heart for lost persons.

Lighthouse Christians know that God works through prayer. When we pray God works! When we don't pray, God limits His working. Andrew Murray states: "God's giving is inseparably connected with our asking. . . . Only by intercession can that power be brought down from heaven, which will enable the Church to conquer the world."[2] Unfortunately, many in the Church today do not believe that. They simply assume that God, being sovereign, will do what He wants to do whether or not we pray.

Elijah knew differently. Elijah knew that God would send rain to the parched land of Canaan because He had promised. But Elijah did not presume that God would do it automatically without his praying. Instead he prayed seven times that God's will would be accomplished. In response to his prayers the rain came (1 Kings 18). God chooses to accomplish His will through the prayers of His people. Lighthouse Christians understand that.

Lighthouse Christians are devoted to prayer. The first Christians were truly devoted to prayer. Their prayers were not short, shallow, bless-me kinds of prayers. Three times in the early chapters of Acts, Luke uses the intense Greek word *proskartere*, often translated as "devoted to," to report on the strength of their commitment to prayer. The word literally means "to occupy oneself diligently with something." It's the word used in Acts 1:14 to describe their first prayer meeting: "These . . . were all continually devoting themselves to prayer" (NASB). It's the word used in Acts 2:42 to characterize their community activities: "they devoted themselves . . . to prayer." It's the word used to explain the decision of their spiritual leaders to "devote [themselves] to prayer" (6:4, NASB). The New Testament writers could not have been clearer. Devotion to prayer was the norm for New Testament Christians.

Unfortunately, most of today's Western church does not share this same devotion to prayer. The quick and easy kinds of prayer, so widely practiced today, will not suffice as the basis for an effective Lighthouse ministry. It takes devotion to prayer, persistence in prayer, and even sometimes wrestling in prayer in order to see God's power and grace released into the lives of our neighbors.

Lighthouse Christians are compassionately concerned for the spiritual well-being of others. When Jesus saw the crowds "he was moved with compassion for them, because they were weary and scattered, like sheep having no shepherd" (Mt. 9:36). Jesus was moved at the very depths of His being at their hopeless spiritual condition. He desperately wanted them to be saved. Lighthouse Christians, like Jesus, care so deeply for those who do not know Christ that they invest themselves in ministries of love and grace in their behalf.

Lighthouse Christians pray for "lost sheep." Scripture underscores the importance of praying for unsaved persons. Jesus speaking of other sheep that were not yet in the fold said, "Them also I must bring, and they will hear my voice" (Jn. 10:16). His desire to reach lost sheep led Him to say to the Father: "I do not pray for these [my disciples] alone, but also for those who will believe in Me through their word" (Jn. 17:20). Paul also set an example in praying for unsaved persons: "My heart's desire and prayer to God for Israel is that they may be saved" (Rom. 10:1). Lighthouse Christians are committed to praying for "the other sheep."

Lighthouse Christians are committed to relationship-building. It's tempting and comfortable to limit our social relationships to a select group of Christian friends. But Lighthouse evangelism will only work in a context where Christians are open to and intentional about building relationships with non-Christians. Jesus modeled this kind of love. He drew to Himself those who were considered to be on the fringes of proper society, the tax collectors and "sinners" of his day. It even came to the point where Jewish leaders muttered, "This man receives sinners and eats with them" (Lk. 15:2). It takes that kind of love to make evangelism work.

Implementing Lighthouse Ministries in a Congregation

Consider the following steps when initiating the Lighthouse ministry in a congregation.

Preach and teach on prayer. Many Christians need to become stronger in prayer if they are to be effective Lighthouse pray-ers. Lay strong foundations for Lighthouse of Prayer ministries by preaching a series of messages on prayer. Teach and train congregational members in prayer also by means of education classes and small groups.

Focus on non-Christians. Urge members of the church to start their prayer list with the names of non-Christians who are relationally closest to them: family members, friends and classmates, and then to go on to think of co-workers, neighbors and acquaintances for whom God would have them pray. Provide a Prayer-Care-Share Card for them to record the names of these persons.

Provide prayer helps. Many Lighthouse intercessors have found the simple BLESS pattern of prayer helpful. In this pattern the letters of the word BLESS represent five important ways to pray for those around us.

B *Body*—health, protection, strength
L *Labor*—work, income, financial security
E *Emotional*—joy, peace, hope, no anxiety
S *Social*—love, marriage, family, friends
S *Spiritual*—salvation, faith, grace

Provide harvest events. Some Lighthouse intercessors will be able to share the gospel one-on-one as the opportunity arises. Others will not. The church should provide times and places where those being prayed for will hear a gospel presentation and be invited to respond.

Questions for Further Thought or Discussion

1. How would you compare the Lighthouses of Prayer holistic, "three core realities" approach to evangelism, to forms of evangelism that specialize in only one or two of these realities?
2. What is the fundamental concept of intercessory prayer that undergirds the Lighthouse ministry? Why is this concept of prayer important?
3. Review the "basic requirements" for Lighthouse evangelism in section three. Are there requirements that could be left out? Are there requirements that should be added?

The author: Alvin J. VanderGriend is Prayer Evangelism Associate for Harvest Prayer

Ministries of Terre Haute, IN. He is the author of *The Praying Church Sourcebook, Love to Pray, A 40-Day Devotional for Deepening Your Prayer Life*, and *The Joy of Prayer, A 40-Day Devotional for Enriching Your Prayer Life.*

SUGGESTED ADDITIONAL READING

Kamstra, Douglas. *The Praying Church Ideabook.* Grand Rapids: CRC Publications, 2001.

Sacks, Cheryl. *The Prayer-Saturated Church.* Colorado Springs: NavPress, 2004.

Small, P. Douglas. *Transforming Your Church into a House of Prayer.* Cleveland, TN: Pathway Press, 2006.

ENDNOTES

1. Ed Silvoso, *Prayer Evangelism* (Ventura, CA: Regal, 2000), p. 35.
2. Andrew Murray, *The Ministry of Intercession* (Minneapolis: Bethany House, 1981), pp. 22-23.

chapter

65

PRAYER AND MISSIONARY MOVEMENTS

Ron Boehme

"Then Jesus made a circuit of all the towns and villages . . . When he looked out over the crowds, his heart broke. So confused and aimless they were, like sheep without a shepherd. 'What a huge harvest!' he said to his disciples. 'How few the workers! On your knees and pray for harvest hands!'" (Mt. 9:37, 38, TMB).

Prayer has always been the fuel of Christian missions. Jesus Himself set the standard when He began His ministry with forty days of fasting and prayer. Afterwards He returned in the "power of the Holy Spirit" and people flocked to His message (Mt. 4:1-25). Later Jesus chose twelve apostles after a night of prayer, and sent them out to share the good news (Lk. 6:12-16, 9:1-6). In the Matthew 9 passage above we see Jesus engaged in mission activity in various towns that made His heart ache and caused Him to exclaim: "What a huge harvest! "How few the workers!" He then announced the key to future success: "On your knees and pray for harvest hands!"

Though we don't fully understand the whys of prayer, we do know that God has designed the moral universe around its efficacy. Without prayer, God doesn't act. Through prayer, people's lives are changed. It might be said that prayer *gives an impartial God a reason to be partial in someone's life.* Prayer is the gunpowder and the work of the Holy Spirit the bullets in God's redemptive arsenal. As our hearts ache over lost individuals and nations as Jesus' did, we will also fall to our knees and pray to the Lord of the harvest. His answer will be to multiply workers (missions) around the world.

The early Church fueled its missions outreach by prayer, beginning with a ten-day prayer meeting and confession time in the Upper Room that brought the fire of the Holy Spirit on Pentecost. Peter preached and thousands were saved (Acts 2:1-41). The disciples continued to pray and daily people were added to the church (2:47). In Acts 4:23-31, Luke records a corporate prayer of the early believers where "the place where they were assembled together was shaken; and they were all filled with the Holy Spirit, and they spoke the word of God with boldness." There's the success equation: People pray—the Holy Spirit comes—powerful outreach ensues. The U.S. Center for World Missions estimates that prayer-propelled missions in the early Church brought the ratio of unbelievers-to-professing Christians to 360:1 by the year 100 A.D.[1]

During the Middles Ages, the power of the Church ebbed because of worldly success which diminished the need for and power of prayer. Its rebirth came in the monastic orders where a life devoted to prayer and Bible-reading eventually became the center of medieval society.[2] From Anthony in Egypt to Patrick in Ireland to the Nestorians in China and eventually the Franciscans, Dominicans and Jesuits traveling the globe, men and women of God began to fervently pray against the evils of their time and share their faith. They came in all shapes, sizes, and espoused various creeds—but their common denominator was a life devoted to prayer. God honored their efforts and much of Europe was Christianized—bringing the global unbelievers-to-professing Christian ratio to 69:1 in 1500 A.D. at the dawn of the Reformation.[3]

Following the renewal of the Church under Martin Luther, John Calvin, and others, Protestant missions emerged in 1727 through a young nobleman named Nicholaus von Zinzendorf who established a community for persecuted believers in Moravia. After years of turbulent growth, God visited the 300-member Moravian community in revival showers that gave birth to a twenty-four hour prayer thrust at "Herrnhut"—the watch of the Lord. This fervent, continuous prayer meeting lasted for more than one hundred years and launched the first Moravian missionaries into Scandinavia, other parts of Europe, the West Indies, and around the world.[4] It was through a Moravian missionary named Peter Buehler that John Wesley found salvation in Christ and launched the Methodist revival in England—all of it fueled by prayer.[5]

On the other side of the Atlantic, the great American theologian, Jonathan Edwards, was spreading revival fire as a part of the American Great Awakening that rocked the colonies from 1734-45. Edwards' long-titled book said it all: *An Humble Attempt to Promote the Agreement and Union of God's People Throughout the World in Extraordinary Prayer For a Revival Of Religion And The Advancement Of God's Kingdom On Earth, According To Scriptural Promises And Prophecies Of The Last Time.* There's the success formula again: *Prayer—Revival—Missions.* William Carey, the English cobbler, would follow in 1792 with his "Humble Attempt" treatise on reaching the heathen around the world. Carey's tireless efforts in India would light the fires of English missions that propelled the English language into prominence as the number one language in global missions.[6]

In 1806, Samuel Mills and four other college students were gathering in a field for prayer near Williams College in Massachusetts when they were overtaken by thunder and torrents of rain. Seeking cover on the leeward side of a haystack, their famous rendezvous with destiny became the "Haystack Prayer Meeting" where they cried out to God to send young American missionaries to the far reaches of Asia. Samuel Mills' famous prayer contained these words: "We can do this if we will!"[7] Over the next few years, powered by the prayers of thousands, the first American missions societies were born and in 1810 the first missionaries were sent—among them was Adoniram Judson, pioneer missionary to Burma. Samuel Mills went on to help found the American Bible Society and thousands of American youths continued to pray while becoming answers to their own prayers.

The next wave in American missions would also center around youth and prayer. In July 1886 Evangelist Dwight L. Moody invited 250 collegians to a thirty-day prayer and Bible conference in Mt. Hermon, Massachusetts where one hundred men volunteered to go into missions. Two of the student volunteers, Robert Wilder and John Forman, traveled to 167 colleges and universities the following year calling the campuses of America to prayer and global evangelization. Their recruitment gave birth to the Student Volunteer Movement which eventually mobilized more than 20,000 young missionaries for overseas service and scores of thousands at home.[8] John Mott, one of the original one hundred volunteers, became chairman of the movement in 1888 and began to preach across the United States "The evangelization of the world in this generation." The Student Volunteer Movement saw many women join the cause of missions for the first time including Lottie Moon and Gladys Aylward in China and Amy Carmichael in India. In its zenith, the Student Volunteer Movement was the largest known missions movement in history, following on the heels of both the American Civil War and the Great (Prayer) Revival of 1857. Through aggressive prayer and outreach, the ratio of unbelievers to professing Christians around the world would shrink to 27:1 by 1900.[9]

The 20th century would see even greater fountains of prayer and evangelistic effort. In 1904 God used a young seminary student named Evan Roberts to bring a powerful revival to Wales known as the Welsh Revival. It was characterized by more than 100,000 conversions, fervent intercession and heart-felt worship. After only a few years of public ministry, Evan Roberts retreated to a life of obscurity where he spent the final forty years of his life in prayer.[10]

On April 14, 1906, in a "tumble-down shack" at 312 Azusa Street in Los Angeles, God poured out His Spirit upon black evangelist William J. Seymour and his followers who were in the middle of ten days of fasting and prayer. Soon hundreds and thousands of people were seeking God, many praying in tongues, and being empowered by the Holy Spirit to share their new-found faith. This was the beginning of the Azusa Street Revival which would birth major denominations including the Church of God in Christ (1907) and the Assemblies of God in 1914.[11] These Pentecostal Christians were fervent in prayer and had a heart to go all over the world with the good news of Christ. By the early 21st century, Pentecostals and Charismatics numbered more than 500 million worldwide—and were at the forefront of global missions.[12] By 1950 the ratio of unbelievers to professing Christians had shrunk to 21:1.[13]

The 1950s to 1980s saw an ever-growing tide of global prayer and world missions. Beginning in the 1940s, Billy Graham preached to scores of millions of people and said that there were three secrets to his ministry: Prayer, prayer, and prayer. In 1950 Bill & Vonette Bright started Campus Crusade for Christ which grew to become the world's largest missionary organization. The engine of their growth was the "Great Commission Prayer Crusade." Loren Cunningham and Youth With A Mission in 1960 led the next wave in a global missions explosion. The foundational principles of YWAM included hearing God's voice and intercession for the nations. By 1990 YWAM had preached the gospel in all 223 geo-political nations on earth.

During this same period, God was pouring out His Spirit upon the Korean people who used prayer grottoes, mountains, and all-night prayer meetings to seek the Lord of the harvest. By 2000 South Korea had become the second largest missionary-sending nation in the world.[14] And perhaps the largest movement of God in any nation in history took place in the latter part of the 20th century in China where the church grew from one million believers in 1900 to 120 million in 2007 (an official state estimate). Fueled by the prayers and passion of an entire generation of house church leaders, China now stands poised in the 21st century to send millions of missionaries across Central Asia to bring the gospel "back to Jerusalem."[15] By 1980 the ratio of unbelievers to professing Christians was down to 11:1.[16]

In the past three decades we see a clear correlation to between increasing prayer and growing outreach. We live in the time where prayer for the nations has exploded around the world. Many nations now have intercessor groups that fast and pray for revival in their own countries. There are 24/7 Prayer Rooms and watches, a National Day of Prayer in the United States and other nations, and prayer focuses that target the Muslim world, the Buddhist world, and other spiritual strongholds. A Global Day of Prayer each spring at Pentecost that originated in southern Africa and has spread around the world.[17] On that one day alone it is estimated that 200 million Christians cry out to God for world evangelism. Certainly the increased temperature of global prayer is producing the following amazing results:[18]

- South of the Sahara Desert, nearly half of the Africa continent expresses faith in the Lord Jesus Christ.
- In 1900 there were 50,000 Protestants in Latin America. Today there are more than 35 million.
- The Church is growing so rapidly in Asia, Africa, and Latin America that by 2020 it is estimated that 70% of the Church will reside in the southern hemisphere.
- 70 churches are started every day; 28,000 people are converted in China every day; 20,000 converts take place in Africa everyday; Worldwide, 70,000 people daily are entering into the joy of eternal life in Christ.

Due to the incredible potency of prayer-fueled missions, the ratio of unbelievers-to-professing Christians has fallen all the way from 360:1 in 100 A.D. to 2:1 today! Over two billion people profess faith in Jesus Christ; an additional two billion have heard the gospel message; and a final two billion have yet to hear. If we're faithful to the Lord of the harvest, and take His words seriously to "go on our knees and pray for harvest hands," then the 21st century just might see the evangelization of the world in this generation. Let's complete the task—through giving ourselves to prayer.

Questions for Further Thought or Discussion

1. Why do you believe there is a specific relationship between prayer and evangelism and missions? Do our prayers really matter? Why or why not?
2. Can you name other figures or movements in history where prayer fueled the advance of the gospel? What biblical examples come to mind?
3. Share one of your own personal stories about how your prayers affected the life or salvation of another person. How can you increase your prayer life for others? What nations or peoples would God have you to focus on in prayer?

The author: Ron Boehme is the Director of U.S. Renewal Ministries for Youth With a Mission, North American Office He is the author of four books including *Leadership for the 21st Century* and *If God Had a Plan for My Life Why Can't I Find It?* He lives in Port Orchard, Washington.

SUGGESTED ADDITIONAL READING

Anderson, Phil. *The Lord of the Ring: Uncovering the Secret Origins of 24/7 Praying.* Ventura, CA: Regal Books, 2007.

Bounds, E. M. *Essentials of Prayer.* New Kennsington, PA: Whitaker House Publishers, 1994.

Johnstone, Patrick and Jason Mandryk. *Operation World.* Pasadena, CA: US Center for World Mission, 2001.

ENDNOTES

1. *Mission Frontiers* (Pasadena: U.S. Center for World Missions, July-August 1994), p. 5.

2. A popular book on this subject is Thomas Cahill's *How the Irish Saved Civilization.*

3. *Mission Frontiers* (Pasadena: U.S. Center for World Mission, July-August, 1994), p. 5

4. A good resource on the Moravians is *A Short Introduction to the History, Customs, and Practices of the Moravian Church* by Herbert Spaugh. www.everydaycounselor.com/archives, 1999.

5. Robert Tuttle, Jr., *John Wesley, His Life and Theology* (Grand Rapids: Zondervan Publishing, 1978), pp. 181-192.

6. See the William Carey Library at www.missionbooks.org.

7. Claude Hickman, *The Haystack Prayer Meeting.* www.svm2.citymaker.com/haystackstory.

8. Christian History Institute, *Glimpses* #81. http://Chi.gospelcom.net/climpsef/glimpses, 2007.

9. *Missions Frontiers* (Pasadena: U.S. Center for World Missions, July-August), 1994, p. 5.

10. There are many sources on the Welsh Revival. A good on-line summary is www.welshrevival.com.

11. Gary McGee, "William J. Seymour and the Azusa Street Revival," *Enrichment Journal*, 2007. www.ag.org/enrichmentjournal.

12. Pentecostalism, Wikipedia.

13. *Missions Frontiers* (Pasadena, CA: U.S. Center for World Missions, July-August), 1994, p. 5.

14. Patrick Johnstone and Jason Mandryk, *Operation World* (Carislile,

UK: Paternoster, 2005), p. 387.

15. There are many works on the Chinese Revival. See *The Heavenly Man*, by Brother Yun, and www.backtojerusalem.com.

16. *Missions Frontiers* (Pasadena: U.S. Center for World Missions, July-August), 1994, p. 5.

17. See www.globaldayofprayer.com.

18. The following statistics are confirmed from a number of mission sources including *The World Christian Encyclopedia* by David Barrett.

chapter

66

STRATEGIC PRAYER FOR GOD'S MISSION AND MISSIONARIES

Mike Barnett

The year was 1982. It was another Wednesday afternoon—stuck in stop-and-go traffic westbound out of Houston on Interstate 10. My destination was Kingsland Baptist Church, Katy, Texas. I was headed to the Wednesday evening meal and prayer service followed by my favorite mid-week activity, choir practice! Cindy and I were blessed to be a part of this new, young church. We were learning much about our faith and God's church. Wednesday evenings served as a mid-week break for me. A time to reflect on spiritual things, enjoy friendships among like-minded believers, and discover more about loving and serving God and His mission.

This was where I first learned to pray for the missionaries. We sat in small groups and prayed by name for every missionary who had a birthday that week. Occasionally someone mentioned a specific prayer need of an individual missionary he or she knew, but usually it was a simple, more generic, somewhat ritualistic recognition before God of those serving Him on foreign fields. “God bless the missionaries!” It was a beginning.

Twenty-five years later, I am pleased to see how far our churches have progressed in their prayers for God’s mission and His missionaries. Some churches still pray for missionaries on their birthdays, “God bless the missionaries!” But increasingly our prayers are better informed and infinitely more strategic. Surely this is a factor in the amazing reports from around the world about the progress of the gospel. What is behind these strategic prayers? Why should we pray for missions and missionaries in the first place? Whom should we pray for? How should we pray? And what happens when we pray? This chapter addresses these critical questions.

Why pray for God’s mission and His missionaries?

Because God answers prayer! Throughout the Old and New Testaments, time after time, God responds to the prayers of His people. On the evening after the dedication of the temple, God reminded Solomon, that when God’s people humbly pray and seek His will, He hears from heaven and answers their prayers (2 Chron. 7:14). God’s mission plan for Israel was to be a “light to the Gentiles,” a witness among all peoples on earth (Isa. 49:6). God’s temple was to be a “house of prayer for all nations” (56:7). Prayer was a vital link between God’s people and His mission.

Almost one thousand years later, Jesus condemned the temple managers for turning God’s temple from a house of prayer for the nations into a “den of thieves” (Mk. 11:17). The next day He debriefed His disciples on the importance of prayer for the kingdom: “Whatever things you ask in prayer, believing, you will receive” (Mt. 21:22). In other words, do not forget that God answers the prayers of His faithful followers. Then Jesus re-instated God’s mission to “make disciples of all nations, baptizing them in the name of the Father, and of the Son, and of the Holy Spirit, teaching them to observe all things that I have commanded” (28:19-20).

The disciples of the early Church understood this power of prayer. They “continued in one accord in prayer” (Acts 1:14). In times of crisis they prayed (Acts 6:4, 13:2-3; Mk. 9:29). In the middle of the mission, they prayed

(Col. 4:2). And God answered. No wonder the gospel of Jesus Christ swept throughout the Roman Empire in such a short time. God's people prayed for His mission and His missionaries. Why? Because they knew that God answers prayer. He did then . . . He does now.

For whom should we pray?

For the "nations" and the missionaries! Before we pray for the missionaries, we need to pray for those they serve. Paul prayed, "for Israel . . . that they may be saved" (Rom. 10:1). Jesus said, "I do not pray for these alone, but also for those who will believe in Me through their word" (Jn. 17:20). As followers of Jesus, committed to His Great Commission, we must pray for all peoples on earth. Especially for those who have yet to hear of Jesus. Even for those "least reached peoples" who have yet to meet a missionary.

In recent years, we have become more effective in praying for the lost peoples on earth. Whereas our traditional prayers for the missionaries seldom connected us with these "nations," today we have access to information about the people groups who have yet to hear the gospel. In the past we received missionary letters full of personal requests related to the well-being of the missionary family. Pray for our health, the children's education, consistent electricity, clean water, a good language learning experience, a suitable house, our elderly parents at home, a new refrigerator, our next care package from home, our crates of personal belongings, and such.

Today we read e-letters from missions teams focused on strategic prayer needs of the local peoples:

- Pray for Ahmed and Mohammed, that God would open their hearts and spirits to the gospel.
- Pray for local tribal leaders and their willingness to meet with believers.
- Pray for Fatima and her sister as they approach their mother with the truths of the gospel.
- Pray for this tribe's deliverance from the bondage of the evil one.
- Pray for a specific mega-city (>1 mil.) and for opportunities for humanitarian projects to provide access to the gospel.
- Pray for local translators working with Bible societies on Bible translation projects.

- Pray for effective radio broadcasts and Jesus film distribution.

Today we are able to pray more strategically for the unreached.

So, do we forget the old prayer, "God bless the missionaries?" Absolutely not! We must continue to pray for the missionaries. But what should we pray for the missionaries? Our western worldview of success and individualism has unduly influenced our church culture. We seem preoccupied with personal comfort and success. Often our view of God is that His sole purpose or His main mission is to take care of us, to make us happy. This is a twisted and dangerous theology.

What do we mean when we ask God to bless the missionaries? Jesus did not pray that God would rescue the disciples from the hardships of the world. He asked the father to "keep them from the evil one" (Jn. 17:15). After Saul's Damascus Road experience, Christ said He would show Paul "how many things he must suffer" for Jesus' name (Acts 9:16). God's call upon the life of a missionary (or any believer for that matter) does not remove the reality of pain, suffering, sickness, and persecution. This theme of serving Christ through persecution and suffering is both a biblical and historical reality. How many of us have heard the testimonies and requests of persecuted house church leaders in China. They plead with us not to pray for the suffering and persecution to end, but rather for God to be glorified through the persecution. With persecution comes kingdom growth. It has always been so. Tertullian said the blood of the Christians is holy seed.[1] Christ said, "If anyone desires to come after Me, let him deny himself and take up his cross, and follow Me" (Mt. 16:24).

So, perhaps we should pray less for the "success," happiness, and comfort of the missionaries and more for their endurance and character as cross-cultural disciplers. In their book, *Called to Reach: Equipping Cross-cultural Disciplers*, Yount and Barnett identify eight characteristics of effective missionaries. When we pray for the missionaries (expatriates and locals), perhaps we should pray that they would:

1. Depend on the Holy Spirit in all they do (spiritual character).
2. Live according to the teachings of the Bible (biblical character).
3. Be good thinkers and teachers across cultural barriers (rational character).

4. Be willing to *suffer with* those they witness to (compassionate character).
5. Endure as they *suffer for* the sake of the gospel (impassioned character).
6. Build lasting, witnessing relationships (relational character).
7. Stay focused on God's mission, not their own (maturational character).

For whom should we pray? Pray for the nations. Pray for the lost of this world, the unreached peoples who receive the witness of our missionaries. Intercede on behalf of the local peoples whom God will use to establish His kingdom in their lands and beyond. And don't forget to pray for the missionaries—that they would endure and be of Christ-like character.

How should we pray?

Pray for God's kingdom to come! The disciples must have asked Jesus how to pray. After coaching them on their motives for prayer, Jesus told them to pray like this: "Father, *Your* name be praised and honored. *Your* kingdom come and *Your* will [Your mission] be done" (Mt. 6:9-10, *italics and paraphrase mine*). Jesus, the son of God, tells us to pray for God! For His glory, His name, His fame, His kingdom, and His mission. God desires our praise. He wants us to participate in His mission of a blessing for all peoples (Gen. 12:3-4) as He establishes His kingdom today on earth and forever in heaven.

So, pray for God to call out His laborers into His harvest fields more than ours. Pray for the establishment of His Church, more than our mission organization or denomination. Pray for the reputation of His name, more than our recognition. It is no accident that the most effective missionaries are often standing in the background, not upfront in the spotlight. Pray for the Holy Spirit to convince unbelievers through His teachings more than our clever arguments. Pray for new believers to obey His commandments more than our traditions. Pray for the new church to find answers from His Word, more than our words. When we pray like this, He inevitably will surprise us. After all, it is His mission. And He will accomplish it.

What happens when we pray?

God's mission proceeds from our prayers! He expands His kingdom! When we pray for God's mission it is like we are praying the gospel to ourselves. And God answers our prayers. He expands the influence of His gospel.

Where there are movements of believers planting churches on earth today, they were preceded by movements of prayer for God to accomplish His mission among those peoples.[2] When we stop praying, when we relegate prayer to the fringes of our church practice like the temple managers of old, God's mission is diminished. More than eighty years ago, Helen Barrett Montgomery said it well,

> Now the Bible, which is the vehicle of the gospel, brings to light an inner message of prayer which is dynamic. The Bible may bring the knowledge of Christ to a nation or individual, but if there is no appropriation of prayer-power there is no life, no movement. It is important that men should know the gospel, it is more important that they should pray the gospel. If they pray, the gospel proceeds; if they do not pray the gospel halts. Its victories are wholly wrought by prayer; its defeats proceed from prayerlessness.[3]

Praying for God's mission and His missionaries is the most strategic endeavor of the church.

Summary

Why pray for God's mission and His missionaries? Because God answers prayer! He always has and He always will. Whom should we pray for? The nations and the missionaries! Pray for the nations to hear and understand the good news of Jesus Christ. Pray for missionaries to endure and develop Christ-like character as they serve. How should we pray? For God's mission to be accomplished! Don't focus so much on our plans, strategies, means, and methods but God's will to be done—His kingdom to come. What happens when we pray? God expands His kingdom! These are the basics of praying strategically for God's mission and His missionaries.

The church we attend today doesn't have a church-wide Wednesday evening Bible study and prayer meeting. We no longer pray for the missionaries on their birthdays. But we do pray for God's mission and His missionaries. God bless the missionaries! Your kingdom come!

Questions for Further Thought or Discussion

1. Why doesn't the church pray more for God's mission and missionaries?
2. What do you think about the statement that says we should pray less for the "success," happiness, and comfort of the missionary?
3. What can you or your group do to become more strategic in praying for God's mission and His missionaries?

The author: Dr. Mike Barnett is Professor of Missionary Church Planting at Columbia International University, Seminary and School of Missions in Columbia, South Carolina. He is a former international missionary and is the co-author of *Called to Reach: Equipping Cross-cultural Disciplers.*

SUGGESTED ADDITIONAL READING

Montgomery, Helen Barrett. *Prayer and Missions.* West Medford, MA: The Central Committee of the United Study of Foreign Missions, 1924.

Garrison, David. *Church Planting Movements: How God Is Redeeming a Lost World.* WigTake Resources, 2004.

Yount, William R. and Mike Barnett. *Called to Reach: Equipping Cross-cultural Disciplers.* Nashville: Broadman & Holman, 2007.

ENDNOTES

1. Robin Daniel, *This Holy Seed: Faith Hope and Love in the Early Churches of North Africa,* (Harpenden Herts: Tamarisk Publications, 1993), p. 33.

2. David Garrison, *Church Planting Movements: How God Is Redeeming a Lost World* (Midlothian, VA: WigTake Resources, 2004), pp. 172-77.

3. Helen Barrett Montgomery, *Prayer and Missions* (West Medford, MA: The Central Committee of the United Study of Foreign Missions, 1924), p. 11.

chapter

67

PRAYERWALKING AS A METHOD OF INTERCESSORY PRAYER

Randy Sprinkle

As the 21st century unfolds, Washington D.C. remains the ultimate power place. Its philosophical force field reaches across the nation validating its ways and drawing to itself ever more Type A's who are driven to achieve and realize.

On a spring morning at the beginning of this new century, two groups arrived in the city. One, completely unnoticed by virtue of its small number (only two), watched as a long line of buses opened their doors. Sleepy riders received signs from the bowels of the buses and energy from their swelling numbers. That evenings' news made no mention of the first group but it did cover the second reporting that it numbered 200,000 and had come to Washington to change administration policy. The group's organizers expected to do that through their marching and their chanting.

Two groups that day at the epicenter of power. Each there with purposes. Each with strategies to achieve those purposes. Each agreeing that Washington needed to change. One, the larger group, was saying by its method, "If it's to be, it's up to me." They believed, and their methods demonstrated, that if change was going to come it would be at their initiative and by their power. The other group believed equally in the need for change and was demonstrating a comparable level of sacrifice to see it realized but their activities demonstrated a method that was foundationally different. They were followers of Jesus and they believed that needed change would not come at their initiative and certainly not through their power. Their methods were saying, "If it's to be, it's *not* up to me." The initiative and the power resided with Another.

The larger group were activists. The smaller group? Prayerwalkers. And at the end of the day it needs to be asked: Which group brought the greater good? And why?

What in the world?

In the early 1970s it was noticed in disparate parts of the world that there were pray-ers who were not in their church buildings and their "prayer closets" where they belonged but out in the streets and neighborhoods of their worlds. Not only were they not praying where they should, they were not praying as they should. Heads were up. Eyes were open. Hands were unfolded. Instead of on their knees, they were on their feet, and they were on the move. "Proper" prayer was under assault but not from the forces of the enemy or the flesh or even the world as some presumed, but from the very Spirit of God. And the assault, while doing some violence to tradition and assumption and habit, had a greater aim—to do violence to the kingdom of darkness. In the process it did not supplant "proper" prayer; it enhanced it and revitalized it.

Before very long it began to be clear, where pray-ers moved out into their worlds, their worlds changed—or better stated—were changed. It wasn't so much that something was happening as it was Someone was happening. Efforts were made periodically to label the movement a fad but they were like yard sale price tags made from Post-it® notes. When the wind blew, they just wouldn't stick. And there was a Wind about this movement. Not only would labels not stick, add-ons and aberrations and even high jacking efforts all were ultimately unsuccessful. This Wind just kept clearing the decks, refilling the sails and pushing the ship ever on course. Along the journey, though, one label did finally stick. It was unremarkable and not at all catchy but apparently quite acceptable to the ship's Master. The label? Prayerwalking.

Where'd this come from?

Those who sought to follow the tracks of the movement back to its beginning found the trail quickly faded out. To understand what was happening and the genius behind it, a different tack would be needed. Rather than looking for its beginning the searchers needed to go back to the beginning. On the surface, prayerwalking looked like an activity or an event but those expressions of it came and went as quickly as, well, a fad. But when they looked at the prayerwalkers they saw something both unique and ancient about them. These unusual intercessors were not just avenues of change they were actually being changed. They were thinking differently and believing differently and (this was the amazing thing) they were actually living differently.

Back at the beginning (Genesis 1-3) the investigators noticed something. God, the One of infinite creativity, actually seemed to be quite uncreative when it came to method. The way He chose was certainly spectacular. He spoke and it was! Wow! But with all the other options available to Him, He seemed methodologically stuck. That is until He came to the epitome of His work, the making of humankind. These would be different by being alike—like Him. And since they would be like Him, in image and in essence, they would be made differently. These He would make by hand. And when He was done, He would crown His work by breathing His life into them. They were not just like Him, they were of Him. And this "of-ness" made possible "with-ness." How did the investigators find this "with-ness" expressed. In what seemed to be the most mundane of ways. Each day God and these first humans walked together.

It was so good until it became so bad. Sin always separates. When sin separated Adam and Eve from God it was not just awful, it was hopeless—until God, in loving mercy and at the right time, sent one who would bridge the separation and make a way back. We were created to walk with God in unhindered intimacy and oneness. Certainly that was lost. But not forever.

The one, Jesus, settled our account, picked up our tab, redeemed us. We can come back. The invitation's been issued. The door is again open. And not only has He redeemed us, He is evermore redeeming us back to that for which we were created. And that is? To walk with God.

Prayerwalking: Passion or Pragmatism?

The one, who is redeeming us back to that for which we were originally created, has also revealed in the calling of His first disciples the way that He is accomplishing this mission. He simply said, "Follow Me." (Mt. 4:19). As we do, He does the shaping, the changing, the making of us into what we are to be. God's predetermined intent is clear: we are to be more and more conformed to the image of His Son (Rom. 8:29). If the disciple is to be like the Master he must be with Him and if we are going to stay with Him then we'll have to follow Him through each day without pause, without straying and without personal agenda.

Minutes after President George Bush was sworn in on January 20th, 2001, he kept one of his campaign promises, issuing Executive Order No. 13199, which created and funded the White House Office of Faith-Based and Community Initiatives. This pleased many church and ministry groups. It also opened a dangerous door. We, as the light of the world, are, of course, to let our light shine in the world. To change metaphors, we are to be leaven in the loaf. But, whenever we walk this way, we find as a new traveling companion the easy option of entangling ourselves "in the affairs of men" and we meet a temptation that is almost atmospheric, that of also adopting "the ways of men." Washington's ways (which are often synonymous with the world's ways) can become our ways.

Pragmatism is a philosophy that determines value or truth by results. "If it works, do it." It is inconsistent with biblical truth, but, surprisingly, it is pervasive in the Church today. How can that be? There are several possible answers, all similar: we don't know the ways of God, we don't want to know the ways of God, or we don't know how to know the ways of God. So we substitute and the substitute is the ways of the world.

In some of His last words before going to the cross, (John 15) Jesus draws the analogy of our lives as branches and His as the vine. In doing this He makes unmistakably plain that our single most important focus is on being not doing. Organically and intimately, we have to remain connected to Him ("abiding"). "With-ness" was God's original intent and our ongoing intent must be the nurturing of this walk with Him. Following the command to stay vitally connected Jesus then makes a startling declaration. If we don't, our lives will be barren. "Without Me (i.e. out there on your own) you can do nothing." (15:5b)

When we fail to live out this truth, either by ignorance or by intent, we reveal a flawed theology which says branches bear fruit. They don't. The vine bears the fruit and it bears it on the branches. This is the only fruit that lasts. And that can happen only as the branch is connected to the vine in such a way that it's life can flow into and through that branch.

Prayerwalking isn't pragmatism in its newest iteration; it is passion for the one who calls us to abide with Him, to walk out a life that is a prayer, one with no "Selah" and no "Amen."

So how does prayerwalking "work"?

God is powerfully impacting our world through an activity that He has authored called prayerwalking. But the impact is coming not as we plan events or learn new techniques but as we come to know Him. As life increasingly becomes a prayerwalk, Jesus increasingly becomes more and more precious to us. His love changes us. The grip of the things of earth is loosened and they do grow strangely dim. Our goals become less important and His goals become more important. Our agendas grow less dominating as His agenda rises in significance and life orienting power. And our praying is transformed. The intercession flows but not out of obligation or guilt but out of a heart that is being enlarged by His heart. Our lives are becoming a prayer.

As we walk out lives that are intimately and practically related to Him, we find ourselves walking more and talking less. In this listening orientation we hear His voice but more deeply we hear His heart and we are moved and we have to respond. Key facets of this response are gratitude, love, willingness, sacrifice, obedience, service. And we begin to intercede as never before. This intercession is powerful for its refined purity and is intensely directed because the one who lives continuously to make intercession is finding in these fellow journeyers, hearts ready to see and hear and receive and believe. Prayerwalkers follow Jesus to the places where He intends to bring blessings.

They see people through His eyes and hear their hurts as He hears them. And they pray out of identification, not first with people but, with Him. Then they and/or others return to those same places in ministry that becomes the actual channels of the Savior's blessing and salvation.

Prayerwalking is a method of coming alongside and praying for hurting, hopeless, people. Really, though, it is better described by a synonym with a nuanced but critical distinctive. A method is a way of doing something. A manner is a way of being that results in a way of doing. The Apostle Paul exhorts, "Walk worthy of the calling with which you were called." (Eph. 4:1). This moment in kingdom history is one in which Jesus is uniquely calling us back to a manner of living—life as prayerwalk. This life has favor with God and with people and for it the world and the enemy have no new answer.

Questions for Further Thought or Discussion

1. Write a definition of prayerwalking and explain why it is more than a pragmatic trend.
2. Identify two or three examples of prayerwalking from the Bible and explain how it can be applied to the work of the Church today.
3. Design a plan for your local congregation that includes a teaching outline, a training method, and a strategy to deploy prayerwalking teams throughout the community.

The author: Dr. Randy Sprinkle is Director of Transformational Leadership for the Baptist Convention of New England, Northborough, Massachusetts. A former missionary to Africa, he is author of *Until the Stars Appear, Follow Me: Lessons for Becoming a Prayerwalker,* and *Strong Walk: Becoming a Lifestyle Spiritual Warrior.*

SUGGESTED ADDITIONAL READING

Sprinkle, Randy. *Follow Me: Becoming a Lifestyle Prayerwalker.* Birmingham, AL: New Hope, 2001.

Hawthorne, Steve and Graham Kendrick. *Prayerwalking: Praying On Site with Insight.* Orlando: Creation House, 1993.

Crawford, Dan and Calvin Miller. *Prayerwalking: A Journey of Faith.* Chattanooga, TN: AMG Publishers, 2002.

chapter

68

PRAYER CALENDARS/ NETWORKS/ COMMUNICATION LINKS

Naomi A. Frizzell

Prayer, prayer calendars and telephone prayer chains were a familiar part of life at the Nazarene Church I attended while growing up in Michigan. Some of my earliest memories of corporate prayer involve Wednesday night prayer meetings kneeling on the hard church sanctuary floor, counting ceiling tiles while trying to stay awake. Although at the time the prayer meetings seemed boring, they left a deep impression on me as I listened to people share burdens with God and each other. In addition to familiar health or employment needs, requests from missionaries in then unfamiliar places like Papua, New Guinea, or Swaziland opened wide my vision for prayer, missions and evangelism.

The priority of personal prayer was reinforced by my parents. Weekdays before dawn, I would catch my mother on her knees interceding both for our family and for her third grade students. During evening devotions my father would lead us in prayer for friends and family who didn't know Christ.

Prayer communication in many churches today still resembles the type of communication I grew up with in the 1960s and 1970s. Bulletin inserts, prayer cards and telephone prayer chains are still widely used because of their accessibility. Yet scores of churches have embraced technology that facilitates prayer among God's people by connecting Christians around the world in a moment's notice. Denominations/associations, churches, para-church ministries and individuals are bringing Christians together as never before around a common vision to pray on a specific day or for a particular area of the world or issue.

"Prayer is communication with God and prayer unites God's people,"[1] says Sarah Plummer, Chair of the Intercession Working Group for the Lausanne Committee for World Evangelization. She believes technology such as the Internet, email and teleconferencing is fostering greater prayer efforts and closer communication and unity among people who pray. Plummer cited the example of Greater Calling (www.greatercalling.org), which connects Christians in prayer, anytime, anywhere in the world via conference calls.

Networks, Days, and Internet Prayer Opportunities

Ethnê to Ethnê (www.ethne.net), which is dedicated to reaching the nearly seven thousand *Unreached People Groups* (UPGs), has prayer resources such as bookmarks, bulletin inserts and MP3 files available in multiple languages.

The Global Prayer Digest (www.global-prayer-digest.org) establishes the daily discipline of praying for UPGs with an overview of an area of the world, its people and the opportunities to reach them with the gospel. *The Global Prayer Digest* is available by mail, email or as a PDA download.

Since 1996, the **International Day of Prayer for the Persecuted Church** (www.persecutedchurch.org) has raised awareness of the needs of the persecuted Church and coordinated intercessory prayer and action on its behalf.

Moms In Touch International (www.MomsInTouch.org) gathers women to pray weekly for their children, the schools they attend and teachers/administrators.

The **National Day of Prayer** (US) (www.nationaldayofprayer.com) focuses on personal repentance and prayer intercession in areas such as the government, media and the family.

The Canadian **40 Day Prayer Ramp** calls Christians to pray for revival so that "men, women and children come to Christ in every community across this land."[2]

"Eliminating geography as a barrier and connecting people of like-mind and passion," is the goal of the **National Pastors' Prayer Network** (NPPN), according to founder Phil Miglioratti. The NPPN (www.nppn.org) began connecting pastor's prayer groups in Chicago in the 1990s and now links pastors and other praying people around the world through email and the Internet. Miglioratti says the NPPN, which includes nearly nine hundred pastors' prayer groups, provides encouragement, information and instruction on prayer and builds relationships and communication among people who pray.

Largest Prayer Event

The Global Day of Prayer (GDOP, www.globaldayofprayer.com) represents one of the most significant examples of using technology to unite Christians who pray, both in promoting the day and during the actual day of prayer.

In July 2000, South African Christian businessman Graham Power envisioned bringing together Christians from all denominations in Cape Town, South Africa for a Day of Repentance and Prayer. His vision grew into a Day of Prayer and Repentance for all of Africa in 2002 and in 2004 Christians from fifty-six African nations participated in the first-ever Day of Repentance and Prayer for Africa. Prayer reports so encouraged and motivated praying Christians around the world that later that year the Global Day of Prayer five-year vision (2005 to 2010) was launched. The GDOP emphasizes ten days of continuous prayer from Ascension Day to the Saturday before the GDOP (Pentecost Sunday)—and 90 Days of Blessing following—as Christians serve and minister in their communities in tangible ways.

The first GDOP (2005) brought together Christians from 156 nations. By 2007, 233 nations participated, including Uganda, where churches gathered in thirty-five stadiums, and Hong Kong, where thirty thousand people prayed together in one stadium.

Satellite and Internet feeds connect participants around the world on the

GDOP. Grace Samson, School of Video Production Leader for the Youth With A Mission Media Village in Cape Town, South Africa, is the GDOP broadcast anchor. Bringing Christians together on the GDOP, says Samson, "demonstrates our unity in Christ as a witness to the world that we are one. We believe God commands His blessings in the place of unity and that when the body of Christ stands together, we can see far greater results as opposed to individually doing our own thing."[3]

The extraordinary GDOP growth is attributed to God's blessing and to the massive distribution of vision videos. "According to Graham Power, GDOP growth is in direct proportion to the production and circulation of videos that document the event and serve as a prototype for those willing to start a prayer network,"[4] says Samson. The videos, produced by Media Village, help unite Christians in prayer because, Samson emphasizes, "there is a sense of the presence of God, capturing the emotions and impact of passionate prayers that brings about a remarkable motivation on viewers. We have received reports of people weeping and having tangible experiences with God through watching those videos."[5]

The GDOP website offers free downloads of Power Point presentations; logos; event/logistics information; examples of promotional merchandise such as hats and t-shirts that groups can produce locally; audio scripts and more. Resources are translated into as many languages as possible. Readily accessible resources encourage participants to make the GDOP reflect their own culture and community.

The GDOP has brought individual Christians, churches and ministries together in an unprecedented manner. By being "open-handed" in sharing resources online, the GDOP has set a new benchmark not only for cooperative prayer, but also for planning global events and facilitating global collaborative ministry.

Prayer Online

The Internet and email offer great potential for connecting God's people in prayer, affirms Plummer, who is helping develop the **Global Prayer-Web** (GPW), a multi-lingual website (launching 2009). She says the website will connect adults and children online by offering simple, clear prayer requests through postings, chat-prayer rooms and more, making it easier for Christians to "pray for other people and nations in a coordinated and relevant way."[6] The GPW is unique in categorizing the world—not just by country or nation, but also by oceans to offer intentional prayer coverage for people working on oil rigs and ships/boats and living on islands. The GPW will emphasize transformational prayer, she adds, to mobilize the Church to talk to God about lost people because "as people pray for the lost, they become bolder to share with lost people."[7] The GPW will also use the Missions Atlas Project and offer Regional Mission Status Maps that provide evangelization updates, progress on *JESUS* Film translation and the status of Bible translation.

One key challenge for the GPW, and other prayer websites and emails, is coordinating prayer for and with Christians in creative access countries (countries hostile to Christianity). Keeping information secure, while also mobilizing prayer, is a delicate balance because events and key issues cannot always be shared globally.

In addition to creating prayer websites, Christians are also ministering on public websites. **SecondLife.com**, a virtual reality world of eight million people (July 2007), offers individuals the opportunity to live a "second life" in virtual reality by taking on a new name, identity and body. Reaction to the implications of living a "second life" online is mixed, yet Christians are responding to the spiritual needs of the millions of people flocking to SecondLife.com. During Easter Week 2007, the SecondLife Christian Leaders Association and churches on SecondLife sponsored *The Redemption Week Tour* to tell the story of the life, death and resurrection of Jesus and highlight SecondLife Christian groups. People shared prayer requests and were prayed for online and while the method may be unconventional, the response to the prayer needs was very real.

Cautions

"We need to remind ourselves that technology is only a tool God is using to bring about His purposes on earth," Samson cautions. "Christians can use technology to communicate, but we must not rely on it as our source of effectiveness. The power of the Holy Spirit is what every believer needs to pray for,"[8] she adds.

In addition to a right perspective on using technology, Christians need to remember the importance of personal connections. Online and email prayers can sometimes lead to a sense of isolation, disconnection and lack of accountability. Prayers can be said anonymously and without any connection to the person being prayed for who may need to know God is moving others to pray for them. Migliarotti points out that "no matter what software or gadgets are developed that remove geography and other barriers to working together in unity,"[9] people need personal, face-to-face prayer with others. Samson agrees: "Media and technology must never replace our fellowship, relationship, personal communication and connection."[10]

Because of the speed of the Internet and email, Migliarotti also says there is a danger of passing along prayer information that is not verified or corroborated. People may distribute unintentionally misleading or not quite true information, he warns, by simply forwarding an email. He cautions people to try to verify the accuracy before sending emails and to respect confidentiality when sharing names or other information. In addition, he urges Christians to pray for discernment in what they share and post online recognizing that, "just because it's out there doesn't mean it's correct or beneficial to forward on."

Christians need to pray for wisdom in determining the appropriate use of technology, concludes Plummer. It can be tempting to use every new means of communication; however, millions of Christians don't have regular email and Internet access because of infrastructure, finances or security issues. Miglioratti also advises being prudent because some generations of leaders are not early adopters of new technology.

Thirty years ago the idea of almost instaneous communication was the stuff of *Star Trek* and *Lost in Space.* Kneeling in that small Nazarene church decades ago I never would have dreamed of receiving instant prayer requests or talking regularly via the Internet with the people I pray for around the world. I thank God for how He has directed the development of prayer communication tools and pray that we use these tools wisely to His honor and glory. Only God knows what the next ten years hold in the area of prayer communications. Yet as we embrace the proper use of technology, "There is one thing we can be sure of when we come to God in prayer. If we ask anything in keeping with what He wants, He hears us" (1 Jn. 5:14)

Questions for Further Thought or Discussion

1. How can Christians use seemingly "non-personal" tools such as the In-

ternet and email for prayer while keeping in mind the need for personal interaction and accountability in prayer?

2. What are some ways Christians who do not have regular access to the Internet or email can be connected with other Christians around the world in prayer?
3. What technology tools can you use to personally enhance your prayer life?

The author: Naomi Frizzell is Director of Communications for the Lausanne Committee for World Evangelization. She lives in Jacksonville, Florida.

SUGGESTED ADDITIONAL READING

Gene Edward Veith Jr. (Series Editor), Christopher L. Stamper. *Christians in a .com World: Getting Connected without Being Consumed.* Wheaton, IL: Crossway Books, 2000.

Higley, Sandra. *A Year of Prayer Events for Your Church.* Terre Haute: IN: PrayerShop Publishing, 2007.

SUGGESTED ADDITIONAL RESOURSES

Note: The websites listed below are only a small representation of the many prayer resources available online. The content of the websites listed in this section and throughout the chapter is the sole responsibility of the sponsoring organization. Inclusion on this list does not necessarily mean an endorsement of all the opinions and views expressed on the website. (URLs correct as of July 2007.)

- 24/7 Prayer—www.global24-7.org
- 30 Days, Loving Muslims Through Prayer—www.30-days.net
- America's National Prayer Committee—www.nationalprayer.org
- Australian Prayer Network—www.ausprayernet.org.au
- Campus Renewal Ministries—www.campusrenewal.org
- Church Prayer Leaders Network—www.prayerleader.com
- Ethnê to Ethnê—www.ethne.net
- Global Day of Prayer—www.globaldayofprayer.com
- Global Mapping—www.gmi.org
- *Global Prayer Digest*—www.global-prayer-digest.org

- Greater Calling—www.greatercalling.org
- Harvest Prayer Ministries—www.harvestprayer.com
- Intercessors for America—www.ifapray.org
- International Day of Prayer for the Persecuted Church—www.persecutedchurch.org
- International Prayer Council—www.ipcprayer.org
- International Renewal Ministries—www.prayersummits.net
- Joel News—www.joelnews.org
- Joshua Project—www.joshuaproject.net
- Lydia Fellowship—www.lydiafellowship.org
- Moms In Touch International—www.MomsInTouch.org
- National Day of Prayer (United States)—www.ndptf.org
- National Pastors' Prayer Network—www.nppn.org
- National Prayer Center (Assemblies of God)—www.prayer.ag.org
- Missions Atlas Project—www.worldmap.org
- Operation World—www.gmi.org/ow
- Pray for China—www.prayforchina.com
- Pray for Denmark—www.prayfordenmark.com
- Pray for Egypt—www.prayforegypt.com
- Pray for Kuwait—www.prayforkuwait.com
- Prayer Connection (North American Mission Board)—www.namb.net/prayer
- Prayer Garden—www.prayerforthenations.com/prayergarden/flash.htm
- Presidential Prayer Team (United States)—www.presidentialprayerteam.org
- Thirty Second Kneel Down—www.30kd.org
- Transformation Africa—www.transformationafrica.com
- U.S. Prayer Center—www.usprayercenter.org
- WayMakers—www.waymakers.org
- World Prayer Center (U.S.)—www.theworldprayercenter.org
- World Prayer Centre (U.K.)—www.worldprayer.org.uk

ENDNOTES

1. From a personal conversation with Sarah Plummer.
2. http://www.40dayprayerramp.com/vision.shtml

3. From a personal conversation with Grace Samson.
4. Sampson.
5. Sampson.
6. Plummer.
7. Plummer.
8. Sampson.
9. From a personal conversation with Phil Migliarotti.
10. Sampson.

chapter

69

PRAYER AND SPIRITUAL WARFARE

Chuck Lawless

Perhaps you remember the book, *This Present Darkness,* written by Frank Peretti and first published in 1986. Set in the fictional town of Ashton, this novel described some believers in the town clashing with demonic forces who sought to take over their community. So popular was this fictional account of spiritual warfare that it remained on the bestseller list for quite some time.

Regrettably, the interest in spiritual warfare popularized by Peretti's work has often resulted in one of the extremes that C. S. Lewis recognized in his familiar work, *Screwtape Letters*: some have become fascinated with the demonic.[1] Much contemporary teaching about spiritual warfare lacks a biblical base, and we should be careful to filter through the scriptures everything written about the topic.

At the same time, the Bible does speak forcefully about the warfare we face as Christians. Jesus warned Peter that Satan demanded permission to "sift you as wheat" (Lk. 22:31). Peter himself later warned believers, "Your adversary the devil walks about like a roaring lion, seeking whom he may devour" (1 Pet. 5:8). The Apostle Paul, who himself experienced "a thorn in the flesh . . . a messenger of Satan" (2 Cor. 12:7), likewise admonished believers to "put on the whole armor of God, that you may be able to stand against the wiles of the devil" (Eph. 6:11). James, too, called believers to resist the devil, presupposing that the enemy would attack (Jas. 4:7).

Were spiritual warfare not real, such recurrent warnings would seem irrelevant and unnecessary. The goal of this chapter is to examine the relationship between this intense battle and the spiritual discipline that is the focus of this book: prayer. Specific attention is devoted to prayer in connection to evangelism and discipleship, with a final discussion of the concept of "warfare prayer."

The Urgency of Praying in the Battle

As noted above, both Peter and Paul knew the ferocity of the enemy's attacks. Hence, it is little wonder that they called believers to be ever alert:

- "Be sober, be vigilant, because your adversary the devil walks about like a roaring lion, seeking whom he may devour." (1 Pet. 5:8)
- "With all prayer and supplication, in the Spirit, being watchful to this end with all perseverance and supplication for all the saints." (Eph. 6:18)

Their words are strong and pointed, as both apostles understood that *all believers* are targets of the enemy. No follower of God is immune from the attacks of the one who will devour whom he can. If the enemy was brazen enough to attack Peter, Paul, and *Jesus Himself* (Mt. 4:11), surely we should not expect anything less. The battle is on, whether we like it or not.

Sometimes the most deceived believers are those who fail to recognize the reality of the battle—and who thus fail to prepare for the battle through prayer. C. S. Lewis is again insightful here, reminding us through the senior demon Screwtape how Satan attacks us: "The best thing, where it is possible, is to keep the patient [the human being] from the serious intention of praying altogether."[2] Indeed, prayerlessness is a primary indicator that a believer may have already lost the battle.

Moreover, we must not miss the Apostle Paul's mandate to pray for all believers with persistence and perseverance. Because the battle is real for all believers, intercessory prayer for each other is a non-negotiable. Most of our praying, however, is more reactive than proactive; that is, we start praying only *after* we learn of a losing battle (e.g., a family is in trouble, a young person is wandering, or a church is divided). The devil aims his arrows, hits his target—and *then* we decide to pray.

Frankly, praying for others is hard work, and discouragement sets in quickly. It is easy to fall asleep on the watch just as Jesus' own disciples did (Lk. 22:45-46). Nevertheless, might the enemy win fewer battles if we strategically, intentionally, and urgently prayed more often for each other?

The Relationship of Prayer, Spiritual Warfare, and Evangelism

In his thorough study of Satan and demons, Sidney H. T. Page indicates that two Pauline passages describe Satan's activities toward unbelievers—2 Corinthians 4:4 and Ephesians 2:2.[3] The former verse describes Satan's primary strategy against unbelievers: "the god of this age" has blinded their minds. Also called the "ruler of this world" (Jn. 12:31) and "prince of the power of the air" (Eph. 2:2). Satan does whatever he can to keep unbelievers in darkness. The unbeliever is by no means guiltless—"for the blindness spoken of is a consequence of unbelief"[4]—but the darkness is deepened by the enemy's efforts to maintain control.

Satan himself is already defeated, yet he still "has the strength to besiege human minds and to incite them to embrace and exalt evil rather than God."[5] While the world (and even the church at times) buys the lies of universalism, pluralism and inclusivism, Satan "transforms himself into an angel of light" (2 Cor. 11:14) and lulls unbelievers into a false sense of spiritual security.

This recognition that evangelism involves a spiritual battle is perhaps the most significant insight offered by writers in the spiritual warfare movement. Evangelism is more than just a strategy, technique, or program; rather, it is taking the gospel into the kingdom of darkness. To evangelize is to march into a spiritual battle.

Foundational to this understanding of evangelism is awareness that evangelism is fruitless without God's power. Apart from the supernatural work of God's grace countering the enemy's hold on non-believers, evangelism produces no converts. For this reason, evangelism must be accompanied with *prayer.* Evangelism is the task, but prayer is the necessary power behind the task.

The Relationship of Prayer, Spiritual Warfare, and Discipleship

Maybe your story is like mine. I became a believer as a teenager, but nobody taught me to be a disciple of Christ. My church told me what I needed to do (like read the Bible, pray, and witness), but it did not show me how. Nobody told me how to walk in truth, righteousness, and faith (see Eph. 6:11-17). As a result, I lived a defeated Christian life for far too many years.

The enemy aims his arrows at young believers who have not been discipled. He strikes them with doubt and discouragement. Sometimes he hits them with loneliness, as they move away from their non-Christian friends and try to fit into a church that is unfamiliar to them. At other times, he lures them with the same temptations they faced as non-believers. Whatever his strategy may be, he wants to strike at new believers before they are solidly planted in the Church.

This issue is related to prayer in at least two ways. First, many new believers are never taught how to pray. What they are told to do, they are not taught to do—and the result is a frustrated believer who longs to pray but does not know how. The enemy thus wins when the new believer gives up trying. This failure to disciple is, in my estimation, a primary cause of prayerlessness in the Church today.

Second, undiscipled believers often live defeated, sinful lives that hinder praying in the first place. Both Isaiah and the psalmist (Isa. 59:1-2, Ps. 66:18) knew that God chooses not to respond to the prayers of those who live in sin. It is the fervent prayer of a *righteous* man that makes a difference (Jas. 5:16), not the prayers of one living in unrighteousness.

How, though, does a new believer know how to stand for righteousness and fight against temptation unless the Church teaches him? An undiscipled believer may realize that his praying is ineffective, yet not know enough to understand *why*—and he gives up on the power of prayer. The enemy again wins.

A brief summary is in order here. The enemy seeks to keep unbelievers blinded to the gospel, thus holding them in bondage. He further schemes against believers, striving to discourage and defeat them so their faith is weakened and their prayers are ineffective. Powerless, prayerless believers make little difference in the war inherent in evangelism.

The Importance of Strategically Teaching Prayer

Paul warned his readers to stand against the "wiles" or schemes of the devil (Eph. 6:11), indicating that the enemy is a strategist who methodically attacks believers. One reason that the enemy so often wins is that he operates strategically, while the Church operates from Sunday to Sunday. With particular reference to this chapter, the Church often has no plan in place to raise up prayer warriors. Listed below are several steps to address this issue.

Teach the Church about prayer. Prayer is a mysterious and magnificent event, a divine encounter with the God of eternity. That this righteous Creator allows us to enter His presence is remarkable indeed. Church members who remain amazed by prayer keep their focus on God—and anything the enemy offers pales in comparison. Teach the Church about prayer through a sermon series on prayer, studies on prayer warriors in the Bible, or other study courses on prayer.

Teach the theology of prayer. Teach not only the magnificence of prayer, but also the power of believing God even when He seems distant. The enemy always wants us to get discouraged and give up; to counter that strategy, teach members to trust God's sovereign plan even when His will involves difficult spiritual conflict and seemingly unanswered prayer. Consider reading together biographies of great prayer warriors who trusted God and "prayed on" through tough times.

Model prayer in mentoring relationships. Just as Jesus taught His disciples to pray (Lk. 11:1). We should teach others in the context of discipling relationships. Exhibit before others holiness that undergirds powerful praying. Show patience in trusting God to respond. Make your praise public when He does answer. Hold yourself accountable to other believers. Let this goal be yours: to pray so relationally, so powerfully, and so effectively that others around you would say, "Please teach us to pray." The enemy is threatened by believers who pray in such a way.

What about warfare prayer?[6]

Some contemporary spiritual warfare leaders have written about "warfare prayer," or praying against high-ranking demons that rule over particular regions or territories. When prayer warriors identify the spirit over a given territory and then pray for that spirit's power to be broken, the area is then considered ready for effective evangelism to follow.

Daniel 10:10-21 are the primary texts given to support this concept. Daniel had prayed, but a supernatural force known as the "prince of the kingdom of Persia" caused a delay in the response to his prayer. Only after the angel Michael intervened did Daniel receive his answer.

Some believe that the "prince of the kingdom of Persia" was a demonic force assigned to the region of Persia. Based on that assumption, some warfare proponents seek to identify territorial spirits and pray that their power be broken over a given area.

Two cautions are important here. While the Daniel passage does seem to show that spirits sometimes influence regions, no mandate is given to name the power or to pray against it. Daniel, in fact, knew nothing about the spiritual battle occurring until *after* Michael had already intervened. We should be cautious not to read into this text a prescription for doing spiritual warfare in this fashion.

Second, some prayer warriors sometimes focus so much on discerning the enemy that they unintentionally miss what God is doing. The words of Daniel 10:10-21 were intended to be comforting to Daniel—the spiritual battle was real, but God victoriously did what was necessary to accomplish His will in Daniel's life. We must also be careful not to get so enamored with the enemy's ways that we miss God's hand in the process. Our focus must remain on the God who answers our prayers as He wishes according to His timing.

Questions for Further Thought or Discussion

1. What strategies does the enemy use to try to keep you from praying?
2. What steps will you take to pray with more urgency?
3. If you were designing a discipleship strategy to teach new believers to pray, what would that strategy include?

The author: Dr. Chuck Lawless is Dean of the Billy Graham School of Missions, Evangelism & Church Growth and Director of Doctorial Studies at the Southern Baptist

Seminary in Louisville, Kentucky. He is author of *Discipled Warriors, Putting on the Armor, Serving in Your Church Prayer Ministry,* and co-author with Thom Rainer of *Eating the Elephant* and with John Franklin of *Spiritual Warfare.*

SUGGESTED ADDITIONAL READING

Arnold, Clinton. *3 Crucial Questions about Spiritual Warfare.* Grand Rapids: Baker, 1997.

Bounds, E. M. *Prayer and Spiritual Warfare.* New Kensington, PA: Whitaker House, 2002.

Franklin, John. *And The Place Was Shaken.* Nashville: Broadman & Holman, 2005.

Gurnall, William. *The Christian in Complete Armour.* Cornwall, UK: Diggory Press, 2007.

Spurgeon, Charles. *Spurgeon on Prayer and Spiritual Warfare.* New Kensington, PA: Whitaker House, 1998.

ENDNOTES

1. C. S. Lewis, *Screwtape Letters* (New York: Macmillan, 1961), p. 3.

2. Lewis, *Screwtape Letters* (Old Tappan, NJ: Revell, 1976), p. 33.

3. Sidney H. T. Page, *Powers of Evil* (Grand Rapids: Baker, 1995), pp. 184-186.

4. Page, p. 184.

5. David Garland, "2 Corinthians," *New American Commentary* (Nashville: Broadman, 1999), p. 211.

6. This section was first published in Lawless's, *Discipled Warriors* (Grand Rapids: Kregel, 2002), pp. 163-164.

chapter

70

MOBILIZING PRAYER ADVOCACY

Eleanor Witcher

I started putting together a puzzle at work—a little space was cleared by the copy machine, a place where one might have a few idle moments as equipment warms up or a printing task is completed. A piece here, another there, and three weeks later, only the frame and one distinctive line of the complicated puzzle was complete. And that's when it happened: I got caught up in finding the trees, then the sky, and then I had to stop before allowing myself to start on the sunflowers which fill two-thirds of the picture.

That is what can happen when a prayer advocate gets involved in global missions activity. A missionary first invites the individual to pray and shares a request here, another there. Weeks later, the intercessor is slowly beginning to see the framework of the missionary's ministry and to learn the names of a few frequently mentioned nationals. Then it happens: the advocate gets caught up in finding ways to minister alongside the missionary, then to share the prayer needs with others, and then . . . well, then they don't want to stop before the picture is complete.

But just how does a missionary find those prayer advocates who will passionately and sacrificially intercede? How do we effectively communicate the strategic prayer needs of the ministry? And how do we nurture the long-term commitment of our prayer network? As a minister, you will play a vital role in helping missionaries find these advocates within your church and encouraging those who go to the mission field from your church to develop intercessory prayer for their mission.

While these principles are written more to an individual who is planning on going to the field, many of the suggestions can be used in your church either as you develop prayer teams for you and other pastors or as you organize prayer for missionaries.

Finding Passionate Prayer Advocates

Jesus consistently prayed over the significant events and people in His life. In His High Priestly prayer recorded in John 17, Jesus prayed for Himself as He anticipated what is irrefutably the most challenging act of service anyone could face—crucifixion. There in the Garden of Gethsemane, He also prayed for His co-laborers that they would be sanctified and equipped for their ministry in the world. And Jesus then prayed for those who would come to salvation through the testimony of His disciples. We must keep our eyes fixed on Jesus as we pray for personal purity, for the co-laborers we invite to join us, and for the lost who will believe on Jesus through the testimony of our words. Where does one begin in mobilizing prayer advocacy? *Start with prayer.* Determine that prayer will be foundational in your ministry and jealously guard your time with the Lord. As your personal prayer life deepens, you will more effectively communicate God's heart for your people group and inspire others to join you.

People gathered around Jesus wherever He went, but Jesus also made a point of gathering particular groups to Himself. As Jesus began His ministry, He selected the twelve disciples and poured His life into these men, training them to teach others. Within their number, Jesus had His inner circle of Peter, James, and John. Following the resurrection, Jesus appeared to the disciples and to a gathering of more than 500 believers. Later, He was also seen by Paul (1 Cor. 15:5-8). As Jesus gathered His witnesses of the resurrection, we, too, can gather advocates who will actively proclaim the good work that God is doing around the world.

Missionaries serving with the International Mission Board (IMB) of the Southern Baptist Convention are encouraged to develop a Comprehensive Prayer Network and categorize their advocates as Prayer Partners, Ministry Partners, and Personal Intercessors. Enlisting five churches to pray regularly and intentionally, missionaries establish their broad base of **Prayer Partners** similar to the gathering of 500 who witnessed the resurrected Jesus and faithfully shared what they had seen. It may be that a church is already praying for the people group or country where a missionary plans to serve. Making connection with that church represents an answer to their prayers and reminds us that God is the one mobilizing prayer advocacy.

Some of these prayer partners develop a stronger bond as they persist in daily intercession for the missionary and for the people group served. They often take volunteer trips to the field to labor alongside the overseas team. These **Ministry Partners**, akin to Jesus' disciples, are always looking for a deeper involvement in the work on the field and are excellent advocates in conveying prayer needs to their church family and association. The partnership and friendship is mutual, encouraging both the missionary and the Ministry Partner.

An even smaller group relates to Jesus' inner circle, those **Personal Intercessors** who are sensitive to the intimate prayer needs of a missionary, his family, and his team. Confidential requests can be communicated without a concern of the information being shared further. Do not force any intercessory relationship. That person who is a close friend may not demonstrate any interest in your adopted foreign culture or the exciting work God has given you. Although such friends will pray, they do not necessarily form this core of personal intercessors. Ask God to reveal a small group of people who are so keenly attuned to the ministry and to the Lord's heart that they will stop whatever they are doing to pray whenever the Holy Spirit prompts them.

All missionaries should mobilize a network of Prayer Partners, Ministry Partners, and Personal Intercessors. Recognize the different levels of interest as well as availability and celebrate the commitment each intercessor brings to your ministry.

It is important not to overlook the avenues available through the sending agency. Although personal contact is invaluable, we can also invest tremendous time, energy and resources in developing newsletters, Blogs, virtual prayerwalks and websites. The IMB asks each field team to submit its top-priority, strategic prayer items monthly. When a team intentionally considers its strategic needs each month, team members are more apt to remain focused on their goals and rejoice in the fruit the Lord has provided. These prayer requests and answers to prayer are posted on CompassionNet, (www.imb.org/compassionnet). Stateside prayer supporters, national believers, and worldwide intercessors can access a ninety-day history of requests submitted by each team, as well as daily view approximately thirty requests from around the world. By taking advantage of the sending agency's resources, a missionary is able to multiply prayer support, provide the most strategic requests, and maintain ministry focus.

Please do not hear me say that there is no place for newsletters, blogs, virtual prayerwalks or websites. Without question, they are critical tools in communicating the prayer needs of individual missionaries, their field teams, and people groups. But no one person can do everything, so maximize the resources available through the sending agency, and then enlist special help for the team. Recruit one or several ministry partners to serve in the unique role of **Stateside Prayer Advocate** (SPA). Although responsibilities vary by team and gifting, an SPA may receive and distribute prayer requests from the field via electronic newsletter and "snail mail," recruit additional prayer partners, organize virtual prayerwalks in local churches or coordinate prayer journeys to the field, and help with the team's publication needs. When an intercessor makes an offer like, "Let me know if you ever need anything," be ready with specific ideas.

SPAs are often former missionaries whose hearts are still on the field. Others are lay people who have a longing to serve as missionaries but life circumstances prevent the opportunity. What bonds them together is the prompting of the Lord which keeps them lifting up the lost of the world, looking toward the day when "their" people group will know the salvation afforded through Jesus Christ. Like Paul, the witness who saw the resurrected Jesus at a later time, a committed SPA will voluntarily serve with unparalleled fervency. Multiply your labors and your prayer network exponentially by locating Stateside Prayer Advocates within those who are already demonstrating a zeal for prayer and missions.

Communicating Effectively

By gathering a prayer advocacy network, missionaries take on the responsibility of communicating their strategic needs effectively. The methods will vary widely and should take into account the needs of the intercessor as well as the predilection of the field. Many intercessors simply prefer a printed prayer letter that can be slipped into their Bible for ready reference. Others get a charge out of logging on to a blog and reading the latest word from the field. Your prayer team wants to hear how God is at work, so be sure to include answers to the requests you have previously shared.

In selecting strategic needs, consider Paul's requests for prayer. In the letter to the Romans, he urged them, "through the Lord Jesus Christ, and through the love of the Spirit, that you strive together with me in prayers to God for me" (Rom. 15:30). And in the letters to the Thessalonians and the Ephesians, Paul asked the brothers to pray "that the word of the Lord may run swiftly and be glorified" (2 Thess. 3:1) and "that words may be given to *Paul* in opening *his* mouth boldly to proclaim the mystery of the gospel" (Eph. 6:19, ESV, *emphasis added*). Intercessors want to hear cultural stories—funny, exotic, poignant—but they are also ready to give themselves in ardent prayer for the sake of the gospel. Strategic prayer needs will communicate the difficulties of ministry clearly and soberly while demonstrating complete trust in the Lord's sovereign ability to answer. Strategic requests may include personal concerns but always keep the focus on the rapid spread of the gospel and a missionary's ability to proclaim with fluency and courage.

Nurturing Long-Term Commitment

By gathering a prayer advocacy network, missionaries also take on the responsibility of communicating regularly. Intercessors that are encouraged by the field through consistent communication of strategic field needs can be counted on as long-term passionate prayer advocates; but failure to keep in touch may convey a sense of disinterest from the field and cause intercessors to feel unnecessary. Monthly updates via a sending agency's website or a team's newsletter will suffice for the broad base of Prayer Partners. Ministry

Partners, however, benefit from more frequent communication. One of my favorite electronic newsletters is a simple calendar format sent daily by the team's SPA with a picture and one sentence. With the knowledge of its overall work gained through the agency's website and its less-frequent personal emails, I am prompted by these daily emails to pray for a different aspect of its ministry. If daily is not possible, a succinct weekly email will keep your ministry partners connected.

Really encourage your intercessors by inviting them to come and visit you on a short-term volunteer trip, placing an occasional phone call from the field, or even dropping a personal letter in the mail. Consider your intercessors a part of the team with differing levels of responsibility and requiring differing levels of interaction. The more intimately involved the pray-er is with the ministry, the more frequent the communication.

Conclusion

Most of us tackle a puzzle by finding all the straight edge pieces and assembling the frame, then we sort the remaining pieces by color or another distinctive characteristic. Assembling a prayer advocate network requires equal commitment to organization and capitalizing on the distinctive gifts others bring to the task. Start with prayer, asking God to help you gather a passionate prayer advocate network. Intentionally ask individuals and churches to partner with you in prayer. Communicate your team's strategic prayer needs effectively by staying focused on proclaiming the gospel. And nurture a long-term commitment from the prayer network by staying in contact regularly.

The puzzle I mentioned earlier has absolutely no priority in our office. Other than the picture not being completed, there will be no adverse consequences if it is not even touched for several days. However, the Christian who fails to make prayer an intentional, integral part of his global strategy plan may find himself "going it alone" and suffering from a fruitless ministry. Prayer cannot be optional; rather it is foundational. Allowing others to come alongside a partner in prayer helps everyone in bearing one another's burdens and in celebrating the great work God is doing around the world.

Questions for Further Thought or Discussion

1. Where does one begin in mobilizing prayer advocacy?

2. What are the three basic categories of partners and how do they relate to a field team?
3. What are the responsibilities of the missionary in gathering a prayer network? How can a pastor help?

The author: Eleanor Witcher is Associate Director of the International Prayer Strategy Office for the International Mission Board of the Southern Baptist Convention, located in Richmond, Virginia.

SUGGESTED ADDITIONAL READING

Drumwright, Minette. *The Life That Prays: Reflections on Prayer as Strategy.* Birmingham, AL: Woman's Missionary Union, 2001.

Hunt, T.W. and Catherine Walker. *Disciple's Prayer Life: Walking in Fellowship with God.* Nashville: Lifeway Press, 1997.

Sanchez, R. Daniel, Ebbie C. Smith and Curtis E. Watke. *Starting Reproducing Congregations: A Guidebook to Contextual New Church Development.* Fort Worth, TX: ChurchStarting.net, 2001.

chapter

71

PRAYING FOR THE UNREACHED PEOPLE GROUPS OF THE WORLD

Ed Cox

If one were to read through 100 sermons on international missions, one would undoubtedly discover that the three most cited Scripture passages would be:

- Isaiah's faithful response to God's call: "Also I heard the voice of the Lord, saying: 'Whom shall I send, and who will go for Us?' Then I said, 'Here am I! Send me'" (Isa. 6:8).
- The Great Commission: "Go therefore and make disciples of all the nations, baptizing them in the name of the Father and of the Son and of the Holy Spirit, teaching them to observe all things that I have

commanded you; and lo, I am with you always, even to the end of the age" (Mt. 28:19-20).

- Christ's last words before He ascended to heaven: "But you shall receive power when the Holy Spirit has come upon you; and you shall be witnesses to Me in Jerusalem, and in all Judea and Samaria, and to the end of the earth" (Acts 1:8).

Literally thousands upon thousands of missionaries have charged into the world's harvest fields with these powerful passages burning in their hearts—reminding them of their call, defining their task, and identifying their own field to harvest.

If one were to expand the list to include a fourth Scripture text, the Lord of the Harvest passage would probably come next: "But when He saw the multitudes, He was moved with compassion for them, because they were weary and scattered, like sheep having no shepherd. Then He said to His disciples, 'The harvest truly is plentiful, but the laborers are few. Therefore pray the Lord of the Harvest to send out laborers into His harvest'" (Mt. 9:36-38).

Not only do these passages challenge, inspire and educate overseas missionary personnel, but they are equally valuable for intercessors who desire to pray faithfully for missionaries and the people groups they hope to reach with the good news of Jesus Christ. This is especially true for pray-ers who intercede strategically for the world's unengaged unreached people groups (UUPGs).

Orville Boyd Jenkins of the International Mission Board (IMB) of the Southern Baptist Convention defines people group as "an ethno linguistic group with a common self-identity that is shared by the various members." He further states that "language is a primary and dominant identifying factor of a people group. Usually there is a common self-name and a sense of common identity of individuals identified with the group. A common history, customs, family and clan identities, as well as marriage rules and practices, age-grades and other obligation covenants, and inheritance patterns and rules are some of the common ethnic factors defining or distinguishing a people. What they call themselves may vary at different levels of identity, or among various sub-groups."[1]

For strategic purposes, the IMB simply defines a people group as being "the largest group through which the gospel can flow without encountering significant barriers of understanding and acceptance."[2]

The IMB considers that an unreached people group (UPG) is any people group in which less than 2 percent of the population is Evangelical Christians.[3]

The IMB's Global Research Department considers that an UPG is unengaged when a church planting strategy consistent with evangelical faith and practice is not under implementation. In this respect, an UPG continues to be unengaged when it has been merely adopted, is the object of focused prayer, or is a part of an advocacy strategy. Another criteria held by many missiologists is that UUPGs have no coordinated evangelical Christian missionary presence among them. Surprisingly enough, as of June 2007, there are still 3,393 UUPGs worldwide, 644 of which have populations greater than 100,000.[4]

I recently sat in on a partner meeting with David Garrison, IMB regional leader for South Asia (Pakistan, Bhutan, Sri Lanka, India, Bangladesh, Nepal and the Maldives), during which I discovered that over one-half (345) of the world's UUPGs of greater than 100,000 population are located within this region. Incredible as it may sound, South Asia's 345 UUPGs number more than 400 million people. More than the entire population of the United States or all of Western Europe![5]

A unified desire to take the gospel to the UUPGs of the world spawned a movement known as Finishing the Task. The partnering agency list reads like a "who's who" in global missions. Their vision is "to see every people group in the world engaged with an indigenously led church planting movement."[6]

Prayer advocacy for these UUPGs is one component of the IMB's contribution toward the fulfillment of this vision. Its International Prayer Strategy Office teams with 11 IMB regional prayer advocates to link Southern Baptist churches and groups with the UUPGs through a prayer advocacy program entitled PRAYERplus Partnership. As churches select an UUPG from a prioritized listing of these people groups, they commit to pray regularly for their people group and to be attentive and obedient to the Holy Spirit's promptings as to the plus that He would lead them to do.

In response to Christ's appeal to His disciples (Mt. 9:38), PRAYER-plusers regularly "ask the Lord of the Harvest to send out workers into His harvest field." Just as the Holy Spirit leads them to pray for their family members, for the lost around them and for their daily needs, He prompts them to be constantly asking God to send out workers to labor among their chosen UUPG. As their passion for their UUPG deepens, they find themselves, much like the neighbor in need of three loaves of bread (Lk. 11:5-13), persistently, shamelessly calling out to the Lord of the Harvest. A customary Saturday morning cup of coffee and the newspaper knocks them to their knees as they come across the name of their people group in their reading. Weeping unabashedly before the Lord, they plead with Him to thrust workers into the harvest fields. Often these prayers come in the form of asking for missionaries from the United States to be called. Increasingly, informed intercessors are learning also to ask God to call out workers from neighboring people groups or nations to answer His call to go and make disciples among their UUPG.

It comes as no surprise to learn that some who voice this prayer to the Father find themselves identifying with Isaiah and saying, "Here am I! Send me." Such was the case for a pastor from Texas. His church committed to a PRAYERplus Partnership for an UUPG. It was not long before the Lord of the Harvest called him into the harvest. He became the answer to his own prayers and is presently serving among this people group, which is experiencing a church planting movement.

Another request PRAYERplusers often lay before the Lord is for the Holy Spirit to prepare the hearts of their people group to receive God's Word, so that when workers arrive to scatter seed, it will fall on fertile soil, where the seed can germinate, sprout and bear luscious fruit (Lk. 8:15).

Each year I have the pleasure of hosting two overseas prayer journeys. Several of these have taken me among people groups who have had little or no access to the gospel. On trips of this nature, I often encounter someone along my route who has never met a Christian, read God's Word or heard of Jesus Christ, but who is very open to the message of God's gift of abundant and eternal life through faith in Jesus Christ. I can readily sense that the Holy Spirit has accomplished the proper soil preparation in them to receive the seed. Without this necessary preparation, the seed falls among the rocks and thorns and rarely, if ever, matures. This truth has come home to me quite clearly during the past couple of years as I find myself digging up faltering perennials that my landscaper hurriedly planted without taking the time and effort to prepare the soil to receive the scores of plants. A little extra time and effort on the front end would have saved me hours and hours of replanting. The same is true in seed sowing. The time and effort expended by intercessors on their knees before the Lord reaps long-term benefits.

Following truths set forth in 2 Corinthians 10:3-5, these intercessors boldly enter into spiritual battle, praying down Satan's strongholds over their UUPG. "For though we walk in the flesh, we do not war according to the flesh. For the weapons of our warfare are not carnal but mighty in God for pulling down strongholds, casting down arguments and every high thing that exalts itself against the knowledge of God, bringing every thought into captivity to the obedience of Christ."

In most cases, Satan has held dominion over these UUPGs through the ages, applying his stranglehold through false religions, governmental structures, cultural traditions and educational systems, to name only a few. Intercessors are encouraged to research every aspect of their people group to unearth the face of Satan's lies in order to pray each one down. PRAYER-plusers are keenly aware of the death grip the Devil has on their people group and earnestly call on God to liberate them from Satan's wiles. "For we do not wrestle against flesh and blood, but against principalities, against powers, against the rules of the darkness of this age, against spiritual hosts of wickedness in the heavenly places" (Eph. 6:12).

Quite naturally, as these intercessors learn more about their people group and labor in prayer on their behalf, the Holy Spirit deepens their love and concern for them. Touching them through newspaper and web-based articles no longer meets their need to know and understand them. They develop a desire to walk among them, to get to know them personally, and to reach out and touch them. These pray-ers want to smell the smells, hear the sounds, and see the land of the people they have come to love. This deepening hunger to experience them in their true environments propels the PRAYERplusers into the plus of their relationship with their UUPG.

No longer content to pray from afar, they organize prayer journeys to their people group's homeland. As they prayerwalk places of government, education, religion, commerce and community, the Holy Spirit gives them keener insights into the satanic strongholds and the needs of the people. Their prayers take on a whole new level of frequency and fervency. Their ministry of prayer to their people group becomes very, very personal. The people in the oft-handled photos now have individual personalities, personal stories and apparent needs. As Christ stood and wept over Jerusalem, these intercessors pray and weep over the people whom they ardently desire to trust in Jesus. They are forever changed. Their prayers will never be the same. They have become God's touch of love to their people. Far from God granting them just a *fleeting* touch, His Spirit keeps that physical and emotional sensation alive deep in their hearts, prompting them to rise early in the morning to pray for the people whom they love so dearly, the people whom God yearns to accept His Son.

Obviously, prayer journeys are only one form that the plus takes as the PRAYERplusers follow the Holy Spirit's leading into involvement with their people group. It is not uncommon for them to organize other types of ministries among their people group—for example, Scripture distribution, humanitarian relief projects, and *JESUS* film distribution/showings.

A statement that David Garrison made during the previously mentioned partner meeting continues to occupy my thoughts. In reference to Acts 1:8, he commented, "For Jesus, *Jerusalem, Judea and Samaria* represented areas where He had traveled and ministered; whereas, *the end of the earth* covered everything else" (*emphasis added*). David further explained, "Jerusalem, Judea and Samaria currently represent areas where the gospel has been preached, the Word of God is available and laborers are currently in the harvest field; whereas, the end of the earth refers to the UUPGs of the world." Pray to the end of the earth! Pray for the unengaged unreached peoples of the world!

Questions for Further Thought or Discussion

1. Identify five or six prayer points that are inspired by Isaiah 6:8, Matthew 28:19-20, Acts 1:8 and Matthew 9:36-38.
2. What distinguishes an unengaged unreached people group from an unreached people group?
3. Do you agree with David Garrison's statement "Jerusalem, Judea and Samaria currently represent areas where the gospel has been preached, the Word of God is available and laborers are currently in the harvest field; whereas, the end of the earth refers to the UUPGs of the world?" If you do, why? If you do not, why not?

The author: Rev. Ed Cox is Director of International Prayer Strategy for the International Mission Board of the Southern Baptist Convention, Richmond, Virginia.

SUGGESTED ADDITIONAL READING

Drumwright, Minette. *The Life That Prays.* Birmingham, AL: Woman's Missionary Union, 2001.

Johnstone, Patrick, and Jason Mandryk. *Operation World: When We Pray God Works.* Carislile, UK: Paternoster, 2005.

Rankin, Jerry. *To the Ends of the Earth: Churches Fulfilling the Great Commission,* Richmond, VA: International Mission Board, SBC, 2005.

ENDNOTES

1. Orville Boyd Jenkins. "What Is a People Group" http://www.imb.org/globalresearch/peoplegroups.asp.
2. www.peoplegroups.org.
3. www.peoplegroups.org.
4. www.peoplegroups.org.
5. www.peoplegroups.org.
6. www.finishingthetask.com.

chapter

72

EQUIPPING THE CHURCH FOR GLOBAL PRAYING

John Quam

As we look at prayer throughout the scriptures, we see many patterns. From calls for help to the Lord of the angel armies to requests for blessing and prosperity, we see God's people encouraged to come to Him at all times and in all circumstances. One of the most important commands issued by Jesus is His call to pray "the Lord of the Harvest to send out laborers into His harvest" (Lk. 10:2). This command by Jesus both reveals God's heart for those who are lost but also the important role of prayer in the mission to seek and save them. If this is of such great importance to Jesus, how can it be of any lesser importance to the local church? In other words, passionate, prayer for the lost, whether across the street or around the world, is not an option for the church. It is God's revealed will.

Getting Started

Once a church has discovered the biblical imperatives for global-sized praying, there are simple steps a church can take in developing a comprehensive prayer strategy. Your church may be well down the road in prayer for world missions or you may have only one or two strategies in place. Following are some building blocks to grow and expand your congregation's commitment to global praying.

Identify leadership. Like any other initiative in a church, good leadership is important to the success of growing a prayer base for missions. Assuming a missions committee already exists, who on that committee most exemplifies the person needed to lead this prayer effort? That person should then recruit a sub-committee or task force (all members do not need to be a part of the missions committee). As a group they should review this information and any other useful material on prayer and missions. If they are in agreement that this is God's assignment for them, they should proceed to the next steps. If there is no missions committee in the church, a pastor or elder can form such a group. In this case, one of the highest prayer priorities would be for the identification of an ongoing missions leadership structure.

Prioritize the strategies you want to implement. As the missions prayer leadership group examines the different prayer strategies, and spends time in prayer together, what seems to leap out as a first or second priority for your church? Do you want to begin with prayer in the worship service or emphasize prayer for missions in your church's small group ministry? Obviously, a church can't do everything at once. Picking some key places to begin and gaining some success in those areas can be very motivating to do more. Perhaps a strategy can be mapped out for the next two or three years so that prayer on ten different levels is being developed.

Communicate and enlist. It is wonderful to have a comprehensive prayer strategy for world missions, but who will actually do the praying? Engage as many as possible in this important effort. Spend time with those who give leadership to other parts of the church's ministry to secure their interest and cooperation. Sunday school leaders need to see how this can be integrated into their overall objectives. Youth leaders need to have up-to-date information to keep the young people engaged, and they need to have answers to prayer that they can share. Most importantly, the pastor should be aware of all that is being developed and should have help in crafting the Missions Moment each Sunday. Personal appointments are needed to help these church leaders see your passion and commitment to prayer for world missions. Ask leadership to try something for six months or a year to see how it works. Once it proves significant, an ongoing commitment and involvement can be secured.

Communicate answers and encourage. Perhaps the area where we are most likely to fail is in communicating how our prayers are making a difference. Of course, we cannot always see the direct impact of our prayers. But we must be faithful to communicate concrete answers when they come. We also need to seek feedback from those we are praying for when that is appropriate. Did the new church get started, did the sick person get well, did the neighbor family come to Christ? We may have to do some research to see if the unreached people group we are praying for has had initial contacts for the gospel. What have been the results? Churches should also chronicle the results of their prayers for missions over a longer period of time. This provides continuity and tells our people both that we prayed and that God answered. In addition to answers to prayer, it is good to encourage those who are serving this prayer effort by acknowledging their work and from time to time. Reward them with a significant book or a registration to a missions or prayer conference that might interest them. While some people will serve for years without being noticed, most people would like to hear a few "well-dones" before they get to heaven. Our little encouragements along the way are much appreciated.

Keep expanding the vision. As was mentioned earlier, no church can begin every kind of prayer initiative at once. Beginning with a few key strategies will help pave the way for other types of prayer. The process for reevaluating the priorities and deciding what's next is an ongoing one. Mapping out a long-term vision is always helpful as long as we hold it lightly and allow God to take us in a different direction if He should so choose.

Linking Arms with Other Kingdom-Minded Churches

Following are some further suggestions for enhancing the missions outreach of the church through prayers for greater cooperation and collaboration.[1]

Partnering increases the power. While doing it on our own is a high value for many, in the Church it is very seldom the best way. God has designed us to work in cooperation for His purposes, not just in one local congregation but all across the Body of Christ. Sometimes that cooperation is expressed in denominational partnership. But God also calls us to a geographic partnership in the city or community where our church exists or in the region/city of the world our church has missionaries or ministries. Paul and Peter often wrote their letters to the churches in a city or region and instructed them to be read in all the different places where the church met. Paul mentions the partnership in the gospel as one church helping another in resources and prayer, asking for doors to be opened, and blessing to result from his preaching. The Global Day of Prayer, held on Pentecost Sunday each year, is an example of a community-based opportunity to pray with other churches for God's global mission.

Discover the common interests of other congregations. While it may not be all that common, it is certainly biblical that one church pray for the missions outreach of another and find out how their strengths might come together to better serve God's kingdom purposes. Do you know the strong missions churches in your city or area? What do they have to offer that you might benefit from in your church? What do you have to offer them? Why not pray for an open door to partner?

Cooperate in training and mentoring. When it comes to world evangelization there is always more to be learned. Often God is revealing a new approach or strategy to someone down the street in another church, across the city, or across the nation or world. It is important to ask God for opportunities to learn and grow. Ask God to direct you to training programs and conferences that will benefit your church. Ask God for the proper equipping opportunities for those your church might be sending out. Ask God to show you what your church has developed that might be of help to another congregation.

Create consortiums and partnerships in financing missions. Sometimes the answer to your prayers for resources is the more effective use of the resources God is giving you. Two churches sending two different people out to do the same task in the same region may not be the best use of resources. Talking together and cooperating can create more effective ways of doing God's work. Some cities have formed consortiums so that when the committee so decides, immediate funding for a missionary or project can be available. Praying for effective ways to partner might be one of the most important tasks of the missions leadership in the church.

Pray in concert over key mission issues. It is helpful if someone in your church subscribes to a key missions oriented on-line news service.[2] They bring regular reports on kingdom issues from around the world and help expand the vision and excitement for prayer among the people of the church. Of course you can't cover all issues but you can pick out the ones most relevant to your own missions program or whichever ones the Holy Spirit lifts out for your attention.

Rejoice together. Some cities have found it very encouraging to have a united, citywide, missions conference where prayer, equipping, and rejoicing can encourage and expand the vision for world evangelization. Today the gospel is making extraordinary advances in very difficult places. A citywide conference can highlight these victories and be of great encouragement. Singers and musicians with a heart for missions can also lift the spirits of the people. Videos and special technical presentations are possible when many churches are working together. Most of all it is God's heart that we work together as one. When we pray together in such a context, we emulate the church in the upper room during that memorable Pentecost when God came in power and many were converted.

Conclusion

As churches create a powerful prayer ministry for world missions, they also create a ministry model that affects the way their missionaries go about their work. "The medium is the message" was a key phrase and the name of a best-selling book a few decades back. Author Marshall McLuhan was convinced that the context and medium of a message influenced its impact as much as the actual words. When prayer is the foundation and framework for our world missions activities, the power of that "medium" will both model the approach and increase the effectiveness of all that is done.

Questions for Further Thought or Discussion

1. Using this statement: "Passionate prayer for the lost, whether across the street or around the world, is not an option for the church, it is God's

revealed will," construct a simple teaching/preaching outline you could use to cast vision for global praying.

2. Identify and explain three or four components of a congregational or prayer group strategy for casting vision and increasing focus on global praying.
3. List an activity or two for each of these focal points of global prayer: Relational, Theological, Geographical, Political, Economical (others?)

The author: John Quam is the National Facilitator for Global Ministries for the Mission America Coalition. He lives in Buffalo, Minnesota.

SUGGESTED ADDITIONAL READING

Johnstone, Patrick, and Jason Mandryk. *Operation World: When We Pray God Works.* Carislile, UK: Paternoster, 2005.

Winter, Ralph, and Steve Hawthorne. *Perspectives on the World Christian Movement, A Reader.* Pasadena, CA: William Carey Library, 1999.

Global Prayer Digest. US Center for World Mission (www.global-prayer-digest.org.)

ENDNOTES

1. For additional help go to www.missionamerica.org and click on the Global Ministries tab.

2. Missions oriented on-line news service include Brigada or Assist News Service.

chapter

73

KINGDOM PRAYING

Minette Drumwright Pratt

What does kingdom praying entail? Kingdom praying includes that dimension of intercession that reaches beyond our immediate surroundings. Praying about personal, local matters often happens more naturally and more consistently for most of us. My problems, my work, my family, my needs, and the concerns of those close to me—these tend to come more spontaneously to my heart and mind. Of course, personal, local praying is valid. In fact, it is essential. God longs for us to bring our personal burdens to Him. Yet kingdom praying is a level of praying that reaches beyond us.

Kingdom praying, then, seeks to discern what God wants to happen in His kingdom, and prays for that to take place. In kingdom praying, we seek to attune our hearts to His heart's desire and pray for its fulfillment.

What is God's heart's desire? He expresses it throughout the Scripture: "that Your way may be known on earth, Your salvation among all nations" (Ps. 67:2). God wants all people saved! Peter expressed it very plainly that our Lord is "not wanting anyone to perish, but everyone to come to repentance"

(2 Pet. 3:9, NIV). Our Lord's heart's desire is for all people to love and worship Him and become a part of His kingdom. Thus, His desire, according to His Word, must become the mission of every follower of Christ, the mission of every church.

The staggering fact before us is that at least two-thirds of the world's population do not know and love God's Son. What can God's people do? Throw up our hands? As a matter of fact, yes, like Moses did—in intercession.

Hear again the psalmist quoting our Lord: "Ask of me, and I will make the nations your inheritance" (Ps. 2:8, NIV). In one of the most astounding statements in the Bible, God makes a connection between our asking and the nations being saved. He declares a direct link between the prayers of His people and the accomplishment of His heart's desire. He reveals that kingdom praying is a priority strategy in making Christ known and loved.

Consider these principles of kingdom praying.

There really is power in our praying. God has chosen to accomplish His purposes in this world in response to the prayers of His people. Does this mean He is powerless without our praying? Not at all. God can do anything He wants at any time in any way He chooses—with or without our prayers. Yet He has made a holy decision to release His power in response to the prayers of His people. Thus, He gives us this awesome role of dynamic partnership with Him. His power does the work that makes the difference, saves, and transforms. But our prayers release His power.

The reach of prayer is total. Prayer can reach into every life and every home in your neighborhood, into every town, city, state, and nation—even into all 237 nations of the world. In response to our intercession, God can turn the hearts of people toward the gospel. Through our partnership with Him in prayer, He will encourage believers we have never seen. Our prayers can reach into places we have never been and never will go and impact them for Christ. God *is* able!

Every believer can have impact for Christ through prayer. Through kingdom praying, every Christian of every age, every race, and every circumstance can have great effect for Christ where we live and around the world. Everyone cannot go to another country to personally introduce people to Jesus. Some can and do, but everyone cannot. Everyone cannot financially have impact for Christ. Some have that ability, but not all. Yet every believer can *pray* and make a difference for Jesus near at hand and around the world. Imagine the extraordinary release of God's power that would take place if all believers of all ages were mobilized in united prayer!

Kingdom praying takes us into the realm of spiritual warfare. "Our struggle is not against flesh and blood, but against the rulers, against the authorities, against the powers of this dark world and against the spiritual forces of evil in the heavenly realms" (Eph. 6:12, NIV).

Surely, no one would argue with Paul about the existence of spiritual forces of evil in the world. Daily we encounter and observe some degree of the unseen, sinister, divisive, deceptive, destructive forces that demonstrate the power of Satan's presence. The "powers of this dark world" constantly clash with the love, power, and will of God. There is no doubt but that Satan seeks the destruction of the people of God and the work of God. There really is a war.

While Satan intends destruction, God intends the spiritual *con*struction of His people. Our loving Lord envisions and desires joyful worship of Himself and transformation of the worshippers. Satan, at the same time, envisions leading each and all who will follow him into disobedience and rejection of God.

Kingdom praying calls forth laborers to go into the fields. Jesus Himself instructed us: "Ask the Lord of the harvest, therefore, to send out workers into this harvest field" (Mt. 9:38, NIV). We desperately need laborers where we live and to the ends of the earth to witness, teach, and live out Christ's love and redemption obediently and faithfully. Surely God is calling more laborers than are hearing and responding. Through employing prayer as strategic kingdom praying, we can do our part in praying forth those whom God is calling.

Kingdom praying is the most crucial work we can do. Kingdom praying is work! It demands our time, our energy, our intentional attention, our focus, our self-discipline. We must recommit ourselves to it every day. Prayer is work, but prayer *works*. More accurately, God works in response to the work of prayer, in response to the prayers of His people.

God's Word, as well as history and our own experiences, teach us that the most powerful work we can do is to be obedient and faithful in the work of prayer.

Employing kingdom prayer as strategy involves all that concerns the heart of our Lord. We can be sure these include:

1. **The lost**—beginning with lost family members in our own homes, moving to those in our neighborhood, and reaching out in concentric circles around the world. Every day we encounter personally those who do not know and love our Lord. Does it enter your mind and heart to pray for them to come to Him?
2. **Missionaries**—those serving in our own country and those assigned around the world. The main purpose of kingdom praying for missionaries is to release God's power and divine energy in their lives, families, and ministries as they seek to bring others into the kingdom. Missionaries desperately need and desire our united, specific praying.
3. **Believers** around the world. While we have traditionally emphasized prayer for missionaries, we have more recently emphasized our responsibility to pray for the growth, development, courage, and boldness of fellow believers in other nations. World evangelization will not take place unless and until local Christ followers take responsibility for evangelizing their own people group and/or nation and discover their role in sharing the gospel even beyond their own borders.
4. **Leaders** of our nation and **officials** around the world. The Scriptures clearly mandate intercession for our own leaders and for government officials in other lands, for officials' decisions can either impede or enhance the spread of the gospel. We must pray increasingly for the leaders of the world, asking God to use for good even those influences that are intended for evil. We can pray strategically when we pray for leaders to do that which will enhance the gospel, knowingly or unknowingly.
5. **More laborers,** here and around the world. Jesus specifically directed prayer for laborers as part of a disciple's responsibility. Pray that those whom God is calling will not only hear but also respond.
6. **Mission strategists.** Missions leaders request prayer for God to give them vision and wisdom as they make crucial decisions impacting many lives and lands. Pray they will discern and know God's heart and plans for reaching the lost. Intercede for leaders of all evangelical missions agencies and prayer movements.
7. **Worldwide revival and spiritual awakening.** A sweeping, incredible movement of prayer has preceded every spiritual awakening

throughout history. One of our greatest prayer burdens is to *pray* that people will pray.

8. **Bible translators.** Another key strategy in fulfilling God's heart's desire is producing the Scriptures in the heart language of the people. Bible translation agencies are working together with a goal of publishing portions of the Bible in every language spoken by more than 250,000 people. With Scriptures another essential strategy in discipling believers and planting churches, pray earnestly for this essential missions ministry.
9. **Christian radio and television broadcasts.** The goal of Christian broadcast agencies is to give opportunity to every person on earth to hear the gospel in a language they can understand. Pray for the agencies pursuing this goal, and ask God to supply the translators they need. Pray for those who even now are hearing the gospel by radio and television.
10. **Persecuted Christ followers.** Believers living in various parts of the world today suffer persecution, even to the power of death, because of their faith. Family and former friends often ostracize them. Pray for Christian sisters and brothers around the world who daily face not just the threat but the reality of persecution.

When we pray, we link hands with Jesus and the Holy Spirit, a powerful threefold linkage. The role of the Holy Spirit is well known: "We do not know what we ought to pray for, but the Spirit himself intercedes for us" (Rom. 8:26, NIV). We are to pray and have confidence that the Holy Spirit will interpret our heart's cry. "Pray in the Spirit on all occasions with all kinds of prayers and requests" (Eph. 6:18, NIV)—meaning pray in the presence and power of the Holy Spirit.

Missionary Ed Pinkston, representing a lifetime of missionary work in West Africa wrote: "When we get to heaven and are able to read God's history book, I believe we will see that the people really responsible for many of the miracles are the unseen, unsung believers who lift to the Father their intercessions on behalf of His people and His work."

Prayer is the ultimate strategy for releasing God's power into our lives, our families, our churches, our world. Prayer is God's strategy for the kingdom.

(The material in this chapter was adapted from the author's previous work, *The Life That Prays,* published by Woman's Missionary Union, Birmingham, AL, 2001 and is used by permission.)

Questions for Further Thought or Discussion

1. How can kingdom prayer become a possible strategy in your life?
2. Why do you think God has chosen to make us His partners in the accomplishment of His purposes in the world?
3. What makes prayer so powerful and crucial?

The author: Minette Drumwright Pratt is the retired Director of the International Prayer Strategy Office, International Mission Board, Southern Baptist Convention, Richmond, VA. She is the author of several books including, *The Life That Prays* and *When My Faith Feels Shallow.* She and her husband Dr. William Pratt reside in Fort Worth, TX.

SUGGESTED ADDITIONAL READING

Foster, Richard J. *Prayer: Finding the Heart's True Home.* San Francisco: Harper, 1992.

Long, Brad and McMurry, Doug. *Prayer That Shapes the Future.* Grand Rapids: Zondervan, 1999.

Jeremiah, David. *The Prayer Matrix: Plugging into the Unseen Reality.* Sisters, OR: Multnomah Publishers, 2002.

chapter

74

PRAYING FOR THOSE IN GLOBAL AUTHORITY

John Lind

In his first epistle to Timothy, couched with all manner of instruction to the Church at Ephesus, the Apostle Paul gives directions to his young protégé on how to lead.

Persuasive Paul offers counsel on women, worship, leaders and much more in this pastoral epistle. But he saves his strongest words for the first few verses of chapter two where he "exhorts" Timothy to stimulate prayer in the Church.

Prayer is to be offered first, for "all men," and then, for "kings and all who are in authority" (1 Tim. 2:1-2). Since our leaders are singled out for prayer, we must heed with intentional intercession for those who carry the responsibilities of our governments on their shoulders and in their hearts, in times of peace and in times of trouble alike.

The terror attacks of September 11, 2001 have painfully engraved themselves on our national memory. Though our recollections fade, who could forget the overwhelming horror, the mass shock and the instant national unity that swept across America—even the world? Churches filled to overflowing with repentant citizens wanting to right their hearts toward God and help their country. They prayed. Everyone prayed. Concerns over separation of church and state dissolved as America returned to her origins of prayer. A worldwide prayer movement known as The Presidential Prayer Team (PPT) began, pointing out the need to pray for our leaders. PPT met a tremendous need by providing weekly prayer requests for the President, his cabinet, the country and our armed forces.

This movement was surprisingly unique. National prayer efforts have been instigated from America's earliest days, ranging from presidential decrees for days of fasting and prayer (George Washington, Abraham Lincoln and others) to presidents actually leading the nation in prayer (Franklin Roosevelt, Dwight Eisenhower and George H.W. Bush, to name three). Non-governmental organizations like the National Day of Prayer and the National Prayer Breakfast have involved millions of people over the years, yet there had never been an effort dedicated specifically to praying for the person occupying the Oval Office.

Whether one intercedes individually or participates in a united group effort like PPT, it is clear that, from the Apostle Paul's perspective, prayer for our leaders is a requirement, not an option, for those leading the Church, and by implication, for all believers. The Presidential Prayer Team is based on this premise.

Comprehensive Prayers

Paul is comprehensive in his urging, calling for prayers of *every* kind for *all* persons.

With such a broad command, not that different from "pray continually," how do we break it down? How, and further, *why* should we pray for those who lead? What did this command mean to Timothy and the believers at Ephesus? What does it mean to spiritual leaders today? Is this just "one more thing" that a busy pastor must do, or is there genuine value in motivating those we lead to pray for those who lead us? Can a Christian be a good citizen without praying for leaders?

Paul's Prayer Principles

Paul writes, "I exhort first of all that supplications, prayers, intercessions, and giving of thanks be made for all men, for kings and all who are in authority, that we may lead a quiet and peaceable life in all godliness and reverence. For this is good and acceptable in the sight of God our Savior, who desires all men to be saved and to come to the knowledge of the truth" (1 Tim. 2:1-4).

Note that Paul says we should **pray first!** Our tendency is to turn in many directions—to cable news, the Internet, newspapers or to "phone a friend." Paul calls for a re-ordering of our inclinations when he exhorts us to **pray first,** in crisis or in calm.

Paul's comprehensive instructions include **supplications, prayers, intercessions** and **thanksgiving**. Not much is left out (Other than imprecation—which some may feel necessary when talking to God about government, but Paul doesn't go there!). Eugene Peterson's *Message* simply paraphrases the passage as, "Pray every way you know how."

Supplications, Intercessions and Prayers. These are prayers for issues and needs in the lives of our leaders, including their health, safety, family, spiritual sensitivities, etc. These prayers also lift up the leader in light of specific challenges or situations like national crises, critical decisions or involvement in summits or other encounters, asking God's intervention and help in ways that only He can.

Prayers. There is an ongoing nature to Paul's "prayers." They are less event-oriented, and more personhood-focused. We hold our leaders in our hearts continuously, bringing their regular concerns (wisdom, protection, good health, clarity, etc.) before the Lord at all times. These prayers are most effective as a daily discipline; some use a prayer reminder to trigger consistency.

Intercession. One who intercedes is a go-between, standing in a gap, bridging the span of lack between a holy God and a human servant just as Jesus prays for us (Heb. 7:25). Prayers of intercession take the concerns of the one being prayed for to heart as if they were one's own. When we intercede, we call to God for mercy, grace and help as our leaders daily do their jobs. We pray for moral courage, divine wisdom and a sense of God's presence as they go about their work.

Thanksgiving. Gratitude is a great provider of perspective. It helps us see the ways God has worked and moved, even through leaders we may question or with whom we disagree. Thanksgiving enables us to express gratitude for the ways and means civil servants have been a conduit for God to achieve His purposes. Paul acknowledges in Romans 13:1 that authorities are placed by God's design and choosing, making Him the one who should receive our thanks for them. So, whether we agree with their policies and decisions or not, one thing is clear—we are to thank God for the leaders He has placed over us.

This brings a beautiful economy in prayer: we ask, request, intercede *and* offer thanks to Almighty God from whom all good things come. This is a natural response to receiving good from God's hand, yet it is easily forgotten in the rush of requests. We are to give thanks for answered prayers and for our leaders.

Pray this way for *whom*?

An examination of those spotlighted for prayer by members of the early church sheds helpful light on our prayers today.

Honor the Emperor. Paul echoes the Apostle Peter when he calls for prayers for all those in authority: "Fear God. Honor the king" (1 Pet. 2:17). Regardless of what rulers and leaders were doing to members of the early Church—persecuting them, seeking to obliterate their new religion or torturing them publicly—it never stopped praying for them. This is particularly moving in light of the fact that Nero—known for his creative means of torturing Christians for amusement and sport—was most likely reigning as Emperor of Rome at the time Paul wrote to Timothy.

So Paul's instructions can't possibly mean that Timothy is to spur the Church to prayer only for those leaders with whom he agrees, or those leaders who create conditions that are friendly to the Church. The prayers of the Church are to be offered for authorities whom God has put in place. This is a high act of selfless love; praying for the good of one who may not respond in kind is in accord with the essence of the gospel. In their humility, poverty and powerlessness, our early brothers and sisters may have been more proficient at this kind of prayer than we are.

We are to pray for our leaders at every level, from the highest centers of government on down, whether they are Red, Blue or Green, Conservative, Tory, Whig or Other. Paul offers no out for those who don't agree with their elected officials—apparently these prayers are much more about serving the greater good than bowing to prevailing cultural or societal grievances.

Peaceful and Quiet Lives. There is an outworking to Paul's directive to pray for our leaders: "That we may live quiet and peaceable and lives." These prayers will work to bring the tranquility and calm that will enable further spiritual growth and depth. There is an implication of both societal and governmental peace, unscathed by rebellion or uprising.

This result would be pleasing enough, but Paul goes on to describe the qualities manifested in those for whom we pray as well as in our own lives.

Godliness and Holiness. In referring to godliness and holiness, Paul is using terms that are difficult for us to grasp, for they describe qualities that few of us have experienced. "Godliness" describes a person who is so utterly balanced that he honors both God and others with temperance and self-control, creating an aura of approachable piety that is pleasing to all. He rises to serve and honor God in spite of trials, difficulties or distractions, never losing sight of this duty, and remaining true to self.

"Reverence" implies dignity in the very act of living, whether worshipping, working or interacting with others. Paul uses this word several times in his pastoral epistles, describing a quality he longs to see in those who lead—deacons, overseers, their wives and older men. Here, however, he says it is an outworking of prayer.

Powerful Results

These are desirable results, regardless of one's political leanings, denominational stripe or economic standing. Though not formulaic, Paul's assurance of "quiet and peaceable lives" rings with a goodness that is pleasing to us as well as to God. Time spent in prayer is surely time well spent, but further, it has the power to change society.

Prayer for our leaders lead to higher ends than griping, lobbying or complaining. For government is "God's minister to you for good" (Rom. 13:3). This also implies that our prayers will impact our world with great significance. Our prayers and our actions are the first and most important means of bringing peace to our communities and our nation; indeed to the world.

Patriotism and Prayer?

So if it is true, as former Senate Chaplain Lloyd Ogilvie often said, "The greatest act of patriotism (and I would add, citizenship) is prayer," we should be compelled to make prayer for our leaders one of the highest priorities of personal and congregational life. It is the one thing we can do, regardless of condition of our country, the popularity of our leaders or the moral state of citizens.

That's part of the beauty of an effort like The Presidential Prayer Team; by praying for people, not for issues, we lay a foundation of prayer across our country and with it a readiness for revival to break out as a ripple effect. For indeed revival needs, as its prerequisite, passionate prayer.

As I've traveled the country and spoken with those involved in PPT, I've seen the difference prayer makes, both in the lives of the leaders for whom we've prayed and in the lives of those who have interceded.

When people are in crisis, whether it's a national disaster or a family member's illness, accident or even relational pain, we've seen them instantly and utterly embrace the efficacy of prayer. Newscasters, press agents, attorneys, or anyone in the public eye, when faced with death or tragedy, don't ask for cookies or a basket of soaps. They ask for prayer! Prayer makes us all stronger in all situations and prepares us for the next challenge.

Though at times our national sensitivity may seem squeamish about prayer, as evidenced by the many efforts to eliminate prayer from the public discourse, we remain "One Nation Under God" with room and freedom for all. The Church will do well to heed the Apostle Paul's counsel to "Pray this way!"

Questions for Further Thought or Discussion

1. The Apostle Paul urges prayer in many situations. Why do you suppose he insists that his young protégé Timothy put such an emphasis on prayer for the Church at Ephesus—especially prayer for rulers and leaders?
2. Do you agree with the analysis that prayer for today's leaders is vital, even when we disagree with their decisions? Why or why not? Would there ever be a time when it was not appropriate to pray for our leaders, according to Paul? According to you? If yes, explain.
3. What would "peaceful and quiet lives" look like in today's world?

The author: John Lind worked for seventeen years with Youth for Christ on the local and national levels and also served with Promise Keepers and ChildHelp USA before becoming President/CEO of *The Presidential Prayer Team* in 2002. He lives in Scottsdale, Arizona.

SUGGESTED ADDITIONAL READING

Hallesby, Ole. *Prayer.* Minneapolis: Augsburg, 1994.

Moore, James P. *One Nation Under God: The History of Prayer in America.* New York: Doubleday, 2005.

Omartian, Stormie. *The Power of a Praying Nation.* Eugene, OR: Harvest House, 2002.

Sheets, Dutch. *Intercessory Prayer.* Ventura, CA: Regal Books, 1996.

chapter

75

PRAYER FOR THE HARVEST

Paula Hemphill

Several women stepped off the bus onto the dusty road leading to the village. Ripe summer wheat fields stretched out on both sides of the path. A family was cutting wheat and stacking the stalks. The field was huge and there were only a few laboring to harvest the crop. Spontaneously the women who had come to prayerwalk through the village sensed an open door. They moved out into the field and offered to help the small family harvest their wheat. After several hours of hot work and many scrapes and scratches from the brittle wheat stalks, the women were invited to lunch in the family's modest home. As the mother prepared the meal, she told of her husband's death several months before. "We did not know how we would harvest our wheat without my husband," she stated. The door was now open for the team to share God's word and His plan for them to be there to help. "God sent you to us today!" the mother exclaimed.

As I debriefed the team later that evening, I thought of Jesus' words to His disciples in Matthew 9:37, "The harvest truly is plentiful, but the laborers are few." Our small group had been divided into teams that day and visited three villages. To our knowledge only one of the villages had ever been visited by Christian workers. Jesus tells us the harvest is enormous. But there is a problem. There are not enough workers to labor in the fields. Jesus identified prayer as God's strategy to thrust laborers into His harvest. What motivated Jesus to teach His disciples to pray for the harvest? What is our challenge to pray for the harvest? What keeps God's children from obeying this call to prayer? This chapter will address these important questions and seek to mobilize intentional prayer for the harvest.

The Motivation to Pray for the Harvest

The first motivation for Jesus' call to prayer for the harvest is the great need of the lost sheep before Him. Jesus *saw* people, multitudes of people (Mt. 9:35). Chapters 5-9 of Matthew are filled with ceaseless activity as Jesus ministered through preaching good news of the kingdom, teaching, and healing. A grieving father (9:18), a woman with chronic bleeding (9:20), the blind and mute men seeking sight and deliverance (9:27-33)—Jesus touched them all. Jesus saw more than their physical needs; He saw their spiritual condition. Seeing with spiritual eyes evokes action.

Jesus' busy ministry was motivated by *compassion*, a gut reaction to the needs before Him (14:14). Earlier in Matthew 9:13 Jesus quoted the prophet Hosea and commanded His disciples, "But go and learn what this means: 'I desire mercy and not sacrifice.' For I did not come to call the righteous, but sinners." Feeling with deep "mercy" or compassion flows from a realistic understanding of the condition of lost sinners. The dictionary defines compassion as "sympathy for the suffering of others, often including a desire to help" (*Encarta* online).

The needs of the lost are expressed with the Old Testament metaphor of sheep without a shepherd (9:36). My husband Ken describes these sheep as "bear bait." Helpless and hopeless sheep are defenseless against predators ready to devour them. Jesus describes the multitudes as weary, dispirited, and harassed. Do you see the lost around you and feel compassion for them at the very center of your being? Do these realities move you to pray and act?

In 1970 I read *Too Hard for God* by C. R. Marsh. He and his wife Pearl served as missionaries in North Africa beginning in 1929. Through his writings I "saw" Muslim women and their spiritual needs for the first time. Early missionary pioneers among Muslims like Lilias Trotter, Samuel Zwemer and the Marshes understood the power of prayer for the harvest. Their writings have fueled my passion to pray and to mobilize intercessors.

One of the tools I have found effective is to introduce women to "Fatima." Wearing indigenous dress, I share a monologue from among the stories of several women I have met who are named "Fatima." Fatima may be the illiterate widow in Afghanistan who is one of the first followers of Isa al Masih among her people group. She is the refugee who attended our ESL class in Fort Worth, Texas. Fatima from North African is tri-lingual and studies mathematics at a university in Europe. After learning about these women's lives, we share a prayer tea and focus intercession on the specific needs of Muslim women and their families. Information and tea resources are available at http://btw.imb.org.

Mission agencies use stories and statistics to help modern day disciples "see and "feel compassion" for the lost. In print and on the web there are adequate resources available for those who seek to pray wisely. The motivation to pray for the harvest has not changed—seeing the spiritual condition of the lost evokes compassion and mobilizes intercessors.

The Promise of the Harvest

God promises a bountiful harvest to those who sow with tears. Indeed their reaping will be with shouts of joy (Ps. 126:5-6). The agricultural picture of a ripe crop ready for harvest is far removed from the day to day experience of most urban Christians. To have a harvest there must be plowing, seed sowing and cultivation. Each worker who prepares the soil, plants seed, cultivates or harvests contributes by fulfilling his task. No task is insignificant (1 Cor. 3:6-9).

Faith is required to see the harvest before the first blade sprouts from the soil. In the parable of the sower, Jesus likens the good seed to the word of God sown into hearts (Mt. 13:19; Lk. 8:11). There are real obstacles to the healthy maturity of a sprouting seed. An adequate water supply is critical for an abundant harvest.

> Prayer is God's ordained means to prepare God's highway through spiritually dry and arid places, and prayer is God's ordained way to bring the refreshing water of God's Spirit to barren lives. The more you pray, the more the water of the Spirit flows. The more you pray the more the seed sown is watered. The prayer you pray has the potential to turn any heart or desert into a garden of the Lord.[1]

Workers must trust the Lord of the harvest to protect the seed as it matures. As Jesus prepared His disciples for their commission to the mission and ministry, He understood the challenge before them (Jn. 4:35; Matthew 10). The promise of a harvest would sustain the workers during times of persecution and difficulty.

Several years ago my husband and I traveled to China with a group of seminary presidents and their wives. We visited several Chinese seminaries and Bible institutes served by the China Christian Council. In Shanghai we also attended worship services in a large registered Protestant church. During our meetings with the staff, questions were asked about the history of the church. The original marker with the name Moore Memorial Methodist Church remained in the courtyard. The missionaries who planted and cultivated the church were forced to leave Shanghai as the Japanese invaded China.

The woman telling the story was the wife of the Chinese pastor who died in a Japanese prison during World War 2. She told of Bibles and hymn books being burned by soldiers in the street. The church building was turned into a stable for the horses of the Japanese army. Every day she lead a small group of women to stand across from the church and pray for God to restore His Church and bring a harvest to China.

Today God is answering her prayers and the prayers of multitudes who interceded for China. The harvest there is unprecedented. People from every tongue and people group are coming to faith in Christ in incredible numbers (Rev. 5: 9). The promise of the harvest is the Lord's promise to His children who labor in His field.

Jesus taught us to pray for His kingdom to come on earth as it is in heaven. His harvest is ready and waiting. We pray in response to the command of God's Word and at the prompting of His Spirit. We pray with confidence in God's promises, knowing that our Sovereign Lord is already at work establishing His Kingdom among all the peoples of the world.[2]

The Challenge of Workers for the Harvest

Harvesting is hard work! Our challenge is to pray for workers who can persevere through drought and hardship. The saying, "many hands make light work" is true in the harvest fields of God's world. The solution to the need for workers is a simple one. Jesus challenges His disciples to beg the Lord of the harvest to meet the demand for laborers. *Beseech*, used in Matthew and Luke in the NASB can also be translated *pray*. The word is a strong one, demanding action, pleading for an answer.

The prayer challenge will demand intercessors with perseverance. Each generation must pray for a fresh shift of workers to serve an ever-increasing world population. As the median age of the world's population drops, as urbanization increases and as many become disillusioned with militant Islam and materialism, the need for workers increases exponentially.[3]

Praying for laborers may impact the intercessor personally. Samuel Zwemer understood the two-fold power of prayer. "The subjective power is on the mind and heart of him who prays. Its objective power is on others for whom we pray or in the realm of the material world."[4] In prayer the presence and power of God stretches "the sinews of the soul and hardens spiritual muscles."[5] The believer is strengthened to contend for those trapped in the darkness and to tear down the spiritual fortresses in the heavenly places (2 Cor. 10:1-6). The challenge of the harvest demands fortitude and tenacity.

The Apostle Paul understood the dependence on prayer in his work as a missionary and church planter. He wrote the Colossians and the Ephesians asking them to participate as partners in the work of harvest (Col. 4:2-4; Eph. 6:18-20). Paul made a three-fold request.

1. Access—An open door for the word of God.
2. Boldness—Boldness to speak the mysteries of the gospel.
3. Clarity—Wisdom in clearly communicating God's Word.

As partners in the harvest today, we can accept Paul's exhortation to devote ourselves to prayer with alert spirits, always expressing thanksgiving to the Lord of the harvest.

Lilias Trotter (1853-1930) served in Algeria and was one of the founders of Arab World Ministries. One day Trotter received a visual picture of the power of vibrations, and she turned the lesson into a parable for the church concerning prayer for the unreached fields of the world. An Arab baker installed himself in the outer gallery of the old house where she lived. The baker's bread was kneaded by the action of a large see-saw powered by two men. The constant vibrations created by hours of swinging back and forth eventually shattered the old masonry and brought the gallery down with a crash. Air and sunlight flooded the once dark interior of the bakery.

Trotter saw in the sudden destruction an object lesson. "Each prayer-beat down here vibrates up to the very throne of God, and does its work through that throne on the principalities and powers around us."[6] The vibrations of faithful, persistent intercession open doors of access for the seed of the word, shed the light of truth in dark places, and shower refreshing waters of the Spirit to yield a bountiful harvest.

In conclusion, God's word and His passion for the lost provide motivation to pray for the harvest. His promise of fruitful reaping challenges His children to obey His call to prayer for laborers in the world's fields.

Questions for Further Thought or Discussion

1. What does it take for the church to see the multitudes as Jesus did?
2. What are helpful ways to pray for laborers in the harvest?
3. What do you see as the greatest challenge for the harvest today?

The author: Paula Hemphill is Women's Mobilization Consultant for the Southern Baptist International Mission Board, Richmond, Virginia. She and her husband, Dr. Kenneth Hemphill reside in Travelers Rest, SC.

SUGGESTED ADDITIONAL READING

Johnstone, Patrick, and Jason Mandryk. *Operation World* 6th Edition. Carlisle, UK: Paternoster, 2005.

Duewel, Wesley. *Touch the World Through Prayer.* Grand Rapids: Zondervan Publishing, 1986.

Winter, Ralph, and Steve Hawthorne. *Perspectives on the World Christian Movement.* Pasadena, CA: Wm. Carey Library, 2000.

ENDNOTES

1. Wesley Duewel, *Touch the World Through Prayer.* (Grand Rapids: Zondervan, 1986), p. 189.

2. Hemphill, *EKG: The Heartbeat of God.* (Nashville: Broadman and Holman, 2004), p. 212.

3. Duewel, p. 18.

4. Samuel Zwemer, *Prayer.* (New York: American Tract Society, 1952), p. 18.

5. Zwemer, p. 19.

6. Rockness, Miriam Huffman, *A Passion for the Impossible: The Life of Lilias Trotter.* (Wheaton, IL: Harold Shaw, 1999), p. 294.

chapter

76

PRAYER JOURNEYS: PRAYING ON LOCATION FOR THE NATIONS

Pat Allen

Our prayer team was introduced to the concept of praying on location for the nations by Marty Lombardo, a missionary to Italy. His main calling to Italy was, however, not as a missionary in typical evangelist fashion, but as an intercessor. He established a regular routine of praying on location—at the Vatican, the Parliament, and the President's Palace.

At first he was persecuted by the police, but an Italian newspaper published an article questioning why the police would be beating on a man of prayer, and ultimately Marty actually became friends with his persecutors. Then there came a day when Parliament was evacuated because of a car bomb parked in the plaza, but Marty refused to leave his prayer assignment. God got the glory as the newspapers reported that the man of prayer kept praying and the car bomb never detonated.

Marty was called to pray for the government, the Mafia, the Catholic Church, and Christian reconciliation. And, while few of his prayers were answered as dramatically as the car bomb incident, he has seen governmental corruption exposed, the Mafia's chokehold broken, the Catholic Church revive, and a genuine move of reconciliation between the Protestants and Catholics.

We were privileged to join Marty's intercessory ministry by taking a prayer journey to Rome in 1995. There we discovered that our intercession was brought to a new level by being present where the need could be seen. This experience of praying "on site with insight"[1] makes the prayer journey a uniquely effective way to pray for the nations.

We have returned to Italy many times since 1995, building relationships, teaching, and even evangelizing. But we were never again called to make a prayer journey to Italy. Instead, God moved on our team to go to other nations, as well as locations in the U.S., to pray "on site with insight."

One of our most memorable prayer journeys was a trip our team took to England and Ireland in 1998. This trip provides an illustration of the elements of a prayer journey.

Go with God's calling.

Just as Paul and Barnabas were called by God for their missionary work while at a prayer meeting in Antioch (Acts 13:2), so a prayer journey must begin with a call from God. The call to go to England and Ireland came to our team members separately and jointly in corporate prayer. Over the next few months the team got a clearer understanding of exactly where to go, but scheduling the trip proved difficult as one suggested date after another was rejected.

It was not until after the date was set and the tickets were bought that the reason for God's timetable became clear. Our team was scheduled to arrive in the midst of a climatic confrontation between the Protestants and Catholics in Northern Ireland. We would never have taken such a risk had not God's call and His timetable been revealed to us.

Go under authority.

Paul and Barnabas did not begin their journey until they had been sent out by the Antioch Church (13:3) and they held themselves accountable to the Antioch Church when they returned (14:27). If Paul submitted himself to his church, how much more should we. Our team operates under the covering of our church elders, and our trips are submitted to their review. Once, when we were planning a prayer journey to Israel, our elders vetoed the trip because the Intifada had broken out. After things had settled down a bit our elders allowed the trip to proceed, and we had a safe and successful journey thanks to the protection of operating under authority.

In addition to our own church, we normally try to obtain an invitation and covering from a pastor or other spiritual authority in the destination nation. This additional covering strengthens our authority in prayer and brings another layer of protection to the team. We have found that many intercessors who experience "backlash," or suffer in the aftermath of a prayer journey, have not submitted themselves to proper spiritual authority prior to undertaking the prayer assignment.

Go in unity.

The great prayer principle of agreement (Mt. 18:19-20) is vital for a successful prayer journey. A time of team bonding, such as the time of worship and fasting at Antioch prior to sending out Paul and Barnabas (Acts 13:2), is necessary to bring the team into agreement. Often a small group will be more successful than a large group because unity is much easier to achieve in a small group.

For our trip to England and Ireland we chose a team of five. Three of the group had prayed together regularly for years and were veterans of other prayer journeys together. The other two members were from the next generation, submitted and willing to learn from the more experienced intercessors.

Bless and do not curse.

We believe that we are called to be a blessing and that our intercessors should bless and not curse (1 Pet. 3:9-11). Some have taught that we should curse the spiritual principalities and powers, but our experience has been that cursing often brings "backlash," in the form of a curse back upon the intercessor. We believe that these principalities exist because the people living in darkness elect to follow them. Prayers of blessing can open the blinded eyes, letting light scatter the darkness.

In the case of our trip to England and Ireland, the darkness we faced was caused by centuries of religious and ethnic violence. We prayed for repentance for both sides and asked God to cleanse the land of its bloodshed. We prayed in places where wars had been launched and battles had been fought, asking God to bring peace to a situation which was poised to explode into violence.

Expect God to meet you there.

Just as Abraham began his journey depending on God to show him where to go (Gen. 12:1), so we begin our prayer journeys depending on God to show us how to pray when we arrive. That is not to say that there is no preparation for a prayer journey. On the contrary, a study of the history and culture of a nation can yield vital clues concerning its prayer needs. However, even the most thoroughly researched journey will depend on God's revelation on site for success.

The England and Ireland trip is a good illustration of the need for God's guidance in the nations because the confrontation in Northern Ireland was unanticipated by the team when the prayer journey was organized. It was on the first leg of the journey, in England, that the team became aware that their prayer assignment was directed toward the conflict which was scheduled to occur as Protestants marched to celebrate the Protestant triumph over the Catholic forces at the Battle of the Boyne in 1690. God's hand was evident as the team realized that they were landing in Dublin, Ireland on the anniversary of the Battle of the Boyne.

The crisis in Northern Ireland deepened as the Protestants assembled in a field with weapons and bombs, preparing to force their way through hostile Catholic neighborhoods. Then, a horrible incident occurred where a child was murdered in a fire bombing. Yet it seemed that this murder brought everyone to their senses.

The Protestant militants abandoned their plans to march. Some even left their weapons and bombs in the field where they had gathered. We had seen a miraculous change take place, as peace emerged from the near disaster. Our prayers, along with many thousands of others, were powerfully answered and peace between the Irish Protestants and Catholics has been advancing since that day, as evidenced by an August 2007 article in *Charisma* magazine titled "Christians Say Prayer Is Behind Peace Deal."

What a joy it was for our team to participate in a prayer assignment where our prayers were added to those of both Protestants and Catholics seeking God's help for reconciliation. Such immediate and dramatic answers to prayer are seldom seen. Most of the time the prayer team is planting seeds: sometimes of evangelism, sometimes of reconciliation, sometimes of forgiveness, sometimes of protection, but always of blessing. God sends others to bring the seeds to fruition, and we rejoice as we see the answers to our prayers manifested in the nations.

God is looking for intercessors who are obedient to His call, working under authority and in unity to bless the nations. God will take such people on prayer journeys that will change the destinies of nations and shake the whole world.

Questions for Further Thought or Discussion

1. Why would God call intercessors from one nation to go pray in another nation?
2. What advantages are there to being present in the nation when you are praying?
3. Can you think of a nation for which you have a prayer burden that could lead to a prayer journey?

The author: Pat Allen is President of Corporate Prayer Resources in Dallas, Texas.

SUGGESTED ADDITIONAL READING

Crawford, Dan and Calvin Miller. *Prayerwalking: A Journey of Faith.* Chattanooga, TN: AMG Publishers, 2002.

Otis, George Jr., ed. *Strongholds of the 1040 Window.* Seattle, WA: YWAM Publishing, 1995.

Richardson, Don. *Eternity in Their Hearts.* Ventura, CA: Regal, 1981.

ENDNOTES

1. The phrase "praying on site with insight" is the subtitle of a book by Steve Hawthorne and Graham Kendrick, entitled, *Prayerwalking: Praying on Site with Insight*, (Orlando, FL: Creation House, 1993).

chapter

77

PRAYER FOUNDATION FOR GLOBAL MINISTRY

Daniel Sanchez

Prayer is indispensable for any type of ministry in which we might be involved.[1] Jesus said: "I will build My church, and the gates of Hades shall not prevail against it" (Mt. 16:18). There are two powerful implications in this statement.[2] First, it is Jesus who builds His church and not those who are involved in global ministries. Since Jesus is the architect, it is very important for those who are involved in global ministry to cultivate the habit of spending time in prayer seeking instruction and guidance from the Lord. Second, global ministry is a spiritual endeavor. The statement, "the gates of Hades shall not prevail against it," reveals the fact that the church is involved in spiritual warfare. In this battle, Jesus gives the picture of the church as advancing even to the strongholds of Satan and liberating people with the power of the gospel.

The Apostle Paul reminds us that "we do not wrestle against flesh and blood, but against principalities . . ." (Eph. 6:12). The person who believes that global ministry is simply a matter of utilizing appropriate strategies and methods is as ill equipped for the battle as a person using bows and arrows against an army with automatic weapons. Those involved in global ministries, therefore, must have a well-defined prayer strategy personally as well as for their intercessors.

Personal Prayer Strategy

Thomas Wade Akins, a missionary who has been instrumental in starting hundreds of churches in Brazil makes the following suggestions concerning a personal prayer strategy.[3]

1. **Praise.** Begin your prayer with praise. Sing hymns to God, sing or read praise choruses, and read passages of prayers in the Bible and personalize each verse. When you praise God you thank Him for who He is.
2. **Thanksgiving.** Gratefulness is thanking God for what He has done.
3. **Confession.** During our time alone with God, the Holy Spirit may bring to mind recent un-confessed sins. We should confess all the sins in our hearts.
4. **Hearing God's voice.** God uses primarily two means to speak to His believers on a daily basis: the Holy Spirit and His Word. It is necessary, therefore, to read and apply the lessons from Scripture continually.
5. **Paraphrasing the Word of God.** Utilizing Ephesians 1:1, for example, you can pray: "I thank You God because You called me to be a disciple of Jesus Christ." Then proceed to the second verse, etc.
6. **Intercession.** This means praying for other people (Eph. 6:18). Make a list of the days of the week and under each place the name of the people for whom you will pray.
7. **Meditation and Scripture memory.** God's purpose is to make Christians conform to the image of Christ (Rom. 8:29). Choose a verse in the Bible each week. Read the verse in its context. Ask God

to show you the spiritual truths in this verse.

8. **Supplication.** This means simply presenting to God our own needs. "Let us therefore come boldly to the throne of grace, that we may obtain mercy and find grace to help in the time of need" (Heb. 4:16).

Intercessory Team Prayer Strategy

In order to be effective, Christians also need to be supported by the fervent, constant, and focused prayers of an intercessory team.

Heavenly Prayer Partners

When those involved in global ministries think about the concept of prayer partners, they are prone to focus only on earthly prayer partners. Wesley Duewel reminds us that we have heavenly prayer partners. "God the Son is your enthroned prayer partner and God the Holy Spirit is your indwelling prayer partner."[4]

Dan Crawford adds:

> As our prayer partner, Jesus prays for us just as He did for His disciples (Lk. 22:23; Jn. 17; Rom. 8:34; Heb. 7:25; Heb. 9:24; 1 Jn. 2:1). As a prayer partner, Jesus affects our prayer life in a least three ways: we learn to pray in agreement with Him, in confidence with Him, and in persistence with Him. . . . The Holy Spirit also acts as a prayer partner. . . . According to Romans 8:26-27, the Holy Spirit "helps our weaknesses," guides us in "how to pray as we should," "intercedes for us," "searches our hearts," and helps us to discern "the will of God.". . . In addition to the Father, the Son, and the Holy Spirit serving as our prayer partners, there is a partnership entered into with the angels. Angels are assigned by God "to render service for the sake of those who will inherit salvation" (Heb. 1:14).[5]

It is reassuring for us to know that we can count on the heavenly prayer partners whom God provided as we are involved in His ministry. This helps us to avoid the feeling that we are alone and that we are the only ones who are praying and seeking God's guidance and help.

Earthly Prayer Partners

In addition to heavenly prayer partners, there are earthly prayer partners who can contribute in a significant way to the effectiveness of our ministry. Jesus encouraged His followers to pray together when He said: "If two of you agree on earth concerning anything they may ask, it will be done for them by My Father in heaven" (Mt. 18:19). Prayer partners can play a key role when they join us in seeking God's will and asking for His power and guidance in a church starting effort.

A crucial question that Christians involved in ministry ask is, where can I find effective prayer partners? Robert Logan makes the following suggestions:

> Make a list of people who: (1) have said they will pray for you; (2) called and ask for prayer requests; (3) asked if you have had answers to their prayers; (4) you know to be a prayer warrior; (5) have received ministry from you where you felt a "chemistry," that is, you liked them and they liked you.[6]

Once the intercessors have been found it is important to help them to understand their role. It is also very important to share prayer requests with them on a regular basis. These requests need to be specific so that both the intercessors and the person involved in ministry can know when prayers have been answered. Asking God to "bless a community" or to bless efforts to "reach a target group" is too vague. Specific prayers, on the other hand, will give the intercessors the opportunity to rejoice when God answers their prayers. It is very helpful also to share information about prayer (e.g., books, articles) with intercessors so that they will continue to grow in their ministry. Encouraging the intercessors to pray for one another as well as for those involved in ministry can also contribute toward their spiritual growth.

The Focus of Our Prayers

Those involved in ministry should be very focused in their personal prayer life and should help the intercessors to focus on prayer requests that relate to specific areas of need.

There are prayers that focus on the well-being of those involved in ministry. This is very important. Often there are needs related to health issues, to travel arrangements, and to security concerns. Many who are involved in ministry can give ample testimony of answered prayers during crucial moments in their lives. It is certainly reassuring to know that people are praying for us when we face difficult circumstances. We should, therefore, be very specific when we ask for prayer related to our well-being.

In addition to these types of prayers, there should be prayer for the people to whom we are going to minister. Paul prayed for the Lord to open doors, for the Lord to guide him as to where he should minister (Bithynia or Macedonia?), and even for boldness to witness in the midst of trying circumstances. If we only pray for our own safety and well-being, we are focusing on only half the task. When we pray for the Spirit of God to touch the hearts of people, to break down walls of resistance, and for Him to work in a miraculous way, we are acknowledging the fact that it is God who paves the way for the spreading of the gospel. A retired missionary was asked to pray for a young couple who was about to leave for the mission field. This is how he prayed: "Father, help this young couple to know that they are not taking You to the mission field, that You are taking them, and that You are already there." This prayer speaks volumes. It recognizes the fact that God is the one who is at work and that we are simply to follow Him. Someone said: "Christian ministry is a team effort and the Holy Spirit is the team captain."

A number of years ago, Randy and Nancy Sprinkle were appointed to go to the country of Lesotho and start a work there. Knowing that they were going to face many challenges, the Sprinkles established an intercessory prayer partnership with the Woman's Missionary Union (WMU) of Missouri. Their concerns were well founded. To start with, the government refused to give them a visa. This became the first prayer request. Their second greatest challenge was to find a house in which to live. Their third concern had to do with Nancy's health. Their fourth concern had to do with the Lord opening a door for the gospel there. As a result of the intensive, focused prayer of the WMU, the government granted the Sprinkles a temporary visa.

Upon entering the country they faced what appeared to be a conspiracy. No one wanted to rent them a house. Their prayer became even more intense when they found themselves living in a hotel room next to a disco which played loud music every night into the wee hours of the morning. After living there for several months with their young children the Lord answered their prayer and a man who was going to leave the country for a year offered to let them rent his home.

Their third prayer concern was answered as the Lord gave Nancy who was suffering from Lupus strength to carry on in a very difficult environment. The Sprinkles then began to see evidence of answered prayer regarding their fourth concern when they were able to start Bible studies in their home and see people respond to the gospel message. Even their first concern received an additional answer when the WMU prayed at the specific time that the Sprinkles were going to visit the government office. While they were there, a government official shook her head and said: "I don't understand this, the impression I had was that our government had decided it would not extend your visa but it has extended it for several years."

A prayer foundation is absolutely essential for those involved in global ministries. They need to have a disciplined prayer life. A recognition that Jesus, the Holy Spirit, and God's angels, are a part of the prayer team can give those involved in ministry a deep sense of confidence and power. The ministry of an intercessory prayer team is also vital to the success of a global ministry effort. Throughout Paul's epistles, we find examples of the prayers that he prayed for his co-workers as well as of his requests for prayer. Paul knew that the spiritual battle inherent in ministry could not be won without the continued fervent prayer of the faithful. Those involved in global ministries should have the same commitment to prayer.

Questions for Further Thought or Discussion

1. Summarize each of the points presented as a personal strategy and attach a scripture (or additional reference) to each one.
2. Explain why a prayer team is an essential part of a prayer strategy.
3. Design a Bible study for a small group/mission team that surveys three or four Old Testament and three or four New Testament scriptures that connect prayer to global ministry.

The author: Dr. Daniel Sanchez is Associate Dean for Masters Degrees and Professor of Missions at Southwestern Baptist Seminary in Fort Worth, Texas. He is the author of books both in English and Spanish including *Starting Reproducing Congregations, Hispanic Realities,* and *Church Planting Movements in North America.* He is a former denominational executive and missionary to Panama.

SUGGESTED ADDITIONAL READING

Sprinkle, Randy. *Follow Me: Becoming a Lifestyle Prayerwalker.* Birmingham, AL: New Hope Publishers, 2001.

Crawford, Dan. *The Prayer Shaped Disciple.* Peabody, MA: Hendrickson Publishing, 1999.

Winter, Ralph, and Steve Hawthorne. P*erspectives on the World Christian Movemen*t. Pasadena, CA: William Carey Library, 1999.

ENDNOTES

1. This is an adaptation of a segment which appears in chapter 5 of Daniel R. Sanchez, Ebbie Smith, *Starting Reproducing Congregations* (Fort Worth: Church Starting Network, 1991). Used by permission.

2. Logan points this out in Robert E. Logan, Steven L Ogne, *The Church Planter's Tool Kit.*

3. Thomas Wade Akins, *Pioneer Evangelism* (Rio de Janeiro: Brazilian Baptist Convention, 1995), pp. 50-56.

4. Wesley Duewel, *Touch the World Through Prayer* (Grand Rapids: Francis Asbury Press, 1986), p. 45.

5. Dan R. Crawford, *The Prayer-Shaped Disciple* (Peabody, MA: Hendrickson Publishers, 1999), pp. 12-13.

6. Logan, *The Church Planter's Toolkit*, pp. 2-6.

78

THE INTERNATIONAL HOUSE OF PRAYER

Gary Wiens

The International House of Prayer Missions Base in Kansas City, Missouri, was conceived in 1983 through a prophetic word given to Mike Bickle, a 27-year old who felt called to plant a church in that city. The essence of this prophetic word was that there would come a day when Mike would give leadership to a twenty-four hour, seven-day-a-week House of Prayer in the spirit of the Tabernacle of David. The focus of this prayer ministry would be the release of revival in Kansas City, the empowering of missions in the nations, and the restoration of Israel to the purposes of God in preparation for the second coming of Jesus.

After sixteen years of daily corporate prayer meetings, release came in 1999 to begin continuous prayer. On May 7 of that year, the doors of IHOP were opened for thirteen hours a day. On September 19, 1999, the schedule expanded to twenty-four hours a day, seven days a week, and has continued in that mode for eight years at the time of this writing. Today, in the fall of 2007, there are approximately 2000 individuals from around the world who have found their spiritual home at the IHOP.

The Biblical Mandate of Intercession for the Nations

I want to suggest two ideas that underscore the necessity of intercession as an irreplaceable component of effective evangelism in the nations of the earth. The first idea is that Scripture gives us compelling reasons to include prayer in the work of missions. Psalm 2 gives voice to the mind of God in this matter: "I will declare the decree: The LORD has said to Me, 'You are My Son, today I have begotten You. Ask of Me, and I will give You the nations for Your inheritance, And the ends of the earth for Your possession'" (Ps. 2:7-8).

The New Testament writers apply these verses to Jesus, and we must therefore consider the fact that Jesus' methodology of reaching the nations of the earth with the gospel was rooted in intercession: "Ask of Me, and I will give You the nations for Your inheritance." It is a simple matter to establish the fact that Jesus' ministry was rooted in prayer,[1] and that His main strategy for the nations was that God would give them to Him in answer to prayer. Since that is the Father's main strategy for Jesus, then surely it is to be part of our strategies as well.

For many in the Body of Christ today, prayer has been seen as being of lesser importance than other strategies for the accomplishment of the task of missions. The simple reality that this book is being written to fill a void in the training process of Christian leaders underscores that fact. At best, prayer has been seen as a way of tapping into the plans of God, to discover what He is planning and doing so that we humans can participate in His plans. That is a wonderful and valid dimension of prayer, but it is incomplete. The Scripture is clear that not only will God reveal His activity to those who pray, but that He will do more in answer to prayer than He would otherwise have done. Consider such passages as these:

> Call upon Me in the day of trouble;
> I will deliver you, and you shall glorify Me. (Ps. 50:15)

> He will be very gracious to you at the sound of your cry;

> When He hears it, He will answer you. (Isa. 30:19)

> Then you will call upon Me and go and pray to Me, and I will listen to you. And you will seek Me and find Me, when you search for Me with all your heart. (Jer. 29:12-13)

> Call to Me, and I will answer you, and show you great and mighty things, which you do not know. (33:3)

> In this manner, therefore, pray: Our Father in heaven, hallowed be Your name. Your kingdom come. Your will be done on earth as it is in heaven. (Mt. 6:9-10)

> Ask, and it will be given to you; seek, and you will find; knock, and it will be opened to you. For everyone who asks receives, and he who seeks finds, and to him who knocks it will be opened. (7:7-8)

In every one of these passages (and there are many more) God is revealing to us that He will do more in answer to prayer than He would do if we do not pray. He is looking for partners on the earth who desire the establishment of His kingdom here, in part as we wait for Jesus' return, and in fullness when He comes to take His place as the King of kings and Lord of lords.

The second idea that emerges from Scripture is the importance of night and day intercessory worship as it relates to missions. As I stated in the introduction, the prophetic word that seeded the House of Prayer was that it would emerge "in the spirit of the Tabernacle of David." Although the thing that burned in King David's heart was the establishment of a place of unceasing worship that he might behold the beauty of the Lord,[2] in the heart of God there was an additional issue. Somehow, there would be a connection between night and day intercessory worship and the spread of the gospel to the nations. This is a compelling component of intercession for the nations, because the Bible declares that God's purpose for David's Tabernacle was precisely the salvation of the nations of the earth. Consider these two passages from Amos 9 and Acts 15 that articulate the plan of God in this matter:

> On that day I will raise up the tabernacle of David, which has fallen down, And repair its damages; I will raise up its ruins, and rebuild it as in the days of old; That they may possess the remnant of Edom, *and all the Gentiles who are called by My name,*" says the LORD who does this thing. (Amos 9:11-12, *emphasis added*)

> After this I will return and will rebuild the tabernacle of David, which has fallen down; I will rebuild its ruins, and I will set it up; *so that the rest of mankind may seek the LORD, even all the Gentiles who are called by My name,*" says the LORD who does all these things. (Acts 15:16-17, *emphasis added*)

Applying These Scriptures at IHOP

The goal of the International House of Prayer is not to duplicate the Tabernacle of David, but to attempt to give a current expression to the reality that was shown to David from heaven.[3] In Revelation 4 and 5, we are given a compelling glimpse into the majesty and wonder of the heavenly worship center. We read of the glory of the Throne of God, the beauty of the emerald rainbow around the Throne, the sounds of the voices and thunderings coming from the Throne. We are impacted by the wonder of the seven lamps which are the seven-fold Spirit of God, by the imagery of the four living creatures, the twenty-four elders, and the throngs gathered in worship on the sapphire sea that stretches out from the Presence of God.

Then, in chapter five, verse eight, we are told that the elders and the four living creatures all have harps, which symbolize worship, and bowls of incense, which are the prayers of the saints. The harp and the bowl represent the weaving together of worship and intercession, rising in unceasing fashion before the Throne of God.

It is this eternal reality that gives rise to the intercessory worship model exercised at IHOP. Worship and intercessory teams engage in prayer non-stop, with new teams coming into place every two hours. The worship leader sets the tone of the prayer meeting, and the intercessors come to the microphone to lead the spoken prayers. Using the apostolic prayers of the New Testament,[4] the Psalms, and passages of Scripture that make prophetic declarations, we set the focus of intercessory worship on the cities and nations of the world.

Through the course of any given week, a number of prayer meetings are focused on individual nations. For example, Tuesdays are given over to praying for the nation of Israel. Every Tuesday from 10 AM to noon, and from 4-6 PM the prayers are directed toward the believers in Israel, that the Holy Spirit would strengthen them and equip them to stand in the pressures of that environment, and to empower and protect them as they preach the gospel in that resistant place. The 4 PM prayer meeting is particularly exciting because they have video connection with a prayer ministry in Jerusalem. The intercessors in Jerusalem plug into the meeting in Kansas City via webstream, and are encouraged and invigorated because of the connection. For example, an intercessor in Kansas City might pray from Paul's second letter to the Thessalonian believers: "Finally, brethren, pray for us, that the word of the Lord may run swiftly and be glorified, just as it is with you, and that we may be delivered from unreasonable and wicked men; for not all have faith" (2 Thess. 3:1-2).

The prayer leader will take short phrases from this prayer (i.e. "let the word of the Lord run swiftly") and restate that phrase in his or her own words. Then, the singers on the worship team, who have spent much time studying these prayers phrase by phrase, begin to respond with spontaneous songs of intercession, all of which are rooted in the Scriptures. There emerges a wonderful dialogue between the prayer leader, the singers, and the congregation as the intercession and worship is woven together. We call upon the Holy Spirit to release the power of these prayers to the believers in Israel, and trust that God will in fact do just that. By praying in this way, we come into unity with the Holy Spirit and with one another concerning God's activity in that land, and the dynamic of the kingdom of God is released in greater measure.

An example of the power of this type of intercession occurred in the early months of 2005. YWAM was planning an extensive evangelism surge in the nation of New Zealand, and John Dawson, the YWAM International President, contacted IHOP for prayer support. For fifty days IHOP pointed the "prayer cannon" at that nation. Every prayer meeting, either totally or in part, was directed at praying for the outreach teams, for the weather patterns, for the people who would attend the meetings—in short, for every conceivable dimension of the outreach.

Each day IHOP would receive updates from a YWAM representative, informing us what was happening in New Zealand in answer to our prayers, and giving us new direction to pray for the immediate needs there. For example, some very strong weather patterns developed over that nation during the time period. Several times, as we prayed over the weather, the skies cleared above the outdoor arena where the meetings were happening, even though the rain continued to fall in areas around the arena. By the end of the fifty days, more than 26,000 people had given their lives to Christ, and the churches of New Zealand were experiencing an unprecedented season of unity and cooperation in the follow-up efforts. Since then, IHOP has engaged with a number of other missions agencies in similar fashion, providing the prayer covering for the evangelistic activities that have been set in place.

Night and day prayer is an integral part of the work of missions. May the fire on the altar never go out, and may the Lamb receive His reward in the nations of the earth.

Questions for Further Thought or Discussion

1. Define the purpose and describe the practice of around-the-clock prayer at the International House of Prayer.
2. Defend this expression of prayer and praise from a scriptural foundation.
3. How can these practices and principles be applied to a single congregation or a weekly prayer gathering?

The author: Rev. Gary Wiens is President of Burning Heart Ministries, Inc. in Gig Harbor, Washington. He was a member of the Senior Leadership Team of the International House of Prayer Missions Base from May 1999, through June 2007, and is the author of *Come to Papa* and co-author with Mike Bickle of *Bridal Intercession* and co-author with his wife, Mary Wiens, for *Reaching Your Power Potential.*

SUGGESTED ADDITIONAL READING

Greig, Peter and David Blackwell. *24/7 Prayer Manual: A Guide to Creating and Sustaining Holy Space in the Real World.* Colorado Springs, CO: Cook Communications, 2005.

Greig, Peter and Dave Roberts. *Red Moon Rising: How 24-7 Prayer Is Awak-*

ening a Generation. Lake Mary, FL: Relevant Books, 2005.

Anderson, Philip. *The Lord of the Ring: Uncovering the Secret Origins of Praying 24/7.* Ventura, CA: Regal Books, 2007.

ENDNOTES

1. See such passages as John 5:19-20; Mark 1:35-38; Luke 6:12ff.
2. See Psalm 27:4; also Psalm 132:1-9.
3. See 1 Chronicles 28:12,19.
4. For a complete list of the prayers of Scripture, visit the IHOP website at www.IHOP.org.

chapter

79

MISSIONARY DYNAMIC AND PRAYER

George W. Peters

The Bible is a record of supernatural manifestations, interventions and activities. Many of these happenings are direct answers to prayers. "It is a noteworthy fact that there are 657 definite requests for prayer in the Bible, not including the Psalms, and 454 definitely recorded answers."[1] Prayer is a prominent subject in the Bible and a most significant exercise of faith by the saints and the church.

> Work backed up by prayer is too often the practice, if not the ideal, of the Church. If the world is to be won, that order must be reversed, and the Church learn to depend on prayer backed up by work. Christian work that thinks and plans and bustles and toils,

> but forgets to pray, is an almost pathetic spectacle. . . .
>
> It is important to realize that prayer . . . is something far more than a subjective spiritual exercise. . . . Prayer is a force which achieves objective results. It actually causes things to happen which otherwise would not happen. The Biblical theory of prayer is that it is a force at work.[2]

"Very effectual [dynamic] in its working is the prayer of a righteous man" (Jas. 5:16, Free Trans.). This is a fact of tremendous significance. It is well documented in the Bible and richly demonstrated in history.

The book of Ezra leads us back many centuries and reports some marvelous experiences of Israel and Judah, the Old Testament people of God. Because of sin and failure the people were given over in judgment to the nations of the world. Nebuchadnezzar had captured and destroyed Jerusalem and the temple. The wealth and prominent tribespeople had been taken to Babylon into captivity. Though the adjustments to Babylon had been difficult (Psalm 137), the people eventually settled down and prospered.

In due time Babylon was subjugated and Medo-Persia became dominant. It is here that the story of Ezra begins.

Cyrus was king of Persia. In a vision the Lord spoke to him and ordered him to build the house of the Lord in Jerusalem. The attitude of Cyrus was commendable. He responded with a challenge to the people of Judah to return to their homeland and build the house of the Lord God of Israel. He also made financial arrangements and provided the means to have the work completed (Ezra 1:1-2, 7-8; 3:7; 6:4, 8).

At the same time the Spirit of the Lord moved upon the people of Judah in captivity and called forth an army of volunteers to return to Palestine and undertake the task as commanded (1:5; 2:64-67). The hands of this volunteer army were strengthened by the goodwill and free gifts of the people who remained behind (1:6; 2:68-70). Thus an open door, the good will of authorities, a volunteer army of builders, a supporting people, and the necessary means were provided for the cause of the Lord. Although the building of the temple did not proceed without difficulty, the work was eventually completed.

The action of Cyrus has been variously interpreted. It has been suggested that the king saw in Egypt his potential rival and that as a good politician he proceeded to build in Judah a friendly and supporting buffer state. It has also been mentioned that Cyrus introduced a more humane treatment of the people of captured states and thus he was returning the captives to their homeland.

It is not impossible that such motives were present in the mind of Cyrus. However, the sacred writer of the record looks behind the curtain of human feelings and thinking and sees the moving of the Holy Spirit and the action of God (1:1, 5). God was present and He was at work. In keeping with Isaiah's prophecy, Cyrus became the Lord's servant (Isa. 44:28; 45:1).

According to Jeremiah's predictions, the time had come to rebuild the temple (Jer. 25:12-13). Thus God moved into history and caused things to happen to fulfill His prophecy and purpose.

We could stop here and praise God for His faithfulness and we would not go amiss in it. God *is* faithful and He *does* stand by His promises. He *does* fulfill His prophecies. His plan and program are assured by Him, and His purposes are certain. However, the biblical record does not view it thus. The mystery of the gracious movements of God in history here are led back one more step.

An elderly and godly man living in Babylon is well known to us. His name is Daniel. Although he is primarily a politician by profession and experience, he is above all a man of God and greatly beloved of the Lord. Time may have dimmed his eyes but not his vision. His concern for his people cannot be measured. His desire for their welfare is difficult to express. His faith in the prophets of God is absolute. His assurance of the faithfulness of God knows no wavering. His experience in answered prayer permits no doubting in God and His purpose, cause and people.

Upon the prayers of Daniel, the mighty and gracious hand of God was moved that stirred the spirit of Cyrus and moved the hearts of the people of the captivity. The mystery of history is unlocked in Daniel 9-10. Here this remarkable man records: "I Daniel understood by books the number of the years, whereof the word of the Lord came to Jeremiah the prophet, that he would accomplish seventy years in the desolations of Jerusalem. And I set my face unto the Lord God, to seek by prayer and supplications, with fasting, and sackcloth, and ashes: and I prayed unto the Lord my God"(9:1-4, KJV).

Then follows one of the most heart-stirring prayers of the Bible. Similar is the experience in chapter 10.

The chronology of the chapters, dates and names is not too difficult to reconcile with the record of Ezra and history. The fact remains: Daniel prayed and, in response to his prayer, God invaded history and moved to accomplish His will and purpose.

Here is the key to many mighty and surprising movings of God in history. Someone prayed and God responded. It could really be that "if there should arise one utterly believing man, the history of the world would be changed."

However, it is a sad fact that unbelief too often clouds our vision and paralyzes us in the way to the highest and the greatest. This was not so in the life of our Lord. "When we think about prayer, we think, as a rule, instinctively of its limitations; the mind of Christ seemed always to be occupied with its possibilities."[3]

Prayer did occupy a very significant part in the life and teaching of our Lord. He is, indeed, *The Man of Prayer* (J.H. Strong). And we are exhorted to pray—persistently (Lk. 18:1-8), in faith (Mt. 21:21-22), in His name (Jn. 14:14; 16:23), in sincerity (Mt. 15:21-28), with fasting (Mk. 9:29; Acts 13:2-3; 14:23), in specifics (Mt. 20:32-22), according to His will (1 Jn. 5:14), for laborers in the harvest (Mt. 9:37-38), and unitedly (18:19).

Prayer in the Book of Acts

The significance of payer is well demonstrated in the book of Acts. While this book may well be entitled as the book of the Acts of the Holy Spirit, it is likewise the book of mighty prayer.

The dispensational setting of Pentecost dare not be minimized. The Old Testament calendar of God had foreshadowed it as an event and as to time. Thus, while Pentecost was not born *by* prayer, it was born *in* an attitude and practice of prayer. For days the disciples had faithfully "waited in Jerusalem" to be equipped for their world task. It is also noteworthy that Pentecost did not become a substitute for prayer. Pentecost intensified prayer. Thus, while from the divine side things happened according to the Holy Spirit, from the human side prayer played a major role. Of this the disciples were deeply conscious. Therefore, when their schedule became too crowded and threatened to interfere with their primary ministry, they called the multitude together and appointed deacons in order that they might give themselves to "prayer and to the ministry of the word" (Acts 6:1-4).

Prayer not only emboldened the witnesses; it also gave them the stamina to suffer. It wrought miracles, and it also brought forth the first missionaries, as recorded in Acts 13:1-4. Prayer becomes the subterranean channel for the flow of spiritual dynamic throughout the pages of the book of Acts. The very fact that it is mentioned more than thirty times in this book is evidence of its theological and practical dominance in the mind and life of the early church.

Prayer in the Ministry of Paul

The missionary significance and dynamic of prayer are best illustrated in Paul. "I bow my knees to the Father of our Lord Jesus Christ" (Eph. 3:14) is typical of Paul. Next to the book of Psalms there is no part of the Bible that contains such wealth of devotion, such depth of adoration, such height of thanksgiving and such width of intercession as Paul's epistles.

Paul prayed for himself, for the brethren, and especially for the churches. No doubt it was Paul's prayer as well as his teaching that produced the quality Christians we read of in the New Testament. The comprehensiveness of his care for the churches can be seen by the petitions in his prayers. He prayed for love (1 Thess. 3:12-13), for sanctification (5:23), for God's good pleasure (2 Thess. 1:11-12), for consolation (2:16), for love and patience (3:5), for corporate perfection (2 Cor. 13:7-9), for unity (Rom. 15:5-6), for hope (15:13), for knowledge of God's will (Col. 1:9-14), for full assurance of knowledge (2:1-3), for the glory yet to come (Phil. 1:15-21), for the triune indwelling (Eph. 3:14-21), for perseverance to the end (Phil. 1:9-11).[4] Thus the great apostle labored in prayer for the churches under his care.

Paul, however, was also deeply conscious of his own needs and of his dependence upon the prayers of the saints. Thus he humbly and persistently asked for the prayers of the churches. "Brethren, pray for us" was his challenge and his plea. And from the various references and requests we can well formulate our missionary prayers. Some of the main references are as follows: Romans 15:30-32; 2 Corinthians 1:10-11; Ephesians 6:18-20; Philippians 1:19; Colossians 4:2-4; 1 Thessalonians 5:25; 2 Thessalonians 3:1-3; Philemon 22.

The requests are comprehensive. The churches are to pray for divine deliverance, for acceptance of Paul's service, for divine guidance, for boldness to speak the mystery of the gospel, for open doors to preach the gospel, for a free course of the word of the Lord. Somehow Paul never found it necessary to pray for finances. Neither did he appeal to the home churches for more missionaries. His toil and prayers produced a quality Christianity which provided both of these necessities for the expansion of the gospel and the growth of the churches.

Prayer and Modern Missions

Prayer has remained the lifeline of missions. Modern missions can be traced to revival in prayer.

The Reformation gave back to the church the missionary message, but it did not give the church the missionary vision. Neither did it generate missionary dynamic. The latter two were born of Pietism. Philip Jakob Spener (1635-1705), August Herman Francke (1663-1727), Count Nicholaus Ludwig Zinzendorf (1700-1760) and the Moravian Brethren at Herrnhut became the true pioneers in modern missions. The movement was deeply rooted in prayer.

Herrnhut greatly influenced the great leaders of Methodism, and a marked revival of payer for the non-Christian world resulted.

In 1723 Robert Millar, a Presbyterian minister of Scotland, published a pamphlet in which he urged prayer as the first known means for the conversion of the heathen world.

In 1744 a call was widely circulated to unite in prayer for the salvation of the non-Christian world. In 1746 a memorial was sent to Boston, inviting all Christians of North America to enter into a concert of prayer for a period of seven years.

In 1747 Jonathan Edwards of Northhampton responded by issuing a call to intercessory prayer on the part of all Christian believers for the spread of the gospel. Thirty-seven years later this stirring pamphlet was introduced into the churches of England by Jon Sutliffe in the Northhamptonshire Association, a gathering of Baptist ministers. Following the reading of the message, he moved that all Baptist churches and ministers set aside the first Monday of each month for united intercessory prayer for the non-Christian world. The motion was adopted and the Reverend John Ryland of Northhampton drew up a plan in which he challenged the churches to regular and earnest intercessory prayer for a world in darkness and sin.

The inevitable consequence of these payer meetings was the organization of the Baptist missionary society known as "The Particular Baptist Missionary Society for Propagating the Gospel among the Heathen." It was founded in 1792 at Kettering, England.

In rapid succession, societies sprang up in Great Britain as well as on the Continent.

The story of Samuel J. Mills and his four loyal comrades and Williams College and the Haystack Prayer Meeting are foundational to American foreign missions. As the five students waited before the Lord in shelter of the haystack, they discussed the spiritual darkness of the vast multitudes without Christ. They debated the possibility of realizing the Lord's command and its bearing in their own lives. Mills proposed that they devote themselves to sending the gospel to the non-Christian world. His immortal words, "We can do it if we will," have characterized much of American missions. Upon these words they knelt in prayer and then quietly went home. The hour was late and no one was aware that a crisis hour in the history of missions had come, an hour that would draw thousands of able-bodied American men and women into the service of world evangelism.

Conclusion

Prayer, indeed, is dynamic and works if exercised in the name of Christ and the Holy Spirit. Christian missions is a supernatural venture. Only supernatural resources can sustain it and make it dynamic. The contact with the Divine is imperative. Prayer is not optional; it is operational and decisive.

The history of missions abounds with evidences of divine intervention and gracious manifestation in behalf of the cause of missions. The history of the vast amount of prayers invested in the venture and the divine response to them will never be recounted on this side of eternity. Only in the blaze of divine light will be see the fullness of divine glory, faithfulness and manifestations. And to our great surprise, most of such manifestations will appear to be a direct response to some prayer. Someone prayed and God acted.

Here is the secret of divine dynamic. Here is the challenge to human helplessness. Here is the key that transforms human limitations into divine limitlessness. Here the Church is on trial before God and the world. Here the Church stands numbed in bankruptcy or filled with miracle and power.

Prayer is the key that unlocks the divine resources of power and supply.

> Now I beg you, brethren, through the Lord Jesus Christ, and through the love of the Spirit, that you strive together with me in prayers to God for me, that I may be delivered from those in Judea who do not believe, and that my service for Jerusalem may be acceptable to the saints, that I may come to you with joy by the will of God, and may be refreshed together with you. Now the God of peace be with you all. Amen. (Rom. 15:30-33)

(This chapter was taken with permission and adapted from *A Biblical Theology of Missions*, Moody Publishers 1972 by George W. Peters.)

Questions for Further Thought or Discussion

1. "Prayer is a force which achieves objective results." What does this mean and how should this insight influence our praying for missions?
2. How has prayer impacted the history of the modern missionary movement?
3. Using Romans 15:30-33 as your text, construct an outline for a teaching or preaching on the role and result so of both individual and corporate prayer for missions.

The author: The late Dr. George W. Peters was Professor of World Missions for many years at Dallas Theological Seminary in Dallas, Texas. Listed in *Who's Who in American Education*, he was the author of *Saturation Evangelism, Indonesia Revival; Focus on Timor, A Theology of Church Growth: Contemporary Evangelical Perspectives* as well as *A Biblical Theology of Missions.*

SUGGESTED ADDITIONAL READING

Terry, John Mark, Ebbie Smith, and Justice Anderson. *Missiology: An Introduction to the Foundations, History, and Strategies of World Missions.* Nashville: Broadman & Holman, 1998.

McQuilken, Robertson. *The Five Smooth Stones: Essential Principles for Biblical Ministry.* Nashville: Broadman & Holman, 2007.

Chester, Timothy. *The Message of Prayer: Approaching the Throne of Grace.* Downers Grove, IL: InterVarsity Press, 2003.

ENDNOTES

1. Edward S. Woods, *Modern Discipleship* (New York: Association Press, n.d.) p. 92.
2. Woods, p. 89.
3. J. H. Oldham, Source unknown.
4. Adapted from Samuel Zwemer, *Into All the World*, p. 164.

80

THE LORD'S MODEL OF PRAYER FOR THE KINGDOM

Darrell W. Johnson

It has been said the petition in our Lord's prayer—"Our Father in heaven . . . Your kingdom come . . . On earth as it is in heaven (Mt. 6:9-10)"—ought to have come with a warning label.

In using the term "kingdom of God," the Hebrew writers of Scripture were not thinking of a place over which God would rule, nor even of an identifiable people over whom God would rule. Rather, "the kingdom of God" or "kingdom of heaven" is a way of saying, "God is acting as King." The Hebrew prophets longed for the day when God would finally impose and establish His kingly-rule over the entire world.

The term "kingdom of God," therefore, refers to a brand new world order, centered in God's Messiah, in which human beings are re-made into the image of God and all of creation *restored* to God's original design.

The Kingdom at Hand

"In this manner, therefore, pray," says Jesus, "Your kingdom come . . . On earth as it is in heaven." Do you see what Jesus is encouraging us to ask God to do? "O God, hasten the coming of the Day of the Lord when Your kingdom will be present in all its fullness." Hasten the day of reversal and restoration! Hasten the day of the new creation!

We mere human beings are given the privilege of inviting in God's glorious future. We are given the privilege of asking heaven to invade and occupy the earth. As amazing as that is, it does not exhaust the meaning of this prayer, for Jesus taught the prayer in the context of the staggering claim He made in His first public sermon.

The essence of His sermon is recorded in Mark 1:15. Jesus says, "The time is fulfilled, and the kingdom of God is at hand."

"The time is fulfilled." The Greek word for "time" used here is *kairos*. The more usual word is the word *kronos*, from which we get our word "chronological." As my uncle, Emmett Johnson, used to put it, *kronos* is "tick-tock" time, time measured by clocks and calendars. *Kairos* time cannot be so measured. It is "opportunity time." *Kairos* time is that unique moment determined by God for the fulfillment of His divine purposes.

Let it astonish you afresh: Jesus came on the scene and the first thing He says is that "the time is fulfilled"—the *kairos* is now! He did not proclaim, "The Day of the Lord has arrived." The "Day" is still to come. What Jesus claimed was that in Him the unique moment for the fulfillment of promise has *begun*. Because of Jesus every day potentially participates in the *kairos*. Since the first Christmas Eve we are living in "fulfillment time," or as the Apostle Paul puts it in, "the fullness of time" (Gal. 4:4).

Every *kronos* moment can be a *kairos* moment. *Kairos* for what? Time for what? For the in-breaking of the kingdom! "The time is fulfilled," and what does Jesus claim next? "The kingdom of God is at hand." That is the good news, the gospel that Jesus preached and calls us to believe: in Him and because of Him the long awaited kingdom of God, the reign of God, God's new world order, has "come near." Does Jesus mean it is just about to arrive, so we should get ready? Or does He mean it is here—so we should grab hold and enter in? As you can imagine there is considerable scholarly debate on this issue and people want to settle on one or the other side of the issue. I believe, following many scholars from the full range of theological traditions, that taken in light of the whole New Testament, the term "at hand" is used in both senses—both "just about to arrive," and "right here, now." Jesus is announcing that in Him and because of Him the future reign of God is both "just about to dawn on the world" and "is dawning right now."

Thus, after freeing a man from demon possession, Jesus says to the Pharisees: "If I cast out demons by the Spirit of God, surely the kingdom of God has come upon you" (Mt. 12:28). The kingdom has come!

On another occasion Jesus said, "The law and the prophets were until John. Since that time, the kingdom of God has been preached" (Lk. 16:16).

This is why after recording Jesus' staggering claim, the gospel writers go on to record a series of Jesus' mighty deeds. Jesus' deeds validate Jesus' claim. Jesus' miracles demonstrate that indeed the future is breaking into the present, but they do more than validate the claim. They give us a picture of what God's kingdom is all about.[1.] Jesus gives sight to the blind—that is the kingdom of God come near. Jesus causes the lame to walk—that is the kingdom of God come near. Jesus touches and cleanses lepers—that is the kingdom of God come near. Jesus liberates those held captive by demonic powers—that is the kingdom, the new order, breaking into the present. Jesus heals the sick—that is the kingdom of God. Jesus befriends prostitutes and one of them comes and washes His feet with her tears—that is the kingdom. Jesus calms the wind and waves—that is the kingdom. Jesus multiplies the loaves to feed the hungry—that is the kingdom. Jesus champions the powerless; He stands in solidarity with the poor—that is the kingdom, God's new world order.

Jesus unites people the world divides. In His company is Simon the Zealot and Matthew the tax collector, two arch enemies. One represents an oppressive foreign government; the other, revolutionary insurgency—he's a terrorist. But in Jesus they become brothers! That is the kingdom of God come near.

Jesus calls women into His company, granting them dignity, and entrusting them with His gospel message. That is the reign of God, the new world order breaking into the present. Jesus has dinner with Zacchaeus, the corrupt tax collector. After the meal, Zacchaeus denounces his corrupt practices and offers to pay back four-fold those he had cheated. That is the kingdom of God come near. "Today salvation has come to this house," says Jesus (Lk. 19:1-10).

Jesus fills ordinary people with the Holy Spirit; that is the kingdom, the blessing of the future breaking into the present. Jesus raises from the dead the daughter of Jairus, and a widow's son, and Lazarus. That is the kingdom of God! Jesus triumphs over the grave, He is resurrected! That is the reign of God, the new order of existence, breaking into the present from the future. Isn't this exciting?

Yet, a number of times in the Gospels we hear Jesus speaking of the kingdom as still to come. In the upper room, during the first Lord's Supper, Jesus says to the disciples, "I say to you, I will not drink of the fruit of the vine until the kingdom of God comes" (Lk. 22:18). It was during the week before that night that Jesus taught the parables of waiting and watching. These parables call us to look forward to the coming reign of God. Jesus' basic exhortation in each of them is, "Watch!" (Mk. 13:37).

What is going on here? We are faced with the tension we encounter again and again in the New Testament, the tension in which the church must live and serve and pray. The tension is expressed in the phrase, "already, not-yet." In Jesus this glorious, redeeming, recreating reign of God is "already, not-yet." In Jesus God's new world order is already present in some form, but not-yet present in the form it will be on the Day of the Lord.

The Kingdom to Come

Now we are getting to the heart of the second position of our Lord's prayer. What is the nature of this "already, not-yet?" It seems that the "already, not-yet" means "partial" versus "complete."[2.] The kingdom of God is already partially here, not-yet completely here. It seems that the tension is "some" versus "all"—already some of the kingdom, not-yet all, of the kingdom. To a certain degree this is a helpful way of seeing it. But "partial" versus "complete" misses the good news in Jesus' "at hand."

The good news is that the "already, not-yet" is a matter of "veiled" versus "visible." The "already, not-yet" is a matter of "hidden" versus "manifest."[3.] The *really* good news is that in Jesus the new order is already among us, but in a veiled, hidden form. It is not-yet among us in a visible, manifest form. That is the mystery of the kingdom which Jesus taught in His parables.

So what is the nature of His "already, not-yet-ness"? Is it a matter of partial versus complete?

No. Jesus Christ is not partially here. He is already completely here. But He is here in *hidden* form. He is *veiled*, or as I should say, ordinarily veiled. Yet hidden and veiled though He may be, He is *really* and *completely* here. The King is here—right where you are—in all His glory, splendor and power: in your home and in your office and in your hospital room. Jesus Christ is at hand, just behind that thin, permeable veil of hiddenness. If God wanted to, He could pull back that veil and we would all be on our knees.

Because the King has come, the kingdom has come. Because the King is still to come, the kingdom is still to come. Because the King is here, the kingdom is here. But the King is here in veiled form, the kingdom is ordinarily present in veiled form. Is that not why Jesus so often speaks of "having eyes to see and ears to hear"? Not everyone recognizes His already-ness. So not everyone will recognize the already-ness of the reign of God.

You can see that the term "second coming" is a bit misleading, for He is not coming from some far away place. He is breaking through from behind the veil of hidden-ness. When He does, the already present, but ordinarily hidden, kingdom of God will be manifest to all and will overcome and replace all other kingdoms.

So, what does it mean to pray, "Your kingdom come, on earth as it is in heaven"? It means something like "Living God, even before the Day of the Lord, reveal what is invisible, manifest what is hidden."

Can you handle that? That is what those words mean. We ought to pray the words standing on tiptoe!

We mere human beings . . . *we* can ask for the unveiling of the kingdom of God? Yes! If the Church of Jesus has been given this privilege then why haven't we exercised it more intentionally? Perhaps it is because we have not understood the privilege. Perhaps it is that we have not wanted to submit our lives to the King. We may have wanted the benefits and blessings of the kingdom but we have not been willing to align our lives with His rule. Or perhaps it is that we know the coming of God's rule means the end of our rule. Perhaps the Church has not fervently prayed for the kingdom because we know it is dangerous to do so; the King just might answer and start turning everything upside-down!

This is what is happening in the world today. The prayer *is* being answered. This is a *kairos* time. The kingdom of God in Jesus Christ is coming, pressing in on the world from every side; unsettling the status quo. We are in what the Apostle Paul called "birth pangs" (Rom. 8:22). The baby has been conceived and is kicking in the womb and is about to be delivered. It is "at hand." We are on the verge of the delivery. And in the mystery of things, praying the Lord's Prayer is part of the process by which it all happens.

What an incredible privilege, to serve the world as midwives, as labor coaches, praying, "your kingdom come." Will you do it today and in the days to come? Will you dare to invite the invasion of heaven on earth?

Will you pray for the kingdom to come *in you*? Will you pray for the kingdom to come through you? Will you pray for the kingdom to come in and through your church and the other churches of your city or town? Will you pray for the kingdom to come among the nations?

This—and so much more—is what it means to pray the second petition of the Lord's Prayer. "Bring it on! Bring on your revolution. *Reverse* the effects of sin. *Restore* broken humanity. Come and reign without rival in all the earth!"

(This chapter is adapted from the author's previous work, *Fifty-seven Words That Changed the World*, Regent College Publishing, © 2005. It is used here by permission.)

Questions for Further Thought or Discussion

1. Describe the author's views of the Kingdom Come and the Kingdom to Come and analyze why understanding this distinction is important in both personal and corporate praying.
2. Based on your reading of this chapter, paraphrase this passage.
3. Explain how you would use this prayer as a format or template for a corporate prayer gathering. Identify each theme and the textual foundation.

The author: Dr. Darrell W. Johnson is Associate Professor of Pastoral Theology at Regent College in Vancouver, British Columbia, Canada and former Adjunct Professor at Fuller Theological Seminary. He is the author of several books including *Discipleship on the Edge: An Expository Journey through the Book of Revelation.*

SUGGESTED ADDITIONAL READING

White, James Emery. *The Prayer God Longs For.* Downers Grove, IL: InterVarsity Press, 2005.

Pritchard, Ray. *And When You Pray: The Deeper Meaning of the Lord's Prayer.* Nashville: Broadman & Holman Publishing, 2002.

Work, Telford. *Ain't Too Proud to Beg: Living through the Lord's Prayer.* Grand Rapids: Eerdmans Publishing, 2007.

Wright, N.T. *The Lord and His Prayer.* Grand Rapids: Eerdmans Publishing, 1997.

ENDNOTES

1. This was the significant insight of New Testament scholar C.E.B. Cranfield in *The Gospel According to St. Mark* (London: Cambridge University Press, 1959), pp. 66-67.

2 Cranfield, p. 66.

3. Cranfield, p. 66.

CONCLUSION

Even though there are approximately one hundred eighty references to prayer in the Book of Acts, the book is not named The Prayers of the Apostles, but rather The Acts of the Apostles. This number represents an average of one reference to prayer for every twenty-three verses in the book. Thus, the acts are preceded, followed, and occasionally accompanied by prayer, demonstrating the balance of Acts 6:4, "prayer and . . . the ministry of the word."

You may remember from the introduction that Acts 6:4 is where this book began. The early Church was following the balance set forth by Jesus when He "appointed twelve, that they might be with Him and that He might send them out to preach" (Mk. 3:14). Not long after the twelve disciples went forth to proclaim the good news, Jesus called them back to be with Him for awhile. The pattern was set—a balance of being with Jesus and ministering in His name. Similarly, the early Church followed the balance through "prayer and . . . the ministry of the word."

This book has focused heavily on prayer—being with Jesus. Even in certain chapters, when an emphasis was on ministry, it was in direct relationship to prayer. However, lest you think that a relationship with Jesus Christ is all about prayer, let us conclude with a challenge to get "off your knees" and "on your feet." A life that is heavy on ministry and light on prayer will result in burn out—growing weary in well doing. On the other hand a life that is heavy on prayer and light on ministry will result in dysfunctional discipleship.

Through the pages of this book you have studied prayer, prayed prayer, and passed on your new knowledge and practice of prayer. Now it is time to minister. So, to the work—the work of the Word—and hundreds of ways to proclaim the good news.

It is our final hope that as you proclaim "the ministry of the Word" in sermons and songs, through teaching and testifying, by writing and witnessing, you will also enter into the presence of our Lord and give yourself "continually to prayer."

Dan R. Crawford

BIBLIOGRAPHY OF BOOKS ON PRAYER

Compiled by Dan R. Crawford

à Kempis, Thomas. *The Imitation of Christ*. Translated by William Creasy. Notre Dame: Ava Maria Press, 1989.

Ahn, Che. *How to Pray for Healing*. Ventura, CA: Regal Books, 2004.

Aldrich, Joe. *Prayer Summits*. Portland: Multnomah Press, 1992.

Archer, J. W. *Teach Us to Pray*. St. Louis: Concordia Publishing House, 1961.

Almquist, Jenny. *KidsGap: Training Children to be Kingdom Intercessors*. Terre Haute, IN: PrayerShop Publishing, 2007.

Allen, Charles L. *All Things Are Possible Through Prayer*. Westwood, NJ: Fleming H. Revell, 1957.

________. *Prayer Changes Things*. Westwood, NJ: Fleming H. Revell, 1964.

Allen, R. Earl. *Prayers That Changed History*. Nashville: Broadman Press, 1977.

Alves, Elizabeth. *Becoming a Prayer Warrior*. Ventura, CA: Regal Books, 1998.

Anderson, Andy. *Fasting Changed My Life*. Nashville: Broadman Press, 1977.

Anderson, Leith. *Praying to the God You Can Trust*. Minneapolis: Bethany House Publishers, 1998.

________. *When God Says No*. Minneapolis: Bethany House Publishers, 1996.

Anderson, Phil. *The Lord of the Ring: Uncovering the Secret Origins of 24/7 Praying*. Ventura,CA: Regal Books, 2007.

Andrew, Brother. *And God Changed His Mind*. Westwood, NJ: Fleming H. Revell, Chosen Books, 1990.

Anson, Elva. *How to Keep the Family That Prays Together from Falling Apart*. Chicago: Moody Press, 1975.

An Unknown Christian. *The Kneeling Christian*. Grand Rapids: Zondervan, 1971.

Appleton, George, ed. *The Oxford Book of Prayer*, 6th edition. NY: Oxford University Press, 1989.

Arensen, Shel. *Come Away: How to Have a Personal Prayer Retreat*. Grand Rapids: Kregel Publishers, 2003.

Arnold, Clinton. *3 Crucial Questions about Spiritual Warfare*. Grand Rapids: Baker, 1997.

Arthur, Kay. *Lord, Teach Me to Pray*. Eugene, OR: Harvest House Publishers, 1995.

Askew, S. H. *Great Bible Prayers*. Atlanta: Board of Women's Work, Presbyterian Church in the United States, n.d.

Austin, Bill. *How to Get What You Pray For*. Wheaton: Tyndale House, 1984.

Aycock, Don M. *Prayer 101*. Nashville: Broadman & Holman, 1998.

Baillie, John. *A Diary of Private Prayer*. New York: Charles Scribner's Sons, 1949.

Bakke, Robert. *The Concert of Prayer: Back to the Future?* Minneapolis: Evangelical Free Church of America, 1992.

Balsinger, David W., Joette Whims and Melody Hunskor. *The Incredible Power of Prayer*. Wheaton: Tyndale House Publishers, 1998.

Balthasar, Hans Urs von. *Prayer*, London: Geoffrey Chapman, 1963. (Also available in paperback from Ignatius Press.)

Banks, Louis Albert. *A Year's Prayer-Meeting Talks*. New York & London: Funk & Wagnalls Company, 1899.

Barclay, William. *A Guide to Daily Prayer*. New York: Harper & Row Publishers, 1962.

Barry, James C. *Ideas for Effective Prayer Meetings*. Nashville: Convention Press, 1988.

Barth, Karl. *Prayer*. Translated by Sara F. Terrien. Philadelphia: Westminster Press, 1949.

Bast, Henry. *The Practice of Prayer.* Grand Rapids: Temple Time, Inc., 1971.

Baughen, Michael. *Breaking the Prayer Barrier: Getting Through to God.* Wheaton: Harold Shaw Publishers, 1981.

Bauman, Edward J. *Intercessory Prayer.* Philadelphia: Westminster, 1958.

Beall, James Lee. *The Adventure of Fasting.* Weatwood, NJ: Fleming H. Revell, 1974.

Beasley-Topliffe, Keith. *Surrendering to God: Living the Covenant Prayer.* Brewster, MA: Paraclete Press, 2001.

Bell, James S, Jr., ed. *Memos to God: A Prayer Journal Based on the Writings of E. M. Bounds.* Chicago: Moody Press, 1994.

Beltz, Bob. *Becoming a Man of Prayer.* Colorado Springs, CO: NavPress, 1996.

Bennett, Arthur G. *The Valley of Vision: A Collection of Puritan Prayers and Devotions.* Carlisle, PA: Banner of Truth, 2003.

Bennett, Rita. *Inner Wholeness Through the Lord's Prayer.* Tarrytown, NY: Chosen Books, Fleming H. Revell Company, 1991.

Bergan, Jacqueline Syrup and S. Marie Schwan. *Surrender: A Guide to Prayer.* Winona, MN: Saint Mary's Press, 1986.

Besnard, A. M. *Take a Chance on God: A Guide to Christian Prayer.* Denville, NJ: Dimension Books, 1977.

Bevington, G.C. *Modern Miracles Through Prayer and Faith.* Salem, OH: Schmul Publishing Co., n.d.

Bewes, Richard. *Talking About Prayer.* Downers Grove, IL: InterVarsity Press, 1979.

Bezek, Cynthia. *Come Away with Me:* Pray! *Magazine's Guide to Prayer Retreats.* Colorado Springs, CO: NavPress, 2008.

Bickersteth, Edward. *A Treatise on Prayer; Designed to Assist in the Devout Discharge of that Duty.* New York: American Tract Society, n.d.

Bickle, Mike. *After God's Own Heart.* Lake Mary, FL: Charisma House, 2004.

________. *Passion for Jesus: Perfecting Extravagant Love for God.* Lake Mary, FL: Creation House, 1993.

Bickel, Bruce, and Stan Jantz. *Bruce and Stan's Pocket Guide to Prayer.* Eugene, OR: Harvest House, 2000.

Biehl, Bob and J. Hagelganz. *Praying: How to Start and Keep Going.* Ventura,

CA: Gospel Light, 1976.

Billheimer, Paul E. *Destined for the Throne.* Fort Washington, PA: Christian Literature Crusade, 1975.

Bisagno, John. *The Power of Positive Praying.* Grand Rapids: Zondervan, 1965.

Blaiklock, E.M. *The Positive Power of Prayer.* Ventura, CA: Regal Books, 1974.

Blackaby, Henry. *Experiencing Prayer with Jesus.* Sisters, OR: Multnomah Publishers, 2006.

________. *Hearing God's Voice.* Nashville: Broadman & Holman, 2002.

________. *A God-Centered Church.* Nashville: Broadman & Holman, 2007.

Blackaby, Henry T and Claude V. King. *Faith Encounter: Experiencing God Through Prayer, Humility and Heartfelt Desire.* Nashville: Broadman & Holman, 1996.

Blackaby, Henry, and Richard Blackaby. *When God Speaks: How to Recognize God's Voice and Respond.* Nashville: LifeWay Publishers, 1995.

Blackwood, Andrew W. *Leading in Public Prayer.* New York: Abingdon Press, 1958.

Blocker, Simon. *How to Achieve Personality Through Prayer.* Grand Rapids: Eerdmans, 1954.

Bloesch, Donald G. *The Struggle of Prayer.* Colorado Springs, CO: Helmers and Howard, 1988.

Boa, Ken. *Face to Face: Praying the Scriptures for Intimate Worship*, 2 vols., Grand Rapids: Zondervan, 1997.

Bondi, Roberta. *To Pray & To Love: Conversations on Prayer with the Early Church.* Fortress Press, 1991.

Bonhoffer, Deitrich. *The Cost of Discipleship.* Translated by R.H. Fuller. New York: Macmillan Publishing Company, 1963.

Borst, James. *Contemplative Prayer: A Guide for Today's Catholic.* Liguori Publications, 1993.

Bounds, E.M. *Power Through Prayer.* Grand Rapids: Baker Book House, 1972.

________. *The Best of E.M. Bounds on Prayer.* Grand Rapids: Baker Book House, 1981.

________. *Prayer and Spiritual Warfare.* New Kensington, PA: Whitaker House, 2002.

________. *Selections: The Compete Words of E.M. Bounds on Prayer,* Grand Rapids: Baker Books: 1990.

________. *Essentials of Prayer.* New Kensington, PA: Whitaker House Publishers, 1994.

________. *Preacher and Prayer.* Chicago: The Christian Witness, n.d.

________. *A Treasury of Prayer.* Minneapolis, MN: Bethany House Publishers, 1981.

Bradshaw, Paul F. *Daily Prayer in the Early Church: A Study of the Origin and Early Development of the Divine Office.* New York: Oxford University Press, 1982.

Brane, Grace Adolphsen. *Receptive Prayer: A Christian Approach to Meditation.* CBP Press, St. Louis, 1985.

Brandt, R.L. *Praying with Paul.* Grand Rapids: Baker Book House, 1966.

Brase, Lee. *Approaching God.* Colorado Springs, CO: NavPress, 2003.

Briggs, Edward. *A Pilgrim's Guide to Prayer,* Nashville: Broadman Press, 1987.

Bright, Bill. *The Transforming Power of Fasting and Prayer.* Orlando: New Life Publications, 1997.

________. *The Coming Revival: God's Call to Fast, Pray and "Seek God's Face."* Orlando: New Life Publications, 1995.

Bright, Vonette and Ben A. Jennings. *Unleashing the Power of Prayer.* Chicago: Moody Press, 1989.

Bringman, Dale S. and Frank W. Klos. *Prayer and the Devotional Life.* Philadelphia: Lutheran Church Press, 1964.

Brown, John. *An Exposition of Our Lord's Intercessory Prayer.* Grand Rapids: Baker Book House, 1980.

Brown, John. *Pious and Elaborate Treatise Concerning Prayer; and the Answer of Prayer.* Edmonton, AB: Still Waters Revival Books, 1745.

Brown, L. B. *The Human Side of Prayer: The Psychology of Praying.* Birmingham, AL: Religious Education Press, 1994.

Brown, Steve. *Approaching God, How to Pray.* Melton Keynes, England: Summit Publications, Ltd., 1996.

Brownson, William C. *Courage to Pray.* Grand Rapids: Baker Book House, 1989.

Brueggemann, Walter. *Praying the Psalms.* Winona, MI: Saint Mary's Press, 1993.

Bryant, Al, compiled and edited. *Sermon Outlines on Prayer.* Grand Rapids: Zondervan, 1956.

Bryant, David. *In the Gap.* Ventura, CA: Gospel Light/Regal Books, 1989.

________. *Concerts of Prayer.* Ventura, CA: Regal Books, 1988.

Bunyan, John. *How to Pray in the Spirit.* L. G. Parkhurst, Jr. ed. Grand Rapids: Kregel, 1991.

________. *Prayer.* London: Banner of Truth Trust, 1965.

Burr, Richard A. *Developing Your Secret Closet of Prayer.* Camp Hill, PA: Christian Publications, 1998.

Buttrick, George A. *So We Believe, So We Pray.* Nashville: Abingdon Press, 1951.

________. *The Power of Prayer Today.* Waco: Word Books, 1970.

________. *Prayer.* New York and Nashville: Abingdon-Cokesbury Press, 1952.

Butts, David. *Upfront: Training Prayer Teams for Ministry* (DVD). Terre Haute, IN: PrayerShop Publishing, 2007.

Butts, David and Kim. *Pray Like the King: Lessons from the Prayers of Israel's Kings.* Terre Haute, IN: PrayerShop Publishing, 2007.

Butts, Kim. *The Praying Family: Creative Ways to Pray Together.* Chicago: Moody Publishers, 2003.

Callahan, William R. *Noisy Contemplation: Deep Prayer for Busy People.* Hyattsville, MD: Quixote Center, Inc., 1982.

Campbell, James M. *The Place of Prayer in the Christian Religion.* New York: Methodist Book Concern, 1915.

Campbell, Wesley and Stacey. *Praying the Bible: The Pathway to Spirituality.* Ventura, CA: Regal Books, 2003.

Carden, John, Compiler. *A World At Prayer: The New Ecumenical Prayer Guide.* Mystic, CT: Twenty-Third Publications, 1990.

Carey, Walter J. *Prayer and Some of Its Difficulties.* London: A.R. Mowbray & Co., 1914.

Carleton, J. Paul. *Rejoicing in Prayer.* Shawnee, OK: Oklahoma Baptist University Press, 1949.

Carroll, B. H. *Messages on Prayer.* Nashville: Broadman Press, 1942.

Carruth, Thomas Albert. *Prayer: A Christian Ministry.* Nashville: Tidings, 1971.

Carse, James P. *The Silence of God.* New York: MacMillan, 1985.

Carson, D.A. *Teach Us to Pray: Prayer in the Bible and the World.* Grand Rapids: Baker Book House, 1989.

________. *A Call to Spiritual Reformation.* Grand Rapids: Baker Book House, 1992.

Carter, Tom. *They Knew How to Pray: 15 Secrets from the Prayer Lives of Bible Heroes.* Grand Rapids: Kregel, 2003.

Carver, W.O. *Thou When Thou Prayest.* Nashville: Broadman Press, 1987.

Casteel, John L. *Rediscovering Prayer.* New York: Association Press, NY, 1955.

Cedar, Paul. *A Life of Prayer.* Nashville: Word Books, 1998.

Celebrate Jesus 2000 Prayer Committee. *Praying Your Friends to Christ.* Alpharetta, GA: North American Mission Board of the Southern Baptist Convention, 1998.

Chadwick, Samuel. *The Path of Prayer.* London: Hodder and Stoughton, 1931.

Chafer, Lewis Sperry. *True Evangelism: Winning Souls Through Prayer.* Grand Rapids: Kregel Publications, 1993.

Chambers, Oswald. *If You Will Ask: Reflections on the Power of Prayer.* Grand Rapids: Discovery House Publishers, 1958.

Chambers, Talbot W. *The New York City Noon Prayer Meeting: A Simple Prayer Gathering That Changed the World.* Wagner Publications, 2002.

Chapell, Bryan. *Praying Backwards: Transform Your Life by Beginning in Jesus' Name*, Grand Rapids: Baker Books, 2005.

Charlesworth, James H., Mark Harding and Mark Kiley eds. *The Lord's Prayer and Other Prayer Texts from the Greco-Roman Era.* Valley Forge, PA: Trinity Press International, 1994.

Chavda, Mahesh. *The Hidden Power of Prayer and Fasting.* Shippensburg, PA: Destiny Image Publishers, 2007.

Chester, Tomothy. *The Message of Prayer: Approaching the Throne of Grace.* Downers Grove, IL: InterVarsity Press, 2003.

Cho, Paul Y. *Prayer: Key to Revival.* Waco: Word Books, 1984.

________. *Praying With Jesus.* Altamonte Springs, FL: Creation House, 1987.

Christenson, Evelyn. *What Happens When Women Pray?* Wheaton: Victor Books, 1985.

________. *What Happens When God Answers.* Waco: Word Publishers: 1986.

________. *What Happens When We Pray for Our Families.* Wheaton: Victor Books, 1992.

________. *Unleashing God's Power: What God Does When Women Pray.* Nashville: Word Books, 2000.

________. *Praying God's Way.* Eugene, OR: Harvest House Publishers, 1996.

Clements, Ronald E. *In Spirit and in Trust: Insights from Biblical Prayers.* Atlanta: John Knox Press, 1985.

Chervin, Ronda De Sola. *Prayers of the Women Mystics.* Ann Arbor, MI: Servant Publications, 1992.

Coleman, Robert E. *Introducing the Prayer Cell.* Huntington Valley, PA: Christian Outreach, 1960.

________. *One Divine Moment*, Old Tappan, New Jersey: Fleming Revell, 1970.

Collins, Donald E. *Like Trees That Grow Beside a Stream: Praying Through the Psalms.* Nashville: Upper Room Press, 1991.

Constable, Thomas L. *Talking to God: What the Bible Teaches about Prayer.* Grand Rapids: Baker Books, 1995.

Copeland, Germaine. *Prayers That Avail Much, Vol. 1.* Tulsa, OK: Harrison House, Inc. 1989.

Cornwall, Judson. *Praying the Scriptures.* Orlando: Creation House. 1998.

________. *The Secret of Personal Prayer.* Altamonte Springs, FL: Creation House, 1988.

Counsell, Michael, Compiler. *2000 Years of Prayer.* Harrisburg, PA: Morehouse Publishing, 1999.

Cove, Gordon. *Revival Now through Prayer and Fasting.* Salem, OH: Schmul Publishing Co., 1988.

Cowan, John F. *New Life in the Old Prayer-Meeting.* New York: Fleming H. Revell Co., 1906.

Cowart, John W. *Why Don't I Get What I Pray For?* Downers Grove, IL: InterVarsity Press, 1993.

Crabb, Larry. *The Papa Prayer: The Prayer You've Never Prayed.* Nashville: Thomas Nelson, 2006.

Crawford, Dan R. and Calvin Miller. *Prayer Walking: A Journey of Faith.* Chattanooga, TN: AMG Publishers, 2002.

Crawford, Dan R. and Al Meredith. *One Anothering: Praying Through Challenges Together.* Webb City, MO: Covenant Publishing, 2000.

Crawford, Dan R. *The Prayer-Shaped Disciple.* Peabody, MA: Hendrickson Publishers, 1999.

Crump, David. *Knocking on Heaven's Door.* Grand Rapids: Baker Academic, 2006.

________. *Jesus the Intercessor: Prayer and Christology in Luke-Acts.* Tübingen: J.C.B. Mohr, 1992. Reprint, Grand Rapids: Baker, 1999.

Curran, Sue. *The Praying Church.* Lakeland, FL: Shekinah Publishing House. 1987.

Cymbala, Jim. *Fresh Wind, Fresh Fire.* Grand Rapids: Zondervan Publishing House, 1997.

________. *Break Through Prayer.* Grand Rapids: Zondervan Publishing House, 2003.

Daily Prayers for the Lord's Hidden Ones. Boston: American Tract Society, n.d.

Daskam, Max F., Editor. *Meditations and Prayers of William L. Sullivan.* New York and Nashville: Abingdon Press, 1961.

Dawson, John. *Taking Our Cities for God.* Lake Mary, FL: Creation House Publishers, 1989.

Dawson, Joy. *Intercession, Thrilling and Fulfilling.* Seattle: YWAM Publishers, 1997.

Day, Albert Edward. *Existance Under God: The Christian's Life of Prayer.* New York and Nashville: Abingdon Press, 1953.

________. *An Autobiography of Prayer.* New York: Harper & Brothers Publishers, 1952.

Dean, Jennifer Kennedy. *Legacy of Prayer.* Birmingham: New Hope Publishers, 2002.

Deitz, Eddie. *What Does Prayer Enable God to Do?* Cherokee, NC: Mountain

Gospel Publishing, 1997.

Demaray, Donald E. *How Are You Praying?* Grand Rapids: Asbury Press, 1985.

________. *Alive to God Through Prayer.* Grand Rapids: Baker Book House, 1965.

DeMoss, Nancy Leigh. *A Place of Quiet Rest: Finding Intimacy with God Through a Daily Devotional Life.* Chicago: Moody Publishers, 2002.

Deweese, Charles W. *Prayer in Baptist Life.* Nashville: Broadman, 1986.

Dilday, Russell H, Jr. *Prayer Meeting Resources.* Nashville: Convention Press, 1977.

Dobson, Shirley. *Certain Peace in Uncertain Times: Embracing Prayer in an Anxious Age.* Portland: Multnomah Publishers, 2002.

Dood, Brian J. *Praying Jesus's Way.* Downers Grove, IL: InterVarsity Press, 1997.

Doohan, Helen and Leonard. *Prayer in the New Testament: Make your Requests Known to God.* Collegeville, MN: The Liturgical Press, 1992.

Dodd, M.E. *The Prayer Life of Jesus.* Wyckoff, NJ: Doran Co., 1923.

Donehoo, Paris. *Prayer in the Life of Jesus.* Nashville: Broadman Press, 1984.

Dossey, *Healing Words: The Power of Prayer and the Practice of Medicine.* San Francisco: HarperSanFrancisco, 1993.

Downame, George. *Godly and Learned Treatise of Prayer.* London: Roger Daniel, 1640.

Drumwright, Huber L. *Prayer Rediscovered.* Nashville: Broadman, 1978.

Drumwright, Minette. *The Life That Prays,* Birmingham, AL: Woman's Missionary Union, 2001.

Duewel, Wesley L. *Touch the World Through Prayer.* Grand Rapids: Asbury Press, 1986.

________. *Mighty Prevailing Prayer.* Grand Rapids: Asbury Press, 1990.

Duke, Dee. *Prayer Quest: Breaking Through to Your God-Given Dreams and Destiny.* Colorado Springs, CO: NavPress, 2004.

Dunnam, Maxie. *The Workbook of Intercessory Prayer.* Nashville: The Upper Room, 1979.

________. *The Workbook of Living Prayer.* Nashville: The Upper Room, 1974.

Dunn, Philip. *Prayer Language of the Soul.* New York: Daybreak Books, 1997.

Dunn, Ronald. *Don't Just Stand There, Pray Something.* Nashville: Thomas Nelson, 1991.

Durham, Maxie D., Compiler. *Prayer in My Life.* Nashville: Parthenon Press, 1974.

Dye, Colin. *Sword of the Spirit: Effective Prayer.* England: Sovereign World Ltd, 1997.

Eastman, Dick. *A Celebration of Praise.* Grand Rapids: Baker Book House, 1984.

________. *Beyond Imagination.* Grand Rapids: Chosen Books, 1997.

________. *Heights of Delight.* Ventura. CA: Regal, 2002.

________. *Love on Its Knees.* Grand Rapids: Chosen Books, 1989.

________. *No Easy Road.* Grand Rapids: Baker Book House, 1971.

________. *Pathways of Delight.* Ventura, CA: Regal, 2002.

________. *Rivers of Delight.* Ventura, CA: Regal, 2002.

________. *The Hour That Changes the World.* Grand Rapids: Baker Book House, 1978.

________. *The Jericho Hour.* Orlando: Creation House, 1994.

Eastman, Dick and Hayford, Jack. *31 Days Meditating on the Majesty of Jesus.* Wheaton: Tyndale House, 2007.

Eaton, Kenneth O. *Men on Their Knees.* New York: Abingdon Press, 1956.

________. *Men Who Talked With God.* New York and Nashville: Abingdon Press, 1964.

Edwards, Jonathan. *A Call to United, Extraordinary Prayer.* Scotland: Christian Focus Public, 2003.

Eims, Leroy. *Prayer: More than Words.* Colorado Springs, CO: NavPress, 1984.

Elliff, Thomas D. *Praying for Others.* Nashville: Broadman, 1979.

________. *A Passion for Prayer: Experiencing Deeper Intimacy with God.* Wheaton: Crossway Publishing, 2001.

Elliott, Norman. *How to Be the Lord's Prayer.* Waco: Word Books, 1968.

Ellul, Jacques. Translated by C. Edward Hopkin. *Prayer and Modern Man.* New York: Seabury Press, 1970.

Elmore, Tim, John D. Hull, and John C. Maxwell. *Pivotal Praying: Connecting With God in Times of Great Need.* Nashville: Thomas Nelson, 2002.

Emmons, Grover Carlton. *Alone with God.* Nashville: The Upper Room, 1945.

Engstrom, Theodore W. *Workable Prayer Meeting Programs.* Grand Rapids: Zondervan Publishing House, 1955.

Epp, Theodore H. *Praying with Authority.* Lincoln, NE: Back to the Bible, 1965.

Erickson, Kenneth A. *Power of Praise.* St. Louis: Concordia, 1984.

Escott, Harry, Ed. *Isaac Watts's A Guide to Prayer.* London: Epworth Press, 1948.

Evans, Mike. *The Unanswered Prayers of Jesus.* Minnneapolis: Bethany House Publishers, 2003.

Ferre, Nels F.S. *A Theology for Christian Prayer.* Nashville: Nashville Tidings, 1963.

Fife, Eric. *Prayer: Common Sense and the Bible.* Grand Rapids: Zondervan Publishing House, 1976.

Finney, Charles G. *Prevailing Prayer.* Grand Rapids: Kregel Publications, 1965.

________. *Principles of Prayer.* Minneapolis: Bethany House Publishers, 1980.

Fisher, Fred. *Prayer in the New Testament.* Philadelphia: Westminster Press, 1964.

Fletcher, Kingsley A. *Prayer and Fasting.* New Kensington, PA: Whitaker House, 1992.

Floyd, Ronnie W. *The Power of Prayer and Fasting.* Nashville: Broadman & Holman, 1997.

________. *How to Pray.* Nashville: Word Publishing, 1999.

Forsyth, P.T. *The Soul of Prayer.* Grand Rapids: Eerdmans, 1960.

Fosdick, Harry Emerson. *The Meaning of Prayer.* New York: Association Press, 1915.

Foster, Richard A. *Meditative Prayer.* Downers Grove, IL: InterVarsity Press, 1983.

Foster, Richard J. *Celebration of Discipline.* San Francisco: Harper Publishers, 1988.

________. *Prayer: Finding the Heart's True Home.* San Francisco: Harper Publishers, 1992.

Freer, Harold Wiley and Hall, Francis B. *Two or Three Together.* New York: Harper & Row, 1954.

Franklin, John, Compiler. *A House of Prayer.* Nashville: Broadman & Holman, 1999.

________. *And the Place Was Shaken: How to Lead a Powerful Prayer Meeting.* Nashville: Broadman & Holman, 2005.

Frizzell, Gregory R. *Local Associations and United Prayer.* Memphis: Riverside Printing, 1996.

________. *How to Develop a Powerful Prayer Life.* Memphis: Master Design, 1999.

Fromer, Margaret and Sharrel Keyes. *Let's Pray Together.* Wheaton, IL: Harold Shaw Publishers, 1974.

Fuller, Cheri. *The One Year Book of Praying Through the Bible.* Wheaton, IL: Tyndale House Publishers, Inc., 2003.

________. *Loving Your Spouse through Prayer (How to Pray God's Word into Your Marriage)* Nashville: Thomas Nelson, 2007.

Gaddy, C. Weldon. *A Love Affair with God; Finding Freedom & Intimacy in Prayer.* Nashville: Broadman & Holman, 1995.

Gesswein, Armin R. *With One Accord in One Place.* Harrisburg, PA: Christian Publications, Inc., 1978.

Getz, Gene A. *Praying For One Another.* Wheaton, IL: Victor Books, 1988.

Gill, Frederick C. *John Wesley's Prayers.* London: The Epworth Press,1951. Reprint, 1959.

Gills, James P. *The Prayerful Spirit: Passion for God, Compassion for People.* Tarpon Springs, FL: Love Press, 1994.

Goetsch, Ronald W. *Power Through Prayer.* St. Louis: Concordia, 1959.

Goldsworthy, Graeme. *Prayer and the Knowledge of God: What the Whole Bible Teaches.* Downers Grove, IL: InterVarsity Press, 2004.

Gooding, Terry. *Paths of Gold: Praying the Way to Christ for Lost Friends and Family.* Colorado Springs, CO: NavPress, 2002.

Gordon, S.D. *Quiet Talks on Prayer.* Westwood, NJ: Fleming H. Revell, 1904.

________. *Five Laws That Govern Prayer.* Westwood, NJ: Fleming H. Revell, 1925.

Goodwin, Thomas. *The Return of Prayers.* Grand Rapids: Baker, 1979.

Goforth, Rosaland. *How I Know God Answers Prayer.* Elkhart, IN: Bethel Publishing, n.d.

Gossett, Don. *There's Dynamite in Praise.* Springfield, PA: Whitaker House, 1974.

Gothard, Bill. *The Power of Crying Out: When Prayer Becomes Mighty.* Portland: Multnomah Publishers, 2002.

Graf, Jonathan. *The Power of Personal Prayer.* Colorado Springs: NavPress, 2002.

Graf, Jonathan and Lani Hinkle. eds. *My House Shall Be a House of Prayer.* Colorado Spring, CO: *Pray!* Books, 2001.

Graham, Billy. *Angels: God's Secret Agents.* Nashville: Thomas Nelson, 2000.

Grant, Peter. *The Power of Intercession.* Ann Arbor, MI: Servant Publications, 1984.

Gray, Donald. *All Majesty and Power: An Anthology of Royal Prayers.* Grand Rapids: William B. Eerdmans Publishing Company, 2000.

Green, Thomas H. *When the Well Runs Dry: Prayer Beyond Beginnings.* Notre Dame, IN: Ave Maria Press, 1979.

Greig, Pete. *God on Mute: Engaging the Silence of Unanswered Prayer.* Ventura, CA: Regal Books, 2007.

Greig, Peter and Dave Roberts. *Red Moon Rising: How 24-7 Prayer Is Awakening a Generation.* Lake Mary, FL: Relevant Books, 2005.

Grenz, Stanley J. *Prayer: The Cry for the Kingdom.* Peabody, MA: Hendrickson Publishers, 1988.

Griffin, Emilie. *Clinging: The Experience of Prayer.* New York: Harper & Row Publishers, 1984.

Grubb, Norman. *Rees Howell Intercessor.* Fort Washington, PA: Christian Literature Crusade, 1967.

Guardini, Romano. *Prayer in Practice.* Garden City, NY: Image Books, 1963.

Guest, John. *Only a Prayer Away.* Ann Arbor, MI: Vine Books, 1985.

Gunsaulus, Frank W. *The Prayers of Frank W. Gunsaulus.* New York: Fleming H. Revell Company, 1922.

Gutzke, Manford. *Plain Talk on Prayer.* Grand Rapids: Baker Book House, 1973.

Haden, Ben. *Pray: Don't Settle for a Two-Bit Prayer Life*. Nashville: Thomas Nelson, 1974.

Hallesby, O. *Prayer*. Minneapolis: Augsburg Publishing House, 1934.

Hallock, E.F. *Always in Prayer*. Nashville: Broadman, 1966.

________. *Prayer and Meditation*. Nashville: Broadman Press, 1940.

Hamilton, Herbet Alfred. *Conversation with God: Learning to Pray*. New York: Abingdon Press, 1961.

Hammond, Peter. *The Power of Prayer Handbook*. Cape Town, South Africa: Christian Liberty Books, 2007.

Handyside, James. *Melt the Icebergs! A Fresh Look at Prayer*. Asheville: Revival Literature, 1977.

Hanne, John Anthony. *Prayer or Pretense*? Grand Rapids: Zondervan Publishing House, 1975.

Harkness, Georgia. *Prayer and the Common Life*. New York: Abington-Cokesbury, 1948.

________. *How to Find Prayer More Meaningful*. Nashville: The Upper Room, 1946.

Harner, Philip B. *Understanding the Lord's Prayer*. Philadelphia: Fortress Press, 1975.

Harper, Steve. *Prayer Ministry in the Local Church*. Grand Rapids: Baker Book House, 1976.

________. *Praying Through the Lord's Prayer*. Nashville: Upper Room Books, 1992.

Harrell Irene. *Prayerables: Meditations of a Homemaker*. Waco, TX: Word Books, 1967.

________. *Prayerables II: Ordinary Days with an Extraordinary God*. Waco, TX: Word Books, 1971.

Harries, Richard. *Prayer and the Pursuit of Happiness*. Grand Rapids: Eerdmans, 1985.

Hart, Dirk J. *Five Sermons on Prayer*. London, ON: 1978.

Hartley, Fred A. III. *Prayer on Fire: What Happens When the Holy Spirit Ignites Your Prayers*. Colorado Springs, CO: *Pray!* Books, 2006.

Harvey, E.F. and L. *Kneeling We Triumph, Book One*. Hampton, TN: Harvey & Tait, 1982.

________. *Kneeling We Triumph, Book Two*. Hampton, TN: Harvey &

Tait, 1992.

________. *Royal Exchange Thirty-one Stimulating Readings on Prayer.* Yanceyville, N.C.: Harvey Christian Publishers, n.d.

Haskin, Dorothy. *A Practical Primer on Prayer.* Chicago: Moody Press, 1951.

Hawkins, Frank. *The Church at Prayer.* Nashville: Broadman, 1986.

Hawthorne, Steve. *PrayerWalk Organizer Guide.* Austin, TX: PrayerWalk, USA, 1996.

________. *Seek God for the City.* Austin, TX: WayMakers 2007.

Hawthorne, Steve and Graham Kendrick. *Prayerwalking: Praying On-Site with Insight.* Orlando: Creation House, 1992.

Hayford, Jack W. *Prayer Is Invading the Impossible.* Jacksonville, FL: Logos International, 1977.

Hellberg, Marilyn Morgan. *Where Soul & Spirit Meet: Praying with the Bible.* Nashville: Abingdon Press, 1986.

Helms, Elaine. *If My People . . . Pray.* Marietta, GA: Church Prayer Ministries, 2000.

Hemphill, Ken. *The Prayer of Jesus.* Nashville: Broadman & Holman, 2001.

Hendrix, John & Ann B. Cannon. *Circle Your World with Prayer.* Nashville: LifeWay Press, 2000.

Henderson, Daniel. *Fresh Encounters: Experiencing Transformation Through United Worship-Based Prayer.* Colorado Springs, CO: NavPress, 2004.

________. *PrayZING! Creative Prayer Experiences from A to Z.* Colorado Springs, CO: NavPress, 2007.

Herman, Bridgid E. *Creative Prayer.* New York: Harper & Row Publishers, n.d.

Herring, Ralph A. *Cycle of Prayer.* Nashville: Broadman, 1966.

Higgs, Mike. *Youth Ministry on Your Knees: Mentoring and Mobilizing Young People to Pray.* Colorado Springs, CO: *Pray!* Books, 2004.

Hiebert, Edmond. *Working with God Through Intercessory Prayer.* Greenville, SC: Bob Jones University Press, 1991.

Higley, Sandra. *A Year of Prayer Events for Your Church.* Terre Haute: IN: PrayerShop Publishing, 2007.

Hinson, E. Glenn. *The Reaffirmation of Prayer.* Nashville: Broadman, 1979.

Holland, Tom. *Talking it Over, Conversations on Prayer.* Brigend, Wales: Bryntirion Press, 1998.

Hollars, James E. *Be Still and Know.* Fort Worth, TX: Taylor Jewell Press, 2006.

Howard, Evan B. *Praying the Scriptures.* Downers Grove, IL: InterVarsity Press, 1999.

Howington, Nelan P. *The Vigil of Prayer.* Nashville: Broadman Press, 1987.

Hubbard, David Allan. *The Practice of Prayer.* Downers Grove, IL: InterVarsity Press, 1983.

Huebsch, Bill. *A New Look at Prayer.* Mystic, CT: Twenty-Third Publications, 1991.

Huegel, F.J. *The Ministry of Intercession.* Minneapolis: Bethany, Dimension Books, 1971.

Huffman, John A, Jr. *Forgive Us Our Prayers.* Wheaton, IL: Victor Books, 1980.

Huggett, Joyce. *Listening to God.* London: Hodder and Stoughton, 1986.

Hughes, R. Kent. *Abba Father: The Lord's Pattern for Prayer.* Wheaton, IL: Crossway Books, 1986.

Hulstrand, Donald. *The Praying Church.* New York: Seabury Press, 1977.

Humphries, Fisher. *Heart for Prayer.* Nashville: Broadman Press, 1980.

Hunt, Art. *Praying With the One You Love.* Sisters, OR: Questar Publishers, Inc., 1996.

Hunt, T. W. *The Doctrine of Prayer.* Nashville: Convention Press, 1986.

Hunt, T. W., Compiler. *Church Prayer Ministry Manual.* Nashville: Baptist Sunday School Board, S. B. C., 1992.

Hunt, T. W. and Catherine Walker. *PrayerLife: Walking in Fellowship with God.* Nashville: Sunday School Board, S. B. C., 1987.

Hunt, T.W. and Claude V. King. *In God's Presence.* Nashville: LifeWay Press, 1994.

Hunter, W. Bingham. *The God Who Hears.* Downers Grove, IL: InterVarsity Press, 1986.

Huss, John. *Paths to Power: A Guide to Dynamic Midweek Prayer Meetings.* Grand Rapids: Zondervan Publishing House, 1958.

Hybels, Bill. *Too Busy Not to Pray.* Downers Grove, IL: InterVarsity Press,

1988, 1998.

________. *Prayer: Opening Your Heart to God.* InterActions Small Group Series. Grand Rapids: Zondervan Publishing House, 1997.

Ironside, H. A. *Praying in the Holy Spirit.* New York: Loizeaux Brothers Publishers, n.d.

Jacobs, Cindy. *Possessing the Gates of the Enemy.* Grand Rapids: Chosen Books, 1991.

Jenkins, David L. *Great Prayers of the Bible.* Nashville: Broadman Press, 1990.

Jennings, Ben. *The Arena of Prayer.* Orlando: New Life Publications, 1999.

Jennings, Jeremy. *The Church on Its Knees: Dynamic Prayer in the Local Church.* London: HTB Publications 1998.

Jeremiah, David. *Prayer: The Great Adventure.* Sisters, OR: Multnomah Publishers, 1997.

________. *The Prayer Matrix: Plugging into the Unseen Reality.* Sisters. OR: Multnomah Publishers, 2002.

________. *What the Bible Says about Angels.* Sisters, OR: Multnomah Publishers, 1998.

Jeremias, Joachim. *The Lord's Prayer*, trans. by John Reumann. Philadelphia: Fortress Press, 1964.

________. *The Prayers of Jesus.* Philidalphia: Fortress Press, 4th printing 1989.

Johnson, Ben Campbell. *To Pray God's Will.* Philadelphia: Westminster Press, 1987.

Johnson, Bill. *When Heaven Invades Earth.* Shippensburg, PA: Destiny Image Publishers, 2005.

Johnson, Jan. *When the Soul Listens.* Colorado Springs, CO: NavPress, 1999.

Johnson, Terry L. *When Grace Comes Alive.* Ross-shire, Great Britain: Christian Focus Publications, 2003.

Johnstone, Patrick, and Jason Mandryk. *Operation World*, 5th Edition. Grand Rapids: Zondervan Publishing House, 1993.

________. *Operation World: 21st Century Edition.* Minneapolis: Bethany House, 2001.

Jones, E. Stanley. *How to Pray.* Nashville: Abingdon Press, 1979.

Jones, Timothy. *Prayer's Apprentice*. Nashville: Word Publishing, 2000.

Jones, Timothy, and Jill Zook-Jones. *Prayer: Discovering What Scripture Says*. Wheaton, IL: Harold Shaw Publications, 1993.

Kamstra, Douglas A. *The Praying Church Idea Book*. Faith Alive Christian Resources, 2001.

Keating, Charles J. *Who We Are Is How We Pray*. Mystic, CT: Twenty-Third Publications, 1987.

________. *Open Mind, Open Heart: The Contemplative Dimension of the Gospel*. Rockport, MA: Element, 1986.

Keller, W. Philip. *A Layman Looks at the Lord's Prayer*. Chicago: Moody Press, 1976.

Kelly, Douglas F. *If God Already Knows, Why Pray?* Brentwood, TN: Wolgemuth & Hyatt Publishers, 1989.

Kelsey, Morton T. *The Other Side of Silence: A Guide to Christian Meditation*. New York: Paulist Press, 1976.

Kemper, Frederick W. *Prayers for the Day*. St. Louis: Concordia Publishing House, 1980.

Kerr, Clarence W. *Pattern for Powerful Praying*. Los Angeles: Cowman Publishing Company, 1958.

Killinger, John. *Bread for the Wilderness, Wine for the Journey: The Miracle of Prayer & Meditation*. Waco: Word Books, 1976.

Kimmel, Jo. *Steps to Prayer Power*. Nashville: Abingdon Press, 1972.

King, Geoffrey R. *Let Us Pray*. Fort Washington, PA: Christian Literature Crusade, n.d.

Kinne, C. J. *Prayer: The Secret of Power*. Kansas City, MO: Nazarene Publishing House, 1913.

Kriegbaum, Richard. *Leadership Prayers*. Wheaton, IL: Tyndale House Publishers, 1998.

Kroll, Woodrow. *When God Doesn't Answer*. Grand Rapids: Baker Book House, 1997.

Knorr, Dandi Daley. *When the Answer Is No*. Nashville: Broadman Press, 1985.

La Haye, Beverly. *Prayer: God's Comfort for Today*. Nashville: Thomas Nelson Publishers, 1990.

Lake, Alexander. *Your Prayers Are Always Answered*. New York: Gilbert

Press, Inc. 1956.

Laubach, Frank C. *Prayer: The Mightiest Force in the World.* Westwood, NJ: Fleming H. Revell, 1946.

Laurie, Greg. *Wrestling with God.* Portland: Multnomah Publishers, 2003.

Lavender, John Allen. *Why Prayers Are Unanswered.* Philadelphia: Judson Press, 1967.

Lawless, Chuck. *Serving in Your Church Prayer Ministry.* Grand Rapids: Zondervan Publishing, 2003.

Lawrence, Brother. *The Practice of the Presence of God.* Westwood, NJ: Fleming H. Revell, 1965.

Lawrence, R. *How to Pray When Life Hurts.* Downers Grove, IL: InterVarsity Press, 1993.

Laymon, Charles M. *The Lord's Prayer.* Nashville: Abingdon Press, 1968.

Leach, Kenneth. *True Prayer.* New York: Harper and Row, 1980.

Lee, R.G. *The Bible and Prayer.* Nashville: Broadman Press, 1950.

LeFevre, Perry. *Understandings of Prayer.* Philadelphia: Westminster Press, 1981.

Lewis, C.S. *Letters to Malcolm: Chiefly on Prayer.* New York: Harcourt, Brace, and World, 1964.

Lindsell, Harold. *When You Pray.* Grand Rapids: Baker Book House, 1969.

Littleton, Mark. *Getting Honest with God: Praying as if God Really Listens.* Downers Grove, IL: InterVarsity Press, 2003.

Lockyer, Herbert. *All the Prayers of the Bible.* Grand Rapids: Zondervan Publishing, 1959.

________. *All the Angels of the Bible.* Peabody, MA: Hendrickson, 1995.

________. *Power of Prayer.* Nashville: Thomas Nelson Publishers, 1982.

Long, Brad and Doug McMurry. *Prayer That Shapes the Future.* Grand Rapids: Zondervan, 1999.

Longenecker, Richard N. Editor. *Into God's Presence: Prayer in the New Testament.* Grand Rapids: Wm. B. Eerdmans, 2001.

Lord, Peter. *Hearing God.* Grand Rapids: Baker Book House, 1988.

Lowder, Paul D., Compiler. *Let us Pray: A Minister's Prayer Book.* Nashville: The Upper Room, 1963.

Lucado, Max, ed. *A Thirst for God: Studies on the Lord's Prayer.* Nashville: Word Publishing. 1999.

Lucas, Daryl J., ed. *107 Questions Children Ask about Prayer.* Wheaton, IL: Tyndale House Publishers, 1998.

Luthi, Walter. *The Lord's Prayer.* London: Oliver and Boyd, 1961.

MacArthur, John Jr. *Jesus' Pattern of Prayer.* Chicago: Moody Press, 1981.

________. *The Disciples' Prayer, Study Notes.* Panorama City, CA: Grace Community Church, 1981.

Macartney, Clarence Edward. *Wrestlers with God: Prayers of the Old Testament.* New York: R.R. Smith Inc., 1930.

________. . *Prayer at the Golden Altar.* Grand Rapids: Zondervan, 1944.

MacDonald, Hope. *Discovering How to Pray.* Grand Rapids: Zondervan Publishing House, 1976.

MacNutt, Francis and Judith. *Praying for Your Unborn Child.* New York: Doubleday, 1988.

Mack, Wayne A. *Reaching the Ear of God.* Phillipsburg: R & R Publishing, 2004.

Maclachlan, Lewis. *21 Steps to Positive Prayer.* Philadelphia: Judson Press, 1978.

Magdalen, Margaret. *Jesus, Man of Prayer.* Downers Grove, IL: InterVarsity Press, 1987.

Magee, John. *Reality and Prayer.* New York: Harper & Brothers, 1957.

Marshall, Catherine, Ed. *The Prayers of Peter Marshall.* New York: McGraw-Hill Book Company, 1954.

________. *Adventures in Prayer.* Old Tappan, NJ: Chosen Books, 1975.

Martin, Catherine. *Six Secrets to a Powerful Quiet Time.* Eugene, OR: Harvest House Publishers, 2006.

Martin, Glen and Dian Ginter. *Power House: A Step-by Step Guide to Building a Church That Prays.* Nashville: Broadman & Holman, 1994.

Martin, Linette. *Practical Praying.* Grand Rapids: Wm. B. Eerdmans Publishing Co., 1997.

Maxwell, John. *Partners in Prayer.* Nashville: Thomas Nelson Publishers, 1996.

McClellan, Keith. *Prayer Therapy.* St. Meinrad, IN: Abbey Press, 1990.

McClure, James G. K. *Intercessory Prayer: A Mighty Means of Usefulness.* Chicago: Moody Press, 1902.

McConkey, James H. *Prayer.* Pittsburg: Silver Publishing Society, 1905.

McDonald, H. D. *The God Who Responds.* Minneapolis: Bethany House, 1986.

McFadyen, John Edgar. *The Prayers of the Bible.* New York: A.C. Armstrong and Son, n.d.

McGaw, Francis. *Praying Hyde.* Minneapolis: Bethany Fellowship, Inc. 1970.

McHenry, Janet Holm. *Prayerwalk: Becoming a Woman of Prayer, Strength and Discipline.* Colorado Springs, CO: Waterbrook Press, 2001.

McIntyre, David. *The Prayer Life of Jesus.* Ross-shire, Scotland: Christian Focus Publications, 1992.

McIntosh, Doug. *God Up Close: How to Meditate on God's Word.* Chicago: Moody Press, 1998.

Mehl, Ron. *A Prayer That Moves Heaven.* Portland: Multnomah Press, 2002.

Merton, Thomas. *Contemplative Prayer.* New York, NY: Doubleday. 1996.

Metz, Johann and Rahner, Karl. *The Courage to Pray.* New York: Crossroad Publishing, 1981.

M'Gill, James. *"Enter Into Thy Closet" or Secret Prayer.* Philadelphia: Presbyterian Board of Publications, 1843.

Michael, Chester and Marie C. Norrisey. *Prayer and Temperament: Different Prayer Forms for Different Personality Types.* Charlottesville, VA: The Open Door Inc., 1984.

Miller, Calvin. *The Table of Inwardness.* Downers Grove, IL: InterVarsity Press, 1984.

________. *Disarming the Darkness: A Guide to Spiritual Warfare.* Grand Rapids: Zondervan, 1998.

________. *The Path of Celtic Prayer.* Downers Grove, IL: InterVarsity Press, 2007.

Montgomery, Helen Barrett. *Prayer and Missions.* West Medford, MA: The Central Committee of the United Study of Foreign Missions, 1924.

Moody, Dwight L. *Prevailing Prayer.* Chicago: Moody, 1962.

Moore, Beth. *Praying God's Word.* Nashville: Broadman & Holman Publishers, 2000.

________. *Living Free: Learning to Pray God's Word.* Nashville: LifeWay Church Resources, 2001.

Moore, James P. *One Nation under God: The History of Prayer in America,* New York: Doubleday, 2005.

Moore, T.M. *The Psalms for Prayer.* Grand Rapids: Baker, 2002.

More, Hannah. *The Spirit of Prayer.* Grand Rapids: Zondervan, 1986.

Morgan, G. Campbell. *The Practice of Prayer.* Westwood, NJ: Fleming H. Revell, 1906.

Morley, Janet, *All Desires Known: Inclusive Prayers for Worship and Meditation.* Harrisburg, PA: Morehouse Publishing, 1988.

Morneau, Roger J. *The Incredible Power of Prayer.* Hagerstown, MD: Review and Herald Publishing Association, 1997.

Morrison, J. G. *The Stewardship of Fasting.* Kansas City, MO: Beacon Hill, n.d.

Morrissey, Kirkie. *On Holy Ground.* Colorado Springs, CO: NavPress, 1983.

Mueller, George. *Answers to Prayer.* Chicago: Moody Press, 1895.

Murphey, Cecil. *Invading the Privacy of God.* Ann Arbor: Servant Publications, 1997.

________. *Prayerobics: Getting Started and Staying Going.* Waco: Word Books, 1979.

Murphy, Ed. *The Handbook for Spiritual Warfare.* Nashville: Thomas Nelson Publishers, 1992.

Murphy, Miriam. *Prayer in Action.* Nashville: Abingdon, 1979.

Murray, Andrew. *The Ministry of Intercessory Prayer.* Minneapolis: Bethany House, 1981.

________. *With Christ in the School of Prayer.* Westwood, NJ: Fleming H. Revell, 1885.

________. *The Believer's School of Prayer.* Minneapolis: Bethany House, 1982.

________. *The Prayer Life.* Springfield, PA: Whitaker House, 1981.

________. *Prayer Power.* New Kensington, PA.: Whitaker House, 1998.

Muto, Susan and Adrian van Kaam. *Practicing the Prayer of Presence.* Mineola, NY: Resurrection Press, 1980.

Myers, Warren and Ruth. *Pray: How to Be Effective in Prayer.* Colorado Springs, CO: NavPress, 1983.

________. *Praise: A Door to God's Presence.* Colorado Springs, CO: NavPress,

1987.

Nee, Watchman. *The Prayer Ministry of the Church*. New York: Christian Fellowship Publishers, 1973.

________. *Let Us Pray*. New York: Christian Fellowship Publishing, 1977.

Nouwin, Henri J. M. *Out of Solitude*. Notre Dame, IN: Ave Maria Press, 1974.

________. *With Open Hands*. Notre Dame, IN: Ave Maria Press, 1972.

Ogilvie, Lloyd John. *Praying with Power*. Ventura, CA: Regal Books, 1983.

________. *Ask Him Anything*. Minneapolis: Grason, 1983.

________. *Conversation with God: Experience Intimacy with God through Personal Prayer*. Eugene, OR: Harvest House Publishers, 1993.

Oglesby, Stuart R. *Prayers for all Occasions*. Richmond: John Knox Press, 1940.

Omartian, Stormie. *The Power of a Praying Wife*. Eugene, OR: Harvest Publications, Inc., 1997.

________. *The Power of a Praying Nation,* Eugene, OR: Harvest House, 2002.

Orr, J. Edwin. *Fervent Prayer*. Chicago: Moody Press, 1974.

Ostrom, Henry. *The Law of Prayer*. Philadelphia: The Praise Publishing Company, 1910.

Otis, George, Jr. *Informed Intercession*. Ventura, CA: Regal Books, 1999.

Packer, J. I. *Praying the Lord's Prayer*. Wheaton: Crossway, 2007.

Packer, J. I. and Nystrom, Carolyn. *Praying: Finding Our Way Through Duty to Delight*. Downers Grove, IL InterVarsity Press, 2006.

Palmer, B.M. *Theology of Prayer*. Harrisonburg, VA: Sprinkle Publications, 1980.

Parker, William R. and Elaine St. Johns. *Prayer Can Change Your Life*. Englewood Cliffs, NJ: Prentice-Hall, 1957.

Parkhurst, Louis Gifford, Jr. *Charles G. Finney's Principles of Pra*yer. Minneapolis: Bethany Fellowship, 1980.

________. Compiler. *The Believer's Secret of Intercession*. Minneapolis: Bethany House Publishers, 1988.

________, ed. *Principles of Prayer*. Minneapolis: Bethany House, 2001.

Parks, Helen Jean. *Holding the Ropes*. Nashville: Broadman Press, 1983.

Paulsell, William O. *Rules for Prayer*. New York: Paulist, 1993.

Payne, Leanne. *Listening Prayer*. Grand Rapids: Baker Book House, 1994.

Pennington, M. Basil. *Call to the Center: The Gospel's Invitation to Deeper Prayer*. Hyde Park, NY: New City Press, 1995.

________. *Centering Prayer*. New York: Image Books Doubleday, 1980.

Perrine, Myra. *What's Your God Language*? Carol Stream, IL: Tyndale House Publishers, 2007.

Peterson, Ben. *Deepening Your Conversation with God*. Minneapolis: Bethany House, 1999.

Peterson, Eugene H. *Earth and Alter: The Community of Prayer in a Self-Bound Society*. Downers Grove, IL: InterVarsity Press, 1985.

Pier, Mac and Katie Sweeting. *The Power of a City at Prayer: What Happens When Churches Unite for Renewal*. Downers Grove, IL: InterVarsity Press, 2002.

Pierson, Arthur T. *George Müller of Bristol and His Witness to a Prayer-Hearing God*. New York: The Baker and Taylor Company, 1899.

Pike, Wentworth. *Principles of Effective Prayer*. Fort Washington, PA: Christian Literature Crusade, 1983.

Pilkington, Evan. *Paths to Personal Prayer*. Mystic, CT: Twenty-Third Publications, 1990.

Piper, John. *A Hunger for God: Desiring God through Prayer & Fasting*, Wheaton, IL: Good News Publishers/Crossway, 1997.

Poinsett, Brenda. *When Jesus Prayed*. Nashville: Broadman Press, 1981.

________. *Reaching Heaven: Discovering the Cornerstones of Jesus' Prayer Life*. Chicago: Moody Publishing, 2002.

Poloma, Margaret M. and George H. Gallup Jr. *Varieties of Prayer: A Survey Report*. Philadelphia, PA: Trinity Press International, 1991. Reprint, 1992.

Postema, Don. *Space for God: The Study and Practice of Prayer and Spirituality*. Grand Rapids: Bible Way, 1983.

________. *Not My Will but Thine*. Nashville: Broadman & Holman, 1998.

Powell, Cyril H. *Secrets of Answered Prayer*. New York: Thomas Y. Crowell Company, 1958.

Prange, Edwin E. *A Time for Intercession*. Minneapolis: Bethany Fellowship, Inc., 1971.

Prater, Arnold. *Learning to Pray*. Nashville: Abingdon Press, 1977.

Pratt, Richard L. *Pray with Your Eyes Open*. Phillipsburg, NJ: Presbyterian and Reformed Publishing Company, 1987.

Prime, Samuel. *The Power of Prayer: The New York Revival of 1858*. Edinburgh, Scotland: Banner of Truth Trust, 1991.

Prince, Derek. *Shaping History Through Prayer and Fasting*. Westwood, NJ: Fleming H. Revell, 1973.

Pritchard, Ray. *And When You Pray*. Nashville: Broadman & Holman, 2002.

________. *Beyond All You Could Ask or Think: How to Pray Like the Apostle Paul*. Chicago: Moody Press, 2004.

Quoist, Michael. *Prayers*. Sheed and Ward, 1963.

Rainsford, Marcus. *Our Lord Prays for His Own: Thoughts on John 17*. Chicago: Moody Press, 1950.

Ramon, Brother. *The Prayer Mountain*. Norwich: Cantebury Press, 1998.

Ravenhill, Leonard. *Revival Praying*. Minneapolis: Bethany House, 1962.

________. Compiler. *A Treasury of Prayer: The Best of E.M. Bounds on Prayer in a Single Volume*. Minneapolis: Bethany House Publishers, 1981.

Reapsome, James. *Effective Prayer: Studies on Prayer Skills*. Grand Rapids: Zondervan Publishing, 1992.

Redding, David A. *If I Could Pray Again*. Waco: Word Books, 1965.

Redpath, Alan. *Victorious Praying*. Chicago: Moody Press, 1970.

Rees, Paul Stromberg. *Prayer and Life's Highest*. Grand Rapids: Wm. B. Eerdmans Publishing Company, 1956.

Reidhead, Paris. *Beyond Petition*. Minneapolis: Bethany Fellowship, Inc., 1974.

Reisinger, John G. *The Sovereignty of God and Prayer*. Fredrick, MD: New Covenant Media, 2002.

Rhymes, Douglas. *Prayer in the Secular City*. Philadelphia: Westminster Press, 1967.

Rice, John R. *Whosever and Whatsoever When You Pray*. Murfreesboro, TN: Sword of the Lord Publishers, 1970.

________. *Prayer: Asking and Receiving*. Murfreesboro, TN: Sword of the Lord Publishers, 1942.

Richards, Larry. *Every Prayer and Petition in the Bible*. Nashville: Thomas Nelson Publishers, 1998.

Richardson, Rick. *Experiencing Healing Prayer: How God Turns Our Hurts into Wholeness*. Downers Grove, IL: InterVarsity Press, 2005.

Ridings, Dean. *The Pray! Prayer Journal*. Colorado Springs, CO: *Pray!* Books, 2003.

Rinker, Rosalind. *Communicating Love through Prayer*. Grand Rapids: Zondervan Books, 1969.

________. *Prayer: Conversing with God*. Grand Rapids: Zondervan Books, 1959.

________. *Praying Together*. Grand Rapids: Zondervan Books, 1968.

________. *Conversational Prayer*. Waco: Word Books, 1970.

Rittelmeyer, Friedrich. *The Lord's Prayer*. New York: The MacMillian Company, 1931.

Robb, John D. and James A. Hill. *The Peacemaking Power of Prayer*. Nashville: Broadman & Holman Publishers, 2000.

Roberts, Howard W. *Learning to Pray*. Nashville: Broadman Press, 1984.

Rodenmayer, Robert N. *The Pastor's Prayerbook*. New York: Oxford University Press, 1960.

Rossetti, Stephen. *I Am Awake: Discovering Prayer*. New York: Paulist Press, 1987.

Roth, Ron. *Prayer and the Five Stages of Healing*. Carlsbad, CA: Hay House, Inc., 1999.

Rubietta, Jane. *Resting Place: A Personal Guide to Spiritual Retreats*. Downers Grove, IL: InterVarsity Press, 2005.

Ruspantini, Anthony J. *Prayersphrases: Priceless Legacies of Prayer*. Binghampton, NY: Prayerphrases, 1997.

Ryle, J. C. *A Call to Prayer*. Grand Rapids: Baker Book House, 1976.

Sacks, Cheryl. *The Prayer Saturated Church*. Colorado Springs, CO: NavPress, 2004.

Sacks, Cheryl and Arlyn Lawrence. *Prayer-Saturated Kids: Equipping and Empowering Children in Prayer*. Colorado Springs, CO: NavPress, 2007.

Saloff-Astakhoff, N. I. *The Secret and Power of Prayer*. Chicago: Good News Publishers, 1948.

Sanders, J. Oswald. *Prayer Power Unlimited*. Grand Rapids: Discovery House, 1977.

________. *Effective Prayer*. Chicago: Moody Press, 1963.

Sandlin, John Lewis. *A Book of Prayers for Youth*. Westwood, NJ: Fleming H. Revell Company, 1966.

Sangster, W.E. *Teach Us to Pray*. London: Epworth, 1951.

Sangster, W.E. and Leslie Dawson. *The Pattern of Prayer*. Grand Rapids: Asbury Press, 1988.

Schaeffer, Edith. *The Life of Prayer*. Wheaton, IL: Crossway Books, 1992.

Schreiber, Vernon R. *Abba! Father*! Minneapolis: Augsburg Publishing House, 1988.

Schuller, Robert H. *Prayer: My Soul's Adventure with God*. Nashville: Thomas Nelson, 1995.

________. *Positive Prayers for Power-Filled Living*. New York: Bantam Books, 1976.

Searcy, Edwin, ed. *Awed to Heaven, Rooted to Earth: Prayers of Walter Brueggemann*. Minneapolis: Fortress press, 2003.

Self, Carolyn Shealy and William L. *Learning to Pray*. Waco: Word Books, 1978.

Seymour, Jack L. *Praying the Gospel of Mark*. Nashville: Upper Room Books, 1988.

Shedd, Charlie W. *How to Develop a Praying Church*. New York: Abingdon, 1964.

________. *The Exciting Church Where People Really Pray*. Waco: Word Books, 1974.

Sheets, Dutch. *Intercessory Prayer*. Ventura, CA: Regal Books, 1996.

________. *Watchman Prayer*. Ventura, CA: Regal Books, 2000.

Sherrer, Quin. *How to Pray for Your Family*. Ann Arbor, MI: Vine Books, 1990.

________. *Miracles Happen When You Pray*. Grand Rapids: Zondervan Publishing House, 1997.

________. *Praying Prodigals Home*. Ventura, CA: Regal Books, 2000.

Sherrer, Quin and Ruthanne Garlock. *How to Pray for Your Children*. Ventura, CA: Regal Books, 1998.

________. *The Spiritual Warrior's Prayer Guide*. Ann Arbor, MI: Servant Publications, 1992.

Shirer, Priscilla Evans. *Discerning the Voice of God: Recognizing When God Speaks*. Chicago: Moody Publishing, 2007.

Shoemaker, Helen Smith. *The Secret of Effective Prayer.* Waco: Word Publishers, 1967.

________. *Prayer & Evangelism.* Waco: Word Books, 1974.

Silvoso, Ed. *That None Should Perish.* Ventura, CA: Regal Books, 1994.

Simpson, A.B. *The Life of Prayer.* Camp Hill, PA: Christian Publications, 1989.

Sims, A. *Mighty Prevailing Prayer.* Grand Rapids: Zondervan Publishing House, n .d.

Simms, George. *In my Understanding.* Philadelphia: Fortress Press, 1982.

Simundson, Daniel J. *Where Is God in My Praying.* Minneapolis: Augsburg Publishing House, 1986.

Sittser, Gerald Lawson. *When God Doesn't Answer Your Prayer.* Grand Rapids: Zondervan, 2003.

Small, P. Douglas. *Transforming Your Church into a House of Prayer.* Cleveland, TN: Pathway Press, 2006.

Smith, Alice. *Beyond the Veil: Entering into Intimacy with God Through Prayer.* Ventura, CA: Regal Books, 1997.

________ . *40-Days Beyond the Veil.* Ventura, CA: Regal Books. 2003.

Smith, David R. *Fasting: A Neglected Discipline.* Fort Washington, PA: Christian Literature Crusade, 1993.

Smith, Eddie and Alice Smith. *The Advocates: How to Plead the Cases of Others in Prayer.* Lake Mary, FL: Charisma House, 2001.

________. *Drawing Closer to God's Heart: A Totally Practical, Non-Religious Guide to Prayer.* Lake Mary, FL: Charisma House, 2001.

________. *Intercessors & Pastors: The Emerging Partnership of Watchmen & Gatekeepers.* Houston: SpiriTruth Publishing, 2001.

Smith, Eddie. *Intercessors: How to Understand and Unleash Them for God's Glory.* Houston, TX: SpiriTruth Publishing, 2001.

________. *How to Be Heard in Heaven: Moving from Need-Driven to God-Centered Prayer.* Minneapolis: Bethany House Publ., 2007.

Smith, Eddie and Michael Hennen. *Strategic Prayer: Applying the Power of Targeted Prayer.* Bloomington, MN: Bethany House, 2007.

Smith, Michael M. *Nurturing a Passion for Prayer.* Colorado Springs, CO: NavPress, 2000.

Spear, Wayne R. *Talking to God: The Theology of Prayer.* Grand Rapids: Baker

Book House, 1979. Pittsburg: Crown & Covenant Publishers, 2002.

Spencer, William David and Aida Besancon Spencer. *The Prayer Life of Jesus, Shout of Agony, Revelation of Love: A Commentary*. Lanham, MD: University Press of America, 1990.

Sponheim, Paul R., Ed. *A Primer on Prayer*. Philadelphia: Fortress Press, 1988.

Sprinkle, Randy. *Follow Me: Becoming a Lifestyle Prayerwalker*. Birmingham, AL: New Hope, 2001.

Sproul, R.C. *Effective Prayer: Making Prayer All It Is Meant to Be*. Wheaton, IL: Tyndale House, 1984.

Spurgeon, Charles H. *Effective Prayer*. Evangelical Press, n. d.

________. *Twelve Sermons on Prayer*. Grand Rapids: Baker Book House, 1996.

________. *The Power in Prayer*. New Kensington, PA: Whitaker House, 1996.

________. *Praying Successfully*. New Kensington, PA: Whitaker House, 1997.

________. *Spurgeon on Prayer and Spiritual Warfare*. New Kensington, PA: Whitaker House, 1998.

St. Teresa of Avila, James M. Houston, ed. *A Life of Prayer*. Multnomah Press, 1983.

Stanley, Charles F. *Handle with Prayer*. Wheaton, IL: Victor Books, 1982.

________. *How to Listen to God*. Nashville: Thomas Nelson, 1985.

Stedman, Ray C. *Jesus Teaches on Prayer*. Waco, TX: Word Publishers, 1975.

________. *Talking to My Father*. Portland: Multnomah Press, 1975.

________. *Spiritual Warfare*. Portland: Multnomah Press, 1975.

Steere, Douglas V. *Dimensions of Prayer*. New York: Harper & Row, 1962.

Stein-Rast. David. *Gratefulness, the Heart of Prayer*. New York: Paulist Press, 1984.

Stewart, George S. *The Lower Levels of Prayer*. New York: Harper & Row, 1962.

Stewart-Sykes, Alister. *Tertullian, Cyprian, and Origen on the Lord's Prayer*. Crestwood, St. Vladimir's Seminary Press Popular Patrisitic Series, 2004.

Stokes, Mack B. *Talking With God*. Nashville: Abingdon Press, 1989.

Storms, Samuel C. *Reaching God's Ear*. Wheaton, IL: Tyndale House Publishers, 1988.

Strauss, Lehman. *Sense and Nonsense about Prayer*. Chicago: Moody Press, 1974.

Strong, John Henry. *Jesus: The Man of Prayer*. Philadelphia: Judson Press, 1945.

Taylor, Jack R. *Prayer: Life's Limitless Reach*. Nashville: Broadman, 1977.

Teykl, Terry. *Encounter: Blueprint for the House of Prayer*. Muncie, IN: Prayer Point Press, 1997.

________. *How to Pray After You've Kicked the Dog*. Muncie, IN: Prayer Point Press, 1999.

________. *Making Room to Pray: How to Start and Maintain a Prayer Room*. Muncie, IN, 1993.

________. *Praying Grace: Training for Personal Ministry*. Muncie, IN: Prayer-Point Press, 2002.

Thielicke, Helmut. *How We Learn to Speak with God*. Nashville: The Upper Room, 1973.

Thomas, J. Moulton. *Prayer Power*. Waco, TX: Word Books, 1976.

Thompson, Ken. *Bless This Desk: Prayers 9 to 5*. Nashville: Abingdon 1976.

Thomson, James G. S. S. *The Praying Christ*. Grand Rapids: Eerdmans, 1959.

Thornbury, John. *Help Us to Pray*. Durham, England: Evangelical Press, 1991.

Thornton, Henry. *Devotional Prayers*. Chicago: Moody Press, 1993.

Thrasher, Bill. *A Journey to Victorious Praying*. Chicago: Moody Press, 2003.

Tiessen, Terrance. *Providence & Prayer*. Downers Grove, IL: InterVarsity Press, 2000.

Tippit, Sammy. *The Prayer Factor*. Chicago: Moody Press, 1987.

________. *Praying for Your Family*. San Antonio: Sammy Tippit Ministries, 2006.

Tirabassi, Becky. *Let Prayer Change Your Life*. Nashville: Thomas Nelson Publishers, 1990.

Tittle, Ernest Fremont. *The Lord's Prayer*. Nashville: Abingdon-Cokesbury

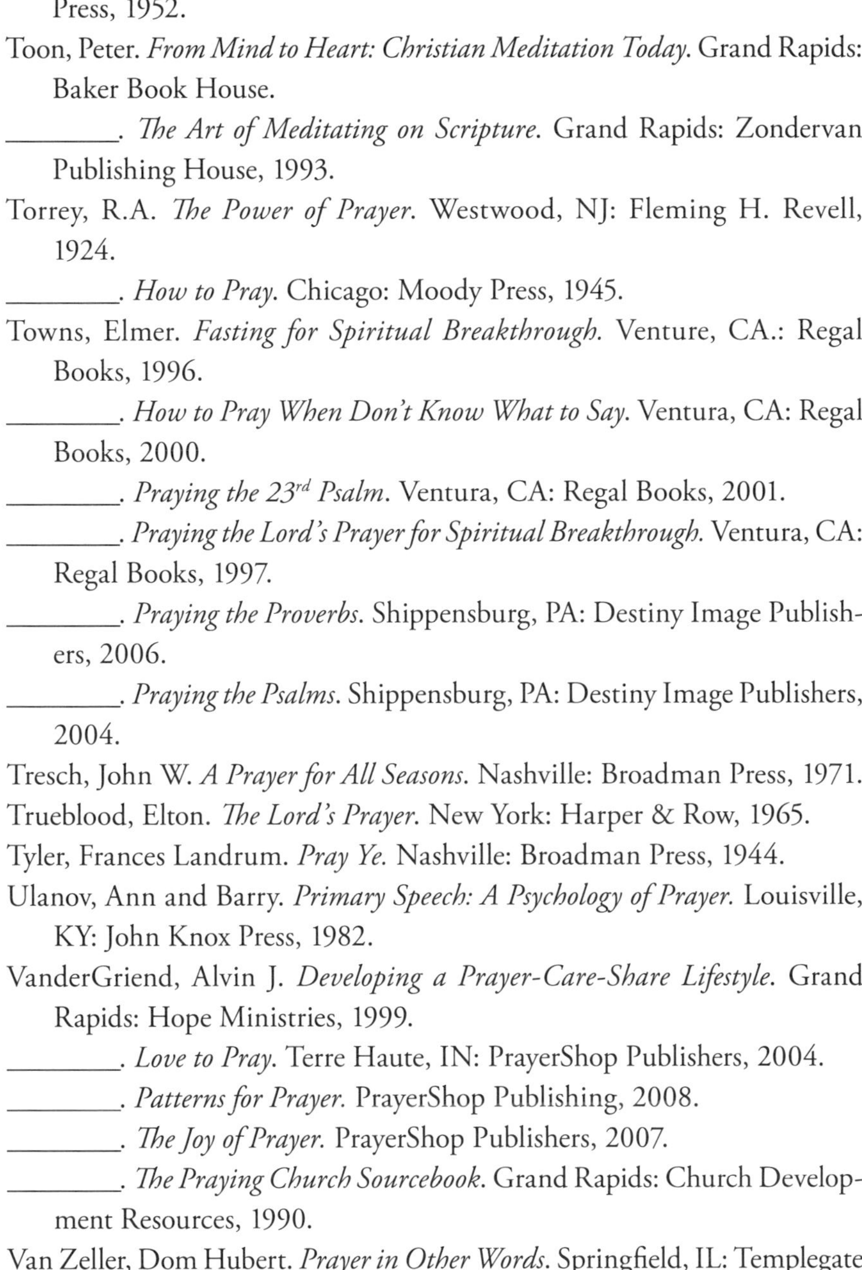

Press, 1952.

Toon, Peter. *From Mind to Heart: Christian Meditation Today*. Grand Rapids: Baker Book House.

________. *The Art of Meditating on Scripture*. Grand Rapids: Zondervan Publishing House, 1993.

Torrey, R.A. *The Power of Prayer*. Westwood, NJ: Fleming H. Revell, 1924.

________. *How to Pray*. Chicago: Moody Press, 1945.

Towns, Elmer. *Fasting for Spiritual Breakthrough*. Venture, CA.: Regal Books, 1996.

________. *How to Pray When Don't Know What to Say*. Ventura, CA: Regal Books, 2000.

________. *Praying the 23rd Psalm*. Ventura, CA: Regal Books, 2001.

________. *Praying the Lord's Prayer for Spiritual Breakthrough*. Ventura, CA: Regal Books, 1997.

________. *Praying the Proverbs*. Shippensburg, PA: Destiny Image Publishers, 2006.

________. *Praying the Psalms*. Shippensburg, PA: Destiny Image Publishers, 2004.

Tresch, John W. *A Prayer for All Seasons*. Nashville: Broadman Press, 1971.

Trueblood, Elton. *The Lord's Prayer*. New York: Harper & Row, 1965.

Tyler, Frances Landrum. *Pray Ye*. Nashville: Broadman Press, 1944.

Ulanov, Ann and Barry. *Primary Speech: A Psychology of Prayer*. Louisville, KY: John Knox Press, 1982.

VanderGriend, Alvin J. *Developing a Prayer-Care-Share Lifestyle*. Grand Rapids: Hope Ministries, 1999.

________. *Love to Pray*. Terre Haute, IN: PrayerShop Publishers, 2004.

________. *Patterns for Prayer*. PrayerShop Publishing, 2008.

________. *The Joy of Prayer*. PrayerShop Publishers, 2007.

________. *The Praying Church Sourcebook*. Grand Rapids: Church Development Resources, 1990.

Van Zeller, Dom Hubert. *Prayer in Other Words*. Springfield, IL: Templegate Publishrs, 1963.

Vaswig, William L. *At Your Word, Lord: How Prayer Releases the Power of God in Your Life*. Minneapolis: Augsburg Publishing House, 1982.

________. *I prayed, He Answered.* Minneapolis: Augsburg Publishing House, 1977.

Vennard, Jane E. *Praying with Body and Soul: A Way to Intimacy with God.* Minneapolis: Augsburg Fortress Publishers, 1998.

Verploegh, Harry. ed. *Oswald Chambers Prayer: A Holy Occupation.* Nashville: Discovery House Books, 1992.

Wagner, C. Peter. *Engaging the Enemy.* Ventura, CA: Regal Books, 1991.

________. *Prayer Shield: How to Intercede for Pastors, Christian Leaders and Others on the Spiritual Frontines.* Ventura, CA: Gospel Light, 1997.

________. *Warfare Prayer.* Ventura, CA: Regal Books, 1992.

Wagner, C. Peter, Stephen Peters and Mark Wilson. *Praying Through the 100 Gateway Cities of the 10/40 Window.* Seattle: YWAM Publishing, 1995.

Wakefield, James. *Sacred Listening.* Grand Rapids: Baker Books, 2006.

Walker, Michael. *Hear Me, Lord.* Old Tappan, NJ: Fleming H. Revell, 1969.

Wallis, Arthur. *God's Chosen Fast.* Fort Washington, PA: Christian Literature Crusade, 1968.

________. *Jesus Prayed.* Fort Washington, PA: Christian Literature Crusade, 1966.

Wangerin, Walter, Jr. *Deepening Your Experience of Prayer.* Grand Rapids: Zondervan Publishing House, 1998.

Water, Mark. *Prayer Made Easy.* Peabody, MA: Hendrickson Publishers, 1999.

Washington, James Melvin. *Conversations with God: Two Centuries of Prayers by African Americans.* New York: Harper, 1995.

Weatherhead, Leslie D. *A Private House of Prayer.* New York: Abingdon Press, 1958.

Weaver, Gary R. *Gentle Words in a Raging Storm: Prayer for all Occasions.* Lima, OH: C.S. Publishing Company, 1991.

Wentroble, Barbara. *Praying with Authority: How to Release God's Authority in Order for His Will to Be Done on Earth.* Ventura, CA: Regal Books, 2003.

Whiston, Charles Francis. *Pray: A Study of Distinctively Christian Praying.* Grand Rapids: Eerdmans, 1972.

________. *When Ye Pray Say Our Father*. Cleveland, OH: Pilgrim Press, 1960.

White, John. *Daring to Draw Near*. Downers Grove, IL: InterVarsity Press, 1977.

White, Thomas B. *The Believer's Guide to Spiritual Warfare*. Ann Arbor, MI: Servant Publications, 1990.

________. *City-wide Prayer Movements*. Ann Arbor: Vine Books, 2001.

White, Reginald E.O. *They Teach Us to Pray*. New York: Harper & Brothers, 1957.

________. *Prayer Is the Secret*. New York: Harper & Brothers Publishers, 1958.

Whitman, Virginia. *The Excitement of Answered Prayer*. Grand Rapids: Baker Book House, 1978.

Whittaker, Colin. *Seven Guides to Effective Prayer*. Minneapolis: Bethany House Publishers, 1987.

Whyte, Alexander. *Lord, Teach Us to Pray*. London: Hodder & Stoughton, 1922.

Wiens, Gary. *Bridal Intercession: Authority in Prayer through Intimacy with Jesus*. Greenwood, MO: Oasis House, 2001.

Wiersbe, Warren W., Compiler. *Classic Sermons on Prayer*. Grand Rapids: Kregel Publications, 1987.

________. *Prayer: Basic Training*. Wheaton: Tyndale House Publishers, 1988.

Wiles, Gordon P. *Paul's Intercessory Prayers*. Cambridge: Cambridge University Press, 1974.

Wilkinson, Bruce. *The Prayer of Jabez*. Portland: Multnomah Publishers, 2000.

Williamson, Robert L. *Effective Public Prayer*. Nashville: Broadman Press, 1960.

Willis, Edward David. *Daring Prayer*. Atlanta: John Knox, 1977.

Winger, Mell, ed. *Fight on Your Knees*. Colorado Springs, CO: NavPress, 2002.

Winward, Stephen. *How to Talk to God*. Wheaton: Harold Shaw Publishers, 1973.

Wolfe, Sam. *The Deeper Secrets of Prayer*. Huntsville, AL: Evangel Publications, 2002.

Wood, Barry. *Questions Christians Ask About Prayer and Intercession.* Old Tappan, NJ: Fleming H. Revel Company, 1984.

Work, Telford. *Ain't Too Proud to Beg: Living Through the Lord's Prayer.* Grand Rapids: Eerdmans Publishing Company, 2007.

Wright, Alan D. *Lover of My Soul.* Sisters, OR: Multnomah Publishing, 1998.

Wright, N.T. *The Lord and His Prayer.* Grand Rapids: Eerdmans Publishing Company, 1996.

Wright, C. Thomas. *Pray Timer: Real Time for Real Prayer.* Alpharetta, GA: North American Mission Board, 2000.

Yancey, Phillip. *Praying: Does It Make Any Difference.* Grand Rapids: Zondervan, 2006.

Zanzig, Thomas. *Learning to Meditate.* Winona, MN: Saint Mary's Press, 1990.